California
HMH SCIENCE DIMENSION

The Living Earth

Watch the cover come alive as you travel through time after an ecosystem disturbance.
Download the Science Dimensions AR app available on Android or iOS devices.

This book belongs to

_____

Teacher/Room

_____

Houghton Mifflin Harcourt™

Stephen Nowicki, Ph.D.

Bass Fellow and Professor
Departments of Biology, Psychology, and Neurobiology
Duke University
Durham, North Carolina

Steve Nowicki has taught at Duke since 1989, where he directed a complete redesign of the introductory biology program. His research explores animal communication and sexual selection from an integrative perspective that includes a wide range of behavioral, ecological, developmental, genetic, and evolutionary approaches. Nowicki's research has been published in more than 120 articles in scientific journals, including *Science, Nature,* and the *Proceedings of the National Academy of Science*. He also coauthored the book *The Evolution of Animal Communication: Reliability and Deception in Signaling Systems*. In 2010, he was elected a Fellow of the American Association for the Advancement of Science.

Cover Credits
fern leaf ©Noorashikin Ismail/Fotolia; *fern fossil* ©Science Stock Photography/Science Source

Copyright © 2020 by Houghton Mifflin Harcourt Publishing Company

Printed in the U.S.A.

ISBN 978-1-328-89609-4

6 7 8 9 10   0868   27 26 25 24 23 22 21 20

4500798051   C D E F G

ACCESS AND EQUITY CONSULTANT

Bernadine Okoro
S.T.E.M. Learning Advocate & Consultant
Washington, DC

ENGINEERING CONSULTANT

Cary I. Sneider, PhD
Associate Research Professor
Portland State University
Portland, Oregon

LAB SAFETY REVIEWER

Kenneth R. Roy, PhD
Senior Lab Safety Compliance Consultant
National Safety Consultants, LLC
Vernon, Connecticut

PROGRAM ADVISORS

Elizabeth A. DeStasio, PhD
Raymond H. Herzog Professor of Science
Department of Biology
Lawrence University
Appleton, Wisconsin

Kim Withers, PhD
Assistant Professor
Department of Life Sciences
Texas A&M University–Corpus Christi
Corpus Christi, Texas

CLASSROOM REVIEWERS

Tamara Marie Alt
Biology Teacher
Apple Valley High School
Apple Valley, California

Heather Garcia
NGSS, AVID, PBIS, and AP Biology
Chino Hills High School
Chino Hills, California

Bridget Gardea
Science Teacher Specialist
Pomona Unified School District
Pomona, California

Stephanie Greene
Science Department Chair
Sun Valley Magnet School
Sun Valley, California

Ryan Hainey
Biological Science Teacher
La Cañada High School
La Cañada Flintridge, California

Joy Lopez, EdD
Director of Technology
Sacred Heart Schools
Atherton, California

Steve Markley
El Camino High School
Sacramento, California

Bonnie Oxley
South High School
Bakersfield, California

Lance Powell
Science Instructional Coach, Teacher
Menlo-Atherton High School
Menlo Park, California

Lisa Snyder
NGSS Coordinator
Manteca Unified School District
Manteca, California

Interacting components can make a system function.

All living things, and many nonliving things, are made up of carbon-based compounds.

Kelp forests are important aquatic ecosystems.

Many species develop unique features that help them survive.

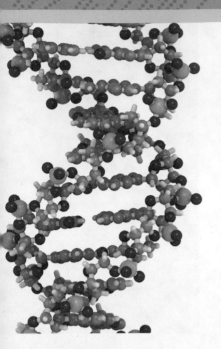

DNA is an essential molecule for all living things.

Behaviors of organisms have different costs and benefits.

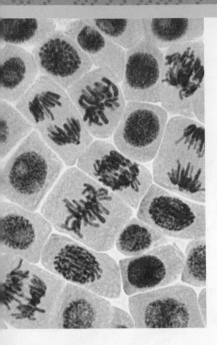

These living cells are in various stages of growth and division.

Transportation networks cover Earth, representing the extent of human development.

Claims, Evidence, and Reasoning

You likely use claims, evidence, and reasoning in your daily life—perhaps without even being aware of it. Suppose you leave a notebook behind in the cafeteria. When you return later, you see a number of similar notebooks on the counter. You say, "I left my notebook here earlier" and pick up one of them. The cafeteria worker says, "Are you sure that one is yours? They all look pretty much alike." You say, "Yes, my initials are right here on the cover." To confirm the fact, you open the notebook to show your full name inside. You also present your student ID to prove that it's your name.

This encounter is a claims-evidence-reasoning interaction. You claimed the notebook was yours, and you showed evidence to prove your point.

CLAIM

A *claim* is your position on an issue or problem. It answers the question "What do you know?"

EVIDENCE

Evidence is any data related to your claim that answer the question "How do you know that?" These data may be from your own experiments and observations, reports by scientists or engineers, or other reliable sources. Scientific knowledge is based on *empirical evidence*, or evidence that is derived from observation or experiment. As you read about science, perform lab activities, engage in class discussions, and write explanations, you will need to cite evidence to support your claims.

REASONING

Reasoning is the use of logical, analytical thought to form conclusions or inferences. It answers the question "Why does your evidence support your claim?" Reasoning may involve citing a scientific law or principle that helps explain the relationship between the evidence and the claim.

Scientists use claims, evidence, and reasoning—or *argumentation*—for many purposes: to explain, to persuade, to convince, to predict, to demonstrate, and to prove things. When scientists publish the results of their investigations, they must be prepared to defend their conclusions if they are challenged by other scientists.

Here is an example of a claims-evidence-reasoning argument.

CLAIM: Ice melts faster in the sun than it does in the shade.

EVIDENCE: We placed two ice cubes of the same size in identical plastic dishes. We placed one dish on a wooden bench in the sun and placed the other on a different part of the same bench in the shade. The ice cube in the sun melted in 14 minutes and 32 seconds. The ice cube in the shade melted in 18 minutes and 15 seconds.

REASONING: We designed the investigation so that the only variable in the setup was whether the ice cubes were in the shade or in the sun. Because the ice cube in the sun melted almost 4 minutes faster, this is sufficient evidence to support the claim that ice melts faster in the sun than it does in the shade.

Construct your own argument below by recording a claim, evidence, and reasoning. With your teacher's permission, you can do an investigation to answer a question you have about how the world works, or you can construct your argument based on observations you have already made about the world.

CLAIM	
EVIDENCE	
REASONING	

 For more information on claims, evidence, and reasoning, see the online **English Language Arts Handbook**.

Lab Safety

Before you work in the laboratory, read these safety rules. Ask your teacher to explain any rules that you do not completely understand. Refer to these rules later on if you have questions about safety in the science classroom.

Personal Protective Equipment (PPE)

- PPE includes eye protection, nitrile or nonlatex gloves, and nonlatex aprons. In all labs involving chemicals, indirectly vented chemical splash goggles are required.

- Wear the required PPE during the setup, hands-on, and takedown segments of the activity.

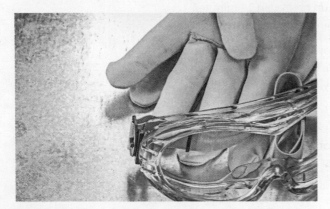

Dress Code

- Secure any article of clothing—such as a loose sweater or a scarf—that hangs down and may touch a flame, chemical, or piece of equipment.

- Wear closed-toe shoes.

- Tie back long hair or hair that hangs in front of your eyes.

- Acrylic fingernails are very flammable and should not be worn when using a flame.

Directions

- Observe all safety icons.

- Know where the fire extinguisher, fire blanket, shower, and eyewash station are located in your classroom or lab, and know how to use them in an emergency.

- Read all directions, and make sure that you understand them before starting the activity.

- Do not begin any investigation or touch any equipment until your teacher has told you to start.

- Never experiment on your own. If you want to try a procedure that the directions do not call for, ask your teacher for permission first.

- If you are hurt or injured in any way, tell your teacher immediately.

Chemical Safety

- If you get a chemical in your eye, use the eyewash station immediately. Flush the eye a minimum of 15 minutes.

- If you get a hazardous chemical on your skin or clothes, use the emergency shower for a minimum of 15 minutes.

- Never touch, taste, or sniff any chemicals in the lab. If you need to determine odor, waft. To waft, hold the chemical in its container 15 cm away from your nose, and use your fingers to bring fumes from the container to your nose.

- Take only the amount of chemical you need for the investigation. If you get too much, ask your teacher how to dispose of the excess. Do not return unused chemicals to the storage container; this can cause contamination.

- When diluting acid with water, always add acid to water. Never add water to an acid.

Heating and Fire Safety

- Keep your work area neat, clean, and free of materials.

- Never reach over a flame or heat source.

- Never heat a substance or an object in a closed container.

- Use oven mitts, clamps, tongs, or a test tube holder to hold heated items.

- Do not throw hot substances into the trash. Wait for them to cool, and dispose of them in the container provided by your teacher.

Electrical Safety

- Never use lamps or other electrical equipment with frayed cords or plugs with a missing ground prong.

- Make sure no cord is lying on the floor where someone can trip over it.

- Do not let a cord hang over the side of a counter or table so that the equipment can easily be pulled or knocked to the floor.

- Never let cords hang into sinks or other places where water can be found.

- Only use a Ground Fault Circuit Interrupter (GFCI) protected circuit receptacle.

Glassware and Sharp-Object Safety

- Use only clean glassware that is free of chips and cracks.

- Use knives and other cutting instruments carefully. Always wear eye protection, and cut away from yourself.

Animal Safety

- Never hurt an animal.

- Wear gloves when handling animals or preserved specimens.

- Specimens for dissection should be properly mounted and supported.

Cleanup

- Follow your teacher's instructions for the disposal or storage of supplies.

- Clean your work area and pick up anything that has dropped to the floor.

- Wash your hands with soap and water after completing the activity.

Safety in the Field

- Be sure you understand the goal of your fieldwork and the proper way to carry out the investigation before you begin fieldwork.

- Do not approach or touch wild animals. Do not touch plants unless instructed by your teacher to do so. Leave natural areas as you found them.

- Use proper accident procedures, and let your teacher know about a hazard in the environment or an accident immediately, even if the hazard or accident seems minor.

Safety Symbols

Safety is the priority in the science classroom. In all of the activities in this textbook, safety symbols are used to alert you to materials, procedures, or situations that could be potentially hazardous if the safety guidelines are not followed. Learn what you need to do when you see these icons, and read all lab procedures before coming to the lab so you are prepared. Always ask your teacher if you have questions.

 ANIMALS Never injure an animal. Follow your teacher's instructions for handling specific animals or preserved specimens. Wash your hands with soap and water after handling animals or preserved specimens.

 APRON Wear a nonlatex apron at all times in the lab as directed. Stand whenever possible to avoid spilling in your lap.

 BREAKAGE Use caution when handling items that may break, such as glassware and thermometers. Always store test tubes in a test tube rack.

 CHEMICALS Always wear indirectly vented chemical splash goggles when working with chemicals. Stand whenever possible when working with chemicals to avoid spilling on your lap. Tell your teacher immediately if you spill chemicals on yourself, the table, or the floor. Never taste any substance or chemical in the lab. Always wash your hands with soap and water after working with chemicals.

 DISPOSAL Follow your teacher's instructions for disposing of all waste materials, including chemicals, specimens, or broken glass.

 ELECTRIC Keep electrical cords away from water to avoid shock. Do not use cords with frayed edges or plugs with a missing ground prong. Unplug all equipment when done. Only use GFCI protected electrical receptacles.

 FIRE Put on safety goggles before lighting flames. Remove loose clothing and tie back hair. Never leave a lit object unattended. Extinguish flames as soon as you finish heating.

 FUMES Always work in a well-ventilated area. Do not inhale or sniff fumes; instead, use your fingers to bring fumes from the container to your nose.

 GLOVES Always wear gloves to protect your skin from possible injury when working with substances that may be harmful or when working with animals.

 HAND WASHING Wash your hands with soap and water after working with soil, chemicals, animals, or preserved specimens.

 HEATING Wear indirectly vented chemical splash goggles, and never leave any substance while it is being heated. Use tongs or appropriate insulated holders when handling heated objects. Point any materials being heated away from you and others. Place hot objects such as test tubes in test tube racks while cooling.

 PLANTS Do not eat any part of a plant. Do not pick any wild plant unless your teacher instructs you to do so. Wash your hands with soap and water after handling any plant.

 SAFETY GOGGLES Always wear indirectly vented chemical splash goggles when working with chemicals, heating any substance, or using a sharp object or any material that could fly up and injure you or others.

 SHARP OBJECTS Use scissors, knives, or razor tools with care. Wear goggles when cutting something. Always cut away from yourself.

 SLIP HAZARD Immediately pick up any items dropped on the floor, and wipe up any spilled water or other liquid so it does not become a slip/fall hazard. Tell your teacher immediately if you spill chemicals.

UNIT 1
Living Systems

YOU SOLVE IT

What is the Most Effective Nature Preserve Design?

 To begin exploring this unit's concepts, go online to investigate ways to solve a real-world problem.

The internal workings of a mechanical watch are an intricate and complex nonliving system.

FIGURE 1: Each sea star in this tide pool is a living system.

Living and nonliving systems are all around you. Nonliving systems help you complete many tasks. For example, cars and buses allow travel to and from school, and cell phones let you keep in touch on-the-go. Organisms, such as sea stars, are examples of living systems. All living and nonliving things are part of larger systems on Earth. For example, the tide pool that sea stars and other organisms live in is an example of an ecosystem, which is a system with both living and nonliving parts.

PREDICT How do you think living systems, such as sea stars, carry out life functions and respond to changes in their environment?

_____

_____

_____

_____

DRIVING QUESTIONS

As you move through the unit, gather evidence to help you answer the following questions. In your Evidence Notebook, record what you already know about these topics and any questions you have about them.

1. How is the Earth system organized?
2. When studying a population, what features or aspects might scientists focus on?
3. How do changes in ecosystems affect ecosystem stability?
4. How have advances in technology influenced the environment and human society?

UNIT PROJECT

Go online to download the Unit Project Worksheet to help plan your project.

California Wetlands at Your Service

Wetlands are ecosystems that have water at or near the soil surface at various times of the year. Why are wetlands important to humans and other organisms in California? Model a local wetland and investigate how the degradation of wetlands changes the composition of populations and ecosystems. What can we do to lessen these impacts?

Language Development

Use the lessons in this unit to complete the chart and expand your understanding of the science concepts.

TERM: system

Definition	Example

Similar Term	Phrase

TERM: biosphere

Definition	Example

Similar Term	Phrase

TERM: ecosystem

Definition	Example

Similar Term	Phrase

TERM: biodiversity

Definition	Example

Similar Term	Phrase

TERM: carrying capacity

Definition	Example
Similar Term	**Phrase**

TERM: resilience

Definition	Example
Similar Term	**Phrase**

TERM: resistance

Definition	Example
Similar Term	**Phrase**

TERM: engineering design process

Definition	Example
Similar Term	**Phrase**

Life in the Earth System

A hornworm caterpillar eats the leaves of a tomato plant.

CAN YOU EXPLAIN IT?

This tomato plant has a big bug problem. A hornworm caterpillar is eating the leaves of the plant. These insects are voracious eaters and can devour an entire plant's leaves, and sometimes even the fruits, in just a few hours. Its camouflaged appearance makes it a particularly irritating visitor in home gardens, as it is often discovered long after it has made the tomato plant its personal buffet.

Some plants that are infested with caterpillars or other insects produce chemicals that repel the insects and attract wasps that eat or parasitize the insects. Neighboring plants that are not infested with insects may start to produce these chemicals, too.

PREDICT How do you think tomato plants detect pests on a neighboring plant so they can protect themselves from infestation?

_____

_____

_____

_____

 Evidence Notebook As you explore the lesson, gather evidence to make a claim about what defines a living system.

Systems and System Models

Throughout history, humans have aimed to understand the world around us. To help make sense of observed phenomena, we organize information and identify patterns. One approach to understanding natural phenomena is called systems thinking. This way of thinking examines links and interactions between components, or parts, of a system to understand how the overall system works.

Properties of Systems

A system is a set of interacting components considered to be a distinct entity for the purpose of study or understanding. Systems exist on all scales, from atoms to the universe, and can be living or nonliving.

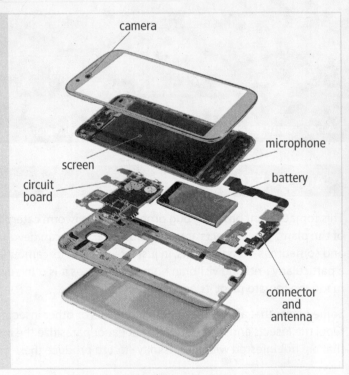

FIGURE 1: To send a text message, a cellular phone requires components, such as a signal receiver and transmitter, a battery, a circuit board, and a screen.

camera
microphone
screen
circuit board
battery
connector and antenna

Collaborate With a partner, answer the following question: What systems could you define in the world around you?

Boundaries and Components

Boundaries define the space of the system, to separate that system from the rest of the universe. A cellular phone is a system of electronics contained in a protective covering. The components are all the parts of the system that interact to help the system carry out specific functions. For example, a cellular phone needs the parts described in the image above to function properly. Together, the components send and receive radio signals and transform them into useful communication, such as text messages.

Inputs and Outputs

The inputs and outputs of different types of systems include energy, matter, and information. Outputs are generated when the inputs are processed in some way. In the case of a cellular phone, a radio signal (an input) is converted to vibrations (an output) that you detect as sound.

Open and Closed Systems

Systems can be categorized according to the flow of inputs and outputs. In an open system, the inputs and outputs flow into and out of the system. In a closed system, the flow of one or more inputs and outputs is limited in some way. An isolated system is a system in which all of the inputs and outputs are contained within the system.

APPLY Is the human body an open, closed, or isolated system?

○ **a.** open   ○ **b.** closed   ○ **c.** isolated

Controls

The components of a system include the controls that help keep the system working properly by monitoring and managing the inputs and outputs. Controls can be automatic, manually set, or a combination of both. An important system control is feedback. Feedback is information from one step of a cycle that acts to change the behavior of a previous step of a cycle. So, feedback is output that becomes input. A feedback loop is formed when an output returns to become an input in the same system that generated the output.

⚬ Systems and System Models

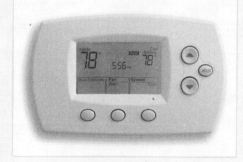

FIGURE 2: A thermostat can be used to control the heating and cooling systems in a home.

Some air conditioners and heaters have a control system called a thermostat. A thermometer inside the thermostat continually measures the temperature in the room. If the air temperature in the room rises above a preset temperature, the thermostat signals the air conditioner to turn on. If the air temperature in the room falls below the preset temperature, the thermostat signals the air conditioner to turn off.

ANALYZE Number these steps in order to illustrate the feedback loop that occurs when the air temperature becomes warmer than the thermostat setting (78 °F)

_____ **a.** The thermostat senses the decrease in air temperature.

_____ **b.** The air temperature reaches 78 °F.

_____ **c.** The air conditioner turns off.

_____ **d.** The thermostat senses the increase in air temperature.

_____ **e.** The air temperature reaches 79 °F.

_____ **f.** The air conditioner turns on.

System Organization

Systems can range in size and in complexity. More complex systems generally have more levels of organization than simpler systems. For example, organisms, or living things, are systems made up of smaller systems, such as organs, tissues, and cells. Two organisms that interact also can make up a system, such as a bird that pollinates a plant. On a larger scale, you are a system that is part of an ecosystem, or a community of organisms, and their physical environment. You also are part of the larger Earth system.

FIGURE 3: Both the hummingbird and the thistle plant are systems that interact with one another. They are part of an ecosystem, such as a city park.

As previously stated, an output of a system can feed back into the system, changing how the system may respond. Similarly, an output of one system can act as an input to a completely different, perhaps even unrelated, system. Think about walking into an air-conditioned building on a hot day. The cool air becomes an input to your body system, as receptors in your skin detect the change in air temperature. You may even begin to shiver slightly: the body's response to generate heat when it senses cold temperatures.

FIGURE 4: A human and scuba gear are both systems.

EXPLAIN The scuba diver is a living system. The scuba gear, or self-contained underwater breathing apparatus, is a system of air exchange. How are these two systems interacting? What are the inputs and outputs of these systems?

_____

_____

_____

_____

_____

System Models

Suppose that an engineering team is designing a new airplane. If they were to build a full-sized airplane for a performance test of each different design, the cost and the time would be impractical. A more practical option would be to use a smaller scale model of the airplane to study and analyze the various components of the system. A model is a pattern, plan, representation, or description designed to show the structure or workings of an object, system, or concept. You might think of a model simply as a smaller scale physical representation of a larger system. However, models are not limited to physical objects. Other types of models include computer simulations, conceptual diagrams, and mathematical equations, as shown in Figure 5.

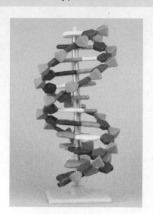

Protein Synthesis

DNA ⟶ RNA ⟶ Proteins

$y = a(1 + r)^x$

y = final population

a = initial population

r = growth rate

x = number of time intervals passed

a **Physical Model**
A smaller or larger copy of an object, such as this large model of a DNA molecule; a physical model built to scale can show the proportional relationship between the model's measurements and the real object's measurements.

b **Conceptual Model**
A diagram or flowchart that shows how parts of a system are related or how a process works; this conceptual model shows the steps of protein synthesis.

c **Mathematical Model**
An equation or set of equations that generates data related to how a system or process works; this mathematical model can help scientists predict the growth rate in a population.

d **Simulation**
Often in the form of a computer model; can be used to test variables and observe outcomes; a computer model can be used to see how a protein in the human body can misfold and potentially cause disease.

Systems Biology

We can apply systems thinking to biology. Systems biology studies biological systems as an integrated whole. This approach allows scientists to consider biological phenomena at different scales and examine how the components of a biological system interact. By considering the larger picture, biologists are better able to identify emergent properties of the system. An *emergent property* is a property that a system has but that its component parts do not have, that is, the sum is greater than its parts. For example, cells are self-contained systems that can function independently. However, when combined, similar cells form tissues, which can perform functions that the individual cells could not.

Language is a more recognizable example of a system with emergent properties. Its basic components are the sounds that combine to form words. The emergent properties are the meaning of the words made from these sounds. Another level of emergent properties comes from combining words into sentences that can convey meaning the words cannot do individually.

Similarly, DNA is a molecule that carries the genetic code of all organisms. The code consists of just four bases represented by the letters A, T, G, and C. The sequence of these bases in DNA provides coded instructions for making thousands of different proteins. Each protein is made of a specific arrangement of amino acids coded for by DNA. The emergent property of DNA is the information that codes for proteins.

 Evidence Notebook How might you model the relationship between a tomato plant and the hornworm caterpillar? Identify the components of the model, including inputs and outputs.

The Earth System

To understand living things better, we can study the systems in which they live. One of these systems is our home planet—Earth. The Earth system includes all of the solids, liquids, and gases; all living and nonliving objects; and all of the different forms of energy within Earth's boundary. Earth is made up of smaller systems, such as the biosphere, where all living things exist and interact. The biosphere in turn includes many smaller subsystems of living things in both aquatic and land environments. Earth itself exists within larger systems, such as the solar system and the Milky Way galaxy.

Matter stays within the Earth system, but energy enters the system in the form of sunlight and exits in the form of heat. In the Earth system, light energy is converted into other forms of energy. This drives the transformations of matter from one form to another as it cycles through the system.

Organization of the Earth System

Scientists use a system model to better understand interactions within the Earth system. The Earth system is organized into five interconnected systems, or spheres: geosphere, hydrosphere, biosphere, atmosphere, and anthrosphere.

The geosphere is all the solid features of Earth's surface, such as mountains, continents, and the sea floor. It also includes everything below Earth's surface. The hydrosphere is all of Earth's water, including water in the form of liquid water, ice, and water vapor. The biosphere is the area of Earth where life exists. The atmosphere is all of the air that envelops Earth's solid and liquid surface. The anthrosphere is the portion of Earth's environment that has been constructed or modified by humans.

FIGURE 6: Scientists organize the Earth system into five spheres.

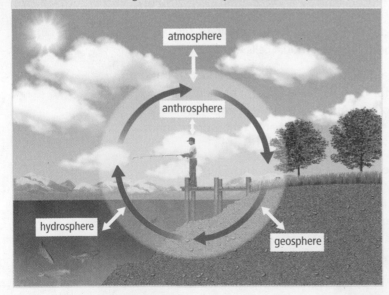

ANNOTATE Where should the biosphere appear in this systems model? Add a label for the biosphere to the diagram. Then use reasoning to explain your answer.

_____

_____

_____

_____

_____

_____

_____

_____

_____

_____

Organization of the Biosphere

Earth's biosphere is made up of ecosystems. An ecosystem includes all of the biotic and abiotic components in a given area. The living components in an ecosystem are called biotic factors. The nonliving components of ecosystems are abiotic factors. Energy and matter cycle through these various components. Similar to other systems, an ecosystem also has feedback mechanisms that keep it balanced and restore it to a balanced state when disrupted.

INFER Write the correct term in the appropriate box:

biome   biosphere   community   ecosystem   organism   population

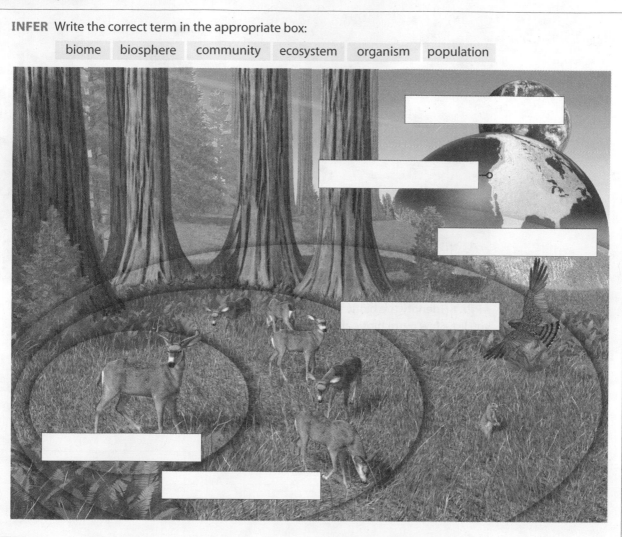

Ecologists can study ecosystems at different scales. They may study an individual organism, such as a mule deer, to learn more about factors that affect that species. They may also study an entire population of mule deer. A population is a group of the same species that lives in the same area. Multiple populations of different species form a community. In the Sierra Nevada, an ecologist may study how a community of mule deer, Belding's ground squirrels, and birds in a certain giant sequoia grove interact with one another.

Not all ecosystems are terrestrial, or land-based. About 71 percent of Earth's surface is covered with water, and it, too, is home to living organisms. These water-based ecosystems are called *aquatic ecosystems*. There are two main categories of aquatic ecosystems: salt water, or marine, and fresh water.

A biome is a major regional or global distribution of organisms, characterized by specific climate conditions and plant communities. There are several different types of biomes. The plants and animals of each biome are adapted to living in that particular environment. Many different ecosystems make up a biome, and each ecosystem has specific biotic and abiotic factors that interact and are interdependent.

FIGURE 7: Taiga, also called the Boreal forest, is a biome characterized by long, cold winters and short, mild, and rainy summers.

APPLY Identify the biotic and abiotic components of the taiga ecosystem shown here. Can you list a few more biotic and abiotic components that might be a part of this ecosystem?

| snow | plants | elk | air | sunlight | insects |

biotic	abiotic

Although biomes can be categorized separately, they are still connected. Each of these broad biome types can be divided into more specific zones. For example, a prairie is a type of temperate grassland. Frozen polar ice caps and snow- and ice-covered mountain peaks are not considered biomes because they do not have specific plant communities.

Evidence Notebook Make a model to illustrate how the biotic and abiotic factors listed above interact in the taiga ecosystem.

Characteristics of Living Things

Scientists use a set of characteristics to define living things. In general, all living things are made up of one or more cells and require an energy source. Living things grow and change over time and reproduce by making copies of themselves or by having offspring. Living things also respond to changes in their environment. *Homeostasis* is the maintenance of constant internal conditions in an organism. Although temperature and other environmental conditions are always changing, the conditions inside organisms usually stay quite stable. Maintaining stable internal conditions is critical to an organism's survival.

The Venus flytrap is a living thing. It is a plant made up of individual cells that work together to perform the functions it needs to survive. It gets its energy from the sun and the nutrients it needs from the insects it digests. A Venus flytrap reproduces both sexually through pollination and asexually by spreading its rhizomes—rootlike stems—underground in the soil.

FIGURE 8: Most plants get nitrogen from the soil. Venus flytraps grow in nitrogen-poor soil and must rely on the insects they catch as their source of nitrogen.

EXPLAIN Describe at least two biological systems. Explain how these systems are independent from and interconnected with each other.

_____

_____

_____

_____

_____

How scientists think about the characteristics of living things undergoes revision as new evidence comes to light. For example, there is disagreement about whether viruses are alive because they do not have all of the characteristics of living things. A virus is not made up of cells, does not maintain homeostasis, and cannot reproduce without a host organism.

Another way to think about life is as an emergent property of a collection of certain nonliving things. As an example, proteins are chemical building blocks in all organisms, but proteins by themselves are nonliving things. However, proteins in combination with other molecules and a complex set of biochemical reactions make up living things.

A virus consists of a strand of genetic material surrounded by a protein coat. But there are some membrane-bound viruses. Over time, could life emerge from the nonliving components of viruses? And there is new evidence that many of the protein folds in viruses are also found in cells from a variety of organisms. Could this mean that viruses used to be alive? The debate continues.

 Evidence Notebook How could the tomato plant's response to being eaten by a hornworm caterpillar be described as a function of homeostasis?

Interactions in Ecosystems

As its name suggests, an ecosystem is a system—it has boundaries, components, inputs, and outputs. Every living thing requires specific resources and conditions. The gray fox requires certain types of food, shelter, temperatures, and other factors to survive.

FIGURE 9: A gray fox emerges from its den.

Gray foxes live in dens located in underground burrows, under rock crevices, or in caves. They eat plants, insects, and small mammals, such as mice and rabbits. Many types of internal and external parasites live on and in gray foxes, including ticks and tapeworms. Coyotes prey upon gray foxes, but the foxes can climb trees to escape.

Habitat and Niche

Gray foxes live throughout North America and parts of South America. They prefer environments that have both trees and open areas. These environmental features are examples of a gray fox's habitat. A *habitat* includes all of the biotic and abiotic factors in the environment where an organism lives. For a gray fox, these factors include things such as the food that it eats, the dens that it uses, and the air temperature.

Many species live in the same habitat, but each species occupies a different ecological niche. An *ecological niche* contains all the physical, chemical, and biological factors that a species needs to survive and reproduce. The factors that make up a species' niche include the following:

Food sources The type of food a species eats, how a species competes with others for food, and where it fits in the food web are all part of a species' niche.

Abiotic conditions A niche includes the range of conditions such as air temperature and amount of water that a species can tolerate.

Behavior The time of day a species is active and where and when it feeds and reproduces also are factors in the niche of a species.

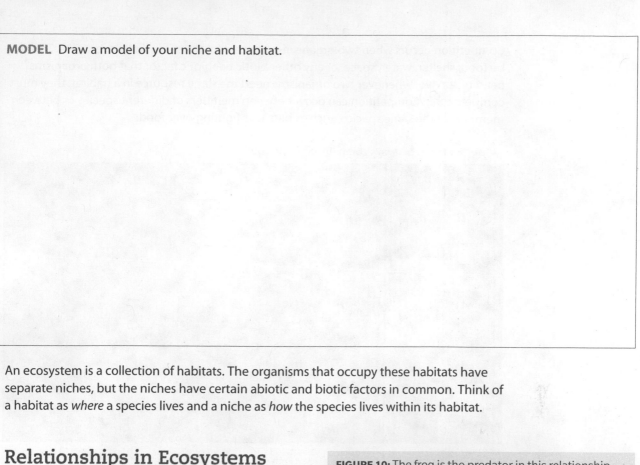

MODEL Draw a model of your niche and habitat.

An ecosystem is a collection of habitats. The organisms that occupy these habitats have separate niches, but the niches have certain abiotic and biotic factors in common. Think of a habitat as *where* a species lives and a niche as *how* the species lives within its habitat.

Relationships in Ecosystems

Each organism in an ecosystem interacts with other organisms as it goes about its daily activities. The gray foxes and other animals prey on mouse, rabbit, and insect populations for food, and they in turn are food for larger carnivores. Plants compete with one another for space, water, and nutrients. Still other organisms form interspecies relationships to provide or gain shelter, get protection, or find food. These interspecies interactions often benefit only one of the organisms in the relationship, but sometimes both organisms benefit.

FIGURE 10: The frog is the predator in this relationship.

Predation and Competition

Predation is the process by which one organism, the predator, captures and feeds upon another organism, the prey. The frog in Figure 10 is the predator, and the insect is its prey. However, if a snake slithered by, the frog might become its prey. Predation is not limited to carnivores. Herbivores that seek out and eat parts of living plants are considered predators, too. The relationship between predator and prey is important for energy transfer in food chains.

APPLY Are humans predators in their ecosystem? Explain your answer.

_____

_____

_____

_____

Competition occurs when two organisms compete for the same limited resource. This may be food, shelter, water, space, or any other biotic or abiotic factor that both organisms need to survive. Whenever two organisms need the same resource in a habitat, they must compete for it. Competition can occur between members of different species or between members of the same species, such as blue jays fighting over food.

FIGURE 11: Two blue jays compete for a food source.

Collaborate With a partner, think of at least two reasons why an organism might compete with another organism of the same species for a limited resource. Explain why two organisms would compete for these limited resources rather than share them.

FIGURE 12: A shrimp cleans the mouth of a fish.

Symbiosis

Symbiosis is a close ecological relationship between two or more organisms of different species that live in direct contact with one another. There are three major types of symbiosis: mutualism, commensalism, and parasitism. Mutualism occurs when both species benefit from the relationship. A shrimp cleaning the mouth of a fish is an example of mutualism. Commensalism is a relationship between two organisms in which one organism receives an ecological benefit from the other, while the other neither benefits nor is harmed. An egret that eats the insects kicked up by a cow as it moves is an example of commensalism. Parasitism is a relationship in which one of the organisms benefits while the other one is harmed. Unlike a predator, which most often quickly kills and eats its prey, a parasite benefits by keeping its host alive for some period of time. A wasp that lays its eggs inside of a caterpillar is an example of parasitism.

 Evidence Notebook How might symbiosis help the stability of an ecosystem? How might it hurt ecosystem stability?

Biodiversity

Coral reefs make up a small percentage of marine habitats, but they contain most of the oceans' species diversity. The more diverse an ecosystem is, the more likely it is to remain stable over the long term. If a disturbance, such as pollution, affects an ecosystem, recovery can happen more quickly if that ecosystem has more biodiversity. Biodiversity is a measure of the number of different species found within a specific area.

FIGURE 13: Coral reefs are marine ecosystems where many different species live.

ANALYZE What are two abiotic and two biotic conditions in a coral reef that provide the conditions necessary for it to have high biodiversity? How could a disturbance affect the biodiversity of the coral reef?

_____

_____

_____

_____

_____

Biodiversity in Ecosystems

The complexity of an ecosystem indicates its biodiversity. An area with a high level of biodiversity, such as a tropical rain forest, has a large assortment of species living near one another. The amount of biodiversity found in an area depends on many factors, including moisture and temperature. The complex relationships in ecosystems mean that a change in a single biotic or abiotic component can have many effects, both small and large, on a number of different species.

Data Analysis

Measuring Biodiversity

There are many different ways to measure biodiversity in an area. Two factors that ecologists often use are species richness and species evenness. Species richness is the number of species per sample of an area. Areas with a high number of different species have high species richness and therefore high biodiversity. Species evenness measures the relative abundances (population sizes) of different species that make up the species richness. Species evenness considers the relative distribution of the numbers of species in an ecosystem.

FIGURE 14: Ecologists analyze species richness (a) and species evenness (b and c) to evaluate ecosystem biodiversity.

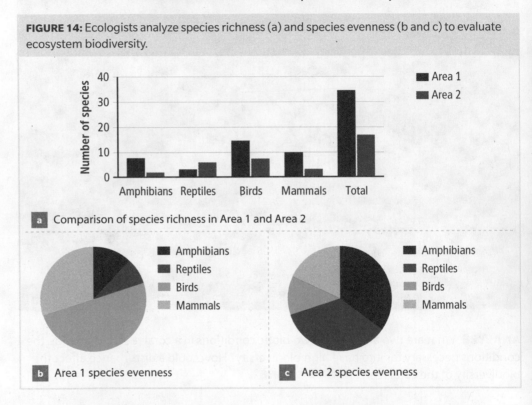

a Comparison of species richness in Area 1 and Area 2

b Area 1 species evenness

c Area 2 species evenness

ANALYZE Use the graphs in Figure 14 to answer the following questions.

1. What might happen to biodiversity in Area 1 if a new bird species moved into the area?

_____

_____

2. How might biodiversity in Area 1 change if the new bird species ate small mammals, lizards, and toads?

_____

_____

3. What conclusions can you draw about species richness and species evenness between the two areas?

_____

_____

_____

FIGURE 15: Scientists have identified more than 30 biodiversity hot spots around the world. Each hot spot often contains unique plant and animal species.

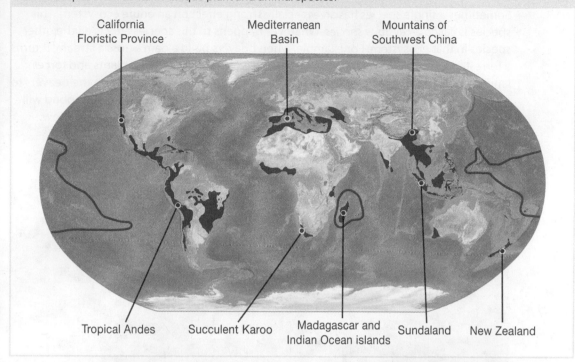

California Floristic Province

Mediterranean Basin

Mountains of Southwest China

Tropical Andes   Succulent Karoo   Madagascar and Indian Ocean islands   Sundaland   New Zealand

A biodiversity hot spot is an area with a very high level of biodiversity. Figure 15 shows a global map of biodiversity hot spots. These locations often contain species that are found nowhere else in the world. One hot spot located in North America is the California Floristic Province, an area with a Mediterranean-like climate that is home to giant sequoia and coastal redwood trees.

Preserving biodiversity hot spots helps to prevent species from going extinct and protects the unique ecosystems as a whole. Maintaining as much biodiversity as possible makes the entire biosphere healthier and provides a more stable habitat for plants, animals, and other species. These areas are also important because they may hold clues to new medicines and new resources, and may further our understanding of the biosphere.

Engineering

Building Artificial Coral Reefs

Earth's coral reefs are critical for the stability of marine ecosystems. Unfortunately, many are classified as threatened because of the effects of human activity. Living corals depend on the limestone deposited by their predecessors to get the minerals necessary to build their own bodies. However, the limestone is being dissolved from existing reefs due to increased ocean acidity caused by climate change. Marine ecologists are now combating this destruction by sinking artificial reefs, such as the one shown in Figure 16, which uses electrical currents to attract the limestone deposits needed by growing coral.

FIGURE 16: Artificial reef

 Evidence Notebook What is the relationship between biodiversity and ecosystem stability? How do artificial reefs affect a marine ecosystem's stability?

Keystone Species

Sometimes a single species has an especially strong effect on an entire ecosystem. This species is called a *keystone species*. Whatever happens to this species affects all the other species in that ecosystem. For example, when beavers build a dam across a stream, it turns a terrestrial ecosystem into a freshwater ecosystem. This kills existing plants and forces land animals to move to new territories. The new pond's inhabitants rely on the beavers to maintain the dam. If the beavers are removed, the dam will eventually fail. The pond will drain and over time, the land will return to a terrestrial ecosystem, such as a meadow.

FIGURE 17: Beavers are a keystone species that make and maintain pond ecosystems.

formation of wetland ecosystem

increased waterfowl population

keystone species

increased fish population

nesting sites for birds

 Collaborate With a partner, discuss why protecting a keystone species can protect a habitat as a whole.

FIGURE 18: Many farmers use pesticides to control insects and weeds in order to increase the amount of harvested crops.

Factors That Affect Biodiversity

Many factors can reduce biodiversity. Human activities can reduce it very quickly. Humans need food, and much of that food comes from crop plants. Large areas of land must be cleared to make fields to grow crops. Developing agricultural land removes most of the native plant and animal species in a region and replaces them with only a few species that are managed as crops. In addition, pesticide use can negatively affect any remaining native organisms. Biodiversity is also lost when land is cleared for human housing and industrial sites.

Introduction of new plants and animals into ecosystems is another serious issue. These species can reduce biodiversity by preying on native species or out-competing native species for resources, such as food or shelter.

 Evidence Notebook How would you describe the relationship between the hornworm caterpillar and the tomato plant? Do they have a symbiotic relationship? Explain your reasoning.

Engineering

Modeling a System

Whether you think about it or not, you interact with systems every day. A school, a classroom, or an athletic team could be modeled as a system.

DESIGN CHALLENGE Model a system that is familiar to you. Then use your model to suggest ways to improve that system. You can choose one of the following school-related systems or come up with one of your own:

- getting food in the cafeteria
- visitors checking in at the front office
- students getting on buses to go home
- cars leaving the parking lot when school is over

You may work on your system model on your own or in collaboration with one or more students.

PLAN What system will you model and why?

_____

_____

_____

Develop a Model

Make a model of the system you have chosen. Your model should illustrate the following:

- the components of the system
- how the components interact
- the inputs and outputs of the system
- the system boundaries
- system controls and feedback loops

In your Evidence Notebook, describe how your model will meet these requirements. Then construct a model for the system you are investigating.

Define the Problem

In your Evidence Notebook, identify a problem with this system for which you could suggest solutions. For example, is there congestion in this system when too many people try to get to a location at the same time?

FIGURE 19: Your school cafeteria can be modeled as a system.

Design Solutions

Brainstorm some solutions to this problem. In your Evidence Notebook, explain how the efficiency of this system could be improved in terms of the following:

- time
- costs
- materials
- inputs and outputs

Choose one of the solutions you suggested, and answer these questions in your Evidence Notebook: How would this proposed solution affect the other parts of the system? Are there any social, cultural, or environmental impacts of your solution?

Optimize

Revise your original model to show how the solution you suggested would be implemented into the system.

> **Language Arts Connection** Prepare a multimedia presentation to persuade people to implement your solution. A multimedia presentation should use graphics, text, music, video, and sound. Include your final model, an explanation of the solution you are proposing, and a discussion of the tradeoffs you considered.

| ECOSYSTEM SERVICES | EXPLORE A LOCAL ECOSYSTEM | LIFE UNDER A MICROSCOPE | Go online to choose one of these other paths. |

Lesson Self-Check

CAN YOU EXPLAIN IT?

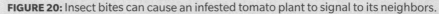

FIGURE 20: Insect bites can cause an infested tomato plant to signal to its neighbors.

When an infested tomato plant produces defensive chemicals, these chemicals can travel directly through the air to other plants. But they can also travel through soil, with the help of fungi. The fungi form a network that connects all the roots of the plants in a given area. A defensive chemical signal can travel through this network from the infested plant to all of its unaffected neighbors. When a plant receives the message that a nearby plant is infested, it can produce its own chemicals as a defense.

 Evidence Notebook Refer to your notes in your Evidence Notebook to explain how tomato plants might be able to detect insects on a neighboring plant and protect themselves from infestation.

1. Make a simple model illustrating your claim about how the components of this system interact. Show how fungi transfer information from insect-infested tomato plants to nearby uninfested tomato plants. Be sure to label any inputs and outputs in the model.

2. In your model, show how the biosphere, geosphere, and atmosphere are all components of this system.

3. How might humans interact with this system in order to produce crop plants with a strong defense against insect infestation?

CHECKPOINTS

Check Your Understanding

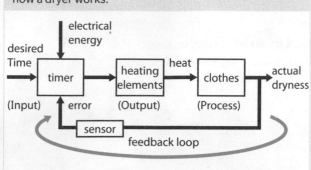

FIGURE 21: This conceptual model shows the basics of how a dryer works.

Use the diagram to answer the next three questions.

1. How does the sensor interact with the other components of this system?
   - a. The sensor detects the heat of the clothes and makes the timer generate more heat.
   - b. The sensor detects the dryness of the clothes and then sends information to the timer.
   - c. The sensor detects whether the heating element is functioning properly and then sends input to the timer.
   - d. The sensor detects how much time is left and sends input to the heating element to increase or decrease the heat.

2. Select the correct term to complete the statement.

   The model of the dryer system represents a(n) open | closed | isolated system because energy enters in the form of heat | electricity and exits in the form of heat | electricity, but matter contained in the dryer, such as the metal casing and electrical wiring, enter and exit | remain in | are often removed from the system

3. Which of these is not a direct input for the timer in this system? Select all correct answers.
   - a. time manually entered by the user
   - b. electrical signals by the sensor
   - c. dryness of the clothes
   - d. heat from the heating element
   - e. electricity from the wall outlet

4. What is an emergent property?
   - a. a property that a system has but that its individual component parts do not have
   - b. a property that a system does not have but that its individual component parts have
   - c. a property that both a system and its individual component parts have
   - d. a property that is not always exhibited by a system

5. Pick two of Earth's spheres (anthrosphere, atmosphere, biosphere, geosphere, hydrosphere), and draw a model showing how these two systems interact. Your model should show components of these systems, at least one way these components interact, and inputs and outputs that move from one system to another.

6. Order the terms according to scale from smallest to largest. Label the smallest term as 1 and the largest as 6.

   _____ a. community

   _____ b. biome

   _____ c. biosphere

   _____ d. organism

   _____ e. population

   _____ f. ecosystem

CHECKPOINTS (continued)

7. Explain what a feedback loop is using the terms *input, output,* and *homeostasis.*

_____

_____

_____

_____

8. Top predators are often keystone species in their habitat. Explain what happens to the biodiversity of an ecosystem when a top predator is deliberately removed from the ecosystem in which it lives.

_____

_____

_____

_____

9. Do you think it is possible for a biome to change due to human activities? Explain a situation in which this might happen.

_____

_____

_____

10. Biodiversity hot spots are found around the world. Why can't scientists come up with a single solution to protect all of these areas?

_____

_____

_____

_____

MAKE YOUR OWN STUDY GUIDE

 In your Evidence Notebook, design a study guide that supports the main ideas from this lesson:
Models can be used to illustrate the relationships between components of living and nonliving systems.

A model can be used to illustrate the hierarchical organization of the Earth system.

Biodiversity is a measure of the number of different species found within a specific area.

Remember to include the following information in your study guide:
• Use examples that model main ideas.
• Record explanations for the phenomena you investigated.
• Use evidence to support your explanations. Your support can include drawings, data, graphs, laboratory conclusions, and other evidence recorded throughout the lesson.

Consider the properties of systems and system models and how systems can be used to model the levels of organization within living organisms.

Analyzing Populations

A sea otter floats in a kelp bed off the coast of California.

CAN YOU EXPLAIN IT?

Sea otters live in aquatic ecosystems. They can be found in ocean habitats off the California coast, from San Mateo County in the north to Santa Barbara County in the south. These sociable fur-covered mammals swim among kelp forests and use the kelp as shelter. Sea otters prey on sea urchins and other invertebrates that eat kelp. At the beginning of the last century, the number of sea otters significantly declined at a relatively rapid pace due to overhunting by humans. By the 1920s, sea otters were nearly extinct. Protection and recovery efforts have helped, but the population of Pacific Coast sea otters is still well below what it once was.

PREDICT What factors contribute to past and present changes in California's sea otter population? How do these changes affect other organisms living in the same ecosystem?

_____

_____

_____

_____

 Evidence Notebook As you explore this lesson, gather evidence for how populations interact in ecosystems.

Population Density and Dispersion

FIGURE 1: Urban cities have dense human populations.

If you have ever traveled from a rural area to a city, you may have noticed a change in population density. Cities have more dense populations, while rural areas have more widely dispersed, or scattered, populations. Species populations are measured in a similar way. What can we learn from population data?

Collaborate With a partner, discuss whether the area where you live has a dense or a dispersed population. Explain your reasoning.

Population Density

You may be familiar with the term *density* in the context of matter. It is the amount of matter in a given space. Population density is very similar: it is the number of individuals living in a defined space. When scientists such as wildlife biologists observe changes in population density over time, they investigate whether the changes are due to environmental changes or natural variations in the life history of the species. Biologists may use this information to decide if it is necessary to make changes to maintain a healthy population.

One tool that biologists can use to make this decision is to calculate the ratio of individuals living in an area to the size of that area. Population density is calculated using the following formula:

$$\frac{\text{number of individuals}}{\text{area (units}^2)} = \text{population density}$$

To calculate this ratio for the deer herd shown in Figure 2, a biologist would first determine the size of the herd's home range. Then the scientist would count all of the individuals in that population within the defined area.

FIGURE 2: Deer gather in a field to graze.

SOLVE A wildlife biologist and her team counted 200 individual deer in an area of 10 square kilometers.

1. What is the population density?_____

2. Ten years later, researchers return to the same area and find that the population density has declined to 5 deer per square kilometer. What might a decrease in the density of a deer population tell scientists about the habitat in the area?

_____

_____

Population Dispersion

You may have noticed that people tend to separate themselves in different ways—some like to hang out in large groups, some gather in twos and threes, while others prefer to be alone. There are also patterns in the way different populations of other organisms separate themselves. There are three main patterns of population dispersal: clumped, uniform, and random.

INFER How would you classify each type of population dispersion? Write the type of dispersion shown in each image in the space provided.

random   clumped   uniform

_____   _____   _____

Clumped dispersion occurs when resources are spread unevenly within an ecosystem. Individuals gather into groups where resources are available. Clumped dispersion helps protect individuals from predators and makes finding a mate easier. Uniform dispersion occurs when individuals of the same species must compete for limited resources and territory. Random dispersion is the least common pattern of distribution. It occurs when individuals are spread randomly within an area or a volume. In plants, this type of dispersion often occurs when seeds are scattered by wind or water, resulting in seeds being dropped randomly. The seeds will only sprout if conditions are right, which increases the randomness of the distribution.

ANALYZE Evaluate the claim that uniform distributions occur only in areas where humans have changed the ecosystem, such as by planting crops or trees. Provide evidence, if any, that refutes this claim.

_____

_____

_____

Population Sizes at Different Scales

The population growth rate of a species may not be the same in every place it is found. Also, the population growth rate of a species may be different in a specific ecosystem when compared to its growth rate on a larger, global scale. Consider the human population. Human population growth rates can be quite different in different parts of the world and the growth rate in any one region may differ from the overall growth rate of the human population on Earth. For example, the human population on the continent of South America is experiencing an overall growth rate of just over 1 percent. However, the South American country of Brazil is experiencing a decline in population growth from 2.9 percent in the mid-1960s to the current rate of 0.8 percent. Populations in other countries in South America, such as Uruguay, Chile, and Argentina, are also growing at rates that are significantly below the world average.

Many factors may contribute to a lower population growth rate of a species in one area in comparison to another area. For example, one ecosystem might experience environmental changes or exposure to disease that another ecosystem does not.

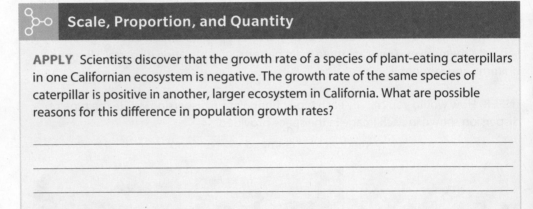

Scale, Proportion, and Quantity

APPLY Scientists discover that the growth rate of a species of plant-eating caterpillars in one Californian ecosystem is negative. The growth rate of the same species of caterpillar is positive in another, larger ecosystem in California. What are possible reasons for this difference in population growth rates?

_____

_____

_____

_____

Measuring Population Size

FIGURE 3: This monarch butterfly is tagged on its wing.

Measuring population size over a large area may seem like an impossible task. Sometimes, a complete count of every individual can be done, particularly if the species lives in an enclosed area. However, what if you needed to count a very large population over many square kilometers? In this case, biologists can use a variety of sampling techniques to estimate the size of a population.

One method scientists use to measure the size of a population of animals is the mark–recapture technique. Biologists capture individuals within a population, tag them, and then release them back into their habitat. After a period of time, a second sample is captured, and biologists look for and count the tagged individuals as well as any newly captured animals. They may also fit animals with radio collars or Global Positioning System (GPS) satellite devices to track their movements.

Calculating Population Size

SAMPLE PROBLEM

Scientists use a formula to calculate population size when they use the mark–recapture method. The formula states that the number of marked recaptured individuals divided by the total number of individuals in the second sample equals the number of individuals initially marked divided by the total estimated population size:

$$\frac{R \text{ (marked recaptured individuals)}}{T \text{ (total individuals in second sample)}} = \frac{M \text{ (initially marked individuals)}}{N \text{ (total population size)}}$$

ANALYZE

In order to solve the equation for N, population size, rearrange the equation so that N is isolated on one side of the equation. The formula will now state that the total estimated population size is equal to the number of initially marked individuals multiplied by the total number of individuals in the second sample, divided by the number of marked recaptured individuals.

$$N = \frac{M \times T}{R}$$

For example, suppose scientists capture 12 yellow-bellied marmots from an alpine meadow. Each captured marmot has measurements taken, is given an ear tag, and is then released. The next year, scientists capture 15 marmots in the meadow and find 10 of them have ear tags.

SOLVE

In this example, 12 marmots were captured and initially tagged with ear tags, so $M = 12$. Then, 15 marmots were captured in the second sample, so $T = 15$. Scientists counted 10 ear tags in the recaptured marmots, so $R = 10$. Plug these values into the formula to solve for N:

$$N = \frac{M \times T}{R} = \frac{12 \times 15}{10} = 18 \text{ yellow-bellied marmots}$$

PRACTICE PROBLEM

SOLVE Suppose you are helping scientists conduct a study of a population of Clear Lake hitch, which is a fish species that lives in Californian lakes. The scientists initially capture 80 hitch from a lake and tag all of them. After 30 days, they capture 100 hitch and count 20 tags. Use the space below to calculate the estimated number of hitch in the lake. Show your work.

Hands-On Lab

Quadrat Sampling

Quadrat sampling is another method used by ecologists to collect data about population sizes in an ecosystem. Quadrats are square or rectangular grids of a known size. Quadrat sampling works best with species that do not change location, such as plants and corals.

RESEARCH QUESTION How can the quadrat sampling method be used to collect data about population sizes in the area where you live?

FIGURE 4: Quadrat sampling is most often used to survey populations of plants.

MAKE A CLAIM

Why does quadrat sampling provide an accurate estimate of a population size within a defined area? Explain your reasoning.

_____

_____

_____

MATERIALS

- nonlatex gloves   • calculator   • meterstick   • quadrat

SAFETY INFORMATION

- Wear nonlatex gloves when handling any plant material.

- Wash your hands with soap and water immediately after completing this activity.

CARRY OUT THE INVESTIGATION

1. Obtain a quadrat frame. Measure, calculate, and record the area of the quadrat on a piece of paper or in your Evidence Notebook.

2. Stand at the edge of the area you will sample and randomly toss your quadrat. Make sure your quadrat does not overlap with another.

3. Count how many individuals of each species are in your quadrat. Record your data in a data table. Repeat this procedure three times.

CALCULATE

1. Combine your data with that of your classmates. Find the average number of each species for all of the samples.

_____

_____

2. Obtain the area of the sampling plot from your teacher. Calculate how many quadrats would fit in the area of the sampling plot. Multiply this value by the average number of each species found in one quadrat to estimate the population of each species.

_____

_____

3. Calculate the density of each species. Which species had the highest density? Which had the lowest? Why do you think that is?

_____

_____

DRAW CONCLUSIONS

1. How can you make sure that your estimate of population size will be as close to the actual population size as possible?

_____

_____

_____

_____

2. Why do scientists only gather data for a part of the population, instead of the entire population? How does this affect the accuracy of the final population count?

_____

_____

_____

_____

 Evidence Notebook Investigating sea otters helped scientists identify a decline in the population. This, in turn, led to efforts to protect the sea otters and work to ensure that the population grows.

1. What methods might scientists have used to study the sea otter population in California?
2. How could these methods have helped scientists identify a problem with the sea otter population? Explain.

Population Growth Patterns

Imagine you leave an apple in your locker over winter break. Upon your return to school, you open your locker door to find a cloud of fruit flies. When you left school, the fly population in your locker was zero—now it's at least 100! Your locker ecosystem had a huge change in its fruit fly population. While this is hopefully not a normal occurrence in your locker, changes in population sizes and densities in ecosystems are normal responses to changes in resource availability.

PREDICT What would happen to the fruit fly population in the locker if the apple were removed from that ecosystem? Give your reasoning.

_____

_____

_____

_____

Population Size

FIGURE 5: A population of elephants has both young and old individuals.

How might biologists track the population size of a species, such as a group of elephants? To accurately track the population over time, they would need to account for four factors: immigration, emigration, births, and deaths.

Immigration and emigration have to do with individuals entering and leaving a population. For example, if a disturbance occurred in a nearby habitat, some elephants might immigrate, or move into, a new population. Then, competition for resources could increase, causing some elephants to move out of the population, or emigrate, to a new area.

Births and deaths also change a population size over time. Individuals have offspring, which adds more members to the population. Some individuals die each year, which reduces the population.

Calculating the Growth Rate

The growth rate of a population can be measured with an equation that takes into account the four factors that affect population size:

$$r = (b + i) - (d + e)$$

In this equation, r = population growth rate, b = birth rate, i = immigration rate, d = death rate, and e = emigration rate. We can apply the four factors to our locker ecosystem example. A small population of fruit flies immigrated into the locker in search of food. The population increased due to the birth of a new group of fruit flies. Those flies that did not die when you swatted them in surprise emigrated from the locker when you threw the apple away.

As part of a long-term elephant study, biologists counted individuals in a population of elephants each spring. In one year, there were 18 males and 34 females. Over the following year, each female gave birth, from which 28 offspring survived. Predators killed 9 elephants. A construction project cleared 50 acres of nearby forested land, causing 5 males and 19 females to immigrate into the study area. Competition for females increased, resulting in the emigration of 10 males to a new territory in search of mates.

SOLVE Find the growth rate of this population. Show your work.

_____ elephants per year

Exponential and Logistic Growth

A population may grow very rapidly, or it may grow slowly over time. Population growth may be positive, negative, or show no changes. Population growth depends on environmental conditions. The rate of growth for a population is directly determined by the amount of available resources. These resources include any of an organism's basic needs such as food, living space, water, and oxygen. If the availability of these resources changes significantly, a change in population growth may result. There are two distinct patterns of population growth: exponential growth and logistic growth.

Exponential Growth

Almost any species that lives in ideal conditions of available resources, space, and other factors will rapidly increase in population size. This type of growth, called exponential growth, occurs when a population size increases dramatically over a relatively short amount of time.

As shown in Figure 6, a graph of exponential growth looks like a J-shaped curve. Exponential growth may occur when a species moves into a previously uninhabited area. A real-world example of exponential growth in a population occurred in 1859, when an Australian landowner brought 24 rabbits into the country for sport hunting and released them into the wild. With no predators, enough space, and plentiful resources, the rabbit population grew exponentially and spread across the country. After many unsuccessful tries to control the population, Australian officials estimate today's population to be between 100 and 200 million rabbits.

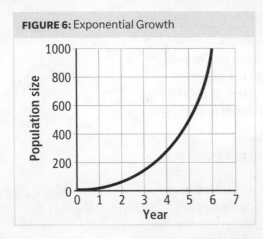

FIGURE 6: Exponential Growth

PREDICT What conditions may occur when a population is in exponential growth? Select all correct answers.

☐ **a.** birth rate is greater than death rate

☐ **b.** birth rate is less than death rate

☐ **c.** immigration rate is greater than emigration rate

☐ **d.** immigration rate is less than emigration rate

Logistic Growth

When a population is growing exponentially, resources are plentiful and there are no factors to interfere with survivability. However, most populations face limited resources and thus show a logistic growth pattern. During logistic growth, a population begins with a period of slow growth followed by a period of exponential growth before leveling off to a stable size. A graph of logistic growth takes the form of an S-shaped curve, as shown in Figure 7. During the initial growth period, resources are abundant, and the population is able to grow at a fast rate. Over time, resources are reduced, and growth starts to slow. As resources become even more limited, the population levels off at a size the environment can support.

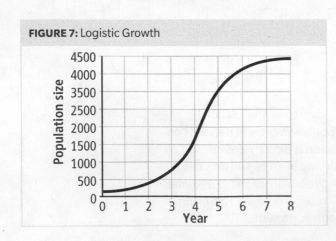

FIGURE 7: Logistic Growth

ANALYZE According to the Logistic Growth graph, in what year did the limited availability of resources cause the population to begin to stabilize?

○ **a.** year 1

○ **b.** year 3

○ **c.** year 5

○ **d.** year 7

Evidence Notebook When the sea otter population began to increase again, the populations of many other species began to change.

1. Which factors should scientists measure to learn how each population changed over time?
2. How would scientists know if populations were increasing or decreasing over time?
3. How might the increase in sea otters change the growth patterns of other species?

Factors That Limit Population Growth

Carrying Capacity

The carrying capacity of an environment is the maximum population size of a species that a particular environment can normally and consistently support in terms of resources. As shown in Figure 8, once a population hits this limit, certain factors keep it from continued growth. These factors include availability of resources such as food, water, and space, as well as competition among individuals. When a population exceeds its carrying capacity, the population reduces in size until it once again is at a level that can be supported by the environment. Then, once the conditions allow, the population can rebound and eventually stabilize. Sometimes the population exceeds the carrying capacity to the point at which the environment is degraded and the population cannot recover. This results in a crash in the population.

Carrying capacity can change at any time. For example, sudden flooding could reduce the availability of food or shelter in an ecosystem. This change would lower the environment's carrying capacity. As a result, the environment would support fewer individuals. When conditions improve, the carrying capacity would increase.

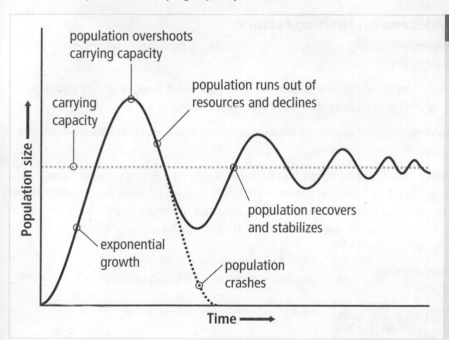

Carrying Capacity

FIGURE 8: An environment's carrying capacity limits the growth of a population.

EXPLAIN Why does the population size of a species rise and fall around the carrying capacity, rather than immediately stop growing and flatten out once the carrying capacity is reached?

_____

_____

_____

_____

Limiting Factors

Many factors can affect the carrying capacity of an environment for a population of organisms. The factor that has the greatest effect in keeping down the size of a population is called a limiting factor. There are two categories of limiting factors—density-dependent and density-independent.

Density-Dependent Limiting Factors

Density–dependent factors are factors that are affected by the number of individuals in an area. The larger the population, the greater the effect. Density–dependent limiting factors include the following:

Competition Both plants and animals compete among themselves for needed resources. As a population becomes more dense, the resources are used up, limiting how large the population can grow.

Predation The relationship between predator and prey in an environment is ongoing and always changing. The number of available prey can limit predator populations, and the prey population can be limited by being caught.

Parasitism and disease Parasites are a type of organism that live off their hosts, weakening and even sometimes killing them. Parasites and disease spread more quickly through crowded, dense populations.

Density-Independent Limiting Factors

Density–independent factors are factors that can impact a population regardless of its density. These factors include things such as:

Weather Any weather-related event such as a drought, flood, frost, or severe storm can wipe out a population or destroy their sources of food, water, or shelter.

Natural disasters Volcanic eruptions, earthquakes, tsunamis, and fires usually result in a sudden decrease in population size.

Human activity Habitats, and sometimes entire ecosystems, are degraded or even completely destroyed by human activities such as forest clearing, draining of wetlands for land development, and habitat fragmentation by roads and fences. Populations can be directly affected by human activities such as hunting or fishing.

FIGURE 9: Forest fires kill living organisms, destroy habitat, and force animal populations to flee.

EXPLAIN Why is fire considered a density–independent limiting factor?

_____

_____

_____

_____

_____

_____

_____

_____

Moose–Wolf Interactions on Isle Royale

For over 50 years, the wolf and moose populations on Isle Royale in Lake Superior served as a classic example of how predator-prey interactions limit population growth. As shown in Figure 10, changes in population size occur in an offset manner. In other words, it takes some time for an increase or decrease in one population to affect the other. Over time, the populations rise and fall in a pattern.

Density-Dependent Limiting Factors

FIGURE 10: Predator–Prey Interactions on Isle Royale

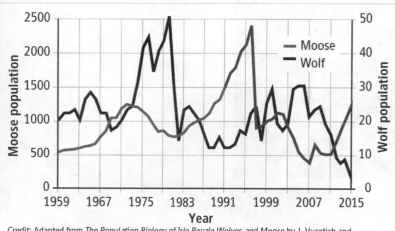

Credit: Adapted from *The Population Biology of Isle Royale Wolves and Moose* by J. Vucetich and R. Peterson. Copyright ©2015 by J. Vucetich and R. Peterson. Adapted and reproduced by permission of John Vucetich and Rolf Peterson.

ANALYZE Use the graph in Figure 10 to answer the following questions.

1. Based on this graph, what is the most likely explanation for the increase in the moose population between 1989 and 1995?

_____

_____

_____

2. In 2016, the wolf population on Isle Royale declined to only two individuals. How will the lack of wolves affect the moose population? Will the moose population grow exponentially? Use past evidence from the graph to support your answers.

_____

_____

_____

_____

 Evidence Notebook What are some density-dependent limiting factors and density-independent limiting factors that may influence the sea otter population as it tries to recover?

Hands-On Activity

Modeling Carrying Capacity

FIGURE 11: Blue heron

In this activity, your group will represent heron families that must catch fish to survive. In each generation, you will calculate the number of surviving individuals based on the amount of food collected. You will then graph the heron population over time to analyze the factors that affected your population.

MAKE A CLAIM

How do changes in environmental factors affect the predation habits of the blue heron?

_____

_____

_____

_____

MATERIALS

For each group
- tray or paper, 21 × 27 cm²
- uncooked beans (50)

For each student
- paper cup

SAFETY INFORMATION

- Immediately pick up any dropped items on the floor so they do not become a slip/fall hazard.

CARRY OUT THE INVESTIGATION

1. Form groups of four students. Assign one member to make a data table to record data for the group.

2. Put 50 "food units" (beans) on the tray.

3. For the first generation, you must collect two food units to survive. Taking turns, collect two food units at a time.

4. Record the number of surviving individuals in your data table. The number of surviving individuals for the first generation should be four.

5. Put all the food units back in the tray.

6. In the next generation, everybody in the group will have one offspring. To survive, you must collect two food units for yourself and two food units for each offspring.

7. Select a different group member to go first this time. Take turns collecting food, two units at a time, until everybody has enough food for themselves and their offspring. Record the number of surviving individuals for this generation (the second generation).

8. Repeat Steps 5–7 eight more times, recording the number of surviving individuals at each generation. The number of offspring that survive each generation depends on the amount of food that is gathered. For example, if your family consists of you and four offspring, but you only collect six food units, two of your offspring will die.

9. In the eleventh generation, runoff with large nutrient amounts causes an algae bloom in the lake. When the algae die and decomposition occurs, the oxygen level in the lake becomes very low, causing fish to die. Put 30 food units in the tray instead of 50.

10. Repeat Steps 6 and 7 and record the number of surviving individuals.

11. In the twelfth generation, the food stock starts to recover. Put 40 food units in the tray.

12. Repeat Steps 6 and 7 and record the number of surviving individuals.

13. In the thirteenth generation, the food stock has fully recovered. Put 50 food units in the tray.

14. Repeat Steps 6 and 7 and record the number of surviving individuals.

15. In the fourteenth generation, predators are abundant. Each person loses two offspring to predators.

16. Repeat Steps 6 and 7 five more times and record the number of surviving individuals.

ANALYZE

1. Graph your data in your Evidence Notebook or on a separate sheet of graph paper. Include a title and appropriate labels. What patterns do you see in your data, if any?

2. How was the amount of food caught by a heron related to changes in biotic and abiotic factors?

_____

_____

3. What limiting factors affect the carrying capacity in this model?

_____

_____

4. How might abundant amounts of food allow herons to reproduce more often?

_____

_____

5. How might the populations of amphibians and small reptiles be affected if the fish population in the lake remained low for an extended period of time?

_____

_____

_____

| LIMITING FACTORS FOR ALGAE | CONTROLLING EXPONENTIAL GROWTH | CAREER: BIOGEOGRAPHER | Go online to choose one of these other paths. |

Lesson Self-Check

CAN YOU EXPLAIN IT?

FIGURE 12: The sea otter population that lives in the coastal waters of California relies on populations of kelp and other organisms that live in their ecosystem.

Sea otters that live off the coast of California are an important species in the area. They prey on sea urchins, which eat kelp. The kelp forests provide shelter, food, and oxygen for a very large number of organisms. In the early 1900s, the sea otter population in the Pacific Ocean dramatically decreased due to overhunting by humans. In fact, the sea otters almost completely died off. As a result, the sea urchin and kelp populations were significantly impacted. Recovery efforts, including legal actions to protect the sea otters, have helped the populations to rebound. Scientists continue to monitor sea otter populations, which continue to rise and fall and are nowhere near what they once were.

 Evidence Notebook Refer to your notes in your Evidence Notebook to explain what factors contribute to past and present changes in California's sea otter population.

1. Make a claim about how changes in the sea otter population affect other organisms that share the same ecosystem.
2. Use what you know about population changes, carrying capacity, and limiting factors as evidence to support your claim.
3. What factors might be preventing the sea otter population from increasing to its historical levels? Explain your answer.

CHECKPOINTS

Check Your Understanding

1. Which of these abiotic factors would contribute to a clumped dispersion pattern in an ecosystem? Select all correct answers.

   ☐ **a.** unlimited water

   ☐ **b.** limited water

   ☐ **c.** high temperatures

   ☐ **d.** moderate temperatures

   ☐ **e.** ample rainfall

   ☐ **f.** limited rainfall

2. An antelope population has a negative population growth rate. Which of the following conditions must also be true for the population growth rate to be negative?

   ○ **a.** births + deaths < immigrations + emigrations

   ○ **b.** births + deaths > immigrations + emigrations

   ○ **c.** births + immigrations < deaths + emigrations

   ○ **d.** births + immigrations > deaths + emigrations

3. A population of yellow warblers, a type of songbird, experiences a period of exponential growth. Which of these factors would be a density-dependent limiting factor that could decrease the carrying capacity of the ecosystem for this population of songbirds?

   ○ **a.** a competing species moves into the forest

   ○ **b.** a period of lower than normal rainfall

   ○ **c.** a developer fills in a wetland to build an office park

   ○ **d.** high winds knock down a quarter of the trees

4. A massive flood displaces a population of deer from their habitat. The flood is an example of

   ○ **a.** a density-dependent limiting factor.

   ○ **b.** carrying capacity.

   ○ **c.** a density-independent limiting factor.

   ○ **d.** survivorship.

5. A group of rodents is introduced on a remote island due to a shipwreck. Eventually, the population of rodents reaches the island's carrying capacity. At this point, the birth and death rates are

   ○ **a.** relatively equal.

   ○ **b.** crashing.

   ○ **c.** increasing.

6. A herd of zebras has 9 males and 62 females. During a one-year period, 22 foals that are born survive and 25 adults die. Six females join the herd. Three males and 11 females leave the herd. Has the herd reached its carrying capacity for this ecosystem? How do you know?

   ○ **a.** The herd has reached its carrying capacity because the growth rate is negative.

   ○ **b.** The herd has reached its carrying capacity because the growth rate is positive.

   ○ **c.** The herd has not reached its carrying capacity because the growth rate is negative.

   ○ **d.** The herd has not reached its carrying capacity because the growth rate is positive.

7. Draw a graph of logistic growth. Label the point at which the resources for the population cannot support exponential growth.

CHECKPOINTS (continued)

8. Describe three advantages an individual organism might have by living in a population with a clumped dispersal pattern.

_____
_____
_____
_____
_____
_____

9. Why might exponential growth occur only for a short period when a new species is introduced to a resource–filled environment?

_____
_____
_____
_____
_____
_____

10. How might a population crash be related to resource availability in the environment or the carrying capacity of the ecosystem?

_____
_____
_____
_____
_____
_____

MAKE YOUR OWN STUDY GUIDE

In your Evidence Notebook, design a study guide that supports the main idea from this lesson:

Populations grow in predictable patterns and are limited by resource availability.

Remember to include the following information in your study guide:
- Use examples that model main ideas.
- Record explanations for the phenomena you investigated.
- Use evidence to support your explanations. Your support can include drawings, data, graphs, laboratory conclusions, and other evidence recorded throughout the lesson.

Consider how ecological factors such as resource availability limit population growth.

Changes in Ecosystems

A small plant grows in a crack in a sheet of bare volcanic rock.

CAN YOU EXPLAIN IT?

Few forces on Earth are as powerful or as destructive as a volcanic eruption. Hot, molten rock erupts through an opening in Earth's crust and flows over the surface as lava. This lava destroys almost everything in its path and eventually cools into thick rock. Shortly after an eruption, it may appear that this rocky, desolate landscape will never again contain life. However, gradually—often over many decades—this seemingly lifeless region can transform into a thriving, vital, and diverse ecosystem.

PREDICT How do you think an ecosystem can reestablish in an area after a disturbance such as a volcano?

_____

_____

_____

_____

_____

 Evidence Notebook As you explore this lesson, gather evidence to explain how ecosystems maintain stability or change over time.

Disturbances in Ecosystems

An ecosystem is a complex web of relationships and interactions among organisms in their environment. In general, an ecosystem can remain relatively constant over a long time under stable conditions. However, a change in one or more of the biotic or abiotic factors can disrupt the ecosystem and cause change. A change brought about by a physical, chemical, or biological agent that impacts population size or community structure is called a disturbance. Disturbances can occur over short or long time frames. The type and size of the disturbance can affect how the ecosystem changes. For example, a tsunami rapidly disrupts a coastal ecosystem by flooding habitats and saturating soil with salt.

FIGURE 1: A tsunami causes devastating flooding.

INFER How might the carrying capacity of a coastal ecosystem change as the result of a tsunami? Explain using one or more examples.

_____

_____

_____

_____

Natural Disturbances

Natural disturbances refer to the damage or destruction to ecosystems caused by nature. Tornadoes, earthquakes, volcanoes, and lightning-caused forest fires are all examples of natural disturbances. These disturbances may affect only a very small area. For example, a tornado causes a natural disturbance along a relatively narrow path where it touches down. However, a forest fire or flood can cause natural disturbances that cover many square miles.

Analyzing the Effects of Drought

One example of a natural disturbance is a drought, a period of very low precipitation. During drought cycles, water levels decrease, the land becomes drier, and the risk of wildfires increases. Scientists can track drought patterns by studying data from tree rings. Scientists know that the relative width of a ring in a tree trunk is a good indicator of the amount of rainfall the tree received in a given year. As shown in Figure 2a, trees produce wider rings in rainy years and narrower rings in dry years. By analyzing data from tree rings, scientists discovered that the three-year period between 2012 and 2014 produced the worst drought conditions in California in at least 1200 years.

Satellite images are an important tool scientists use to study how conditions and landscapes change over time. Increasing temperatures have resulted in limited snowfall in the Sierra Nevada mountains. Using satellite images, the snow coverage on the Sierra Nevada mountains in a wet year (Figure 2b) can be compared to that of a drought year (Figure 2c). The mountains had visibly less snow in 2015 than they did in 2010. To confirm their hypothesis, scientists again analyzed data from tree rings. They found that the amount of snow in 2015 was the lowest it had been in 500 years.

FIGURE 2: Scientists can study the effects of drought using tree-ring data and satellite images.

rainy season

drought

scar from forest fire

a Sample tree ring

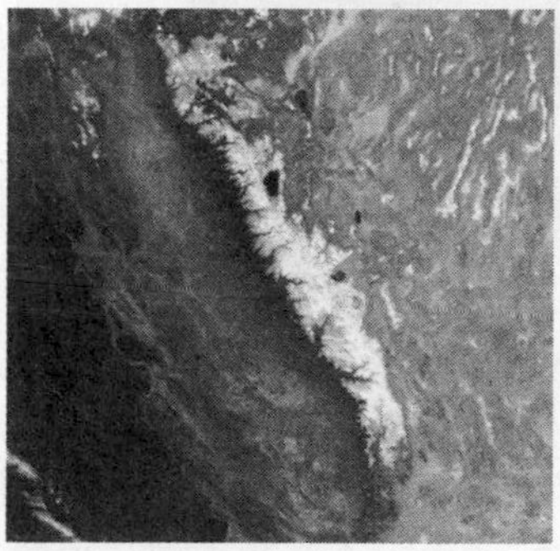

b Snow coverage in the Sierra Nevada mountains (2010)

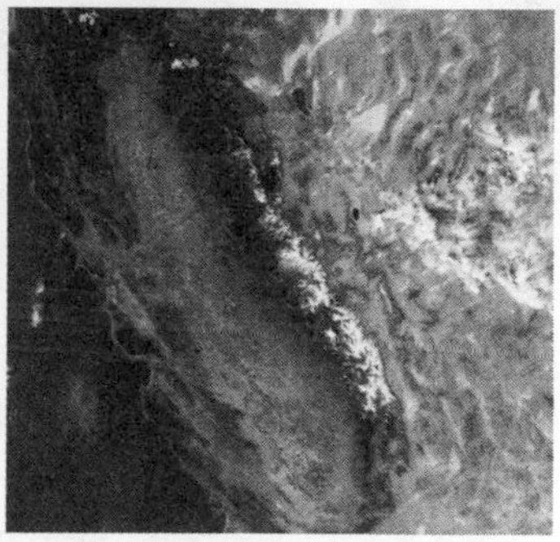

c Snow coverage in the Sierra Nevada mountains (2015)

EXPLAIN Melted snow from the Sierra Nevada mountains and other mountain ranges is an important water source for much of California. Using evidence, explain why a lack of snow in the mountains could make drought cycles worse over time.

_____

_____

_____

ANALYZE How could scientists use data from tree rings to learn more about ecosystems in the past? Use evidence from the tree ring in Figure 2a to support your answer.

_____

_____

_____

Human-Caused Disturbances

People live in the environment, and many of our actions affect ecosystems. Human-caused disturbances include human settlements, agriculture, air and water pollution, clear-cutting forests, and mining. Like natural disturbances, human-caused disturbances can affect both small and large areas. They destroy habitats, wipe out populations of organisms, and contribute to a loss of biodiversity. However, some disturbances are unique to humans because the changes are more or less permanent. For example, roads and highways can permanently fragment an ecosystem, changing the way populations of species interact with their habitat and altering the way abiotic factors cycle through an ecosystem.

FIGURE 3: Clear-cutting a forest means removing all the trees.

Analyzing the Effects of Urbanization

As the human population grows, the amount of land used for human development increases. One phenomenon currently being studied by ecologists is urbanization. Urbanization refers to the process by which human developments, such as cities and towns, are established and develop as more people begin living in central areas. In general, as urbanization increases, biodiversity in that area decreases.

Habitat fragmentation refers to a situation where a large continuous habitat is broken up into many smaller habitats. As cities expand, habitat fragmentation worsens, and biodiversity decreases.

Scale, Proportion, and Quantity

EXPLAIN Make a claim about the affect urbanization has on biodiversity. Does urbanization always decrease biodiversity? Use evidence to support your claim and explain your reasoning. Address the following questions in your answer:

• What are the main factors that lead to biodiversity loss in urban areas?
• How is the size of a habitat related to its biodiversity and its stability?
• Can an ecosystem in an urban area ever return to its previous state?

_____

_____

_____

_____

_____

ANALYZE How does urbanization affect your life and the area in which you live?

_____

_____

_____

_____

Ecosystem Stability

Urbanization and other human activities can cause large changes to an ecosystem that can cause the ecosystem to become unstable. All ecosystems are in a constant state of change. Temperature and other environmental conditions fluctuate over time, and species can be introduced to the ecosystem. A stable ecosystem can bounce back from these normal disruptions, maintain the proportions and diversity of its species, and sustain the natural processes that cycle nutrients to support the growth and development of organisms. However, when a disruption causes a large change within a stable ecosystem, the ecosystem can destabilize, which could threaten the long-term viability of the ecosystem.

FIGURE 4: This old-growth forest has been stable for many years.

ANALYZE Old-growth forests have remained undisturbed for hundreds of years or more. From what you see in the photo above, what are some characteristics of a stable ecosystem?

_____

_____

Ecosystem Resilience

Ecologists define ecosystem resilience as the ability of an ecosystem to recover after it has undergone a disturbance. This means that even though the structure of the ecosystem is affected in some way, the ecosystem can recover quickly and return to functioning as it did before the disturbance. For example, a grassland that has regular fires is considered resilient because the grasses quickly regrow and the animals return very soon after a fire ends.

The resilience of an ecosystem is determined in part by its level of biodiversity. A complex ecosystem with many populations of species that perform the same function, such as plants, is more resilient than one that has a limited number of species that perform each function. Consider two forests, one a single-species stand of mature pine trees and the other a multispecies stand of old and young conifers. If both stands are impacted by identical severe wind events, the stand of mature pines will be more severely affected by breakage and uprooting than the mixed stand. The mixed stand, with its variety of wood characteristics and ages, will have more trees left after the wind event. It will recover and continue to function as a forest much more quickly than the single-species stand of pines.

Biodiversity improves the resilience of an ecosystem, but only to a point. Genetic diversity in each species in an ecosystem is also important. Genetic diversity refers to the amount of genetic variability within a species. Genetic variation allows for different traits to be present in a species. Human activities that alter biodiversity or increase the rate of change, such as using pesticides and antibiotics, fishing, and destroying rain forests, reduce genetic diversity. A reduction in genetic diversity decreases the chance that populations can adapt to abiotic disturbances in an ecosystem.

Explore Online ▶

Hands-On Lab

Simulating Fire in a Forest Ecosystem Develop or use an existing simulation to examine how fire affects forest species. How might prescribed burns be used to manage the biodiversity in a forest, including threatened or endangered species?

Evidence Notebook What similarities would you expect to find in highly resilient ecosystems?

Ecosystem Resistance

Even the most resistant ecosystem can be stressed beyond its ability to recover. Between 2010 and 2016, an unprecedented 102 million trees died in California forests due to a combination of extreme drought, the rise in destructive bark beetles, and warming temperatures due to climate change. Resistance is the ability of an ecosystem to resist change from a disturbance. Some ecosystems are highly resistant to change, while others have little resistance. Highly resistant ecosystems remain essentially unchanged when a disturbance occurs.

Resistance and Resilience in Ecosystems

FIGURE 5: Resistant ecosystems remain unchanged after a disturbance occurs, while a resilient ecosystem quickly rebounds.

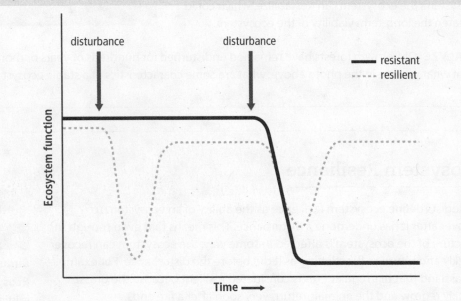

Collaborate With a partner, discuss how the concepts of resistance and resilience shown in the graph can be applied to humans, as well. For example, advancements in medical technology have allowed scientists to develop effective vaccines and antibiotics to treat and prevent diseases caused by pathogens. Does this make humans more or less resilient as a species? Does it make humans more or less resistant? Explain your reasoning to your group.

Resistant ecosystems initially show little impact caused by disturbances. However, if disturbances become too intense, ecosystem structure and function may be severely impacted. Figure 5 shows a simplified version of how ecosystem function might respond to disturbances in a resistant and a resilient ecosystem. In this example, after a second disturbance, the resistant ecosystem is not able to recover as easily. A resilient ecosystem is often Immediately impacted by even low-intensity disturbances, but it can quickly recover structurally and functionally to levels approaching the conditions before the disturbance occurred.

 Evidence Notebook Think back to the volcanic eruption on the island. Once the lava cooled, plants began to grow. Is this an example of a stable ecosystem? Use evidence from the discussion of resilient and resistant ecosystems to support your answer.

Stability and Change in Ecosystems

Species depend on resources from their habitat to survive. When the habitat changes, the survival of the species can be affected. Habitat change can occur on a small or a large scale. Pollution of a small pond can make the pond uninhabitable for some of the species that live there. Deforestation by the lumber and the construction industries has eliminated large areas of the world's forests. In the 1980s, approximately 137 269 square kilometers of the world's tropical forests were removed by deforestation each year.

The Scale of Ecosystems

True to their name, small-scale ecosystems, like ponds and tidal pools, cover a relatively small region of Earth. Fallen trees can also contain a small ecosystem within the larger forest. When a tree in a forest dies and falls to the ground, it attracts bacteria, fungi, and other decomposers. These organisms feed on the wood from the tree and release nutrients from the tree into the ecosystem. The decomposing tree is a fertile place for mosses and other small plants to grow. These plants attract herbivorous insects and small mammals. Small predators, such as snakes, frogs, and birds, use the fallen tree as shelter and feed on these insects and small animals. Fallen trees have been removed by humans for use as firewood or to decrease wildfire risk, which causes habitat loss for these organisms. Over time, it can reduce the biodiversity of the forest.

FIGURE 6: This fallen tree provides shelter and a source of nutrients for a variety of organisms.

Many forests depend on occasional wildfires to maintain ecosystem balance. These fires remove harmful invasive species and recycle nutrients throughout the ecosystem. Some plant species have even evolved to release seeds during wildfires. However, human settlement has caused wildfires to become more frequent. Humans have converted large portions of the Amazon rainforest into farmland by chopping down trees and burning the remaining shrubs. Poor control of these fires has led to the unintentional destruction of surrounding areas of the forest. These bare regions that were once shaded by thick trees become more prone to natural wildfires triggered by the intense heat of the sun.

Language Arts Connection How has the rise in human settlement in California contributed to habitat changes in small-scale ecosystems (like fallen trees) and large-scale ecosystems (like forests)?

Research the trend in human settlement in California. Make a claim to address the question. Cite specific text evidence from several scientific sources to support your claim and explain how the evidence supports your claim. Use these questions to guide your research:

- How has human settlement in California changed over time?
- What risks do humans pose to natural California ecosystems?
- Does human intervention affect small-scale ecosystems differently than large-scale ecosystems?
- What steps are being taken to reduce the damage in these ecosystems?

Primary Succession

The area surrounding the Kilauea volcano on the island of Hawaii is a prime example of what happens when an ecosystem undergoes a devastating disturbance. What was once a lush tropical ecosystem is now covered in bare volcanic rock. Over time, this new volcanic rock will undergo a series of changes. Ecological succession is the sequence of biotic changes that creates a community in a previously uninhabited area or restores a damaged community. Two types of ecological succession occur: primary and secondary. Primary succession is the establishment and development of an ecosystem in an area that was previously uninhabited, usually a bare rock surface.

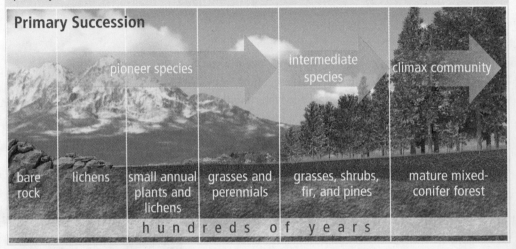

FIGURE 7: Volcanic eruptions, retreating glaciers, and landslides all begin the process of primary succession.

APPLY Place the following steps of primary succession into the correct order.

_____ **a.** Pioneer species, such as lichen and moss spores, are blown in by wind. As they grow, they break up the rock further. When they die, their remains mix with the rock pieces to form a thin layer of soil.

_____ **b** Different tree species take root in the shade and eventually replace the original trees, which need direct sunlight to thrive.

_____ **c.** Bare rock is exposed. Wind, rain, and ice begin to break down the surface of the rock, forming cracks and breaking the rock into smaller pieces.

_____ **d.** As the soil continues to increase in depth and gain nutrients, small trees take root, and different animals move into the area. These trees provide shade.

_____ **e.** Over time, seeds are blown into the area or are dropped by birds. Small flowers and hardy shrubs grow from these seeds. These new plants provide habitat for small animals, break up the rock further with their roots, and add material to the soil when they die.

The burning of fossil fuels and other human activities are contributing to a rise in average global temperatures. In Alaska and other cold regions, these rising temperatures are leading to melting glaciers, a phenomenon known as glacial retreat. In Kenai Fjords National Park in Alaska, retreating glaciers have exposed rock, giving scientists an up-close view of primary succession at work. The most recently exposed rock is still bare; however, rocks that have been exposed longer are covered in moss and lichens. In regions that have been uncovered for longer periods of time, small plants and shrubs are growing. In areas that have been exposed for decades, cottonwood trees grow. Cottonwoods are shade-intolerant trees that grow rapidly. In regions that have been exposed for at least 100–200 years, a climax community with a wide variety of trees and plants grow.

ANALYZE How do human societies influence natural processes such as primary succession?

_____

_____

_____

_____

_____

_____

_____

_____

Explore Online ▶

Hands-On Lab

Using GPS in Ecological Surveys Explore how technology can improve ecological sampling and examine how natural and human disturbances might affect an ecosystem.

 Scale, Proportion, and Quantity

Scale of Time and Ecosystems

The rounded domes, high peaks, and canyons in the Sierra Nevada region are the result of millions of years of geological processes. The mountains contain granite rock that formed from magma over 100 million years ago. Around 10 million years ago, this granite was pushed upward, forming the Sierra Nevada mountain range. Since its formation, these mountains have experienced four periods of glacial activity that covered the granite peaks with thick layers of ice. Over the last century, increasing temperatures have accelerated the melting of these glaciers, exposing the granite rock. Today, signs of life have returned to the exposed areas.

FIGURE 8: Glacial retreat in the Sierra Nevada mountains.

 Evidence Notebook How can a model help to show the scale of change that occurred in the Sierra Nevada region over time? In your answer, discuss how the model can explain changes that cannot be seen with the naked eye.

Secondary Succession

Secondary succession is the reestablishment of an ecosystem in an area where the soil was left intact, such as after a fire or flood. Because soil is already present in the ecosystem, secondary succession reaches the climax community stage more rapidly than primary succession. The plants, seeds, and other organisms that remain after the disturbance occurs begin the process of regrowth.

FIGURE 9: Secondary Succession

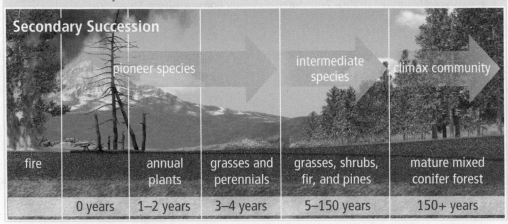

fire	annual plants	grasses and perennials	grasses, shrubs, fir, and pines	mature mixed conifer forest
0 years	1–2 years	3–4 years	5–150 years	150+ years

As with primary succession, biodiversity of the ecosystem typically increases as secondary succession progresses. One reason for increased biodiversity is the return of animals as the plant population grows. In addition, animals bring in seeds from plants in other ecosystems on their fur and in their waste, which will establish new plant populations if conditions are favorable for growth.

FIGURE 10: Secondary succession resulting from a forest fire

a Immediately after a forest fire, there is very little plant growth.

b After two years, pioneer species like grasses and annual plants return.

 Evidence Notebook Make a model that shows the difference between primary and secondary succession. Make sure your model explains how long each step takes and why.

FIGURE 11: The amount of species richness in an ecosystem is related to its stage of succession.

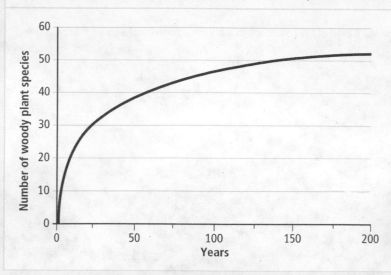

The graph shows how the number of woody plant species—which includes trees, shrubs, and long-stemmed vines—changes over time in an example ecosystem. Refer to the graph to answer the following questions.

INFER When does species richness increase at the fastest rate? Why is this possible?

_____

_____

_____

_____

ANALYZE Why does the species richness not continue to increase over time? Explain.

_____

_____

_____

Succession is an ongoing process. Even after the climax community is reestablished, changes continue to occur. Small disturbances, such as a tree falling, restart the process. For this reason, an ecosystem is generally never really permanently established—the processes of succession are always causing changes in an ecosystem.

 Evidence Notebook How does ecological succession affect biodiversity? Use evidence gathered from this lesson to support your claims.

Language Arts

FIGURE 12: A specially designed air tanker drops a load of fire retardant to slow the progress of a California wildfire.

Should Forest Fires Be Suppressed?

Forest fires can cause considerable damage to forest ecosystems; therefore, wildland firefighters work hard to contain and put out forest fires. They use heavy equipment, such as bulldozers, to stop the spread of wildfires. Sometimes airplanes and helicopters carrying water or fire retardant are also used to put out the fires.

Fire is a natural part of many ecosystems. It cycles nutrients back into the soil from plants. In some forests, shrubs growing underneath the trees are removed by naturally occurring fires. In most cases, these fires leave the trees and other organisms living in the ecosystem unharmed. With increased efforts to prevent and stop forest fires, shrubs and other understory species grow thick. When a fire does occur, it burns extremely hot and catches the trees on fire. This can have a catastrophic impact on the forest as a whole.

After major forest fires in the late 1800s, early conservationists became concerned about the effect of wildfire on future timber supplies. In 1905, they convinced the U.S. government to establish the U.S. Forest Service. This agency developed fire-protection practices in an effort to conserve what came to be known as national forests.

Just five years later, a series of fires burned 3 million acres over a three-state region. The "Big Blowup," as it was called, changed national thinking about fire management. State and Federal forest officials decided the best way to protect the national forests was to completely suppress any and all wildfires. To that end, policies were enacted that were designed to stop fires completely when possible and put out any fire that did occur as rapidly as possible.

At the time, conservationists and foresters did not understand fire's ecological importance to a forest ecosystem. Their concern focused on the damaged timber, an economically important resource. As a result, they banned the use of fire to clear underbrush and improve soil. They also constructed roads, watchtowers, and ranger stations to make it easier to detect and reach any forest fire quickly.

In the 1930s, a firefighter corps was established that could be sent anywhere a forest fire occurred. As technology advanced, airplanes and helicopters were added to the ground equipment to drop firefighters and fire-suppression chemicals wherever they were needed. Today, the National Interagency Fire Center (NIFC) coordinates and supports the deployment, training, and certification of firefighters, equipment, and support staff nationwide.

Through continued research, scientists found that fire can actually be helpful to some ecosystems, and Forest Service officials began to realize that fire suppression created a buildup of shrubs and other understory, or fuel that made fires much more hazardous when they did break out. This led to a change in policy that allowed for prescribed burns to manage fuel loads in certain forests and other wildlands, based on the ecological needs of the area.

How do officials decide where and when a wildfire should be fought instead of being allowed to burn? Ecosystem characteristics play a major role in these decisions. For example, stands of Rocky Mountain lodgepole pines need regular exposure to fires severe and intense enough to wipe out the stand and allow a new one to grow in its place. Other plants depend on fire as part of their reproductive strategies. For example, the cones from sequoia trees need fire to open and release their seeds. Fire also exposes bare soil, where the seeds can take root, and opens the forest canopy, allowing light to reach the seedlings, which helps them grow. On the other hand, wildfires in zones near human populations require active suppression to protect life and property. As human development takes over what were once wild spaces, the potential for widespread catastrophe increases.

Climate affects fire-management policy as well. Naturally occurring events, such as the yearly Santa Ana winds that blow along coastal Southern California and northern Baja California, contribute to the outbreak and spread of wildfires. Lightning strikes, heat waves, and droughts also increase the occurrence of wildfires. Climate change is beginning to increase the severity of weather phenomena that contribute to wildfires. These fire events increase the amount of stored carbon released into the atmosphere. All of these factors require officials to be flexible in their policy decisions.

Last of all, cost figures into the development of fire-management policies. Fighting wildfires is expensive in terms of hours worked, transportation, and equipment costs. Wildfires also cause economic damage to communities and endanger lives. Officials must weigh these factors when determining whether to practice fire-suppression policies.

FIGURE 13: Forest fires can cause significant economic damage to cities and towns in their path.

Language Arts Connection Some policymakers think that natural wildfires should be allowed to burn or that prescribed burns should be used as a forestry management tool. Others argue that the risk of letting fires burn or starting prescribed burns poses a hazard to forests and people.

Select a position on whether or not to allow prescribed burns. Research to learn about the pros and cons of prescribed burns. Gather information and write a one-page position paper. Your paper should discuss your viewpoint and cite evidence from your research to support your claims.

After completing your research and writing your position paper, you will take part in a classroom debate. In the debate, you will have an opportunity to state and defend your position using the information you gathered in your research. Be sure to listen to the students who agree with your position and those who disagree as you make your own arguments.

After the debate, did you change your mind based on any new information presented in the debate? Explain your answer. In your opinion, what were the strongest arguments that your opponents had to support their position?

| CASE STUDY: MOUNT ST. HELENS | SUCCESSION IN ECOSYSTEMS | USING GPS IN ECOLOGICAL SURVEYS | Go online to choose one of these other paths. |

Lesson Self-Check

CAN YOU EXPLAIN IT?

FIGURE 14: A lone small plant begins the process of colonizing a field of lava.

Volcanic eruptions play an important role in the formation of new ecosystems, but the resulting lava flows leave behind a hard rock surface that cannot support life. Nevertheless, living things will gradually begin to grow and thrive on this rock surface as it undergoes chemical and physical weathering. Over time, the bare rock will no longer be visible as it becomes covered in soil and plant life.

The Hawaiian Islands began to form more than 70 million years ago following volcanic eruptions in the middle of the Pacific Ocean. As time passed, the process of succession created unique tropical ecosystems. Succession from bare rock to highly diverse vegetation takes a great deal of time. When new eruptions occur, the process of succession begins again, and eventually a stable ecosystem returns.

 Evidence Notebook Refer to your notes in your Evidence Notebook to explain whether or not an ecosystem would return to its previous state after a major disturbance.

1. Make a claim about the process of succession. What is the role of pioneer species and other organisms?
2. Do you think this ecosystem will return to its previous state? What types of evidence would you need to support your claim?
3. How do you think scientists study the effects of disturbances such as a volcanic eruption? How do they apply their research results to make predictions about future disturbances to ecosystems?

CHECKPOINTS

Check Your Understanding

1. After an extensive forest fire, an affected region of the forest shows signs of ecological succession. Place the steps of succession in the correct order.

   _____ **a.** The community of diverse organisms approaches a relatively steady state, and a climax community is established.

   _____ **b.** Larger herbivores and carnivores become more prevalent as taller trees enter the region. These taller trees shade out some of the shorter plants.

   _____ **c.** Diversity of plant life begins as short grasses enter the region. Insects and other small animals begin to diversify in the region.

   _____ **d.** Shrubs and small conifer trees start to grow in the region.

   _____ **e.** Fireweed seeds sprouts in the existing soil. With no competition with other plants, these plants grow quickly and produce many seeds.

2. Which of the following are factors in determining the stability of a community? Select all correct answers.

   ☐ **a.** the process by which it recovers after a disturbance

   ☐ **b.** the ability to function during a disturbance

   ☐ **c.** whether a disturbance is natural or human-made

   ☐ **d.** the rate of recovery after a disturbance

   ☐ **e.** multiple populations of predators

3. Which of these are pioneer species for primary succession? Select all correct answers.

   ☐ **a.** moss

   ☐ **b.** grass

   ☐ **c.** shrubs

   ☐ **d.** lichen

4. Scientists monitored a coral reef for several decades. As the temperature steadily increased, the coral was able to maintain consistent populations of organisms. However, when the temperature increased to its peak point, the number of species in the ecosystem drastically declined. Even after the temperature stabilized, the ecosystem showed few signs of recovery. Which statement best describes this ecosystem?

   ○ **a.** The ecosystem was resistant but not resilient.

   ○ **b.** The ecosystem was resilient but not resistant.

   ○ **c.** The ecosystem was both resilient and resistant.

   ○ **d.** The ecosystem was neither resilient nor resistant.

5. Which of these best describes a climax community that results from succession?

   ○ **a.** a forest of hardwood trees

   ○ **b.** a mixture of pine trees and oak trees

   ○ **c.** trees that are all mature

   ○ **d.** depends on the biome

6. Select the correct terms to complete the statement about ecosystem disturbance.

   If an ecosystem is resilient | resistant, it is generally stable unless drastically changed by a disturbance. When a disturbance causes a change, the ecosystem quickly recovers when it is resilient | resistant.

7. If you look closely at an image of a clear-cut forest, you can see that clear-cutting does more than just remove trees from an ecosystem. What other effects will clear-cutting have on this ecosystem? Select all correct answers.

   ☐ **a.** Runoff will affect the stream ecosystem.

   ☐ **b.** Erosion will remove nutrient-rich topsoil.

   ☐ **c.** Nutrients continue to cycle into the soil.

   ☐ **d.** Some animal populations will move away.

CHECKPOINTS (continued)

8. Ecosystem A and Ecosystem B have the same eight species, but Ecosystem A has a more even distribution of species than Ecosystem B. Which ecosystem is more diverse? Explain your reasoning.

_____

_____

_____

9. Ecological succession after a disturbance usually takes hundreds of years in the Pacific Northwest. However, succession after the Mount St. Helens eruption in 1980 has progressed much more rapidly because some plants and animals were in protected areas when the hot ash and pumice fell. What conclusion can you draw about the pace of succession from this example?

_____

_____

_____

_____

10. Discuss why foresters might choose to clear-cut a forest rather than use another method to get wood for human needs. What are the pros and cons of clear-cutting?

_____

_____

_____

_____

_____

MAKE YOUR OWN STUDY GUIDE

 In your Evidence Notebook, design a study guide that supports the main ideas from this lesson:

Within an ecosystem, organisms interact with each other and with their environment.

The stability of the ecosystem is determined by its biodiversity, resilience, and resistance to change.

Remember to include the following information to your study guide:

- Use examples that model main ideas.
- Record explanations for the phenomena you investigated.
- Use evidence to support your explanations. Your support can include drawings, data, graphs, laboratory conclusions, and other evidence recorded throughout the lesson.

Consider how water pollution affects the ecosystem in a small pond as well as the larger forest that surrounds the pond.

Environmental Engineering

A burrowing owl perches near a geothermal power plant.

CAN YOU SOLVE IT?

Burrowing owls are found in different parts of the United States, including California. As their name suggests, they live in underground tunnels, often in burrows that were dug by other animals such as ground squirrels. There are significant threats to the owls' habitat in the Imperial Valley region due to increased human activity, such as land development for agriculture, mining, and geothermal power production purposes.

PREDICT Power plants were built in the Imperial Valley as a means to harness power from geothermal resources. However, the construction of these power plants has led to the loss of habitat for burrowing owls. How can engineers and scientists solve the problem of habitat loss for burrowing owls and other wildlife?

_____

_____

_____

_____

_____

 Evidence Notebook As you explore this lesson, gather evidence about how engineering is used to solve environmental problems.

Technology and Living Systems

When you think about the term *technology*, you probably think of a cell phone or a tablet computer. Technology is the application of scientific knowledge for practical purposes. Technology does include advanced machines, such as computers and robotic equipment. It also includes simpler items you may not have thought of, such as sunglasses, scissors, and pencils.

Collaborate Discuss the following questions with a partner:

1. Name at least three technologies that you used as you prepared for school today.

_____

_____

_____

2. Choose an item and describe the materials that were used to make it.

_____

_____

_____

3. How does the construction or function of this item impact the environment?

_____

_____

_____

Technology and the Environment

Over the course of human history, advancements in science and technology arose through the process of engineering. The concepts of engineering can be applied to living things and the environment. Through engineering and scientific advancements, technology has been developed for environmental applications. Earth's ever-growing human population has led to an increase in human-caused environmental issues, and the demand for engineering solutions is high.

Analyzing Benefits, Risks, and Costs

Every new technology has benefits, risks, and costs. Engineers must analyze these tradeoffs when considering how new or improved technologies can impact living systems. Decisions must be made about whether a new technology's benefits outweigh the associated costs and risks. Benefits are the favorable effects of the solution, while the costs and risks are the unfavorable effects. For example, consider the design of a new wind turbine. A benefit could include a decreased dependence on fossil fuels. A risk could be the impact on bird and bat populations in the region. A cost might include the amount of time necessary to construct a new turbine. Engineers must balance the benefits, risks, and costs of each design solution.

ANALYZE Sort the phrases below as benefits or risks of using satellite tracking devices to monitor wildlife. Place each phrase in the appropriate column.

| highly accurate data collection | frequent collection of data | high initial cost | require capture of wildlife |

Benefits	Risks

Advancement in technology lets scientists who study the environment, such as ecologists and biologists, collect data about populations within different ecosystems across the globe.

Devices such as Global Positioning System (GPS) satellite collars, tags, and other remote trackers provide information about an animal through the use of satellite signals from or to a device carried by the animal. For example, the GPS tag on the California condor shown in Figure 1 collects and transmits data about the bird's flight patterns. Scientists can use this information to build a detailed picture of the tracked animal's habitat use and requirements. This information, in turn, can be used by stakeholders such as land developers, local governments, or conservation groups when they need to make decisions that affect the ecosystems in which these animals live.

FIGURE 1: There are risks and benefits to using technology such as tracking devices.

Scientists and engineers continue to modify technology to meet the needs and demands of society. This often involves increasing the benefits of technology while reducing the costs and risks. Since the introduction of the GPS device, engineers have already increased its benefits by improving data storage and retrieval and increasing the longevity of the device. They have also worked with scientists to decrease the need to directly handle the animals, which reduces risk. For example, collars can be programmed to automatically fall off the animal at a set time, rather than requiring the scientists to recapture the animal to remove it themselves. In addition, engineers may find new materials to make batteries that reduce the impact on the environment and reduce the overall cost of the device.

Research and Development

Scientists ask questions to learn more about a phenomenon, and engineers design solutions to problems related to that phenomenon. This back-and-forth between scientists and engineers is part of a process known as research and development. The studies and testing performed during this process often lead to the development and improvement of technologies.

In the case of the GPS monitoring device, scientists ask questions to learn more about the phenomena of wildlife monitoring. For example, scientists might ask, "What kind of data will help us learn the most about a wildlife population?" or "What kind of device is the least intrusive on an animal's natural behaviors?" Engineers can use this information to design a GPS device based on the requirements from wildlife biologists in the field.

Technology and Society

Technology has greatly influenced society, and society has influenced progress in technology. New technologies change our lifestyles, our environment, and our living spaces. Likewise, as social trends, economic forces, and cultural values change, including values about the environment, new technologies emerge that support these changes.

Consider the advances in computing equipment. Prior to the 1970s, computers were massive machines that took up huge amounts of space in corporate and government offices. These giant computers required huge teams of engineers to keep them running. Today, society relies on computer technology for countless tasks, including collecting data in the field. Advancements in computing equipment has solved many problems.

FIGURE 2: Environmental scientists rely on advancements in computing equipment to do their job.

a When computers were first introduced, the equipment filled up an entire room.

b Modern computers, such as laptop and tablet computers, can be taken into the field to record data.

EXPLAIN How have advancements in computer technology most directly influenced our knowledge of wildlife and the ecosystems in which they live?

_____

_____

_____

_____

All new technologies come with risks and costs to people and society, no matter how great the benefits. For example, wildlife monitoring technology lets scientists collect almost unlimited data, which helps them better understand how to preserve and protect the natural function of ecosystems. However, there are some people who find the process intrusive or unnecessary. Educating the public about current monitoring programs and their importance can help reduce this conflict.

In some cases, by solving one problem, advances in technology can cause new social and economic problems. Advancements in GPS tracking have made remote downloading of data possible, thereby reducing human handling of animals. But the upfront cost for GPS tracking systems is high. The environment also is a concern when it comes to new technologies. Wildlife monitoring technology requires batteries that may harm the environment if they are disposed of incorrectly.

Clean Drinking Water

FIGURE 3: Societies around the world gain access to clean drinking water through new engineering designs, such as improved devices to transport water and new wells.

Many people in the world do not have access to clean drinking water. They must walk miles to and from wells to bring water to their homes. Once they carry the water home, it often needs to be filtered to avoid water-borne diseases, such as cholera. In response, environmental engineers developed better water filtration systems in wells, making the water cleaner and safer. Engineers also developed devices to make it easier to transport water over long distances, as shown on the left in Figure 3. Getting water can be a full day's work and is often the job of women and young girls. By decreasing the time spent obtaining water, women and girls have more time to devote to other tasks, such as furthering their education.

ANALYZE If you were to design a device to transport water, such as the rollers shown above, what are some societal, cultural, and environmental factors you should consider?

_____

_____

_____

_____

APPLY How does this example of technology show how science and engineering influence human society? Explain your answer.

_____

_____

_____

Evidence Notebook Wildlife monitoring technology is an important part of protecting our ecosystems and the populations that live within them. How do you think advancements in this kind of technology could help protect burrowing owl populations?

Engineering in Life Science

Engineering and scientific inquiry both involve a set of principles and a general sequence of events. Scientists use the scientific method to ask questions, make predictions, and develop an experiment or series of experiments to answer their questions. Engineers use a process similar to the scientific method to create solutions to problems.

The Engineering Design Process

The engineering design process is a method used to develop or improve technology. The process is iterative, meaning it uses repeating steps. Engineers do not always apply these steps in the same order. They may skip some steps or perform other steps more than once.

FIGURE 4: The engineering design process is a set of steps that lead to designing or improving a solution to a problem.

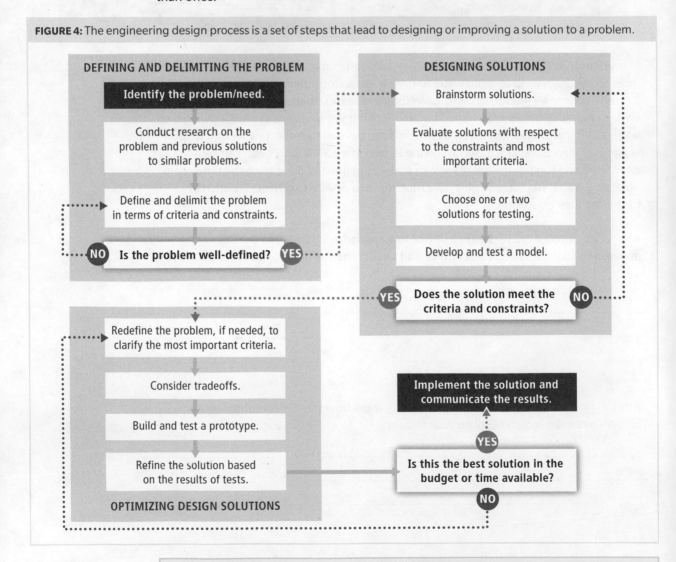

DEFINING AND DELIMITING THE PROBLEM

Identify the problem/need.

Conduct research on the problem and previous solutions to similar problems.

Define and delimit the problem in terms of criteria and constraints.

NO Is the problem well-defined? **YES**

DESIGNING SOLUTIONS

Brainstorm solutions.

Evaluate solutions with respect to the constraints and most important criteria.

Choose one or two solutions for testing.

Develop and test a model.

YES Does the solution meet the criteria and constraints? **NO**

Redefine the problem, if needed, to clarify the most important criteria.

Consider tradeoffs.

Build and test a prototype.

Refine the solution based on the results of tests.

OPTIMIZING DESIGN SOLUTIONS

Implement the solution and communicate the results.

YES

Is this the best solution in the budget or time available?

NO

 Collaborate Discuss the following questions with a partner: How is the engineering design process similar to the scientific method? How do the two processes differ?

ANALYZE How does the diagram in Figure 4 show that the engineering design process is an iterative, or repeated, process?

_____

_____

_____

_____

EVALUATE Why is it necessary for engineering processes to be iterative, instead of following a fixed sequence of steps?

- **a.** It encourages engineers to skip steps that do not seem necessary when time and budget are limited.

- **b.** It helps to ensure that the problem is well defined, criteria and constraints are met, and the best solution is chosen.

- **c.** It encourages engineers to follow the most efficient path to a solution as possible.

- **d.** It ensures that no mistakes are made in any of the three main stages of the engineering design process.

Following a well-defined set of steps ensures that engineers take a thoughtful and complete approach when designing a solution to a problem. In this process, engineers must first identify and define the problem or need. In doing so, they may need to perform research or analyze data to learn more about the problem. They must identify aspects that are desired in a final solution as well as the limits on the solution. Next, engineers will begin to design solutions. During this stage, they will evaluate several different solutions and choose only one or two options to begin testing. In the testing, or optimizing, stage, designs are tested using computer simulations and prototypes. Based on the results of these tests, the designs may be accepted or refined. The engineers may even decide to choose a different solution and start the process over.

Defining and Delimiting the Problem

The first step in the engineering design process is to define the problem. Engineers ask questions to help them understand the criteria for the design. The criteria (singular _criterion_) set a standard on which a solution can be based. Criteria identify the "wants" for the solution by identifying what the solution will do and how well it will do it. Criteria can include many different aspects of a design, but often safety, reliability, cost, and aesthetics are considered when defining the problem.

Then, engineers delimit the problem. Delimiting is the process of defining the limitations, or constraints, of the solution. Constraints are the limitations that a design or solution must stay within. Constraints can include things such as cost, weight, dimensions, available resources, time, and the environment in which the solution must function or exist. Any solution that does not meet the constraints of the design is not considered.

Engineers must balance the benefits, risks, and costs of each design solution. They may accept some risks in exchange for greater benefits. Or they may give up one benefit in favor of another to avoid a potential risk. A tradeoff is an exchange for one thing in return for another. Consider the devices used to monitor wildlife. Some less expensive devices often weigh more and have greater potential to interfere with an animal's natural behaviors than better designed, more expensive devices. The benefit of a tradeoff will depend on the problem defined by the engineer.

Influence of Science, Engineering, and Technology on Society and the Natural World

Fish Passage Improvement Program

FIGURE 5: Fish use a ladder to swim around a dam.

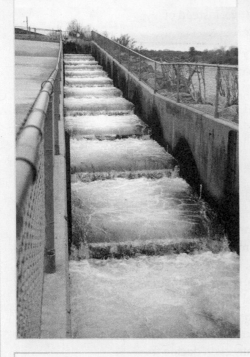

Sometimes when engineering is used to solve problems, new issues result. Consider the construction of dams. They provide water for irrigation and help prevent potentially disastrous floods. Because they form large lakes, dams also can provide places of recreation for people. But dams obstruct waterways, which prevents fish from migrating up and down rivers. One solution to this problem has been to construct fish ladders. A fish ladder is a structure that provides a passageway for fish to swim over or around an obstacle on a river. Another solution has been to completely remove dams. This has been done primarily in areas where dams were constructed for recreational purposes.

IDENTIFY What are some criteria and constraints an engineer should consider when designing a new technology to solve a problem that protects a natural resource such as fish? Select all correct answers.

☐ **a.** ability of technology to appear natural
☐ **b.** cost to design, build, and maintain technology
☐ **c.** whether or not the design matches others like it
☐ **d.** safety of technology for people who maintain it
☐ **e.** safety of technology for the natural resource using it

FIGURE 6: Engineering solutions can have a variety of tradeoffs.

Solution	Fish ladders	Dam removal
Safety	Puts some stress on fish.	Requires heavy equipment; can add pollutants to the water.
Environmental Impact	Appears to have minimal impact, but ladders are in place indefinitely.	Short-term impact is strong, but the ecosystem eventually returns to its natural state.
Aesthetics	Ladders are noticeable and do not blend into the environment.	Causes a lot of disruption to the area, but this is temporary. Over time, ecosystem returns to its natural state.
Cost	Costs are typically in the millions of dollars.	Costs are typically in the millions of dollars.

ANALYZE Consider the tradeoffs between each of the solutions listed in the table in Figure 6. What is one question an environmental engineer might ask to help a community pick the technology that best addresses their needs and wants?

____

____

Engineers prioritize criteria by deciding which ones are most important for a given problem. They make tradeoffs between them to begin brainstorming solutions to the problem. Engineers may even redefine the problem to clarify the most important criteria before beginning to design and test a solution. Remember, if a proposed solution does not meet the constraints of the problem, it will not move forward in the engineering design process.

Designing Solutions

After engineers have identified the criteria and constraints for solving a problem, the next step is to brainstorm design ideas for a solution. Usually, engineers and other specialists work in teams when brainstorming. The group leader presents the problem to be solved and encourages all ideas to be suggested, even if they seem outrageous.

Once the team has brainstormed several ideas, they may use a decision matrix, or Pugh chart, to evaluate each solution against the criteria of the problem. In a decision matrix, each criterion is given a number, or weight, based on how important that criterion is. The more important the criteria, the greater the weight assigned to it. Then, each design is rated based on how well it meets those criteria. The scores for each design are multiplied by their respective weights, and the products are totaled so engineers can determine how well the design meets the criteria. They may choose to take the design with the highest score to the next phase, or they may choose to brainstorm new ideas if no designs meet the requirements.

FIGURE 7: An example decision matrix for three water filtration system designs, weighted on a scale from 0 to 5.

Design Criteria	Weight	Design 1	Design 2	Design 3
Safety	5	4	1	5
Reliability	4	2	3	4
Cost	2	1	2	1
Aesthetics	1	1	1	0
Total Points		31	22	43

The table in Figure 7 shows how a decision matrix can be filled out for three engineering designs. In this example, each column represents a different design for a new water filtration system people can use in their homes. Safety is weighted at a 5, meaning it is extremely important. Aesthetics are weighted very low, meaning they are not as important. To determine how to weight each design, engineers may choose to make a model or run computer simulations to see how each design would work in a typical situation.

EXPLAIN Select the correct terms to complete the statement about decision matrices.

Engineers will often use a decision matrix to evaluate different models | solutions and how well they meet the cost | criteria of a design. Each criterion is given a weighted number, and more important criteria are given higher | lower weights. If no designs are acceptable based on the score of the matrix, engineers will brainstorm new designs, making this a(n) fixed | iterative process.

An environmental engineer may use a decision matrix to evaluate a technology, such as a new design for a wildlife tracker. These trackers are worn by animals in the wild and range from simple leg bands to sophisticated remote tracking such as the GPS tracking system discussed earlier in the lesson. The criteria for a new tracking technology device would likely include safety to the animal and reliability of data, but also may include environmental impacts and ease of use.

FIGURE 8: Different types of technology are used to track wildlife.

a Colorful leg bands may be used to track smaller animals such as birds.

b Radio collars are one way to remotely track larger animals.

c A tiny microchip tracks the movement of honey bees.

d Satellite tracking is a fairly advanced method of wildlife monitoring.

DRAW In the space provided, make a decision matrix for the four wildlife-tracking methods shown in Figure 8. What criteria do you think are important for choosing which method to use? How would you weight them?

Once a number of solutions are proposed, they are evaluated against the criteria and constraints set out for the desired solution. Solutions that do not meet the constraints must be redesigned if they are to be considered. In general, one or two ideas that best meet the criteria and all constraints are selected, and these ideas enter the optimization phase of the design process.

Optimizing Design Solutions

When one or two solutions have been chosen, engineers may build a prototype of the technology to further test the capabilities and effectiveness of the design. A prototype is the first build of a design and may not be built to scale or with the final materials.

Because the results from prototype testing may require design changes, prototypes are often built with cheaper materials. This way, engineers can run many tests and build many versions of their designs. As the design is refined and finalized, engineers may begin to use the final materials to ensure the solution will work as expected.

 Engineering

Optimizing Wind Turbine Design

One of the biggest challenges faced by engineers is the need to think creatively and to seriously consider new designs. While not traditional, these new designs may be what are required to solve a problem or improve an existing product. Machines that harvested the wind were once relatively short, inefficient structures. As shown below, wind turbine design and the materials used to make them have changed over the years. The present day design is streamlined to harness wind much more efficiently.

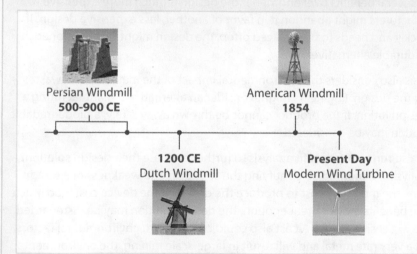

Persian Windmill
500-900 CE

American Windmill
1854

1200 CE
Dutch Windmill

Present Day
Modern Wind Turbine

FIGURE 9: Wind turbine design has improved over time.

 Collaborate Discuss the following questions with a partner: How have windmill and wind turbine designs changed over time? What factors may have influenced scientists and engineers to continually revise the design of these structures?

Testing is an important part of the engineering design process, as it lets engineers get feedback on the design. Data collected from tests will tell engineers if their design is working as expected. The data also may show design problems that were not seen in early stages of the process. Engineers will review these issues and determine which ones need to be fixed. Considering tradeoffs is an important part of the optimization process. Issues that do not seriously impact important criteria or constraints may not be corrected if the tradeoff is undesirable, such as increasing the cost of the design. However, if the issue is important enough, engineers may need to change the design or brainstorm new designs to address the concern.

FIGURE 10: Engineers may return to a design or a prototype during the optimization process.

ANALYZE What types of information can be gained from building a prototype that is not an exact model of the final product?

_____

_____

_____

_____

_____

_____

_____

_____

_____

_____

_____

Life cycle analyses are another way to evaluate a design. A life cycle analysis attempts to evaluate the real cost of a new technology or design. It takes into account the materials and energy used to manufacture, transport, use, and dispose of a product. Perhaps one design has several benefits over another. If the design is much more expensive to produce, manufacturers might abandon it in favor of another, less expensive design. If it wears out quickly and needs to be replaced often, the design might be abandoned in favor of a more durable alternative.

Life cycle analysis also considers the environmental impact of the materials and wastes from producing the design. Engineers might consider an alternative if manufacturing a design produces pollution. If the product cannot be thrown away safely, a biodegradable or recyclable option may be considered.

Engineers may also run a cost-benefit analysis to further evaluate their design solution. A cost-benefit analysis is a method of identifying the strengths and weakness of a design. The cost could be the monetary cost to produce the design. If the device costs too much to make and the benefits are not great enough, the design solution may be disregarded in favor of a less expensive design. A cost also could be related to environmental factors. If a design uses a very rare metal and will result in large-scale mining, the environmental impact may outweigh the benefits, especially if a different material could be used.

When a final design has been chosen and fully tested, engineers will communicate their results. This may just involve presenting the final solution to the client to begin production. If the design is new or groundbreaking or has important implications within their field or to society at large, the engineering team may publish a journal article detailing the design to the scientific community.

 Evidence Notebook How do you think the engineering design process has been used to solve the problem faced by the burrowing owl population and the loss of their natural burrowing sites?

Engineering Activity

Building a Habitat For Burrowing Owls

Burrowing owls nest underground, typically in burrows already excavated by mammals such as ground squirrels. Like many species, burrowing owl populations are declining as habitat is lost due to human development. In the case of the burrowing owl, this includes the loss of mammals that build the burrows the owls inhabit. One solution to this problem is to build human-made burrows in areas that burrowing owls would inhabit.

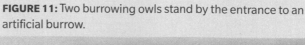

FIGURE 11: Two burrowing owls stand by the entrance to an artificial burrow.

DESIGN CHALLENGE Consider how the project criteria might differ for building human-made owl burrows in an urban area as opposed to a nature preserve.

DEFINE THE PROBLEM

What problem does your design need to solve?

_____

_____

_____

What criteria and constraints are associated with designing potential habitat space for burrowing owls?

_____

_____

_____

_____

DESIGN SOLUTIONS

Based on the identified criteria for burrowing owl habitat space, select a potential urban site for artificial owl burrows. Demonstrate how project criteria for burrow installations at this site can ensure the needs of both owls and humans are met.

_____

_____

_____

_____

_____

Draw a scale model of your solution, including the owl burrow and a potential urban site to install the burrow.

CONSTRUCT AN EXPLANATION

Why is it important to preserve burrowing owl populations? Explain your answer in terms of stability and change in ecosystems.

_____

_____

_____

_____

_____

COMMUNICATE

In your Evidence Notebook, make a decision matrix that could be used to evaluate potential burrow solutions in an urban environment. Explain why specific criteria were chosen.

_____

_____

_____

_____

_____

_____

_____

 Evidence Notebook How might criteria and constraints for an artificial burrow built in a nature preserve compare to one built in an urban area?

Careers in Engineering

Environmental Engineer

Environmental engineering focuses on the relationship between humans and the environment to develop solutions to environmental problems. Environmental engineers may use concepts from biology, chemistry, physics, mathematics, or soil science. They solve problems related to solid waste and wastewater management, water supply and quality, air quality, and public health. For example, an environmental engineer might design desalination equipment to help provide more drinking water in an area.

Desalination removes salt from seawater or brackish groundwater. The water produced can be treated to meet water quality standards for human consumption. Desalination plants require a source of water to treat and a place to dispose of the salts and other contaminants removed during this process. Desalination plants help increase the water supply of an area. Water shortages due to drought led to the construction of a desalination plant in Carlsbad, California.

The first task in designing a desalination plant is to define the problem and identify the social, technical, and environmental criteria and constraints that could limit potential solutions. The engineer would research background information on the project site, past and current water supply issues, the government permits required for this type of project, potential community involvement, and much more.

Once the problem is defined, an environmental engineer may be asked to design potential solutions. Solutions often build off of existing technology. An engineer might study existing desalination plants and make adjustments based on the unique limitations for the project.

Next, modeling may be used to determine if the system will work as expected and what, if any, environmental or societal impacts can be expected from the solution. An engineer could make a mathematical model of the desalination process to determine the efficiency of the design.

FIGURE 12: This desalination plant in Carlsbad, California was built to provide fresh water to the San Diego region.

Finally, an environmental engineer would communicate the solution through presentations and reports. For a desalination project, this could include an explanation of why the proposed solution will be effective and suitable for solving the water supply problem.

Language Arts Connection You are part of a team of 3-4 environmental engineers consulting on a project. The client needs a reliable source of water in a remote desert location without surface water. Groundwater salinity is triple that of seawater. Electricity is not readily available. The client is considering whether desalination is a possible option or if another method for accessing water is recommended. Present your solution as an email to the client.

- Identify the criteria and constraints.
- Include the steps you will take to solve the problem.
- Identify one or more solutions.
- Explain how your best proposed solution could be tested.

Biology in Your Community Interview and write a short article about an environmental engineer whose work has benefited your community.

USING DRONES TO MONITOR WILDLIFE   DEVELOPING A LAND-USE MODEL   BIOMIMICRY   Go online to choose one of these other paths.

Lesson Self-Check

CAN YOU SOLVE IT?

FIGURE 13: A geothermal power plant dominates this burrowing owl's habitat.

Unlike many owls that nest in trees, burrowing owls nest underground in burrows. Due to human activity, there are significant threats to the owls' burrowing sites. Often, solutions to one problem lead to new problems. The construction of geothermal power plants has helped solve problems related to the need for renewable energy sources. However, land development comes at the cost of habitat for burrowing owls and also affects other components of an ecosystem. Artificial burrows are one possible solution, but the criteria and constraints of a design must be considered in order to properly evaluate each situation and design.

 Evidence Notebook Refer to your notes in your Evidence Notebook to explain how engineering can help to design solutions to habitat loss for burrowing owls and other wildlife.

1. Make a claim about the role of the engineering design process in solving the problem of habitat loss for burrowing owls and other wildlife.
2. How might scientists and engineers work together to develop a solution? Identify the processes that they might use to coordinate a solution.
3. How would you define and delimit the problem of habitat loss? What steps would need to be taken to optimize the solution? Explain your answers.

CHECKPOINTS

Check Your Understanding

1. Computers are one of the most influential technologies of our time. They have revolutionized the way in which we live. What are some of the negative impacts of computer technology on society and the environment? Select all correct answers.

   ☐ **a.** Computers save people time on some activities, which frees up time for other activities.

   ☐ **b.** Computers are made with metals and are difficult to dispose of.

   ☐ **c.** People often focus more on computers and less on direct social interactions.

   ☐ **d.** More electricity is consumed when computers are left on around the clock.

2. Imagine that you are an engineer who designed a prototype for a client. After testing the prototype, you discover it does not address the client's needs. What might be the best possible next step in the process?

   ○ **a.** evaluate the prototype against the criteria and constraints

   ○ **b.** define and delimit the problem

   ○ **c.** build a new prototype

   ○ **d.** refine the solution

3. An environmental engineer is developing a portable aerial device designed to monitor wildlife in remote areas. She made a list of criteria and constraints for the new device. Which of these should be classified as criteria? Select all correct answers.

   ☐ **a.** the device must be developed within 12 months

   ☐ **b.** one person can fly it without assistance

   ☐ **c.** the device uses a rechargeable battery

   ☐ **d.** the body of the device is made of waterproof material

   ☐ **e.** the budget is $10 000

   ☐ **f.** the device produces minimal sound to reduce impact on wildlife

4. Which of the following technologies would likely involve an environmental engineer to design and build? Select all correct answers.

   ☐ **a.** tablet computer

   ☐ **b.** wastewater treatment plant

   ☐ **c.** surgical robot

   ☐ **d.** compostable product packaging

   ☐ **e.** fish passageway

5. You and a partner have brainstormed a design for a desalination device to help remove salt from ocean water. What should be the next step in the design process?

   ○ **a.** test on a sample of ocean water

   ○ **b.** build a working model

   ○ **c.** revise the design

   ○ **d.** evaluate the plans for the design

6. Select the correct term or phrase to complete the statement about the engineering design process.

   Suppose engineers defined a problem, brainstormed a solution, and built and tested a model. They discover that the model does not meet the most important criteria. According to the engineering design process, they move forward | repeat previous steps in order to optimize the solution. This is an example of how the process is iterative | fixed.

7. How might building a prototype of a negative-emissions machine help engineers get funding for moving the design up to a larger scale?

   ○ **a.** The prototype demonstrates the proof of concept and proves that the technology is functional.

   ○ **b.** The prototype functions exactly like the end product.

   ○ **c.** Building a prototype allows engineers and investors to evaluate the design against set criteria and constraints.

   ○ **d.** The prototype shows potential investors that the design has been optimized.

CHECKPOINTS (continued)

8. One of the ways in which society impacts technology is through government regulations. Describe how government regulations have both positive and negative impacts on technology.

_____

_____

_____

_____

_____

_____

9. A client engages an engineering firm to develop environmentally-friendly packaging for the sports drink that they manufacture. What questions would you ask to define and delimit the problem?

_____

_____

_____

_____

10. Why is it useful for engineers to use a decision matrix when designing solutions to environmental problems?

_____

_____

_____

_____

MAKE YOUR OWN STUDY GUIDE

In your Evidence Notebook, design a study guide that supports the main ideas from this lesson:

Engineering is the application of the engineering design process to develop and modify solutions for the needs of society.

Environmental engineers design and evaluate solutions to environmental problems.

Remember to include the following information in your study guide:

- Use examples that model main ideas.
- Record explanations for the phenomena you investigated.
- Use evidence to support your explanations. Your support can include drawings, data, graphs, laboratory conclusions, and other evidence recorded throughout the lesson.

Consider how new technologies for solving problems can impact society and the environment in expected and unexpected ways.

Technology Connection

Computer Systems Computers and people have more in common than you might think. Computers are nonliving systems that use internal hardware and software to store, manipulate, and analyze data. People are living systems that use smaller internal systems, such as organs and cells, to survive and reproduce. Just as computers and people have internal similarities, they can also both be part of larger systems, such as networks and ecosystems.

> Make a diagram of a computer system that describes its smaller internal systems, its linkages to external larger systems, and how information and energy flow through the system. Make a list of questions you would ask about the relationship between people and computers based on the diagram you develop.

FIGURE 1: Computers, such as this laptop, are made up of many components.

Art Connection

Conservation Photography Conservation photographers use pictures to highlight environmental problems. These images are used to invoke a response in the public and to advocate for conservation outcomes. When devastating changes in ecosystems are documented in visual ways, it can strengthen public understanding and involvement in critical environmental issues.

> Prepare a multimedia presentation that features a California photographer who specializes in conservation photography. Include selections of his or her work and explanations of the conservation issues highlighted.

FIGURE 2: This photograph could be used to highlight the impact of climate change on polar bear populations.

Social Studies Connection

Environmental History Human impacts on the environment during the last several centuries have been extensively studied and documented. It is clear that humans have changed and destabilized many modern ecosystems. There is also evidence that ancient peoples, such as the Maya, the Nazca, and the Rapa Nui, changed the landscape in dramatic ways. These changes may not have been on the scale of modern human impacts, but the changes may have resulted in destabilization of ecosystems that led to the downfall of these civilizations.

> Write a report that evaluates the claims and evidence that environmental changes led to the disappearance of a particular ancient society. Include an illustration of the potential impacts the society had on the environment with a model, graph, map, or other method.

FIGURE 3: These Mayan ruins in Cozumel, Mexico show the impact their buildings had on the environment.

A BOOK EXPLAINING
COMPLEX IDEAS USING
ONLY THE 1,000 MOST
COMMON WORDS

RANDALL MUNROE
XKCD.COM

HOW FORESTS COME BACK

How trees and flowers and animals fill in the land again after a big change

After a disturbance in an ecosystem, biotic changes regenerate the damaged community or create a new community in a previously uninhabited area. Take a look at this process of change and rebirth.

THE STORY OF CHANGING FORESTS

FORESTS ARE ALWAYS CHANGING.

OH, HI! YOU MUST BE NEW HERE.

THERE ARE BIG CHANGES, LIKE WHEN A WHOLE FOREST IS BURNED OR CUT DOWN...

WE SHOULD HAVE OUR PICNIC ANOTHER DAY.

...AND SMALL CHANGES, LIKE WHEN A BIG TREE FALLS OVER AND LEAVES AN OPEN AREA IN THE FOREST.

SOME ANIMALS AND FLOWERS, AND TREES WAIT FOR THESE CHANGES, AND SPRING UP AS SOON AS THEY HAPPEN WHILE OTHERS TAKE HUNDREDS OF YEARS TO GROW.

NOW'S MY CHANCE!

WHEN WE CUT DOWN OLD FORESTS AND NEW FORESTS GROW UP IN THEIR PLACE, THE NEW FORESTS AREN'T THE SAME AS THE OLD ONES. THEY'RE MADE OF THE KINDS OF TREES THAT LIKE CHANGE.

WE LIKE TO THINK OF FORESTS AS WILD PLACES, BUT THEY'RE SHAPED BY PEOPLE AND THE CHOICES WE MAKE. WE CHANGE THE LAND, WATER, AND AIR, AND WE MOVE LIVING THINGS AROUND THE WORLD. THE THINGS WE DO HELP DECIDE WHICH KINDS OF ANIMALS CAN LIVE IN THE WORLD AROUND US, AND WHICH THINGS WE'LL FIND GROWING AFTER A FOREST FALLS DOWN.

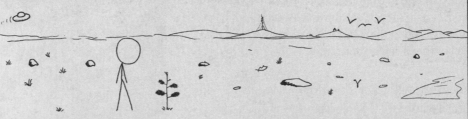

THINGS THAT HAPPEN TO FORESTS

Sometimes, big things happen to forests that clear out lots of the old trees and animals that live there. When these things happen, lots of new trees and flowers come in to fill in the space. After a while, big trees can grow back.

Here are a few of the things that can happen to forests:

FIRE

In some forests, there are fires every so often that burn lots of the plants and trees, along with dead sticks and leaves lying on the ground.

PEOPLE

People cut down forests to make room for stuff or because they want to use the wood. Most of Earth's old forests have been cut down over the years.

WIND

When there's a really big storm, wind can push over lots of trees, especially if the storm happens when the trees have leaves on them.

GETTING EATEN

Most animals that eat trees get eaten by other things. If something that eats trees moves to a new part of the world where nothing eats it, it can eat whole forests.

TREE-EATING ANIMAL

SMALL HOLES IN THE FOREST

Some forests have little animals that like to build their houses in pools. If they can't find a pool to use, they make a new one by cutting down trees and building a wall across the river.

The water covers part of the forest, and the trees that are covered with water die. When the animals move away, the wall falls apart.

When the water in the pool goes away, it leaves an open area among the trees. Over the years, this area fills with green things and becomes a forest again.

RIVER

HOUSE WALL WATER

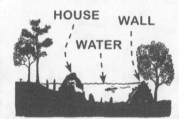

BIGGER PROBLEMS

Life doesn't just come from nowhere. When forests are cleared and grow back, some of the new trees grow from parts in the ground that are still alive. Other green things move in from the edges or are carried by the wind or birds.

But if there's a really big change, there might not be any life left in the area to grow back. Sometimes, on land out in the sea, hot fire comes out of the ground and the rocks get hot and run like water. If this happens, nothing grows back until new life is carried there from across the sea.

BOOM

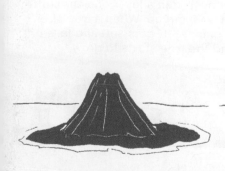

A FOREST AFTER A FIRE

WHAT STARTS FIRES?

Many forest fires are caused by people. Sometimes, people drop burning things on the ground and forget about them, or they start fires to sit around and then don't put them out.

Other fires start without help from people. Most of those are caused by flashes of power from big storms, but some are caused by hot rocks that come out of holes in the tops of mountains.

SPACE ROCKS

Big rocks falling from space can start fires, but that doesn't happen very often. As far as we know, there haven't been any of these fires since people started writing down things that happened.

FIRE STARTER
Fires aren't usually started by people who are bad at flying space boats, but it could happen!

If there are a lot of dry sticks or dead branches on the ground, fires can get big and hot. These fires can spread to the tops of trees and burn down forests.

These small fires can be good for a forest, because they burn away the leaves and sticks before too many of them pile up.

If it goes a long time without raining, all the dry stuff makes fires bigger and hotter.

Some fires burn the dead leaves and sticks on the ground but don't really bother the big trees.

TREE EGGS
These things fall off of trees. Then they open up and new trees grow out of them.

BABY TREES (INSIDE)

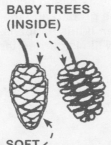

SOFT STUFF

Fires clear away the tall trees that block light from the ground. Some trees make tree eggs that stay closed until there's a fire, so they can get lots of light and grow quickly.

These tree eggs are covered in a layer of clear stuff that keeps them from opening up. When a tree egg gets hot in a fire, the clear stuff gets soft and falls off, the egg opens up, and the tree starts to grow.

TREE EGGS ON THE GROUND

TREES THAT DON'T MIND FIRE

Some trees are good at living through fires. Their strong, thick skin keeps them safe from heat, and some keep most of their branches near the top to keep their leaves away from the burning stuff on the ground.

GREEN THINGS RETURN

The first things to grow up after a fire are grasses and flowers, like the things you pull up from your garden. They're good at spreading and grow very fast.

Go online for more about *Thing Explainer*.

TREE FIGHTS

Some trees try to be the first to grow up in the clear space after a fire. If a tree grows taller than the ones around it, it can block the sun's light from the other trees and keep more light for itself.

BIRDS DROPPING TREE EGGS AS THEY FLY AROUND

HIDING TREES

Some trees and green things live through fire even if their top parts burn down. They can grow back up out of the parts left in the ground.

BIRDS THAT EAT SMALL ANIMALS

Some birds that eat small animals like to fly over open fields like this or sit in trees near the edge. When they see something running in the grass, they try to catch it.

Since these birds like areas where forests meet open areas, they're often spotted in trees by the side of big roads.

FAST TREES

In the first twenty or thirty years after the forest is cleared away, fast trees grow up. They block the sun's light from reaching the ground, which makes the grasses and small plants die off. These are young forests.

BIRDS THAT EAT OTHER BIRDS (HIDING)

Different animals like different kinds of forest. In some areas, as the trees get bigger, different kinds of birds move in. Some birds are good at flying through trees to catch other birds. Since these birds usually stay away from the edges of forests, people don't see them as often.

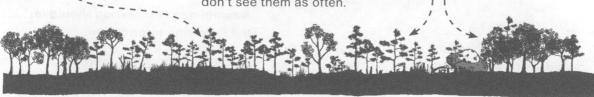

SLOW TREES

After the first trees grow up, new kinds of trees start to grow. These newer trees grow slowly, and they don't need as much sun, so they can grow up in the shadows of the faster trees.

OLD FORESTS

Slow trees grow up and take the place of the fast trees. This takes a very long time—longer than a person's life.

Forests that are many times older than the oldest humans are special. They have different kinds of trees and animals than young forests have. Many of those older forests have been cut down, and some people are trying to save the ones that are left.

Analyzing Red Squirrel Populations

The Mount Graham red squirrel (*Tamiasciurus hudsonicus grahamensis*) is an endangered red squirrel subspecies that is endemic to the Pinaleño Mountains in southeastern Arizona. Population data for this squirrel is shown in the table. Use this information and independent research to determine population trends for the red squirrel. Investigate whether the red squirrel habitat is declining and what natural or human-caused disturbances may be responsible for fluctuations in the red squirrel population. Based on your investigation, decide whether you think the Mount Graham red squirrel population is resistant or resilient to disturbance.

1. ASK A QUESTION

Develop a set of questions to help guide your research and data analysis. Focus your inquiry on population trends, how those trends relate to habitat loss, and how the causes of the habitat decline are affecting the red squirrel population.

2. CONDUCT RESEARCH

Investigate the Mount Graham red squirrel population. Use library and Internet resources to explore how this species has fared over the last half-century.

3. ANALYZE DATA

Analyze your research and the population data provided. Graph the population data in order to visualize the red squirrel population trends. Is there evidence of disturbances, ecosystem decline, or the resilience or resistance of the squirrel population?

4. CONSTRUCT AN EXPLANATION

Use your analysis to answer your questions and construct an explanation for the changes in the population of the Mount Graham red squirrel and its habitat.

5. COMMUNICATE

Present your findings about the Mount Graham red squirrel and its habitat. Be sure to include whether you think the squirrel population is resilient or resistant to disturbances. Your presentation should include images and data to support your claims.

Average Mount Graham Red Squirrel Population, 1987–2010			
Year	Average population estimates	Year	Average population estimates
1987	242	1999	530
1988	202	2000	484
1989	174	2001	270
1990	275	2002	292
1991	391	2003	293
1992	332	2004	276
1993	375	2005	289
1994	419	2006	285
1995	407	2007	305
1996	381	2008	273
1997	392	2009	259
1998	566	2010	216

Source: U.S. Fish and Wildlife Service. 2011. Draft Recovery Plan for the Mount Graham Red Squirrel (*Tamiasciurus hudsonicus grahamensis*), First Revision. U.S. Fish and Wildlife Service, Southwest Region, Albuquerque, NM. 85 pp. + Appendices A-D.

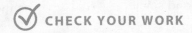 CHECK YOUR WORK

A complete presentation should include the following information:

- guiding questions that are answered in the final presentation
- a graph that shows changes in the population size of Mount Graham red squirrels over time
- an explanation of the current status of the squirrel and its habitat, as well as a discussion of disturbances that may have affected the squirrel population and whether or not the squirrel population has shown resilience or resistance to disturbances
- images and data that further support your explanation

Name _____   Date _____

SYNTHESIZE THE UNIT

In your Evidence Notebook, make a concept map, other graphic organizer, or outline using the Study Guides you made for each lesson in this unit. Be sure to use evidence to support your claims.

When synthesizing individual information, remember to follow these general steps:

- Find the central idea of each piece of information.
- Think about the relationships among the central ideas.
- Combine the ideas to come up with a new understanding.

DRIVING QUESTIONS

Look back to the Driving Questions from the opening section of this unit. In your Evidence Notebook, review and revise your previous answers to those questions. Use the evidence you gathered and other observations you made throughout the unit to support your claims.

PRACTICE AND REVIEW

1. What is the relationship between population number and carrying capacity in a stable population?
   - a. They match exactly through births, deaths, immigrations, and emigrations.
   - b. They oscillate around each other as resources and population growth rates change slightly over time.
   - c. They both increase when resources are scarce and decrease when resources are abundant.
   - d. They are inversely proportional. An increase in carrying capacity will be accompanied by a decrease in population numbers.

2. An invasive species moves into three niches that were once occupied by three different native species and outcompetes the native species, producing larger population numbers than the three native species combined. What happens to the biodiversity of the ecosystem?
   - a. It increases because the number of individuals increases.
   - b. It decreases because only native species count toward biodiversity in an area.
   - c. It remains the same because the same ecological niches are still filled.
   - d. It decreases because the number of species decreases.

3. A fire occurs in a conifer forest. Plants begin to grow shortly after the fire occurs. This ecosystem is said to be
   - a. resilient.
   - b. resistant.

4. Which statement is *not* true about systems thinking?
   - a. It can apply to living and nonliving entities.
   - b. The boundary of a system is scalable.
   - c. The interactions between components of a system are never included in systems thinking.
   - d. A system may be open, closed, or isolated.

5. A solution for a problem scores high for all criteria but violates one of the constraints. What is the relationship between the solution and the problem?
   - a. The solution will work for the problem because it does not have to satisfy every constraint.
   - b. The solution may work for the problem if there is a tradeoff between criteria and constraints.
   - c. The solution is not viable for the problem as it is currently defined and delimited.
   - d. The solution will never be successful and should be abandoned.

6. Why is the spread of disease considered a density-dependent limiting factor?

_____

_____

_____

_____

_____

7. Give an example of how technology and society interact to improve each other.

_____

_____

_____

_____

_____

_____

8. How does the scale of what you are studying affect how you might organize, or model, the system? Think about the differences in organizing a system in these two ways: biosphere/geosphere/hydrosphere/atmosphere/anthrosphere model or an individual/population/community/ecosystem model.

_____

_____

_____

_____

_____

_____

_____

UNIT PROJECT

Return to your unit project. Prepare your research and materials into a presentation to share with the class. In your final presentation, evaluate the strength of your claim, evidence, and conclusions.

Remember these tips while evaluating:

- Was your claim supported by your evidence?
- Look at the evidence you gathered from your wetland model. Does the evidence support your claim and reasoning regarding how wetlands influence the stability of populations and neighboring ecosystems?
- Consider if the evidence and reasoning are logical. Does your research contradict any evidence you have seen?

UNIT 2

Carbon in the Earth System

California's giant sequoias are perhaps the most efficient carbon sinks in the world.

FIGURE 1: Earth's atmosphere as seen from space

Earth's atmosphere is composed of 78% nitrogen, 21% oxygen, and 1% other gases. The makeup of the atmosphere is an important part of what makes life on Earth possible. Earth's early atmosphere was composed largely of carbon dioxide that would be toxic to most organisms living today. The evolution of photosynthetic green plants changed the makeup of Earth's atmosphere.

PREDICT How did photosynthesis and cellular respiration affect Earth's atmosphere?

_____

_____

_____

_____

DRIVING QUESTIONS

As you move through the unit, gather evidence to help you answer the following questions. In your Evidence Notebook, record what you already know about these topics and any questions you have about them.

1. What do plants need to survive? How do plants obtain energy?

2. How do living things store energy not needed for immediate use? How is this energy later released?

3. What is the relationship between photosynthesis and cellular respiration?

UNIT PROJECT

Go online to download the Unit Project Worksheet to help plan your project.

Modeling Earth's Atmosphere

How has Earth's atmosphere changed over time and how have these changes affected other Earth systems? Discover more about the coevolution of Earth's systems. Use models to show how the composition of gases in Earth's atmosphere changed over time as life on Earth evolved.

Language Development

Use the lessons in this unit to complete the chart and expand your understanding of the science concepts.

Definition	Example

Similar Term	Phrase

Definition	Example

Similar Term	Phrase

Definition	Example

Similar Term	Phrase

Definition	Example

Similar Term	Phrase

TERM: cellular respiration

Definition	Example

Similar Term	Phrase

TERM: aerobic

Definition	Example

Similar Term	Phrase

TERM: anaerobic

Definition	Example

Similar Term	Phrase

TERM: mitochondrion

Definition	Example

Similar Term	Phrase

Photosynthesis

Most plants harness and convert energy from the sun.

CAN YOU EXPLAIN IT?

Scientists are looking for clean energy sources to minimize the human impact on the planet. Plants are the most efficient solar power collectors in the world, operating at nearly 100% efficiency—most solar cells operate at only about 12% efficiency. As a result, researchers are interested in capturing energy from plants to produce electricity.

PREDICT Do you think it is possible to capture energy from photosynthesis for human use? How might this technology work?

_____

_____

_____

_____

A "cell" in a solar panel captures energy directly from sunlight and converts it to electricity. If the electricity is not needed immediately, it can be stored as chemical energy in a battery. When the battery is used, the chemicals react and produce electricity. This process is not very efficient and a lot of energy is lost. To improve the process of harnessing the sun's energy, scientists must first understand more about how plants capture energy.

 Evidence Notebook As you explore the lesson, gather evidence to describe the inputs and outputs of matter and the transfer and transformation of energy in photosynthesis.

Carbon in Living Things

Living and nonliving things are all made of matter. To understand the complex interactions and processes in living systems, we need to explore the composition of living things at a molecular level. All organisms depend on a variety of chemicals and chemical reactions. The study of living things relies on a basic understanding of chemistry.

Atoms, Elements, and Compounds

Every physical thing, living or not, is made of incredibly small particles called atoms. An atom is the smallest basic unit of matter. Trillions of atoms could fit in a space the size of the period at the end of this sentence. All atoms share the same basic structure.

FIGURE 1: Atoms consist of three types of particles. Protons have a positive charge, electrons have a negative charge, and neutrons have no charge.

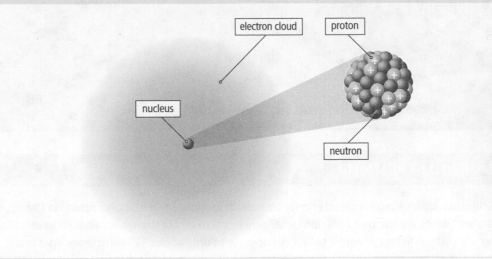

FIGURE 2: Salt forms when a sodium (Na) atom transfers one electron to a chlorine (Cl) atom, forming NaCl.

An element is a substance made up of one type of atom and cannot be broken into simpler substances by ordinary chemical means. All the atoms of a given element have a specific number of protons. Different elements have different numbers of protons. For example, all hydrogen (H) atoms have one proton, and all carbon (C) atoms have six protons.

Atoms tend to have the same number of electrons as protons, which makes them stable. Atoms that lack the same number of electrons and protons become charged and bond with other atoms to become more stable. Chemical bonds form when electrons are transferred or shared between atoms.

Compounds are substances composed of atoms of two or more different elements bonded together in specific ratios, such as table salt. Common compounds in living things include carbon dioxide (CO_2) and water (H_2O). The chemical formula of a compound shows the number of atoms present for each element. A molecule is two or more atoms bonded by shared electrons.

MODEL Identify and label the following terms on the models: *compound, element,* and *chemical formula.*

carbon dioxide

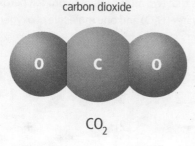

CO_2

water

H_2O

When examining the chemical formulas for compounds, look closely at the ratios of the atoms of the elements in the compound. For example, water (H_2O) has two hydrogen atoms for each oxygen atom. If the ratio of oxygen to hydrogen changes, a new compound with new properties results. Hydrogen peroxide (H_2O_2), for example, has two hydrogen atoms and two oxygen atoms. The same elements are present, but in a different ratio. As a result, this compound has a different chemical formula and different properties than water.

Chemical Reactions

Chemical reactions are important to all living things. Plant cells make compounds by linking simple sugars together. Plant and animal cells break down sugars to get usable energy. These and other chemical reactions change materials into different substances by breaking chemical bonds and forming new ones, rearranging atoms in the process.

 Collaborate With a partner, think about the last food you ate. How do you know that the chemical bonds in your food were broken and the atoms were rearranged?

To understand chemical reactions, we need to know the inputs and outputs. Reactants are the initial substances in a chemical reaction. As the reaction proceeds, the bonds of the reactants are broken and rearranged to form the products of the reaction. The products of a chemical reaction are different from the reactants. All the same atoms are still present, but their rearrangement produces substances with properties that are different from those of the starting materials.

Chemical equations model what happens in a chemical reaction. In a chemical equation, the reactants are on the left side of the equation and the products are on the right side. Chemical reactions also demonstrate the conservation of matter. This means that in chemical reactions, atoms are not created or destroyed, only rearranged. All the atoms from the reactants will still be present in the products once the reaction is complete.

FIGURE 3: This chemical reaction shows that two molecules of hydrogen peroxide (H_2O_2) break apart to form two molecules of water (H_2O) and one molecule of oxygen (O_2).

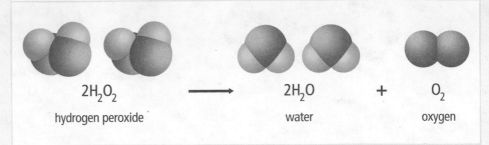

$2H_2O_2$ ⟶ $2H_2O$ + O_2

hydrogen peroxide   water   oxygen

INFER How are the atoms in hydrogen peroxide rearranged in this chemical reaction?

_____

_____

GATHER EVIDENCE What are the inputs and outputs of the reaction?

_____

_____

_____

EXPLAIN Complete the statement by selecting the correct terms.

Before the reaction, there are two | four | eight | oxygen atoms, and after the reaction, there are two | four | eight | oxygen atoms. The same is true for hydrogen atoms. So, atoms are | are not created or destroyed. This supports | refutes the claim that matter is conserved during a chemical reaction.

FIGURE 4: In this firefly, chemical reactions take place that give off energy in the form of light, which allows the insect to attract a mate.

All chemical reactions involve changes in energy. The reactants must absorb energy to break their chemical bonds. When new bonds form to make the products, energy is released. During a chemical reaction, energy is both absorbed and released. Some chemical reactions absorb more energy than they release, while other reactions release more energy than they absorb. Whether a chemical reaction absorbs or releases more energy depends on the bond energy of the reactants and products.

Properties of Carbon

Carbon atoms continually cycle through organisms, the biosphere, atmosphere, geosphere, and hydrosphere in a process called the carbon cycle. Carbon is the basis of most molecules that make up organisms and is involved in nearly all of the processes that support life. The atomic structure of carbon allows it to make covalent bonds with up to four other atoms by sharing its electrons. In addition to forming single bonds, carbon atoms can also form double, or even triple bonds. In organic molecules, carbon is most commonly bonded to the elements hydrogen, oxygen, nitrogen, and phosphorus.

FIGURE 5: Carbon-based molecules can have many different structures, including straight chains, branched chains, and rings.

Straight Chain	Branched Chain	Ring
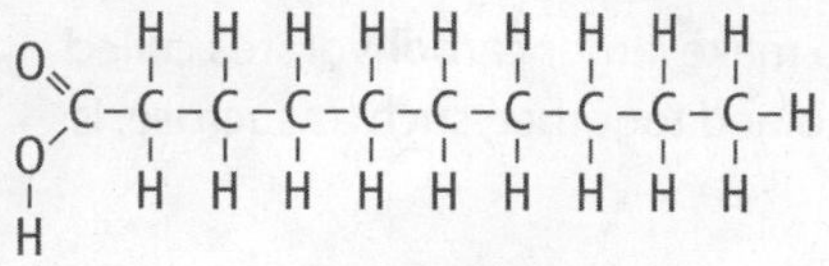	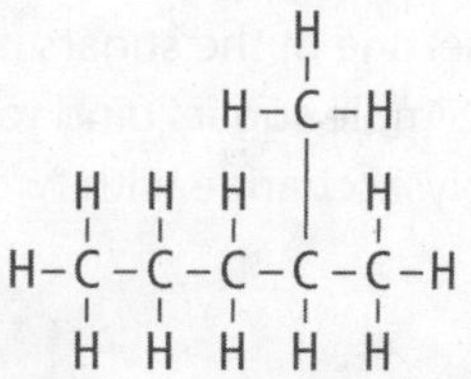	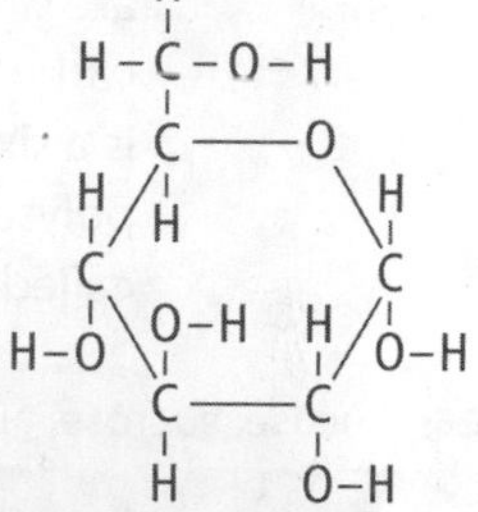
CAPRIC ACID	**ISOHEXANE**	**GLUCOSE**
Capric acid is a fatty acid found in some plant oils, as well as in the milk of some mammals. It has been shown to have antibacterial and anti-inflammatory properties.	Isohexane is a clear liquid used to make gasoline and glues, and as a solvent for extracting oils.	Glucose is a simple sugar that is a critical energy source for living organisms.

ANALYZE According to the models of carbon-based molecules, how many chemical bonds does carbon form?

_____

INFER Carbon atoms can form many different molecules with many different shapes. Why is this beneficial to living things? Select all correct answers.

☐ **a.** Carbon can bond to many different elements.

☐ **b.** Carbon is always bound to oxygen, which is essential to all living things.

☐ **c.** Carbon is a central element in most of the molecules that make up living things.

☐ **d.** Living things require a variety of different molecules to form tissues and cells.

☐ **e.** Living things require elements that can have four bonds.

Chemical reactions in the cells of living things break chemical bonds between atoms. These atoms are rearranged to make the major classes of compounds that living things need to build structures and carry out functions necessary for life. The ability of carbon to make so many different kinds of molecules allows for millions of carbon-based compounds to exist. Of those compounds, there are four main groups that comprise all living things: lipids, proteins, nucleic acids, and carbohydrates.

Lipids, such as fats and oils, are made of fatty acids containing carbon, hydrogen, and oxygen. Lipids are used for storing energy and to make up structures such as cell membranes. Proteins consist of long chains of amino acids, which are primarily formed from carbon, hydrogen, oxygen, and nitrogen. Proteins comprise many body structures, such as muscles, and carry out functions such as relaying messages and transporting molecules throughout the body. Nucleic acids are made of nucleotides, which are composed of sugars, nitrogen-containing bases, and phosphates. Nucleic acids carry genetic information important for reproduction and heredity. Carbohydrates contain carbon, hydrogen, and oxygen. They include sugars and starches, and are primarily used as sources of energy.

Carbohydrate Structure and Function

Carbohydrates are made of carbon, hydrogen, and oxygen. The most basic carbohydrates are simple sugars, or monosaccharides. Many simple sugars have either five or six carbon atoms. Glucose, one of the sugars made by plant cells during photosynthesis, is a six-carbon sugar. Simple sugars bind together to make larger carbohydrates called polysaccharides. A polysaccharide with two sugars joined together, such as sucrose, is called a disaccharide.

FIGURE 6: Glucose, sucrose, and cellulose are all carbohydrates.

Monosaccharide	Disaccharide	Polysaccharide
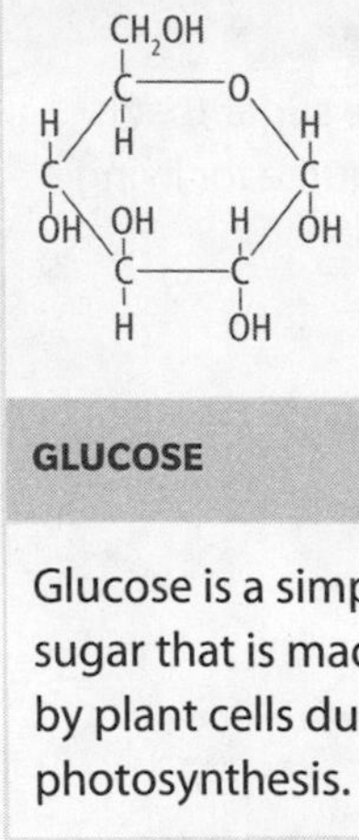	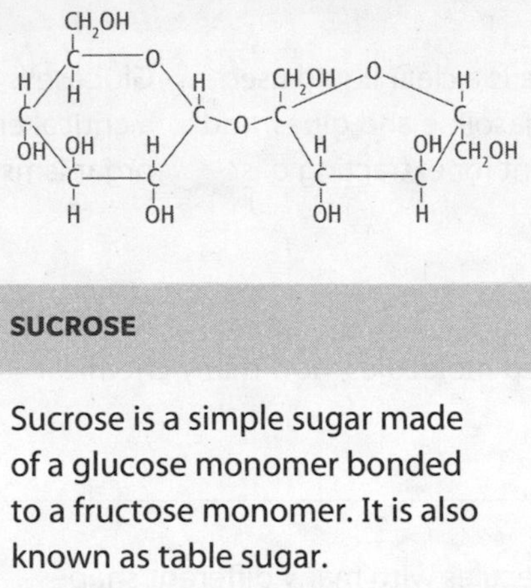	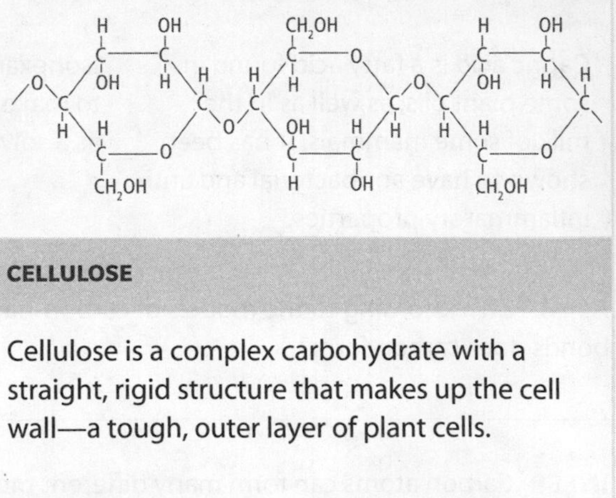
GLUCOSE	SUCROSE	CELLULOSE
Glucose is a simple sugar that is made by plant cells during photosynthesis.	Sucrose is a simple sugar made of a glucose monomer bonded to a fructose monomer. It is also known as table sugar.	Cellulose is a complex carbohydrate with a straight, rigid structure that makes up the cell wall—a tough, outer layer of plant cells.

EXPLAIN Why does it take longer for your body to break down complex carbohydrates than simple carbohydrates?

○ **a.** Complex carbohydrates have stronger bonds than simple carbohydrates, so they are harder to break.

○ **b.** Complex carbohydrates have more subunits than simple carbohydrates, so there are more bonds to break.

○ **c.** Complex carbohydrates have a higher proportion of carbon than simple carbohydrates, and carbon is difficult to break down.

○ **d.** Complex carbohydrates always have a ring structure, which is harder to break down than the structure of simple carbohydrates.

The energy contained in carbohydrate molecules can be released and used for essential cell processes. Foods such as vegetables, fruit, bread, pasta, and sweeteners contain many carbohydrate molecules that your body breaks down to release usable energy. Simple carbohydrates like glucose and sucrose can be quickly broken down and absorbed by your body. Complex carbohydrates are made up of longer chains of molecules and are broken down more slowly. Sources of complex carbohydrates include vegetables, whole grains, and potatoes. Complex carbohydrates are often rich in cellulose, or fiber, which is not broken down in your digestive system.

Chemical Energy and ATP

Where do organisms get the energy to break down food molecules and rearrange the atoms to make new molecules? The energy for practically every chemical reaction that takes place in living things comes from one molecule—ATP.

ATP, or adenosine triphosphate, is a molecule made up of subunits called adenine and ribose, as well as three phosphate groups. The bonds between the phosphate groups are high-energy bonds that store chemical energy in a form that cells can use. Although it has a carbon compound, ribose, as an anchor, the important parts of ATP are the phosphate groups.

Cells use energy from the breakdown of carbon-based molecules to make ATP. ATP then travels among cells, carrying energy in its phosphate bonds. Where energy is needed, ATP transfers one of its phosphate groups to another molecule. When the bond between the phosphate groups is broken, the energy is released. ATP becomes ADP, or adenosine diphosphate, a lower-energy molecule. The energy released can be used to power cell processes such as transporting materials, carrying out reactions, and producing new molecules.

FIGURE 7: ATP is made up of adenine, ribose, and three phosphate groups. The "tri" in triphosphate signifies that there are three phosphate groups in this molecule.

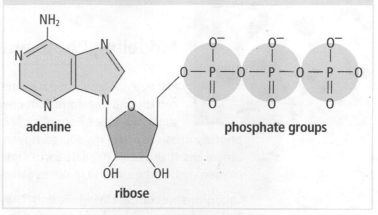

FIGURE 8: Cells use energy from the breakdown of carbon-based molecules to add a phosphate group to ADP. This forms ATP, a higher-energy molecule. When a phosphate group is removed from ATP, energy is released for cell processes.

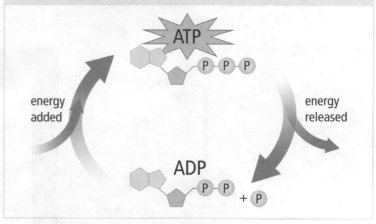

 Language Arts Connection Make an analogy to explain the role of ATP in storing energy and releasing energy for cell processes.

 Evidence Notebook Use evidence to support or refute the claim that living things break down and rearrange carbon-based molecules. What is the role of green plants?

Matter and Energy in Photosynthesis

FIGURE 9: This panda is a consumer that gets its energy and nutrients from eating leaves.

Living systems take in energy and matter and convert them to forms they can use. For example, plants are very efficient producers that capture light energy and convert it to chemical energy to carry out cell processes within the plant. The chemical energy takes the form of chemical bonds in sugar molecules. When a consumer, such as a panda, eats plant matter, it obtains this energy and other nutrients it needs for cell processes and growth through the process of digestion. Any matter that cannot be digested is excreted as waste.

Modeling Photosynthesis

Plants, algae, and some bacteria use a process called photosynthesis to capture and transform light energy from the sun and store it in high-energy sugar molecules. Both plant cells and animal cells use sugars made by photosynthesis as an energy source. However, photosynthesis is not just important to organisms. It also helps regulate Earth's environment. Photosynthesis produces the oxygen we breathe and also removes carbon dioxide from Earth's atmosphere.

Organisms are complex living systems. They live and interact in ecosystems, which are systems within the biosphere. All organisms play different roles in the cycling of matter and the transfer of energy in their ecosystem. To better understand the relationship between organisms and the environment, scientists collect many different types of data.

FIGURE 10: This setup shows a plant in a closed system. Sensors are measuring carbon dioxide and oxygen concentrations in the bottle. The gas concentrations are shown in parts per thousand (ppt).

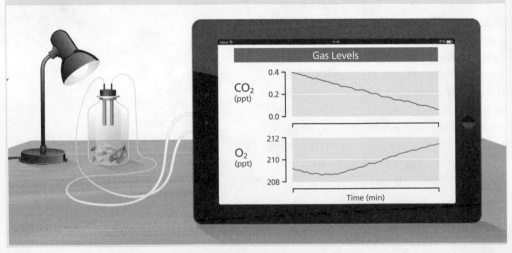

 Evidence Notebook Identify inputs and outputs for this system. How can the data help scientists understand the relationship between plants and the environment?

Photosynthesis is important to life on Earth. Nearly all organisms on Earth depend on this process. Understanding the relationship between organisms and photosynthesis is critical. Using equipment to measure the rate of photosynthesis, for example, is one way to study the impact that organisms have on the process. Using models is another way to understand photosynthesis. Scientists can use models to study the relationship between the inputs and outputs of the process.

 Energy and Matter

The process of photosynthesis can be modeled in various ways. For example, a chemical equation is one way to represent photosynthesis.

$$6CO_2 + 6H_2O \xrightarrow{\text{enzymes}} \rightarrow \xrightarrow{\text{light}} 6O_2 + C_6H_{12}O_6$$

This model shows the inputs and outputs as reactants and products. The multiple arrows indicate that the process of photosynthesis has many steps. Light and enzymes must be present for this reaction to take place, and these are often placed around the arrows. In this equation, carbon dioxide and water are reactants and oxygen and glucose are products. Plant cells use glucose to form complex carbohydrates, such as starch and cellulose, which the plant uses for growth and maintenance.

Evidence Notebook Draw a plant and label the inputs and outputs of photosynthesis. When making your model, consider how each compound enters or leaves the plant system.

Light and Photosynthesis

Light is a form of energy known as electromagnetic radiation. Electromagnetic radiation travels in waves of various lengths. Of the different wavelengths, plants absorb only visible light to use for photosynthesis. Visible light consists of different wavelengths that correspond to different colors of light that humans can see. However, plants do not absorb all of the wavelengths in the visible portion of the electromagnetic spectrum.

FIGURE 11: Visible light is a small portion of the electromagnetic spectrum.

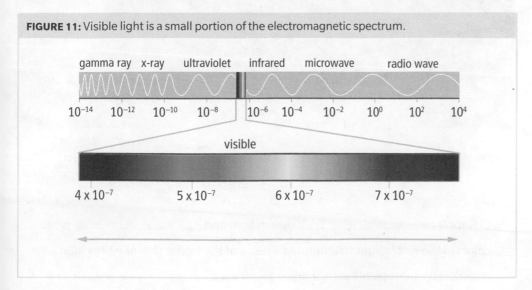

Investigating Light Sources and Photosynthesis Design an experiment to investigate the effect of different light sources on the rate of photosynthesis.

In plant cells, light absorption and photosynthesis take place inside an organelle called a chloroplast. Inside the inner membrane of the chloroplast are stacks of disc-shaped sacs called thylakoids, which contain pigment molecules called chlorophyll.

FIGURE 12: The area inside the chloroplast is the stroma. The area inside the thylakoid sac is the lumen. Photosynthesis occurs along the thylakoid membrane that separates the stroma and the lumen.

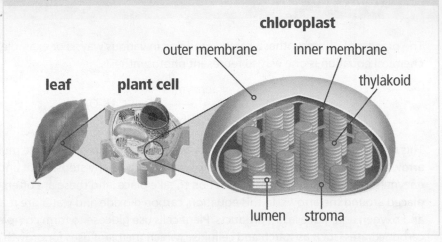

Different types of chlorophyll absorb different wavelengths of light, transforming the light energy into chemical energy through photosynthesis. The plant's pigments reflect unabsorbed wavelengths, and our eyes detect these wavelengths as the plant's color.

FIGURE 13: Chloroplasts are distributed in a plant cell. Chlorophyll is a pigment molecule in chloroplasts. Plants have two main types of chlorophyll: chlorophyll *a* and chlorophyll *b*. The type of plant pigment determines which wavelength of visible light is absorbed.

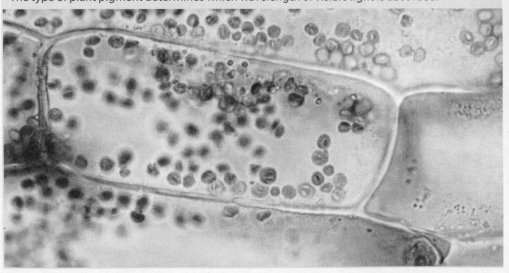

INFER Which colors of light are absorbed and which colors do most plants reflect?

absorb   reflect

Chloroplasts _____ green light and _____ other colors of the visible light spectrum. As a result of the interaction of visible light with chloroplasts, most plants appear green to our eyes.

Photosynthesis and Earth's Atmosphere

The atmosphere on Earth has not always had the oxygen-rich conditions we experience today. Billions of years ago, the atmosphere was made up of gases such as methane, ammonia, and carbon dioxide.

About 3.5 billion years ago, aquatic, single-celled photosynthetic organisms called cyanobacteria evolved. About 2.3 billion years ago, the organisms began to use visible light and produce oxygen during photosynthesis. These organisms were so abundant and diverse that they contributed significant amounts of oxygen to the atmosphere. This change in atmospheric oxygen concentration is known as the Great Oxidation Event. As shown in Figure 14, oxygen levels peaked again around 300 million years ago at the end of the Carboniferous period.

Data Analysis

CO_2 and O_2 Concentrations in the Atmosphere

FIGURE 14: The concentrations of carbon dioxide and oxygen in Earth's atmosphere compared to the present atmospheric level (PAL).

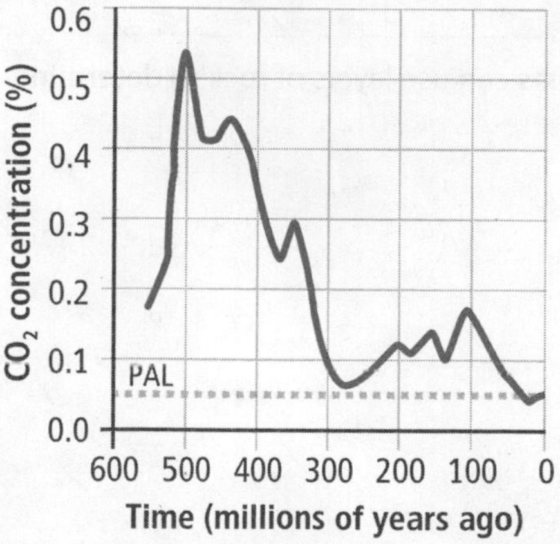

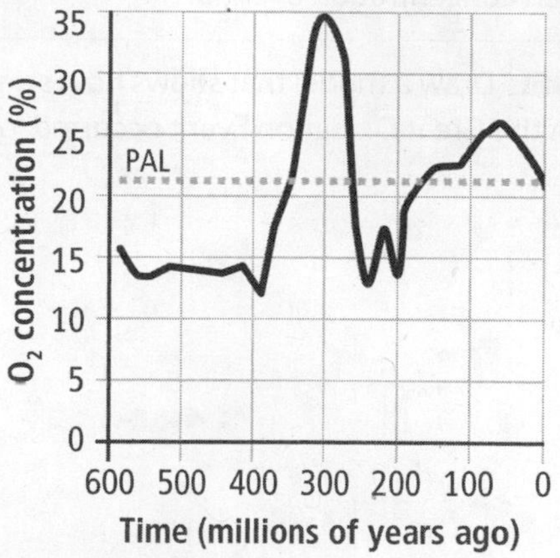

Credit: Adapted from "Atmospheric Oxygen, Giant Paleozoic Insects and the Evolution of Aerial Locomotor Performance" by Robert Dudley from Journal of Experimental Biology, Volume 201: 1043-1050. Copyright © 1998 by The Company of Biologists Ltd. Adapted and reproduced by permission of The Company of Biologists Ltd.

ANALYZE Review the graphs in Figure 14. What trend do you notice about the relative amount of carbon dioxide in the atmosphere over time? And for oxygen?

_____

_____

_____

EXPLAIN What factors could cause changes in the carbon dioxide and oxygen gas levels in Earth's atmosphere?

_____

_____

_____

FIGURE 15: Cyanobacteria were the first photosynthetic organisms.

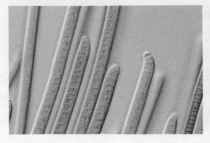

a Cyanobacteria

b Stromatolites

c Banded iron formation

Cyanobacteria can grow in mats. These mats formed unique mounds, called stromatolites, in shallow oceans about 3.5 billion years ago. The first cyanobacteria lived in an oxygen-poor, or anaerobic, environment. As they photosynthesized, they depleted the surrounding water of carbon dioxide and increased the oxygen concentration.

The free oxygen produced by cyanobacteria reacted with elements in the ocean, such as iron, and became trapped in rock layers. This reaction led to layers of iron-rich deposits that settled on the ocean floor. Known as banded iron formations, these rock layers gave scientists the evidence they needed to make conclusions about changes in atmospheric oxygen concentration over time.

MODEL Draw a model that shows how scientists can use layers of rock to determine when the Great Oxidation Event occurred.

As life on the planet evolved, the number and variety of photosynthetic organisms increased. Today, cyanobacteria, algae, and plants carry out photosynthesis. They take in carbon dioxide from the atmosphere and produce oxygen that is released into the atmosphere. Single-celled aquatic organisms in the ocean produce about half of the oxygen in Earth's atmosphere. This activity significantly contributes to the oxygen we breathe today. In addition, the oxygen from photosynthesis contributes to the formation of a layer of ozone high in the atmosphere. This layer protects life on Earth from harmful ultraviolet radiation.

 Evidence Notebook Use evidence to evaluate the role photosynthetic organisms, such as cyanobacteria, had on the formation of Earth's atmosphere.

Transforming Light Energy

So far, you have seen that plants transform energy from sunlight into chemical energy stored in the chemical bonds of sugar molecules. But how does this transformation of energy happen? It all comes down to electrons and ions.

Electrons are negatively charged particles in atoms. Ions are charged atoms or molecules. For example, when a water molecule is split into one oxygen atom and two hydrogen atoms, the bonds in the molecule that joined the atoms together are broken. Now each of the hydrogen atoms has a positive charge because they each lost the negatively charged electron they shared with oxygen, so they are called hydrogen ions (H^+).

Electrons can move through tiny spaces such as cell structures. Energy from the electrons is used to make molecules that act as energy carriers. These energy carriers are ATP and another molecule called NADPH. ATP and NADPH transfer energy between the two stages of photosynthesis.

Stages of Photosynthesis

Photosynthesis can be broken into two major stages—the light-dependent reactions and the light-independent reactions. The light-dependent reactions take place within and across the membrane of the thylakoids, which are stacked inside the chloroplast. The light-independent reactions take place in the stroma, the area outside the thylakoids.

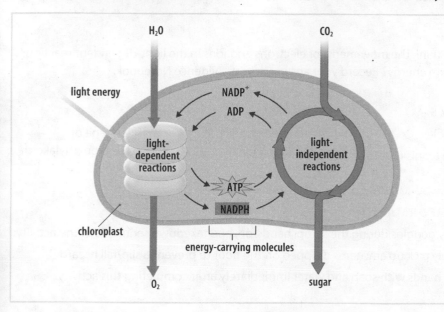

FIGURE 16: The two stages of photosynthesis, light-dependent reactions and light-independent reactions, occur in the chloroplast.

EXPLAIN Complete the statement by selecting the correct terms.

In the light-dependent reactions, H_2O and light energy are inputs, and CO_2 | O_2 | H_2O | sugar is an output. In these reactions, an energy-carrying molecule, CO_2 | ATP | ADP | sugar, and an electron carrier, NADPH, are produced and sent to the light-independent reactions. In the light-independent reactions, CO_2 | O_2 | ADP | sugar is an input, and CO_2 | O_2 | ATP | sugar is an output. ADP and $NADP^+$ return to the light-dependent reactions.

Hands-On Activity

Modeling Reactions in Photosynthesis

The main function of the light-dependent reactions in photosynthesis is to capture the energy in light and transform it into energy that can be used in cells to build biological molecules. Light is absorbed by chlorophyll and other pigments in a group of molecules called photosystem II. This light energy activates the free electrons, which are released by the breaking of the bonds in water molecules.

The Electron Transport Chain

Once electrons are activated in photosystem II, they move through what is called an electron transport chain to another group of molecules called photosystem I. (The two photosystems are named for the order in which they were discovered, not the order in which they occur.) While the electrons are in the electron transport chain, their energy is used to pump hydrogen ions (H^+) into the thylakoid, making a buildup of ions. In photosystem I, the electrons are recharged again, and continue on to the end of the chain, where $NADP^+$ picks them up, becoming NADPH. Meanwhile, the high concentration of hydrogen ions inside the thylakoid also builds up. The pressure of the hydrogen ion gradient on one side of the membrane drives the ions to pass through an enzyme in the membrane called ATP synthase, which makes ATP.

MAKE A CLAIM

How do you think the movements of electrons and ions in the light-dependent reactions help transform energy? Record your answer in your Evidence Notebook.

MATERIALS

- safety goggles
- balls, table tennis (10–15) [electrons]
- crumpled paper (15) [hydrogen ions]
- masking tape or painter's tape [thylakoid membrane]

SAFETY INFORMATION

- Wear safety goggles during the setup, hands-on, and takedown segments of the activity.
- Immediately pick up any items dropped on the floor to prevent a slip/fall hazard.
- Wash your hands with soap and water immediately after completing this activity.

CARRY OUT THE INVESTIGATION

Part A: Light-Dependent Reactions

1. Form groups of 13–15 students. Then assign roles to each group member: ADP (1–2 students), ATP Synthase, Chlorophyll in Photosystem I, Chlorophyll in Photosystem II, Electron Transport Chain (2–3 students), $NADP^+$ (5 students), Solar Energy, and Water.

2. Place two rows of masking tape or painter's tape on the classroom floor to represent the thylakoid membrane. Decide which side of the membrane will be the lumen and which side will be the stroma.

3. Position each group member inside and around the thylakoid membrane in such a way that they represent the light-dependent reaction process. Start by putting "chlorophyll in photosystem II" on the farthest left end of the thylakoid membrane. Place five hydrogen ions in the stroma and the rest in the lumen. Use the diagram in Figure 17 for reference if needed.

4. Give "solar energy" seven electrons and "water" three electrons.

5. Once your process is physically in place, ask "solar energy" to start the reactions by passing one electron to "chlorophyll in photosystem II." Have "solar energy" model how the light photons kick the electron into an excited state by gently moving the hands of the person receiving the electron above her or his head.

6. Pass the electrons down the electron transport chain until they get to "chlorophyll in photosystem I." "Solar Energy" gives "chlorophyll in photosystem I" a high five to represent the electron being excited again.

7. Pass the excited electron along to the first electron receptor, "NADP$^+$." Once this person has collected two electrons, she or he can also take a hydrogen ion from the stroma to become "NADPH."

8. Note that hydrogen ions are moving from the stroma into the lumen, increasing the number of hydrogen ions in the lumen. This is called a concentration gradient, which stores energy to be used by ATP synthase during ATP formation.

9. Once all of the electrons from "solar energy" are used up, consider where else electrons could come from and keep the reaction going.

10. While the reaction is occurring, "ATP synthase" picks up a hydrogen ion from the lumen, moves it to the stroma, and high-fives "ADP" to represent ATP formation.

FIGURE 17: Energy from light is captured in the light-dependent reactions. Explore Online ▶

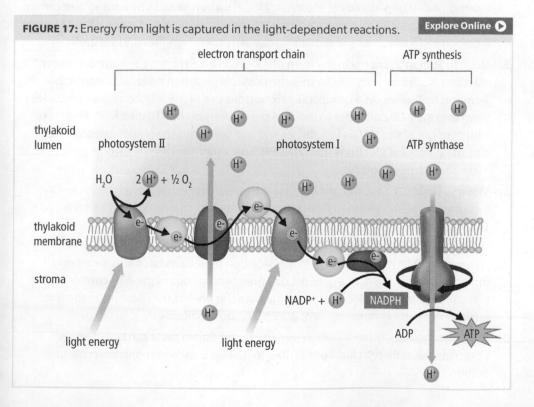

Answer the following questions in your Evidence Notebook.

1. Aside from solar energy, what else could provide electrons?

2. What are the end products of the light-dependent reactions?

3. Review Figure 17. What is the function of the hydrogen ion concentration gradient? How could you model the gradient, as discussed in Step 8?

The Calvin Cycle

The second stage of photosynthesis uses energy from the light-dependent reactions, mainly ATP and NADPH, to make sugars. As the name for this stage implies, the light-independent reactions—also known as the Calvin cycle—do not need sunlight. The Calvin cycle is the synthesis part of photosynthesis.

MATERIALS

- safety goggles
- buttons, medium (12) [NADPH/NADP$^+$]
- buttons, small (18) [ATP/ADP]
- containers, small (6)
- foam balls, black (24) [carbon atoms]
- foam balls, red (6) [oxygen atoms]
- toothpicks [covalent bonds]

CARRY OUT THE INVESTIGATION

Part B: Light-Independent Reactions

1. In Part B, you will work in groups of six. At Station 1, make three 5-carbon molecules, using the toothpicks to attach the foam balls together. Make three CO_2 molecules by attaching two red balls to one black ball. The Calvin cycle begins with three 5-carbon molecules already in the cycle. The Calvin cycle "fixes" carbon into organic molecules. It does this by attaching the carbon atom from molecules of carbon dioxide to the 5-carbon molecules already in the cycle. Model carbon fixation by adding one carbon molecule from each CO_2 molecule to each 5-carbon molecule to make a total of three 6-carbon molecules. Pair the remaining oxygen atoms together and set aside.

2. Move to Station 2. Energy in the form of ATP and NADPH from the light-dependent reactions is used by enzymes to split the unstable 6-carbon molecules into stable 3-carbon molecules. As a group, take six buttons out of the ATP container and place them into the ADP container to indicate the conversion of ATP into ADP. Then take 6 buttons out of the NADPH container and put them into the NADP$^+$ container to indicate the loss of electrons from NADPH. Split apart the three 6-carbon molecules to make six 3-carbon molecules.

3. Move to Station 3. One student holding a 3-carbon molecule leaves the cycle. One 6-carbon molecule is formed from every two 3-carbon molecules that exit the cycle. Therefore, it takes two turns of the Calvin cycle to build a single 6-carbon sugar. The students holding the remaining five 3-carbon molecules should move to Station 4.

4. Energy from ATP is used to change the 3-carbon molecules back into 5-carbon molecules. At Station 4, as a group, take three buttons out of the ATP container and place them into the ADP container to indicate this energy use. Rearrange the five remaining 3-carbon molecules into three 5-carbon molecules.

5. Now that there are three 5-carbon molecules, the Calvin cycle can begin again. Complete the activity at least once more to make a 6-carbon sugar molecule at Station 3.

ANALYZE

Answer the following questions in your Evidence Notebook.

1. How many carbon dioxide molecules are needed to make one 6-carbon sugar molecule? Use evidence from the activity to explain your answer.

2. What molecules provide the energy and electrons for making the molecules in the light-independent reactions? Where did they come from?

3. How does the Calvin cycle act as a bridge between carbon in the atmosphere and carbon-based molecules in the food you eat? Use evidence from your model to support your answer.

DRAW CONCLUSIONS

Write a conclusion in your Evidence Notebook that addresses the points below.

Claim How do the light-dependent reactions help transform energy and capture it in a usable form? How does the transformed energy capture and store carbon from the atmosphere into sugars that are used to build the plant?

Evidence Which aspects of photosynthesis were portrayed by the model you developed? Give specific examples from your model to support your claim.

Reasoning Explain how the evidence you gave supports your claim. Describe, in detail, the connections between the evidence you cited and the argument you are making.

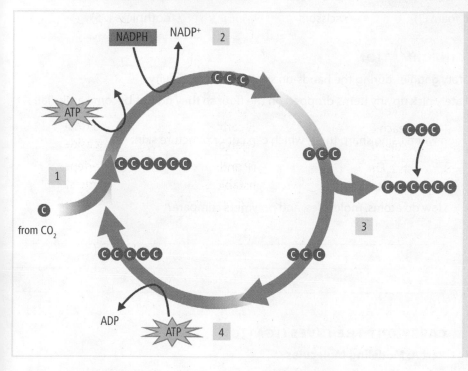

FIGURE 18: Energy in the form of ATP and NADPH is used to make sugars in the light-independent reactions.

 Evidence Notebook Develop a model to illustrate how photosynthesis transforms light energy into chemical energy. In your model, show how energy from sunlight is converted to energy in sugars, and identify the inputs and outputs for each stage of the process.

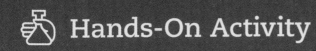

Hands-On Activity

Modeling Biochemical Compounds

Atoms bond together to make molecules. Many molecules can also bond together to form bigger molecules. Molecules that make up living organisms are often large and complex. For example, many biologically important carbon-based molecules are polymers, which are composed of many simpler subunits called monomers. Starch is a polymer composed of many simple sugar units bonded together. Proteins are made of many amino acids bonded together. Nucleic acids, such as DNA, are made of long strands of subunits called nucleotides.

Scientists often use models to help study and understand atoms and molecules. Biochemists use computers to make molecular models in which all the atoms and atomic bonds of a molecule are included. In this lab, you will use ordinary materials to model small molecules and polymers.

MATERIALS

- safety goggles
- ball, black foam (9)
- ball, red foam (3)
- construction paper
- protractor
- scissors
- tape, clear, 50 cm
- tape, double-sided, 6 cm
- toothpicks (25)

SAFETY INFORMATION

- Wear safety goggles during the hands-on segment of the activity.
- Immediately pick up any items dropped on the floor so they do not become a slip/fall hazard.
- Use caution when using sharp tools, which can cut or puncture skin.

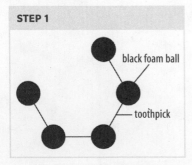

STEP 1

black foam ball

toothpick

MAKE A CLAIM

How do atoms, molecules, and polymers compare?

_____

_____

_____

CARRY OUT THE INVESTIGATION

Part A: Modeling Molecules

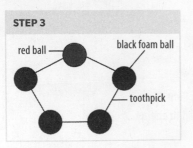

STEP 3

red ball

black foam ball

toothpick

1. Make a simple model of a glucose molecule's ring structure. Glucose is composed of a ring of five carbon atoms and one oxygen atom. Obtain five black foam balls. These will represent carbon atoms. Use toothpicks to "bond" the atoms together at ~120° angles.

2. Use toothpicks to attach a red foam ball (oxygen) to complete the ring structure of glucose. Glucose is a simple sugar, or monosaccharide.

3. Build a model of another simple sugar, fructose. Fructose contains a ring of four carbon atoms and one oxygen atom bonded together. As with the model of glucose, additional hydrogen and oxygen atoms bonded to the ring will not be included in your model. Connect four black foam balls together with toothpicks at ~108° angles. Complete the ring with toothpicks and a red foam ball.

4. Make a model of sucrose (a disaccharide) by bonding the glucose to the fructose. Connect one of the carbon atoms that is next to the oxygen atom in your glucose model to another oxygen atom, as shown. Connect a red ball (oxygen) to the glucose model. Insert a toothpick into the new oxygen atom. Use it to connect the oxygen to a carbon that is next to the oxygen in the fructose model.

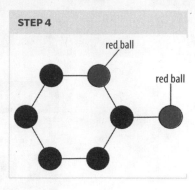
STEP 4
red ball
red ball

Part B: Modeling Polymers

5. Make glucose models out of paper by drawing several hexagons on construction paper. Use the scissors to carefully cut the hexagons out of the paper. Connect several glucose molecules together to model the polysaccharide called starch.

6. Tape a toothpick to one corner of each hexagon, so that most of it extends beyond the paper.

7. Tape the toothpick from one glucose hexagon to the end of another glucose hexagon. Be sure that you attach the toothpick to the end that is opposite to that hexagon's toothpick. Keep connecting the hexagons until they are all linked together to form a model of part of a starch molecule.

- -

ANALYZE

1. How are glucose and fructose similar? How are they different?

_____

_____

2. How are starch and sucrose similar? How are they different?

_____

_____

3. When photosynthetic organisms use energy from the sun to convert carbon dioxide and water into simple sugars, such as glucose, what happens to each molecule?

_____

_____

4. Describe the strengths and weaknesses of using these models to represent atoms and molecules.

_____

_____

_____

| ARTIFICIAL PHOTOSYNTHESIS | | THE BLUE-GREEN OCEAN | | LIGHT AND PHOTOSYNTHESIS | Go online to choose one of these other paths. |

Lesson Self-Check

CAN YOU EXPLAIN IT?

FIGURE 19: How might photosynthesis be used to generate energy for human use?

To use solar energy to make electricity, researchers are exploring ways to capture energy from plants, the world's most efficient solar collectors. Today, researchers are attempting to develop technology that collects energy generated through photosynthesis before the plants can make use of it, allowing the energy to instead be used to run low-powered electrical devices.

 Evidence Notebook Refer to your notes in your Evidence Notebook to explain the flow of matter and energy in the process of photosynthesis.

1. Do you think it's possible to capture energy from photosynthesis for human use? Use the information in your Evidence Notebook and what you have explored in this lesson to make and support your claim.

2. What criteria and constraints are associated with using photosynthesis to generate energy on a large scale for human use?

3. Why might it be important to consider alternative energy solutions for humans? Use evidence and reasoning to support your answer.

CHECKPOINTS

Check Your Understanding

1. Select the correct terms to complete the statement.

   | ATP | photosynthesis | glucose |

   Some living things, such as plants and algae, transfer energy from sunlight to

   _____ molecules. This process

   is known as _____ . Virtually all

   living things transfer energy from these molecules

   to another molecule called _____

   which provides the energy for cell processes.

2. Which of the following result from producers performing photosynthesis? Select all correct answers.
   - ☐ **a.** oxygen is produced
   - ☐ **b.** carbon dioxide is transferred back to the atmosphere
   - ☐ **c.** energy is transferred from sunlight to consumers
   - ☐ **d.** carbon is cycled through the biosphere

3. Select the correct terms to complete the statement.

   | ATP | thylakoids | chlorophyll |

   | chloroplasts | electrons |

   Light energy is absorbed by

   _____ found in the membranes

   of _____ , which are saclike

   structures inside _____ . The light

   energy excites _____ , which are

   used to make NADPH . Energy from this process is

   used to make _____ .

   Carbon dioxide and energy are used to make

   sugars, which the plant stores or uses for energy.

4. How do the two photosystems work together to capture energy from sunlight?
   - ○ **a.** Photosystem I captures energy from sugars, which energizes electrons. The electrons are passed along to photosystem II, which absorbs more energy and adds it to the electrons.
   - ○ **b.** Photosystem II takes energy from ATP, which energizes electrons. The electrons are passed along to photosystem I, which produces ATP.
   - ○ **c.** Photosystem II absorbs energy from sunlight, which energizes electrons. The electrons are passed along to photosystem I, which absorbs more energy and adds it to the electrons.
   - ○ **d.** Photosystem I harnesses energy from carbon dioxide, which energizes electrons. The electrons are then passed to photosystem II, which generates water.

5. How does the stability of an ecosystem depend on its producers?
   - ○ **a.** Producers create energy, which is necessary for the proper functioning of an ecosystem.
   - ○ **b.** Producers transfer energy from light to molecules that living things can eat.
   - ○ **c.** Producers transfer energy from sugars to other types of carbon-based molecules.
   - ○ **d.** Producers eat other organisms, which helps transfer matter through the ecosystem.

6. Which of these evidence statements should you include in an explanation of the relationship between carbon, amino acids, and proteins? Select all correct answers.
   - ☐ **a.** Amino acids are polymers made up of proteins.
   - ☐ **b.** Proteins are polymers made up of amino acids.
   - ☐ **c.** Proteins and amino acids are polymers, because they contain multiple carbon atoms.
   - ☐ **d.** Amino acids are monomers made up mostly of carbon, hydrogen, nitrogen, and oxygen.

CHECKPOINTS (continued)

7. In what ways is ATP like a fully charged battery?

_____

_____

_____

_____

_____

8. A common misconception is that the bulk of a plant's material comes from soil or water. Explain where the carbon in sugars actually comes from, citing evidence from the Calvin cycle to support your answer.

_____

_____

_____

_____

_____

9. How do the processes of light-dependent and light-independent reactions help the cell conserve energy and matter?

_____

_____

_____

_____

_____

_____

_____

MAKE YOUR OWN STUDY GUIDE

In your Evidence Notebook, design a study guide that supports the main idea from this lesson:

Photosynthesis is a process used by most producers to transform light energy into stored chemical energy.

Remember to include the following information in your study guide:

- Use examples that model main ideas.
- Record explanations for the phenomena you investigated.
- Use evidence to support your explanations. Your support can include drawings, data, graphs, laboratory conclusions, and other evidence recorded throughout the lesson.

Consider how photosynthesis transforms light energy into stored chemical energy.

Cellular Respiration

Fireworks exploding in the night sky release carbon dioxide, heat, and light.

CAN YOU EXPLAIN IT?

A firework explosion is a fast series of chemical reactions. The fuel is powdered charcoal (carbon) that reacts with other chemicals, such as potassium nitrate (KNO_3) resulting in an explosive reaction. When heat is added, the charcoal and other chemicals packed inside the firework casing combust, or burn and release heat. This reaction occurs very quickly, and releases energy in the forms of heat and light—which is the explosion we see from the firework.

PREDICT How is the process of combustion in a firework similar to the way the cells in your body release stored energy?

_____

_____

_____

_____

_____

Evidence Notebook As you explore this lesson, gather evidence that bonds are broken and new bonds are formed in the process of cellular respiration.

Matter and Energy in Cellular Respiration

FIGURE 1: Glucose structure and appearance

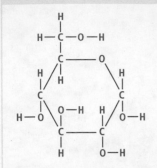

a A glucose molecule is made of six carbon, 12 oxygen, and six hydrogen atoms.

b Glucose, a simple sugar, is one of the fuel sources used by organisms.

Fuel is any material that reacts with other materials to release energy to be used for work. There are many types of fuels, each with a different chemical structure. Some fuels, such as wood, peat, and charcoal, contain carbon, hydrogen, and oxygen atoms. Other fuels, such as natural gas and petroleum, only contain carbon and hydrogen. Compounds that contain only carbon and hydrogen are called *hydrocarbons*. Most fireworks use charcoal as a fuel. Most living things use a simple sugar called glucose as a fuel.

Energy in Living Systems

Almost all the energy on Earth has its origin in the sun. In the process of photosynthesis, plants transform light energy from the sun into chemical energy in the form of glucose. Chemical bonds in a glucose molecule must be broken for stored energy to be released. In cells, a process called cellular respiration releases chemical energy from sugars and other carbon-based molecules to make ATP when oxygen is present. These chemical reactions are essential to the survival of living organisms.

All chemical reactions involve changes in energy. The reactants must absorb energy to break their chemical bonds. When new bonds form to make the products, energy is released. During a chemical reaction, energy is both absorbed and released.

Activation energy is the amount of energy needed to start, or activate, a chemical reaction. Chemical reactions are classified by the difference between the amount of energy absorbed and the amount of energy released. When a chemical reaction releases more energy than it absorbs, it is called an *exothermic reaction*. The excess energy is often given off as heat or light. In contrast, when a chemical reaction absorbs more energy than it releases, it is called an *endothermic reaction*.

Exothermic Reaction

FIGURE 2: Activation energy is the energy needed to start a chemical reaction. An exothermic reaction releases more energy than it absorbs. Cellular respiration is an exothermic reaction.

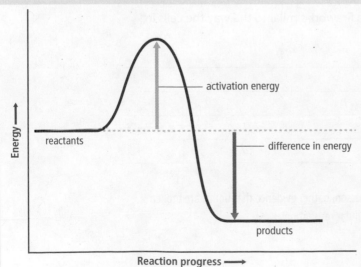

 Evidence Notebook Use the graph in Figure 2 to explain why cellular respiration is an example of an exothermic reaction.

Energy Content in Food

Unlike a firework, which releases all of its energy at once, cellular respiration releases energy in small bursts. The fuel comes from food molecules, such as proteins, carbohydrates, and fats that organisms eat. The energy used to make these molecules is stored within their chemical bonds. The amount of energy each of these macromolecules provides is measured in kilocalories (Calories), where one Calorie is the amount of energy needed to raise the temperature of one kilogram of water one degree Celsius. Once ingested, macromolecules are broken down into simpler molecules, such as glucose. During cellular respiration, the breakdown of glucose and other carbon-based molecules releases energy stored in their chemical bonds. The stored energy is transferred to ATP and used to power many processes in the body. Energy in the form of heat is also released.

FIGURE 3: The energy humans need to survive and grow comes from food.

EXPLAIN Select the correct terms to complete the statement about chemical energy.

The chemical energy of food molecules provides the heat | fuel | ATP for cellular respiration. Food molecules are broken down and the energy in their bonds is released | absorbed. This energy is transferred to heat | fuel | ATP and used throughout the body. Some energy is released as heat | fuel | ATP.

All living things store energy because resources may not always be available. Plants convert glucose into starch, which is stored in the chloroplasts. Animals convert glucose into glycogen, which is stored in the liver and in muscle tissues. Animals also store fat in a type of connective tissue called adipose tissue.

The Process of Cellular Respiration

Cellular respiration is an aerobic process, which means that it requires oxygen to take place. Some organisms can produce small amounts of ATP through anaerobic processes, which are processes that do not require oxygen. However, the presence of oxygen allows cellular respiration to produce far more ATP from each glucose molecule.

ANNOTATE Write the inputs and outputs of cellular respiration on this diagram.

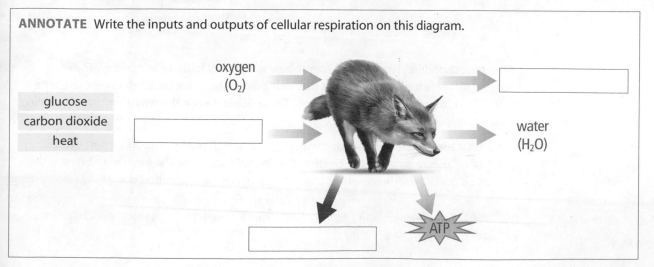

oxygen
(O₂)

glucose
carbon dioxide
heat

water
(H₂O)

ATP

The balanced chemical equation for cellular respiration is:

$$C_6H_{12}O_6 + 6O_2 \rightarrow \rightarrow \rightarrow 6CO_2 + 6H_2O + heat + ATP$$

APPLY How does this equation represent the law of conservation of matter—that matter cannot be created or destroyed?

_____

_____

EXPLAIN How does this equation represent the law of conservation of energy—that energy cannot be created or destroyed? Consider the role of photosynthesis in your answer.

_____

_____

_____

Mitochondria

In eukaryotic cells, cellular respiration takes place inside an organelle called the mitochondrion (plural *mitochondria*), shown in Figure 4. Mitochondria release the chemical energy required to make ATP. Both plant and animal cells contain mitochondria, because both plants and animals carry out cellular respiration.

FIGURE 4: Mitochondria are bean-shaped organelles that provide energy to the cell.

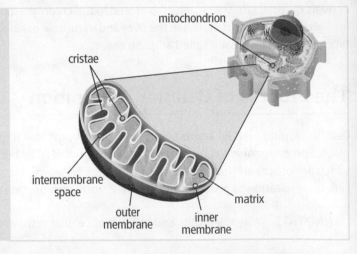

The mitochondrion has an inner membrane with many folds, called cristae. The cristae increase the surface area of the membrane. The outer membrane separates the mitochondrion from the rest of the cell. The space between the two membranes is called the intermembrane space.

The inner membrane is embedded with proteins, which play an important part in the final step of cellular respiration, the electron transport chain. Inside the inner membrane is the matrix, a gel-like substance where the first step of cellular respiration occurs.

 Collaborate With a partner, cite evidence that supports the claim that mitochondria are the "powerhouses of the cell."

Cellular Respiration and Photosynthesis

ANNOTATE Use the correct terms to complete this diagram showing the reactants and products for each chemical reaction.

| CO_2 | $C_6H_{12}O_6$ | H_2O | O_2 |

Photosynthesis

light energy

REACTANTS

PRODUCTS

Cellular Respiration

REACTANTS

PRODUCTS

heat   ATP

Almost all energy for living things comes from photosynthesis, either directly or indirectly. Producers absorb light energy from the sun and use photosynthesis to transform it to a usable form of energy, or food. This energy is then passed from producers to consumers. Although only producers carry out photosynthesis, both producers and consumers carry out cellular respiration. Photosynthesis stores energy from sunlight as chemical energy. In contrast, cellular respiration releases stored chemical energy as ATP and heat.

Evidence Notebook Photosynthesis and cellular respiration work together as a cycle. Review the two chemical reactions to compare the processes. What is the relationship between photosynthesis and cellular respiration?

Hands-On Lab

Modeling Photosynthesis and Cellular Respiration

Design an experiment to determine which organisms—pond snails and *Elodea*—produce carbon dioxide and which use carbon dioxide.

POSSIBLE MATERIALS

- indirectly vented chemical splash goggles, nonlatex apron, nonlatex gloves

- beaker, 100 mL

- bromothymol blue indicator in dropper bottle

- glass vials with screwcap lids (8)

- light bulb and power source

- marker

- pond snails (4)

- straw, individually wrapped·

- sodium hydroxide (NaOH) solution in dropper bottle

- sprigs of *Elodea* (4)

- tap water

- tape, labeling

SAFETY INFORMATION

- Wear indirectly vented chemical splash goggles, a nonlatex apron, and nonlatex gloves during the setup, hands-on, and takedown segments of the activity.

- Wash your hands with soap and water when you are finished handling plant samples.

- Use only GFI protected circuits when using electrical equipment, and keep away from water sources to prevent shock.

- Sodium hydroxide is corrosive. Avoid contact with the skin.

- Do not inhale through the straw while it is in the solution. If you need to take a breath, first remove your mouth from the straw. Do not share straws with other students.

MAKE A CLAIM

How does the presence of light affect the cycling of matter between organisms that carry out photosynthesis and cellular respiration?

_____

_____

_____

indirectly vented chemical splash goggles

PLAN THE INVESTIGATION

1. In your Evidence Notebook, draw a diagram illustrating how matter cycles between photosynthesis and cellular respiration. Include the organisms that carry out each process, and the names or chemical formulas for the specific molecules exchanged.

2. In your Evidence Notebook, make a data table to record your observations for Steps 3-4. For each step, record the color of the indicator solution, and write an explanation of what the color indicates about the presence or absence of carbon dioxide.

3. Place 30 mL of tap water into a small beaker. Add 7 drops of bromothymol blue (BTB) indicator. BTB indicator is blue when there is no carbon dioxide present in a solution. If your solution is not blue, add one drop of NaOH solution and stir. Add drops only until the solution is blue. Record your observations.

4. Insert a straw into the beaker and gently blow through the straw until the solution stops changing color. Record your observations.

5. In your Evidence Notebook, draw or describe an experimental design to determine which organism produces carbon dioxide and which organism uses carbon dioxide. For example, you could examine how much carbon dioxide is produced by each organism under light and dark conditions.

6. When planning the experimental design, you should include enough experimental setups so that you can observe how matter cycles in different scenarios. Be sure to have a control setup.

7. Show your teacher your written procedure for approval.

CARRY OUT THE INVESTIGATION

1. Obtain the vials and prepare each one to fit your experimental design.

2. All vials should be filled to one-quarter inch from the top with water. Some pond snails breathe through gills and others through lungs. Air needs to be at the top of the vial so the snails with lungs can go to the top periodically for air. Use pieces of *Elodea* equal to the length of the vial. All caps should be screwed on loosely.

3. Label each vial with your name and the test conditions. Make a data table in your Evidence Notebook to record your daily observations. Record your observations for today, Day 1, and then place the vials in the areas designated by your teacher. Let them remain undisturbed overnight.

4. After 24 hours have elapsed, examine the vials and record your observations in your Evidence Notebook.

5. Empty all vials of pond water, *Elodea*, and snails in the place designated by your teacher. Follow the cleanup procedure as instructed by your teacher. Wash your hands before leaving the lab.

ANALYZE

1. Summarize your results for the setups that contained only plants and the setups that contained only animals. How did the conditions you tested affect the use and production of carbon dioxide by the plants? By the animals? What does this indicate about whether photosynthesis and/or cellular respiration occurred in each vial?

_____

_____

_____

_____

_____

_____

2. Summarize your results for the setups that contained both plants and animals. How did your test conditions affect the use and production of carbon dioxide? What does this indicate about whether photosynthesis and/or cellular respiration occurred in each vial?

_____

_____

_____

3. What was your control setup in this experiment? How did your observations of the control influence your analysis of the results?

_____

_____

_____

DRAW CONCLUSIONS

Write a conclusion that addresses each of the points below.

Claim Make a claim about which organism(s) used carbon dioxide and which organism(s) produced carbon dioxide. How did your test conditions affect the cycling of matter between plants and animals?

Evidence Describe specific observations from your experiment to support your claim.

Reasoning Did your observations support your claim? Describe, in detail, the connections between the evidence you gave and the claim you are making.

_____

_____

_____

_____

_____

_____

_____

_____

_____

_____

 Evidence Notebook How is the combustion reaction of a firework similar to and different from the reactions shown by the living organisms in this lab? What are the inputs and outputs for the reaction?

Using Chemical Energy

One way that organisms maintain stable body conditions is through cellular respiration. This process releases energy to carry out cell processes and helps maintain body temperature. Bonds in food molecules and oxygen molecules are broken and new molecules form. These new molecules transfer energy in arrangements that the organism can use. Cellular respiration transfers chemical energy stored in the bonds of glucose and other molecules to ATP, which is the cell's "energy currency."

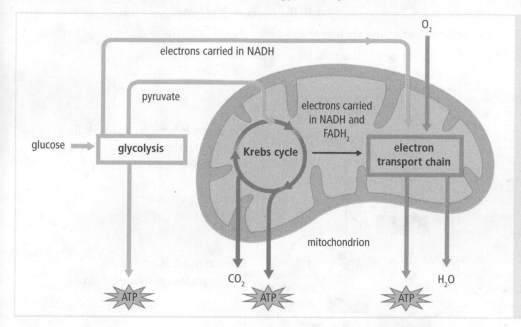

FIGURE 6: The process of glycolysis occurs before the two main stages of cellular respiration: the Krebs cycle and the electron transport chain.

Glycolysis and the Stages of Cellular Respiration

Before cellular respiration can take place in the mitochondria, glucose must be broken down into compounds the mitochondria can use. This process, called glycolysis, occurs in the cytoplasm of the cell. Glycolysis is an anaerobic process that breaks glucose into two three-carbon molecules, called pyruvate. Mitochondria use the pyruvate molecules to fuel cellular respiration. Glycolysis also produces two NADH molecules, which are electron carriers, and two molecules of ATP for every one glucose molecule.

FIGURE 7: Glycolysis occurs in all living organisms.

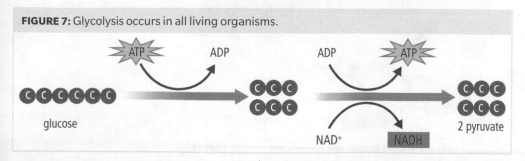

Evidence Notebook Summarize evidence that bonds are broken and new bonds are formed in glycolysis.

Krebs Cycle

The Krebs cycle, also called the citric acid cycle, is the first set of reactions in cellular respiration. The function of the Krebs cycle is to complete the breakdown of glucose started in glycolysis and fuel the production of ATP. This is done by transferring high-energy electrons from the carbon bonds in the pyruvate molecules to the electron transport chain. The two electron-transporting molecules formed in the Krebs cycle are NADH and FADH$_2$.

EXPLAIN Use the correct terms to complete the statement about the Krebs cycle.

Energy in the chemical bonds of carbon-based molecules is released | absorbed when those bonds are broken | formed. In the process, high-energy electrons | protons are transferred to molecules such as FADH$_2$ and NADH | CO$_2$. These molecules carry the high-energy electrons to the next stage of cellular respiration.

FIGURE 8: The Krebs cycle is the first stage of cellular respiration.

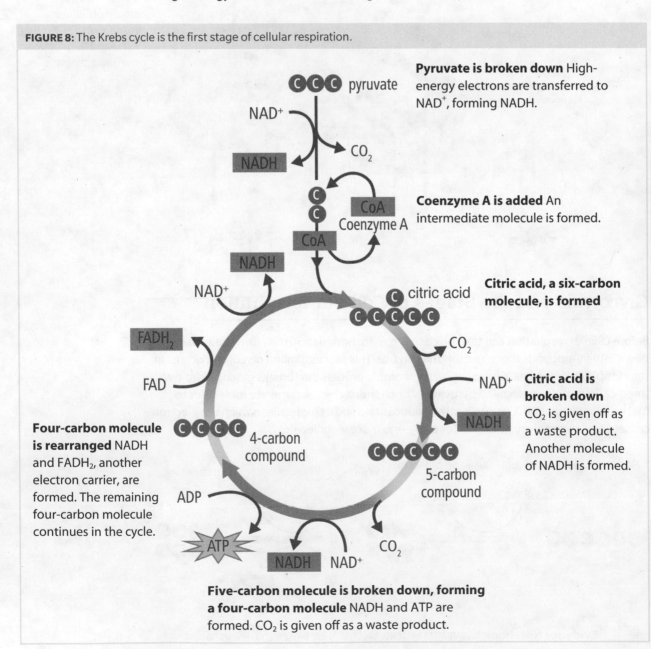

Pyruvate is broken down High-energy electrons are transferred to NAD$^+$, forming NADH.

Coenzyme A is added An intermediate molecule is formed.

Citric acid, a six-carbon molecule, is formed

Citric acid is broken down CO$_2$ is given off as a waste product. Another molecule of NADH is formed.

Four-carbon molecule is rearranged NADH and FADH$_2$, another electron carrier, are formed. The remaining four-carbon molecule continues in the cycle.

Five-carbon molecule is broken down, forming a four-carbon molecule NADH and ATP are formed. CO$_2$ is given off as a waste product.

The Electron Transport Chain

The second stage of cellular respiration is the electron transport chain. It is similar to the electron transport chain stage of photosynthesis. In eukaryotes, this process uses proteins embedded in the inner membrane of the mitochondrion. In prokaryotes, this process occurs in the cell membrane. The energy carried by the NADH and FADH$_2$ molecules produced in the Krebs cycle is used to make ATP. Every time an electron is transferred, energy is released. A number of enzymes are also involved in this process.

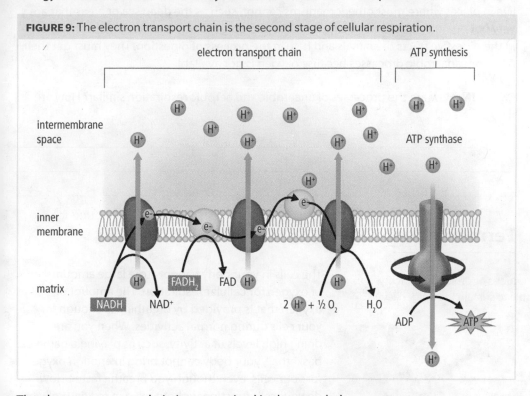

FIGURE 9: The electron transport chain is the second stage of cellular respiration.

The electron transport chain is summarized in the steps below.

1. **Electrons are transferred** Proteins embedded in the inner membrane of the mitochondrion take high-energy electrons from NADH and FADH$_2$.

2. **Hydrogen ions are transported** High-energy electrons travel from protein to protein in the electron transport chain. Each time two electrons are passed down the chain, a hydrogen ion is transported across the inner membrane to the intermembrane space where the ions build up. Eventually, there are more hydrogen ions in the intermembrane space than in the matrix, which produces a gradient.

3. **ATP is produced** The flow of hydrogen ions is used to make ATP. Due to the gradient, hydrogen ions return to the matrix through a channel in the enzyme ATP synthase. As a hydrogen ion moves through the channel, ATP synthase adds phosphate groups to ADP to make ATP.

4. **Water is formed** Oxygen picks up the now low-energy electrons and hydrogen ions to form water. The water molecules are given off as a waste product.

Together, glycolysis and cellular respiration produce up to 38 ATP molecules for every glucose molecule.

 Collaborate In two large groups, work together to make a model of the electron transport chain. Present your model to the other group.

Anaerobic Respiration

Not all organisms rely on oxygen for cellular respiration. Life on Earth originally evolved in an environment that lacked oxygen. These organisms instead had to use anaerobic processes to get the energy they needed to survive. The evolution of cyanobacteria and the subsequent increase in atmospheric oxygen was key to the eventual evolution of single-celled organisms and multicellular organisms that used aerobic respiration. Organisms that use anaerobic respiration have an important role in ecosystems. They can live in places where most other organisms cannot, such as the deep sea or areas that are very hot or highly acidic. For example, some microorganisms, such as bifidobacteria, live in the digestive tracts of animals and help in the process of digestion. They must get their ATP from anaerobic processes because oxygen is not available.

EXPLAIN How are the processes of anaerobic and aerobic respiration similar? How are they different?

_____

_____

_____

Fermentation

FIGURE 10: During strenuous or prolonged activity, athletes may not be able to sustain the oxygen levels their bodies need.

The cells in your body cannot store large amounts of oxygen for cellular respiration. The amount of oxygen that is provided by breathing is enough for your cells during normal activities. When you are doing high levels of activity, such as playing a game of basketball, your body cannot bring in enough oxygen for your cells, even though you breathe faster. How do your cells function without oxygen to keep cellular respiration going?

When oxygen is unavailable, ATP is made through the process of fermentation. Scientists originally thought fermentation was an aerobic process. However, experiments by French scientist Louis Pasteur in the 1850s provided evidence that fermentation was indeed an anaerobic process. Fermentation includes glycolysis, which makes ATP, and other reactions that remove electrons from NADH. This is important because glycolysis, just like cellular respiration, needs the electron carrier NAD^+ to pick up electrons.

The role of fermentation is simply to provide the process of glycolysis with a steady supply of NAD^+. If you've ever felt your muscles "burn" during hard exercise, that is a result of fermentation. Lactic acid is a waste product of fermentation that builds up in muscle cells and causes that burning feeling. Once oxygen is available again, your cells return to using cellular respiration. The lactic acid is quickly broken down and removed from the cells.

Evidence Notebook Summarize the evidence that you have gathered to explain how molecules are rearranged and energy is transferred in the process of cellular respiration.

1. Cite evidence to support the claim that bonds are broken and new bonds are formed in each stage of cellular respiration.
2. Explain how energy is transferred from the bonds of food molecules to cellular processes.

Applications in Wastewater Treatment

Wastewater is water that contains waste from homes, industry, and sometimes from storm runoff. Wastewater can contain chemicals, soap, food scraps, and human waste. Wastewater treatment plants filter and treat water to make the water clean enough to return to the city water supply or a river, lake, or ocean where it becomes part of the water cycle again. In areas subject to unpredictable drought events and increased human population, wastewater treatment and recycling reduces the burden on water reservoirs.

Wastewater Treatment

Treating wastewater is critical for human and ecosystem health. If untreated wastewater enters a body of water, it can cause many problems for humans and ecosystems. In addition to disease-carrying organisms, untreated wastewater carries nutrients, which can lead to harmful algae blooms. In turn, the increase in plant and algae populations decreases the dissolved oxygen and nutrient levels in the water and affects other organisms, such as fish. Wastewater can also contain heavy metals and other toxic compounds that are poisonous to humans and other organisms. Untreated sewage has the potential to pollute drinking water supplies, and close fisheries and other industries that depend on the water. Once polluted, it is difficult to completely remove pollutants from the water, or remediate the affected ecosystem. It is also very expensive, requiring anything from simple biological processes to sophisticated engineering techniques.

FIGURE 11: Runoff is captured by storm drains in urban areas and flows untreated into a lake, river, or ocean. Dumping trash, chemicals, or other wastes in storm drains is illegal because they can have harmful effects on the aquatic environment and water quality.

Engineering

Fermentation Technology

Fermentation is an anaerobic process that has been used for centuries as a biotechnology. Organisms including some bacteria, cyanobacteria, yeasts, algae, and fungi are used to develop products that humans use. There are many fields of industry that use fermentation in product development. For example, engineers and scientists have designed processes to produce biofuels as an alternative fuel for cars. The industrialized fermentation of penicillin has improved treatment of many infectious diseases on a global scale. Fermentation is used in a variety of other industries including food and textiles.

 Evidence Notebook Synthetic biology is an emerging area of research that combines biology and engineering to develop or redesign systems based on biological systems. What are the benefits to applying natural processes, such as fermentation, in an industrial manufacturing process? What are the challenges?

Modeling Wastewater Treatment

Wastewater treatment is an important aspect of California cities. Many treatment processes use microbes to help remove dissolved organic matter from wastewater. There is usually an aerobic component, where bacteria undergo cellular respiration. In this lab, you will model the aerobic part of the wastewater treatment process by using yeast to represent bacteria and glucose to represent pollution.

MAKE A CLAIM

Make a claim predicting the effect that yeast will have on glucose levels. Make a second claim predicting the effect that adding more yeast will have on the changing glucose levels.

_____

_____

_____

MATERIALS

- indirectly vented chemical splash goggles, nonlatex apron, nonlatex gloves
- active dry yeast, 1 package
- aquarium aerator with tubing and aeration stone (5)
- beaker, 100 mL (5)

- beaker, 500 mL (1)
- distilled water, 500 mL
- Erlenmeyer Flask, 250 mL
- glass stirring rod
- glucose, 48 g
- glucose test strips

- hot pad/plate
- markers
- scale
- table sugar, 4 g
- tape, labeling
- thermometer, digital

SAFETY INFORMATION

indirectly vented
chemical splash
goggles

- Wear indirectly vented chemical splash goggles, a nonlatex apron, and nonlatex gloves during the setup, hands-on, and takedown segments of the activity.

- Immediately wipe up any spilled water on the floor so it does not become a slip/fall hazard.

- Use caution when working with hot plates, which can cause skin burns or electric shock.

- Use caution when working with glassware, which can shatter if dropped and cut skin.

- Use only GFI protected circuits when using electrical equipment, and keep away from water sources to prevent shock.

- Wash your hands with soap and water immediately after completing this activity.

CARRY OUT THE INVESTIGATION

Part A

1. Activate the yeast. Using a hot plate and an Erlenmeyer flask, heat 150 mL of distilled water to 40 °C. Add the contents of the packet of yeast and 4 g of table sugar. Stir. Let sit for 10 minutes. If the solution contains bubbles, the yeast is alive and good to use.

2. While you wait for the yeast to activate, add 250 mL of distilled water and 24 g of glucose to a beaker. Then, make sure the aeration stone is connected to the tubing and the aerator, and insert the stone into the bottom of the beaker. Turn on the aerator.

3. In your Evidence Notebook, make a data table to record your findings.

4. Measure the amount of glucose in the water using a glucose test strip. To use the test strip, dip it in the glucose solution for a few seconds, then wait about three minutes. Compare the color of the strip to the scale on the test strip box or bag and record the concentration of glucose in the water.

5. Add 50 mL of the activated yeast solution to the glucose solution.

6. Measure the concentration of glucose in the beaker after five minutes. For the first 20 minutes, record the concentration of glucose every five minutes. After that, record glucose concentrations every 10 minutes until the end of class (a total of 40-60 minutes).

7. In your Evidence Notebook, set up a graph to plot your data.

Part B

While you are waiting for measurements for Part A, begin Part B.

1. Label the five smaller beakers A, B, C, D, and E. Repeat the setup used in Part A Step 2, dividing the fresh glucose solution evenly across the beakers (50 mL per beaker).

2. Repeat Part A Step 3 for the five Part B beakers.

3. Add the yeast to the beakers as follows:
   - no yeast solution to beaker A
   - 10 mL of the yeast solution to beaker B
   - 20 mL of the yeast solution to beaker C
   - 30 mL of the yeast solution to beaker D
   - 40 mL of the yeast solution to beaker E

4. Repeat Part A Step 5 for each Part B beaker, recording your results for each beaker.

5. Dispose of waste according to your teacher's instructions.

ANALYZE

After making your tables and graphing the data, answer the following questions in your Evidence Notebook.

1. Summarize the results in the large beaker.

2. Summarize the results in the smaller beakers. Is there a pattern in the data? What will happen if the yeast percentage continues to increase?

DRAW CONCLUSIONS

Write a conclusion in your Evidence Notebook that addresses the points below.

Claim How do microorganisms contribute to the process of wastewater treatment?

Evidence Describe specific observations from your experiment to support your observations.

Reasoning Explain how the observations you cited support your claim. You may also use evidence from the text to support your observations.

FIGURE 12: Aerobic microorganisms in aerated tanks break down small particles in the water by using oxygen during cellular respiration.

Aerobic Water Treatment

The aerobic part of wastewater treatment is often called secondary treatment, and takes place in large, aerated tanks that mix the water. This lets aerobic bacteria "breathe" so they can continue to break down the organic matter that is dissolved in the water. This common technique also contributes to the cycling of carbon. After this stage, the water can be passed on to tertiary treatment, which removes even finer particles, or disinfects the water.

FIGURE 13: Anaerobic microorganisms digest small particles in settling tanks, helping clean the wastewater of organic matter and breaking down the particles to make them more accessible to the global carbon cycle and aerobic bacteria.

Anaerobic Water Treatment

Some water treatment facilities have an anaerobic component called primary treatment, which uses microorganisms such as bacteria to break down small particles. Often, these bacteria use methane instead of carbon dioxide to conduct cellular respiration. After the larger solid wastes are filtered out of the sewage, the water goes into a sedimentation tank where the remaining solid particles sink down to the bottom of the tank to be digested. The sludge that is left over from this process can be cleaned and used as fertilizer for non-food crops or sterilized and used for anything that requires rich compost.

Energy and Matter

APPLY Explain how the following statement applies to wastewater treatment plants: Energy cannot be created or destroyed.

_____

_____

_____

_____

 Evidence Notebook Summarize the evidence you have gathered that wastewater treatment uses cellular respiration to help clean the water. Cite evidence from the text in your answer.

Language Arts

Food and Energy

Have you ever heard the saying, "You are what you eat"? In many ways, this is true! Living things are made up of different types of organic, or carbon-based, molecules. When we eat food, our digestive system breaks down the food into smaller molecules that can be used by the body. When digestion is complete, nutrients are absorbed by the body and transported by the circulatory system and lymphatic system to all the cells.

Once food enters the body, it can be broken down further to harness energy and form new types of molecules. For example, sugar molecules contain the elements necessary to produce many other types of organic molecules. These elements can be rearranged and combined with other elements through chemical reactions to form new products such as proteins, fats, and DNA.

The information on a food label can help you make good choices and compare the values of different foods. The label shown in Figure 14 is for cereal.

Serving size and number This measurement varies from one product to another. In this case, one serving equals 3/4 of a cup of cereal.

Calories The numbers listed on the label are for one serving only. If you eat your cereal with milk, you will have a different number of Calories.

Nutrients to limit Americans usually consume too much saturated fat, trans fat, cholesterol, and sodium. Trans fat is a type of fat that can cause cell damage. A diet high in these nutrients is linked to obesity, which affects more and more Americans of all ages. Too much sodium can raise blood pressure by causing the body to retain water.

Nutrients to target People need to consume enough fiber, vitamins, and other nutrients each day. Notice that this product is low in Vitamin A and Vitamin C, but high in iron.

FIGURE 14: Nutrition labels contain information about the nutrients in your food.

The guidelines for what makes up a healthy diet have changed over time based on new evidence or new understandings of existing evidence from ongoing research. For example, you may have seen a balanced diet described as a food pyramid, which has carbohydrates at the base of the pyramid, and fats, oils, and sweetened foods at the top of the pyramid. More recently, a plate with four main sections for vegetables, proteins, grains, and fruits has been used as a model of a balanced diet.

Language Arts Connection Research current nutritional guidelines using scientific and government sources. Consider the following when conducting your research:

- What is a balanced diet? How can it be modeled?
- How have nutritional guidelines changed over time?
- How is diet related to cellular processes? How does the energy content in nutrients such as carbohydrates, fats, and proteins affect dietary choices?

Use your research to develop an informational pamphlet to share with your peers.

WASTEWATER PLANT MANAGER   **AEROBIC AND ANAEROBIC RESPIRATION IN YEAST**   **MODEL CARBON MOVEMENT**   Go online to choose one of these other paths.

Lesson Self-Check

CAN YOU EXPLAIN IT?

FIGURE 15: Fireworks undergo a combustion reaction.

A firework explosion is an exothermic reaction. The reactants are a fuel and an oxidizing agent. The products of the reaction include carbon dioxide, heat, and light. When the bonds in the reactant molecules break apart, the energy in the bonds is released as heat and light, and cause an explosion. One way to represent the chemical reaction in a firework is

$$6KNO_3 + C_7H_4O + 2S \rightarrow K_2CO_3 + K_2SO_4 + K_2S + 4CO_2 + 2CO + 2H_2O + 3N_2 + \text{heat} + \text{light}$$

In contrast, cellular respiration is a slower process, with energy being released over a series of several steps. This makes it possible to capture and store the energy as ATP, which is then available for use whenever cells of the body need it to carry out cellular activities.

$$C_6H_{12}O_6 + 6O_2 \rightarrow \rightarrow \rightarrow 6CO_2 + 6H_2O + \text{heat} + \text{ATP}$$

 Evidence Notebook Refer to your notes in your Evidence Notebook to explain how cellular respiration is similar to the combustion reaction in a firework. Using this information, answer the following questions:

1. Make a claim about similarities and differences between the two processes. What are the main reactants and products of each? How are these reactants and products similar?

2. Compare the process by which energy is released in the firework to that of cellular respiration. Where does the energy come from? How are bonds broken and rearranged? Use evidence and reasoning to support your claim.

CHECKPOINTS

Check Your Understanding

1. How does carbon flow between photosynthesis and cellular respiration?
   - ○ **a.** Photosynthesis produces carbon dioxide from glucose made by the process of cellular respiration.
   - ○ **b.** Cellular respiration produces carbon dioxide from glucose made by the process of photosynthesis.
   - ○ **c.** Photosynthesis produces carbon dioxide from ATP made by the process of cellular respiration.
   - ○ **d.** Cellular respiration produces carbon dioxide from ATP made by the process of photosynthesis.

2. Which of the following items are the main inputs, or reactants, in cellular respiration? Select all correct answers.
   - ☐ **a.** pyruvate
   - ☐ **b.** glucose
   - ☐ **c.** carbon dioxide
   - ☐ **d.** oxygen

3. Which of the following items are the main outputs, or products, of cellular respiration? Select all correct answers.
   - ☐ **a.** water
   - ☐ **b.** energy
   - ☐ **c.** oxygen
   - ☐ **d.** carbon dioxide

4. Before cellular respiration, glucose must be broken down by the process of
   - ○ **a.** photosynthesis.
   - ○ **b.** glycolysis.
   - ○ **c.** electron transport.
   - ○ **d.** fermentation.

5. Cellular respiration is a three-part process. Number the processes in the correct order.
   - _____ **a.** electron transport chain
   - _____ **b.** Krebs cycle
   - _____ **c.** glycolysis

6. Which processes provide evidence for the claim that energy is transferred during cellular respiration? Select all correct answers.
   - ☐ **a.** the electron transport chain
   - ☐ **b.** carbon dioxide is released
   - ☐ **c.** hydrogen ions move down the concentration gradient across the inner membrane
   - ☐ **d.** transfer of electron carriers such as NADH and $FADH_2$
   - ☐ **e.** water is formed

7. Is oxygen always necessary for the production of ATP in your cells?
   - ○ **a.** Yes, ATP is only produced during the electron transport chain, which requires oxygen.
   - ○ **b.** No, ATP is only formed during anaerobic processes.
   - ○ **c.** Yes, cellular respiration is aerobic and it produces ATP.
   - ○ **d.** No, ATP is also formed during glycolysis, which can continue without oxygen for a limited time period.

8. Which of the following groups of organisms use cellular respiration in mitochondria to produce ATP for their energy needs?
   - ○ **a.** plants only
   - ○ **b.** eukaryotes
   - ○ **c.** animals only
   - ○ **d.** prokaryotes

CHECKPOINTS (continued)

9. How do you know that energy and matter are conserved during the process of cellular respiration? Explain.

_____

_____

_____

_____

_____

_____

_____

_____

_____

10. How are photosynthesis and cellular respiration related?

_____

_____

_____

_____

_____

_____

_____

_____

_____

_____

MAKE YOUR OWN STUDY GUIDE

In your Evidence Notebook, design a study guide that supports the main idea from this lesson:

Cellular respiration is a process that breaks down food molecules to release energy to fuel cell processes in living organisms.

Remember to include the following information in your study guide:

- Use examples that model main ideas.
- Record explanations for the phenomena you investigated.
- Use evidence to support your explanations. Your support can include drawings, data, graphs, laboratory conclusions, and other evidence recorded throughout the lesson.

Consider how bonds are broken, molecules are rearranged, and energy is transferred during the process of cellular respiration.

Engineering Connection

Carbon Fiber Carbon fiber is stronger than steel, but weighs much less. These long chains of carbon atoms can be added to other materials, such as plastics, to increase their strength while keeping the material lightweight. Carbon fibers are used in airplanes, cars, and even electronics. The application of carbon fiber technology has been significant in the advancement of prostheses for athletes.

Write a magazine article about the history of prosthetics in sports and the influence of carbon fiber. Research ways that engineers use carbon fiber to design prostheses that more closely mimic the way a limb performs. How has carbon fiber changed the way athletes perform in competitive activities, such as sprinting?

FIGURE 1: This carbon fiber prosthetic leg compresses like a spring and rebounds, mimicking a normal leg.

Art Connection

Chemistry of Pigments Pigments are colored substances that can be used to color other materials. Pigments have been used for thousands of years to add color to artwork, clothing, skin, textiles, decorations, and other materials. Each pigment, whether organic or inorganic, natural or synthetic, has unique chemical properties that determine the pigment's color, durability, binding, and other attributes. People using pigments and dyes carefully select those with the characteristics most appropriate and useful for the application at hand.

Research the chemical properties and historical uses of pigments. Using your favorite pigments, make your own work of art, such as a painting, a print, or another format. Prepare a narrative that describes the chemistry and history of the pigments you chose to accompany your artistic work.

FIGURE 2: A collection of pigments

Earth Science Connection

Runaway Greenhouse Effect The atmosphere on Venus is about 96% carbon dioxide and 3% nitrogen, with small amounts of water vapor and other gases. Carbon dioxide, in combination with methane and water vapor, acts like the glass in a greenhouse to trap heat. Due to this greenhouse effect, the temperatures on Venus can reach 471 °C.

Some scientists hypothesize that the atmosphere on Venus was once similar to the current atmosphere on Earth. Research this claim and find evidence that either supports or refutes this hypothesis. Make an infographic that explains the role of the runaway greenhouse effect in the development of the current atmosphere on Venus.

FIGURE 3: The extreme temperatures on Venus are due to the greenhouse effect.

A BOOK EXPLAINING COMPLEX IDEAS USING ONLY THE 1,000 MOST COMMON WORDS

TINY BAGS OF WATER YOU'RE MADE OF

The very tiny parts of people and other animals

RANDALL MUNROE
XKCD.COM

You've learned that a cell is the basic unit of life. Organisms are made of one or more cells, need energy for all of their functions, respond to their environment, and reproduce by passing their genetic information to offspring. Here's a description of animal cells in simple language.

THE STORY OF WHAT LIVING THINGS ARE MADE OF

EVERYTHING THAT'S ALIVE IS MADE OF TINY BAGS OF WATER. SOME LIVING THINGS ARE MADE OF JUST ONE BAG OF WATER. THOSE THINGS ARE USUALLY TOO SMALL TO SEE.

OTHER THINGS ARE MADE OF A GROUP OF BAGS STUCK TOGETHER. YOUR BODY IS A GROUP OF LOTS AND LOTS OF THESE BAGS THAT ARE WORKING TOGETHER TO READ THIS PAGE.

THESE BAGS ARE FULL OF SMALLER BAGS. LIFE USES LOTS OF BAGS.

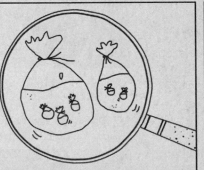

ALL LIFE IS MADE FROM DIFFERENT KINDS OF WATER, AND A BAG KEEPS THE STUFF INSIDE IT FROM TOUCHING THE STUFF ON THE OUTSIDE. BY USING BAGS, LIVING THINGS CAN KEEP DIFFERENT KINDS OF WATER IN ONE PLACE WITHOUT IT ALL COMING TOGETHER.

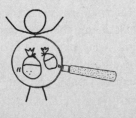

OH MY!   SO SORRY!   AFTER YOU!

SOME OF THE LITTLE BAGS YOU SEE HERE WERE ONCE LIVING THINGS ON THEIR OWN. LONG AGO, SOME LITTLE GREEN BAGS LEARNED TO GET POWER FROM THE SUN. THEN THEY GOT STUCK INSIDE OTHER BAGS, AND THOSE BECAME FLOWERS AND TREES. THE GREEN COLOR OF LEAVES COMES FROM THE CHILDREN OF THOSE LITTLE GREEN BAGS.

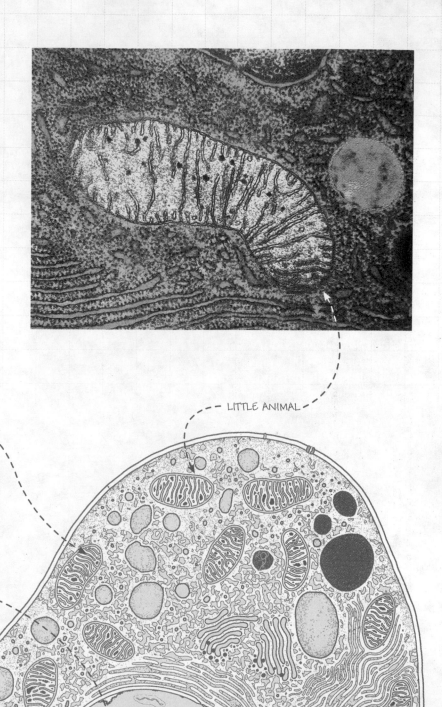

SIZE

These bags are almost always too small to see. In fact, they're almost as small as the waves of light we see with:

BLUE
GREEN
RED

LITTLE ANIMALS

These are living things (not really "animals") that got stuck in our bags of water a long time ago, like the green things in tree leaves. Now we can't live without each other. They get food and air from our bodies and turn them into power for our bags.

INFORMATION

The information for how to make different body parts is stored here.

READERS

These machines read the information about how to make parts and write it on little notes, then send them out through the holes in the wall.

MACHINE MAKER

This part makes the little machines that sit outside the control area.

LITTLE ANIMAL

TINY BAGS OF WATER YOU'RE MADE OF

OUTSIDE WALL
The water bags that make up animals have soft walls. The bags in trees and flowers, which don't need to move around as much as us, have a less soft outside layer.

GETTING IN AND OUT
Some things can go through the bag's wall on their own. Other things can only go through if the bag helps them, either by letting them through an opening, or by making part of the wall into a new bag to hold them.

BAG FILLER
This machine fills little bags with stuff and then sends them out into the water. Some stuff gets sent out of the big bag to another part of your body.

The machine also fills bags with death water, marking them very carefully before sending them out so they don't get used in the wrong place.

BAG SHAPERS
The space between bag parts is full of lots of very thin hair-like lines. These are like bones for the bag; they help hold its shape, and do some other things.

Some of these shapers also have holes down the middle, and can carry things from one part of the bag to another.

STRANGE BOXES
There are lots of these little boxes in our water bags. We don't know what they do.

BAGS OF DEATH WATER
These little bags are full of a kind of water that breaks things into tiny pieces. If something is put inside them, the water breaks it down into whatever it's made of.

If something goes wrong, these little bags tear open and all their bad water falls out. That makes the whole bag around it fall to pieces and die.

"Bags falling to pieces" sounds bad, since bags are what you're made of. But if a bag was having problems, it could hurt you. The death water helps clear it away so your body can make a new one.

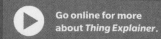
EMPTY POCKETS

This part of the bag has pockets to hold stuff that it might need later. It also makes a few things.

One of the things it makes is that stuff that helps your arms and legs get stronger. Sometimes, people who want to run or ride fast will put bottles of that stuff into their body and then lie about it.

CONTROL AREA

This area in the middle holds information about how to make the different parts of your body. It writes this information in notes and sends them out into the bag.

Bags make more bags by breaking in half. When this happens, the control area also breaks in half, and each half gets a full set of the bag's information.

Not all bags have these control areas. The bags in human blood don't (which means blood can't grow) but the bags in bird blood do.

This control area may have once been a living thing on its own, just like the green things in leaves.

CONTROL AREA HOLES

Notes and workers go out through these openings.

LITTLE BUILDERS

This area is covered in little building machines that build new parts for the bag. The builders sit just outside the control area, reading the notes from inside that tell them what to build.

After the builder makes a part, the part falls away into the bag. Each part has a job to do. Maybe its job is to tell another part it's time to stop working. Maybe its job is to turn one kind of part into another. Maybe it makes another part do something different. Or maybe it has a job, but waits until it sees *another* part before it starts working.

The strange thing is, no one tells the part where to go. It just falls out into the room with all the other parts, and hangs around until it runs into whatever part it's supposed to grab. (Or until another part grabs *it!*) This sounds strange, and it is! There are so many parts, and they're all grabbing each other and stopping each other and helping each other.

The insides of these bags are harder to understand than almost anything else in the world.

STOP IT!

THINGS THAT MAKE YOU SICK

These tiny things can get into your bags and take control of them. When they do that, they use the bag to build more of them.

When the kind shown here gets into you, your body gets hot, your legs hurt, and you have to lie down. Your whole body feels bad, and it makes you hate everything. You feel like you're going to die but usually don't.

We say all life is made of bags, but these things aren't. They also can't make more of themselves; they have to get a bag to make them. So we don't know if it makes sense to say they're "alive." They're more like an idea that spreads itself.

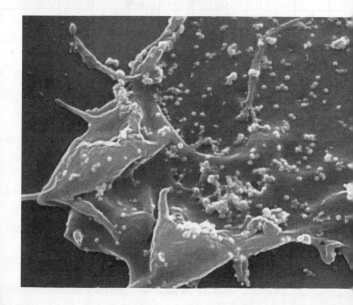

Modeling Carbon Sinks

California's giant sequoias and coastal redwood trees are some of the largest and tallest trees in the world. They start as seeds only a few millimeters in length and grow to towering giants over 50 meters tall. The tallest giant sequoia, known as General Sherman, is 83 meters tall and over 11 meters in diameter. Sequoias are known for their extremely long lifespans. General Sherman is estimated to be about 2000 years old, but other sequoias are estimated to be over 3000 years old. These trees are not just national treasures. They are among the most efficient carbon sinks in the world. A *carbon sink* is anything that takes in more carbon than it releases. Logging and development pressures are increasing, placing these forests in danger.

FIGURE 4: Only growth on a massive scale could have transformed these tiny seeds into such a giant tree.

a These sequoia seeds are only a few millimeters in length.

b A mature sequoia can reach well over 50 meters tall and more than 6 meters in diameter.

1. ASK A QUESTION

Make a list of questions to guide your research and develop your model to explain the importance of carbon sinks. Focus on why sequoias and redwoods are considered to be such efficient carbon sinks.

2. CONDUCT RESEARCH

With your team, investigate giant sequoia and redwood forests. Explore the relationship between the life cycle of these trees and the amount of carbon they take in during their lifetime. How do you think giant sequoias and redwood trees affect the amount of carbon dioxide in the atmosphere?

3. DEVELOP A MODEL

Using your research, develop a model that demonstrates how sequoia and redwood trees function as carbon sinks. Your model should explain how the trees take in carbon dioxide, how they store the carbon, and the importance of their long lifespans.

4. COMMUNICATE

Present your findings and your model of giant sequoias and redwood trees. Be sure to explain why carbon sinks are an important part of controlling the amount of carbon in the atmosphere. Your presentation should include images and data to support your claims.

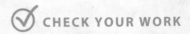 **CHECK YOUR WORK**

A complete presentation should include the following information:

- data that shows, on average, how much carbon giant sequoias and redwoods collect over time
- an explanation of what a carbon sink is and why sequoias and redwoods are effective carbon sinks
- images and data that further support your claims and model
- revisions to strengthen the writing and refine the model based on a practice run with a partner

Name _____   Date _____

SYNTHESIZE THE UNIT

In your Evidence Notebook, make a concept map, other graphic organizer, or outline using the Study Guides you made for each lesson in this unit. Be sure to use evidence to support your claims.

When synthesizing individual information, remember to follow these general steps:

- Find the central idea of each piece of information.
- Think about the relationships among the central ideas.
- Combine the ideas to come up with a new understanding.

DRIVING QUESTIONS

Look back to the Driving Questions from the opening section of this unit. In your Evidence Notebook, review and revise your previous answers to those questions. Use the evidence you gathered and other observations you made throughout the unit to support your claims.

PRACTICE AND REVIEW

1. Although photosynthesis only occurs in certain producers, how does this process contribute to the survival of other organisms, including humans? Select all correct answers.

   ☐ **a.** Photosynthesis produces sugars that are required to fuel cellular respiration, without these sugars, humans would not be able to produce energy for cellular functions.

   ☐ **b.** Photosynthesis produces oxygen, without which cellular respiration does not occur.

   ☐ **c.** Photosynthesis produces chlorophyll, which humans must consume to survive.

   ☐ **d.** Without oxygen, cells could only undergo lactic acid fermentation. After a prolonged period of time, cells would begin to die from a build up of lactic acid and a lack of ATP.

2. Select the correct terms to complete the statement about photosynthesis and cellular respiration.

   Plants transform chemical energy | light energy

   into chemical energy | light energy by the

   process of photosynthesis | cellular respiration.

   This process stores that energy as glucose | water

   molecules and other sugar molecules. These molecules provide the energy content in all foods, including the consumers that eat the plants.

3. Select the statement that best describes the relationship between photosynthesis and cellular respiration in terms of energy and matter.

   ○ **a.** The overall reactants and products produced in photosynthesis are used in cellular respiration and vice versa.

   ○ **b.** Photosynthesis and cellular respiration consume and produce the same reactants and products.

   ○ **c.** The processes of storing energy in carbon-based molecules during photosynthesis and breaking down those molecules to release energy during cellular respiration both occur in the same organelle.

   ○ **d.** All of the energy and matter produced during photosynthesis is consumed during cellular respiration and vice versa.

4. Which of the following statements best describes chemical reactions?

   ○ **a.** Chemical reactions can only occur between compounds.

   ○ **b.** Chemical reactions do not affect the bonds between atoms in the reactants.

   ○ **c.** Chemical reactions break and rearrange the bonds of the reactants.

   ○ **d.** The number and types of atoms in the product of a chemical reaction are different than were present in the reactants.

5. Why is breaking and rearranging bonds in the processes of photosynthesis and cellular respiration important?

_____

_____

_____

6. How does photosynthesis contribute to the survival of humans?

_____

_____

_____

7. Using evidence from this unit, explain the effect cyanobacteria had on the early atmosphere of Earth and the evolution of life.

_____

_____

_____

_____

8. Solar panels capture energy from sunlight and convert it to electricity. As light hits the silicon atoms in a solar cell, the energy is transferred to electrons. The electrons are emitted from silicon atoms, and an electric field organizes the electrons into an electric current. Compare the way a solar cell works to the way a chloroplast works to capture and transfer energy.

_____

_____

_____

_____

UNIT PROJECT

Return to your unit project. Prepare your research and materials into a presentation to share with the class. In your final presentation, evaluate the strength of your claim, evidence, and conclusions.

Remember these tips while evaluating:

- Was your claim supported by your evidence?

- Look at the evidence you gathered to make your model. Does the evidence support your claim and reasoning regarding how Earth's atmosphere changed over time?

- Consider if the evidence and reasoning are logical. Does your research contradict any evidence you have seen?

Ecosystem Interactions and Energy Flow

YOU SOLVE IT

How Can Bioreactors Maximize Algae Production For Fuel?

To begin exploring this unit's concepts, go online to investigate ways to solve a real-world problem.

Kelp forests are important aquatic ecosystems.

FIGURE 1: These terrariums are self-sustaining environments.

Many terrariums are closed, self-sustaining systems. The organisms in these terrariums are able to recycle all of the materials needed for survival. Earth is also a closed system in terms of matter. Very little matter is added to or lost from the Earth system.

PREDICT How do plants and animals grow if no new matter is added to the system?

_____

_____

_____

_____

DRIVING QUESTIONS

As you move through the unit, gather evidence to help you answer the following questions. In your Evidence Notebook, record what you already know about these topics and any questions you have about them.

1. How do animals obtain energy to grow?
2. How are energy and matter transferred between organisms and their environment?

UNIT PROJECT

Go online to download the Unit Project Worksheet to help plan your project.

Bottle Biome

How do energy and matter cycle through a closed system? How do the plants and animals survive? Make your own closed biological system inside a bottle, and investigate how the plants and animals survive with no materials being added to the system. Can you explain how the bottle represents Earth?

Language Development

Use the lessons in this unit to complete the chart and expand your understanding of the science concepts.

TERM: food chain

Definition	Example

Similar Term	Phrase

TERM: food web

Definition	Example

Similar Term	Phrase

TERM: biomass

Definition	Example

Similar Term	Phrase

TERM: energy pyramid

Definition	Example

Similar Term	Phrase

TERM: biomass pyramid

Definition	Example

Similar Term	Phrase

TERM: pyramid of numbers

Definition	Example

Similar Term	Phrase

TERM: reservoir

Definition	Example

Similar Term	Phrase

TERM: fossil fuel

Definition	Example

Similar Term	Phrase

Energy and Matter in Ecosystems

An algae bloom in Copco Reservoir.

CAN YOU EXPLAIN IT?

The gloppy looking green stuff in this reservoir in Northern California is an algae bloom. Large amounts of nutrient runoff into bodies of water allow algae to grow in dense, visible patches near the surface.

In 2015, an algae bloom occurred off the coastlines of Alaska and California in the North Pacific Ocean. This bloom was dominated by the algae *Pseudo-nitzschia*, which produces a neurotoxin called domoic acid. Many large marine animals died during this algae bloom, including sea lions, whales, and birds. Some evidence suggests that these deaths were related to domoic acid poisoning.

PREDICT The marine animals affected by the bloom do not eat algae. How could domoic acid have poisoned these organisms?

_____

_____

_____

_____

_____

> **Evidence Notebook** As you explore the lesson, gather evidence to explain how matter and energy flow through ecosystems.

Explore Online ▶

FIGURE 1: Chlorophyll concentration is an indicator of algae growth. Darker green areas indicate a high amount of algae.

Chlorophyll concentration (mg/m³)

0   0.05   30

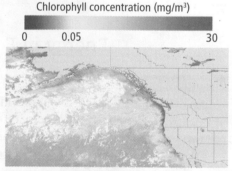

a North Pacific algae growth, 2002

b North Pacific algae growth, 2015

Flow of Energy and Matter in Ecosystems

All organisms need a source of energy to survive. Energy is essential for metabolism, which is all of the chemical processes that build up or break down materials in an organism's body. The law of conservation of energy states that energy cannot be created or destroyed. The form of energy may change, but the amount of energy does not.

MODEL How does energy flow in this terrarium? Draw arrows to show how light energy, chemical energy, and heat are transferred in terms of photosynthesis and cellular respiration.

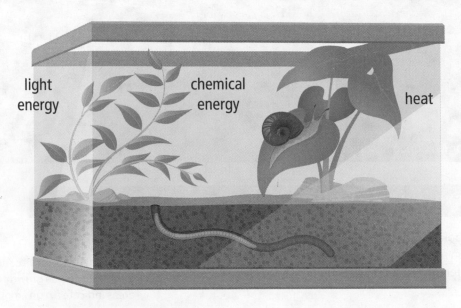

light energy

chemical energy

heat

Energy in Ecosystems

Explore Online ▶

FIGURE 2: A kingfisher dives underwater to catch a fish.

A kingfisher and a fish are components of an ecosystem. Each organism has a role in the transfer of energy and matter within the ecosystem. Within each organism, biomolecules continually change form as they are broken down and rearranged. Energy and matter can change form as they cycle through an ecosystem, but they are not destroyed.

Energy and Matter

APPLY Starting with the source of energy, order the components to show how energy and matter cycle through the kingfisher's ecosystem.

_____ **a.** aquatic invertebrates   _____ **d.** aquatic plants

_____ **b.** kingfisher   _____ **e.** fish

_____ **c.** sunlight

An ecosystem is a complex web of interconnected biotic and abiotic components. Changing one component in an ecosystem can affect many others. Imagine what would happen if a chemical spill occurred in the lake that the kingfisher depended upon as a source of food. If the spill killed the plants, it could negatively affect the insects that eat the plants, the fish that eat the insects, and the kingfisher that eat the fish. This one change could destabilize the entire ecosystem.

Humans, like other species, are part of ecosystems and rely on the environment for survival. If residents of a local town also ate fish from this ecosystem, the changes caused by the chemical spill would negatively impact them as well. All species are affected by changes to the biotic and abiotic factors in an ecosystem.

Food Chains

Feeding relationships are a major component of the structure and dynamics of an ecosystem. Food chains and food webs are useful ways to model the complex structure of an ecosystem and to better understand how energy is transferred between organisms. The simplest way to look at the transfer of food energy in an ecosystem is through a food chain.

FIGURE 3: Food chains help scientists understand the transfer of energy in an ecosystem.

a Producer   b Herbivore   c Carnivore

A food chain is a sequence that links species by their feeding relationships. This simple model follows the connection between one producer and a single chain of consumers within an ecosystem.

Not all consumers are alike. Herbivores are organisms that only eat plants. Carnivores only eat animals. Omnivores are organisms that eat both plants and animals. In a desert ecosystem, western diamondback rattlesnakes are carnivores that eat desert cottontails, which are herbivores. Kangaroo rats are omnivores that eat both seeds and insects. Detritivores are organisms that eat detritus, or dead organic matter. Earthworms are detritivores that feed on decaying organic matter in soil.

Earthworms are also decomposers. Decomposers are organisms that break down organic matter into simpler compounds. Other examples of decomposers include blow flies, fungi, and certain microbes in the soil. Decomposers are important to the stability of an ecosystem because they return vital nutrients back into the environment for other organisms to use.

FIGURE 4: Decomposers, such as this mushroom, break down dead organic matter.

 Evidence Notebook Draw a food chain that includes organisms in the area where you live. Identify the producers and consumers, and describe the flow of energy in the food chain. Identify a decomposer that would interact with this food chain. What might happen in your area if all of the decomposers were suddenly removed?

Trophic Levels

Trophic levels are the levels of nourishment in a food chain. The first trophic level is occupied by the producer. The second level is occupied by the primary consumer, usually an herbivore. The third and fourth levels contain secondary and tertiary consumers, and so on, which can be omnivores or carnivores.

FIGURE 5: Each organism in a food chain occupies a different trophic level.

a Producer

b Primary consumer

c Secondary consumer

d Tertiary consumer

Energy flows up the food chain from the bottom trophic level to the top. Food chains are limited in length because energy is lost as heat to the environment at each trophic level. Organisms use the remaining energy to carry out life functions such as cellular respiration and growth. In this way, less and less energy is available for the next organism in the chain. Eventually, there is not enough energy to support another trophic level.

 Data Analysis

Population Size and Trophic Levels

A scientist sampled a small cross section of a grassland ecosystem. Her data for each trophic level are shown in the table.

Trophic Level	Producers	Primary Consumers	Secondary Consumers	Tertiary Consumers
Population Count	6 025 682	723 082	98 541	4

ANALYZE How does the population size change at each trophic level?

_____

_____

EXPLAIN What is the relationship between trophic level and population size?

_____

_____

PREDICT What would happen if a quaternary consumer were added to this ecosystem?

_____

_____

_____

Food Webs

Food chains are not isolated units but are linked together in food webs. Each organism in an ecosystem may feed on or be eaten by several other organisms and may be part of many different food chains within the food web.

FIGURE 6: A food web is made up of many different food chains.

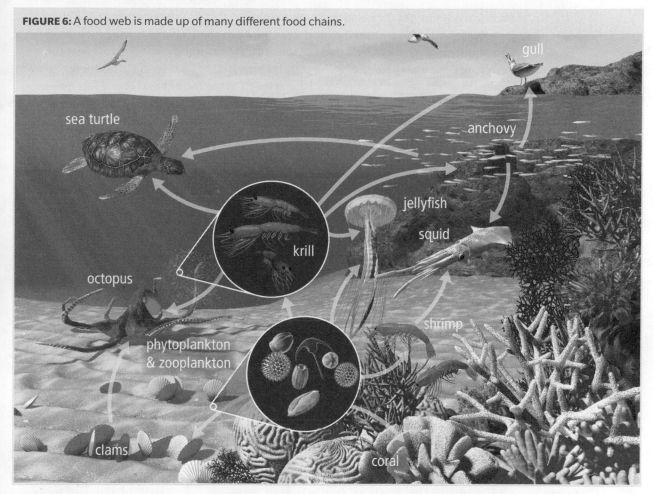

A food web models the complex network of feeding relationships between trophic levels within an ecosystem. A food web represents the flow of energy within and sometimes beyond the ecosystem. The stability of any food web depends on the presence of producers, as they form the base of the food web. In the case of a marine ecosystem such as a coral reef, the algae living in coral as well as floating phytoplankton are producers that play this important role.

 Collaborate With a partner, discuss how the food web would be affected if all the krill were removed from the ecosystem. What about if phytoplankton were removed?

An ecosystem has many different food chains. However, some food chains have one or more organisms in common. A food web shows how the different food chains within an ecosystem are related and gives a better idea of how energy and matter are transferred between organisms and trophic levels within the ecosystem.

 Evidence Notebook How would knowledge of North Pacific ocean food webs help scientists understand what was happening to organisms during the algae bloom in 2015?

Distribution of Energy and Matter in Ecosystems

Most ecosystems get their energy from sunlight. Producers use energy from the sun to make food. Herbivores eat the producers but burn some energy in the process. This energy is given off as heat that escapes into the environment. Carnivores eat the herbivores, but again, some of the energy is converted to heat, leaving the energy unavailable for use by the carnivore. Higher levels in the food chain receive less overall energy than the levels below them. For example, a desert cottontail gets more energy from the grass it eats than the rattlesnake will get by eating the rabbit because there is less available energy at each higher level in the food chain. The sun provides a constant flow of energy into the system and allows life to continue.

FIGURE 7: Energy and matter are transferred between trophic levels, but some energy is lost to the environment as heat.

heat   heat   heat

Reduction of Available Energy

When a consumer eats food, the energy it contains undergoes a transformation. Some energy is used for metabolic processes, which provide energy for movement and maintenance of the organism. Some energy is converted to new biomass, allowing growth of the organism. Of the remaining energy, some is released to the environment as heat, and the rest is excreted as waste. Although energy changes to different forms during this process, the total amount of energy remains unchanged, or is conserved.

MODEL How does the amount of energy at each trophic level compare to the amount of energy at the other levels? Using the organisms shown in the figure above, draw a model that compares the amount of mass and energy available at each trophic level.

Energy Calculations

SAMPLE PROBLEM

Energy can be measured using calories (cal), kilocalories (kcal), and joules (J). A caterpillar consumes 1000 J of energy from the plant it eats. However, the caterpillar cannot digest all the plant matter, so 500 J of energy are lost as bodily waste. Additionally, 320 J of energy are converted to heat or used for metabolism. What percentage of energy remains for the caterpillar to use for biomass, or growth?

FIGURE 8: A large amount of the energy a caterpillar consumes is excreted as waste or converted to heat via metabolism.

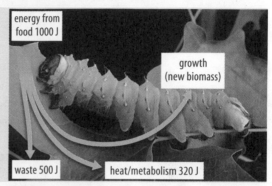

energy from food 1000 J

growth (new biomass)

waste 500 J   heat/metabolism 320 J

ANALYZE

To determine the amount of energy left for the caterpillar to use, subtract the amounts converted to heat and excreted as waste from the total amount consumed:

$$1000 \text{ J} - 500 \text{ J} - 320 \text{ J} = 180 \text{ J}$$

The caterpillar has 180 J left over to convert into biomass.

SOLVE

To determine the percentage of energy that is usable, divide the amount of available energy by the total amount of energy and multiply by 100 percent:

$$\frac{180 \text{ J}}{1000 \text{ J}} \times 100\% = 18\%$$

So 18 percent of the total energy consumed by the caterpillar is available for growth, and 82 percent of the energy is converted to other forms. Only a small percentage of the energy in the food was converted to new biomass.

PRACTICE PROBLEMS

SOLVE A chipmunk consumes 1000 J of energy from food, excretes 177 J as waste, and converts 784 J to heat via metabolism.

Use the information above to complete the problems.

1. How many joules of energy are available to convert into new biomass?

   _____ J

2. What percentage of the total energy was available to become new growth?

   _____ %

3. What percentage of the total energy consumed was converted to forms that were unusable to the chipmunk?

   _____ %

4. Write an equation that supports the idea that energy is conserved in this example.

   _____

Pyramid Models

The same patterns of energy and matter distribution at the organism level also occur at the ecosystem level. Diagrams called pyramid models can show these patterns.

INFER What information can a pyramid model tell a scientist about an ecosystem? How might such models be used?

_____

_____

_____

_____

Pyramid models are useful for showing the productivity of an ecosystem and can illustrate an ecosystem's distribution of energy, biomass, or number of organisms. Productivity is the percentage of energy entering the ecosystem that is incorporated into biomass at a particular trophic level. Modeling ecosystem productivity with a pyramid allows scientists to compare the distribution of energy, biomass, or number of organisms between trophic levels within the same ecosystem and also between different ecosystems.

Energy Pyramid

Trophic efficiency is the percentage of energy transferred from one trophic level to the next. Remember that energy transfer from one organism to another is not efficient.

An energy pyramid models the transfer of energy beginning with producers and working up the food chain to the top-level consumer. The pyramid illustrates how available energy is distributed among trophic levels in an ecosystem. A typical energy pyramid has a very large section at the base for producers, with progressively smaller sections of consumers above. Because energy is converted to heat and released to the environment at each level of the pyramid, the more levels there are in the ecosystem, the greater the loss of energy from the ecosystem. The energy used by producers far exceeds the energy used by the consumers they support.

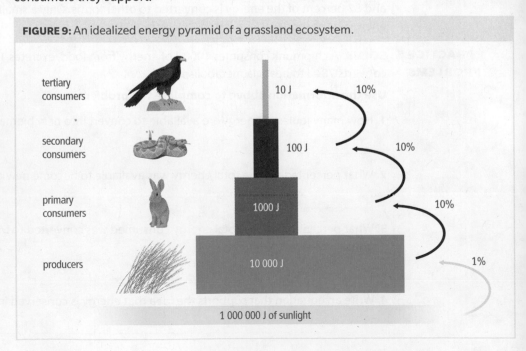

FIGURE 9: An idealized energy pyramid of a grassland ecosystem.

tertiary consumers — 10 J — 10%

secondary consumers — 100 J — 10%

primary consumers — 1000 J — 10%

producers — 10 000 J — 1%

1 000 000 J of sunlight

In the idealized energy pyramid shown in Figure 9, energy flows from one trophic level to the next. In this example, only 10 percent of energy produced is transferred to the next trophic level. Notice that only 0.1 percent of the energy in the producer level transfers to the tertiary consumer level.

Math Connection

Refer to the energy pyramid shown in Figure 9 to complete the problem.

CALCULATE According to this idealized model, if the producer level contained 5000 J of energy, how many joules would be present at the tertiary consumer level?

_____

An idealized pyramid is based on a trophic efficiency of 10 percent for each link in the food chain. A simplified pyramid like this can help scientists make models and hypotheses. In reality, the energy transfer between trophic levels, or trophic efficiency, can range from 5 to 20 percent, depending on the type of ecosystem.

Producers convert only about 1 percent of the energy available from sunlight into usable energy. This is because not all of the sunlight hits the leaves of a plant, not all wavelengths of light are absorbed, and photosynthesis requires large quantities of energy.

When a desert cottontail eats grass, some of the plant material is used to make new cells or tissues. What cannot be used, such as roots or woody stems, is excreted. The majority of the energy the rabbit gets from digesting its food is used to maintain body temperature and fuel the rabbit's metabolism and daily activities. When the rattlesnake eats the rabbit, there is much less energy available to fuel the rattlesnake's own life processes.

Energy efficiency differs among organisms. For example, animals that maintain their own body temperature, such as desert cottontails, use about 98 percent of the energy they take in to fuel their metabolism. Animals that do not maintain their body temperature, such as rattlesnakes, require much less metabolic energy and can use more energy to fuel other activities, such as growth or reproduction.

EXPLAIN Why is there a limit on the number of trophic levels that can exist within an ecosystem?

○ **a.** The number of trophic levels is limited by the amount of available energy.

○ **b.** There would not be enough space for more organisms.

○ **c.** There would be too much competition among organisms.

○ **d.** There is no limit to the number of trophic levels that can be added within an ecosystem.

Biomass Pyramid

A biomass pyramid compares the biomass at different trophic levels within an ecosystem. It illustrates the mass of producers needed to support primary consumers, the mass of primary consumers required to support secondary consumers, and so on. Recall that biomass is measured as the total dry mass per unit of area. The biomass measurement includes living organisms and dead organic matter. As organisms die and decompose, the nutrients and matter in their bodies are cycled back into the biomass pyramid by decomposers such as fungi and earthworms.

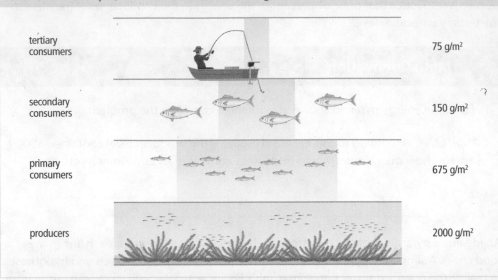

FIGURE 10: A biomass pyramid depicts the total dry mass of organisms found at each trophic level. In this example, the biomass is measured as g/m².

tertiary consumers	75 g/m²
secondary consumers	150 g/m²
primary consumers	675 g/m²
producers	2000 g/m²

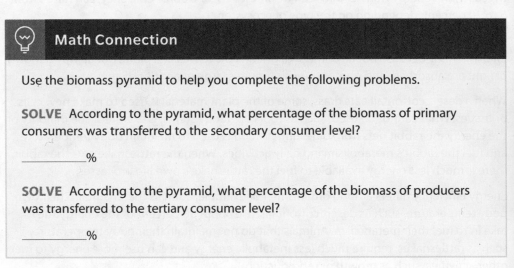

Math Connection

Use the biomass pyramid to help you complete the following problems.

SOLVE According to the pyramid, what percentage of the biomass of primary consumers was transferred to the secondary consumer level?

_____%

SOLVE According to the pyramid, what percentage of the biomass of producers was transferred to the tertiary consumer level?

_____%

The amount of energy and biomass decreases in a biomass pyramid as you move up the trophic levels. In an energy pyramid, the percentage of energy transferred from one trophic level to the next is approximately the same at every level. In a biomass pyramid, the percentage of biomass transferred to the next trophic level depends on the types of organisms present in each trophic level and the level of consumption by those organisms. For example, a population of pronghorn may eat more grass in an area than a population of prairie dogs. It also depends on the availability of biomass for consumption at each level. For example, leaf biomass is more available and useful for herbivores than wood.

Pyramid of Numbers

A pyramid of numbers shows how many individual organisms are present at each trophic level in an ecosystem. This type of pyramid is effective in showing the vast number of producers required to support even just a few top-level consumers. Ecosystems vary in the number and types of organisms in each level. These organisms also vary in their rates of growth and reproduction, as well as in the amount of biomass each species needs to sustain life and growth. A trophic level with organisms that reproduce and grow rapidly often has less biomass at any one time than one in which reproduction and growth rates are slow. The size of the organisms also plays a role in the shape of the various pyramids. The larger the size of the individual organisms, the fewer that are needed to support the next trophic level.

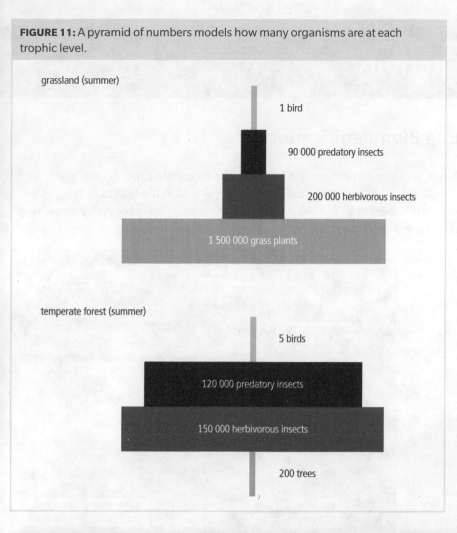

FIGURE 11: A pyramid of numbers models how many organisms are at each trophic level.

grassland (summer)

1 bird

90 000 predatory insects

200 000 herbivorous insects

1 500 000 grass plants

temperate forest (summer)

5 birds

120 000 predatory insects

150 000 herbivorous insects

200 trees

ANNOTATE Draw lines around each of the pyramid of numbers models to identify its basic shape.

Data Analysis

INFER What can you infer about the available matter and energy at each level? How does this influence the shape of each pyramid?

_____

_____

_____

ANALYZE How do the population sizes at each trophic level compare between the two ecosystems?

_____

_____

_____

 Evidence Notebook What might the shape of a biomass pyramid of an ocean ecosystem experiencing an algae bloom look like? Explain your answer.

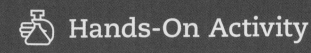

Hands-On Activity

Modeling Biomagnification

Harmful chemicals enter aquatic ecosystems from the runoff of silt, pesticides, and fertilizers. These chemicals enter the food chain and build up in the bodies of organisms through a process known as biomagnification. Scientists study this process by measuring the amount of chemicals in each trophic level in parts per million (ppm).

FIGURE 12: Biomagnification in an aquatic ecosystem.

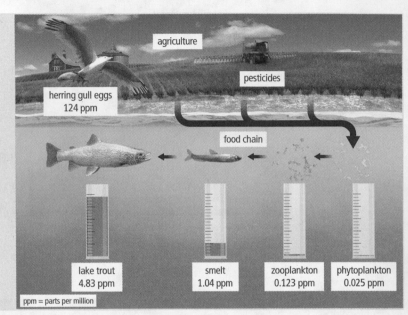

MATERIALS

- safety goggles, nonlatex apron, nonlatex gloves
- beads, large (16)
- beaker, 500 mL
- marker
- paper cups (4 small, 2 medium, 1 large)
- pencil, sharpened
- salt
- tape, masking
- tray, large

SAFETY INFORMATION

- Wear safety goggles, a nonlatex apron, and nonlatex gloves during the setup, hands-on, and takedown segments of the activity.
- Immediately pick up any dropped items on the floor so the items don't become a slip/fall hazard.
- Use caution when using sharp tools, which can cut or puncture skin.
- Wash your hands with soap and water immediately after completing this activity

MAKE A CLAIM

Read the procedure and write a prediction in your Evidence Notebook about how the beads, or pollutants, will transfer between the cups. How are contaminants magnified up the food chain?

CARRY OUT THE INVESTIGATION

1. Label the small cups "Smelt," the medium cups "Trout," and the large cup "Gull." With just the pencil tip, punch one or two small holes in the bottom of each cup, and cover them with tape.

2. Fill each of the cups halfway with salt. Add four beads to each small cup.

3. Hold each of the small cups over the beaker and remove the tape. Allow the salt to flow through the holes into the beaker. Place the tray underneath the beaker to collect any salt that misses the beaker.

4. Pour the remaining contents of two small cups into one medium cup. Pour the contents of the other two small cups into the second medium cup. Repeat Step 3 with the medium-sized cups.

5. Pour the remaining contents of both of the medium cups into the large cup.

ANALYZE

1. What were you modeling when you allowed the salt to flow out of each cup?

_____

_____

_____

_____

_____

2. What pattern did you notice for the transfer of pollutants between trophic levels?

_____

_____

_____

_____

DRAW CONCLUSIONS

Write a conclusion in your Evidence Notebook that addresses the points below.

Claim How are contaminants magnified up the food chain? Was your prediction correct?

Evidence Why would tertiary or higher level consumers have the highest concentration of toxins? What evidence from the activity supports your claim?

Reasoning What role(s) do humans play in biomagnification? Use evidence from this activity to explain your reasoning.

| USING A COMPUTER MODEL | WHAT DO ALLIGATORS EAT? | AQUATIC PRIMARY PRODUCTIVITY | Go online to choose one of these other paths. |

Lesson Self-Check

FIGURE 13: Some algae blooms produce toxic chemicals.

a Algae blooms occur in aquatic ecosystems of different sizes, including ponds, lakes, and oceans.

Chlorophyll concentration (mg/m³)

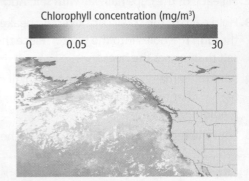

b North Pacific algae growth, 2002

c North Pacific algae growth, 2015

Warm waters combined with the upwelling of nutrients caused the North Pacific algae bloom of 2015. This bloom was significant because of its size and toxicity. Many marine animals, such as pelicans and sea lions, were found washed up on shore, either dead or with symptoms of domoic acid poisoning. These animals are all part of North Pacific food webs.

 Evidence Notebook Refer to your notes in your Evidence Notebook to explain how the marine animals affected by the algae bloom could have been poisoned by domoic acid. Using this information, answer the following questions:

1. Make a claim about how the algae population could impact the marine animals in the North Pacific ecosystem.
2. What evidence supports your claim? For example, how could domoic acid move from algae to sea lions or pelicans? What role do humans play in the cycle?
3. How does an ecosystem maintain stability when a disturbance, such as an algae bloom, is introduced? Your explanation should include a discussion of the flow of energy and matter in ecosystems.

CHECKPOINTS

Check Your Understanding

1. In a prairie ecosystem, which of the following populations has the most stored energy for use by other organisms?
   - ○ **a.** hawks
   - ○ **b.** bison
   - ○ **c.** prairie dogs
   - ○ **d.** prairie grasses

2. Which food chain correctly shows the direction that energy and matter can flow through a temperate forest ecosystem?
   - ○ **a.** fruit $\longrightarrow$ insect $\longrightarrow$ sparrow $\longrightarrow$ hawk
   - ○ **b.** hawk $\longrightarrow$ fruit $\longrightarrow$ insect $\longrightarrow$ sparrow
   - ○ **c.** insect $\longrightarrow$ sparrow $\longrightarrow$ hawk $\longrightarrow$ fruit
   - ○ **d.** insect $\longrightarrow$ hawk $\longrightarrow$ fruit $\longrightarrow$ sparrow

3. Think about the flow of matter and energy in a pyramid model with a producer level, a primary consumer level, a secondary consumer level, and a tertiary consumer level. Select all correct answers.
   - ☐ **a.** The sun is the ultimate source of energy in an ecosystem.
   - ☐ **b.** Matter flows and is often conserved within or among ecosystems.
   - ☐ **c.** Energy flows through ecosystems, but only a certain amount of energy is transformed into biomass.
   - ☐ **d.** Energy flows through ecosystems, but some is lost to the environment as heat.
   - ☐ **e.** Matter and energy are completely conserved and transformed into biomass within an ecosystem.

4. What is the relationship between a food chain and trophic levels?
   - ○ **a.** A food chain demonstrates how the organisms at the highest trophic levels have the most energy.
   - ○ **b.** Food chains illustrate the flow of energy from one trophic level to the next.
   - ○ **c.** A food chain models the energy flow within a single trophic level.

5. A consumer eats 1500 J of food energy. The consumer uses 15 percent of the food energy for new biomass and the rest for metabolic processes and waste. Use this information to answer the following questions in the spaces provided:

   a. How many joules of food energy were converted into new biomass? _____ J

   b. How many joules of food energy are converted to heat and excreted as waste? _____ J

   c. What percentage of the food energy was converted to heat and excreted as waste? _____ %

6. Select the correct terms to complete the statement about the efficiency of an herbivorous diet.

   Herbivores, such as rabbits, eat plants, which are producers. Most producers obtain energy from other plants | the sun | water. When a hawk eats a rabbit, the hawk is getting a small amount | large amount of energy stored in the rabbit.

7. An aquatic ecosystem contains 15 000 algae, 1000 freshwater shrimp, 80 perch, 10 northern pike, and 1 osprey. Draw a pyramid of numbers that represents this ecosystem.

CHECKPOINTS (continued)

8. A student thinks that populations higher in a food chain are larger because they deplete the populations of organisms lower in the food chain. Using evidence from this lesson, explain why this student's thinking is incorrect.

_____

_____

_____

_____

_____

_____

_____

9. Describe how energy and matter flow, interact, and change forms throughout the Earth system.

_____

_____

_____

_____

_____

_____

_____

_____

MAKE YOUR OWN STUDY GUIDE

In your Evidence Notebook, design a study guide that supports the main ideas from this lesson:

Life in an ecosystem requires a source of energy.

Energy and matter change forms as they flow through ecosystems.

The flow of energy and matter in an ecosystem can be modeled by food chains, food webs, and pyramid models.

Remember to include the following information in your study guide:
- Use examples that model main ideas.
- Record explanations for the phenomena you investigated.
- Use evidence to support your explanations. Your support can include drawings, data, graphs, laboratory conclusions, and other evidence recorded throughout the lesson.

Consider how food chains, food webs, and pyramid models show the flow of energy and matter through trophic levels in an ecosystem. Predict the transformations that occur as energy and matter flow through an ecosystem.

Cycling of Matter in Earth's Spheres

Biosphere 2 is a research facility located in Arizona.

CAN YOU SOLVE IT?

The curious-looking buildings shown in the photo above are part of a research facility located in Arizona called Biosphere 2. The tightly sealed glass and steel structure currently serves as a place where scientists study Earth's ecosystems to better understand carbon and oxygen cycles, coral reef health, water recycling, and more.

On September 26, 1991, eight research scientists began a two-year adventure living in Biosphere 2. The researchers, known as "Biospherians," were completely sealed off from the outside environment to simulate living in a closed ecosystem. But the results of the experiment were unexpected. The Biospherians had to cope with inadequate food, decreasing oxygen levels, and increasing carbon dioxide levels. The imbalances resulted in many plants and animals dying, providing evidence that ecosystems are much more complex and dynamic than originally thought.

PREDICT Why did problems with low oxygen levels and increasing carbon dioxide levels develop in Biosphere 2? How would you solve these problems?

_____

_____

_____

 Evidence Notebook As you explore the lesson, gather evidence for how matter and energy change form as they cycle through ecosystems.

Matter Cycles Through Ecosystems

Earth is an open system in terms of energy, as it constantly gains energy from the sun. In contrast, Earth is a closed system in terms of matter. All of the matter on Earth has more or less been here for billions of years. Matter and energy cannot be created or destroyed, only transformed into other forms.

PREDICT Matter and energy move through ecosystems between different organisms. How does matter travel through an ecosystem and through Earth's spheres?

_____

_____

_____

Energy and Matter in the Earth System

The Earth system includes all of the matter, energy, processes, and cycles within Earth's boundary with space. Energy from the sun drives the cycling of matter in Earth's spheres and in the many ecosystems within those spheres. Producers use only about one percent of the sun's energy that enters Earth's atmosphere.

 Math Connection

Solar Radiation

When solar radiation enters Earth's atmosphere, about 23 percent is absorbed in the atmosphere and about 48 percent is absorbed at the surface. The rest is reflected back into space.

SOLVE If energy is conserved, what percent of the solar energy should be reflected back into space?

○ **a.** 71%   ○ **c.** 100%

○ **b.** 12%   ○ **d.** 29%

FIGURE 1: Earth's atmosphere absorbs and reflects energy.

23%

48%

Like energy, matter in the Earth system cycles within and among Earth's spheres: the atmosphere, geosphere, hydrosphere, biosphere, and even the anthrosphere. A relatively small amount of matter is lost into space from the very top of the atmosphere, but scientists generally think of the Earth system as closed in terms of matter.

 Collaborate Discuss this question with a partner: How do you think Earth's ecosystems would be different if more or less solar radiation was reflected by the atmosphere?

EXPLAIN Use the correct terms to complete the statement about Earth's spheres.

FIGURE 2: This glass globe models the Earth system.

| atmosphere | biosphere | geosphere | hydrosphere |

Energy from the sun fuels the cycling of matter. For example, water in the _____ evaporates to the _____. Water returns to Earth's surface, or the _____, as precipitation. Organisms in the _____ use water to carry out cell processes.

Matter changes form as it cycles through the Earth system, but like energy, it cannot be destroyed. For example, organisms metabolize food using chemical reactions. These reactions break bonds and form new chemical bonds among the same atoms to make new compounds. An organism can use these new compounds for growth and cell processes. Some matter is excreted as waste, which is recycled in the environment. The total amount of matter in the system remains unchanged.

Using food webs and pyramid models, you can show how matter cycles through different trophic levels in an ecosystem. As one organism consumes another, that matter is transferred into higher trophic levels. When organisms die, their matter is cycled back through lower trophic levels. In this way, no new matter is created, but matter continually moves through and between ecosystems.

The Water Cycle

Scientists model specific cycles to better understand the cycling of matter in the Earth system. The hydrologic cycle, also known as the water cycle, is the pathway of water on Earth.

ANALYZE Water moves by different processes and is stored in reservoirs. Determine whether each item is a reservoir or a process.

clouds
reservoir | process

precipitation
reservoir | process

evaporation
reservoir | process

freshwater lake
reservoir | process

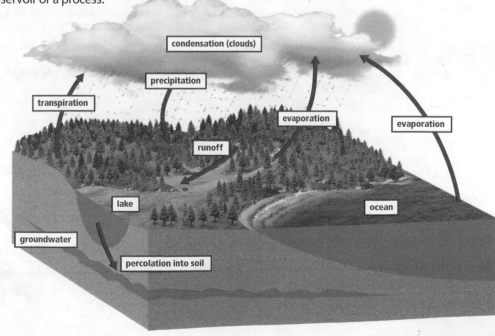

condensation (clouds)

precipitation

transpiration

evaporation

evaporation

runoff

lake

ocean

groundwater

percolation into soil

Earth's Cycles and Weathering Plan and conduct an investigation to see how water can dissolve certain substances, then apply your knowledge to investigate interactions between water and rock in the Earth system.

Within the hydrologic cycle, water moves between reservoirs by different processes. A reservoir is any location where cycling matter is stored. Water molecules might be stored in a reservoir for a long period of time, such as in a glacier, or for shorter periods of time, such as in a cloud. Precipitation is an example of a process that moves water between reservoirs.

In the hydrologic cycle, heat from the sun causes water to evaporate from reservoirs such as the ocean and to evaporate from plant leaves through transpiration. As water vapor rises into the atmosphere, it cools and condenses into clouds. Water then falls back to Earth in the form of precipitation, such as rain, snow, or hail. Precipitation seeps into the ground or flows into streams or rivers. Water ends up in a reservoir where it is stored until the process starts again.

 Collaborate With a partner, discuss this question: If the total amount of water on Earth does not change, why are there concerns about global freshwater shortages?

Cycles of Matter on Earth

Many elements are essential for the functioning and growth of organisms. Elements such as carbon interact chemically as they cycle through Earth's spheres. Like water, these elements cycle through the Earth system, ecosystems, and organisms. The sun and the heat from within Earth provide energy that drives these cycles. The matter in these cycles flows between reservoirs where it is stored for a period of time. As matter cycles, bonds are broken, and atoms are rearranged into new molecules.

The Oxygen Cycle

Most of the oxygen cycling on Earth occurs among the biosphere, hydrosphere, and atmosphere by way of photosynthesis, respiration, and decomposition. When you think about oxygen, you may think of oxygen gas (O_2) in the atmosphere, the form of oxygen that all organisms need. Oxygen is also found in the atmosphere as part of carbon dioxide, and in very small quantities as other gases such as ozone (O_3) and nitrogen oxides (NO and N_2O). In the oceans, it is part of water (H_2O) but also occurs as dissolved gases such as oxygen and carbon dioxide and ions such as bicarbonate (HCO_3^-).

MODEL Select the correct labels to complete the model of the oxygen cycle.

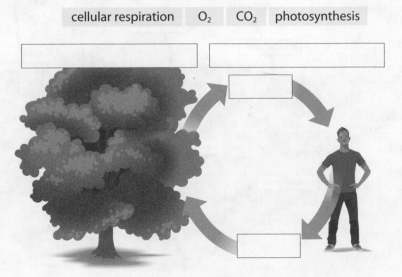

cellular respiration O_2 CO_2 photosynthesis

Oxygen that is taken in by plants and animals is converted into almost every type of biological molecule, including carbohydrates, fats, and proteins. Each cycle on Earth interacts with other cycles. For example, the water cycle interacts with the oxygen cycle, because water is necessary for photosynthesis.

 Evidence Notebook In the Biosphere 2 project, oxygen levels decreased over time and carbon dioxide reached dangerous levels. Describe a possible solution to this problem, and explain how it relates to processes in the oxygen cycle.

The Nitrogen Cycle

About 78 percent of Earth's atmosphere is composed of nitrogen gas (N_2). However, most organisms are not able to use nitrogen in this form to build organic molecules. The nitrogen must be fixed, or incorporated into other molecules that organisms can use. Bacteria, which are involved in many steps of the nitrogen cycle, fix nitrogen into ammonia, nitrite, nitrate, and other chemicals that organisms can use. Much of the nitrogen cycle takes place below ground.

FIGURE 3: The nitrogen cycle is made up of many processes that move nitrogen from the atmosphere to the biosphere and back again.

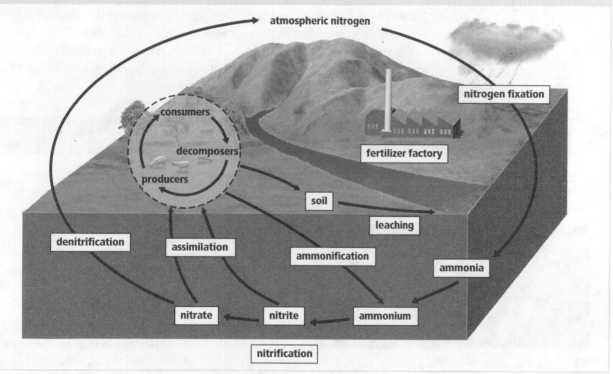

Certain types of bacteria convert gaseous nitrogen into ammonia (NH_3) through a process called nitrogen fixation. Some of these bacteria are aerobic, which means they use oxygen. Other bacteria are anaerobic, which means they do not use oxygen. In aquatic ecosystems, a few types of cyanobacteria perform this task. Some nitrogen-fixing bacteria on land live in small outgrowths, called nodules, on the roots of plants such as beans and peas. Other nitrogen-fixing bacteria live freely in the soil. The ammonia released by these bacteria is transformed into ammonium (NH_4^+) by the addition of hydrogen ions found in acidic soil. Plants take up some ammonium, but most is used by nitrifying bacteria as an energy source. These bacteria change ammonium into nitrite (NO_2^-) and then nitrate (NO_3^-) through a process called nitrification.

Explore Online ▶

Hands-On Lab

Nitrogen Fixation
Investigate the role of nitrogen-fixing bacteria by observing prepared slides of legume root nodules.

EXPLAIN Bacteria are microscopic organisms, but they are essential to life on Earth. Using evidence from the nitrogen cycle, explain how the microscopic fixation of nitrogen can have such a large impact on life.

_____

_____

Nitrates released by soil bacteria are taken up by plants through assimilation, which converts them into organic compounds such as amino acids and proteins. Nitrogen continues along the cycle as animals eat plant or animal matter. When decomposers break down animal excretions or dead animal and plant matter, nitrogen is returned to the soil as ammonium in a process called ammonification. Denitrifying bacteria use nitrate as an oxygen source, releasing nitrogen gas back into the atmosphere as a waste product via denitrification.

Nitrogen fixation can occur through biological processes carried out by special types of bacteria, but it can also occur through industrial processes such as the production of fertilizer. Some nitrogen also enters the soil as a result of atmospheric fixation by lightning. Energy from lightning breaks apart nitrogen molecules in the atmosphere. Nitrogen recombines with oxygen in the air, forming nitrogen monoxide. The combination of nitrogen monoxide with rainwater forms nitrates, which are absorbed by the soil. Nitrates in the soil may be moved by water, eventually settling at the bottom of lakes, swamps, and oceans in a process called leaching.

Energy and Matter

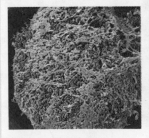 

FIGURE 4: Rhizobia bacteria have a symbiotic relationship with plants in the legume family.

a Rhizobia bacteria are nitrogen-fixing bacteria that live in pea plant nodules (colored SEM).

b Pea plant nodules develop on the roots of the plant.

Rhizobia Bacteria

Nitrogen-fixing bacteria live symbiotically, or in close relationship, with certain types of plants, particularly those in the legume family. Rhizobia bacteria live in the nodules on the roots of legumes. The plant provides essential nutrients to the bacteria and, in return, the bacteria fix nitrogen into ammonia, which the plant absorbs. Most of the ammonia made by the bacteria is kept by the plant and very little is released into the soil until the plant dies. Then, decomposers convert the ammonia molecules into other nitrogen compounds and release some of that nitrogen back into the atmosphere as nitrogen gas.

APPLY Legumes are often planted and harvested as crops. When this happens, the plants are not left to decompose into the soil. How does removing the legumes from the ecosystem affect the nitrogen cycle?

_____

_____

_____

The Phosphorus Cycle

Phosphorus is an important element for living things. It is a component of phosphate groups in ATP, DNA, and phospholipids in cell membranes. Phosphorus occurs in the form of phosphate salts found in ocean sediments and rocks. Geologic processes expose these rocks, and water and wind break them down, making them available to plants and animals.

FIGURE 5: The phosphorus cycle interacts with the rock cycle through processes such as geologic uplift and weathering.

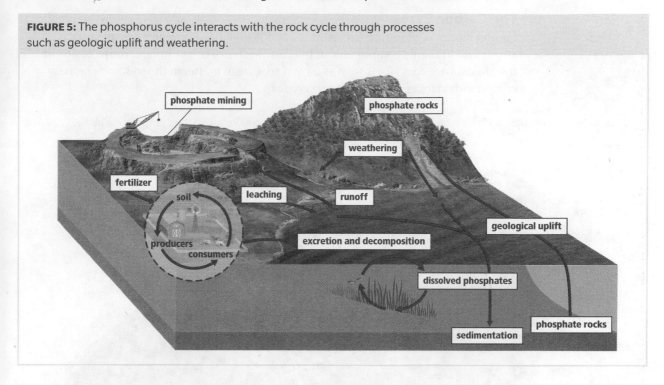

Weathering of phosphate rocks by rain releases phosphate compounds in soil and water. On land, plants can take up phosphate compounds from the soil, and consumers gain phosphorus by eating the producers. Decomposers then return phosphorus to the soil and water when they break down the organic matter and wastes of the producers and consumers.

Water can transport phosphorus to aquatic ecosystems through runoff and leaching. Phosphorus compounds dissolve into phosphates, where they can be taken up by algae and then consumed by other aquatic organisms. Some dissolved phosphates settle at the bottom of oceans in a process called sedimentation, becoming phosphate rocks over millions of years.

Certain geologic processes expose the phosphate rocks at the bottom of the ocean to the atmosphere. The rocks then undergo weathering, releasing phosphate compounds back into the ecosystem and continuing the phosphorus cycle. Humans also introduce phosphates into the ecosystem by mining them to make fertilizers and cleaners. Excess phosphates from human activities can enter aquatic ecosystems through runoff and leaching. Very little phosphate is naturally available in most bodies of water, and any increases can lead to significant changes in the ecosystem.

INFER Which statements are true about the phosphorus cycle? Select all correct answers.

☐ **a.** Phosphate flows from the atmosphere to the geosphere.

☐ **b.** Phosphorus is stored in only abiotic reservoirs.

☐ **c.** Weathering releases phosphate from rocks.

☐ **d.** Phosphate is taken up by producers in aquatic ecosystems.

> **Evidence Notebook** When the water at Biosphere 2 became polluted with too many nutrients, researchers treated the water by running it over mats of algae. Why did they do this, and how does it relate to the nitrogen and phosphorus cycles?

The Carbon Cycle

Carbon is present in most chemical compounds that make up living things. Carbon is also stored in abiotic components of the Earth system. For example, carbon dioxide in the atmosphere, fossil fuels such as oil and coal, dead matter in the soil, and chemical compounds in rocks are all carbon reservoirs.

FIGURE 6: Processes such as photosynthesis, cellular respiration, and combustion drive the cycling of carbon.

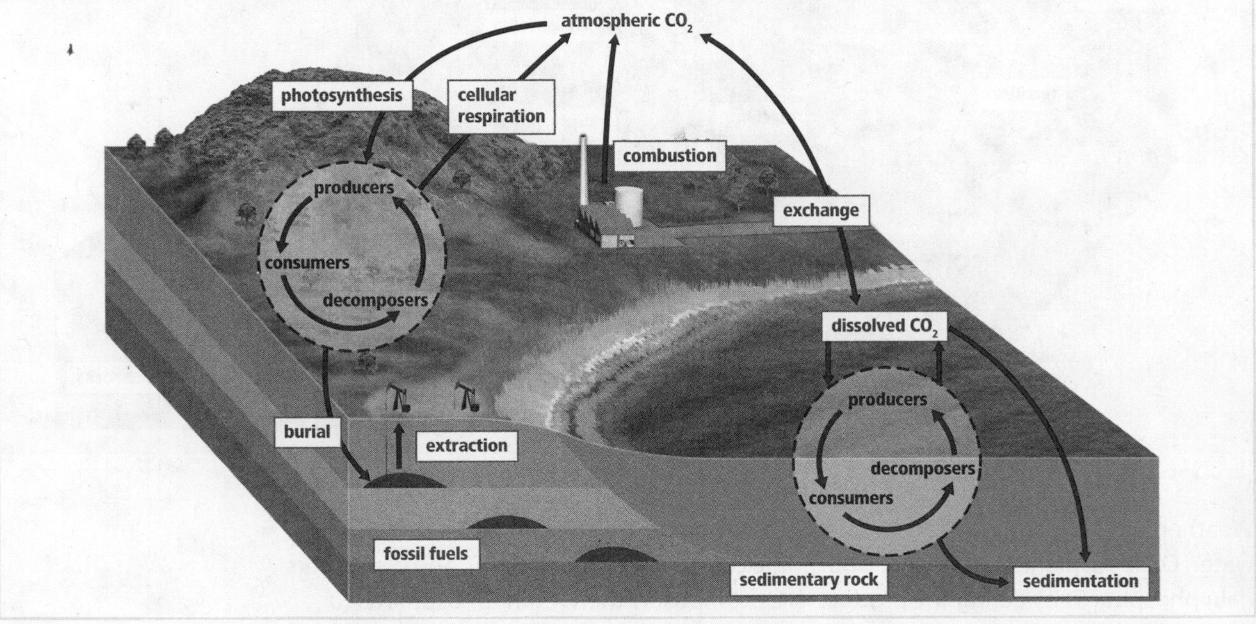

Producers remove CO_2 from the atmosphere through photosynthesis. Photosynthetic organisms incorporate the carbon into carbohydrates to store in their tissues. When consumers eat producers, they obtain the carbon, storing some of it in their tissues and releasing some back into the atmosphere through cellular respiration. When the consumers die, decomposers break down the organic matter and release carbon back into the atmosphere through cellular respiration. Carbon is also released into the soil.

Some of the carbon in organic matter may become fossilized. Under certain conditions, the burial process stores that carbon in Earth's crust where, over millions of years, it becomes fossil fuel. Since the 1800s, humans have extracted this carbon and combusted it, releasing large amounts of carbon back into the atmosphere.

Carbon dioxide diffuses into the ocean from the atmosphere. Oceans are carbon sinks that absorb and hold large amounts of carbon. Carbon enters the aquatic biotic cycle when algae and phytoplankton convert it during photosynthesis. Some dissolved CO_2 is used in the processes of sedimentation and burial to form different types of sedimentary rock. These processes are very slow, taking millions of years, but they form extremely large carbon reservoirs.

> **Evidence Notebook** How do the hydrologic cycle and the different cycles of matter relate to one another? How can a change in one cycle affect all of the other cycles?

Modeling the Carbon Cycle

Carbon appears in many different forms in Earth's systems. It is found in solid form in coal, it is dissolved in seawater, and it appears in gaseous form in the air that we breathe in and out. Carbon is found in the tissues of all life forms. It is also part of the gases in the atmosphere that keep Earth's temperatures warm enough to support life.

The Cycling of Carbon

The impact of the processes that cycle carbon between Earth's systems depends on the time scale and rate at which these processes operate. Natural processes that move carbon between the hydrosphere, atmosphere, and biosphere work on a time scale of a few hundred years. Therefore, these processes can have a more immediate impact on the Earth system than processes that move carbon in and out of the geosphere.

PREDICT How would the processes and reservoirs of the carbon cycle change over time if photosynthesis stopped?

_____

_____

_____

_____

FIGURE 7: Different processes function to cycle carbon on land and in the oceans.

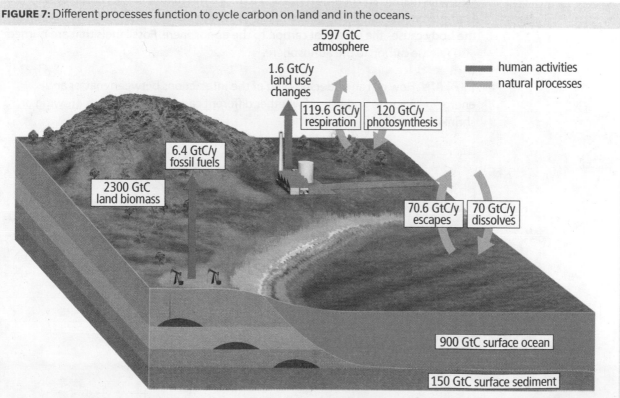

Credit: Adapted from *Climate Change 2007: Working Group I: The Physical Science Basis* by Denman et al. Copyright ©2007 by Cambridge University Press. Adapted and reproduced by permission of Intergovernmental Panel on Climate Change.

In the biosphere, photosynthesis, cellular respiration, and decomposition are processes that cycle carbon between systems. These processes are constant, cycling carbon through plants, animals, and soil organisms such as fungi and bacteria.

The ocean and the atmosphere are also constantly exchanging gases, including carbon dioxide. This exchange of gases is shown by the curved arrows above the ocean in Figure 7. The curved arrows on the land show that photosynthesis and respiration roughly balance each other, but move some carbon toward longer term reservoirs, such as the wood in forests.

Human activities move carbon into the atmosphere from long-term storage in the biosphere and geosphere. The model in Figure 7 shows an additional 8 gigatons (Gt) per year of carbon moving into the atmosphere from human activities. A gigaton is equal to one billion tons.

Measuring Carbon

It is extremely difficult to measure carbon precisely. Different types of measurements give varying results. The amounts also change over time. Numbers in models can also differ, because reservoirs can be grouped differently. For example, in some models, soil is included with biomass, while in others it is included with sediment. Some models show the entire ocean as one reservoir, while others divide it up into two reservoirs: the surface and the deep ocean. Different models can be used together to explain current changes and predict future changes.

Energy and Matter

Carbon is matter, and energy is needed to move this matter in the carbon cycle. Energy from the sun allows plants to use carbon to make biomass. Energy burned in the body causes the release of carbon to the atmosphere. Fossil fuels that are burned also release carbon to the atmosphere.

EXPLAIN How can an understanding of the interactions between matter and energy help you to understand whether different carbon reservoirs are growing or shrinking?

_____

_____

_____

_____

_____

_____

_____

Hands-On Lab

Ocean Acidification

The increased levels of CO_2 in the atmosphere seem to have an adverse effect on marine organisms—specifically those that have exoskeletons of calcium carbonate. Some have a more difficult time building shells, and some existing shells break down more easily. Why is this happening? How does the generation of CO_2 affect the pH of water? In this lab, you will both explore the impact of increased concentrations of dissolved CO_2 on the acidity of water and how that affects the shells of some marine organisms.

MAKE A CLAIM

How does increased concentration of dissolved CO_2 lead to increased acidity of water? Record your answer in your Evidence Notebook

MATERIALS

- indirectly vented chemical splash goggles, nonlatex apron, nonlatex gloves
- baking soda and vinegar (optional)
- beaker, 200 mL

- bromothymol blue indicator solution, 50 mL per test
- candle and matches (optional)
- device with Internet access

- heat source
- pH probe (optional)
- sodium chloride
- straw
- thermometer
- yeast (optional)

SAFETY INFORMATION

- Wear indirectly vented chemical splash goggles, a nonlatex apron, and nonlatex gloves during the setup, hands-on, and takedown segments of the activity.

- Immediately pick up any items dropped on the floor so they do not become a slip/fall hazard.

- Use caution when working with caustic chemicals (acids). They can burn skin.

- Use caution when working with heating sources. They can burn skin.

- Keep burning candles away from combustible materials to avoid causing a fire.

- Do not inhale and suck the indicator solution up the straw. Only exhale and blow out through the straw.

- Use caution when working with glassware, which can shatter if dropped and cut skin.

- Use only GFI protected circuits when using electrical equipment, and keep away from water sources to prevent shock.

- Wash your hands with soap and water immediately after completing this activity.

indirectly vented chemical splash goggles

CARRY OUT THE INVESTIGATION

Part A

1. Pour 50 mL of indicator solution into a beaker. Record the color in your Evidence Notebook.

2. Exhale into the straw to add CO_2 from your breath to the beaker.

3. Stop exhaling once a color change has occurred. Colors will range from green to yellow—yellow indicates a lower pH and green a higher pH. Record the color the solution changed to in your Evidence Notebook.

Part B

1. Think about events that generate CO_2. Brainstorm with your group to come up with at least three different ways that CO_2 could be generated in your lab. If necessary, use the Internet to research ideas for simple CO_2 generation, or ask your teacher for suggestions.

2. As a group, decide which method of CO_2 generation you will use. Then, design an experiment that uses an indicator solution or a pH probe (if available) to explore how CO_2 affects pH. In your Evidence Notebook, explain how you will test the effect of CO_2 on pH.

3. The focus of this investigation is the impact of ocean acidification on marine life. Adapt your experiment to investigate the effect of salinity on the ability of CO_2 to dissolve in the water. In your Evidence Notebook, explain how you will alter your experiment.

4. Rising global temperatures and the parallel rise in the average ocean temperature can also affect marine life. Research how much the average ocean temperature has risen in the last 100 years and then adapt your experiment to investigate the effect of this temperature rise on the ability of CO_2 to dissolve in the water. In your Evidence Notebook, explain how you will alter your experiment.

DRAW CONCLUSIONS

Write a conclusion in your Evidence Notebook that addresses each of the points below.

Claim How does increased concentration of dissolved CO_2 lead to increased acidity of water? Was your prediction correct?

Evidence Use these questions to guide your answer. How does salinity affect the ability of CO_2 to dissolve in water and how does that affect pH levels? How does temperature affect the ability of CO_2 to dissolve in water and how does that affect pH levels?

Reasoning How is the CO_2 level in the atmosphere related to the amount of CO_2 in water? How is rising global temperature related to the amount of CO_2 in water? Why does increased CO_2 affect the shells of some marine animals?

 Evidence Notebook How can understanding a simple model of the carbon cycle help you understand a complex model that shows changes in carbon dioxide concentration in the atmosphere?

Human Impact on Earth's Cycles

Easter Island, located in the southeastern Pacific Ocean, was first inhabited between 400 CE and 700 CE. The human colony grew quickly over the next 1000 years, cutting down the forests for lumber and for building boats. The forests were cleared faster than they could grow back, and eventually the island was left with no trees. Without trees, there was no wood for shelter or boats, the soil washed away, and habitat for the island's animal populations was lost. With no food and the island resources nearly gone, the Easter Islanders disappeared. Today, a small population of people lives on the island. The stone monuments placed by the first inhabitants are a major tourist attraction.

FIGURE 8: These stone figures stand in the open areas of Easter Island.

PREDICT What effect did the human population have on Easter Island? How did they change the island's natural cycling of matter and energy?

_____

_____

_____

Air Pollution

Without human activity, the cycling of carbon, phosphorus, and nitrogen in the Earth system would be in a relatively steady state. Each year humans add synthetic chemicals and materials to Earth, and many of these chemicals cannot be integrated into normal ecosystem functions. The harmful effect of these pollutants can be immediate or delayed, but these effects may add up over time and can disrupt ecosystem functions.

FIGURE 9: Engine combustion contributes to air pollution.

The most common air pollution comes from the waste products produced by burning fossil fuels, such as gasoline and oil that contain carbon, nitrogen, and phosphorus. Burning fossil fuels releases carbon dioxide, methane, nitrous oxide, and other chemicals that pollute the air. Smog is a type of air pollution caused by the interaction of sunlight with pollutants produced by fossil fuel emissions. The nitrogen dioxide in smog reacts with oxygen to produce ozone, O_3. The ozone produced by reactions of nitrogen dioxide and oxygen tends to stay close to the ground, where it can be harmful to human health and ecosystem functions. However, ozone also exists naturally in the upper atmosphere. There, it acts as a shield protecting Earth's biosphere against harmful ultraviolet rays found in sunlight.

 Evidence Notebook As you read, record evidence to support or refute the idea that atoms are rearranged during cycles of matter as a result of human activities.

Climate Change

Carbon dioxide emissions released from the burning of fossil fuels have led to a substantial increase in atmospheric CO_2. The rate at which carbon dioxide enters the atmosphere as a result of human activities is much faster than the rate at which it is removed by other processes. Combusting fossil fuels and clear-cutting forests are two examples of human activities that lead to increased carbon dioxide levels in Earth's atmosphere.

Atmospheric CO_2 at Mauna Loa Observatory

FIGURE 10: Atmospheric carbon dioxide levels have risen substantially since 1960.

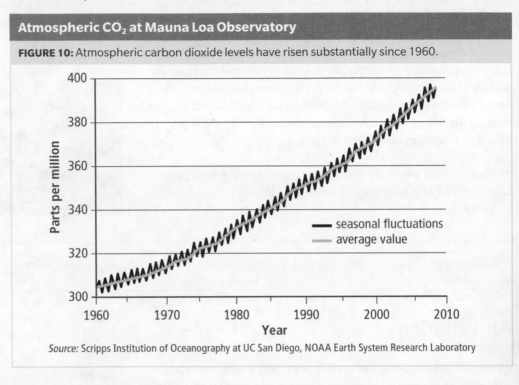

Source: Scripps Institution of Oceanography at UC San Diego, NOAA Earth System Research Laboratory

INFER As carbon dioxide is added to the atmosphere, more carbon dioxide also enters the ocean through diffusion. Carbon dioxide reacts with water to produce carbonic acid, which lowers the pH of the water. What effects do you think this might have on marine life?

_____

_____

_____

_____

Carbon dioxide is one of several greenhouse gases. These gases act in a similar way as a greenhouse for growing plants. They allow sunlight to pass through and provide energy for plant growth, but keep infrared radiation, or heat, from escaping. Increasing the amount of carbon dioxide in the atmosphere has been linked to increasing global temperatures, which can have a devastating effect on ecosystems. Some species have already been observed moving into new areas, because the changes in the climate make it difficult for these species to continue living in their natural range. Increased carbon dioxide levels have also led to shrinking of the polar ice caps, destroying the habitat for polar bears and other animals that live there.

Agricultural Runoff

The production of fertilizers through industrial nitrogen fixation and phosphate mining has increased greatly over the last few decades. Fertilizers are used to enrich the soil and stimulate plant growth. When crops are overfertilized, rain causes excess nitrogen and phosphorus to run off into nearby water bodies. The addition of these chemicals alters the nutrient balance in the water and can stimulate growth of aquatic producers such as algae, called an algae bloom. Similarly, pesticides can be transported by rain into nearby water bodies, impacting the water quality.

Erosion is the movement of rock, soil, and sand by wind and water. Eroded soil washes into nearby waterways. Most farming methods increase the rate of soil erosion. Plowing loosens the soil and removes plants that hold the soil in place. When water runs off the land, it carries some of the soil with it.

FIGURE 11: Agricultural runoff introduces nutrients to groundwater and waterways.

EXPLAIN Use the correct term to complete the statement about agricultural runoff.

Agricultural runoff can affect the overall health of an ecosystem. In the case of aquatic ecosystems, algae blooms, and the bacteria that break down the dead algae, can deplete the oxygen | nitrogen | carbon that fish and other organisms need to survive. Fish-eating birds and other animals are impacted because they rely on the fish for food.

Mining Runoff

Rock formations in the environment are often buried beneath thick layers of soil within ecosystems such as forests or grasslands. To obtain minerals from this rock, soil and vegetation are removed. This exposes the rock to air and water. Water and wind erode the rock and transport nutrients to nearby waterways. Excess amounts of nutrients, such as phosphorus, and soil erosion can impact ecosystems.

FIGURE 12: Mining runoff negatively affects aquatic ecosystems.

EXPLAIN Use the correct terms to complete the statement about mining runoff.

water   soil erosion   reservoir

Both rock and bodies of water are considered a type of

_____ in cycles of matter. When rock is exposed for mining,

_____ can readily transport nutrients from rock to aquatic

ecosystems. Runoff that carries excess nutrients can cause algae blooms. The effects of

_____ also increase water pollution and can clog waterways.

Evidence Notebook Many scientists worry that the influence humans have on hydrologic and other cycles of matter will cause lasting damage to Earth. Make a list of the activities you perform in a day that may impact one of these cycles. Explain how you are interacting with the cycle and how that could be affecting your local ecosystem. What can you do to decrease your impact?

Careers in Science

Oceanographer

The ocean is a large system with many different components. Matter, such as minerals and gases are dissolved in the water. A vast array of organisms live in this huge aquatic ecosystem, from single-celled plankton to Earth's largest animal, the blue whale. The ocean also contains energy absorbed from the sun and energy from Earth's interior.

Oceanography is the study of the ocean system. Because the ocean system is so huge, oceanographers must study many different parts of the system. For example, to answer questions about scalding hot thermal vents on the deep ocean floor, different oceanographers work together to observe, collect, and examine vent organisms, measure the temperature and pressure of the seawater, and analyze the chemistry of water and rock on the seafloor.

Octavio Aburto-Oropeza is an associate professor of marine biology at the Scripps Institution of Oceanography at UC–San Diego. His research focuses on marine reserves and commercially-exploited marine species and their fisheries.

Among the sites that Aburto-Oropeza studies is Cabo Pulmo Marine National Park, located in the Gulf of California. Prior to its establishment in 1995, the region had been severely overfished. The protected region now has a strict "no-take" policy that prohibits fishing.

In a recent assessment of the reserve, Aburto-Oropeza and his colleagues found that between 1999 and 2009, the reserve's biomass showed an increase of 465%, which translates to a ton of new fish produced each year. The results of their study indicate that, with proper management, fish communities can recover to a level comparable to areas that have never been fished before.

ASK List questions that you have about how changes to coral reefs could affect human society.

_____

_____

_____

_____

FIGURE 13: Oceanographer Octavio Aburto-Oropeza dives near the San Benito Islands off Baja California.

Understanding natural systems often requires the work of many scientists in different fields, such as biology, geology, chemistry, and oceanography. Different types of oceanographers study different components and processes in the ocean system. Biological oceanographers study marine organisms and ecosystems. Geological oceanographers study the rock, sediments, landforms, and processes such as volcanic eruptions and earthquakes on the seafloor. Chemical oceanographers study the components of seawater and the chemical reactions that occur in seawater. Physical oceanographers study characteristics such as temperature and pressure and ways that ocean water moves and interacts with outside forces such as wind and gravity.

If you are trying to answer questions related to a coral reef community, why is it important to consider the work of different types of scientists? What contributions towards research could be made by the different types of oceanographers?

COLLABORATE Share your questions about the interactions between humans and coral reefs with a partner. Together decide on one question that you want to focus on.

_____

_____

PREDICT What type or types of oceanographer would be most likely be involved in answering your question? Explain the role of each type of oceanographer.

_____

_____

MODEL With your partner, discuss how to model a system that relates to your question. For example, how would you model the relationship between humans and coral reefs?

_____

_____

_____

_____

PLAN With your partner, write a statement that summarizes a plan to address your question about the relationship between humans and coral reefs.

_____

_____

_____

_____

Language Arts Connection Work with your partner to develop a research plan to answer your question. Include specific steps for conducting the research and cite the sources you will use to address your question. Also, focus on the human connections to the question.

 **HUMAN EFFECTS ON EARTH'S SYSTEMS**   **MODELING A CHEMICAL CYCLE**   **LUNGS OF THE PLANET**   Go online to choose one of these other paths.

Lesson Self-Check

CAN YOU SOLVE IT?

FIGURE 14: The Biosphere 2 project taught scientists many lessons about the cycling of matter and energy.

Not long after the Biosphere 2 experiment began, carbon dioxide levels rose to dangerous levels. Biospherians were so starved for oxygen, they panted as they climbed stairs. Analysis of the Biosphere 2 systems showed that huge amounts of compost had been added to soils at the beginning of the experiment. This allowed soil bacteria to multiply at stunning rates, pumping out vast amounts of carbon dioxide and tilting the balance in the Biosphere 2 atmosphere. To restore the balance, oxygen eventually had to be pumped into the facility.

 Evidence Notebook Refer to your notes in your Evidence Notebook to explain why scientists had problems with low oxygen levels and increasing carbon dioxide levels in Biosphere 2. Use the following questions to develop your explanation:

1. How do matter and energy cycle through Earth's spheres? Use a model to illustrate the cycling of matter and the flow of energy within and between Earth's spheres.
2. Why do you think researchers had problems with low oxygen in Biosphere 2? Use a model that includes trophic levels in your explanation.
3. How would you solve this problem with Biosphere 2? How would your solution work on a global scale?

CHECKPOINTS

Check Your Understanding

1. Place these events in the correct order to show the cause-and-effect relationships that lead to algae blooms.

   _____ **a.** decomposers that break down dead algae take in oxygen for cellular respiration

   _____ **b.** lack of oxygen causes fish and other aquatic organisms to die

   _____ **c.** excess nutrients from fertilizer are transported by rain to nearby bodies of water

   _____ **d.** people overfertilize crops and lawns

   _____ **e.** algae overgrow, become overcrowded, and die

   _____ **f.** excess nitrogen and phosphorus leads to overgrowth of algae

2. Place these steps in the correct order to explain how carbon moves between the atmosphere and the biosphere in the carbon cycle.

   _____ **a.** Organisms carry out cellular respiration, which converts glucose and oxygen to carbon dioxide and water.

   _____ **b.** Plants use water and carbon dioxide from the atmosphere to make glucose and oxygen through photosynthesis.

   _____ **c.** Some animals eat plants and store chemical energy from the plants in their bodies.

   _____ **d.** Carbon dioxide is released by organisms and moves into the atmosphere.

3. Which statement describes a difference between the nitrogen and carbon cycles?
   - ○ **a.** The carbon cycle involves only plants.
   - ○ **b.** The nitrogen cycle requires a process called nitrogen fixation that is carried out by certain bacteria.
   - ○ **c.** The carbon cycle requires freezing temperatures.
   - ○ **d.** The nitrogen cycle occurs entirely in the ocean.

4. Which of the following are common to all of the chemical cycles? Select all correct answers.
   - ☐ **a.** reservoirs and processes
   - ☐ **b.** an atmospheric component
   - ☐ **c.** photosynthesis and respiration
   - ☐ **d.** living things as a reservoir
   - ☐ **e.** the sun as a source of energy
   - ☐ **f.** can be affected by human activities

5. Recently, some areas in the United States have seen an increase in trees due to reforestation efforts. How might the carbon cycle be altered after a large-scale reforestation effort? Select all correct answers.
   - ☐ **a.** Atmospheric carbon dioxide levels would decrease because the new trees would absorb carbon dioxide during photosynthesis.
   - ☐ **b.** Atmospheric carbon dioxide levels would stay the same because the new trees would absorb as much carbon dioxide as they produce.
   - ☐ **c.** Atmospheric carbon dioxide levels would decrease as trees grew larger and more carbon was stored in wood.
   - ☐ **d.** Atmospheric carbon dioxide levels would increase as new trees allowed ecosystems to support an equal number of new animals.

6. The following are processes in the water cycle. Which of these processes are driven by energy from the sun? Select all correct answers.
   - ☐ **a.** runoff
   - ☐ **b.** evaporation
   - ☐ **c.** percolation
   - ☐ **d.** melting
   - ☐ **e.** transpiration

CHECKPOINTS (continued)

7. There is evidence that the increasing carbon dioxide levels in the atmosphere are causing oceans to become more acidic. Ocean acidification may negatively impact species of phytoplankton, which are microscopic photosynthetic organisms that live in surface waters. Explain how the carbon cycle might be affected if phytoplankton populations were to decrease.

_____

_____

_____

_____

_____

_____

_____

8. Decomposers are an important part of many chemical cycles. Some carry out aerobic respiration, and some use anaerobic respiration as they break down organic matter. Explain why decomposers are so crucial for the cycling of matter in ecosystems.

_____

_____

_____

_____

_____

_____

_____

MAKE YOUR OWN STUDY GUIDE

 In your Evidence Notebook, design a study guide that supports the main ideas from this lesson:

Cycles of matter are processes that move matter through and among Earth's spheres. These cycles can be impacted by human activity.

Modeling changes to the carbon cycle allows us to predict future impacts on ecosystems.

Remember to include the following information in your study guide:
- Use examples that model main ideas.
- Record explanations for the phenomena you investigated.
- Use evidence to support your explanations. Your support can include drawings, data, graphs, laboratory conclusions, and other evidence recorded throughout the lesson.

Consider how energy allows matter in the closed Earth system to cycle between Earth's spheres.

Engineering Connection

Algae Biofuels Cars combust fossil fuels, releasing large amounts of carbon dioxide into the atmosphere. Carbon dioxide gas is one of the leading contributors to greenhouse gases, which increase global temperatures. To counteract this effect on the environment, engineers in California and around the world have been researching alternative fuels, such as algae biofuels, that do not release greenhouse gas emissions. Certain strains of algae trap, transform, and store solar energy as oil through the process of photosynthesis. The oil can then be processed into biofuel.

Research algae biofuels and write a blog entry explaining the potential uses of algae biofuels in your community. What impact could biofuels have on human-driven greenhouse gas emissions?

FIGURE 1: Algae biofuel production

Social Studies Connection

BFFs: Black-Footed Ferrets As European settlers moved to the Great Plains, they converted prairie land into farmland. These farmers and ranchers found the prairie dogs that lived on the land a nuisance and killed them off in large numbers. The black-footed ferrets (BFFs), which feed almost exclusively on prairie dogs, were also eradicated in the process. BFFs are a key species in the ecosystem, and their health is a primary indicator of the overall health of that ecosystem.

Research the story of the BFF and what its return into the ecosystem means. Make a pamphlet to document the history of the BFF, and explain any implications for local ranchers and farmers.

FIGURE 2: Black-footed ferrets released into the wild

Computer Science Connection

Computational Ecology Recent advances in computer modeling software and processor speed have expanded the ability of scientists to study the complexity of ecosystems. Historically, food webs were presented as a web of energy arrows connecting producers and consumers. But now, scientists can model hundreds of interactions between species and build a complete ecosystem network.

Review the ecosystem network shown here. What are the pros and cons of such a detailed model of an ecosystem? Do you think a human could analyze this network without a computer? Make a list of questions that you would ask based on this model. Compare your questions with your partner or group.

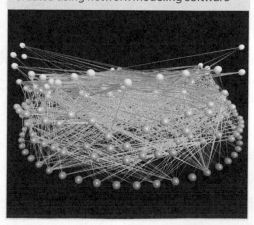
FIGURE 3: A complex ecosystem network created using network modeling software

THING EXPLAINER BY RANDALL MUNROE

A BOOK EXPLAINING COMPLEX IDEAS USING ONLY THE 1,000 MOST COMMON WORDS

TREE
A tree and the living and not living things around it

You know that a tree is a complex living thing. Trees also provide important habitats for a large variety of other living things, a biotic community. These symbiotic components make up the ecosystem in a tree. Here's an overview in simple terms.

RANDALL MUNROE
XKCD.COM

THE STORY OF A TREE AND ITS NEIGHBORS

A TREE IS A LIVING THING THAT GROWS BOTH UP AND DOWN. MOST TREES LIVE AS LONG AS US, BUT SOME OF THEM CAN LIVE MUCH LONGER.

TREES GIVE FOOD, AIR, AND A LOT OF OTHER STUFF TO LIVING THINGS.

PEOPLE USE TREES TO BUILD HOUSES OUT OF THE WOOD.

THEY ALSO BURN WOOD TO HEAT THOSE HOUSES.

YOU KNOW, I DON'T THINK WE REALLY THOUGHT THIS THROUGH.

THIS IS HOTTER THAN I EXPECTED!

OTHER LIVING THINGS MAKE THEIR HOMES INSIDE, ON, UNDER, AND NEAR TREES.

HI THERE!

GROWING UP

Trees grow taller only by making the ends of their branches longer. The spot where a branch joins the main part of the tree is never lifted higher.

LEAVES

Trees make power from the Sun's light using leaves. The green stuff in leaves eats light (and the kind of air we breathe out) and turns it into power (and the kind of air we breathe in).

POINTY CAT

This animal walks around slowly, climbing trees and eating leaves and sticks. It's covered in sharp points that can stick in your skin, so most animals don't bother it.

GRAY TREE-JUMPER

These little animals sleep in big round houses made of sticks and leaves high up in the branches.

QUIET NIGHT CATCHER

These birds fly very quietly and have big eyes to catch animals on the ground in the dark.

People think of them as knowing a lot of things, although that may just be because they're quiet and have big eyes.

BIRD HOLES

Some birds make holes, but a lot of them just use holes other birds make.

DRINK HOLES

These were made by a head-hitting bird looking for tree blood to drink.

TREE-EATING FLOWERS

This flower makes holes in trees and steals food and water from inside them. If the flowers get big, they can kill the branches they're growing on, or even kill the whole tree.

When people stand under this flower at a party, other people tell them to kiss.

LOUD JUMPERS

These two kinds of tiny animals make loud noises and are known for jumping. One has bones.

HEAD-HITTING BIRD

This kind of bird hits trees with its head, making holes in the wood with its sharp mouth. They make holes to find things to eat, and some also make holes to live in.

STORM BURN

When flashes of power from storms hit a tree, they can burn a line in the wood.

TREE

SKIN BURNER

These leaves have stuff on them that makes your skin turn red. It gives you a really bad feeling, like you need to rub your skin with something sharp, but doing that only makes it worse.

This leaf-flower grows in long lines across the ground or up trees. Sometimes it grows into the air like a small tree of its own. Like many things, its leaves come in groups of three.

BROKEN BRANCH HOLE

When a tree gets hurt, like if a branch breaks off, the place where it got hurt grows differently, just like when skin gets cut. Sometimes animals get in through these spots and make the hole bigger.

DIRT BRANCHES

Trees grow branches down into the ground, like the ones in the air. The air branches get light from the Sun, while the ground branches get water and food from the dirt. They spread way out—often farther than the air branches—but usually not very deep.

BIRD HOUSE

FIRE HOLE

These holes are from fires long ago. The leaves and sticks on the ground burned, and the wind blew the fire against this side of the tree. The burned spot grows in a different way and can sometimes turn into a large hole.

ANIMAL HILL

This is the dirt the walking flies took out of the ground while making their holes.

DOOR

TINY DOG

LONG-EAR JUMPERS

WALKING FLIES

These tiny animals live in big groups and make holes. Most of them don't have babies; each family has one mother who makes all the new animals for the house.

They usually don't fly, and they're not much like house flies. They're in the same group with the kinds of flies whose back end has a sharp point that can hurt you.

LONG BITERS WITHOUT ARMS OR LEGS (SLEEPING)

These long thin cold-blooded animals don't usually hang out together, and sometimes eat each other.

During the winter, though, lots of different kinds come together and sleep all wrapped up together in big holes under the ground where it's warmer.

LONG-HOLE MAKERS

Go online for more about *Thing Explainer*.

SKIN

The outer skin of trees is where growing happens and where they carry food up and down. Cutting off a ring of skin all the way around a tree will kill it.

Trees grow by adding new layers, and grow differently in different parts of the year. If you cut open a tree, you can see old layers, and count them to tell how many years old the tree is.

OLD METAL

When people use metal to stick signs to trees, sometimes the tree grows around the metal and eats it up.

Then, many years later, if someone needs to cut down the tree, their saw can hit the metal and send tiny sharp pieces flying everywhere.

TREE-FOOD STEALER

Instead of growing dirt branches of their own, these flowers grow onto the dirt branches of other trees and steal food from them.

Some of these little flowers don't even have green leaves and can't make their own food from light.

LITTLE HOLE-MAKERS

BIG HOLE-MAKERS

DIRT-BRANCH LIFE

Most trees and flowers have life growing on their dirt branches. This life helps them talk to the other trees and flowers around them. They can even use this life to share food or attack each other.

If something tries to eat one tree, it can tell other trees through messages carried by this ground life, and the other trees can start making bad water and other things to make themselves harder to eat.

TALL AND WIDE TREES

The same kind of tree can grow tall or wide. If there are other trees around, they'll grow mostly up, each one trying to get above the others to reach the Sun's light. If a tree is growing alone in a field, it will spread branches out to the sides so it can catch more light.

FIELD TURNING INTO FOREST

When people cut down a forest, sometimes they leave a few trees—to make a cool shadow area, or because the tree looks nice—and those trees will grow out into the new space.

If the forest grows back, the new trees—fighting with each other as they grow—will be tall and thin.

If you find a forest of tall thin trees with one wide tree with low branches in the middle, it might mean the forest you're in was someone's field a hundred years ago.

FOREST ABOVE WATER

DIRT BRANCHES

Analyzing Water Pollution

The small town of Lakeview is located on the shores of Piper Lake. The town relies on the lake for trout fishing, eagle watching, and recreational activities. Recently, a fertilizer plant, H.T.C. Fertilizers, was built upstream on Eagle River, which feeds into Piper Lake. Townspeople have noticed an increase in algae blooms in the lake. They are concerned the fertilizer plant is dumping too much nitrogen into the river, and people's livelihood could be affected. Are they right? Does the plant need to control the waste it puts into the river?

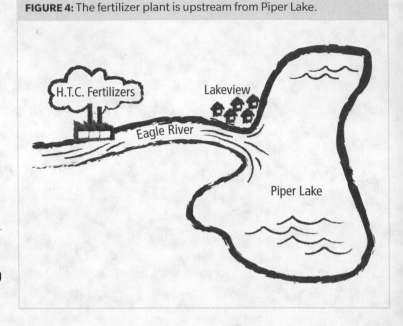

FIGURE 4: The fertilizer plant is upstream from Piper Lake.

1. DEFINE THE PROBLEM

With your team, write a statement outlining the problem you've been asked to solve. Record any questions you have about the situation and the information you need to solve the problem.

2. CONDUCT RESEARCH

With your team, investigate the cause-and-effect relationship between nitrogen, algae blooms, and fish populations. Could the fertilizer plant be responsible for the changes the town is experiencing?

3. ANALYZE DATA

On your own, analyze the problem you have defined along with your research. Make a model that demonstrates how excess nitrogen cycles through the aquatic ecosystem. Your model should also show any effects the nitrogen may have on the ecosystem using a food web, energy pyramid, biomass pyramid, or pyramid of numbers.

4. COMMUNICATE

Present your findings to the town and the fertilizer company. Explain whether or not the runoff from the fertilizer plant is adversely affecting the lake ecosystem. Your presentation should include images and data to support your claims. Try to anticipate your audience's reaction and be ready to answer their questions.

✓ CHECK YOUR WORK

A complete presentation should include the following information:

- A clearly defined problem with supporting questions that are answered in the final presentation.
- A model of the effect of the fertilizer runoff.
- A recommendation that explains how to solve the problem and uses evidence to support the solution.
- Images and data that further support your solution.

Name _____

Date _____

In your Evidence Notebook, make a concept map, other graphic organizer, or an outline using the Study Guides you made for each lesson in this unit. Be sure to use evidence to support your claims.

When synthesizing individual information, remember to follow these general steps:

- Find the central idea of each piece of information.
- Think about the relationships among the central ideas.
- Combine the ideas to come up with a new understanding.

Look back to the Driving Questions from the opening section of this unit. In your Evidence Notebook, review and revise your previous answers to those questions. Use the evidence you gathered and other observations you made throughout the unit to support your claims.

PRACTICE AND REVIEW

1. In a pyramid of numbers, the highest-order organism has the smallest number of individuals in an ecological community. What might happen if the population of this organism increased significantly? Select all correct answers.

   ☐ **a.** The population would eventually die off, because they would over-hunt the lower-ordered organisms.

   ☐ **b.** The population would thrive, because they have no predators.

   ☐ **c.** The populations of lower-ordered organisms would dramatically decrease and may go extinct in the area due to the increased predation.

2. Why are decomposers an essential part of an ecosystem? Select all correct answers.

   ☐ **a.** Plants rely on decomposers as a source of energy to carry out photosynthesis.

   ☐ **b.** If decomposers did not exist, dead organic matter would not be broken down.

   ☐ **c.** Decomposers help cycle nutrients, such as carbon and nitrogen, in ecosystems.

   ☐ **d.** Ecosystems that support decomposers have fewer plants and more animals, which increases biodiversity.

   ☐ **e.** Decomposers convert essential nutrients into forms that other organisms can use.

3. Explain how changes to the carbon cycle affect the cycling of carbon in other chemical cycles. Select all correct answers.

   ☐ **a.** An increase in atmospheric carbon dioxide causes an increase in global temperatures. The increased temperature cause greater evaporation in the hydrologic cycle.

   ☐ **b.** Extracting fossil fuels causes more sediment to be available for geological uplift in the phosphorus cycle.

   ☐ **c.** An increase in atmospheric carbon dioxide can cause plants to die. As certain plants die, so do the nitrogen-fixing bacteria in their roots, removing a large component of the ammonification process in the nitrogen cycle.

   ☐ **d.** Forests are carbon sinks, which collect carbon in their biomass. Deforestation results in less carbon being removed from the atmosphere and less oxygen being produced during the oxygen cycle.

4. In a pyramid of numbers, 90% of the energy can be lost as heat between trophic levels. Suppose the producer level has 50 000 J. Approximately how much energy is available to the secondary consumers in this energy pyramid?

   ○ **a.** 5 J   ○ **c.** 500 J

   ○ **b.** 50 J   ○ **d.** 5000 J

5. Forest fires release into the atmosphere the carbon, nitrogen, phosphorus, and sulfur that were collected in the biomass of the trees. Make a model to illustrate how the carbon, phosphorus, and nitrogen cycles are affected by the forest fire.

Explain how the changes in these cycles affect the local ecosystem.

_____

_____

_____

_____

_____

6. How do scientists use models to study the relationships between all of the components in an ecosystem? How does this help them understand ecosystem changes?

_____

_____

_____

_____

_____

UNIT PROJECT

Return to your unit project. In your final presentation, evaluate the strength of your prediction, experiment, data collection, and conclusions.

Remember these tips while evaluating:

- Look at the empirical evidence—evidence based on observations and data. Does the evidence support the explanation?

- Consider whether the explanation is logical. Does it contradict any evidence you have seen?

- How could you revise your setup and procedure to further test your prediction, model, or the evidence you collected?

UNIT 4

Evidence for Evolution

A bee collects pollen from a native California poppy.

FIGURE 1: This creosote ring in the Mojave Desert is estimated to be 11 700 years old. This makes it one of the oldest living organisms on Earth.

The creosote bush is thought to be the most drought-tolerant plant in North America. It has a variety of adaptations to its desert environment, including its reproductive tendency to clone outward in rings rather than rely solely on seed production. The plant's leaves are coated in a foul-tasting resin that protects it from water loss through evaporation and from grazing. It only opens its stomata in the morning to pull in carbon dioxide for photosynthesis from the more humid air and closes them as the day's temperature increases. It also has a root system that consists of both an exceptionally long tap root and a vast network of shallow feeder roots. Creosote bushes exhibit two different shapes to fit different microclimates. In drier areas, the plant has a cone shape in which stems funnel rainwater into the taproot. In wetter areas, the bush has a more rounded shape that provides shade to its shallow feeder roots.

PREDICT How do species change over time to adjust to varying conditions?

_____

_____

_____

DRIVING QUESTIONS

As you move through the unit, gather evidence to help you answer the following questions. In your Evidence Notebook, record what you already know about these topics and any questions you have about them.

1. How can we learn about life on early Earth?
2. How can we trace the lines of descent between species?
3. What are the mechanisms of natural selection, and how do they lead to changes in species over time?

UNIT PROJECT

Go online to download the Unit Project Worksheet to help plan your project.

Investigating the Evolution of Eyes

Eyes are complex organs. Simple eyes let organisms sense light while complex eyes, such as those in humans, let organisms see images. Explore how small changes over time can lead to the development of unique features, such as eyes. How can you explain the evolution of eyes?

Language Development

Use the lessons in this unit to complete the chart and expand your understanding of the science concepts.

TERM: fossil

Definition	Example

Similar Term	Phrase

TERM: geologic timescale

Definition	Example

Similar Term	Phrase

TERM: tectonic plate

Definition	Example

Similar Term	Phrase

TERM: evolution

Definition	Example

Similar Term	Phrase

TERM: natural selection

Definition	Example

Similar Term	Phrase

TERM: adaptation

Definition	Example

Similar Term	Phrase

TERM: artificial selection

Definition	Example

Similar Term	Phrase

TERM: heritable

Definition	Example

Similar Term	Phrase

Geologic Time

Red Rock Canyon State Park is made up of hills with distinctive layers of rock.

CAN YOU EXPLAIN IT?

Red Rock Canyon State Park in Southern California is known for the dramatic, colorful bands that run through the cliffs. The stripes in the cliffs are different layers of rock that were exposed over time. Within these layers, scientists have discovered more than 100 species of extinct plants and animals that lived from about 12 to about 8 million years ago. Red Rock Canyon has produced one of the most diverse arrays of fossil organisms in Western North America.

PREDICT How do you think the rock layers and fossils found in Red Rock Canyon can provide evidence for Earth's geologic history? What types of information can scientists learn from fossils?

_____

_____

_____

_____

_____

 Evidence Notebook As you explore this lesson, gather evidence to explain how the history of life on Earth is revealed through rock and fossil records.

Sedimentary Rock and Fossils

Rock is natural, solid, nonliving material that makes up Earth's crust and much of its interior. Most rock is composed of combinations of one or more minerals. Properties of a particular type of rock—such as color, texture, and mineral composition—are a result of how the rock formed. Through the rock cycle, rocks undergo physical and chemical changes. Other natural cycles are related to the rock cycle. For example, in the water cycle, moving water erodes weathered rock fragments and deposits them in new places where sedimentary rock layers can then form. Water also causes chemical changes as it dissolves rocks such as limestone and marble.

 Evidence Notebook How do you think the characteristics of rock can be used to determine how it formed and what Earth was like at the time and place where it formed?

The Formation of Sedimentary Rock

Running water, flowing ice, wind, and gravity move pieces of rock, called sediment, from one place to another over Earth's surface. Particles of rock settle out of water and air and accumulate as sediment on Earth's surface. Over time, sediments are buried and compressed. Water moving through pores between the grains of sediment deposits natural cement that glues the grains together. A sedimentary rock forms.

FIGURE 1: Grand Staircase Escalante National Monument, Utah

INFER Which layers of sedimentary rock at Grand Staircase Escalante National Monument do you think are the oldest? Use evidence to support your claim.

_____

_____

_____

Explore Online ▶

Hands-On Lab

Determining the Relative Age of Rock Strata Model core sampling and how large-scale forces change rock strata.

Sedimentary layers are deposited on top of each other. Unless the layers have been disturbed, the oldest rocks are at the bottom and the youngest are at the top. Sediments are also deposited in relatively flat layers. For example, when a river floods, mud, sand, and gravel are deposited in horizontal layers. Over time these layers are compacted and cemented together into hard rock. The top layer makes up the surface of Earth. However, uplift and erosion can expose the layers below the surface. For example, a river can carve into an uplifted sequence of layers and expose them in the canyon or valley walls.

Fossil Formation

A fossil is the trace or remains of an ancient organism that is preserved in rock or sediment. Bones, shells, plant fragments, and bacteria can all be fossilized.

ANALYZE Use Figure 2 to order the steps involved in the process of fossilization.

_____ **a.** Erosion reveals the layer of rock in which the animal was buried.

_____ **b.** An organism dies and begins to decay. If the organism is not buried soon after death, scavengers may feed on the flesh or microbes may break down carbon-rich molecules in the animal.

_____ **c.** With the soft tissues gone, only hard parts like bones, teeth, and shells remain and these remains are buried within a layer of sediment.

_____ **d.** Fossilization of the animal remains occurs over time.

Explore Online ▶

Hands-On Lab

Explore the Water and Rock Cycles Plan and conduct an investigation to explain a process that involves the water cycle and rock cycle.

FIGURE 2: Bones, teeth, footprints, and other traces of life can be fossilized or preserved. The processes involved in fossil formation take place on the scale of millions of years.

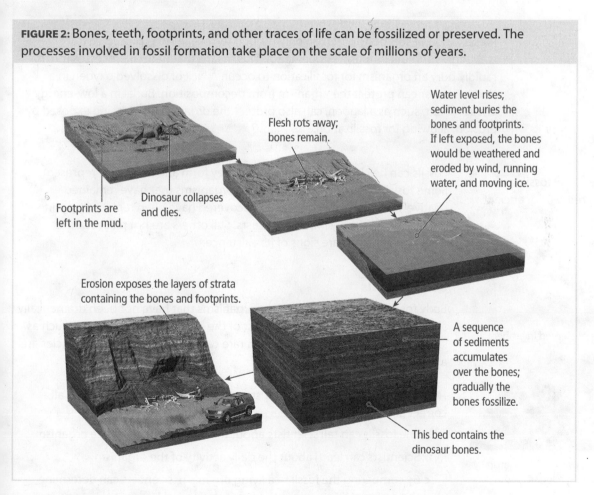

Footprints are left in the mud.

Dinosaur collapses and dies.

Flesh rots away; bones remain.

Water level rises; sediment buries the bones and footprints. If left exposed, the bones would be weathered and eroded by wind, running water, and moving ice.

Erosion exposes the layers of strata containing the bones and footprints.

A sequence of sediments accumulates over the bones; gradually the bones fossilize.

This bed contains the dinosaur bones.

Uncountable organisms have existed on Earth over time, but very few have been fossilized. Instead, the bodies of most organisms have decomposed, and their footprints and burrows have been washed away. Specific conditions must exist and certain processes must occur for an organism or its traces to become fossilized.

Probability of Fossilization

The chances that an organism dies and becomes a fossil depend on complex interactions. This is especially true when talking about a soft-bodied organism, an organism without an internal or external skeleton, or the soft body parts (such as tissues) of organisms with skeletons.

APPLY What makes soft tissue different from hard tissues? Use evidence to support your answer.

_____

_____

_____

_____

Preservation of soft body parts can only occur if the organism is protected from scavengers and decomposers upon death. This means that natural processes must rapidly bury an organism for fossilization to occur. A lack of dissolved oxygen in a body of water can protect the organism from decomposition. Burial in a low-energy environment, such as a lagoon, can also protect the organism from being exposed by erosion, allowing for fossilization.

FIGURE 3: Body fossils are physical remains of ancient organisms.

a Ants preserved in amber

b Beetle preserved in naturally occurring asphalt

c Mammoth preserved in frozen soil

Fossils can be classified based on how they form and what they represent. Some fossils are the actual parts of the organisms that have remained relatively unchanged. Most fossils discovered have been replaced by mineral crystals, or are simply imprints or casts. Still others are not pieces of the organism at all, but are signs of its existence.

Body Fossils

Body fossils are remains of ancient organisms that have not been dramatically altered. Body fossils generally consist of the hard parts of organisms, such as shells, bones, teeth, and cellulose. In rare cases, soft parts such as muscles are also preserved.

INFER What evidence can scientists collect from body fossils? Select all correct answers.

☐ **a.** The fossils can tell scientists about the size and shape of the organism.

☐ **b.** Scientists can learn about the daily activity of the organism.

☐ **c.** By comparing the fossil to a living organism, scientists can determine the group of living things the fossil was part of.

☐ **d.** Scientists can learn about how the organism functioned when it was alive.

Complete and well-preserved fossils, such as those shown in Figure 3, are rare. More commonly, body fossils consist of parts of organisms. Individual teeth or bones, broken or abraded bones and shells, or small fragments of wood are more commonly discovered.

Molds, Casts, and Imprints

If the body of an organism decays or dissolves after it has been buried, a three-dimensional impression of an organism may form. This is known as a *mold*. Although molds do not preserve the organism itself, important surface features can be preserved. Once a hollow mold forms, fluids may flow through it, slowly filling it with minerals, forming a *cast*. Casts can also be made of fine sediments that have filled the mold.

 Collaborate Molds and casts are imprints of body parts, but do not contain actual body fossils. With a partner, discuss what evidence scientists can gather from molds and casts. What kind of information can they not determine using these types of fossils?

FIGURE 4: Casts and imprints provide evidence for the shape and size of an organism.

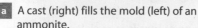

a A cast (right) fills the mold (left) of an ammonite.

b Compression has preserved the delicate structures of this leaf.

Sometimes all that remains of an organism is a dark *imprint* covered in a thin carbon-rich film. These two-dimensional fossils form when soft material and organisms such as leaves and insects are squeezed or compressed between layers of sediment. Over time most of the organic material decomposes and is removed.

Trace Fossils

Unlike body fossils, trace fossils are not actual pieces, molds, or impressions of organisms. Instead, *trace fossils* are preserved signs of the activity or behavior of an organism. There are a wide variety of trace fossils. Some, such as dinosaur tracks and worm trails, provide evidence for how an organism moved. The size and depth of dinosaur tracks can be used to estimate the animal's size, while the spacing between footprints can be used to infer how fast the animal walked or ran. Coprolites—pieces or pellets of fossilized feces—can provide information about the diet of ancient organisms. Fossilized burrows, shown in Figure 5, are evidence for where and how an organism lived. In addition, like other trace fossils, they can also provide information about the environment where they formed. The existence of some organisms can be inferred only from tracks and other trace fossils.

FIGURE 5: *Chondrites* looks like plant roots or coral, but it is actually fossilized burrows.

 Evidence Notebook A scientist examines the body fossil and trace fossils left by an ancient vertebrate species in Red Rock Canyon. What could the scientist learn about this species from each type of fossil? Give specific examples in your answer.

The Geologic Timescale

Rock formations, and the fossils within them, hold the key to unlocking Earth's 4.6 billion-year history. By determining the relative and actual ages of rocks, scientists assembled the geologic timescale, which separates Earth's history into distinct divisions of time.

 Collaborate Make a list of questions scientists might ask about types of fossils, where they are found, and how that information could help them understand the history of Earth. Discuss your list of questions with a partner.

The Fossil Record

In the early 1800s, scientists studying layers of rock in Europe made two very important observations. First, in a set of sedimentary layers, the combination of fossils changes vertically from layer to layer. Second, the groupings of fossils and the order of combinations are mostly consistent from place to place. These observations gave rise to the principle of *faunal succession*. Scientists soon recognized that they could use this principle to connect layers of rock that are separated by long distances.

ANALYZE Scientists can use the specific combinations of fossils in rock layers to correlate layers in different parts of the world. Draw lines connecting the European and Australian layers that are the same age.

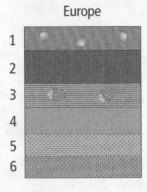
Europe
1
2
3
4
5
6

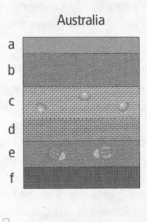
Australia
a
b
c
d
e
f

EXPLAIN How does the principle of faunal succession support the claim that a rock layer on one continent formed at the same time as a layer on another continent? What is the evidence and reasoning behind this?

_____

_____

_____

Index Fossils

Using the principle of faunal succession, scientists began to recognize that they could organize rock layers into broad groups by age. For example, the lowest and oldest layers, rich with trilobites, were classified as Paleozoic, meaning "ancient life." The middle layers containing ammonites and dinosaur bones were called Mesozoic, or "middle life." And the top and youngest layers, with mammal fossils, were called Cenozoic, or "new life."

FIGURE 6: *Tropites* existed for only about 20 million years.

As scientists were correlating and classifying layers based on faunal succession, they also noticed that some fossils were particularly useful for inferring the relative age of a rock layer. These species are known as *index fossils* because they can be reliably used to date rock layers. For example, *Tropites*, a species of ammonite, existed during the Mesozoic, sometime between 230 and 208 million years ago.

INFER Identify whether each instance would make a good or poor index fossil.

a. Fossil is abundant in rock layers. good | poor

b. Fossil is similar to other fossils. good | poor

c. Organism became extinct. good | poor

d. Organism lived in a concentrated area. good | poor

e. Organism lived on Earth for hundreds of millions of years. good | poor

To be useful as an index fossil, a fossil must meet a few important requirements. The organism must have lived over a relatively short period of geologic time—hundreds of thousands to a few million years—and then become extinct. The organism must have been widespread on Earth, not just in one small area. The fossil must be easy to identify and distinguish from similar fossils. The fossil should be abundant in rock layers. Finally, the organism represented by the fossil lived in a wide variety of sedimentary environments.

Tropites is a particularly good index fossil. They were widespread over Earth, evolved and thus changed quickly over time, and are very easy to identify and distinguish from similar fossils. Other important index fossils include different species of trilobites, which lived during the Paleozoic.

Visualizing the Geologic Timescale

Scientists have combined information from fossil evidence all over the world to build a geologic timescale of Earth's history. The geologic timescale divides Earth's history into intervals based on evidence found in layers of rock and the appearance and extinctions of organisms. There is no one place on Earth where you can find rocks representing the complete geologic timescale.

APPLY How can scientists use the fossil record and faunal succession from locations around the world to determine the geologic timescale?

_____

_____

_____

FIGURE 7: Scientists use the geologic timescale to understand Earth's long history.

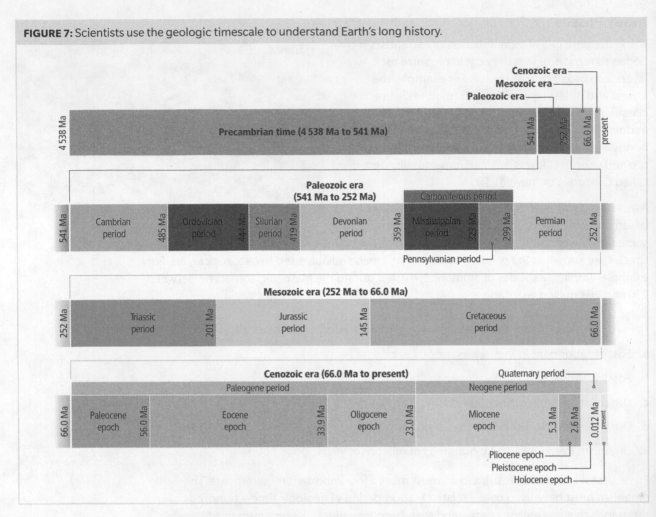

Geologists have interpreted the rock and fossil record to show that Earth's history can be organized like a calendar into time divisions of different lengths. The largest divisions of geologic time are *eons*, and the first three eons together are sometimes referred to as the Precambrian. Eons are divided into *eras*, which are smaller time segments. The Paleozoic era, the Mesozoic era, and the Cenozoic era followed Precambrian time. The three eras are divided into *periods*, which may be further divided into *epochs*.

MODEL Scientists often explain geologic time in terms of a clock. Using this analogy, model the Precambrian time and the Paleozoic, Mesozoic, and Cenozoic eras in terms of a 12-hour clock face.

 Evidence Notebook Vertebrate fossils found in Red Rock Canyon are from species that existed between about 12 and 8 million years ago. How could scientists have determined this? What can you learn about these fossils from the geologic timescale?

History of Life on Earth

The fossil record provides evidence for the evolution of life on Earth, but scientists can also use fossils to determine how the environment of a region has changed over time. For example, scientists can determine if the area was an aquatic or a terrestrial environment based on the types of organisms found in the rock layers.

Evidence Provided by the Fossil Record

We know that organisms alive today have specific features that make them adapted to particular environments. We can assume that the same was true for ancient organisms. Not only are fossils useful for correlating and estimating the ages of rock layers, they can also provide information about environments in which ancient organisms lived.

ANALYZE What could you conclude about the behavior and environment of a saber-toothed cat by comparing its features with those of modern big cats, such as leopards?

_____

_____

_____

_____

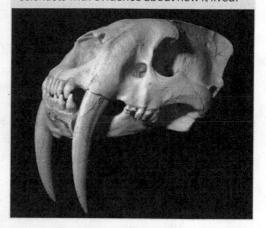

FIGURE 8: This fossil of a saber-toothed cat from the Pleistocene epoch can provide scientists with evidence about how it lived.

Earth's ecosystems are in a constant state of change. When an environment changes significantly, some species may not be able to adapt to the new environment. Eventually, these species will become extinct. Scientists use modern organisms to make inferences about extinct organisms. They study relationships of bone to muscle, of teeth to diet, and of the shapes of stems and leaves to climate. Examining modern organisms helps scientists to interpret evidence from fossils.

Scientists can evaluate fossils as well as patterns of erosion and deposition to determine past climates. Microfossils are fossils of microscopic bacteria, single-celled protists, invertebrate animals, and plant spores and pollen. These fossils can provide information about environment and climate. Fossils of shells and corals provide evidence of the past conditions of the ocean and atmosphere.

Evidence of Tectonic Plate Movement

The fossils of _Mesosaurus_, a freshwater reptile that lived about 270 millions years ago, are found in parts of South America and Africa. Scientists do not think _Mesosaurus_ could have evolved in both locations, nor could it have crossed the saltwater Atlantic Ocean.

Collaborate With a partner, discuss possible explanations for why scientists find fossils of the _Mesosaurus_ in both South America and Africa. What questions might scientists ask to learn more about the conditions of Earth at this time?

FIGURE 9: Locations of *Mesosaurus* fossil discoveries

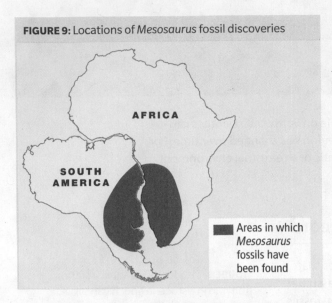

Areas in which *Mesosaurus* fossils have been found

If you put these landmasses together, as shown in Figure 9, you would find that they fit together like puzzle pieces. There are distinct patterns in the geographical range of each fossil. Patterns like this suggest that the organisms existed when these regions were connected in one landmass.

Many others fossils have also been discovered across different continents. Evidence from the fossil record has helped to show that Earth's surface has moved over time. Earth's outer surface is made of large pieces of rock called tectonic plates. Due to convection currents and the motion of rock from beneath Earth's surface, these tectonic plates are always moving. This movement causes the continents to change position over time.

Unicellular and Multicellular Life Forms

There is little direct evidence about climate during the Precambrian. It is likely that soon after Earth's formation, temperatures were quite high with a slow cooling throughout much of the time period. Until the late Precambrian, all organisms were single-celled and lacked a nucleus or other membrane-bound organelles. Recall that cyanobacteria were one of the most important influences on early Earth's atmosphere and climate. They used carbon dioxide and produced oxygen during photosynthesis. By about 2.3 billion years ago, they had produced enough oxygen to cause the Great Oxidation Event.

As a result of removing so much carbon dioxide from the air, Earth cooled dramatically and glaciers formed. Sea-ice covered most or all of the ocean and glaciers covered most of the land, resulting in the mass extinction of unicellular organisms. The oxygen-producing organisms took a long time to recover.

After a gap of almost a billion years, photosynthetic organisms caused another spike in oxygen production. Scientists have inferred that this second oxygenation event supplied enough oxygen to allow for the evolution of organisms with cells with organelles, called eukaryotes, and multicellular organisms.

 Language Arts Connection There are several theories focused on eukaryotic evolution, including the theory of endosymbiosis. Research at least two theories and record evidence that supports or refutes each theory. Prepare a presentation describing which theory you think has the most support.

As scientists continue their research, new evidence for the history of life on Earth becomes available all the time. Recent studies of fossils in Gabon, Africa and China, indicate that colonial cells—cells living together but not part of the same organism, may have originated as long ago as 2.1 billion years. Colonial cellular organisms are thought to be one step toward multicellular organisms. The trend toward multicellular organisms was one of the most important transitions in the history of life.

The Cambrian Explosion

One of the greatest evolutionary changes in life forms in Earth's history started about 540 million years ago during the Cambrian period. Within about 40 million years, almost all major animals groups present on Earth today evolved.

FIGURE 10: These fossils are from the Cambrian period.

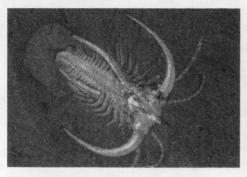

a · *Marrella splendens* is an ancient arthropod.

b · *Modocia typicalis* is a type of trilobite.

INFER Do you think the two organisms in Figure 10 belong to the same group? How could scientists determine whether these organisms are related?

_____

_____

_____

At the start of the Paleozoic era, all life was found in the ocean. Among the earliest vertebrates was a group of jawless fishes. Marine invertebrates, such as the trilobites, were especially abundant. The first complex trace fossils are also found in the fossil record from Cambrian sediments. Some of these trace fossils provide evidence that organisms were developing new ecological interactions, such as burrowing into soft sediment and predation. At the end of the Cambrian period, one of Earth's major mass extinction events changed everything. Evidence suggests that an oxygen crash in combination with poisonous hydrogen sulfide killed off the majority of the period's plant and animal populations.

 Stability and Change

Coevolution in the Fossil Record

Following the Cambrian–Ordovician extinction event, life became dramatically different. During the Ordovician, marine ecosystems expanded in a uniform climate, and high sea levels produced shallow seas all over Earth. These conditions favored Paleozoic marine invertebrates. Ecological diversity was expanded by the evolution of large predators. This evolution affected trilobites, which developed spines and other features that allowed them to avoid predation. This is an example of coevolution.

EXPLAIN How do the evolutionary developments of the trilobites represent stability over the long term, and change over the short term?

_____

_____

_____

_____

The Paleozoic era ended with the most catastrophic mass extinction event in Earth's history, approximately 252 million years ago. It is thought that the extinction resulted in the death of 81% to 96% of marine organisms, and 70% of land organisms. This mass extinction event marked the transition into the Mesozoic era, during which dinosaurs rose to become the dominant animals on the planet.

The Rise of Land Plants

The first land plants appeared during the Ordovician period. By the Devonian, which began about 419 million years ago, forests of club mosses, horsetails, and ferns covered the land. Land plants continued to become more diverse and abundant. By the Carboniferous period, about 359 million years ago, vegetation accumulated in coastal swamps. When this vegetation was buried in a place where oxygen was limited or not present at all, the organic matter in the plant material was converted into the rich coal deposits that are still being mined today.

INFER Complete the statement by selecting the correct terms.

The coal deposits currently being used as an energy resource formed billions | millions | thousands of years ago. Plants grew in swamps and their remains, underwater, were cut off from oxygen | carbon dioxide | water. As a result, the carbon stayed in place and did not cycle back into the atmosphere as oxygen | carbon dioxide | water—the remains became coal deposits.

FIGURE 11: A fossil impression of a Mesozoic angiosperm, *Glossopteris browniana*.

Angiosperms, also known as flowering plants, developed about 125 million years ago during the Cretaceous period. Scientists studying the angiosperms have suggested two possible origins. One origin suggests that the earliest angiosperms were woody plants—trees similar to modern magnolias and laurels. This hypothesis is supported by several lines of evidence, and is favored by scientists today. The other hypothesis suggests that the earliest angiosperms were small herb-like plants. Research continues to try to determine which of these hypotheses may be more accurate.

Collaborate Insects went through an evolutionary explosion in response to the evolution of flowering plants. An increase in the variety of insects caused more types of flowering plants to evolve. With a partner, discuss why you think these groups of organisms evolved together.

The Age of Dinosaurs

The Mesozoic era is known as the age of dinosaurs, or, often, the age of reptiles. This era began around 250 million years ago and lasted until around 66 million years ago. In the early Mesozoic, mammal-like reptiles were the dominant terrestrial vertebrates. By the late Triassic, dinosaurs and their reptile relatives had replaced them as the principal land animals on the planet. Dinosaurs and other reptiles continued to evolve and diversify through the Mesozoic, expanding their range to include marine environments and the air.

The first true birds emerged from bird-like dinosaurs during the Jurassic period, though their fossils are rare. Primitive mammals also evolved during the late Triassic period, but they appear to not have evolved and diversified throughout the Mesozoic era as much as reptiles. The Mesozoic ended with another mass extinction, during which dinosaurs died out, as did marine reptiles and dominant invertebrates.

Connecting Ancient Dinosaurs to Modern Birds

Archaeopteryx has been called both the first bird and a "feathered dinosaur" because it shares features of both birds and dinosaurs. It is considered to be a transitional fossil, meaning it is an intermediate between dinosaurs and modern birds. Only twelve very detailed and well-preserved fossils have been found since it was first discovered in 1860.

Archaeopteryx lived around 150 million years ago in the late Jurassic period. This bird-like dinosaur was about the size of a modern-day raven. It had broad, rounded wings and a long tail. Unlike modern birds, it also had a jaw with sharp teeth, three fingers with claws, and a curved "killing claw" on each of its second toes.

In the 1970s, scientists observed that *Archaeopteryx* shared many unique features with a group of dinosaurs known as theropods. Theropods were dinosaurs that walked on two legs, such as *Tyrannosaurus rex*. Due to shared features, scientists hypothesized that theropods were ancestors of modern-day birds.

FIGURE 12: Theropods are an extinct group of dinosaurs that are thought to be the ancestors of modern birds.

In the 1990s, scientists discovered theropod fossils with feathers. They first appeared over 200 million years ago during the Triassic period. This important discovery showed that feathers did not originate as an adaptation for flight. These theropods were covered with feathers, but they did not have wings. They were running animals. This means that feathers originally had another function in theropods.

GATHER EVIDENCE What patterns in anatomical structures provide evidence of a link between dinosaurs and modern birds?

_____

_____

_____

ANALYZE What additional evidence would help support the claim that these organisms share a common ancestor?

_____

_____

_____

FIGURE 13: A modern bison grazing.

The Rise of Grasses

Today, grass grows all over the world, but that wasn't always the case. Fossil evidence suggests that grasses first appeared during the Mesozoic era. They started to spread during the Cenozoic era as Earth cooled. The increase in grasses gave rise to the evolution of grazing animals. These animals evolved to have adaptations such as high-crowned teeth to improve their ability to eat grass, and stomachs with multiple compartments to digest grass. Grasses also contributed heavily to the development of human agriculture. As humans transitioned from primarily hunting and gathering to growing their own food, grasses became a primary source of food for both humans and livestock. Scientists often use the pollen from grasses to date discoveries to this time period.

ANALYZE How might scientists study modern animals, such as bison, to learn more about the organisms that lived in grasslands during the Cenozoic era?

_____

_____

_____

The Age of Mammals

The first mammals evolved during the Mesozoic era. After the mass extinction at the end of the Mesozoic era, mammals became the dominant group on Earth. During the early Cenozoic era, about 4000 species of mammals evolved in about 10 million years. By the early Eocene epoch, most of the major groups of mammals living today had evolved.

FIGURE 14: A Columbian mammoth found in the La Brea tar pits in California.

The Pleistocene epoch is notable for its megafauna—large mammals of a particular region or habitat. Some examples of megafauna include mammoths, saber-toothed cats, and giant ground sloths. Skeletons of these organisms, and many others, have been preserved in the La Brea tar pits in Los Angeles, California. Animals entered the pits, became trapped in the tar, and died. Sometimes, carnivores and scavengers followed these animals into the pits, also becoming trapped. Plants, insects, pollen, and other microfossils have also been found at La Brea. These fossils provide important evidence about the climate in California and the rest of North America during this time.

Most of these large mammals became extinct at the end of the ice age when Earth began to warm, around 10000 years ago. Humans also spread to different continents during this time and hunted these organisms for food and other resources. Over time, the populations of megafauna dwindled until they eventually became extinct.

The Age of Humans

Modern-day humans evolved relatively recently compared to other species on the planet. Hominins—a general term that groups humans and our extinct ancestors—are commonly placed in two genera: *Homo* and *Australopithecus*. *Australopithecus afarensis* lived 4 million to 3 million years ago in Africa. *Homo habilis*, which lived in Africa 2.4 to 1.5 million years ago, is the earliest known hominin to make stone tools.

One of the most recent hominin relatives to modern humans was *Homo neanderthalensis,* which lived from 430 000 to about 40 000 years ago in Europe and the Middle East. Some evidence suggests that *Homo neanderthalensis* coexisted with modern *Homo sapiens.* Fossil evidence reveals that *Homo sapiens* evolved between 200 000 and 100 000 years ago in what is now Ethiopia in Africa. However, many of their features were different than those of modern humans. Neanderthals had many distinct features, such as angled cheekbones and a wide nose that was adapted to humidifying the cold, dry air in their environment.

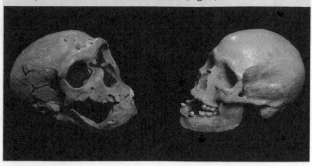

FIGURE 15: The skull of *Homo neanderthalensis* (left) compared with a skull of a human (right).

 Collaborate What type of evidence could support the claim that *Homo sapiens* and *Homo neanderthalensis* coexisted? Discuss your answer with a partner.

Fossil evidence suggests that *Homo sapiens* began to leave Africa to inhabit other continents approximately 60 000 years ago. It's unknown what exactly caused this migration, but one possible explanation could have been a change in climate that occurred during the final portion of the ice age. As humans spread and populated different continents, they began to influence both the evolution and extinction of organisms in other ecosystems. Some species were hunted to extinction, while humans transported other species from one continent to another, both unintentionally and intentionally.

Engineering

Designing Solutions for Endangered Species

Scientists think that we are currently living through another mass extinction event. Evidence suggests humans are part of the cause. Human activity has often been behind the extinction or endangering of many species. People, though, are taking steps to try to prevent the extinction of some species.

California condors are a species of large bird dating from the Pleistocene epoch. Human activities, such as the use of the pesticide DDT and the construction of power lines, reduced the number of these birds to only 22 individuals by the 1980s. Organizations in California placed the remaining birds in captivity and started breeding programs. Using practices such as artificial incubation, these organizations hatched enough condors to release some birds into protected California habitats. Due to these efforts, there are now over 400 California condors.

EXPLAIN How might you use engineering, either by designing a device or process, to help reduce the impact of human activity on a local species?

_____

_____

 Evidence Notebook Fossils discovered in Red Rock Canyon have been dated to many different eras. What additional evidence could help scientists date these fossils?

Data Analysis

The Absolute Age of Rocks

Determining absolute time involves making measurements and calculations that are based on changes and rates of change in natural systems. However, the most accurate and precise method for measuring time relies on changes that happen to individual atoms. This method of measuring time is called *radiometric dating*.

Radiometric Dating

FIGURE 16: Carbon-14 Decay

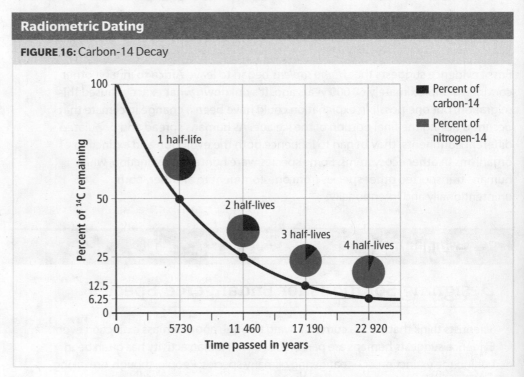

Scientists can determine the age of some fossils through the process of radiometric dating. This technique uses calculations that are based on a radioisotope's steady rate of decay. Isotopes are atoms of the same element that have different numbers of neutrons. For example, all carbon atoms have six protons, but the number of neutrons may vary. The most common carbon isotope has six neutrons in its nucleus. Because the atomic mass of an atom is equal to the sum of protons and neutrons in its nucleus, this isotope is known as carbon-12, or ^{12}C. In the isotope carbon-14, or ^{14}C, there are still six protons but eight neutrons, which add up to 14.

Many elements have multiple isotopes, most of which are stable. However, some isotopes are unstable, or radioactive. This means that they give off radiation as they decay, or break down over time. Decay rates differ widely and are known for each isotope. Figure 17 lists a few radioactive isotopes that are used in radiometric dating.

The decay of any radioisotope happens at a known, constant rate and is expressed as the isotope's half-life. A *half-life* is the amount of time it takes for half of the original mass of the isotope to decay into the product, or daughter isotope. By measuring the amount of parent isotope remaining along with the amount of daughter isotope remaining, you can calculate a ratio.

FIGURE 17: Isotopes used in radiometric dating.

Isotope (parent)	Product (daughter)	Half-life (years)	Isotope (parent)	Product (daughter)	Half-life (years)
rubidium-87	strontium-87	48.8 billion	potassium-40	argon-40	1.3 billion
uranium-238	lead-206	4.5 billion	carbon-14	nitrogen-14	5730

The isotope ^{14}C is commonly used to date recent remains. Organisms absorb carbon through eating and breathing, so ^{14}C is constantly being resupplied. When an organism dies, its intake of carbon stops, but the decay of ^{14}C continues.

The half-life of ^{14}C is roughly 5700 years. This means that after 5700 years, half of the ^{14}C in a fossil will have decayed into ^{14}N, its decay product. The other half remains as ^{14}C. After 11 400 years, or two half-lives, 75% of the ^{14}C will have decayed. Only 25% of the original ^{14}C remains.

The predictability of radiometric dating gives scientists a reliable tool to calculate the age of almost any fossil or rock sample. The oldest known rocks were found in Australia and dated using radioisotopes. They contained small mineral crystals that were calculated to be about 4.4 billion years old. The rate of error for this technique is very low—less than one percent. However, this means that for a sample that is 4.4 billion years old, the error could be up to 40 million years.

Scientists have used radiometric dating to determine Earth's age. Because Earth constantly undergoes erosion and rock recycling, rocks on Earth do not remain in their original state. Unlike Earth's rocks, meteorites—which are mostly pieces of rock and iron that have fallen to Earth's surface from space —do not get recycled or undergo erosion. Meteorites are thought to have formed at about the same time as Earth. Therefore, meteorites provide an unspoiled sample for radiometric dating. Uranium-to-lead isotope ratios in many meteorite samples consistently estimate Earth's age at about 4.5 billion years.

ANALYZE Use the figures to answer the following questions.

1. If a rock contains 75% of the decay product, how many half-lives have passed?

_____

_____

2. If you measured the age of a fossil using ^{14}C dating and determined its age to be about 17 000 years old, how much of the rock should be made of ^{14}N?

_____

_____

3. If you are examining rock layers that are suspected to be about 20 million years old, which radioactive isotope would you use? Explain your answer.

_____

_____

 INVESTIGATING PLATE TECTONICS   **BUILD YOUR OWN TIMESCALE**   **INVESTIGATING COASTAL EROSION**   Go online to choose one of these other paths.

Lesson Self-Check

CAN YOU EXPLAIN IT?

FIGURE 18: The fossiliferous Dove Spring Formation is exposed in the hills of Red Rock Canyon State Park.

The geology of Red Rock Canyon reveals a fascinating look at a Cenozoic world that no longer exists. To biologists, however, the rocks of the Dove Spring Formation are particularly fascinating. These rocks are formed from sediments, lava flows, and ash that were deposited in an ancient valley. This valley no longer exists, but tectonic plate movement along the El Paso Fault elevated these rocks, exposing them to the elements. Thousands of individual fossils have been found in the rocks of the Dove Spring Formation. Most of the fossils found in the canyon come from species that lived between about 12 and 8 million years ago.

 Evidence Notebook Refer to your notes in your Evidence Notebook and the information above to explain how Red Rock Canyon provides evidence for Earth's geologic history.

1. Make a claim about how the rock layers and fossils exposed in the walls of Red Rock Canyon provide evidence for Earth's geologic history.
2. What is the significance of the fossils preserved in the Dove Spring Formation to our understanding of Earth's history?
3. How does rock and fossil evidence help us to gain an understanding of Earth's history?

CHECKPOINTS

Check Your Understanding

1. Select the correct terms to complete the statement about trace fossils.

   Trace fossils are preserved signs of the activity or behavior | mineralized remains | soft parts of an organism rather than actual pieces, molds, or impressions of organisms. While fossilized imprints | bones | footprints and tracks | muscles and tissues are not the only kind of trace fossil, they are the best known.

2. Which of the following statements about the principle of faunal succession is true? Select all correct answers.

   ☐ **a.** It relies on radiometric dating techniques.

   ☐ **b.** It assumes that rock layers are deposited on top of one another.

   ☐ **c.** It assumes that rock layers are deposited beneath one another.

   ☐ **d.** It assumes that specific combinations of organisms were living only at a certain time in Earth's history.

3. Match the evidence to what scientists can learn from that evidence.

dinosaur tracks/worm trails ○	○ animal's pace
size and depth of dinosaur tracks ○	○ diet of ancient organisms
spacing between footprints ○	○ how an organism moved
coprolites ○	○ size of an organism

4. Which of the following shows the correct progression of organisms on the planet?

   ○ **a.** reptiles, fish, hominins

   ○ **b.** fish, reptiles, hominins

   ○ **c.** prokaryotes, angiosperms, gymnosperms

   ○ **d.** reptiles, mammals, fish

5. Which of the following would make the *best* index fossil?

   ○ **a.** An insect that only existed in one small forest for about 100 million years.

   ○ **b.** An aquatic animal that existed all over the world for about 15 million years.

   ○ **c.** A single-celled organism that lived in a widespread region for about 25 million years.

   ○ **d.** A plant species that lived in a specific geographic region for about 5 million years.

6. Select the correct terms to complete the statement about early life on Earth.

   When life first evolved on Earth, there was virtually no oxygen in the atmosphere. The earliest prokaryotes were likely anaerobic | aerobic meaning they did not require oxygen to produce energy. Over time, photosynthetic | chemosynthetic prokaryotes evolved, which made energy from the sun. The chemical reactions involved in this process released carbon dioxide | oxygen | nitrogen into the atmosphere. This allowed for the evolution of eukaryotes.

7. Which of the following statements are true about the Cambrian Explosion around the transition between the Precambrian and the Paleozoic era? Select all that apply.

   ☐ **a.** Life-forms evolved from unicellular organisms to more complex organisms.

   ☐ **b.** Photosynthesizing organisms first appeared in the fossil record.

   ☐ **c.** Most major groups of animals first appeared during this time period.

   ☐ **d.** The Cambrian Explosion occurred over a very long span of time.

CHECKPOINTS (continued)

8. How does the presence of similar fossils on different continents support the idea of tectonic plate movement? Use evidence to support your claim.

_____
_____
_____
_____
_____
_____
_____

9. How did the spread of early _Homo sapiens_ from Africa to other continents likely influence populations of other organisms?

_____
_____
_____
_____
_____
_____
_____

10. Why is the late Cambrian thought of as the period of the greatest evolutionary change in life forms in Earth's history?

_____
_____
_____
_____
_____
_____
_____

MAKE YOUR OWN STUDY GUIDE

 In your Evidence Notebook, design a study guide that supports the main idea from this lesson:

The fossil record provides much of the evidence to support evolution.

Remember to include the following information in your study guide:

- Use examples that model main ideas.
- Record explanations for the phenomena you investigated.
- Use evidence to support your explanations. Your support can include drawings, data, graphs, laboratory conclusions, and other evidence recorded throughout the lesson.

Consider how scientists use patterns to analyze and draw conclusions about rock layers and fossils.

Lines of Evidence for Evolution

A long-tailed pangolin perches on a tree.

CAN YOU EXPLAIN IT?

Long-tailed pangolins are truly unique animals. Each of these tree-dwelling creatures is covered in large, scale-like armor that makes it look like a walking pine cone. Although it may be mistaken for a reptile at first glance, the long-tailed pangolin also shares characteristics with mammals. It has fur on its face, abdomen, and the underside of its legs. As the name implies, it has an extremely long tail that is used to grip and move about trees where it feeds on ants, termites, and other insects. A long nose and sharp claws help the pangolin dig out ants from their nests. The fascinating combination of characteristics make this animal one of the most unusual creatures on Earth.

PREDICT Pangolins share many characteristics with different types of animals. How do scientists determine the evolutionary relationships between different organisms?

_____

_____

_____

_____

_____

 Evidence Notebook As you explore this lesson, gather evidence used to support common ancestry and evolutionary relationships among different species.

Developmental and Anatomical Evidence

Scientists have gathered geological evidence to piece together Earth's history. Geologic evidence, such as the fossil record, has also helped to explain the evolution of species. Evolution is the process of biological change by which descendants come to differ from their ancestors. Biological evidence is used to evaluate and identify relationships between species. An example of biological evidence is shown in Figure 1.

FIGURE 1: Barnacles and copepods look similar during their larval stage.

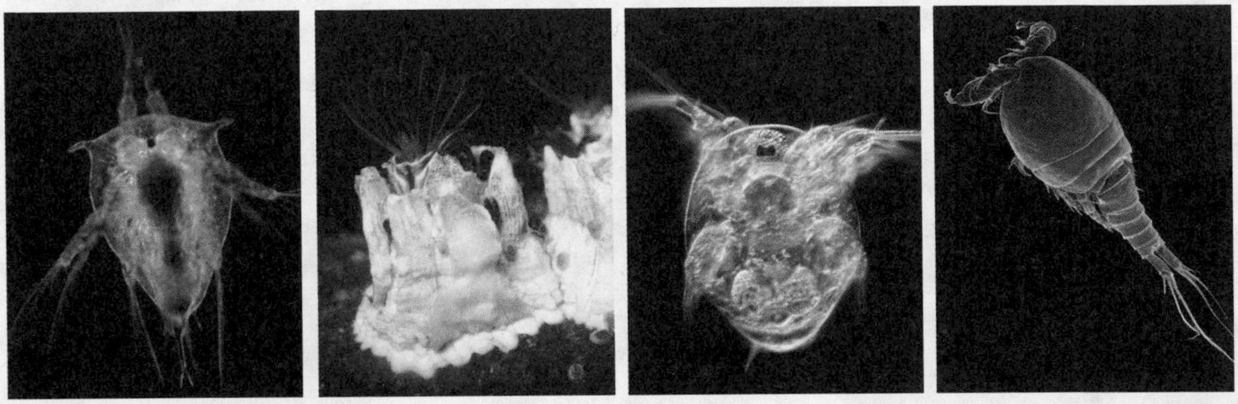

| a Larval barnacle | b Adult barnacles | c Larval copepod | d Adult copepod (SEM) |

PREDICT How can biological evidence such as what is shown in Figure 1 be used to determine evolutionary relationships between different species?

_____

_____

_____

Developmental Similarities

Invertebrates have an initial larval stage in which many species look quite similar. For example, barnacles and copepods are both types of crustaceans. These animals show striking similarities as larvae even though as adults they take on very different body forms and behaviors. Barnacles become stationary animals, attaching to solid structures or larger animals. They must rely on their food to come to them. Microscopic copepods, on the other hand, use their swimming legs to move around and capture food.

EXPLAIN Select the correct terms to complete the statement about developmental similarities among invertebrates.

The larval | adult stage of invertebrates is a very early stage of development in which there are often obvious differences | similarities in body form. This evidence suggests that many invertebrates have common | different ancestors.

All vertebrates, animals with an internal segmented backbone, have three basic body features as embryos—a tail, limb buds, and pharyngeal arches. Note these common features in all four vertebrate embryos shown in Figure 2. Human embryos have a tail and pharyngeal arches, just as fish do. Structures that appear very similar in early development eventually differentiate in both structure and function. For example, in adult fish pharyngeal arches become gills. In mammals, however, pharyngeal arches develop into ear and throat structures. Biologists use shared developmental patterns as evidence of common ancestry.

FIGURE 2: All vertebrates go through a stage of development with common features.

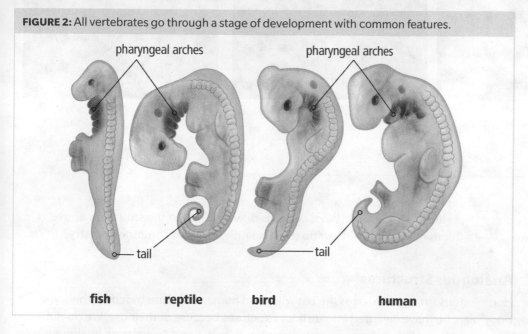

pharyngeal arches

pharyngeal arches

tail

tail

fish   **reptile**   **bird**   **human**

ANALYZE How does the pattern of similarities in vertebrate embryos help support common ancestry?

_____

_____

_____

_____

Anatomical Evidence

In addition to evaluating developmental similarities, scientists use anatomical evidence to support the concept of common ancestry and evolutionary theory. Anatomical evidence involves the study of similar structures found among different species. If different species have multiple structures in common, it suggests that the species share a common ancestor.

Homologous Structures

There are different types of anatomical structures that scientists study to determine evolutionary relationships. Homologous structures are features found in different organisms that share structural similarities but may have very different functions. Their appearance across different species offers strong evidence for common descent. It would be unlikely for many species to have such similar anatomy if each species evolved independently. For example, all four-limbed vertebrates, or tetrapods, share homologous bones in their forelimbs.

ANNOTATE Use colored pencils or markers to color in the homologous structures in each x-ray image.

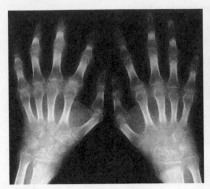

a Human hands

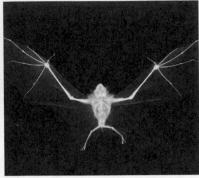

b Bat wings

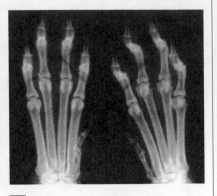

c Dog feet

 Evidence Notebook What patterns do you notice in the structures above in terms of similarities? How do the similarities support common ancestry?

Analogous Structures

Homologous structures such as the bat wing and human hand are based on the same body plan, but have diverged into distinct structures because of their use. We do not use our arms and hands the same way that a bat uses its wing. In contrast, analogous structures are structures that perform a similar function but are not similar in origin. Compare the wings of the parrot to those of the dragonfly in Figure 3. Both bird and insect wings have similar shapes and structures because they are both used for flight. However, wings develop differently in birds and insects, and they are made of different tissues. For example, bird wings have bones. In contrast, insect wings do not have bones, only membranes. The similar function of wings in birds and flying insects evolved separately.

FIGURE 3: Bird wings and dragonfly wings are examples of analogous structures.

a Parrot wings

b Dragonfly wings

EXPLAIN Use the correct terms to complete the statement about homologous and analogous structures. Terms can be used more than once.

different   similar

Homologous structures may be used for _____ functions but have

_____ developmental patterns and basic structure. Analogous

structures may look _____ in appearance but

evolved from _____ structures. Homologous structures are

evidence of common ancestry.

Vestigial Structures

Anatomical comparisons can shed light on evolutionary relationships between species. Common body structures can become more similar or less similar over time. But what about structures that seem to serve no function at all? Early scientists had trouble explaining why flightless birds have wings or why humans have a tailbone. What we now know is that these vestigial structures are remnants of once-important structures that gradually have lost all or most of their function over time. Vestigial structures provide clues to an organism's evolutionary past. Consider the traces of pelvic bones present in the humpback whale, as shown in Figure 4. The pelvis normally sits near leg bones, such as the femur in humans.

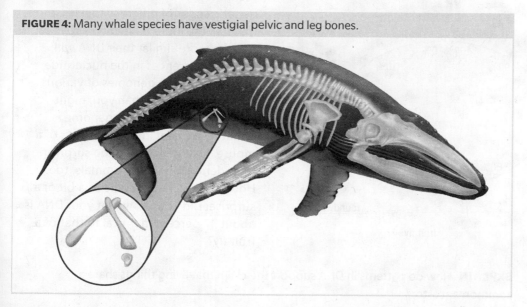

FIGURE 4: Many whale species have vestigial pelvic and leg bones.

ANALYZE How does the evidence shown in the illustration support the idea that whales evolved from land mammals?

_____

_____

_____

 Evidence Notebook What similarities in anatomical structures provide evidence of a link between pangolins and other animals? What additional evidence would help support the claim that the pangolin shares a common ancestor with other animals?

Molecular and Genetic Evidence

Developmental and anatomical similarities provide scientists with visual evidence of common ancestry among organisms. As technology and analytical techniques have advanced, so too has our ability to analyze evolutionary relationships between different organisms. Scientists now use molecular and genetic data to support claims about evolutionary relationships among species. By examining DNA and other biomolecules of living things, scientists can determine relationships among organisms based on the molecular information they have in common. This evidence helps to strengthen our understanding of evolution.

Molecular Similarities

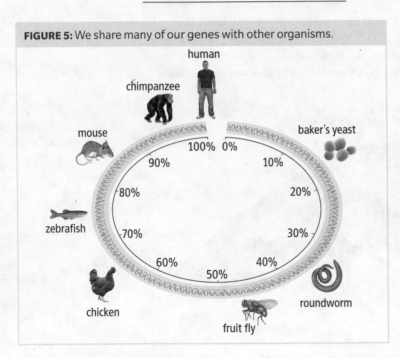

FIGURE 5: We share many of our genes with other organisms.

All living things on Earth share DNA as their genetic code. We all have the same four basic nucleotides that make up our genome. Through DNA sequencing technology, scientists can compare the genetic codes of different species. In general, the more related two species are, the more similar their DNA will be. The differences in the nucleotide sequences in the genomes of various species are smaller than you might think. For example, your genome is about 88 percent identical to that of a mouse. That may not be too surprising considering mice are mammals, too. However, this might come as a bit of a surprise: Did you know that your DNA is about 47 percent identical to that of a fruit fly?

EXPLAIN How do patterns in DNA support the claim that living things share a common ancestor?

_____

_____

_____

Molecular Clocks

Molecular clocks are models that use mutation rates to measure evolutionary time. The rate of mutations is the "ticking" that powers a molecular clock. The more time that has passed since two species have diverged from a common ancestor, the more mutations will have built up in each lineage, and the more different the two species will be at the molecular level.

Mitochondrial DNA

Recall that mitochondria are the energy factories of cells. These organelles have their own DNA, called mitochondrial DNA (mtDNA). The mutation rate of mtDNA is about ten times faster than that of nuclear DNA, which makes mtDNA a good molecular clock for closely related species. And mtDNA is always inherited from the mother because the mitochondria in a sperm cell are lost after fertilization. Scientists use the fact that mtDNA is passed down unshuffled from mother to offspring to trace mutations back through many generations in a single species.

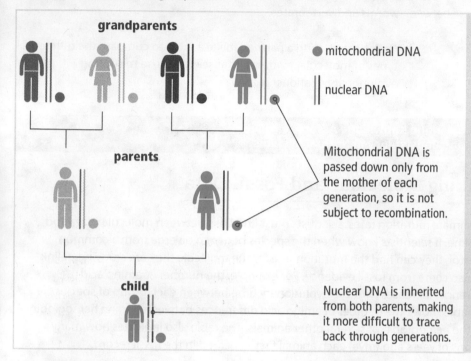

grandparents

● mitochondrial DNA

❘❘ nuclear DNA

parents

Mitochondrial DNA is passed down only from the mother of each generation, so it is not subject to recombination.

child

Nuclear DNA is inherited from both parents, making it more difficult to trace back through generations.

FIGURE 6: Inheritance of mitochondrial DNA compared to nuclear DNA.

ANALYZE Why might an evolutionary biologist benefit from studying mtDNA rather than nuclear DNA as evidence for evolution?

○ **a.** mtDNA mutates at a slower rate, so there are fewer changes to an organism's DNA over time.

○ **b.** mtDNA is inherited from both parents, providing a wider view of inheritance and possible common ancestry.

○ **c.** mtDNA is only passed on to females, so scientists are able to better focus their evidence on one sex.

○ **d.** mtDNA is only inherited from the mother, making it easier to trace lines of descent.

Ribosomal RNA

Ribosomes, which manufacture proteins in cells, contain ribosomal RNA (rRNA). When studying the relationships among species over longer time scales, it is best to use a molecule like rRNA since it has conservative regions that accumulate mutations at a low rate relative to most DNA. Over long periods of geologic time, mutations that do build up in the rRNA of different lineages are relatively clear and can be compared.

Pseudogenes

Pseudogenes also provide evidence of evolution. Pseudogenes are genes that no longer function but are still carried with functional DNA. They can also change through mutation as they are passed on, so they provide another way to determine evolutionary relationships.

Predicting Evolutionary Relationships
Analyze similarities in a protein common to bacteria and eukaryotes. Then use the results of your analysis to draw conclusions about similarities among species.

Protein Sequences

Comparing proteins can also reveal similarities among cell types across organisms. A unique set of proteins is found in specific types of cells. Digital databases of protein sequences can identify similar sequences in different species. Cells from different species that have the same proteins most likely have a common ancestor. For example, the proteins of light-sensitive cells in a brain-like structure of an ancient worm closely resemble proteins in the cells of the vertebrate eye. This shows a shared ancestry between worms and vertebrates.

 Collaborate With a partner, make a table to compare the different types of molecular evidence that scientists use to support evolutionary relationships.

Scientific Knowledge Assumes an Order and Consistency in Natural Systems

Linking Molecular and Fossil Data

To estimate mutation rates, scientists must find links between molecular data and real time. If scientists know when the species began to diverge from a common ancestor, they can find the mutation rate for the molecule they are studying. A link can also come from fossil evidence. For example, the number of amino acid differences increases with the evolutionary time between each group of species. The table shows the number of amino acid differences between human hemoglobin and the hemoglobin of several other animals. The table also indicates how many millions of years ago (mya) each animal first appeared in the fossil record.

ANALYZE Which two animals in this table are least related to humans?

☐ **a.** horse

☐ **b.** mouse

☐ **c.** shark

☐ **d.** frog

Animal	Amino Acid Differences Compared with Humans	Appearance in the Fossil Record (mya)
Mouse	16	70
Horse	18	70
Bird	35	270
Frog	62	350
Shark	79	450

EXPLAIN How does the data in the table support the use of molecular data and the fossil record as evidence for common ancestry across species? Use specific information from the table in your answer.

_____

_____

_____

_____

_____

_____

Body Plan Expression

As an animal develops, its genes guide the formation of organs and the arrangement of body parts. If we have much of our DNA in common with other organisms, such as mice or birds, why then does a bird's body plan look so different from our own? From a very early stage, certain types of genes, called *Hox* genes, help to guide the process that results in the development of an organism's characteristic body plan. The process begins by instructing embryonic cells where in the body they will be located—head, midsection, or tail. From there the genes define the location and number of eyes and limbs, the location of the gut, the development of a wing instead of a leg, and so forth. If a random change, or mutation, arises in these genes, drastic changes can occur in the body plan of the animal. Scientists think that random mutations in these kinds of genes over time account for the incredible diversity of body types seen today.

FIGURE 7: Differences in fruit fly and human body plans arise from variations in *Hox* genes.

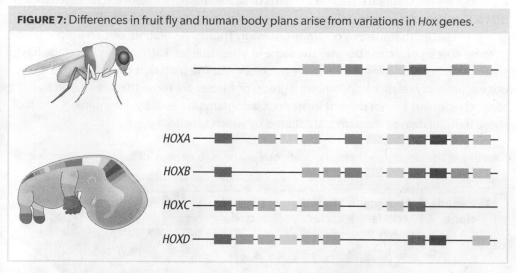

HOXA

HOXB

HOXC

HOXD

INFER What patterns do you see in the similarities and differences between *Hox* genes in humans and in fruit flies? How do your observations support the claim that humans and fruit flies share a common ancestor?

_____

_____

_____

_____

Vertebrates have multiple sets of the same *Hox* genes that insects and other arthropods have. For example, the *Hox* genes that direct the organization of the vertebrate body plan are actually just different versions of the *Hox* gene that directs the body plan in fruit flies and other insects. The difference suggests that over time, mutations have caused the original *Hox* gene to be copied repeatedly, forming a series of similar genes along a chromosome. Mutations in these genes are typically duplications, and with each duplication, the developing organism may show slightly different traits.

 Evidence Notebook What types of cellular or molecular evidence might a scientist study in order to determine the evolutionary relationship between the pangolin and other animals?

The Tree of Life

Scientists can use multiple lines of evidence to build evolutionary histories of organisms. Phylogenetics is the study of the evolutionary history and relationships of organisms. A phylogenetic tree visually represents the relationships among species.

Interpreting a Cladogram

A cladogram is a diagram based on patterns of shared traits, or inherited characteristics, that shows the evolutionary relationships between groups of organisms. A clade is a group of species that shares a common ancestor. Through evolution, certain traits change in some species of a clade but stay the same in other species. Each species in a clade has some traits from its ancestors that have not changed. The traits that can be used to figure out evolutionary relationships among a group of species are those that are shared by some species but are not present in others. Cladograms are built by determining which of these traits, or *derived characters,* are shared by which species.

FIGURE 8: This cladogram shows the relationships among tetrapods, or four-limbed animals.

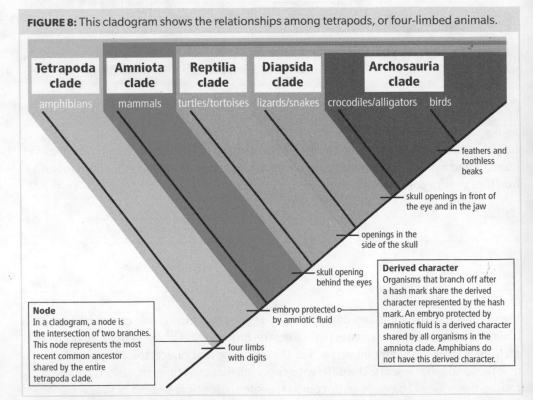

ANALYZE In this cladogram, what derived character is shared by organisms such as turtles and tortoises, but not by organisms such as mammals? Use the diagram to explain your answer.

_____

_____

_____

The tips of the branches on a phylogenetic tree indicate the group being studied and can range from a single species to an entire order. The lines are the branches. How branches split throughout the phylogenetic tree gives information about how the species are related. The point where branches meet is called a node and represents speciation points, or points of evolution of two or more species from one ancestral species. Fewer nodes between species indicates a higher degree of relatedness. An ancestor and all of its descendants represent a clade.

Taxonomic Classification

Scientists use a classification hierarchy, called taxonomic classification, to place organisms into groups based on similarities. In this system, groups that have the largest number of organisms are called domains. Each higher level within the hierarchy is broken down into smaller levels with fewer organisms in each level. The levels after domain from largest to smallest are kingdom, phylum, class, order, family, genus, species.

PREDICT Suppose scientists discover a new species that does not fit into any of the current kingdoms. How will scientists likely address this new discovery?

○ **a.** Scientists will propose a new kingdom only after discovering more new species.

○ **b.** Scientists will modify all of the levels of taxonomy so they can fit the new species into the existing system.

○ **c.** Scientists will either make minor changes to the criteria for one existing kingdom or propose a new kingdom.

○ **d.** Scientists will classify the new species into the kingdom that has the fewest number of species.

FIGURE 9: The number of kingdoms used to classify organisms has changed over time.

1753 Two kingdoms　**1866** Three kingdoms　**1938** Four kingdoms　**1959** Five kingdoms　**1977** Six kingdoms

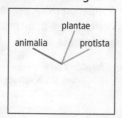
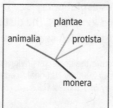
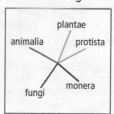
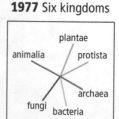

As with all branches of science, ideas about taxonomy change as new technology develops and new discoveries are made. In the original system developed in the 1700s, domains did not exist and there were only two kingdoms—Plantae and Animalia, or plants and animals. A third kingdom called Protista was proposed in the 1860s. This kingdom was meant to contain all single-celled organisms. In 1938, a fourth kingdom called Monera was established. This kingdom contained prokaryotes, which are single-celled organisms that lack membrane-bound nuclei or organelles. As scientists learned more about the nutrition of different organisms, a fifth kingdom, Fungi, was recognized in 1959. This kingdom includes molds and mushrooms. In 1977, rRNA research revealed two genetically different groups of prokaryotes, splitting Monera into two separate kingdoms: Bacteria and Archaea.

 Collaborate With a partner, discuss the following question: Why is the classification of life considered a work in progress?

Classification Today

When Carl Woese proposed splitting kingdom Monera into the kingdoms of Archaebacteria and Eubacteria in 1977, the domain category of classification did not yet exist. His proposal for the new kingdoms was based on discoveries of new organisms that live in extreme environments. Previously, scientists did not know that life could exist under conditions of extreme heat, acid, and salt. These organisms were initially classified as bacteria. However, evidence related to biochemical characteristics and DNA sequencing revealed that the organisms were, in fact, very different from bacteria. Based on his work and the work of other scientists, Woese established the domain category of classification, which is above the kingdom level. In this system, there are three domains: Bacteria, Archaea, and Eukarya. This is the system that is currently used and is known as the tree of life model.

FIGURE 10: The tree of life model divides organisms into three domains.

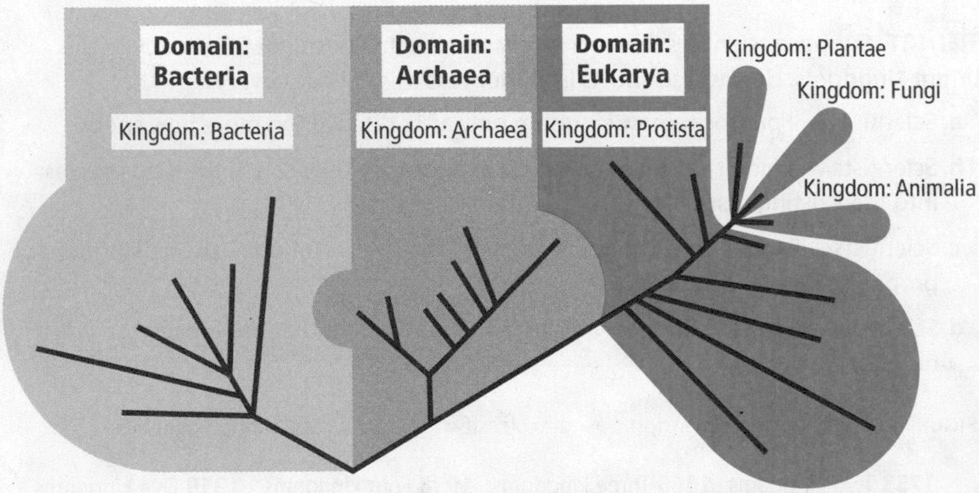

Scientists constructed this evolutionary tree by comparing rRNA sequences from species in each of the six recognized kingdoms. The distances between branches are proportional to the number of differences in rRNA sequences among these species.

Credit: Adapted from "Interpreting the universal phylogenetic tree" by Carl R. Woese from *PNAS*, Vol. 97, No. 15, 8392-8396. Copyright © 2000 by National Academy of Sciences, U.S.A. Adapted and reproduced by permission of National Academy of Sciences, U.S.A.

ANALYZE How have technological advances and our knowledge of evolutionary relationships impacted taxonomy over time?

_____

_____

_____

_____

_____

_____

Evidence Notebook Considering its unique characteristics, what challenge do you think you might encounter if you were to make a phylogenetic tree that includes the pangolin? How would you overcome this challenge?

Guided Research

Tracing the Evolution of Modern Humans

Evidence indicates that physical and behavioral traits shared by all humans originated from apelike ancestors. We evolved into modern humans over a period of approximately six million years. Developmental, anatomical, molecular, and genetic similarities support the idea that modern humans are closely related to apes. In fact, both humans and apes belong to the same classification group, primates. We share a common ancestor with the larger apes of Africa—chimpanzees and gorillas. It is thought that this common ancestor lived between 8 and 6 million years ago.

Fossil evidence of intermediate forms of humans shows the progression of our body form over millions of years. The common ancestor of humans and apes was a primate that lived in the African grasslands, never moving far from trees. Then around 3 million years ago, these primates branched out and gave rise to an early group known as *Australopithecus*. Although they had many apelike features, this group of primates walked on two legs and used tools. Further branching over time led to the evolution of more human-like features and behaviors, such as a larger brain and the use of fire.

Fossil evidence also indicates that humans first evolved in Africa, with most of human evolution occurring there from 6 to 2 million years ago. Eventually, humans migrated to Asia and then Europe, making their way to the Americas between 20 000 to 30 000 years ago. So, modern humans became widespread throughout the world only relatively recently.

With the advancement of technology and analytical techniques, scientists continue to learn more about human evolution and how we, as a species, have changed over time. New discoveries of fossils and improvements in dating techniques have helped us gain a better understanding of when and how humans evolved. Future discoveries will undoubtedly deepen our knowledge of human evolution.

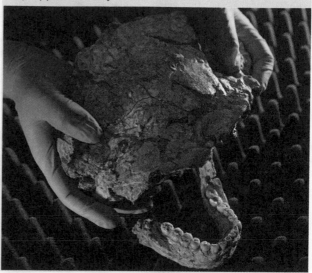

FIGURE 11: A partially-crushed fossil *Homo sapiens* skull is prepped for analysis.

Language Arts Connection   Using credible print or online resources, conduct research about new developments in our knowledge of human evolution. Use the following questions as a starting point for the development of a research-based paper and informative presentation. With your teacher's approval, you may choose to explore your own research questions.

- When and where was the first fossil of *Australopithecus* discovered?
- When and where was the first fossil of the modern human (*Homo sapiens*) discovered?
- How have scientists' ideas of human evolution changed over time?
- Have there been any recent discoveries that have led to changes in these ideas?
- Does molecular evidence support fossil evidence? If so, how?

| EVOLUTIONARY BIOLOGIST | WHALE EVOLUTION | PREDICTING EVOLUTIONARY RELATIONSHIPS | Go online to choose one of these other paths. |

Lesson Self-Check

FIGURE 12: The long-tailed pangolin is a unique creature.

Long-tailed pangolins are animals with unique characteristics. They are covered in large, scale-like armor similar to reptiles. However, pangolins also have characteristics common to mammals, such as hair, mammary glands, and a jaw used to chew food. The pangolin has fur on part of its body and a long tail that is used to grip and move about trees where it feeds on insects such as ants.

This interesting combination of features prompts ongoing questions about how pangolins are related to other organisms. Scientists had thought these animals might be related to anteaters, sloths, and armadillos. New evidence suggests pangolins may actually be more closely related to hyenas, bears, and wolves.

 Evidence Notebook Refer to your notes in your Evidence Notebook to explain how scientists can use evidence to determine the evolutionary relationships between different organisms.

1. Make a claim about the evolutionary relationship between the long-tailed pangolin and other organisms.
2. How would you organize your evidence to support your claim? What evidence would be most useful to support your claim?
3. Why is the classification of organisms considered a work in progress? Use the pangolin as an example in your explanation.

CHECKPOINTS

Check Your Understanding

1. By examining the fin of a primitive fish, scientists have found similarities in bone structure to that of modern day reptiles, birds, and mammals. What type of evidence does this describe?
   - ○ **a.** vestigial structures
   - ○ **b.** embryonic structures
   - ○ **c.** analogous structures
   - ○ **d.** homologous structures
   - ◉ **e.** molecular structures

2. The *Astyanax mexicanus* is a species of tetra fish that lives in bodies of water deep inside caves. Even though they cannot see, these fish still have small, non-working eyes. Their eyes are examples of
   - ○ **a.** vestigial structures.
   - ○ **b.** embryonic structures.
   - ○ **c.** analogous structures.
   - ○ **d.** homologous structures.
   - ○ **e.** molecular structures.

3. How can a comparison of proteins help scientists identify a common ancestor between two species?
   - ○ **a.** It can reveal similar patterns in DNA sequences.
   - ○ **b.** It can help scientists identify similarities among cell types.
   - ○ **c.** It can confirm the presence of similar homologous structures.
   - ○ **d.** It can show similarities and differences in embryonic or larval development.

4. Select the correct terms to complete the statement.
   As embryos, all vertebrates share certain features such as pharyngeal arches | lungs. This provides developmental | molecular | vestigial evidence of a common ancestor among all vertebrate species.

5. The similarity in homologous structures between different species is evidence that they
   - ○ **a.** share a common ancestor.
   - ○ **b.** are members of the same genus.
   - ○ **c.** use the similar structures in the same way.
   - ○ **d.** evolved from each other.

6. Birds and snakes share a common ancestor from over 250 million years ago, but now they show many physical differences. These differences are most directly the result of
   - ○ **a.** coevolution between species.
   - ○ **b.** molecular clocks ticking at different rates.
   - ○ **c.** the long-term accumulation of mutations.
   - ○ **d.** differences in the alleles of the ancestor.

FIGURE 13: Approximate Percentage of Shared DNA with Humans

Organism	Zebrafish	Chicken	Roundworm	Chimpanzee
Shared DNA (%)	70	60	21	98

7. According to the table, humans share the most DNA with which of the following animals?
   - ○ **a.** zebrafish
   - ○ **b.** chicken
   - ○ **c.** roundworm
   - ○ **d.** chimpanzee

CHECKPOINTS (continued)

8. How are genes and proteins similar to homologous structures when determining evolutionary relationships among species?

_____

_____

_____

_____

_____

9. The hummingbird is more closely related to a lizard than it is to a dragonfly. Explain why two species that look similar are not necessarily that closely related.

_____

_____

_____

_____

_____

10. You have discovered the fossil remains of three organisms. One is mammalian, one is reptilian, and the third has both mammalian and reptilian characteristics. What techniques could you apply to determine possible relationships among these organisms?

_____

_____

_____

_____

_____

MAKE YOUR OWN STUDY GUIDE

 In your Evidence Notebook, design a study guide that supports the main idea from this lesson:

Multiple lines of evidence support common ancestry and evolution.

Remember to include the following information in your study guide:

- Use examples that model main ideas.
- Record explanations for the phenomena you investigated.
- Use evidence to support your explanations. Your support can include drawings, data, graphs, laboratory conclusions, and other evidence recorded throughout the lesson.

Consider how patterns among the traits of different species are identified using developmental, anatomical, and molecular techniques.

Theory of Natural Selection

An Anna's hummingbird, native to Southern California, uses its long bill to feed from a flower.

CAN YOU EXPLAIN IT?

Within its narrow, needle-like bill is a hummingbird's even longer tongue. Both of these specialized structures help the Anna's hummingbird reach the nectar found within the trumpet–shaped flowers it feeds from. Both hummingbirds and flowers benefit when a hummingbird stops by a flower to feed, making theirs a mutualistic relationship. The hummingbird gets nutrient-rich nectar and the flower gets pollinated as the hummingbird moves from one flower to another of the same species.

PREDICT How do you think the hummingbird evolved traits, such as bill shape, that make certain flower species ideal food sources? And how did these flower species evolve the traits necessary to attract hummingbirds?

_____

_____

_____

_____

_____

_____

 Evidence Notebook As you explore the lesson, gather evidence for how natural selection results in species that are adapted to their environment.

Hands-On Lab

Modeling Natural Selection: Owls and Field Mice

a Barn owls are predators.

b Mice are prey for barn owls.

We know from molecular, anatomical, and fossil evidence that species have changed over time. This change is called evolution. But how does evolution actually occur in nature? In this lab, you will model one mechanism of evolution called natural selection. You will represent the predator, an owl in search of field mice. Your group will "consume" all the field mice that you can easily see until only 25 percent of the population remains. These surviving field mice will then reproduce. As with the hummingbird, the mice will pass on an important trait for survival to their offspring. You will continue the process for several generations of mice, with some being consumed and others surviving to pass on the traits that made them successful.

MAKE A CLAIM

How does a population change as a result of natural selection?

_____

_____

MATERIALS

- construction paper, five colors
- piece of fabric

CARRY OUT THE INVESTIGATION

1. On the tabletop, spread out the fabric habitat given to you.

2. Count out 20 pieces of each of the five different colors for a total of 100 pieces. This will be your initial population of field mice.

3. One person should spread the pieces out randomly over the entire fabric habitat, making sure that none of the pieces covers the others. The remaining members of the group should not watch this process.

4. The remaining members of the group are now owls. They should pick up 75 pieces (field mice) as they see them, one by one, until a total of 25 field mice remain in the habitat. Be sure to count carefully.

5. Carefully shake off the habitat to remove the surviving mice (a total of 25).

6. Group the survivors by color, and record the numbers in your data table.

7. Next assume that each survivor has three offspring. Place three additional pieces of the same color with each survivor. Record the number of each color in the table. Note that there should again be 100 total pieces.

8. Mix up the new set of pieces. Have a different person spread them over the habitat.

9. Repeat the entire process (Steps 3 to 8) two more times, making a total of three generations of field mice that are preyed upon.

COLLECT DATA

Data Table 1: Effect of Predation on Field Mice Populations Over Time	Color 1	Color 2	Color 3	Color 4	Color 5
Number at start	20	20	20	20	20
Number after first predation					
Number after first reproduction					
Number after second predation					
Number after second reproduction					
Number after third predation					
Number after third reproduction					

ANALYZE

1. Graph your data in the space provided.

2. What patterns can you identify in the graphed data?

   _____

   _____

   _____

3. Which traits appear to be most beneficial for survival in this environment? Explain your answer.

   _____

   _____

   _____

   _____

4. Explain why the number of some mouse varieties increased over time while others decreased.

_____

_____

_____

_____

5. How do you think the data would have changed if the experiment were continued until a total of five generations of field mice were preyed upon?

_____

_____

_____

_____

6. What do you think would happen if you changed the environmental conditions and then ran the experiment again?

_____

_____

_____

_____

FIGURE 2: Female mice can have 5–10 litters per year. Over the span of a year, a single mouse may produce 25–60 offspring.

Mice can reproduce rapidly. In fact, their population could increase exponentially if given enough resources and few predators. However, the greater the population, the more individuals must compete for resources, such as food, water, and mates. In addition, mice must escape predators to survive long enough to pass on their traits to their offspring. Any traits that help them survive and pass on their genes are considered beneficial in this environment. Natural selection is a mechanism by which individuals that have inherited beneficial adaptations show differential reproductive success.

If the environment were to change, the traits that are beneficial could also change. If the grass in a field were to change colors due to a change in weather, different traits would be "selected for." This does not mean that nature actually "chooses" traits. It simply means that some traits are passed down more often than others, because organisms with those traits are better able to survive and reproduce than others in their population that lack those traits.

Evidence Notebook Apply the concepts from this activity to the hummingbird example.

1. Identify traits that help the hummingbird survive in its habitat.
2. What kinds of resources might hummingbirds compete for?
3. What types of traits would give a hummingbird an advantage over other members of its own species?

Developing the Theory of Natural Selection

Charles Darwin is the scientist most people connect with evolution. However, the concept of evolution had been discussed for more than 100 years before Darwin proposed his theory of evolution by natural selection.

Early Ideas About Evolution

Early scientists observed relationships among organisms, and how they seemed to be well adapted for specific environments. Darwin built upon the work of these scientists to develop a theory for how evolution occurs. A *theory* is a proposed explanation based on evidence that has been repeatedly confirmed through experiment or observation. Today, we have a wide body of evidence that supports Darwin's theory of natural selection.

FIGURE 3: Ideas about evolution have developed over time.

1735 *Systema Naturae* Carolus Linnaeus proposed a new system of organization for plants, animals, and minerals based upon their similarities.

1794-1796 *Zoonomia* Darwin's grandfather, Erasmus Darwin, considered how organisms could evolve through mechanisms such as competition.

1809 *Philosophie Zoologique* Jean-Baptiste Lamarck presented evolution as occurring due to environmental change over long periods of time.

1749 *Histoire Naturelle* Georges-Louis Leclerc, Comte de Buffon, discussed important ideas about relationships among organisms, sources of biological variation, and the possibility of evolution.

1798 An Essay on the Principle of Population Thomas Malthus argued that the increasing human population would challenge the world's ability to supply enough food for everyone.

1830 *Principles of Geology* Charles Lyell proposed the theory of uniformitarianism. This theory states that both gradual and catastrophic geological changes have occurred at a constant rate on Earth and are ongoing.

 Collaborate Discuss with a partner how the information in the timeline supports the idea that theories change as new evidence is discovered.

Darwin's Voyage

In 1831, the ship HMS *Beagle* set sail from England on a five-year journey to map the coast of South America and the Pacific islands. The ship captain saw it as an opportunity to collect specimens and study natural history. An invitation was extended to Charles Darwin, a recent graduate from the University of Cambridge. To prepare for the trip, Darwin collected scientific tools, as well as books, one of which was Lyell's *Principles of Geology*, which he read during his travels.

FIGURE 4: Darwin's journey on the HMS *Beagle*.

FIGURE 5: Galápagos tortoises (*Geochelone elephantopus*) had variations in their traits that seemed to match their environment.

a The high shell edge of saddle-backed tortoises allows them to stretch their long necks.

b Domed tortoises have a short neck and short legs.

The first stop occurred at the Cape Verde Islands, where Darwin noticed a band of sea shells on a cliff high above the shoreline. He was curious about how the shells ended up there. During the following year, the young naturalist explored the rain forest to collect specimens of plants, animals, and rocks. As he worked, Darwin kept a diary, recording each new observation. This approach let him make comparative studies, such as noting the differences between fossils found on a later stop in the Falkland Islands and those found on the coast of South America. Darwin also noted geological phenomena that made him wonder how environments changed.

Near the end of his journey, the *Beagle* arrived at the Galápagos Islands, located off the coast of Ecuador. During this stop, Darwin would make some of his most well known observations that are still studied today. Darwin noted that the species found on one island looked different from those on nearby islands and those on the mainland. He was struck by the variation of traits among similar species. Some of these traits seemed well suited to the animals' environments and diets.

PREDICT Select the correct terms to complete the statement about variation of traits.

The saddle-backed | domed tortoise would most likely live in an environment with short | tall plants such as grasses. The saddle-backed | domed tortoise would live in an area with short | tall plants.

Among all of Darwin's observations, the most cited are those of the Galápagos finches. These small birds, sometimes known as "Darwin's finches," are closely related, but have significant differences. These observations led Darwin to infer that species must somehow be able to adapt to their surroundings. An adaptation is a feature that lets an organism survive and reproduce in its environment. It was this analysis that eventually helped shape Darwin's theory about how organisms change over time.

FIGURE 6: Different populations of Galápagos finches have traits that vary.

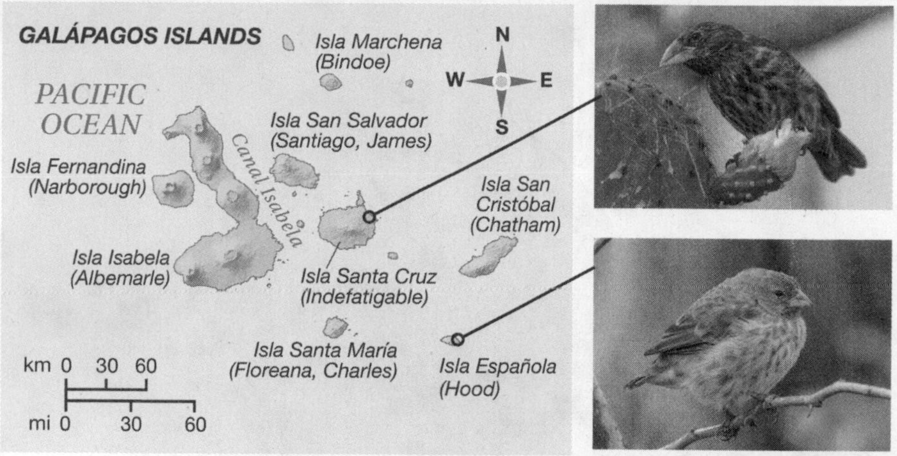

GALÁPAGOS ISLANDS

Isla Marchena (Bindoe)

PACIFIC OCEAN

Isla San Salvador (Santiago, James)

Isla Fernandina (Narborough)

Canal Isabela

Isla San Cristóbal (Chatham)

Isla Isabela (Albemarle)

Isla Santa Cruz (Indefatigable)

Isla Santa María (Floreana, Charles)

Isla Española (Hood)

km 0 30 60
mi 0 30 60

a Large cactus finch (*Geospiza conirostris*)

Species in the genus *Geospiza* have thick beaks and can feed on large, hard seeds that require strength for crushing.

b Small tree finch (*Camarhynchus parvulus*)

Species in the genus *Camarhynchus* have biting strength at the tips of their beaks, which is useful for tearing vegetation.

EXPLAIN How do these finches' adaptations help them survive and reproduce in their environment? What type of beak would you expect to see on a finch that eats insects? Explain your answer.

_____

_____

_____

_____

Since Darwin's time, the evolution of populations on islands has been studied in many living organisms, such as fruit flies and honeycreepers, a type of bird on the Hawaiian Islands. Many of the same patterns have emerged. Island species appear closely related to mainland species, but they have adaptations matched to the conditions on the islands where they live. Adaptations are often very different in related species on islands that may be very close to each other, but have different habitats. Darwin was the first scientist to establish the relationship between island and mainland species. Today this is an important principle of biogeography, which is the study of the distribution of organisms around the world.

APPLY A species of finch on the mainland has a long, thin beak. It lives in swamps and its main food is insects. A closely related species of finch lives on an island near the mainland. This island has many trees that produce small, hard seeds. What kind of adaptation most likely became common in the island population, in response to its different environment?

○ **a.** an even longer and thinner beak

○ **b.** a medium-sized, thick beak

○ **c.** a very large, thick beak

○ **d.** a beak with a sharp tip

Several years before Darwin landed in the Galápagos, the *Beagle* anchored near Bahía Blanca in Argentina. While there, hunters brought back an armadillo. This was Darwin's first introduction to this strange, armored animal. While on a fossil-hunting trip in the area, he found fossils of huge animals, including *Glyptodon*, a giant armadillo. The fact that these fossils looked like the living species suggested that modern animals might have some relationship to fossil forms. These fossils suggested that in order for such changes to occur, Earth must be much older than previously thought.

FIGURE 7: Darwin found fossils of *Glyptodon*, which resembles the modern armadillo. Illustrations not drawn to scale.

Glyptodon

armadillo

ANALYZE Which of these statements are supported by the *Glyptodon* fossil? Select all correct answers.

☐ **a.** *Glyptodon* has a very hard shell, which is not present in any modern species.

☐ **b.** *Glyptodon* has similar features to the modern armadillo.

☐ **c.** *Glyptodon* looked exactly like modern day armadillos.

☐ **d.** *Glyptodon* is not present on Earth today.

During his voyage, Darwin also found fossil shells of marine organisms high up in the Andes Mountains. Darwin later experienced an earthquake during his voyage and noted the effects on the surrounding land. The land that had been underwater was moved above sea level, the result of a process called geologic uplift. This experience explained what he saw in the Andes. Darwin's observations on his voyage supported Lyell's theory that daily geologic processes can add up to great change over a long period. Darwin later extended the ideas of an old Earth and slow, gradual change to the evolution of organisms. These observations led to the concept of evolutionary gradualism. According to this concept, evolutionary changes occur slowly over time, rather than all at once.

EXPLAIN Which types of natural processes could account for fossils of marine organisms being found on top of modern-day mountain ranges? Select all correct answers.

☐ **a.** plate-tectonic forces   ☐ **c.** sedimentation

☐ **b.** geologic uplift   ☐ **d.** erosion

After his voyage, Darwin spent more than 20 years building on his research and knowledge of how evolution occurs. Although he had traveled the world, Darwin also found great insight in his home country of England. One important influence on Darwin's research was the work of farmers and breeders.

Artificial Selection

In England, Darwin observed a lot of variation in domesticated plants and animals. Farmers explained to him that, for example, some cows grew big and strong and produced a lot of milk. Others would be smaller and produce far less milk. The farmer would only breed those cows that were larger and that produced more milk. These productive traits were then passed on to the following generations. Through selection of certain traits, breeders could produce a great amount of diversity within an animal group.

The farmers and breeders were not causing one cow to be more productive than another. Rather, they were controlling which cows would be used to breed offspring. The process of changing a species by breeding it for certain traits is called artificial selection. In this process, humans make use of the genetic variation in plants and animals by acting as the selective agent. Humans determine which traits are favorable and then breed individuals that show those traits.

Humans have been using artificial selection to select for desirable traits in plants and animals for thousands of years. Virtually all of the fruits and vegetables we eat have been greatly altered from their wild forms through the process of artificial selection.

APPLY Select the correct terms to complete the statement about artificial selection.

A dog breeder wants to produce a breed of dog that can rescue people from a snowy mountain. The breeder chooses the largest | smallest puppies with the thickest | thinnest fur, and breeds only those dogs over many generations to produce more effective rescue dogs.

FIGURE 8: Domesticated dogs evolved through artificial selection. The common ancestor for domesticated dogs is the gray wolf.

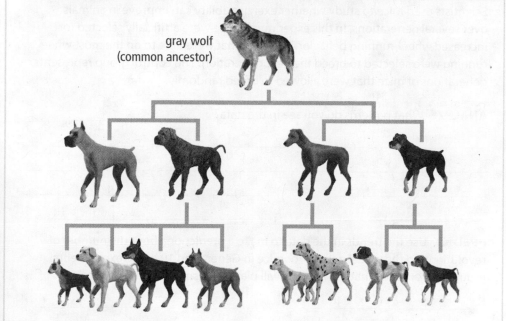

gray wolf
(common ancestor)

Although Darwin had no knowledge of genetics, he observed that, with human intervention, certain individuals could be selected to produce offspring with desirable traits. When selected and allowed to breed, these individuals would pass their traits on to their offspring. For artificial selection to occur, the trait must be heritable. A heritable trait has the ability to be passed down from one generation to the next.

Darwin related what he learned about breeding to his ideas on adaptation. In artificial selection, individuals with desired traits are bred over generations, but only if the traits are advantageous to breeders. However, breeders also might select against features that are not desirable or "useful." During artificial selection, humans act as the selective agent. In nature, however, the environment generates the selective pressure that determines if a trait is passed on or not.

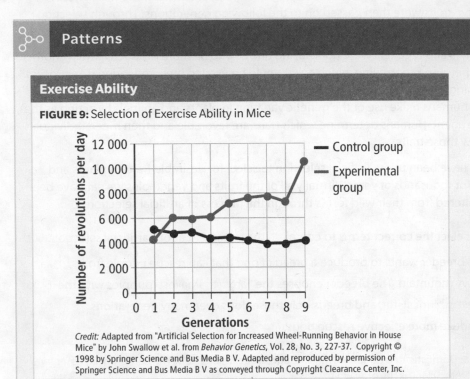

Patterns

Exercise Ability

FIGURE 9: Selection of Exercise Ability in Mice

Credit: Adapted from "Artificial Selection for Increased Wheel-Running Behavior in House Mice" by John Swallow et al. from *Behavior Genetics*, Vol. 28, No. 3, 227-37. Copyright © 1998 by Springer Science and Bus Media B V. Adapted and reproduced by permission of Springer Science and Bus Media B V as conveyed through Copyright Clearance Center, Inc.

Scientists used mice to study whether exercise ability can improve in animals over several generations. In this experiment, mice were artificially selected for increased wheel-running behavior. The mice that were able to do the most wheel running were selected to breed the next generation. The control group represents generations of mice that were allowed to breed randomly.

ANALYZE What patterns do you see in the data?

_____

_____

_____

_____

PREDICT Use the trends in the data to make a prediction about the number of revolutions on the wheel per day for mice in Generation 10 of the experimental group. Do you think that the number will plateau at some point? Explain.

_____

_____

 Evidence Notebook In many bird species, males are brightly colored, while females are dull in color. How might this adaptation become more common over time?

Principles of Natural Selection

Charles Darwin was not the only person to develop a theory to explain how evolution may take place. An English naturalist named Alfred Russel Wallace independently developed a theory very similar to Darwin's. Both Darwin and Wallace had studied the huge diversity of plants and animals in the tropics, and both had studied the fossil record. They also were both influenced by the work of Thomas Malthus and his principles of economics.

Malthus published a book in 1798 in which he discussed how increasing human populations would challenge the world's ability to produce enough food for everyone. Both Darwin and Wallace applied Malthus's ideas to the pressures experienced by plants and animals as populations increased. They noted that no species dominated the world, because some resource limited their ability to reproduce and survive. In an environment where resources are limited, individuals must compete for them. Those organisms that compete successfully go on to reproduce and pass on their characteristics.

EXPLAIN Select the correct terms to complete the statement about resource limitations.

Malthus described how resources limit the growth of plant | human | bacteria
populations. Darwin and Wallace applied the ideas of Malthus, to state that limited
resources could improve | limit the ability of some individuals to pass on their
characteristics through adaptation | extinction | reproduction.

In 1858, the ideas of Darwin and Wallace were presented to an important group of scientists in London. In 1859, Darwin published his ideas in the book *On the Origin of Species by Means of Natural Selection*. The theory of natural selection explains how evolution can occur. Natural selection is a mechanism by which individuals that have inherited beneficial adaptations show differential reproductive success. This theory is built on the premise that more individuals are produced in each generation than can survive in any environment where resources are limited.

Genetic Variation

Darwin's theory of evolution by natural selection was based on observed patterns among plants and animals that he and others studied. What he did not understand was how these changes occurred. About six years after the publication of *On the Origin of Species*, a little-known monk named Gregor Mendel published his research on genetics and the basic principles of heredity.

Mendel's work showed that heritable factors, or traits, are passed down from parents to offspring. We now know that traits are coded for by genes, which are portions of a DNA molecule. Different variations of the same gene are called alleles. The jaguar cub shown in Figure 10 inherited a combination of alleles that resulted in it having a different fur color than its mother. Therefore, there is variation in coat color in the jaguar population, and some variations may prove more beneficial than others in a given environment. Variation in the alleles between individual organisms within a population is called *genetic variation*. Genetic variation is the basis for natural selection.

FIGURE 10: Variation in coat color can be seen in jaguars and their offspring.

Genetic variation is increased by a process called meiosis and sexual reproduction. Meiosis is the type of cell division that results in sex cells: eggs in females and sperm in males. Genes are separated during meiosis. If the genes are not linked, they will separate independently. As genes are lined up and shuffled in different ways during meiosis, various combinations of genetic material are made, as shown in Figure 11.

FIGURE 11: Chromosomes separate independently during meiosis. As a result, sex cells have many different combinations of genes.

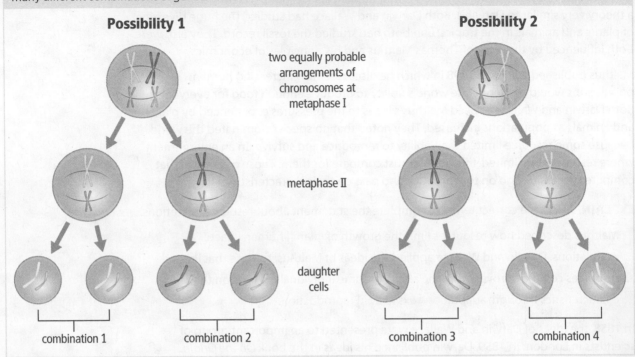

Possibility 1   two equally probable arrangements of chromosomes at metaphase I   Possibility 2

metaphase II

daughter cells

combination 1   combination 2   combination 3   combination 4

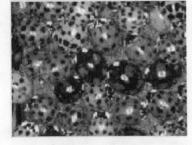

FIGURE 12: Sexual reproduction increases genetic variation.

In sexual reproduction, the offspring receives two forms of each gene, one from each parent. In this way, sexual reproduction produces an organism with a unique combination of inherited traits. A species that reproduces using sexual reproduction will end up with populations of unique individuals that possess all kinds of traits. For example, Figure 12 shows the variation that can be seen in color patterns in a population of Asian beetles. It is this type of variation that natural selection acts on.

Mutations can also increase genetic variation. If a mutation occurs in a sperm or egg cell, it can be passed on to an organism's offspring and increase genetic diversity within a population.

Keep in mind that natural selection acts on physical traits rather than on the genetic material itself. New alleles are not made by natural selection—they occur by genetic mutations. In addition, these mutations must be heritable, or passed down to offspring. Only mutations that occur in sex cells are passed on to offspring.

MODEL Explain how you could have modeled a new trait arising from a mutation in the owl and mouse simulation of natural selection.

_____

_____

_____

_____

Overproduction

The work of Thomas Malthus inspired many of Darwin's ideas about modification by natural selection. In his work, Malthus pointed out the potential of human populations to grow exponentially if there was a constant birth rate and ideal conditions. Such conditions would include unlimited resources and an absence of disease. However, populations do not grow in an unchecked way. As Malthus pointed out, human populations are limited by many factors, such as disease, war, and limited resources.

Human Population Growth

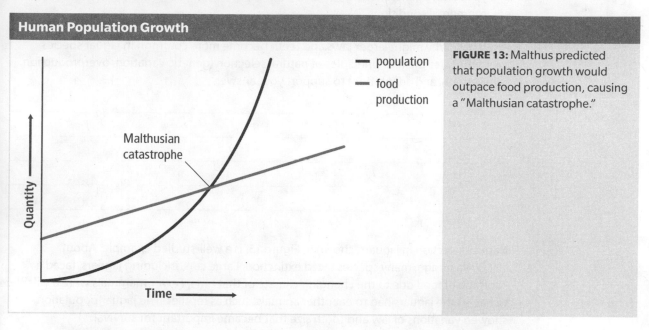

— population
— food production

Malthusian catastrophe

Quantity

Time

FIGURE 13: Malthus predicted that population growth would outpace food production, causing a "Malthusian catastrophe."

EXPLAIN Select the correct terms to complete the statement about population growth. Not all words will be used.

exponential   linear   resources   competition

Most populations do not experience _____ growth because the

_____ in a given environment are often limited, which increases

_____ among individuals.

Competition

Darwin noted that more offspring are born than can survive and that, without limits, any one species might overrun Earth. However, environments place limits on population growth, where some individuals are more successful at survival than others. Those individuals that survive and produce offspring will have their traits passed on to later generations.

Building on Malthus's ideas that there are limits to human population growth, Darwin reasoned that a similar struggle for resources took place in nature. The challenge is for each individual to be better at obtaining available resources, such as food, water, and shelter.

FIGURE 14: In competition for resources, some individuals will out-compete others.

Adaptation

Sometimes, a certain variation lets an individual survive better than other individuals it competes against in its environment. More successful individuals are "naturally selected" to live longer and to produce more offspring that share those adaptations. Over time, natural selection will result in a species population with adaptations that are well suited for survival and reproduction in their environment. More individuals will have the trait in every following generation, as long as the trait continues to be beneficial in the existing environmental conditions.

PREDICT Why might larger jaws and teeth become more common in jaguar species over time? Use the four principles of natural selection (genetic variation, overproduction, competition, and adaptation) to support your answer.

_____

_____

_____

_____

Natural selection in jaguars, shown in Figure 15, is a well-studied example. About 11 000 years ago, many species faced extinction. Large cats, including jaguars, faced a shortage of food due to the changing climate of that time. Fewer mammals were available to eat, so the jaguars had to eat other animals, such as reptiles. The jaguar population showed variations of jaw and tooth size that became important for survival.

FIGURE 15: Natural selection has led to changes in the jaguar species over time.

skull 1   skull 2

a Like many other species, jaguars can produce more offspring than can be supported by the environment. Some jaguars may be born with slightly larger jaws and teeth (skull 1) due to natural variation in the population.

b Jaguars with large jaws and teeth are able to eat armored animals, such as shelled reptiles. These jaguars are more likely to survive and to have more offspring than jaguars that can eat only mammals.

In biology, the term fitness is a measure of the ability of an organism to survive and produce more offspring relative to other members of the population in a given environment. An individual with high fitness is well adapted to its environment. After the change in climate, jaguars that had larger teeth and jaws had a higher fitness than other jaguars in the population. Jaguars that ate less did not necessarily all die or stop reproducing altogether. They just reproduced a little less.

It is important to note that fitness does not simply mean being the biggest and strongest individual. For example, being small is beneficial for some types of male spiders. Their lower body weight makes it easier for these males to cast a strand of silk into the air and be carried by the wind to a new location. As a result, these males have more opportunities to find mates and pass on their genes.

Understanding Natural Selection

To fully understand the theory of natural selection, it is important to consider how changes in the environment can influence fitness. It also is useful to examine some of the common preconceptions about how natural selection occurs.

Changing Environments

As an environment changes, different traits will become beneficial. Ecologists Peter and Rosemary Grant observed an example of natural selection acting on existing traits within a population of medium ground finches on Daphne, one of the Galápagos islands. A drought in 1977 reduced the amount of small, soft seeds that the finches preferred. However, there were still plenty of large, tough-shelled seeds.

The two graphs shown in Figure 16 represent the number of birds with each size of beak. In 1976, a total of 751 birds were measured. The distribution of beak size is shown in the histogram on the left. After the drought, the Grants again measured the beak sizes of the 1978 survivors. Ninety birds were measured to construct the histogram on the right.

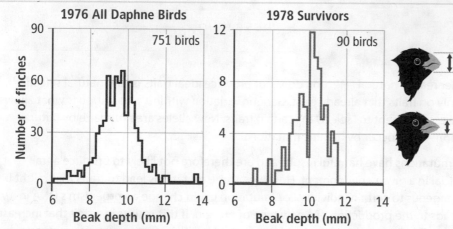

FIGURE 16: The data in these graphs show finch beak size before and after a drought.

Credit: Adapted from *Ecology and Evolution of Darwin's Finches* by Peter R. Grant. Copyright © 1998 by Princeton University Press. Adapted and reproduced by permission of Princeton University Press as conveyed through Copyright Clearance Center, Inc.

INFER What can you infer about how the finch population changed after the drought? Select all correct answers.

☐ **a.** The number of finches with small beaks increased.

☐ **b.** The number of finches with large beaks increased.

☐ **c.** Large-beaked finches were better able to crack large, tough seeds.

☐ **d.** Small-beaked finches were better able to crack large, tough seeds.

The numbers of large-beaked finches on this Galápagos island kept rising until 1984, when the supply of large seeds decreased after an unusually wet period. These conditions favored production of small, soft seeds and small-beaked birds were now better adapted for the changed environment. With evolution, a trait that is an advantage today may be a disadvantage in the future.

Addressing Preconceptions About Natural Selection

It is tempting to assume that any feature on an organism must be the ideal trait for that organism's environment. However, not all traits are adaptations. For example, most vertebrate animals have red blood. Other animals might have blood that is blue, green, yellow, or even purple in color. However, animals with red blood do not survive better than animals with a different color of blood. Instead, blood color results from its chemical makeup. While the chemistry might be a result of an adaptation, the color itself is not.

It also is important to keep in mind that natural selection does not produce individuals who are perfectly suited to their environment. This is partly because organisms have combinations of traits that result from complex sets of tradeoffs. For example, having large horns may help an organism fight successfully for mates, but they may make it difficult for the animal to escape predators as effectively as it could with lighter horns. It would be difficult for selective pressures to produce "ideal" traits, because a trait that is ideal for one function may be less than ideal, or even harmful, in other situations.

FIGURE 17: Large horns provide some benefits, but also come with costs.

APPLY Describe at least two ways in which the large horns on the sheep shown in Figure 17 could reduce their fitness.

_____

_____

_____

_____

_____

_____

Another reason natural selection does not produce ideal traits is that natural selection acts only on traits that already exist. Genetic variation within a population is what allows for the environment to "select" for certain traits. New alleles are not made by natural selection—they occur by genetic mutations.

Many mutations have harmful results and are therefore not likely to produce a trait that is beneficial in a given environment. However, some mutations lead to traits that might be advantageous to certain individuals. A mutation could change an organism's DNA in a way that leads to the production of a new type of protein. If this results in a trait that increases an organism's fitness, this trait would be selected for. Therefore, new traits can occur, but they are not made through natural selection.

Another common preconception about natural selection is that individuals can adapt to their environment. Natural selection leads to changes in populations, not in individual organisms. Evolution is a change in the proportion of alleles in a population over many generations. Therefore, individuals do not adapt to their environment over the course of one lifetime. Adaptations occur in populations, and those adaptations evolve over time through the process of natural selection. This process may take millions of years, or it may occur very quickly, as it does in single-celled organisms, such as bacteria.

Evidence Notebook Plants that attract hummingbirds often produce nectar that is high in sucrose. This is a key nutrient that supports a hummingbird's high metabolism. Use the principles of natural selection to explain this trait in certain plants.

Data Analysis

Antibiotic-Resistant Bacteria

Antibiotics are medicines used to kill disease-causing bacteria. Studies have shown that certain species of disease-causing bacteria have evolved to be resistant to various antibiotics. The Centers for Disease Control and Prevention (CDC) found that doctors were prescribing antibiotics when they weren't necessary. Additionally, patients were not taking their full antibiotic doses. Both practices have led to bacteria developing antibiotic resistance.

The bacterium *Neisseria gonorrhoeae* causes gonorrhea. This infection affects organs of the reproductive system, as well as parts of the urinary tract. If left untreated, an infected person may lose the ability to produce children. These bacteria are transferred from one person to another through sexual activity.

N. gonorrhoeae has now developed varying levels of resistance to most antibiotics, including penicillin and tetracycline. The bacteria is also developing resistance to other antibiotics. Cefixime is starting to show susceptibility to resistance. It is recommended that cefixime be used with other antibiotics so the bacteria do not become fully resistant to it.

The *N. gonorrhoeae* resistance graph in Figure 18 shows a dramatic increase in the resistance of *N. gonorrhoeae* to

fluoroquinolone antibiotics since around 2000. This resistance can be attributed to the increased use of this antibiotic during this time period. The graph also shows that

the bacteria has been resistant to both penicillin and tetracycline since the late 1980s and continues to be resistant.

N. gonorrhoeae Resistance, United States, 1987-2011

FIGURE 18: *N. gonorrhoeae* shows some level of resistance to many types of antibiotics.

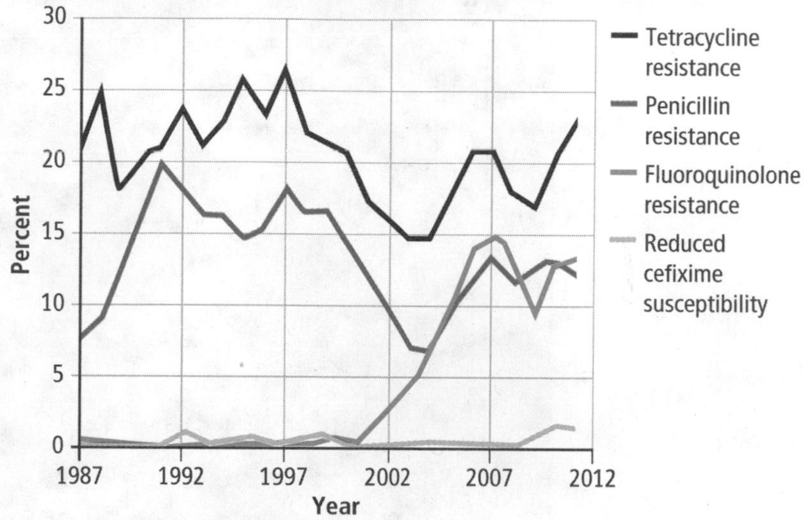

Tetracycline resistance

Penicillin resistance

Fluoroquinolone resistance

Reduced cefixime susceptibility

Source: The Gonococcal Isolate Surveillance Project (GISP), quoted in "Antibiotic Resistance Threats in the United States, 2013" (CDC)

Evidence Notebook Answer the following questions in your Evidence Notebook.

1. What happened to the bacteria's penicillin resistance from 1987 to 1990?
2. Make a model to show the changes in resistant traits in the population of bacteria over time as they were exposed to antibiotics.
3. Why is it important that a patient complete their entire course of antibiotics, even if their symptoms appear to disappear?
4. Why do scientists need to continually develop new antibiotics to treat bacterial diseases such as gonorrhea?

MODELING NATURAL SELECTION **NATURAL SELECTION TODAY** **BIOMECHANICS OF STAG BEETLE JAWS** Go online to choose one of these other paths.

Lesson Self-Check

CAN YOU EXPLAIN IT?

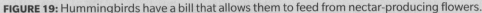

FIGURE 19: Hummingbirds have a bill that allows them to feed from nectar-producing flowers.

Hummingbirds have a variety of adaptations, including uniquely-shaped bill and tongue structures that allow them to effectively feed from nectar-producing flowers. The flowers, in turn, have adaptations that make them especially attractive to the hummingbirds. These adaptations include bright coloration, slender shapes matched to the curve of a hummingbird's bill, and the production of sugar-rich nectar. These flowers are often odorless, which makes them less attractive to bees or other insects that rely on their sense of smell to find food sources.

Research indicates that hummingbirds and the flowers they feed from evolved together. As hummingbirds changed over time, so too did the flowers. Evolution isn't a one-way street. Instead, changes in one species can have a profound effect on an entirely different species, as is the case with hummingbirds and flowering plants.

 Evidence Notebook Refer to your notes in your Evidence Notebook to construct an explanation for how adaptations in hummingbird populations influenced adaptations in the flower populations from which they feed, and vice versa.

1. Make a claim about how natural selection influences the traits in the hummingbird and flower population over time.
2. What evidence supports your claim? Consider how the shape of the hummingbird's bill may have influenced changes in the shape of flowers that it feeds from.
3. Explain how natural selection might affect the hummingbird population if an environmental change affects the flower populations in its habitat.

Check Your Understanding

1. Which of these traits are most likely to be adaptations for butterfly caterpillars in a butterfly population that lives in a meadow? Select all correct answers.

   ☐ **a.** bright coloration that makes them highly visible

   ☐ **b.** thin skin that easily absorbs pesticides

   ☐ **c.** mouthparts that easily chew grass leaves

   ☐ **d.** behavior that causes them to stop moving when predators are near

2. If the climate were to change in an environment, it is more likely that some individuals within a population will survive if

   ○ **a.** the individuals stop reproducing.

   ○ **b.** the individuals are genetically identical.

   ○ **c.** there is genetic variation within the population.

   ○ **d.** the individuals reproduce asexually.

3. Use the correct terms to complete the statement about natural selection.

   Natural selection acts on traits | chromosomes

   in a(n) individual | population.

4. Which of the following are key elements of Darwin's theory of evolution by natural selection? Select all correct answers.

   ☐ **a.** genetic variation

   ☐ **b.** genetic engineering

   ☐ **c.** fitness

   ☐ **d.** adaptation

   ☐ **e.** independent assortment

5. How do mutations lead to genetic variation?

   ○ **a.** Mutations directly result in changes in an organism's traits.

   ○ **b.** Mutations produce random changes in an organism's DNA.

   ○ **c.** Mutations lead to a random arrangement of chromosomes during meiosis.

   ○ **d.** Mutations decrease the variety of traits observed in a population.

6. Use the correct terms to complete the statement about natural selection.

   overproduction   competition

   adaptation   genetic variation

   Natural selection can be modeled by representing "beaks" with plastic forks, knives, and spoons. Participants use their beaks to obtain as many beans as possible from a plate of beans. In this simulation, the different utensils represent _____,

   and trying to obtain beans represents

   _____ over

   limited resources. This is typically the result of

   _____, as more

   individuals are born than can survive. Having more participants take on the form of beak that was most successful at obtaining food is one way to

   represent _____.

7. Match each piece of evidence to the way in which it influenced Darwin's theory of natural selection.

artificial selection ○	○	Organisms are adapted to their environment.
fossils of extinct organisms ○	○	Geological forces have changed Earth over time.
Galápagos tortoises ○	○	Humans can serve as the selective agent.
sea shells above the seashore ○	○	Species have changed over time.

CHECKPOINTS (continued)

8. Explain how longer necks in giraffes might be selected for by natural selection over time. How might this adaptation benefit giraffes?

_____

_____

_____

_____

_____

9. How did the work of farmers and breeders in England influence the work of Charles Darwin? Use examples to support your explanation.

_____

_____

_____

_____

_____

10. What effect did Darwin's travels to the Galápagos Islands have on the development of his theory of natural selection?

_____

_____

_____

_____

_____

_____

MAKE YOUR OWN STUDY GUIDE

 In your Evidence Notebook, design a study guide that supports the main ideas from this lesson:

Many scientists made observations and developed ideas about evolution, but it was Charles Darwin who developed the theory of evolution by natural selection.

Natural selection is a process in which overproduction, variation, and competition lead to the adaptation of populations over time.

Remember to include the following information in your study guide:
- Use examples that model main ideas.
- Record explanations for the phenomena you investigated.
- Use evidence to support your explanations. Your support can include drawings, data, graphs, laboratory conclusions, and other evidence recorded throughout the lesson.

Consider how the evidence Darwin and other scientists collected supports the idea that natural selection changes traits in populations over time.

Earth Science Connection

Biogeography The study of the geographical distribution of organisms and ecosystems over space and time is called biogeography. The concept of biogeography is used to support the idea that species change over time due to evolution through natural selection. For example, what might be indicated by the fact that marsupials only exist in the Americas and Australia?

> How does the geographical distribution of closely related species, and the distribution of similar but not related species, provide evidence for evolution? Select a biogeographical example that provides a line of evidence for evolution. Then make a conceptual model to represent your example, and explain your model in a short story.

FIGURE 1: Female marsupials, such as this tree kangaroo, care for their undeveloped young in special pouches outside their bodies until the young gain independence.

Social Studies Connection

Human Relationships As humans evolved, so did their societies. Human society began as small groups of hunter-gatherers. Over time, some groups have shifted to post-industrial societies. Such societies minimize the number and quality of relationships that are common in other societies. For example, electronic socializing has taken the place of other forms of communication, such as phone calls, letters, and in-person conversations.

> Research the social relationships that characterize hunter-gatherer, agricultural, industrial, and post-industrial societies. Make a claim about whether electronic socializing is affecting the quality of relationships today. Use evidence from the evolution or changing nature of relationships in human societies to explain your answer.

FIGURE 2: Social networking may actually reduce social connections with peers.

Technology Connection

Digital Imaging Scanning and digital imaging technologies have revolutionized the field of paleontology. Surface scanning and tomography allow the creation of detailed 3D digital casts that can then be virtually manipulated and easily shared with colleagues across the globe. Digital imaging allows virtual repair of breakage, replacement of missing pieces, and even reversal of deformations without risk of damage to the original fossil.

> Research the study of a specific species or the efforts of a particular paleontology team at a California university or museum. Prepare a multimedia report of your findings, emphasizing aspects of their research that were only achievable through the use of digital technologies.

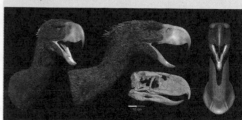

FIGURE 3: Fossil remains were used to make a digital reconstruction of the head of *Andalgalornis steulleti*, an extinct flightless bird species.

A BOOK EXPLAINING
COMPLEX IDEAS USING
ONLY THE 1,000 MOST
COMMON WORDS

RANDALL MUNROE
XKCD.COM

EARTH'S PAST
Everything* that has happened here so far

The geologic time scale provides a framework for understanding the processes that shape our planet. Here's a look at Earth's geological history, layer by layer.

*NOT QUITE EVERYTHING

THE STORY OF EARTH, ONE LAYER AT A TIME

WE LEARN ABOUT THE HISTORY OF THE EARTH FROM ROCKS.

SO, DOES ANYONE HAVE ANY QUESTIONS?

ROCKS ARE LAID DOWN IN LAYERS, AND BY LOOKING AT THE LAYERS FROM DIFFERENT PARTS OF THE WORLD, WHICH ARE ALL DIFFERENT AGES, WE CAN PIECE TOGETHER A SINGLE HISTORY THAT GOES BACK ALMOST TO THE START OF THE WORLD.

THIS PICTURE SHOWS WHAT IT WOULD LOOK LIKE IF YOU COULD SEE THE WHOLE HISTORY OF EARTH IN A SINGLE SET OF LAYERS, WITH EVERY YEAR AS THICK AS EVERY OTHER. IN REAL LIFE, NO SINGLE PLACE HAS ALL THESE LAYERS TOGETHER, AND THERE ARE NO LAYERS AT ALL FROM THE OLDEST PART OF EARTH'S HISTORY.

I WONDER IF WE CAN FIND WHEN THAT SPACE ROCK HIT EARTH!

COOL! CHECK OUT THESE BIG STRANGE ANIMALS!

WHERE ON EARTH DID THESE LAYERS GO?

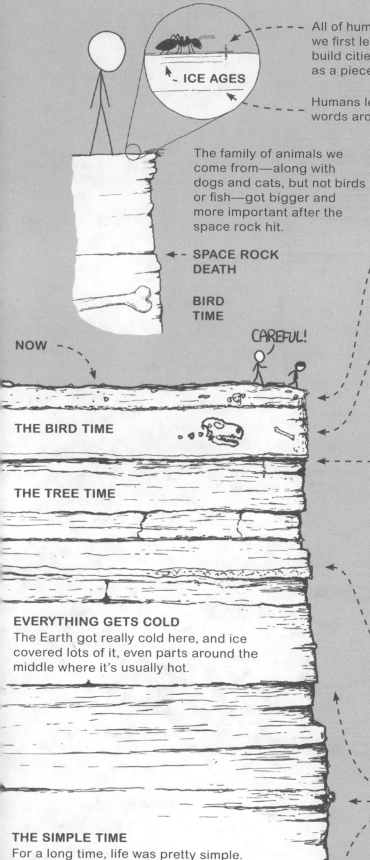

All of human history, since we first learned to write and build cities, is a layer as thin as a piece of paper.

ICE AGES

Humans learned to use words around this time.

YOU ARE HERE

The family of animals we come from—along with dogs and cats, but not birds or fish—got bigger and more important after the space rock hit.

← SPACE ROCK DEATH

BIRD TIME

NOW

CAREFUL!

THE BIRD TIME

THE TREE TIME

EVERYTHING GETS COLD
The Earth got really cold here, and ice covered lots of it, even parts around the middle where it's usually hot.

THE SIMPLE TIME
For a long time, life was pretty simple. There were no animals. Most life was small, either made of single bags of water moving around alone, or big groups of bags growing in big piles on the sea floor.

SPACE ROCK HITS THE EARTH
A big rock hit the Earth, and lots of the animals died. Some groups lived, like birds, some kinds of fish, and our parents.

THE BIRD TIME
A big, well-known group of animals lived during this time. Today's birds are the only animals from that family alive now, but many other animals came from it in the past—like big ones with long necks and bitey ones with huge teeth.

THE GREAT DYING
Almost everything died here, and we're not sure why. There were lots of strange changes in the air and the sea, and around that time a huge layer of hot rock came up out of the Earth and covered a large part of the land. So whatever happened, it was pretty bad.

"The Great Dying" sounds like a name made up to use simple words, but it's not; serious people call it that.

LIFE GETS BIG AND STRANGE
Around this time, big animals started to appear. If you find rocks from this time, you can see lots of strange things in them.

LAND COMES TOGETHER AND BREAKS UP
Right now, Earth's land is broken up into five or six big areas with water in between, but before that, it was pushed together. We think this breaking up and pushing together happened a few times, although it's hard to tell how many.

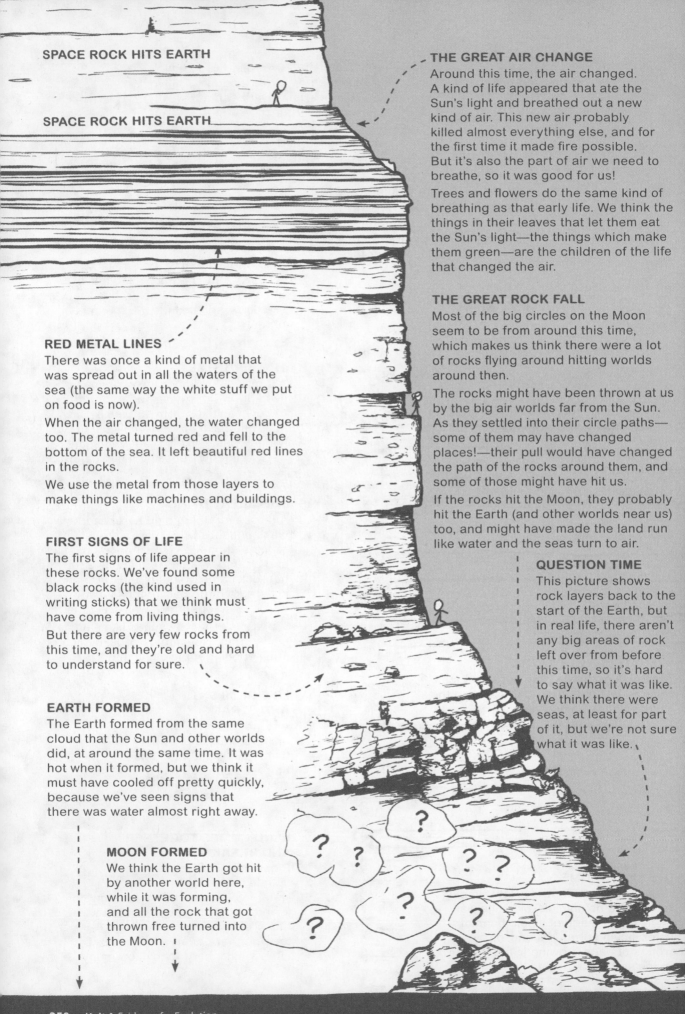

SPACE ROCK HITS EARTH

SPACE ROCK HITS EARTH

RED METAL LINES

There was once a kind of metal that was spread out in all the waters of the sea (the same way the white stuff we put on food is now).

When the air changed, the water changed too. The metal turned red and fell to the bottom of the sea. It left beautiful red lines in the rocks.

We use the metal from those layers to make things like machines and buildings.

FIRST SIGNS OF LIFE

The first signs of life appear in these rocks. We've found some black rocks (the kind used in writing sticks) that we think must have come from living things.

But there are very few rocks from this time, and they're old and hard to understand for sure.

EARTH FORMED

The Earth formed from the same cloud that the Sun and other worlds did, at around the same time. It was hot when it formed, but we think it must have cooled off pretty quickly, because we've seen signs that there was water almost right away.

MOON FORMED

We think the Earth got hit by another world here, while it was forming, and all the rock that got thrown free turned into the Moon.

THE GREAT AIR CHANGE

Around this time, the air changed. A kind of life appeared that ate the Sun's light and breathed out a new kind of air. This new air probably killed almost everything else, and for the first time it made fire possible. But it's also the part of air we need to breathe, so it was good for us!

Trees and flowers do the same kind of breathing as that early life. We think the things in their leaves that let them eat the Sun's light—the things which make them green—are the children of the life that changed the air.

THE GREAT ROCK FALL

Most of the big circles on the Moon seem to be from around this time, which makes us think there were a lot of rocks flying around hitting worlds around then.

The rocks might have been thrown at us by the big air worlds far from the Sun. As they settled into their circle paths—some of them may have changed places!—their pull would have changed the path of the rocks around them, and some of those might have hit us.

If the rocks hit the Moon, they probably hit the Earth (and other worlds near us) too, and might have made the land run like water and the seas turn to air.

QUESTION TIME

This picture shows rock layers back to the start of the Earth, but in real life, there aren't any big areas of rock left over from before this time, so it's hard to say what it was like. We think there were seas, at least for part of it, but we're not sure what it was like.

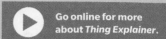
Go online for more about *Thing Explainer*.

YOU ARE HERE

OLDER LIFE?

All life is part of one family, and the information stored in our water bags changes over time, as animals have children and those children have children. By looking at the information stored in the water bags of living things, doctors can figure out how long ago their shared parents lived.

When people have tried to work out how old life's shared parent is, they sometimes come up with a number that's a little *older* than the great rock fall.

But we think the seas turned to air and the rocks to fire, and it's hard to understand how anything could have lived through that.

Investigating Evolution in a Cave

FIGURE 4: These unique organisms were found in Movile Cave.

 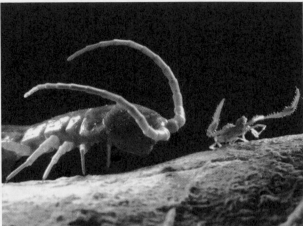

Movile Cave in Romania is closed to the public. In fact, fewer than 100 people have ever entered the cave. Those who have been inside returned with reports and images of translucent organisms, many without eyes, that have extra-long antennae and can breathe in the toxic atmosphere. What do you think is happening in this cave, and what explains the unique appearance of these organisms?

1. ASK A QUESTION

With your team, make a list of questions you have about the organisms and the environment in Movile Cave. Identify the factors you will research to answer these questions.

2. CONDUCT RESEARCH

Investigate Movile Cave in Romania. What makes this cave unique, and what has contributed to the evolution of unique organisms within the cave?

3. DEVELOP A MODEL

Make a model that explains a likely sequence of events that led to the current organisms inhabiting Movile Cave.

4. CONSTRUCT AN EXPLANATION

Use your research and model to construct an explanation for how the organisms in Movile Cave changed and evolved over time. What traits were selected for and how are they advantageous in the environment in which they live?

5. COMMUNICATE

Present your research and your model as a multimedia presentation that explains how evolution and natural selection led to unique organisms in Movile Cave.

 CHECK YOUR WORK

A complete presentation should include the following information:

- a set of questions about what caused the evolution of unique traits in organisms in Movile Cave
- an explanation supported by evidence that details how the organisms changed and evolved over time
- a model to accompany your explanation that explains a likely sequence of events that led to the appearance and behavior of the current organisms inhabiting Movile Cave

Name _____ Date _____

SYNTHESIZE THE UNIT

In your Evidence Notebook, make a concept map, other graphic organizer, or outline using the Study Guides you made for each lesson in this unit. Be sure to use evidence to support your claims.

When synthesizing individual information, remember to follow these general steps:

- Find the central idea of each piece of information.
- Think about the relationships among the central ideas.
- Combine the ideas to come up with a new understanding.

DRIVING QUESTIONS

Look back to the Driving Questions from the opening section of this unit. In your Evidence Notebook, review and revise your previous answers to those questions. Use the evidence you gathered and other observations you made throughout the unit to support your claims.

PRACTICE AND REVIEW

1. DNA nucleotides are said to be universal because they are the same for all known organisms. What is this evidence of? Select all correct answers.
   - ☐ **a.** common ancestry
   - ☐ **b.** fossil record
   - ☐ **c.** evolution
   - ☐ **d.** natural selection

2. How did fossils contribute to Darwin's ideas about changes in species over time?
   - ○ **a.** Fossils supported Darwin's ideas about common ancestry and the relationship of living species to fossil species.
   - ○ **b.** Fossils showed that all species are the result of gradual changes over time.
   - ○ **c.** Fossils explained how species develop different traits.
   - ○ **d.** Fossils showed how humans had affected the traits of organisms for thousands of years.

3. What characteristics make index fossils useful for identifying the relative ages of the layers in which they are found? Select all correct answers.
   - ☐ **a.** Index fossils are widespread.
   - ☐ **b.** Index fossils are abundant.
   - ☐ **c.** Index fossils occur over a long geologic timespan.
   - ☐ **d.** Index fossils are found in diverse habitats.
   - ☐ **e.** Index fossils are easily identifiable.

4. Which statement best describes the relationship between natural selection and variation?
   - ○ **a.** All variations are acted upon by natural selection.
   - ○ **b.** Variations evolve during natural selection to make a species better adapted to its environment.
   - ○ **c.** Natural selection acts on variations that are selected for or against based on the environment.
   - ○ **d.** Natural selection makes variations that are selected for or against based on the environment.

5. Which factor is not required for natural selection to take place?
   - ○ **a.** adaptation
   - ○ **b.** competition
   - ○ **c.** overproduction
   - ○ **d.** sexual reproduction
   - ○ **e.** variation

6. A type of fossil evidence that indicates the presence of ancient organisms without representation of their physical form is known as a
   - ○ **a.** cast fossil.
   - ○ **b.** body fossil.
   - ○ **c.** trace fossil.
   - ○ **d.** mold fossil.
   - ○ **e.** imprint fossil.

7. Why is the fossil record an imperfect line of evidence for evolution?

_____

_____

_____

_____

8. Charles Darwin's reflection on observations made in and around the Galápagos Islands led to his development of the theory of evolution by natural selection. What features of the Galápagos region contributed to the uniqueness of its organisms? Is it reasonable to assume that similar observations could not have been made elsewhere? Why or why not?

_____

_____

_____

_____

9. A classmate makes a claim that genetic mutations are always a negative force in nature. Use evidence and reasoning to explain whether or not you agree with his or her claim.

_____

_____

_____

_____

10. Does the presence of homologous structures in different species provide evidence of common ancestry? How does this compare with the presence of analogous structures?

_____

_____

_____

_____

UNIT PROJECT

Return to your unit project. Share your explanation and supporting model of the evolution of the eye with your class. In your final presentation, evaluate the strength of your predictions, analysis, and conclusions about the evolution of eyes.

Remember these tips while evaluating:

- Look at the empirical evidence—evidence based on observations and data. Does your line of evidence support the idea that eyes have evolved over time?

- Consider if the explanation is logical. Does it contradict any evidence you have seen?

- Is there enough evidence to answer all reasonable questions? How might you develop tests for any additional questions?

UNIT 5

Mechanisms of Inheritance

YOU SOLVE IT

Do Heart Diseases Run in Families?

 To begin exploring this unit's concepts, go online to investigate ways to solve a real-world problem.

DNA is an essential molecule for all living things.

FIGURE 1: Children inherit traits from each of their parents.

In families, children often share similar physical features, such as hair color, hairline, and facial shape, with one or both of their parents. Traits such as these and others are inherited, or passed from parents to offspring. Because of these shared features, it is often possible to tell that two people are closely related as siblings, parent and child, or even grandparent and grandchild. However, except in the case of identical siblings, even closely related individuals have unique features. Some children may share distinctive features of their parents—a father's chin shape or a mother's eye color—but not all children inherit the same sets of features.

PREDICT Why do you think siblings don't look exactly the same if all of their DNA comes from the same mother and father?

_____

_____

_____

_____

DRIVING QUESTIONS

As you move through the unit, gather evidence to help you answer the following questions. In your Evidence Notebook, record what you already know about these topics and any questions you have about them.

1. How are traits passed from parents to offspring? Why do the offspring of the same two parents all look different from each other?

2. How does diversity in traits arise over generations? How can we determine the probability that an organism's expressed version of a trait will be passed on to its offspring?

3. How did scientists determine the structure of DNA?

4. How does the information in DNA get transferred into observable traits?

5. How is the flow of information from DNA regulated?

UNIT PROJECT

Go online to download the Unit Project Worksheet to help plan your project.

Investigating the Heredity of Disease

Many traits and conditions can arise from either genetic or environmental causes. Explore the heredity of Huntington's disease. Based on your analysis, determine the likely cause or causes of Huntington's disease and the role that genetic and environmental factors may play.

Language Development

Use the lessons in this unit to complete the chart and expand your understanding of the science concepts.

TERM: chromosome

Definition	Example
Similar Term	**Phrase**

TERM: meiosis

Definition	Example
Similar Term	**Phrase**

TERM: genetic variation

Definition	Example
Similar Term	**Phrase**

TERM: trait

Definition	Example
Similar Term	**Phrase**

TERM: gene

Definition	Example

Similar Term	Phrase

TERM: DNA (deoxyribonucleic acid)

Definition	Example

Similar Term	Phrase

TERM: protein synthesis

Definition	Example

Similar Term	Phrase

TERM: gene expression

Definition	Example

Similar Term	Phrase

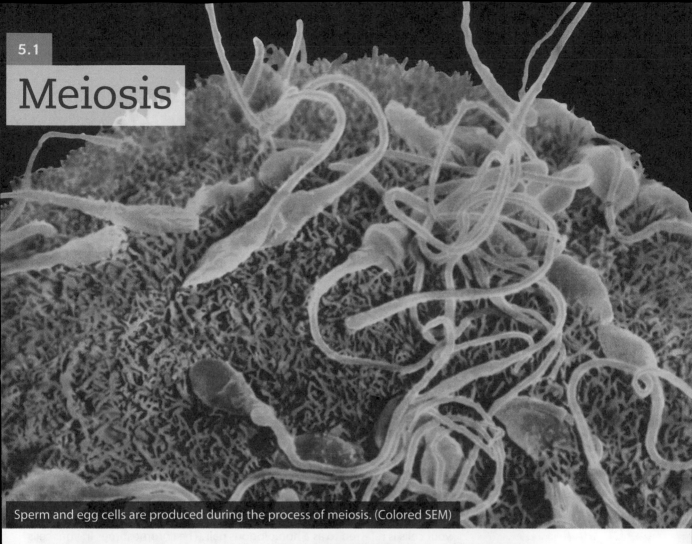

Meiosis

Sperm and egg cells are produced during the process of meiosis. (Colored SEM)

CAN YOU EXPLAIN IT?

Humans have unique versions of traits that cause us to look and act differently from one another. Take a look at the people around you. Are they all the same? Aside from identical siblings, such as identical twins or triplets, there is great variety in physical traits from one person to the next.

PREDICT What do you think accounts for such a large amount of genetic variation within the human population?

_____

_____

_____

_____

_____

_____

 Evidence Notebook As you explore this lesson, gather evidence to explain how meiosis and sexual reproduction increase genetic diversity.

Chromosomes and Meiosis

DNA is the genetic material in organisms. It codes for proteins and contains the information that determines when proteins are made. In complex organisms, long strands of DNA are packaged together with a few particular proteins into chromosomes in the nucleus of the cell. A chromosome is one long continuous thread of DNA that consists of many genes. A gene codes for proteins. Your body cells have 46 chromosomes each. If stretched out straight and laid end to end, the DNA in just one of your cells would be about 2 meters long! How does something so big fit inside the nucleus of a tiny cell?

Chromosome Structure and Function

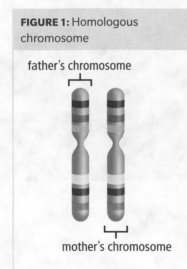

FIGURE 1: Homologous chromosome

father's chromosome

mother's chromosome

Each species has a characteristic number of chromosomes per cell. However, the number of chromosomes does not seem to be related to the complexity of the organism. For example, yeast have 32 chromosomes which occur in 16 pairs. A fern holds the record for the most chromosomes–more than 1200. Each of your body cells contains 46 chromosomes, which occur in 23 pairs. Homologous chromosomes are two chromosomes—one inherited from the mother, one from the father—that have the same set of genes. An example of homologous chromosomes is shown in Figure 1. Each gene is represented by a colored band. While the genes are the same on each homologous chromosome, the version of the gene may differ. Each pair of chromosomes in your cells is referred to as a homologous pair. The chromosomes in your cells are genetically identical to each other, unless mutations have occurred.

When a cell prepares to divide, each homologous chromosome is duplicated. Each half of the duplicated chromosome is called a chromatid, and both halves are referred to as *sister chromatids*. The sister chromatids are attached to one another by the centromere. Each chromatid is a copy of the other. Homologous pairs do not attach to one another. Often, images of chromosomes, such as those in Figures 3b and 3c, display duplicated chromosomes. Remember, if you see an X-shaped chromosome, these are sister chromatids and not homologous pairs.

PREDICT Why do you think DNA is duplicated before a cell divides? Why do you think the sister chromatids are attached to one another?

_____

_____

_____

_____

_____

_____

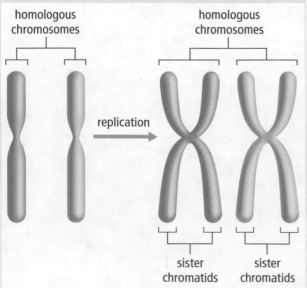

FIGURE 2: Homologous chromosomes duplicate and remain attached to one another.

homologous chromosomes

homologous chromosomes

replication

sister chromatids

sister chromatids

Autosomes and Sex Chromosomes

Scientists are able to directly study chromosomes using a karyotype, such as the one shown in Figure 3a. A karyotype shows each homologous pair of chromosomes in a cell. The chromosomes are stained using chemicals, which produces a pattern of bands on the chromosomes. The sizes and locations of the bands are very consistent for each chromosome, but the bands differ greatly among different chromosomes. Karyotypes can show changes in chromosomes, such as when a person has too many chromosomes. In Down syndrome, for example, a person has an extra copy of at least part of chromosome 21. In XYY syndrome, a male has an extra Y chromosome.

FIGURE 3: Humans have 23 pairs of chromosomes. The chromosomes that make up pair 23 determine whether an individual is male or female.

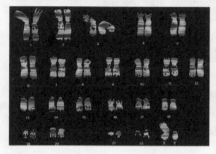
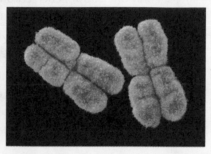
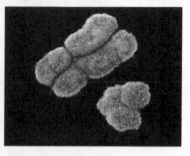

a This colored image shows all of an individual's chromosome pairs.

b Females have two X chromosomes. (Colored SEM)

c Males have one X and one Y chromosome. (Colored SEM)

 Collaborate With a partner, discuss the following questions: What patterns do you observe in the image of human chromosomes? What differences do you see between the chromosomes shown in Figure 3a and those shown in Figures 3b and 3c?

Together, chromosome pairs 1 through 22 make up your autosomes, which are chromosomes that contain genes for characteristics not directly related to the sex of an organism. These chromosomes are numbered by size, with chromosome 1 indicating the largest pair and 22 indicating the smallest pair.

Most sexually reproducing species also have sex chromosomes that directly control the development of sexual characteristics. In most mammals, including humans, an organism's sex is primarily determined by the XY system. An organism with two X chromosomes is female. An organism with one X and one Y chromosome is male. Although the X and Y chromosomes pair up with each other, they are not homologous. The X chromosome is the larger sex chromosome and contains numerous genes, including many that are unrelated to sexual characteristics. The Y chromosome is the sex chromosome that contains genes that direct the development of the testes and other male traits. It is the smallest chromosome and carries the fewest genes.

Cause and Effect

ASK What questions do you have about the relationship between chromosomes and DNA in terms of how traits are inherited?

_____

_____

_____

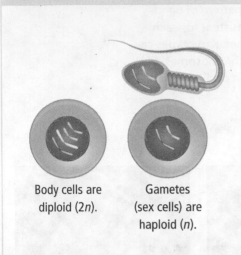

FIGURE 4: Gametes have half the chromosomes of body cells. (Cells are not drawn to scale.)

Body cells are diploid (2*n*).

Gametes (sex cells) are haploid (*n*).

Body Cells and Germ Cells

The 23 pairs of chromosomes you analyzed earlier are from a body, or somatic, cell. Your body cells are called diploid cells because they contain two copies of every chromosome. However, the two copies are not exact copies because one is from your mother and one is from your father. Diploid cells can be represented as 2*n*. In humans, the diploid chromosome number is 46.

In addition to body cells, you also have germ cells located in your reproductive organs. Germ cells form gametes, or sex cells. The male sex cells, formed in the testes, are sperm. The female sex cells, formed in the ovaries, are eggs. Unlike body cells, gametes have only one copy of each chromosome. These cells are called haploid and can be represented as *n*. Human gametes thus contain 23 chromosomes.

Each human egg or sperm cell has 22 autosomes and 1 sex chromosome. In the egg, the sex chromosome is always an X chromosome. In the sperm cell, the sex chromosome can be an X chromosome or a Y chromosome. Only DNA in gametes is passed down to the organism's offspring. The DNA in body cells is not.

EXPLAIN Make a claim explaining why it is important for gametes to be haploid. What would happen if gametes were diploid? Use evidence to support your claim.

_____

_____

_____

_____

_____

_____

Sexual reproduction involves the fusion of two gametes of different types, resulting in offspring that are a genetic mixture of both parents. The joining of these two gametes is called fertilization. When fertilization occurs, the nuclei of the egg and sperm fuse to form a single nucleus.

Maintaining the correct number of chromosomes is important to the survival of all organisms. Typically, a change in chromosome number is harmful. However, increasing the number of sets of chromosome can, on occasion, give rise to a new species. This type of event has occurred in many groups of plants, but is very rare in animals.

Evidence Notebook Answer the following questions about body cells and gametes.

1. What is an example of a body cell in your body?
2. Body cells have 46 chromosomes each, half from the mother, half from the father. How does this number compare to gametes? What is the role of gametes in increasing genetic variation?

The Process of Meiosis

DNA that is passed on to offspring is contained in the gametes, which are formed by germ cells in reproductive organs. So, how exactly are gametes made? Germ cells undergo an essential process called meiosis to form gametes. Meiosis is a form of nuclear division that divides one diploid cell into four haploid cells. There are two rounds of cell division—meiosis I and meiosis II. This process divides the DNA and reduces each resulting cell's chromosome number by half.

INFER Meiosis divides one cell into four cells, but the resulting cells have half the amount of DNA as compared to the original cell. How do you think this is possible?

○ **a.** The DNA is copied twice before cell division.

○ **b.** The DNA is copied once before cell division.

○ **c.** The DNA fuses in two of the cells.

○ **d.** The cell divides twice and fuses once.

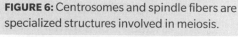

FIGURE 5: Meiosis has many stages and produces four haploid cells from one diploid cell.

Chromosomes and Replication

To understand meiosis, it is necessary to distinguish between homologous chromosomes and sister chromatids. Homologous chromosomes divide during meiosis I, and sister chromatids are split and separated into new gametes during meiosis II.

In addition to chromosomes and chromatids, specialized structures called centrosomes are involved in meiosis in animal cells. As shown in Figure 6, the centrosome is a small region of the cell that produces protein fibers called microtubules. Centrioles are cylinder-shaped cell structures made of short microtubules. Before an animal cell divides, the centrosome, including the centrioles, doubles, and the two new centrosomes move to opposite ends of the cell. Microtubules grow from each centrosome, forming spindle fibers. These fibers attach to the DNA and help it divide between the two cells.

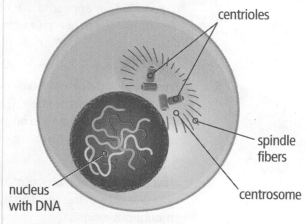

FIGURE 6: Centrosomes and spindle fibers are specialized structures involved in meiosis.

centrioles

spindle fibers

centrosome

nucleus with DNA

EXPLAIN What might happen if the DNA is not divided evenly between cells?

_____

_____

_____

_____

Meiosis I

Before meiosis begins, the cell makes a copy of its DNA. Meiosis I separates homologous chromosomes, producing two haploid cells with duplicated chromosomes. Meiosis I can be described in four distinct phases, each of which is a series of gradual changes.

FIGURE 7: Meiosis I

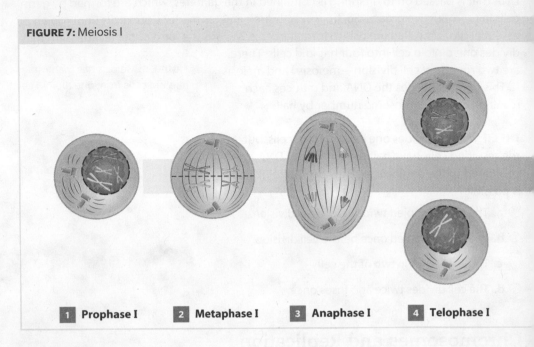

| **1** Prophase I | **2** Metaphase I | **3** Anaphase I | **4** Telophase I |

1. Prophase I
During this first phase of meiosis, the membrane around the nucleus breaks down, the centrosomes and centrioles move to opposite sides of the cell, and spindle fibers start to assemble. The duplicated chromosomes condense, and homologous chromosomes begin to pair up. They appear to pair up precisely, gene for gene, down their entire length. The sex chromosomes also pair with each other, and some regions of their DNA appear to line up.

2. Metaphase I
The homologous chromosome pairs randomly line up along the middle of the cell, or the cell equator, by spindle fibers. The result is that chromosomes—some from the father, some from the mother—are lined up along each side of the cell equator. This arrangement mixes up the chromosomal combinations and helps create and maintain genetic differences.

3. Anaphase I
Next, the paired homologous chromosomes separate from each other and move toward opposite sides of the cell. The sister chromatids remain together during this step and throughout meiosis I.

4. Telophase I
The membrane around the nucleus forms again, the spindle fibers break apart, and the cell divides into two daughter cells.

EXPLAIN Complete the statement about the model of meiosis I.

The products of meiosis I are two | four | six | eight cells with identical | different combinations of chromosomes. One advantage | disadvantage of this model is that it shows the phases of meiosis I very clearly. One advantage | disadvantage is that it does not show the full set of 46 chromosomes found in a human body cell.

Meiosis II

Meiosis II separates sister chromatids, which results in cells with chromosomes that are not doubled. The diagram of this process applies to both of the cells produced in meiosis I. The end result of meiosis II is four haploid cells. It is important to note that DNA is not copied between meiosis I and meiosis II.

Meiosis II

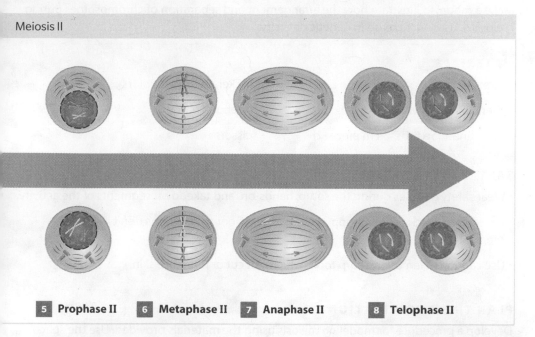

| 5 Prophase II | 6 Metaphase II | 7 Anaphase II | 8 Telophase II |

5. Prophase II
The membrane around the nucleus breaks down, centrosomes and centrioles move to opposite sides of the cell, and spindle fibers assemble.

6. Metaphase II
Spindle fibers align the 23 chromosomes at the cell equator. Each chromosome still has two sister chromatids at this stage.

7. Anaphase II
Next, the sister chromatids are pulled apart from each other and move to opposite sides of the cell.

8. Telophase II
Finally, nuclear membranes form around each set of chromosomes at opposite ends of the cell, the spindle fibers break apart, and the cell divides into two daughter cells.

ASK What questions do you have about how the chromosomes are sorted during meiosis? Discuss the answers to your questions with a partner.

_____

_____

_____

_____

 Evidence Notebook According to this model of meiosis, do all the gametes produced by an organism have the same genetic material? Use evidence to support your claim.

Hands-On Activity
Modeling Meiosis

Make a model to illustrate how the arrangement and separation of chromosomes during meiosis causes an increase in genetic diversity.

MATERIALS

- safety goggles
- chenille stems, white (4)
- hook-and-loop tabs, 2-cm piece (2)
- markers, assorted colors
- notebook paper
- scissors

SAFETY INFORMATION

- Wear safety goggles during the setup, hands-on, and takedown segments of the activity.
- Immediately pick up any dropped items on the floor so the items don't become a slip/fall hazard.
- Use caution when using sharp tools, which can cut or puncture skin.

PLAN THE INVESTIGATION

Develop a procedure for modeling meiosis using the materials provided. Use the space below to develop your ideas, then write your procedure in your Evidence Notebook. Your teacher may request that you submit your procedure for review before you begin designing your model.

1. How does the genetic material on two sister chromatids compare? How does the genetic material on the homologous chromosomes compare?

_____

_____

_____

2. Which aspects of meiosis are not represented in your model? What changes could you make to show these processes?

_____

_____

_____

3. Refer to your model to explain why meiosis is also called "reduction division." Use the words _diploid_ and _haploid_ in your explanation.

_____

_____

_____

4. Explain how sexual reproduction increases genetic diversity.

_____

_____

_____

DRAW CONCLUSIONS

Write a conclusion in your Evidence Notebook that addresses each of the points below.

Claim Make a claim about the effects of chromosomes not separating properly during either phase of meiosis.

Evidence What evidence from your model supports your claim? Work through your model again, and model a chromosome that failed to separate—what is the end result?

Reasoning How do you think this affects the development of a fertilized cell, in terms of the traits that are in the offspring?

Gametogenesis

The haploid cells produced by meiosis are not able to be fertilized until they go through additional changes to produce mature gametes. The final stages of this process, called gametogenesis, differ between the sexes.

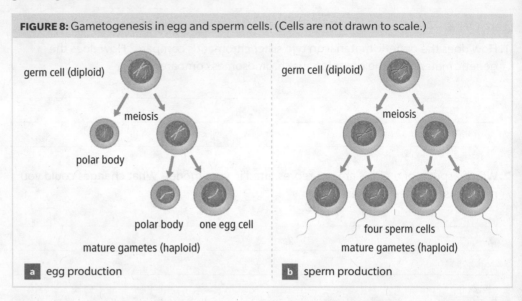

FIGURE 8: Gametogenesis in egg and sperm cells. (Cells are not drawn to scale.)

germ cell (diploid)

meiosis

polar body

polar body   one egg cell

mature gametes (haploid)

a egg production

germ cell (diploid)

meiosis

four sperm cells

mature gametes (haploid)

b sperm production

INFER Use the model of gametogenesis to infer which descriptions below accurately compare and contrast the production of sperm cells and the production of egg cells in gametogenesis. Select all correct answers.

☐ **a.** Both sperm and egg production involve meiosis.

☐ **b.** Gametogenesis results in more eggs per germ cell than sperm per germ cell.

☐ **c.** The sperm cell is much larger than the egg cell.

☐ **d.** Both sperm and egg production begin with diploid cells.

☐ **e.** Sperm production results in diploid cells and egg production results in haploid cells.

The formation of an egg, the female gamete, begins before birth inside the developing body of a female embryo. The process is not finished until a sperm fertilizes that egg many years later. Only one of the cells produced by meiosis actually makes an egg. The other cells produced are called polar bodies and are not typically able to be fertilized. Nearly all of a zygote's cell structures, including mitochondria, and in plants, chloroplasts, come from the egg. Because mitochondria carry their own DNA, the mitochondrial DNA in the embryo is identical to the mother's.

The sperm cell, the male gamete, is much smaller than the egg. The sperm cell's main contribution to an embryo is DNA. Yet it must swim to an egg to fertilize it, so the ability to move is critical. Sperm formation starts with a round cell and ends by making a streamlined cell that can move rapidly. During this process, significant changes occur. DNA is tightly packed and much of the cell body is lost, resulting in a compact head. The sperm cell develops a whip-like flagellum that acts as a propeller and a neck region with mitochondria that provide the energy needed to move the cell's flagellum.

 Evidence Notebook According to the models of meiosis and gametogenesis, do all the gametes produced by an organism have the same genetic material? Use evidence to support your claim.

Meiosis and Genetic Variation

One of the advantages of meiosis and sexual reproduction is the resulting increased genetic diversity within a species. Genetic variation refers to the differences in the genetic material of individuals in a population.

Mechanisms of Genetic Variation

Meiosis and sexual reproduction increase genetic diversity, or genetic variation, within a population. Gametes have different combinations of genes than their parent cells due to independent assortment and crossing over, which both occur during meiosis.

FIGURE 9: Genetic variation is responsible for the different versions of traits you see in this cat's offspring.

Independent Assortment

When homologous chromosomes pair up in metaphase I of meiosis, the chromosomes from your father and the chromosomes from your mother line up randomly on either side of the cell's equator. This assortment of chromosomes is a matter of chance. The arrangement of any one homologous pair does not depend on the arrangement of any other homologous pair. Therefore, it is referred to as independent assortment.

Explore Online ▶

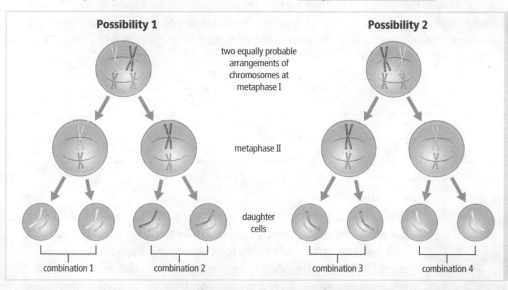

FIGURE 10: Independent assortment results in many different genetic combinations.

Possibility 1 | Possibility 2

two equally probable arrangements of chromosomes at metaphase I

metaphase II

daughter cells

combination 1 | combination 2 | combination 3 | combination 4

Problem Solving

To determine the number of possible chromosome combinations that can result from independent assortment, you can use this formula:

$$\text{Combinations} = 2^n$$

where n = number of different chromosomes.

APPLY What is the approximate number of possible chromosome combinations for a human cell with 23 different chromosomes?

_____

Evidence Notebook
How does your answer to the Problem Solving question support the claim that independent assortment increases variation in an organism's offspring? How could this affect the evolution of a species?

Crossing Over

The exchange of chromosome segments between homologous chromosomes is called crossing over. It happens during meiosis. It occurs during prophase I in meiosis I, and it is a regulated process. At this stage of meiosis, each chromosome has been duplicated, the sister chromatids are still connected, and homologous chromosomes have paired up. Some of the chromatids are very close to each other. Part of one chromatid from a chromosome may break off and reattach to the other chromosome. Crossing over can happen many times within the same pair of homologous chromosomes. Because crossing over results in new combinations of genes, it is another source of genetic recombination.

FIGURE 11: Crossing over increases genetic variation.

Explore Online ▶

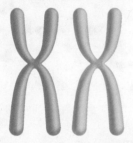 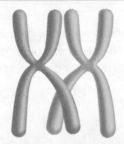 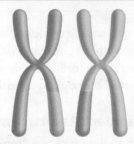

1 Two homologous chromosomes pair up with each other during prophase I in meiosis.

2 In this position, some chromatids are very close to each other and segments cross.

3 Some of these segments break off and reattach to the other homologous chromosome.

EXPLAIN Use the model of meiosis that you made earlier in the lesson to explain how crossing over contributes to genetic diversity. How did you modify your model? How do you think crossing over affects the expression of certain traits compared to the cells where crossing over didn't occur?

_____

_____

_____

_____

FIGURE 12: Fertilization results in a genetically unique organism. (colored SEM)

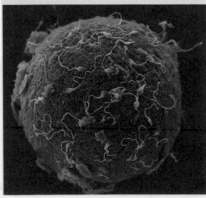

Fertilization

Once mature gametes have formed during the process of gametogenesis, the gametes are ready for fertilization. In fertilization, two gametes of different types fuse, producing a zygote with a complete set of DNA—half from one parent and half from the other. The resulting zygote will have a unique combination of genes. The mixing and matching of genetic material during meiosis and fertilization is responsible for the genetic variation in sexually reproducing organisms.

For example, in humans a sperm cell with one of 2^{23} chromosome combinations fertilizes an egg cell, which also has one out of 2^{23} chromosome combinations. If sperm cells and egg cells were combined at random, the total number of possible combinations is the product of $2^{23} \times 2^{23}$, or more than 70 trillion. So, a human couple can produce a child with one of about 70 trillion different combinations of chromosomes.

 Evidence Notebook Use evidence you have gathered about meiosis and sexual reproduction to construct an explanation for why offspring are not exact replicas of their parents. In your answer, include a discussion of sexual reproduction, independent assortment, and crossing over.

Guided Research

Gene Duplication and Genetic Variation

In metaphase I of meiosis, homologous chromosomes exchange DNA segments via crossing over. This leads to genetic variation in the offspring of sexually reproducing organisms. Sometimes during crossing over, homologous chromosomes do not align with each other properly. If this happens, the two segments crossing over may be different in size. As a result, one chromosome may have two copies of a gene or genes, which is called gene duplication. The other chromosome may have no copy of the gene or genes, known as a gene deletion. This can lead to mutations in the organism, which could be beneficial or lethal for an organism.

Gene duplication has occurred many times over millions of years of eukaryotic evolution. For example, domesticated sunflowers have a duplicated gene that lengthens the plants' growing period. Interestingly, this gene duplication is not the result of domestication. Evidence shows that the duplication occurred long before Native Americans began breeding the plants as a part of their horticultural practices. This variation of sunflower was simply preferred by Native Americans.

FIGURE 13: Gene duplication has influenced the traits of domestic sunflower plants.

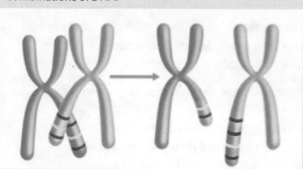

FIGURE 14: Gene duplication results in new combinations of DNA.

Language Arts Connection Conduct research to construct an argument for how gene duplication increases genetic variation. Start by choosing a specific species to research, and look for materials explaining how gene duplication has affected this species. As you conduct your research, evaluate your sources carefully to be sure they are reliable. Do they present verifiable facts? Are the opinions those of an expert or experts in this field? Is there enough evidence to support the claims being made?

Using your own words, write an argument explaining how gene duplication from unequal crossing over has influenced genetic variation in a certain species. Be sure to cite specific evidence to support your claim. Use these questions to guide your research:

1. Which species will you research, and what evidence exists that gene duplication has occurred in this species?
2. How did gene duplication influence the traits of this species?
3. What is the connection between gene duplication and the evolution of this species?

 INVESTIGATING MEIOSIS   **INVESTIGATING GENETIC LINKAGE**   **GATHERING EVIDENCE FOR GENETIC DIVERSITY**   Go online to choose one of these other paths.

Lesson Self-Check

CAN YOU EXPLAIN IT?

FIGURE 15: A unique individual results from the fertilization of an egg by a sperm cell. (colored SEM)

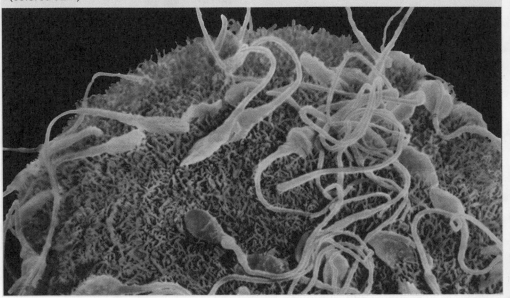

Now that you have learned about meiosis and genetic variation, think again about why there are so many differences among people in any given population. According to some estimates, the number of possible gene combinations made by meiosis is trillions of times more than the number of people who have ever lived on Earth. Independent assortment alone makes millions of possible combinations of chromosomes. Each chromosome contains anywhere from hundreds to thousands of genes. When those genes are shuffled during meiosis, an astounding number of combinations is possible. Multiply this by the probability that the gametes that formed you would merge, and it's no wonder there is so much variation in the human race.

Evidence Notebook Refer to your notes in your Evidence Notebook to explain how meiosis and sexual reproduction increase genetic diversity. Your explanation should include a discussion of sexual reproduction, meiosis, independent assortment, and crossing over.

1. Make a claim about the relationship between meiosis, sexual reproduction, and genetic diversity.
2. Cite evidence to support your claim. Include models and examples as necessary.
3. Explain how the evidence you cited supports your claim. For example, consider the number of possible chromosome combinations made by independent assortment. How would this evidence support the claim you are making?

1. Label each item as a description of a haploid or a diploid cell.

_____	is described as 2*n*
_____	is described as *n*
_____	has single chromosomes, each from one parent
_____	somatic cell
_____	makes fertilization possible
_____	results from meiosis
_____	fertilized zygote

2. A student uses string to model four pairs of homologous chromosomes in a parent cell. Each chromosome pair is a different color. Which model would best show the genetic makeup of a daughter cell that is produced by meiosis?

○ **a.** two strings, each a combination of different colors
○ **b.** two strings, each the same color
○ **c.** four strings, each a combination of different colors
○ **d.** four strings, each the same color

3. Meiosis in human males results in

○ **a.** three haploid cells and one diploid cell.
○ **b.** three diploid cells and one haploid cell.
○ **c.** four haploid cells.
○ **d.** four diploid cells.

4. Fruit fly gametes each have four chromosomes representing 2^4, or 16, possible chromosome combinations. How many chromosome combinations could results from fertilization between a fruit fly egg and a sperm cell?

_____ combinations

5. Trisomy 21, or Down Syndrome, is a genetic condition in which an individual has three copies of chromosome 21. This occurs when homologous chromosomes do not separate during anaphase of meiosis. What would an image of this individual's chromosomes look like if he were male? Select all correct answers.

☐ **a.** Chromosome 23 would consist of two X chromosomes.
☐ **b.** Chromosome 23 would consist of an X and a Y chromosome.
☐ **c.** Chromosome 21 would have a set of three chromosomes.
☐ **d.** Chromosome 3 would have a set of 21 chromosomes.
☐ **e.** Chromosome 21 would consist of a set of two chromosomes.

6. Complete the statement about genetic variation.

Meiosis contributes to genetic variability when the chromosomes line up randomly during metaphase I | anaphase I | prophase I. This random line-up means that when the cell divides, the number of chromosomes in each cell is the same, but the contents are not. This process is called independent assortment | gene linkage | crossing over. During meiosis, gene linkage | independent assortment | crossing over increases genetic variation because it shuffles portions of chromosomes around.

7. Why are genes that are on two different chromosomes said to exhibit independent assortment? Select all correct answers.

☐ **a.** The chromosomes are physically unconnected to the spindle.
☐ **b.** The chromosomes are replicated independently of each other.
☐ **c.** The chromosomes become aligned on opposite poles of the cell.
☐ **d.** The chromosomes end up in the same gamete by random chance.

CHECKPOINTS (continued)

8. Explain how crossing over provides evidence to support the claim that meiosis increases genetic variation.

_____

_____

_____

_____

9. Describe two pieces of evidence to support the claim that sexual reproduction increases genetic variation.

_____

_____

_____

_____

10. Why is it important that human gametes have half a set of DNA instead of a full set of DNA? Use evidence and scientific reasoning to support your claim.

_____

_____

_____

_____

_____

MAKE YOUR OWN STUDY GUIDE

 In your Evidence Notebook, design a study guide that supports the main ideas from this lesson:

Heritable genetic variations result from new genetic combinations made through meiosis and sexual reproduction.

Independent assortment and crossing over are processes that contribute to genetic variation within a species.

Remember to include the following information in your study guide:
- Use examples that model main ideas.
- Record explanations for the phenomena you investigated.
- Use evidence to support your explanations. Your support can include drawings, data, graphs, laboratory conclusions, and other evidence recorded throughout the lesson.

Consider how the models and explanations in this lesson can be used to support a claim for how meiosis and sexual reproduction increase genetic variation.

Mendel and Heredity

The different colors of California poppies is just one example of the endless variation found in nature.

CAN YOU EXPLAIN IT?

The flowers in the photo are all the same species—so why don't they all look exactly the same? Now, think about all the different people you know. Everyone looks different. Even siblings with the same parents often look different from each other and their parents. Variation, such as flower color, ear shapes, or type of fur occurs in organisms in different ways. How does this happen?

PREDICT How do you think characteristics such as flower color, ear shape, or hair type are determined in different organisms?

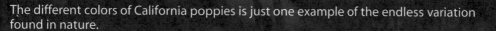

_____

_____

_____

_____

_____

_____

_____

 Evidence Notebook As you explore this lesson, gather evidence to explain how traits are inherited through genes passed down from parents to offspring.

Mendel's Groundwork for Genetics

FIGURE 1: These cats show a variety of inherited traits.

One of the critical outcomes of sexual reproduction is the variety in traits that results from a shuffling of genes. These traits are distinguishing characteristics that are inherited. Scientists have known for a long time that traits in organisms vary, and that offspring often, but not always, look similar to their parents. What remained a mystery was why traits vary.

> **Collaborate** With a partner, identify three traits that vary among the cats in Figure 1.

Genetics is the study of biological inheritance patterns and variations in organisms. Geneticists study and make predictions about inherited traits. They conduct experiments to reveal the causes of genetic variation and show how variation is transmitted through generations.

INFER What does it mean for a trait to be inherited?

○ **a.** The trait is present and is passed from sibling to sibling.

○ **b.** The trait is heavily influenced by the environment.

○ **c.** The trait is passed from parents to offspring.

○ **d.** The trait is present in all the members of a population.

Mendel's Experimental Design

Our current understanding of heredity comes from a foundation laid in the mid-1800s by an Austrian monk named Gregor Mendel. Mendel's detailed experiments using pea plants led to some important changes in the way scientists viewed the transmission of traits. Scientists of the time commonly thought that parents' traits were blended in offspring, like mixing two colors of paint. However, this idea failed to explain how specific traits on one end of the trait spectrum are observed throughout many successive generations without all being blended or "diluted."

Mendel worked with pea plants due to their fast rate of reproduction and their many different varieties and because he could easily control their pollination. He began with purebred plants as the parent generation. Purebred means, for example, that a purple-flowering pea plant produces offspring that have only purple flowers when allowed to self-fertilize. During his experiments, Mendel controlled which plants were able to reproduce. He crossed plants with specific traits by interrupting the self-fertilization process. He then observed the results of each cross. Mendel also used mathematics to analyze the experimental data gathered from hundreds of pea plant crosses.

Explore Online ▶

Hands-On Lab

Investigating Traits and Heredity Plan and conduct an investigation to determine how albinism is inherited in tobacco plants.

Mendel's Experimental Design

FIGURE 2: Mendel removed the male parts of flowers and then fertilized the female parts with pollen from a different plant.

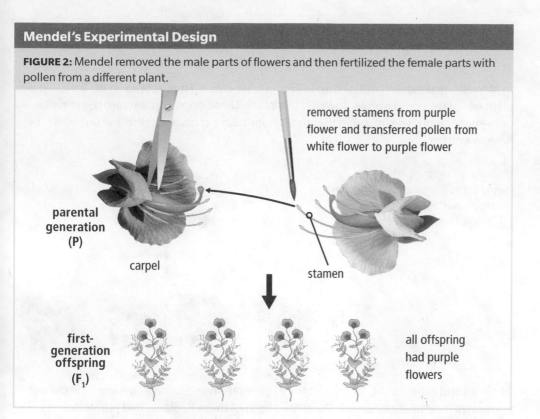

removed stamens from purple flower and transferred pollen from white flower to purple flower

parental generation (P)

carpel

stamen

first-generation offspring (F₁)

all offspring had purple flowers

Mendel's Observations

During his experiments, Mendel observed seven traits in the pea plants. We now know that these specific traits are associated with genes on different chromosomes or are far enough apart on the same chromosome to allow for crossing over. The traits Mendel studied show a simple "either/or" characteristic; they do not show an intermediate form. For example, the plant is either tall or short, but not medium in height. The selection of these traits that occur in the "either/or" fashion played a crucial role in helping Mendel identify the patterns he observed. Had he chosen different traits or a different species for his experiments, he may not have come to the same conclusions.

Evidence Notebook
What is one question you would ask about how these traits are passed down from one generation to another?

FIGURE 3: Mendel worked with seven traits in pea plants for his experiments.

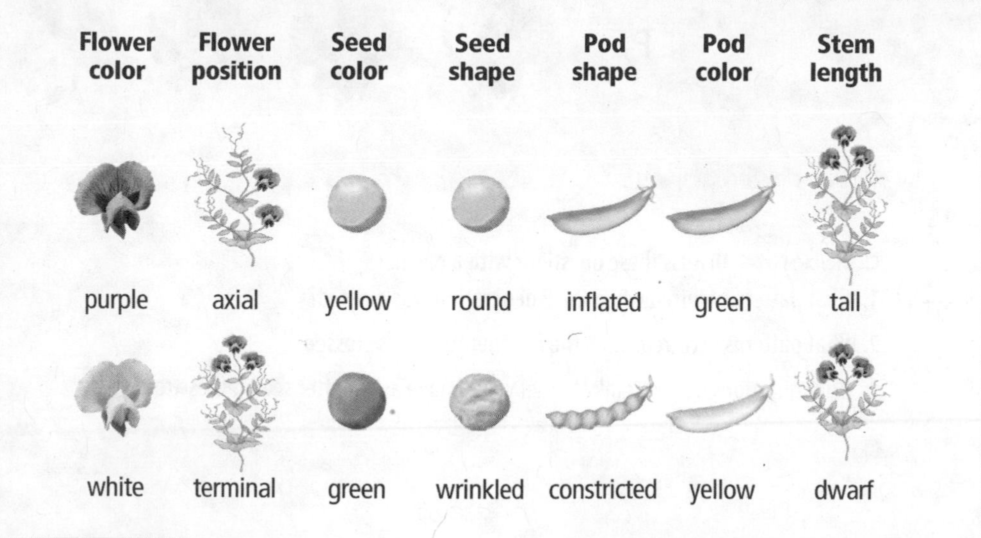

Flower color	Flower position	Seed color	Seed shape	Pod shape	Pod color	Stem length
purple	axial	yellow	round	inflated	green	tall
white	terminal	green	wrinkled	constricted	yellow	dwarf

A genetic cross is the mating of two individuals. When Mendel pollinated a specific female flower of a plant with the pollen from another plant, he carried out a cross. Through his experiments, Mendel was able to observe the results of specific crosses.

In Mendel's first experiment, shown in Figure 4, he crossed a purebred white-flowered pea plant with a purebred purple-flowered pea plant. These original plants are the parental—or P—generation. The offspring that result from such a cross are called the first filial—or F$_1$—generation.

FIGURE 4: Purebred white- and purple-flowered plants were crossed to make the F$_1$ generation.

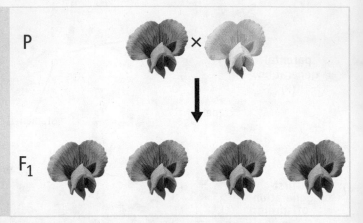

In his second experiment, Mendel let the F$_1$ generation self-fertilize, meaning he did not control their pollination himself. Recall that both of these F$_1$ plants had purple flowers. The offspring from these crosses are referred to as the F$_2$ generation. The F$_2$ plants had a different set of traits, shown in Figure 5.

FIGURE 5: Purple-flowered plants of the F$_1$ generation self-pollinated to make the F$_2$ generation.

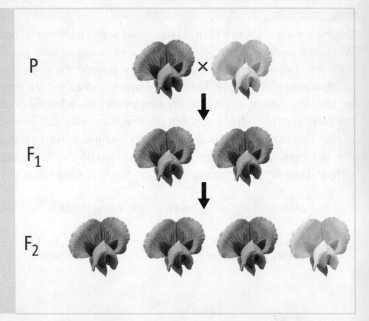

Collaborate Discuss these questions with a partner:
1. What pattern occurred when the P generation was crossed?
2. What patterns occurred when the F$_1$ generation was crossed?
3. What questions do you think Mendel would have asked after seeing these results?

Mendel's Data

Mendel performed similar crosses with other F_1 plants. Each time, he crossed plants showing different versions of a trait and observed parental traits that were absent in the F_1 generation in the F_2 plants. In all cases, the offspring of these crosses showed many plants with one version of a trait and some plants with the alternate version.

FIGURE 6: Mendel observed parental traits when he allowed the F_1 plants to self-fertilize.

Traits	Parental Cross	F_1 Generation	F_2 Generation	Ratio
Seed shape	round × wrinkled	all round	5474 round 1850 wrinkled	2.96:1
Seed color	yellow × green	all yellow	6020 yellow 2001 green	3.01:1
Flower color	purple × white	all purple	705 purple 224 white	3.15:1
Stem length	tall × short	all tall	787 tall 277 short	2.84:1

ANALYZE What patterns do you notice in Mendel's data?

_____

_____

_____

Mendel's Conclusions

Based on his observations and data, Mendel realized that certain traits, such as white flowers, did not disappear, but were temporarily masked. They also were not altered by other traits or blended to form a new trait. Mendel concluded that traits are inherited as discrete "factors" that pass from the parental generation to the offspring. Recall that during meiosis, each gamete receives one copy of each gene. When the gametes fuse during fertilization, the resulting organism has two copies of each gene, one from each parent. This knowledge, unknown to Mendel, parallels his experimental results and his conclusions about inheritance. The separation of genes during gamete formation became known as the law of segregation.

 Evidence Notebook During anaphase I of meiosis, copies of the same gene are separated as homologous chromosomes and move to opposite sides of the cell. These chromosomes may or may not contain the same genetic information. Use evidence from meiosis to explain how gene separation occurs and why gametes have only one copy of each gene. How does this process support the law of segregation?

FIGURE 7: Anaphase I

Genes, Alleles, and Traits

We know a lot about DNA and genes today, but this information was discovered long after Mendel's time. However, Mendel did correctly hypothesize that there was a hereditary factor that carried genetic information. We now call those factors genes. In all organisms, DNA is a long string of genetic material that contains information that determines an organism's inherited characteristics. Specific portions of DNA are divided into genes. The DNA strand is coiled up tightly into the structure we call a chromosome.

FIGURE 8: A chromosome is one long continuous thread of DNA segments which make up many genes. Every gene has a locus, or specific position on a chromosome.

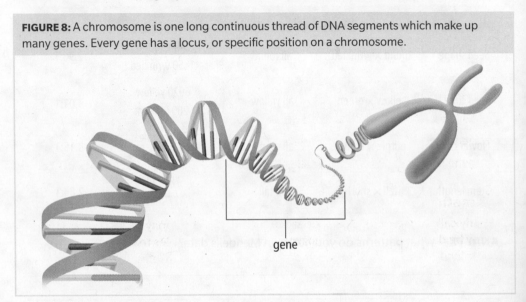

gene

EXPLAIN How are genes, DNA, and chromosomes related? Select all correct answers.

☐ **a.** DNA is made up of genes.

☐ **b.** Genes are made of DNA.

☐ **c.** A gene contains the code that holds the information for a particular protein.

☐ **d.** A chromosome is a tightly coiled string of DNA.

Genes and Alleles

A gene is a piece of DNA that provides a set of instructions to a cell to make a certain protein. Each gene has a locus, which is a specific location on a pair of homologous chromosomes. You can think of the locus as the "address" that tells where a gene is located on a chromosome. Genes located on chromosomes, which get passed on to offspring during reproduction, are the basis for heredity. What Mendel essentially revealed is that it is not the traits that are passed from one generation to the next, but rather the genes that are responsible for those traits.

Genes contain genetic information, but this information can vary widely from one organism to another. An allele is any of the alternative forms or versions of a gene that may occur at a specific locus.

Human cells have two alleles for each gene, which are found on homologous chromosomes. You receive one allele from one parent and one allele from your other parent. The same is true for almost all organisms that reproduce sexually, including pea plants. Asexual organisms of the same species may also carry different alleles of genes even though each organism or cell is haploid. The traits observed in Mendel's experiments, such as flower color or stem height, resulted from varying alleles.

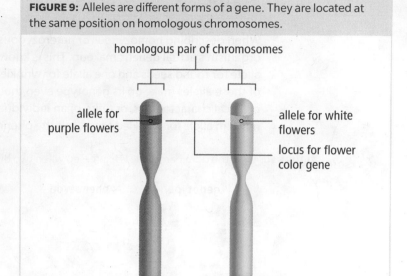

FIGURE 9: Alleles are different forms of a gene. They are located at the same position on homologous chromosomes.

homologous pair of chromosomes

allele for purple flowers

allele for white flowers

locus for flower color gene

ANALYZE How is a gene related to an allele?

○ **a.** An allele is the location of a gene on a chromosome.

○ **b.** An allele is one possible form of a gene.

○ **c.** A gene is used to produce an allele in the cell.

○ **d.** A gene is a small segment of an allele.

Combinations of Alleles

Your body cells contain two alleles for each gene. These alleles may be the same, or they may be different. The term *homozygous* describes two alleles that are the same at a specific locus. The term *heterozygous* describes two different alleles at the same locus. For example, you may inherit an allele for freckles from one parent and an allele for no freckles from your other parent. The same holds true for pea plants. A pea plant may have a purple-flower allele and a white-flower allele, making it heterozygous for that trait.

APPLY Label each set of chromosomes with the correct alleles.

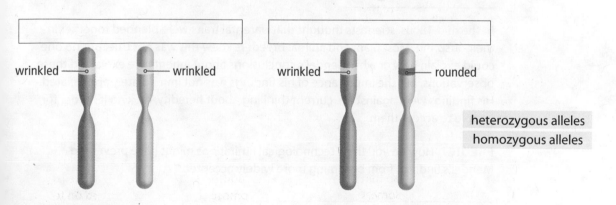

wrinkled —— wrinkled

wrinkled —— rounded

heterozygous alleles

homozygous alleles

GATHER EVIDENCE What is one question you could ask about how traits are expressed when an organism has heterozygous alleles for a trait?

_____

_____

_____

_____

Traits

When describing homozygous or heterozygous pairs of alleles, we are referring to an organism's actual genetic makeup. This is known as its genotype. If a pea plant has one allele for round seeds and one allele for wrinkled seeds, it is said to be heterozygous. Both of these alleles make up its genotype even though one trait will be masked. The actual physical characteristics, or *traits*, of an individual make up its phenotype. The plant might have an allele for wrinkled seeds, but the phenotype expressed is for round seeds.

FIGURE 10: Only the dominant allele is expressed when two different alleles for a gene are present.

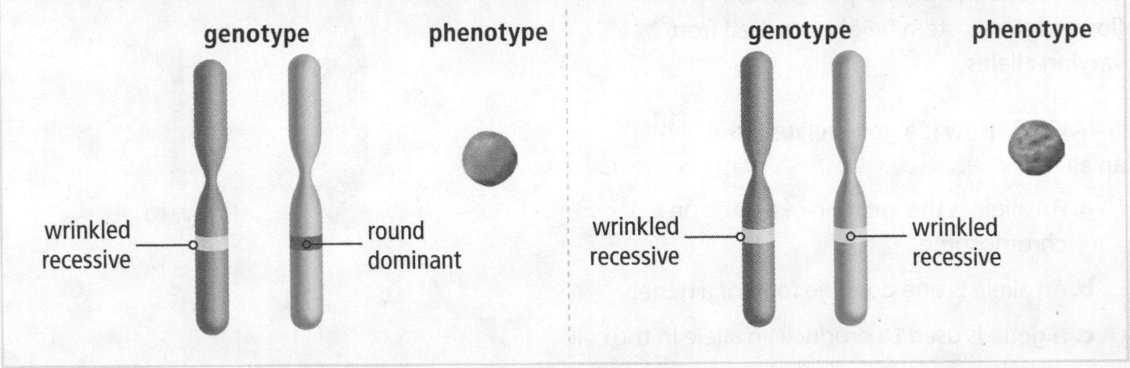

genotype   phenotype   genotype   phenotype

wrinkled   round   wrinkled   wrinkled
recessive   dominant   recessive   recessive

EXPLAIN Based on what you know about Mendel's studies on purple and white flowers, why is genotype sometimes different than phenotype?

Science is a Human Endeavor

Mendel's Legacy

In the mid-1800s, scientists thought that parental traits were blended together in their offspring. Most plant and animal breeders knew this was not true, but no one could explain how or why. Mendel's conclusions about inheritance explained these observations, but the importance of his findings was not immediately appreciated. His findings went against the current thinking about heredity, making it harder for people to accept them.

PREDICT How do you think technological limitations might have prevented Mendel's findings from becoming more widely accepted?

Language Arts Connection Build a timeline showing how Mendel's findings eventually became widely accepted. Consider how technology, scientific breakthroughs, and changes in societal thinking resulted in our current understanding of inheritance.

Sometimes only one allele in the pair will affect the trait. As Mendel's results demonstrated, in some cases one allele may be dominant over another allele. A dominant allele is the allele that is expressed when two different alleles or two dominant alleles are present. A recessive allele is the allele that is only expressed when two recessive copies occur together.

The allele combination, or genotype, of an organism is often represented by a set of letters. Because each body cell contains two alleles per gene, two letters are needed to represent each allele in the pair. Uppercase letters represent dominant alleles, and lowercase letters represent recessive alleles.

In the chromosomes shown comparing genotype and phenotype in Figure 10, the dominant allele, R, codes for round peas. The recessive allele, r, codes for wrinkled peas. The round phenotype will occur if one or two copies of the dominant allele are present. So, plants that are homozygous dominant (RR) or heterozygous (Rr) will have round peas. The wrinkled phenotype, on the other hand, occurs only when two copies of the recessive allele are present. Only plants with the homozygous recessive (rr) genotype will have wrinkled peas.

ANALYZE In pea plants, T represents the allele for a tall plant, which is a dominant trait, and t represents the allele for a dwarf—or short—plant, which is the recessive trait. Using the terms listed below, match the genotypes to their corresponding phenotypes (short or tall), then label each as homozygous dominant, homozygous recessive, or heterozygous.

| short | tall | homozygous recessive | heterozygous | homozygous dominant |

Genotype	Phenotype	Alleles
Tt		
TT		
tt		

All living things have a genetic code. Genes contain the code. Each gene, which can occur in different versions (alleles), has a specific location (locus) on a chromosome. During meiosis, chromosomes are rearranged. As a result of sexual reproduction, chromosomes from each parent are combined, resulting in offspring that have different combinations of alleles.

For a dominant allele, an organism's phenotype does not necessarily give away whether the genotype is homozygous dominant or heterozygous for the trait. For example, in California poppies, the yellow allele, C, is dominant over the white, c, allele. So, a field of yellow poppies might contain flowers with two yellow alleles (CC), and flowers with a yellow and a white allele (Cc).

 Evidence Notebook Write two questions you could ask to learn more about how genetic variation in California poppies, such as petal shape, petal color, or stem height, is passed from parents to offspring.

Traits and Probability

FIGURE 11: The F₁ generation self-pollinated to produce the F₂ generation.

P

F₁

F₂

Gregor Mendel's trials with purebred white-flowered *(pp)* and purple-flowered *(PP)* pea plants yielded a heterozygous purple *(Pp)* F_1 generation. When the F_1 plants self-pollinated, the white flowers reappeared. The F_2 plants were one-fourth *PP*, one-half *Pp*, and one-fourth *pp*.

Collaborate If you crossed two plants from the F_2 generation, what procedure would you follow to determine the genotypes of the next generation? Discuss your answer with a partner.

Modeling Genetic Crosses

In the early 1900s, several British scientists expanded upon Mendel's work. One scientist, R. C. Punnett, explored genetic crosses with chickens and other species. The model he developed tracks the alleles each parent can donate to predict the outcome of crosses.

FIGURE 12: The common vizsla has smooth hair, but the wirehaired vizsla has a wiry coat.

a Smooth vizsla

b Wirehaired vizsla

Coat texture in dogs is a heritable characteristic. Some dogs, like the vizsla, can have a smooth coat or a wiry coat, and this trait is controlled by one gene. The wire-coated allele is dominant, noted as *W*, and the smooth-coated allele is recessive, noted as *w*.

Imagine a dog breeder wants to cross two wirehaired vizslas and that both dogs are heterozygous for the trait. This means each parent has two different alleles for coat texture. The alleles are separated into gametes during meiosis. There are two possible gametes for each parent, one for each allele he or she carries.

EXPLAIN What alleles can each heterozygous vizsla parent pass on in his or her gametes? Select all correct answers.

☐ **a.** *Ww*   ☐ **b.** *WW*   ☐ **c.** *ww*   ☐ **d.** *W*   ☐ **e.** *w*

The genotype of an organism indicates which alleles the organism carries for a certain characteristic. Each gamete contains one allele for each trait in an organism's DNA. Punnett recognized a relationship between parental gametes and the genotypes of offspring. He used this relationship to develop a simple table, now known as a Punnett square, that predicts all possible offspring genotypes resulting from a specific cross. This model is a quick and easy way to determine the probable outcome of a cross.

Because each parent donates one gamete to each offspring, gametes will have either a dominant, wire-coated allele (W) or a recessive, smooth-coated allele (w).

To complete a Punnett square, divide a square into four equal sections. Write the alleles of each parent on the outside of the square, one set above the columns and one set to the left of the rows. Write the dominant allele first.

Next fill in each box in the Punnett square with the parent allele from the top of the column and the parent allele from the beginning of the row. When complete, each box will contain one allele from each parent.

The completed Punnett square shows three possible genotypes for coat type: homozygous dominant (WW), heterozygous (Ww), or homozygous recessive (ww). From these genotypes, we can predict that there is a one in four chance that the WW genotype will occur. There is a two in four chance that the Ww genotype will occur. Finally, there is a one in four chance that the ww genotype will occur.

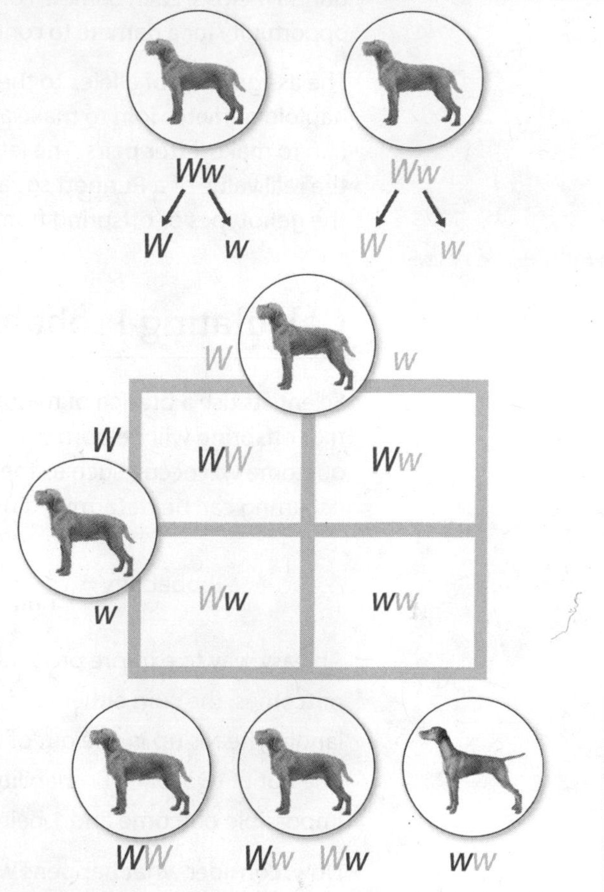

In this cross, both the homozygous dominant and heterozygous genotypes will have wire coats. Only the homozygous recessive genotype will have a smooth coat.

FIGURE 13: A Punnett square is used to model the cross between two parents with known genotypes.

Explore Online ▶

Math Connection

ANALYZE Use the Punnett square to answer the question. The wire-coated allele (W) is dominant to the smooth-coated allele (w).

	W	w
W	WW	Ww
w	Ww	ww

1. What percentage of puppies would have the same genotype as the parents, Ww? _____%

2. What percentage of puppies would have the wire coat phenotype? _____ %

3. What percentage of puppies would have the smooth coat phenotype? _____ %

A Punnett square models complex processes by focusing on individual traits rather than a genome. Separating the letters representing the parental genotype and placing them along the outside of the Punnett square models the segregation of homologous chromosomes during meiosis. Each gamete contains only one version of the gene, and there is an equal opportunity for a gamete to contain either allele.

The assignment of alleles to the empty boxes models fertilization. During fertilization, haploid gametes join to make a diploid zygote. In the Punnett square, the parental alleles join to make letter pairs. The letter pairs represent potential offspring genotypes. This is the real value of a Punnett square. Modeling these processes makes it possible to predict the genotypes of offspring from a specific cross.

Calculating Probabilities

Scientists use a branch of mathematics called probability to determine the likelihood that offspring will be born with certain characteristics. *Probability* is the chance that an outcome will occur, such as the birth of a dog with a wire coat. The probability of an event occurring can be determined using the following equation:

$$\text{Probability} = \frac{\text{number of occurrences of a specific outcome}}{\text{number of total possible occurrences of all outcomes}}$$

An easy way to explore probability is by flipping a coin. Each flip has two possible outcomes: the coin either lands heads up or it lands tails up. The probability of the coin landing heads up is one out of two, or $\frac{1}{2}$. The probability of the coin landing tails up is also one out of two, or $\frac{1}{2}$. Probability is usually expressed on a scale of 0 to 1, with 0 being an impossible outcome and 1 being a certain outcome.

Now, consider what happens when you flip two coins at the same time.

FIGURE 14: A Punnett square reflects the probability of two independent events occurring at the same time.

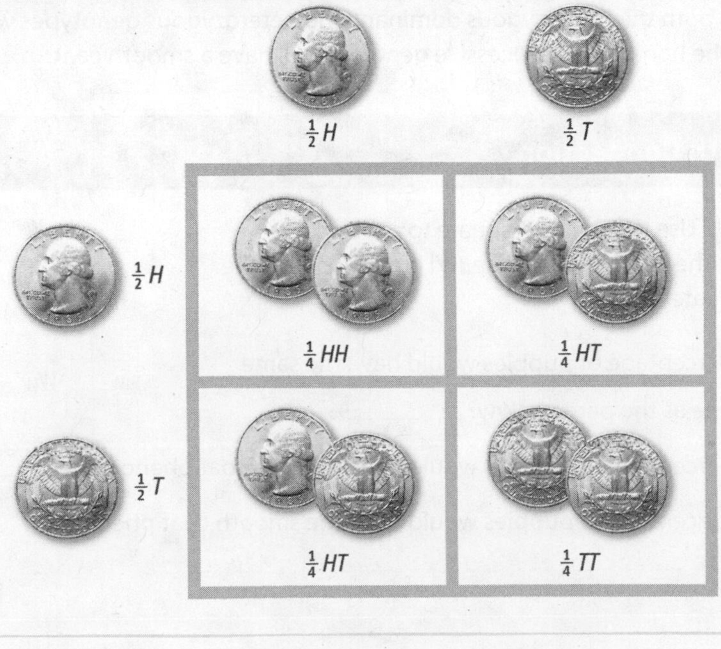

The results of the two coin flips are independent, so the result of one coin flip does not impact the result of the other. Both coins are free to land heads up or tails up. To calculate the probability of two independent events occurring together, multiply the probability of the individual events. The probability of flipping heads is $\frac{1}{2}$. Therefore, the probability of flipping two heads together is $\frac{1}{2} \times \frac{1}{2} = \frac{1}{4}$.

Probabilities are averages, not exact numbers. If you flip a coin twice, you will not always get one heads and one tails. You may get two heads or two tails. The more you repeat an event, the closer you will get to the average described by probability.

Math Connection

SOLVE Analyze the wirehaired dog cross again and determine the probability for each of these possible outcomes. Write your probabilities as fractions.

1. What is the probability of a *Ww* genotype? _____

2. What is the probability of a *WW* genotype? _____

3. What is the probability of a dog with smooth hair being born? _____

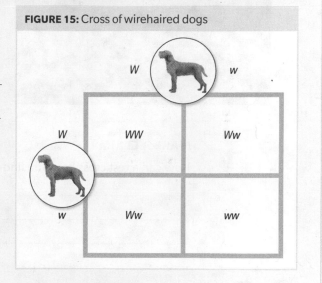

FIGURE 15: Cross of wirehaired dogs

In the cross modeled in the heterozygous Punnett square in Figure 15, what events would have to occur to produce a heterozygous puppy? The father could donate the dominant allele *(W)* and the mother could donate the recessive allele *(w)*. The reverse could also occur. Both of these events would produce a heterozygous puppy, and both are equally likely to occur.

The probability of an event that can occur in more than one way is equal to the probability of the individual events added together. So, the probability of a sperm with a dominant allele fertilizing an egg with a recessive allele is $\frac{1}{4}$. The probability of a sperm with a recessive allele fertilizing an egg with a dominant allele is also $\frac{1}{4}$. So, the probability of producing offspring with a heterozygous genotype can be calculated as $\frac{1}{4} + \frac{1}{4} = \frac{1}{2}$. In other words, there is a one in two chance that a puppy will be born that is heterozygous *(Ww)* for a wire coat.

 Patterns The pattern of inheritance observed in sexually reproducing organisms is explained by chance. This makes probabilities particularly useful for some of the mathematics behind inheritance. How can understanding these patterns be useful for scientists studying inheritance?

Hands-On Activity

Determining a Genotype

FIGURE 16: Peaches and nectarines are the same species, *Prunus persica.*

Peaches have fuzzy skin. A nectarine is a variety of smooth-skinned peach. A dominant allele, *G*, causes fuzzy skin. All peaches have at least one copy of this allele. Nectarines come from trees that are homozygous recessive (*gg*) for fuzz.

Imagine your company sells peach and nectarine seedlings. You developed a new type of peach tree that is very popular. To meet demand, you must learn the genotypes of your breeding stock. You determine them by setting up a test cross between an individual that has a dominant phenotype but an unknown genotype, and an individual with a homozygous recessive genotype.

MAKE A CLAIM

How can a test cross help you find the unknown genotype of the plant?

_____

_____

_____

MATERIALS

- paper
- pencil

CARRY OUT THE INVESTIGATION

1. Plant A produces peaches. You need to determine its genotype. Plant B produces nectarines that have smooth skin and a known genotype of *gg*. You cross Plant A with Plant B.

2. The resulting cross yields twelve plants. Six plants produce peaches upon the first fruiting, and six plants produce nectarines upon the first fruiting.

3. Use Punnett squares to determine the genotype of Plant A.

ANALYZE

Answer the following questions in your Evidence Notebook:

1. What is the genotype of Plant A? Explain how you arrived at your answer.

2. Plant A is crossed with a plant that has a genotype of *GG*. What are the possible genotypes and phenotypes of the offspring?

3. Plant A is crossed with a plant that has a genotype of *Gg*. What is the ratio of dominant to recessive phenotypes of the offspring?

4. In terms of genotype, is Plant A the best plant to produce as many peach seedlings as possible? Why or why not? Which genotype would be best?

Analyzing the Inheritance of One Trait

In most horse breeds, a smooth coat is dominant to a curly coat. The recessive allele is responsible for naturally curly coats that occasionally appear in some horse breeds. Because the gene is recessive, these occurrences are rare. In a few horse breeds, such as the Bashkir horse, the curly-coat allele, *C*, is dominant and the smooth-coat allele, *c*, is recessive.

FIGURE 17: The gene that codes for a curly coat is dominant in Bashkir horses.

All of the genetic crosses discussed so far have involved one trait, from flower color in pea plants to coat texture in dogs. A cross that examines one trait is a *monohybrid cross*. There are three basic types of monohybrid crosses: a homozygous-homozygous cross, a heterozygous-heterozygous cross, and a heterozygous-homozygous cross.

Homozygous-Homozygous Cross

A homozygous-homozygous cross occurs when a homozygous dominant parent crosses with a homozygous recessive parent. Imagine that a Bashkir horse that is homozygous dominant for curly hair *(CC)* is crossed with a Bashkir horse that is homozygous recessive for smooth hair *(cc)*.

SOLVE Record the genotypes of each possible offspring.

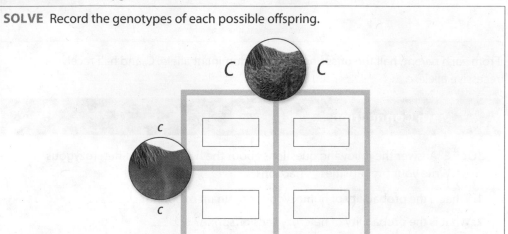

As the Punnett square shows, a homozygous-homozygous cross always results in heterozygous offspring. This is because one parent can donate only dominant alleles and the other can donate only recessive alleles. The sole possible outcome of the cross is one dominant allele and one recessive allele, which is a heterozygous combination. For the cross shown, all of the offspring would have the heterozygous genotype, *Cc*. They would have curly coats because the dominant curly-coat allele, *C*, is present in all genotypes. Each offspring would also carry the recessive smooth-coat allele, *c*.

Math Connection

SOLVE Probability is measured on a scale from 0 to 1. Determine the probabilities of each of the following possible outcomes of a homozygous recessive-homozygous dominant cross:

1. Probability of homozygous recessive offspring _____

2. Probability of homozygous dominant offspring _____

3. Probability of heterozygous offspring _____

Heterozygous-Heterozygous Cross

Imagine you wish to cross two curly-coated, heterozygous Bashkir horses. Each horse has the genotype *Cc* and can pass on either the dominant allele for curly hair, or the recessive allele for smooth hair. The probability of each parent donating a dominant allele to the offspring is $\frac{1}{2}$. The probability of each parent donating a recessive allele to the offspring is also $\frac{1}{2}$.

SOLVE Record the genotypes of each possible offspring.

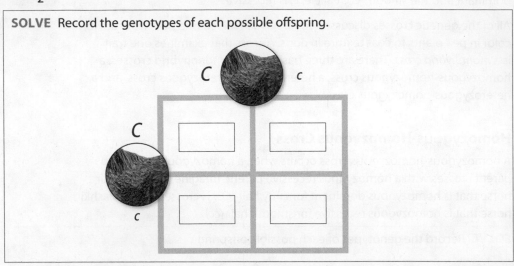

From each parent, half the offspring receive a dominant allele, *C*, and half receive a recessive allele, *c*.

> ## Math Connection
>
> **SOLVE** Answer the following questions about the heterozygous-heterozygous cross. Write your probabilities as fractions.
>
> **1.** What is the probability of homozygous dominant offspring? _____
>
> **2.** What is the probability of heterozygous offspring? _____
>
> **3.** What is the probability of homozygous recessive offspring? _____

This type of cross for a single trait always results in a genotypic ratio of 1:2:1. This means that $\frac{1}{4}$ of offspring will have the homozygous dominant genotype, $\frac{2}{4}$ will have the heterozygous genotype, and $\frac{1}{4}$ will have the homozygous recessive genotype. The phenotypic ratio is 3:1 of dominant:recessive phenotypes. In other words, of the potential offspring phenotypes, $\frac{3}{4}$ will have the dominant phenotype and $\frac{1}{4}$ will have the recessive phenotype.

Heterozygous-Homozygous Cross

Now, imagine a heterozygous-homozygous cross between a heterozygous Bashkir horse with curly hair *(Cc)* and a homozygous recessive Bashkir horse with smooth hair *(cc)*. From the homozygous parent, the offspring receive a recessive allele, *c*. From the heterozygous parent, the offspring can receive either a dominant allele, *C*, or a recessive allele, *c*.

SOLVE Record the genotypes of each possible offspring.

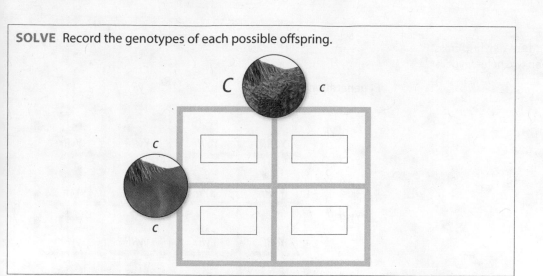

Math Connection

SOLVE Answer the following questions about the heterozygous-homozygous cross. Write your probabilities as fractions.

1. What is the probability of offspring with a heterozygous genotype _____

2. What is the probability of offspring with a homozygous recessive genotype? _____

A heterozygous-homozygous cross always produces parental genotypes in a 1:1 genotypic ratio. For this heterozygous-homozygous cross, the probability of offspring with the heterozygous genotype and the probability of offspring with the homozygous-recessive genotype are both $\frac{1}{2}$. The phenotypic ratio in this instance is also 1:1 because the probability that each coat type will occur is $\frac{1}{2}$. So, in this cross, half of the potential offspring will have curly coats, and half will have smooth coats.

Collaborate Complete a cross between a heterozygous horse and homozygous-dominant horse. Were your results the same as the cross between a heterozygous horse and a homozygous-recessive horse? Discuss the similarities and differences with a partner.

Analyzing the Inheritance of Two Traits

A *dihybrid cross* examines the inheritance of two different traits, such as Mendel's observations of pea color and shape in his plants. For pea color, the yellow allele, *Y*, is dominant to the green allele, *y*. For pea shape, the round allele, *R*, is dominant to the wrinkled allele, *r*. To follow both characteristics at once, Mendel set up a dihybrid cross between a purebred dominant plant (*YYRR*) and a purebred recessive plant (*yyrr*). This homozygous-homozygous cross resulted in all heterozygotes in the F_1 generation (*YyRr*).

Once the genotypes of the gametes have been determined, a larger Punnett square can be used to predict the genotypic and phenotypic ratios in the offspring. A Punnett square for a dihybrid cross has four columns and four rows with sixteen empty cells.

FIGURE 18: Phenotype of peas

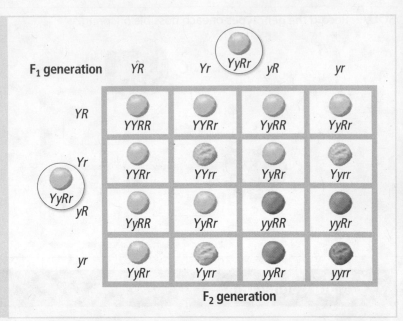

FIGURE 19: A dihybrid cross between two heterozygous pea plants

ANALYZE Use the Punnett square to answer the following questions.

1. What is the probability that the cross will produce a plant that is heterozygous for both traits? What is the probability of producing a plant with yellow and round peas? Why are these two probabilities different?

_____

_____

2. Determine the number of possible phenotypes in the dihybrid cross. What is the ratio for all the possibilities?

_____

_____

3. In your Evidence Notebook, make a Punnett square for the dihybrid cross *YyRr* and *yyrr*. How are the probabilities of this cross different from those in Question 1?

_____

_____

In this cross, the chance of producing offspring that exhibit both dominant traits (yellow and round) is $\frac{9}{16}$. The chance of producing offspring that exhibit one dominant trait and one recessive trait (yellow and wrinkled or green and round) is $\frac{6}{16}$. Finally, the chance of producing offspring that exhibit both recessive traits (green and wrinkled) is $\frac{1}{16}$. Using the Punnett square, you can see these possibilities. In the case above, a heterozygous-heterozygous dihybrid cross results in a phenotypic ratio of 9:3:3:1.

Evidence Notebook Why are Punnett squares a useful model for scientists studying traits? How could a scientist determine the genotypes of different colored poppies?

Careers in Science

Primate Genomicist

Genomics is a branch of biology that analyzes the DNA sequence of one organism and compares it to the DNA sequences of other organisms. One of its main goals is to gain information about a gene's particular function. A career in genomics requires a strong background in molecular biology and a solid foundation in math and statistics. Genomicists use computers to aid in the analysis and presentation of vast amounts of data. Genomics research can involve lab technicians, research scientists, computer programmers, and mathematicians across many different disciplines, including biology and medicine.

Genomics is an important part of the research conducted by Christopher Schmitt, an assistant professor of anthropology and biology at Boston University. In his current research, Schmitt studies the links between genomic variation, morphology, and obesity in primates.

Schmitt's research has taken him to places such as Costa Rica, Ecuador, The Gambia, and Peru. His current fieldwork occurs in South Africa. There, he and a team of scientists trap, anesthetize, measure, and collect genomic data on South African vervet monkeys. The team collects data by taking blood and tissue samples, swabbing for bacterial samples, and making biometric measurements, as shown in Figure 20. Schmitt and his team are using these data to understand how climate and human activities influence the monkeys' metabolism, growth, and development.

As someone who grew up poor and is also gay, Schmitt is especially committed to making science more accessible to groups who have been traditionally underrepresented in both academia and biological fieldwork. He is a founding member of the steering committee for the American Association of Physical Anthropologists' group for LGBTQ+ biological anthropologists and has been profiled by 500 Queer Scientists and LGBT STEM.

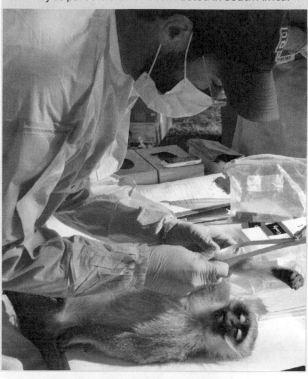

FIGURE 20: Schmitt takes measurements of a vervet monkey as part of fieldwork conducted in South Africa.

Language Arts Connection Write a brief report answering the following questions:

- Why do you think studying the genome of other organisms might provide valuable information?
- In what ways do you think the field of genomics has improved human lives?
- How might changes in technology change the way we study the genomes of organisms?

Biology in Your Community Research a scientist who works in the field of genomics. Develop a profile for this person that explains what the person studies, what questions the person hopes to use research to answer, and how this scientist collaborates with others in the field.

PEDIGREES | EXTENDING MENDELIAN GENETICS | SEQUENCING YOUR OWN GENOME | Go online to choose one of these other paths.

Lesson Self-Check

CAN YOU EXPLAIN IT?

FIGURE 21: The color of California poppies is inherited.

Genes play a large role in shaping who we are, what we look like, and even some behavioral characteristics. You learned how Mendel used pea plants to trace how certain traits are passed from parent to offspring. You also explored how to use probability and tools like Punnett squares to predict how likely it is to see a trait in a given generation.

Scientists are still uncovering how genes are passed on and what other factors affect gene expression. In fact, the California poppy has a relatively small genome, so it is used as a model organism in many evolutionary development studies. These studies focus on how genetic material has been altered over time to evolve into the organisms we see today.

 Evidence Notebook Refer to your notes in your Evidence Notebook to explain how traits are determined in different organisms. Using this information, answer the following questions:

1. Make a claim about how dominant-recessive relationships influence which trait is expressed in the phenotype of an organism. Give an example.
2. What evidence supports your claim? For example, what is the relationship among DNA, genes, alleles, and chromosomes? What role does each play in patterns of inheritance?
3. What tools can be used to model how traits are generally passed from parents to offspring? Give an example.

CHECKPOINTS

Check Your Understanding

1. Why did Mendel remove the stamens, or male reproductive structures, of some pea plants during his first experiments? Select all correct answers.

   ☐ **a.** to prevent reproduction from occurring

   ☐ **b.** to control which parent plants were allowed to reproduce

   ☐ **c.** to prevent self-fertilization of the pea plants

   ☐ **d.** to allow the pea plants to reproduce asexually

2. What do the letters on the top and side of a Punnett square represent?

   ○ **a.** the potential genotypes of the offspring

   ○ **b.** the possible gametes each parent can donate

   ○ **c.** fertilization and the formation of a diploid zygote

   ○ **d.** the phenotype of each parent

3. What are the possible gametes that can be formed by a heterozygous plant with the genotype *YyRr*?

   ○ **a.** *Y, y, R, r*

   ○ **b.** *Yy, Rr, YR, Yr*

   ○ **c.** *YR, Yr, yR, yr*

   ○ **d.** *YyRr, YyRr, YyRr, YyRr*

   ○ **e.** *YR, yr*

4. Which of the following best describes why a recessive trait is not observed in the offspring of a cross between a homozygous dominant and a homozygous recessive parent?

   ○ **a.** The offspring will be heterozygous, and the dominant allele masks the appearance of the recessive allele.

   ○ **b.** Recessive alleles are blended with dominant alleles to make an intermediate trait.

   ○ **c.** The offspring will likely be homozygous dominant for this trait and therefore show the dominant trait.

   ○ **d.** The dominant alleles will destroy the recessive alleles.

5. For each pair listed below, calculate the probability of producing a homozygous recessive genotype. Then, place the pairs in order of increasing probability with the least probable at the top of the list and the most probable at the bottom.

   _____ **a.** *Aa × aa*

   _____ **b.** *aa × aa*

   _____ **c.** *Aa × Aa*

6. Imagine a plant can have striped flower petals or solid flower petals. Solid coloring (*Z*) is dominant to stripes (*z*). Which parental cross would yield the following ratio of offspring: 1 homozygous dominant (*ZZ*):2 heterozygous (*Zz*):1 homozygous recessive (*zz*)?

   ○ **a.** homozygous dominant-homozygous recessive

   ○ **b.** homozygous dominant-homozygous dominant

   ○ **c.** homozygous dominant-heterozygous

   ○ **d.** heterozygous-heterozygous

7. In California poppies, the yellow allele, *C*, is dominant to the white allele, *c*. Make a Punnett square of a heterozygous-heterozygous cross to answer the questions.

   a. What percentage of offspring would have the same genotype as the parents, *Cc*?

   _____ %

   b. What percentage of offspring would have the yellow petal phenotype? _____ %

   c. What percentage of offspring would have the white petal phenotype? _____ %

CHECKPOINTS (continued)

8. Two heterozygous, wirehaired vizslas were crossed. Use the Punnett square to answer the following questions. Express ratios using a colon, such as 2:1 or 3:1.

	W	w
W	WW	Ww
w	Ww	ww

   a. What is the phenotypic ratio of wire-coated:smooth-coated offspring?
   _____

   b. What is the genotypic ratio of homozygous dominant to heterozygous to homozygous recessive offspring? _____

   c. Which genotype has a 100% chance of expressing a recessive allele? _____

9. Why is a recessive allele only expressed when the organism is homozygous? Use an example to support your claim.

   _____
   _____
   _____
   _____
   _____

10. Why is the known genotype in a test cross always homozygous recessive? Provide an example to support your claim.

   _____
   _____
   _____
   _____

MAKE YOUR OWN STUDY GUIDE

In your Evidence Notebook, design a study guide that supports the main ideas from this lesson:

Mendel's observations laid the groundwork for understanding how alleles interact and traits are passed from parents to offspring.

The principles of probability, through Punnett squares and other modeling tools, are critical in understanding the role of alleles and genes in determining traits.

Remember to include the following information in your study guide:
- Use examples that model main ideas.
- Record explanations for the phenomena you investigated.
- Use evidence to support your explanations. Your support can include drawings, data, graphs, laboratory conclusions, and other evidence recorded throughout the lesson.

Consider how algebraic thinking is useful in predicting the effect of different genes on the inheritance of traits.

DNA Structure and Function

Advancements in technology, such as computer modeling, have helped scientists to better visualize the structure of DNA.

CAN YOU EXPLAIN IT?

Making conclusions about something you cannot see has been a challenge throughout the history of science. Sometimes scientists must use indirect evidence. Understanding the structure and function of DNA is one such case. Early biologists recognized that characteristics were passed from one generation to the next, but the molecules responsible for this phenomenon were too small to be seen at the time. Biologists pieced together evidence about the structure of these molecules responsible for the unique characteristics of each organism. Over time, scientists built on the work of others, and technology continued to improve. We now have a much clearer understanding about DNA—the molecule that contains the code for life.

PREDICT Based on the images shown in Figure 1, how do you think scientists used evidence from research to build an understanding of the chemical and structural nature of DNA?

_____

_____

_____

_____

_____

FIGURE 1: DNA observations

a Purified DNA sample

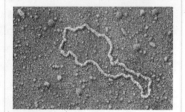

b Bacterial DNA (colorized TEM)

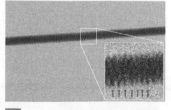

c Bundle of DNA strands (TEM)

 Evidence Notebook As you explore this lesson, gather evidence to explain how scientists determined the function and structure of DNA.

DNA Function

FIGURE 2: Unique traits are observable among humans.

You are one of a kind and like no other—unless you have an identical sibling, of course! How is it that you are so unique? You have a set of traits, or distinguishing characteristics, such as hair color, eye color, and face shape that are passed from one generation to the next. Early scientists noticed that offspring had traits similar to those of their parents. But a question remained: How are traits passed from one generation to the next?

Codes For Proteins

The molecule that stores the genetic information for all organisms is called DNA, or deoxyribonucleic acid. DNA is heritable, which means it can be passed from parent to offspring. This explains why offspring may look like their parents and why individual organisms within a species share many of the same characteristics. Scientists understood that traits were heritable long before they identified DNA and its key role in inheritance.

ANALYZE As you can see in Figure 2, humans have many observable traits that set us apart from each other. What are some traits you have?

_____

_____

_____

DNA does not act alone to pass on genetic information. The information from DNA is used to build another nucleic acid called RNA, or ribonucleic acid. RNA carries the information from DNA needed to build proteins. This concept of information flow from DNA to RNA to proteins is known as the *central dogma* of molecular biology.

Proteins play a crucial role in body functions. Proteins called enzymes help regulate chemical reactions. Other proteins provide structural support for cells. Proteins in the cell membrane transport nutrients across the membrane in response to changing conditions inside or outside the cell. Each protein has a unique structure and function in the cell, so proper coding in the DNA and RNA is critical for building each protein.

Mechanism for Heredity

Genetics is the study of biological inheritance patterns and variation in organisms. Gregor Mendel was an early contributor to our understanding of genetics. Mendel's revolutionary experimentation with breeding pea plants identified factors that controlled traits. He correctly predicted that traits can be inherited as discrete units passed from parents to offspring. However, it would take the work of several different scientists over many years to discover DNA and explain how it codes for the inheritance of individual traits. Results from experiments led by these scientists supported the conclusion that DNA is the molecule of inheritance.

Griffith's Experiments

In 1928, the British microbiologist Frederick Griffith was investigating two types of pneumonia-causing bacteria. One type, called S, has a smooth outer coating made from carbohydrates. The other type, called R, has a rough outer surface.

Cause and Effect

When Griffith injected mice with one or the other type of bacteria, only the S-type killed the mice. When Griffith injected mice with heat-killed S bacteria, they were unaffected. However, when he injected the mice with a combination of heat-killed S bacteria and live R bacteria, the mice died. Even more surprising, he found live S bacteria in a blood sample taken from these dead mice. Unable to identify the factor that transformed harmless R bacteria into disease-causing S bacteria, Griffith called the mystery material the *transforming principle*. This mystery would be a question for other scientists to explore.

PREDICT Use the information in the paragraph above and the terms below to identify the final result for each experiment.

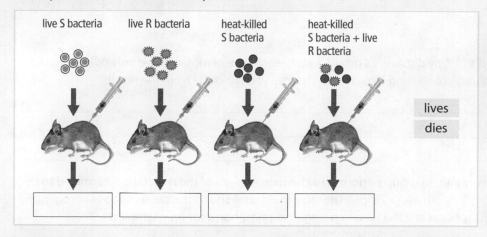

EXPLAIN What evidence suggested that there is a transforming principle?

_____

_____

ASK What further questions would you ask based on Griffith's experimental results?

_____

_____

Avery, McCarty, and MacLeod's Experiments

Canadian and American scientists Oswald Avery, Maclyn McCarty, and Colin MacLeod were intrigued by Griffith's transforming principle. Avery's team worked for more than ten years to answer the question of what transformed the R-strain. The scientists started with heat-killed S bacteria cells. They used a detergent to break down the bacteria, which resulted in an extract that contained only molecules of protein, DNA, and RNA. Initial experiments showed that this extract contained the transforming principle. Avery's team then used enzymes to break down each of the molecules separately. Once degraded, each sample was mixed with R-strain bacteria to test for transformation to S-strain.

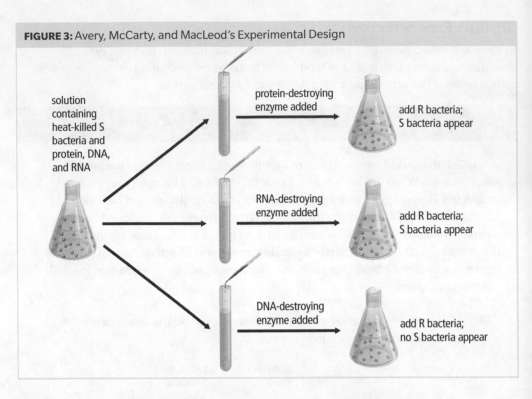

solution containing heat-killed S bacteria and protein, DNA, and RNA

protein-destroying enzyme added → add R bacteria; S bacteria appear

RNA-destroying enzyme added → add R bacteria; S bacteria appear

DNA-destroying enzyme added → add R bacteria; no S bacteria appear

INFER Why did Avery's group destroy each type of molecule before adding it to the solution containing R bacteria? What can you conclude from the results?

_____

_____

_____

Avery and his group performed a chemical analysis of the molecule determined to be the transforming principle. The table in Figure 4 shows the percentage of nitrogen and phosphorus and the ratio of nitrogen to phosphorus for four samples.

Data Analysis

FIGURE 4: Chemical Analysis of the Transforming Principle

	% Nitrogen (N)	% Phosphorus (P)	Ratio of N to P
Sample A	14.21	8.57	1.66
Sample B	15.93	9.09	1.75
Sample C	15.36	9.04	1.69
Sample D	13.40	8.45	1.58
Known value for DNA	15.32	9.05	1.69

ANALYZE How do the data in the table support the claim that DNA is the transforming principle?

○ **a.** The %N is very close to the known value for DNA.

○ **c.** The %P in DNA is less than the %N in DNA.

○ **b.** The %N does not match the known value for DNA.

○ **d.** The %P and %N in DNA are both less than 50%.

Avery's group performed standard chemical tests that showed DNA was present in the extract and protein was not. They also used enzymes to destroy different molecules, such as lipids and carbohydrates. Each time a molecule was destroyed, the transformation from R to S bacteria still occurred—until they destroyed DNA. When DNA was destroyed, the transformation did not occur.

In 1944, Avery and his group presented the evidence to support their conclusion that DNA must be the transforming principle, or genetic material. However, the scientific community remained skeptical as to whether the genetic material in bacteria was the same as that in other organisms. Despite Avery's evidence, some scientists insisted that his extract must have contained protein. Further testing remained to be done.

Hershey and Chase Experiments

In 1952, two American biologists, Alfred Hershey and Martha Chase, were researching different viruses that infect bacteria. These viruses, called bacteriophages, are made up of a DNA core surrounded by a protein coat. To reproduce, the bacteriophages attach themselves to bacteria and then inject material inside the cell. Hershey and Chase thought up a clever procedure that used the chemical elements found in protein and DNA. Protein contains sulfur but very little phosphorus, while DNA contains phosphorus but no sulfur. The researchers grew phages in cultures that contained radioactive isotopes of sulfur or phosphorus. Hershey and Chase then used these radioactively tagged phages in two experiments.

In the first experiment, bacteria were infected with phages that had radioactive sulfur atoms in their protein molecules. Hershey and Chase then used a kitchen blender and a centrifuge to separate the bacteria from the parts of the phages that remained outside the bacteria. When they examined the bacteria, they found no significant radioactivity. In the second experiment, they repeated the procedure with phages that had DNA tagged with radioactive phosphorus. This time, radioactivity was present inside the bacteria.

EXPLAIN Select the correct terms to complete the conclusion from the results shown in Figure 5.

When bacteriophages with radioactively labeled proteins infected the bacteria, radioactivity did | did not enter the cell. When bacteriophages with radioactively labeled DNA infected the bacteria, radioactivity did | did not enter the cell. Therefore, the material that is being injected into the bacteria is DNA | protein.

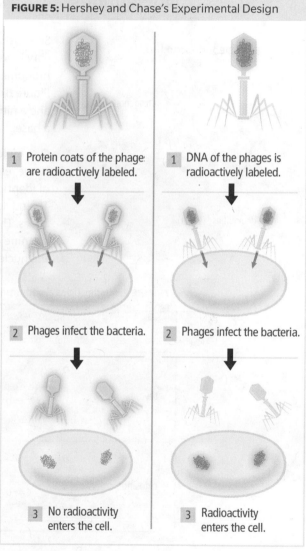

FIGURE 5: Hershey and Chase's Experimental Design

1 Protein coats of the phages are radioactively labeled.

2 Phages infect the bacteria.

3 No radioactivity enters the cell.

1 DNA of the phages is radioactively labeled.

2 Phages infect the bacteria.

3 Radioactivity enters the cell.

Evidence Notebook How did the work of scientists described in this section contribute to our knowledge of DNA? Did that work support the results from Mendel's experiments with pea plants? Explain.

DNA Structure

Once Hershey and Chase completed their experiments with bacteriophages, it was clear that DNA was responsible for the inheritance of traits. What scientists did not yet understand, however, was how DNA stored genetic information. To understand this, they first needed to understand the molecular structure of DNA.

Nucleotides

FIGURE 6: Nucleotide structure

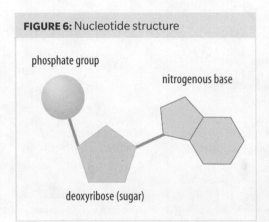

phosphate group

nitrogenous base

deoxyribose (sugar)

Scientists have known since the 1920s that the DNA molecule is a very long polymer, or chain of repeating subunits. The subunit, or monomer, that makes up DNA is called a nucleotide. As shown in Figure 6, a nucleotide is made up of a sugar, a phosphate group, and a nitrogen-containing—or nitrogenous—molecule, called a base.

One molecule of human DNA contains billions of nucleotides. However, if you were to divide all of those nucleotides into groups of identical nucleotides, you would end up with just four groups. The nucleotides that make up DNA differ only in their nitrogenous bases. The bases are cytosine (C), thymine (T), adenine (A), and guanine (G). The letter abbreviations refer both to the bases and to the nucleotides that contain the bases.

FIGURE 7: Nucleotides are identified by their nitrogenous base.

PYRIMIDINES			PURINES		
Name of base	Structural formula	Model	Name of base	Structural formula	Model
thymine	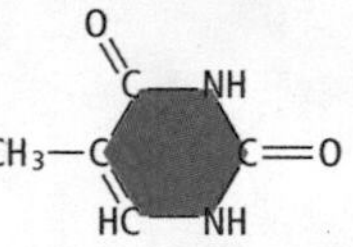 CH_3 structural formula	 T	adenine	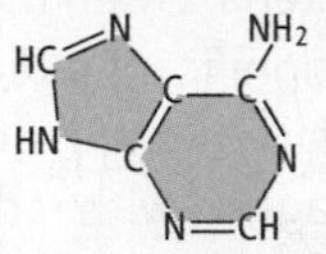 structural formula	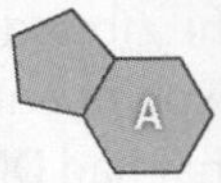 A
cytosine	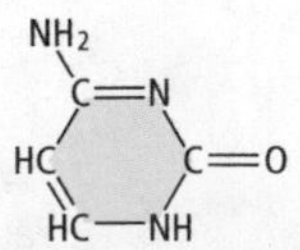 NH_2 structural formula	 C	guanine	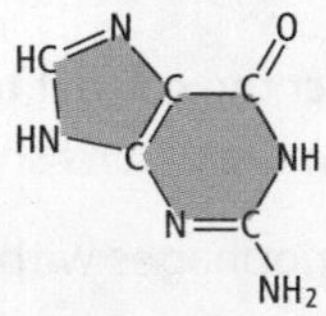 structural formula	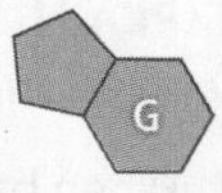 G

INFER Which of the following statements describes the structure of nucleotides that make up DNA? Select all correct answers.

☐ **a.** All nucleotides have the same base.

☐ **b.** All nucleotides have a phosphate group and deoxyribose.

☐ **c.** Adenine has one more carbon-nitrogen ring than thymine.

☐ **d.** Purines have one carbon-nitrogen ring.

☐ **e.** Pyrimidines have one carbon-nitrogen ring.

Determining DNA Structure

For a long time, scientists assumed that DNA was made up of equal amounts of the four nucleotides and that the DNA in all organisms was therefore exactly the same. That assumption made it difficult to convince scientists that DNA was the genetic material. They reasoned that identical molecules could not carry different instructions across all organisms. However, in 1950, Erwin Chargaff conducted a set of experiments that challenged this assumption.

Chargaff's Experiments

Chargaff changed the thinking about DNA by analyzing the DNA of several different organisms. He found that the same four bases are found in the DNA of all organisms, but the proportion of the four bases differs from one organism to another.

 Data Analysis

Comparing Nucleotide Ratios

FIGURE 8: Nucleotide ratios in different organisms

Source	Adenine to Guanine	Thymine to Cytosine	Adenine to Thymine	Guanine to Cytosine	Purines to Pyrimidines
Human	1.56	1.75	1.00	1.00	1.00
Chicken	1.45	1.29	1.06	0.91	0.99
Salmon	1.43	1.43	1.02	1.02	1.02
Wheat	1.22	1.18	1.00	0.97	0.99
Yeast	1.67	1.92	1.03	1.20	1.00
E. coli	1.05	0.95	1.09	0.99	1.00

ANALYZE The numbers shown in the table are ratios. For example, the ratio of adenine to guanine in humans is 1.56 to 1, or 1.56:1. The 1 is assumed, and not shown. What do you observe about these ratios? Select all correct answers.

☐ **a.** The ratio of cytosine to guanine is nearly 1:1.

☐ **b.** The ratio of cytosine to thymine is nearly 1:1.

☐ **c.** The ratio of adenine to guanine is nearly 1:1.

☐ **d.** The ratio of adenine to thymine is nearly 1:1.

EXPLAIN Chargaff found that the proportion of adenine, guanine, cytosine, and thymine varied from organism to organism. How does Chargaff's work support the idea that DNA is the molecule of inheritance?

_____

_____

_____

_____

FIGURE 9: Rosalind Franklin's x-ray diffraction image was critical in the development of our understanding of DNA's shape.

a Rosalind Franklin   b Photo 51

Franklin's X-ray Photographs

In the early 1950s, British scientist Rosalind Franklin was using a technique called x-ray crystallography to determine the three-dimensional shape of molecules. She used a similar technique, called x-ray diffraction, to examine the shape of DNA. When a sample is bombarded with x-rays, the atoms diffract the x-rays in a pattern that can be captured on film. Franklin's x-ray photograph of DNA, known as Photo 51, showed an *X* surrounded by a circle. The pattern and angle of the *X* suggested that DNA consists of two strands, spaced at a consistent width apart, and twisted into a helical shape.

 Collaborate Rosalind Franklin's results made her conclude that the DNA molecule was a helical, or a spiral shape. With a partner, discuss what questions about the structure of DNA still remained.

Watson and Crick's Model of DNA

At about the same time that Franklin was working with x-ray crystallography, American geneticist James Watson and British physicist Francis Crick were also studying DNA structure. Their interest was sparked by the earlier work of Hershey, Chase, and Chargaff as well as biochemist Linus Pauling. Pauling discovered that the structure of some proteins was a helix, or spiral. Watson and Crick hypothesized that DNA might also be a helix. Maurice Wilkins, one of Franklin's colleagues, shared Photo 51 with Watson and Crick without her knowledge. This image, along with Franklin's calculations, gave them the clues they needed to put together a physical model of DNA.

Watson and Crick began working with their model to determine the structure of DNA. They knew they had to be able to twist their model to account for the evidence provided by Franklin's x-rays. They placed the sugar-phosphate backbones on the outside and the nitrogenous bases on the inside. At first, Watson reasoned that A might pair with A, T with T, and so on. But the bases A and G are about twice as wide as C and T, so this made a helix that varied in width. This arrangement was not supported by Franklin's data, which showed that the width of the molecule was constant. Finally Watson and Crick found that if they paired doubled-ringed nucleotides with single-ringed nucleotides, the bases fit together like a puzzle.

ANALYZE Using Watson and Crick's reasoning, which nucleotides pair with one another? How do Chargaff's results support their DNA model?

_____

_____

_____

_____

Watson and Crick built a double-helix model in which the two strands were complementary—that is, if one strand is ACACAC, the other strand is TGTGTG. The pairing of bases in their model was inspired by Chargaff's results. These A–T and C–G relationships became known as Chargaff's rules.

In April 1953, Watson and Crick published their DNA model in the journal *Nature*. In 1962, Watson, Crick, and Wilkins were awarded a Nobel Prize for Physiology or Medicine for their discovery. Rosalind Franklin, who died in 1958, would not be recognized for her contributions to the DNA model until much later.

Current DNA Model

The current model represents DNA nucleotides of a single strand joined together by covalent bonds that connect the sugar of one nucleotide to the phosphate of the next nucleotide. The alternating sugars and phosphates form the sides of a double helix, or the sugar-phosphate backbone of the molecule. The DNA double helix is held together by hydrogen bonds between the bases in the middle. Individually, each hydrogen bond is weak, but together, they maintain DNA structure. The complementary nature of the bases that make up DNA is essential to the process of DNA replication.

FIGURE 10: DNA structure

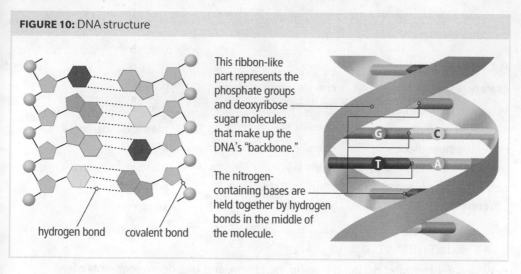

This ribbon-like part represents the phosphate groups and deoxyribose sugar molecules that make up the DNA's "backbone."

The nitrogen-containing bases are held together by hydrogen bonds in the middle of the molecule.

hydrogen bond   covalent bond

EXPLAIN Examine the model of DNA shown in Figure 10. Select the correct terms to complete the description of the structure of the molecule.

The base pairs are found in the middle | sides of the DNA molecule. The base pairs are held together by hydrogen | covalent bonds, which are relatively weak. The deoxyribose sugars and phosphates are found in the middle | sides of the DNA molecule. The sugars and phosphates are connected by hydrogen | covalent bonds, which are relatively strong.

 Evidence Notebook How did technological advances improve scientists' understanding of DNA during Watson and Crick's time?

Hands-On Activity
Modeling DNA

FIGURE 11: DNA model

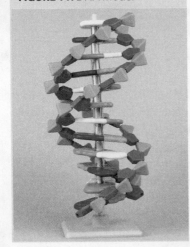

In this activity, you will choose from available materials to build a three-dimensional model of DNA. After building your model, you will manipulate it to determine how a change in the structure of DNA could possibly change its function.

MAKE A CLAIM

How will changes in the base pairs affect the structure of DNA?

_____

_____

_____

_____

MATERIALS

- safety goggles
- chenille stem pieces, black (8)
- chenille stem pieces, blue (4)
- chenille stem pieces, green (4)
- chenille stem pieces, orange (4)
- chenille stems, red (4)
- chenille stem pieces, white (16)
- chenille stem pieces, yellow (4)
- paper
- pencils, colored
- plastic beads, small, black (8)
- plastic beads, small, white (16)
- scissors

SAFETY INFORMATION

- Wear safety goggles during the setup, hands-on, and takedown segments of the activity.
- Immediately pick up any items dropped on the floor so they do not become a slip/fall hazard.
- Use caution when using sharp tools, which can cut or puncture skin.
- Wash your hands with soap and water immediately after completing this activity.

CARRY OUT THE INVESTIGATION

1. Using the available materials, build your DNA model. The model must show the following: a phosphate backbone, correct base pairings, deoxyribose sugar molecules, hydrogen bonds between the bases, and a twisted double-helix shape.

2. Make a sketch of your model in your Evidence Notebook and label it to show which materials represent which parts of the DNA molecule.

3. Take apart at least four of the base pairings and switch them so that the bases are mismatched. Observe how this affects the structure of DNA.

1. How did you use the available materials to build your model of DNA?

_____

_____

_____

_____

2. How did changing the base pairs affect the structure of the model DNA?

_____

_____

_____

_____

3. How do you think changing the base pairs affects the function of DNA?

_____

_____

_____

_____

_____

_____

4. Write at least one testable or researchable question that you still have about the structure and function of DNA.

_____

_____

_____

_____

_____

 Evidence Notebook How do models of DNA, such as the one you made in this activity, help you better understand the structure and function of DNA? What are disadvantages of these models?

DNA Replication

The process by which DNA is copied is called replication. In prokaryotes, such as bacteria, DNA replication occurs in the cytoplasm of the cell. In eukaryotes, such as humans, this process takes place inside the nucleus of a cell. Replication ensures that every cell has a complete set of identical genetic information.

DNA Replication Process

DNA stores genetic information. However, it does not copy itself. Enzymes and other proteins do the work of replication. When the process is finished, the result is two complete molecules of DNA, each exactly like the original double strand.

DNA Unzips

At the beginning of replication, an enzyme called *helicase* binds to the DNA molecule and unzips the strands. This occurs at many places along the chromosome, called the origins of replication. The hydrogen bonds connecting base pairs are broken, the original molecule separates, and the bases on each strand are exposed. Other proteins, called stabilizing proteins, bind to and stabilize the separated strands. The process of unzipping DNA proceeds in two directions simultaneously, rather like unzipping a suitcase.

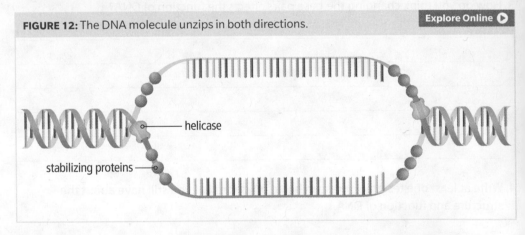

FIGURE 12: The DNA molecule unzips in both directions.

Explore Online ▶

helicase

stabilizing proteins

EXPLAIN Why are stabilizing proteins needed to keep the DNA strands separated?

○ **a.** Hydrogen bonds normally cause the DNA strands to stick together.

○ **b.** The wrong nucleotides can mistakenly pair up on the templates.

○ **c.** The two strands can coil around each other preventing replication.

○ **d.** Without stabilizing proteins, the DNA strands can fragment.

Nucleotide Pairing

Once the DNA is unzipped, the process of adding nucleotides to the single-stranded templates begins. An enzyme called *primase* makes an RNA primer, a short nucleotide segment that begins the synthesis process. The RNA primer segment is necessary because nucleotides can only be added to an existing strand.

Similar to the unzipping process, replication takes place at both forks simultaneously. One by one, free nucleotides pair with the bases exposed as the template strands unzip. Starting at the primer, enzymes called *DNA polymerases* bond the nucleotides together and form new strands using DNA nucleotides that are complementary to each template. Both eukaryotes and prokaryotes use these enzymes, although the specific type and number of enzymes differ between the two types of organisms. Figure 13 shows the types of DNA polymerases used by prokaryotic cells. Although the specific enzymes differ, the general process of replication is very similar in both eukaryotes and prokaryotes.

INFER Why might DNA replication in eukaryotes require more enzymes than DNA replication in prokaryotes?

_____

_____

Because the two strands of the DNA molecule are positioned in opposite directions, there are differences in how each strand is copied. On the *leading strand*, highlighted in the top image in Figure 13, DNA replication begins at the primer and proceeds in one direction (referred to as 5' to 3') as DNA polymerase adds new nucleotides. On the *lagging strand*, highlighted in the bottom image in Figure 13, replication occurs in a discontinuous, piece-by-piece way in the opposite direction. On the lagging strand, primers attach at multiple locations so multiple molecules of DNA polymerase can add nucleotides to each primer at the same time.

FIGURE 13: DNA polymerases bond nucleotides together to form the new strands.

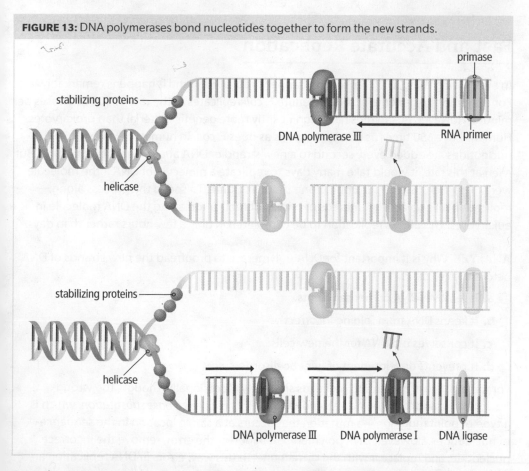

Once the open regions on both strands are filled in, a different DNA polymerase removes the RNA primers from both strands and replaces them with DNA nucleotides. On the lagging strand, the fragments are then bound together by an enzyme called *ligase*.

Two Identical DNA Molecules

When replication is complete, there are two identical molecules of DNA. Each molecule contains one strand of DNA from the original molecule and one new strand. This type of replication is called *semiconservative* because each new molecule of DNA conserves, or keeps unchanged, one strand of DNA from the original molecule.

FIGURE 14: Replication results in two identical molecules of DNA.

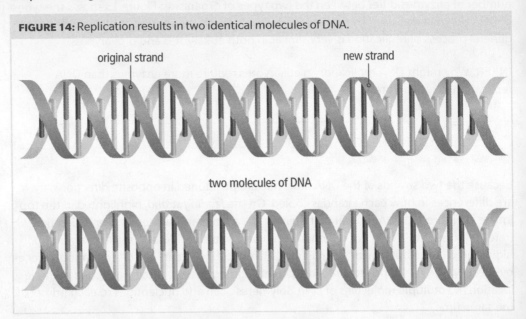

original strand

new strand

two molecules of DNA

Fast and Accurate Replication

In every living thing, DNA replication happens repeatedly, and it happens remarkably fast. For example, the genome of the bacterium *E. coli* replicates at the rate of 100 000 bases per minute. However, eukaryotes have significantly more genetic material than prokaryotes. Humans have 650 times as many base pairs as does *E. coli*. In human cells, about 50 nucleotides are added every second to a new strand of DNA at an origin of replication. But even at this rate, it would take many days to replicate a molecule of DNA if the molecule were like a jacket zipper, unzipping one tooth at a time. To speed the process along, replication takes place at hundreds of origins of replication along the DNA molecule in eukaryotes. This allows replication to be completed in only a few hours rather than days.

ANALYZE Why is it important for DNA polymerase to proofread the new strands of DNA before the cell divides?

○ **a.** It removes RNA primer segments.

○ **b.** It keeps DNA from folding incorrectly.

○ **c.** It conserves old DNA for the new cells.

○ **d.** It prevents development of genetic disorders.

For the most part, replication proceeds smoothly. Occasionally, though, the wrong nucleotide is added to the new strand of DNA. This is called a *base substitution*, which is a type of point mutation—a mutation that occurs at a single location in the sequence of nucleotides. However, DNA polymerase can detect the error, remove the incorrect nucleotide, and replace it with the correct one. In this way, errors in DNA replication are limited to about one error per 1 billion nucleotides. If the substitution is not repaired, it may permanently change the organism's DNA. Sickle-cell anemia is an example of a genetic disorder that results from a base-substitution point mutation.

Replicating Genes

Thanks to advancements in technology, scientists are able to turn a single copy of a gene into thousands, and even millions or billions of copies—all within hours! The process that lets scientists replicate genes is called polymerase chain reaction, or PCR.

PCR requires a polymerase enzyme in order to make new strands of DNA using existing strands as templates. *Taq* polymerase, which is isolated from heat-tolerant bacteria, is the polymerase that is usually used in PCR. As with other DNA polymerases, *Taq* polymerase needs a primer as a starting point for DNA synthesis. Thus, the essential materials needed for a PCR reaction are *Taq* polymerase, primers and nucleotides, and an existing DNA template. These components are put together in a test tube and are exposed to repeated cycles of heating and cooling that result in DNA synthesis.

Although PCR and natural DNA replication are similar in that they use a DNA template, primer, and polymerase, there are differences. For example, in PCR, the DNA to be copied is separated using extreme temperature cycles. In natural replication, an enzyme separates the DNA. And in PCR, only small fragments of DNA can be effectively replicated. In organisms, entire genomic DNA is routinely replicated.

The goal of PCR is usually to make enough of the targeted region of DNA to analyze it further or use it in an application, such as DNA cloning, medical research and diagnostics, or analysis of DNA as criminal evidence.

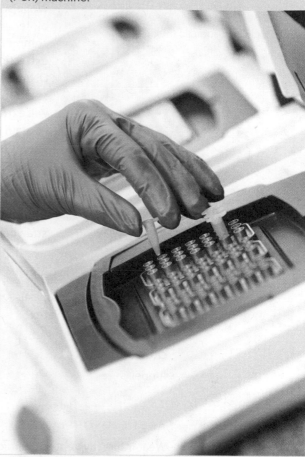

FIGURE 15: A scientist uses a polymerase chain reaction (PCR) machine.

EVALUATE What makes PCR a useful method for investigating genes?

_____

_____

_____

_____

_____

_____

 Evidence Notebook Does DNA replication ensure that every cell in the body has a complete set of identical genetic information? Explain your answer.

🧪 Hands-On Lab

Extracting DNA

FIGURE 16: Strawberries have eight copies of each chromosome in their cells.

While scientists use DNA extraction kits available from biotechnology companies, you can actually extract DNA using common ingredients found in your own home. During a DNA extraction, a detergent is used to burst open cells so that the DNA is released into solution. Then alcohol is added to the solution to cause the DNA to precipitate. In this activity, you will extract DNA from a strawberry. Unlike human cells, which contain two copies of each chromosome, a strawberry has eight copies of each chromosome in its cells.

MAKE A CLAIM

In your Evidence Notebook, predict what the DNA extracted from a strawberry will look like.

MATERIALS

- indirectly vented chemical splash goggles, nonlatex apron, nonlatex gloves
- cheesecloth
- funnel
- isopropyl alcohol, 91%
- dish soap, liquid
- salt
- strawberry (1 per student)
- teaspoon
- test tube with stopper
- water
- wood skewer
- zipper bag, plastic, quart size

SAFETY INFORMATION

indirectly vented chemical splash goggles

- Wear indirectly vented chemical splash goggles, a nonlatex apron, and nonlatex gloves during the setup, hands-on, and takedown segments of the activity.
- Immediately pick up any dropped items on the floor so the items don't become a slip/fall hazard.
- Never eat any food items used in a lab activity.
- Do not inhale or sniff alcohol fumes.
- Wash your hands with soap and water immediately after completing this activity.

CARRY OUT THE INVESTIGATION

1. Place the isopropyl alcohol in a freezer 24 hours before beginning the lab.

2. Put the strawberry in a plastic zipper bag. Zip the bag closed.

3. Gently crush the strawberry by squeezing it inside the closed bag for 2 minutes.

4. Carefully open the bag and add 1 teaspoon water, 1 teaspoon liquid dish soap, and a pinch of salt. Zip the bag closed. Knead for 1 minute.

5. Pour the strawberry mixture into a cheesecloth-lined funnel that is set into a test tube to filter out the solids.

6. Remove the isopropyl alcohol from the freezer. Tilt the test tube in your hand. Very slowly, pour a small amount of alcohol down the inside of the test tube just until there is a thin layer of alcohol floating on top of the solution.

7. Observe the test tube. You should see a band of white, gooey material forming just beneath the layer of alcohol. Gently put the skewer into the test tube and twirl it in the white material in one direction only. Wind the material around the skewer, then carefully draw it up and out of the test tube.

8. Record your observations.

- -

ANALYZE

1. Describe the appearance of your DNA sample.

_____

_____

_____

_____

_____

2. How is your DNA sample similar to and different from the various models you have seen in this lesson?

_____

_____

_____

_____

3. The sample of DNA came from many strawberry cells. Do you think you would have been able to get the same result from your experiment if you had extracted DNA from a single cell? Explain your answer.

_____

_____

_____

_____

| EVIDENCE FOR DNA STRUCTURE AND FUNCTION | TELOMERES AND AGING | THE ART OF DNA FOLDING | Go online to choose one of these other paths. |

Lesson Self-Check

CAN YOU EXPLAIN IT?

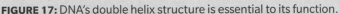

FIGURE 17: DNA's double helix structure is essential to its function.

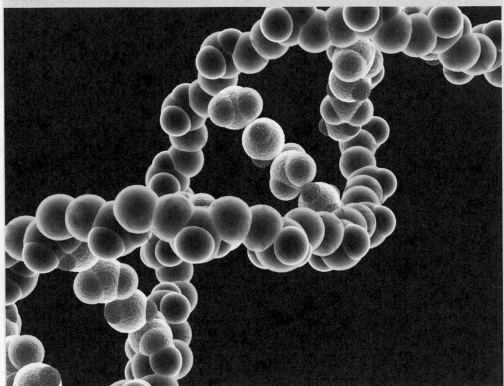

In the past, scientists had to use indirect evidence to support their ideas about DNA structure and function. Although these scientists understood the basic concept that characteristics were passed from one generation to the next, the molecules responsible for this phenomenon were too small to be seen at the time. As technology advanced, scientists were able to better observe DNA's structure. Now, with even more technological advancements, scientists have a much deeper understanding of DNA and how its structure is closely related to its function.

 Evidence Notebook Refer to your notes in your Evidence Notebook to explain how scientists used evidence from research to build an understanding of the chemical and structural nature of DNA.

1. Make a claim about the structure and function of DNA. How is its structure related to its function?

2. How has scientists' knowledge of DNA changed over time? Use evidence from experiments, models, and technology used to support your claim. Consider developing a timeline to illustrate the progress of understanding DNA structure and function.

3. Why were scientists able to learn more about DNA over time?

Check Your Understanding

1. How does the central dogma connect DNA, RNA, and proteins?
   - ○ **a.** DNA codes for proteins, which code for RNA.
   - ○ **b.** DNA codes for RNA, which codes for proteins.
   - ○ **c.** RNA codes for DNA, which codes for proteins.
   - ○ **d.** Proteins code for RNA, which codes for DNA.

2. What is the complementary DNA strand for a strand with the nucleotide sequence AACCCGGTTTG?
   - ○ **a.** GGAAATTCCCT
   - ○ **b.** TTAAACCGGGA
   - ○ **c.** TTGGGCCAAAC
   - ○ **d.** CCGGGTTAAAT

3. What knowledge did scientists gain based on the x-ray diffraction image taken by Rosalind Franklin?
   - ○ **a.** the sequence of nucleotides
   - ○ **b.** how nucleotide bases form a template
   - ○ **c.** the role of DNA in genetic mutations
   - ○ **d.** the double-helix structure of DNA

4. Which part of the replication process helps reduce the chance for genetic mutation?
   - ○ **a.** insertion of RNA primer sequences
   - ○ **b.** sealing the gaps between fragments
   - ○ **c.** opening multiple origins of replication
   - ○ **d.** proofreading new DNA strands

5. Select the correct terms to complete the statement about DNA replication.

   Once DNA replication is complete, there are two identical | unlike molecules of DNA.

   Each new molecule of DNA conserves one strand | changes both strands of DNA from the original molecule.

6. Occasionally, a substitution occurs during DNA replication and the wrong base pairing occurs. Place the events of this example in the correct order to show how a substitution is repaired.

   _____ **a.** DNA polymerase detects an error.

   _____ **b.** Guanine is replaced with adenine.

   _____ **c.** Guanine is added to the new DNA strand to pair with thymine.

7. Match each conclusion about the role of DNA as the molecule of inheritance to the correct experiment.

Experiment		Main Conclusion
Griffith's experiments with mice and S- and R-type bacteria	○ ○	The genetic material injected by viruses is DNA.
Avery, MacLeod, and McCarty's extraction experiment	○ ○	DNA is the transforming principle.
Hershey and Chase's radioactively tagged bacteriophages	○ ○	A "transforming principle" determines traits.

CHECKPOINTS (continued)

8. How do the base-pairing rules explain how a strand of DNA acts as a template during DNA replication?

_____

_____

_____

_____

9. Think about the variety of experiments, models, labs, and activities you explored in this lesson. How does all the information and evidence you gathered clarify your understanding of scientific processes? What questions do you still have about scientific processes and research?

_____

_____

_____

_____

_____

_____

_____

_____

10. How does scientific knowledge build over time? Why might collaboration in the scientific community be important?

_____

_____

_____

_____

MAKE YOUR OWN STUDY GUIDE

 In your Evidence Notebook, design a study guide that supports the main ideas from this lesson:

Our understanding of DNA's structure and function has changed over time.

DNA stores genetic information and is responsible for an organism's traits.

Remember to include the following information in your study guide:
- Use examples that model main ideas.
- Record explanations for the phenomena you investigated.
- Use evidence to support your explanations. Your support can include drawings, data, graphs, laboratory conclusions, and other evidence recorded throughout the lesson.

Consider how the unique structure of DNA allows it to be copied and to transmit traits from parent to offspring.

Protein Synthesis

Like computers that use code to do tasks, DNA uses code to make proteins.

CAN YOU EXPLAIN IT?

When a person types a command into a keyboard, they are "talking to" the computer. However, computers and humans do not speak the same language. Rather than using words to communicate, computers use a language called binary code. Binary code is made up of zeros and ones, which represent the states "on" and "off." Every number, letter, and keyboard symbol are represented by a combination of zeros and ones. People use programming languages to translate between the user and the computer's binary code. These languages allow computers to be programmed to perform many different tasks.

DNA also uses a simple code made up of only four components, which are represented by the letters A, T, G, and C. This "four-letter code" allows cells to produce thousands of different proteins that are used to build body structures or perform life processes.

PREDICT If DNA code consists of only four components, how can it produce so much variety among organisms of the same species?

_____

_____

_____

_____

 Evidence Notebook As you explore this lesson, gather evidence to explain how DNA code affects the structure of proteins.

Introduction to Protein Synthesis

Soon after helping to discover the structure of DNA, Francis Crick defined what he called the *central dogma* of molecular biology. Crick stated that genetic information flowed from DNA to proteins, but not in the other direction. This flow of information from DNA to proteins is referred to as protein synthesis. Crick proposed that in the first step, information flowed from DNA to an intermediate molecule of RNA. In the second step, information was transferred from RNA to build a protein molecule.

Genes Codes for Proteins

Each protein is coded for by a section of DNA called a *gene*. Humans have around 19 000 protein-coding genes. However, the number of genes is not necessarily related to the complexity of the organism. For example, grape plants are not particularly complex organisms, but they have over 30 000 genes, according to the most recent count.

Genes are the most basic unit of heredity. They determine the traits of an organism, because the proteins carry out the work of the cell. Proteins are the connection between DNA and traits. Proteins carry out most of the tasks in the cell, and, as a result, greatly influence the cell's structure and function. Whether they are catalyzing chemical reactions, transporting molecules, or helping fight infections, proteins are essential components of the cell system. Variations in the code of a gene can change the structure of a protein. This leads to different traits.

FIGURE 1: A gene is a section of DNA that codes for a certain protein.

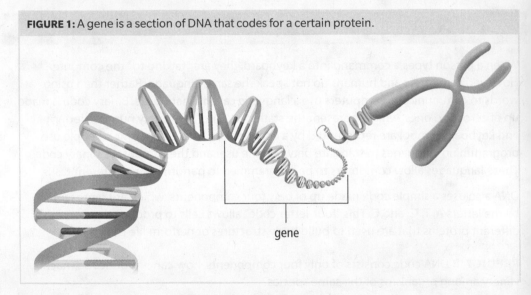

gene

The proteins that your genes code for are responsible for your inherited traits. For example, two genes on chromosome 15 play a major role in the color of human eyes. These two genes produce and regulate proteins that control melanin production in the eyes. Melanin is a pigment that adds color to skin, hair, and the iris of the eyes. In brown-eyed people, these genes allow them to produce more of this pigment, which leads to darker-colored eyes. Blue-eyed people produce less of this pigment, which gives them lighter-colored eyes.

Protein Structure and Function

A protein is a molecule made up of amino acids linked together in a chain. There are a number of different amino acids, but organisms use only 20 to build proteins. Amino acids are molecules that contain carbon, hydrogen, oxygen, nitrogen, and sometimes sulfur. Our bodies can make 12 of these standard amino acids. The others come from foods you eat, such as meats, beans, and nuts.

FIGURE 2: Protein Structure

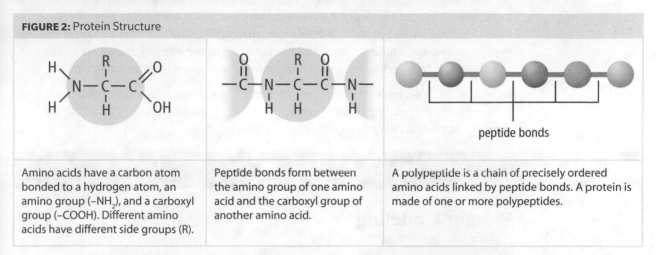

Amino acids have a carbon atom bonded to a hydrogen atom, an amino group (–NH₂), and a carboxyl group (–COOH). Different amino acids have different side groups (R).	Peptide bonds form between the amino group of one amino acid and the carboxyl group of another amino acid.	A polypeptide is a chain of precisely ordered amino acids linked by peptide bonds. A protein is made of one or more polypeptides.

ANALYZE Select the correct terms to complete the statement about the relationship between proteins and amino acids.

A protein is made up of monomers | polymers called amino acids. Proteins differ in the number and order of amino acids. The specific sequence of amino acids determines a protein's structure and function. A chain of linked amino acids is a monomer | polymer. One or more of these chains makes up a protein. Proteins may have three, and sometimes four, levels of structure: primary, secondary, tertiary, and quaternary.

FIGURE 3: There are four possible levels of protein structure.

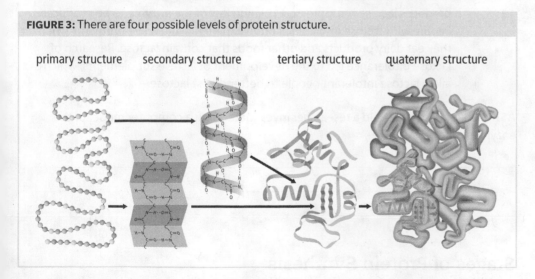

primary structure   secondary structure   tertiary structure   quaternary structure

The primary structure of a protein is the sequence of amino acids in the polypeptide. Hydrogen bonds between amino acids cause the chain to fold into zig-zag-shaped sheets and spirals, which make up the secondary structure. The tertiary structure is the 3D shape of the protein. Many proteins contain multiple polypeptide chains, or subunits, which combine to form the quaternary structure.

PREDICT Would a change to the primary, secondary, or tertiary structure have the greatest effect on a protein's function? Explain your answer.

_____

_____

Many proteins function as enzymes, which help regulate chemical reactions within organisms. Enzymes are involved in almost every process in our bodies, from breaking down food to building proteins. For example, during digestion, an enzyme called amylase in your saliva begins to break down starches in food. In the intestines, another enzyme called maltase breaks down the sugar maltose into individual glucose molecules.

Enzyme structure is important, because each enzyme's shape allows only certain reactants to bind to the enzyme. If pH or temperature exceeds the normal ranges for a cell, the shape of its proteins may change, disrupting their function.

 Engineering

Protein Modeling

FIGURE 4: This computer model can be used to study the enzyme maltase.

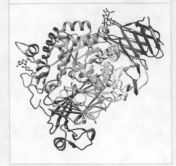

Scientists can use computer-modeling software to study a protein's structure and determine how different conditions affect its function. For example, the structure of maltase allows it to perfectly bind to maltose. If the structure of maltase is altered due to a change in the environment or a genetic mutation, it may not be able to bind to maltose at all. Understanding the structure of enzymes can eventually lead to better treatments for certain medical conditions.

Many adults develop lactose intolerance as they age. The gene that produces lactase is suppressed, causing less of the enzyme to be produced. People with lactose intolerance often experience digestive problems when they eat dairy products and other foods that contain lactose. Research of lactose intolerance led to the development of lactase supplements, which allow lactose intolerant people to better digest lactose.

ASK What questions could a researcher investigate using a computer model of the enzyme maltase?

_____

_____

_____

Stages of Protein Synthesis

Evidence Notebook
How could a change in DNA affect the way a protein is made? Could this affect the expression of the trait?

The process of constructing proteins based on the DNA code has two main stages: *transcription* and *translation*. Transcription is the process of copying a sequence of DNA into an intermediate molecule called mRNA, or messenger RNA. mRNA is like a disposable copy of the DNA message. During translation, the mRNA message is converted into a polypeptide. One or more polypeptides make up a functional protein.

Comparing DNA and RNA

mRNA acts as a messenger, carrying information from DNA in the nucleus to the ribosome for protein synthesis. mRNA is a temporary code made from a gene. A molecule of RNA is similar to a molecule of DNA, but with some distinct differences. The models of DNA and RNA in Figure 5 illustrate how the structures of these molecules compare. For example, DNA contains a sugar called deoxyribose, whereas RNA contains a sugar called ribose. RNA has the nitrogenous base uracil, whereas DNA has thymine.

FIGURE 5: DNA and RNA have some similarities and differences in their structure.

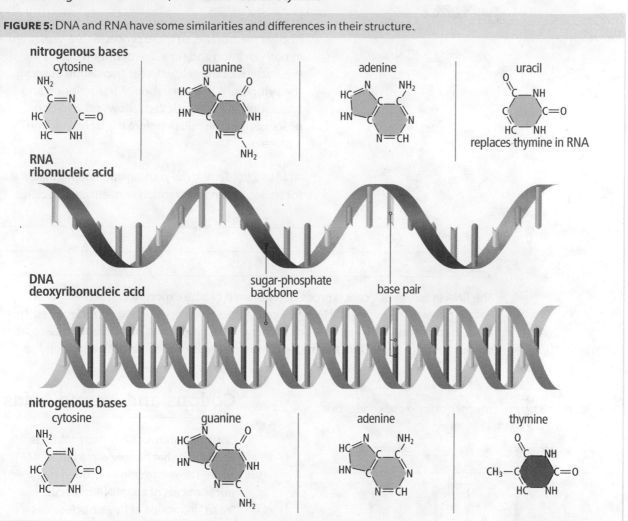

ANALYZE Determine whether the following items are found in DNA, RNA, or both.

DNA	RNA	both

_____ sugar is deoxyribose   _____ sugar is ribose

_____ uracil   _____ single-stranded

_____ nucleic acids   _____ thymine

_____ sugar-phosphate backbone   _____ double-stranded

 Collaborate Think of an analogy to explain the roles of DNA and RNA in protein synthesis. How would you represent the process of protein synthesis and the roles of DNA and RNA? Write your answers, and then compare them with a partner's answers.

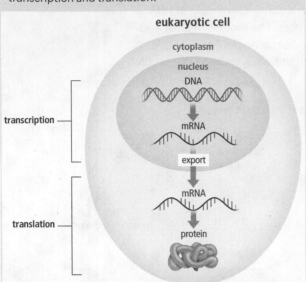

FIGURE 6: Protein synthesis includes the processes of transcription and translation.

eukaryotic cell

cytoplasm

nucleus

DNA

transcription

mRNA

export

mRNA

translation

protein

Prokaryotic and Eukaryotic Cells

Recall that a prokaryotic cell does not have a nucleus; instead, DNA "free-floats" within the cell. Thus, in these cells, transcription and translation all occur in the cytoplasm at approximately the same time. The translation of mRNA begins while the mRNA is still being transcribed.

In eukaryotic cells, however, DNA is located inside the nuclear membrane, so these processes are separated in both location and time. Transcription occurs in the nucleus of the cell, whereas translation occurs in the cytoplasm. The separation of transcription and translation in eukaryotic cells allows for additional processing of the mRNA before it is translated into a protein.

ANALYZE Identify the starting and ending materials for transcription and translation in eukaryotic cells.

_____

_____

_____

The RNA in eukaryotic cells is processed before it can be exported out of the nucleus. Before translation occurs, mRNA is "spliced" into a new combination of nucleotides. This extra modification of the mRNA code allows for the production of different proteins from a single stretch of DNA. Thus, the mRNA transcript can be edited before translation.

FIGURE 7: A codon is a sequence of three nucleotides that code for an amino acid.

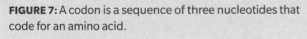

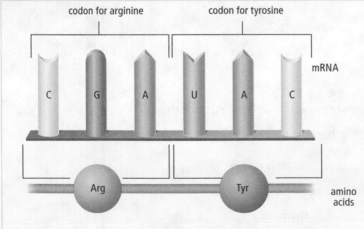

codon for arginine   codon for tyrosine

mRNA

C   G   A   U   A   C

Arg   Tyr

amino acids

Codons and Amino Acids

The translation of RNA into protein is similar to what happens in a computer code. The information encoded in the nucleic acids of an mRNA molecule is "read" in groups of three nucleotides called codons. This is similar to the way a computer interprets the zeroes and ones of binary code strings into a program you can use. A codon is a three-nucleotide mRNA sequence that codes for an amino acid.

SOLVE Suppose an mRNA molecule in the cytoplasm had 300 nucleotides. How many amino acids would be in the resulting polypeptide?

Number of amino acids: _____

Scientists have determined what each combination of nucleotides in RNA code says about a protein and used this information to develop codon charts. A codon chart is used to identify which mRNA codons code for which amino acids. To read a circular codon chart, begin in the center and work outward. Start with the first letter of the codon, and pick the correct letter in the middle of the circle. Then, select the second letter of the codon, follow to the third letter of the codon, and select the appropriate amino acid. Notice that many amino acids are coded for by more than one codon.

FIGURE 8: A codon chart shows which mRNA codons code for which amino acids.

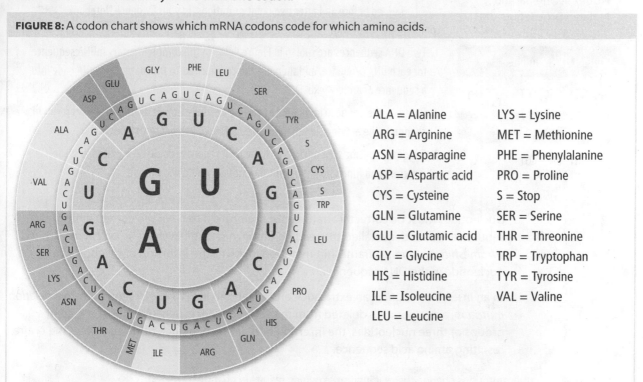

ALA = Alanine   LYS = Lysine
ARG = Arginine   MET = Methionine
ASN = Asparagine   PHE = Phenylalanine
ASP = Aspartic acid   PRO = Proline
CYS = Cysteine   S = Stop
GLN = Glutamine   SER = Serine
GLU = Glutamic acid   THR = Threonine
GLY = Glycine   TRP = Tryptophan
HIS = Histidine   TYR = Tyrosine
ILE = Isoleucine   VAL = Valine
LEU = Leucine

APPLY There is one start codon, AUG, which identifies where translation will begin. Which amino acid corresponds to the start codon?

○ **a.** alanine   ○ **c.** methionine

○ **b.** isoleucine   ○ **d.** glycine

The genetic code is shared by almost all living organisms, as well as viruses. For example, that means that the codon UUU codes for phenylalanine when that codon occurs in an armadillo, a cactus, a yeast, or a human. The common nature of the genetic code suggests that organisms arose from a common ancestor. It also means that scientists can insert a gene from one organism into another organism to make a functional protein. For these reasons, we say that the genetic code is nearly universal. There are, however, a few exceptions to the genetic code. For example, in one species of bacterium, UGA codes for tryptophan instead of functioning as a stop codon.

Mutations and Proteins

Sometimes a mutation changes the sequence of nucleotides in an organism's DNA. When a mutation occurs in a gene, it can change the codon structure of the mRNA, which can ultimately lead to a change in the amino acid structure of the protein. Mutations that occur during replication can be classified as point mutations or frameshift mutations. In a *point mutation*, one nucleotide is replaced with a different nucleotide.

The Effects of Mutation

FIGURE 9: Original and Mutated DNA Sequences (shown 3' to 5')

Original DNA Sequence
TAC AGA GGC CGT

Mutated DNA Sequence
TAC AG**T** GAC CGT

Evidence Notebook Determine the amino acid sequence that would be formed before and after two point mutations. In your Evidence Notebook, complete the following:

1. Two DNA sequences are shown in Figure 9. Write the complementary mRNA sequence for each DNA sequence, and then use the codon chart to translate the mRNA code into a sequence of amino acids.

2. Based on the amino acid sequences you wrote, does a point mutation always result in a change to the amino acid sequence? Support your answer with evidence.

3. Suggest a specific scenario in which the DNA sequence could be mutated, but the structure and function of the resulting protein would not change.

Nucleotides must be correctly arranged for the protein to have the correct amino acid sequence. This order is called the reading frame. A change in the reading frame is called a *frameshift mutation*. A frameshift mutation involves the insertion or deletion of a nucleotide in the DNA sequence.

In an *insertion mutation*, an extra nucleotide is added into the DNA sequence. In a *deletion mutation*, a nucleotide is deleted from the DNA sequence. Because mRNA is read in groups of three nucleotides, the insertion or deletion of a nucleotide can affect the entire resulting amino acid sequence.

FIGURE 10: Frameshift mutations change the reading frame, which results in changes in the sequence of amino acids.

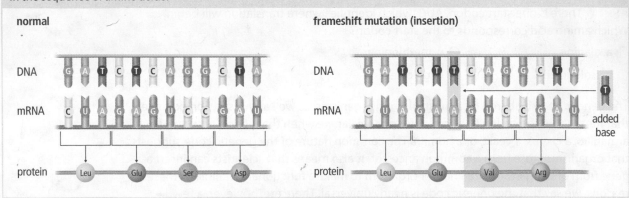

ANALYZE Could there be a frameshift mutation that would not affect the structure and function of the resulting protein? Explain your answer.

_____

_____

_____

 Evidence Notebook How is the formation of mRNA similar to how a computer processes information from a user?

Hands-On Activity

Modeling Protein Synthesis and Mutations

A mutation creates slightly different versions of the same genes. Mutations can result in differences between individual traits, such as hair color, eye color, skin color, height, and even susceptibility to disease. Mutations create variations in protein-coding portions of genes, as well as the codons that act as 'switches,' controlling when and where a protein is made. Genetic variations can change populations over time. Most mutations are reversed or repaired by fixing mismatched nucleotides and splicing broken DNA strands.

MATERIALS

- safety goggles
- beads (blue, green, purple, yellow)
- chenille stems
- pencils, colored (blue, green, purple, yellow)

SAFETY INFORMATION

- Wear safety goggles during the setup, hands-on, and takedown segments of the activity.
- Immediately pick up any dropped items on the floor.
- Wash your hands with soap and water immediately after completing this activity.

CARRY OUT THE INVESTIGATION

1. Use the codon chart to translate the following mRNA sequence into amino acids:
   AUG UUU CUU AUU ACG UAU UCU AAA GUU UGG AGU AGC CAU GAG CAA UGA

FIGURE 11: A codon wheel chart and corresponding amino acids

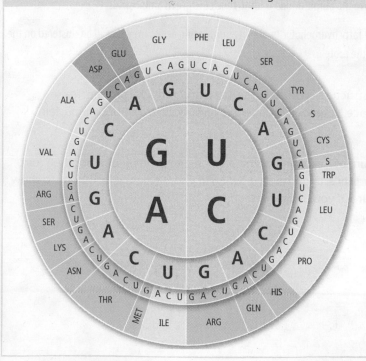

ALA = Alanine	LYS = Lysine
ARG = Arginine	MET = Methionine
ASN = Asparagine	PHE = Phenylalanine
ASP = Aspartic acid	PRO = Proline
CYS = Cysteine	S = Stop
GLN = Glutamine	SER = Serine
GLU = Glutamic acid	THR = Threonine
GLY = Glycine	TRP = Tryptophan
HIS = Histidine	TYR = Tyrosine
ILE = Isoleucine	VAL = Valine
LEU = Leucine	

2. Match each amino acid to the color shown in the codon chart. Build a model of a polypeptide by placing beads of the correct colors on a chenille stick. Use the same color bead that corresponds to the codon chart. When you reach the stop codon, do not place any more beads on the chenille stick.

3. Proteins fold into specific shapes that match their function. Use the following folding instructions to fold your polypeptide into a protein:

   a. Twist one-half of your protein model around a pencil to make a spiral. This spiral region is called an alpha helix.

   b. Bend the other half of your protein molecule into a zigzag shape by making a bend in the opposite direction at each bead. This zigzag region is called a beta-pleated sheet.

   c. The alpha helix and beta-pleated sheet represent the secondary structure of a protein.

4. Make a drawing in your Evidence Notebook modeling the secondary structure of your protein. Label the alpha helix region and the beta-pleated sheet region on your drawing.

5. Twist your protein into a 3D shape according to these protein folding rules:

Protein Folding Rules	
Amino Acid Bead Color	Properties and Guidelines
Blue	These are hydrophilic (water-loving) amino acids. They should be clustered on the outside of the protein.
Green	These are positively charged amino acids that are attracted to negatively charged amino acids. Move the green amino acids to touch the purple amino acids.
Purple	These are negatively charged amino acids that are attracted to positively charged amino acids. Move the purple amino acids to touch the green amino acids.
Yellow	These are fatty hydrophobic (water-fearing) amino acids. They should be clustered on the inside of the protein.

6. The resulting twisted structure is called the tertiary structure of a protein. Make a drawing in your Evidence Notebook to show the tertiary structure of your protein model.

7. The quaternary structure of a protein is formed when one protein joins another. Join your protein with a partner's, and make a drawing in your Evidence Notebook to show the quaternary structure of your protein model.

ANALYZE

1. Determine a point mutation that would change the amino acid sequence of your protein. List the new mRNA codon and amino acid resulting from the point mutation in the space provided. Then, replace the bead that would change in your protein model, and try re-folding your protein.

_____

_____

_____

_____

_____

2. Did this mutation change the structure of the protein? If so, how?

_____

_____

_____

_____

_____

3. How might this change in structure affect the protein's function?

_____

_____

_____

_____

_____

4. If a new nucleotide were inserted into the first codon of the DNA sequence, how would this change the structure of the resulting protein? Use evidence and examples to explain your answer.

_____

_____

_____

_____

_____

Evidence Notebook How well did this process model protein synthesis? How could you improve this model to obtain more accurate results?

Transcription

Before a protein is made, a temporary copy of the DNA code is needed. This first stage of protein synthesis is called transcription. Transcription is the process of copying a sequence of DNA to produce a complementary strand of RNA. In eukaryotes, transcription occurs in the cell's nucleus.

> **Collaborate** Transcribe means "to write". With a partner, discuss why we would use the word *transcribe* to describe the process of making a complementary RNA sequence from a DNA template.

Steps of Transcription

Transcription is the first step in building a protein. During transcription, a gene is transcribed into an RNA message. Transcription is catalyzed by RNA polymerases, which are enzymes that bond nucleotides together in a chain to make a new RNA molecule.

FIGURE 12: In transcription, enzymes use the DNA template to make a complementary strand of RNA.　**Explore Online** ▶

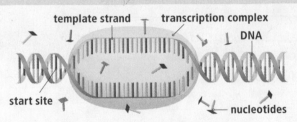

template strand　transcription complex
DNA
start site
nucleotides

1 In eukaryotic cells, a large transcription initiation complex consisting of RNA polymerase and other proteins assembles on the DNA strand and begins to unwind a segment of the DNA molecule. The complex assembles at a specific sequence of nucleotides along the DNA molecule called a promoter.

RNA polymerase moves along the DNA

2 RNA polymerase, using one strand of DNA as a template, strings together a complementary strand of RNA nucleotides. RNA base pairing follows the same rules as DNA base pairing, except that uracil, not thymine, pairs with adenine. So, U pairs with A, and G pairs with C. The growing RNA strand hangs freely as it is transcribed, and the DNA helix zips back together.

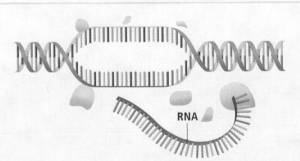

RNA

3 Transcription continues until an entire gene has been converted to RNA. The RNA strand detaches completely from the DNA.

> **Structure and Function** During transcription, the structure of the DNA molecule determines the structure of the mRNA molecule. DNA serves as the template, and the composition of this nucleic acid is complementary to the composition of mRNA, a single-stranded nucleic acid that serves as the code from which the protein is made. This is the central dogma.

Transcription can produce thousands of copies of mRNA, depending on the cell's needs. Transcription enables a cell to adjust to changing demands by making a single-stranded complement of only a segment of DNA and only when that particular segment is needed. Many RNA molecules can be transcribed from a single gene at the same time to help produce more protein. Once RNA polymerase has transcribed one portion of a gene and has moved on, another RNA polymerase can attach itself to the beginning of the gene and start the transcription process again. This process can occur over and over again.

FIGURE 13: Many RNA strands can be transcribed from a single DNA strand.

EXPLAIN How is the ability to produce multiple transcripts simultaneously related to the maintenance of homeostasis in the cell? Select all correct answers.

☐ **a.** It allows many copies of an RNA strand to be transcribed from a single gene.

☐ **b.** It allows the cell to generate more ATP to power cell processes.

☐ **c.** Limiting the number of RNA molecules maintains stable conditions in the cell.

☐ **d.** It allows for the rapid production of mRNA transcripts when needed.

Transcription produces three main types of RNA molecules, each with a unique function. Only mRNA actually codes for proteins, but the others play roles in protein synthesis. Once mRNA is bound to ribosomal RNA (rRNA) in a ribosome, it is read by transfer RNA (tRNA) molecules that carry amino acids to bind to the developing protein.

FIGURE 14: Transcription produces three main types of RNA.

Type of RNA	mRNA	rRNA	tRNA
Model		ribosome: large subunit, binding sites, small subunit	amino acid, tRNA, anticodon
Function	An intermediate message that is translated to form a protein.	Forms subunits of ribosomes, which are the cell's protein factories.	Carries, or "transfers," amino acids to the ribosomes to help make the growing protein.

APPLY Model transcription by matching each part of the DNA sequence to its complementary mRNA sequence.

DNA sequence	TCA	GGT	ACG	CTT
mRNA	_____	_____	_____	_____

The next main stage of protein synthesis, translation, can begin once transcription is complete. However, the RNA strand must be processed before it can exit the nucleus in eukaryotes. This step occurs during, or just after, transcription.

 Evidence Notebook Transcription and DNA replication are often compared to one another, because they have many similarities. However, they do not have the same functions. Make a graphic organizer to compare and contrast DNA replication and transcription in terms of their functions, inputs, and final products.

Translation

To complete protein synthesis, the language of mRNA must be translated into the language of proteins. How does a language consisting of only four characters translate into a language of 20 amino acids? Just as letters are strung together in the English language to make words, nucleotides are strung together to code for amino acids.

 Collaborate In everyday language, translation means to express words in another language. With a partner, write a message that would need to be translated.

So far, you have learned that transcription uses DNA to produce a complementary strand of RNA. In eukaryotes, this stage of protein synthesis occurs in the nucleus. Once the RNA is processed and leaves the nucleus through pores, it enters the cytoplasm. This is where the process of translation decodes the mRNA to produce a protein. The translation occurs in the cytoplasm of both prokaryotic and eukaryotic cells.

Ribosomes

Once it is in the cytoplasm, the mRNA binds to organelles called ribosomes, which are made of ribosomal RNA (rRNA) and proteins. In plant and animal cells, ribosomes may be found floating free in the cytoplasm of the cell. They may also be attached to an organelle called the rough endoplasmic reticulum (rough ER). As proteins are being made, they enter the rough ER. Once inside, the proteins fold into their three-dimensional shapes, and some are modified by the addition of carbohydrate chains.

Animal Cell

FIGURE 15: The rough endoplasmic reticulum, ribosomes, Golgi apparatus, and vesicles are involved in translation.

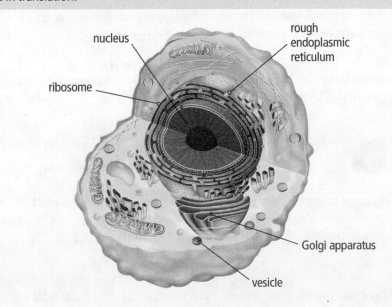

From the ER, proteins generally move to the Golgi apparatus to be processed, sorted, and delivered. Some packaged proteins are stored within the Golgi apparatus for later use. Others are transported to different organelles within the cell. Still others are carried to the membrane, where the vesicles carrying the proteins merge with the cell membrane, releasing the protein outside the cell.

INFER Use the correct terms to complete the statement about transcription.

| Golgi apparatus | nucleus | ribosomes | rough ER |

During transcription, a strand of mRNA is made based on the DNA template in

the _____. The mRNA then leaves the nucleus and binds to

_____ found on the _____ or in the

cytoplasm. Ribosomes translate the mRNA message into proteins, which may enter

the ER to be modified. Proteins move to the _____ to be

processed and are then delivered to other locations in the cell or stored for later use.

> **Evidence Notebook** Draw a flow chart to show the sequence of RNA and proteins through the cell during protein synthesis.

Steps of Translation

Recall that three types of RNA are involved in the process of protein synthesis. Ribosomes, which contain rRNA, have a large and small subunit that fit together and pull the mRNA strand through as translation proceeds. The small subunit holds onto the mRNA strand, and the large subunit holds onto the growing protein.

Transfer RNA (tRNA) acts as a sort of translator between mRNA and amino acids. One end of the tRNA molecule is attached to a specific amino acid. The other end of the tRNA molecule, called the anticodon, recognizes a specific codon on the mRNA molecule. An anticodon is a set of three nucleotides that is complementary to an mRNA codon. For example, the anticodon CCC pairs with the mRNA codon GGG.

EXPLAIN Use the model of the steps of translation in Figure 16 to complete this statement about how the different types of RNA interact during protein synthesis.

| anticodons | codons | mRNA | tRNA |

The ribosome binds to a strand of _____. This nucleic acid has

three-nucleotide codes called _____. The three-letter codes

are complementary to _____ on _____

molecules. Each of these molecules brings with it an amino acid, which will become

part of the growing polypeptide.

FIGURE 16: Translation converts an mRNA transcript into a polypeptide to build a protein.

Explore Online ▶

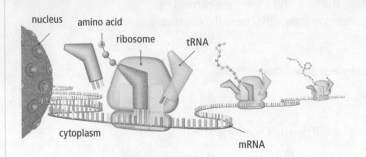

nucleus
amino acid
ribosome
tRNA
cytoplasm
mRNA

1 Before translation begins, a small ribosomal subunit binds to an mRNA strand in the cytoplasm. Then a tRNA with methionine attached binds to the AUG start codon. This binding signals a large ribosomal subunit to join. The ribosome pulls the mRNA strand through itself one codon at a time. The tRNA acts as a translator between mRNA and amino acids.

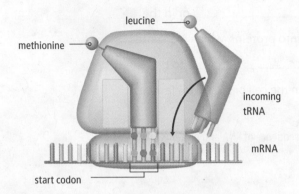

leucine
methionine
incoming tRNA
mRNA
start codon

2 The exposed codon in the first site attracts a complementary tRNA molecule carrying an amino acid. The tRNA pairs with the mRNA codon, bringing it very close to the other tRNA molecule.

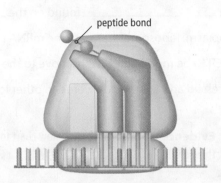

peptide bond

3 The ribosome catalyzes (helps form) a peptide bond between the two amino acids and breaks the bond between the tRNA and its amino acid.

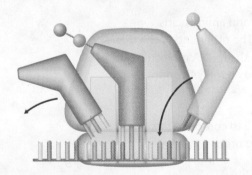

4 The ribosome pulls the mRNA strand along the length of one codon. The first tRNA is shifted into the exit site, where it leaves the ribosome and returns to the cytoplasm to pick up another amino acid. The first site is empty again, exposing the next mRNA codon.

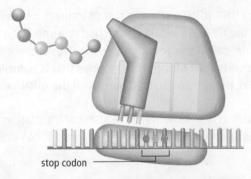

stop codon

5 The ribosome continues to translate the mRNA strand, attaching new amino acids to the growing protein, until it reaches a stop codon. Then the ribosome lets go of the new protein and breaks apart.

 Evidence Notebook Summarize what you have learned so far to explain how the "language" of DNA is translated into the "language" of proteins. Construct a graphic organizer to compare the process of transcription and translation to a computer receiving information from a user.

Language Arts

Loss-of-function Mutations

Gene mutations are sometimes categorized by the effects they have on proteins. Gain-of-function mutations occur when the mutation causes the protein to have a new or enhanced function. Loss-of-function mutations limit the function of a protein or prohibits the protein from forming. Loss-of-function mutations occur in people with cystic fibrosis.

Cystic fibrosis is an inherited disease that affects the respiratory and digestive systems. Airways and some organs are naturally lined and protected by a layer of mucus. Cystic fibrosis causes abnormal, sticky mucus secretions to form. Symptoms include coughing, wheezing, and digestive problems. When untreated, the most common cause of death for a person with cystic fibrosis is a fatal lung infection.

The Cystic Fibrosis Transmembrane Conductance Regulator (*CFTR*) gene codes for the protein that regulates mucus secretion in the respiratory, reproductive, and digestive systems. In Figure 17a, a normal version of the *CFTR* gene produces a protein that acts as a channel to move chloride ions across the cell membrane in mucus-producing cells. Chloride ions move across the cell membrane and accumulate on the outside of the cell, making an ionic gradient. This causes water to move outside of the cell, which maintains mucus of a normal consistency.

A healthy, watery mucus layer traps particulates and bacteria. The cilia of the cell are then free to move and sweep away this foreign matter before they can harm the cell.

In cystic fibrosis, a mutated *CFTR* gene results in a different amino acid sequence resulting in a mutated protein that disrupts the chloride channels, shown in Figure 17b. The irregular protein cannot transport chloride ions across the cell membrane. A higher concentration of chloride and sodium ions form inside the cell compared to outside of the cell. This causes water to move into the cell, drying out the mucus layer. The thick, sticky mucus prevents the cilia from moving and clearing debris. The increased presence of debris and pathogens causes increased infections in individuals with cystic fibrosis.

> **Language Arts Connection** Write an argument about the role of genetic mutations in the genetic variation of organisms, using cystic fibrosis as an example. Your argument should explain how the mutation affects protein structure, and how this protein structure relates to the expression of the trait. Present your findings in a short paper. Follow your teacher's instructions for the formatting of your paper and submit a list of resources.

FIGURE 17: Cystic fibrosis is caused by a mutated CFTR protein.

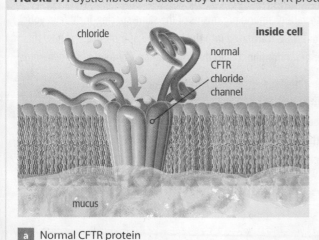

a Normal CFTR protein

b Mutated CFTR protein

MAKING SYNTHETIC CELLS   EXPLORING PROTEIN CRYSTALLIZATION   RETROVIRUSES   Go online to choose one of these other paths.

Lesson Self-Check

CAN YOU EXPLAIN IT?

FIGURE 18: Computer code is the instruction that computers use to perform tasks. Similarly, DNA is the genetic code that cells use to build proteins.

You have explored the cellular process that produces proteins from DNA code. In many ways it is similar to the way that humans translate our language into a language that computers can understand. The binary code that computers understand is made up of zeros and ones, sometimes called machine code. However, computer programmers do not typically write programs directly in this binary code. Instead, they use programming languages that act as translators between the programmer and the computer.

 Evidence Notebook Refer to your notes in your Evidence Notebook to explain how the DNA code can produce so much variety among organisms of the same species. Include in your discussion how the language of DNA is translated into the language of proteins, and how this process compares to computer programming. Using this information, complete the following:

1. Make a claim explaining how the four-letter DNA language encodes instructions for making thousands of different proteins.
2. What evidence supports your claim? For example, which molecules act as the translators in the process of protein synthesis?
3. How is the process of protein synthesis similar to the process of programming a computer? How is it different?

Check Your Understanding

1. Which of the following is evidence that would support the claim that transcription of DNA has been completed?
   - ○ **a.** A disposable copy of the DNA has been produced.
   - ○ **b.** A temporary copy of RNA from the DNA has been produced.
   - ○ **c.** An exact, permanent copy of the DNA has been produced.
   - ○ **d.** A permanent copy of RNA that replaces DNA has been produced.

2. A student is planning to draw a model of DNA and RNA. Which of the following should the student include in the DNA model and *not* the RNA model?
   - ○ **a.** a double-helix
   - ○ **b.** the nucleotide uracil
   - ○ **c.** the sugar ribose
   - ○ **d.** a phosphate group

3. Which statement correctly compares the impact of frameshift mutations and point mutations on polypeptides?
   - ○ **a.** Point mutations have a greater impact because they always change the resulting protein.
   - ○ **b.** Frameshift mutations have a greater impact because they always substitute the first nucleotide in a codon.
   - ○ **c.** Frameshift mutations have a greater impact because they usually shift the entire sequence following them.
   - ○ **d.** Point mutations have a greater impact because they always cause a change in the amino acid sequence.

4. Which flow chart best summarizes the process of protein synthesis?
   - ○ **a.** rRNA ⟶ DNA ⟶ mRNA
   - ○ **b.** Protein ⟶ mRNA ⟶ DNA
   - ○ **c.** mRNA ⟶ DNA ⟶ protein
   - ○ **d.** DNA ⟶ mRNA ⟶ protein

5. Place the stages in the proper order to describe the process of transcription.
   - _____ **a.** The complex of RNA polymerase and proteins breaks apart.
   - _____ **b.** RNA polymerase uses the DNA strand as a template to synthesize a complementary strand of RNA.
   - _____ **c.** The DNA is unwound and a specific sequence of nucleotides is sequenced along the promoter.
   - _____ **d.** A large complex consisting of RNA polymerase and other proteins assembles on the DNA strand.
   - _____ **e.** The RNA strand grows until an entire gene has been transcribed.

6. Use the correct terms to complete the statement.

   | amino acids | DNA | polypeptide | ribosomes |

   Protein synthesis is made up of two stages.

   Transcription occurs within the nucleus and uses

   the _____ template to make

   a complimentary strand of mRNA. This molecule

   leaves the nucleus and enters the cell's cytoplasm

   where _____ read along

   the strand of nucleotides. Transfer RNA molecules

   bearing _____ enter the

   ribosome. The subunits are linked together to

   make a _____, which is

   modified to make the final protein.

CHECKPOINTS (continued)

7. Describe the different functions of mRNA, rRNA, and tRNA. How are their structures related to their functions?

_____

_____

_____

_____

_____

8. Explain how mutations can affect protein synthesis, and how that can affect the expression of a trait.

_____

_____

_____

_____

9. Robinow syndrome is a rare genetic condition, resulting in short limbs and structural abnormalities in the head, face, and vertebrae. Some cases are likely caused by a frameshift mutation. Explain how a frameshift mutation could cause the traits described, and identify two questions that could guide research.

_____

_____

_____

_____

_____

_____

MAKE YOUR OWN STUDY GUIDE

 In your Evidence Notebook, design a study guide that supports the main idea from this lesson:

Protein synthesis consists of two stages. In the first stage, the DNA code is transcribed to make an mRNA strand. The mRNA strand is then translated into a sequence of amino acids.

Remember to include the following information in your study guide:

- Use examples that model main ideas.
- Record explanations for the phenomena you investigated.
- Use evidence to support your explanations. Your support can include drawings, data, graphs, laboratory conclusions, and other evidence recorded throughout the lesson.

Consider how models of protein synthesis can be used to determine the inputs and outputs at each step, as well as where each step of the process occurs in the cell.

Gene Expression and Regulation

The human genome has 3 billion base pairs. The fruit fly genome has 165 million.

CAN YOU EXPLAIN IT?

If you've ever left fruit on the counter for a while, you've probably seen a fruit fly. Fruit flies are small insects, and yet they have thousands of genes. And even though fruit flies and humans could not seem less alike, they actually share some of the same genes.

Homeobox genes are an example of a group of genes shared by fruit flies, humans, and most other organisms. Most animals share a subset of homeobox genes called *Hox* genes. This subset of genes is important in embryo development. Mutations in the *Hox* genes can cause developmental disorders. In the mutant fly shown in Figure 1b, legs have developed where antennae should be.

PREDICT How might changes in genes be responsible for mutations, such as the mutation that causes legs to grow in place of antennae in a fruit fly?

_____

_____

_____

_____

_____

 Evidence Notebook As you explore this lesson, gather evidence for how gene expression is regulated in cells and how this knowledge can be used to manipulate genes for scientific endeavors.

FIGURE 1: Fruit fly development

a Wild-type fruit fly (colored SEM)

b Mutant fruit fly (colored SEM)

Regulating Gene Expression

Most of the cells that make up your body have the same DNA. This is true of the muscle cells that help your heart pump blood, the skin cells on your arm, and most other cells in your body. If all of these cells have the same DNA, how can they differ so widely in structure and function?

EXPLAIN How are genes, proteins, and cell processes related?

○ **a.** Genes code for proteins, which carry out the work of the cell.

○ **b.** Proteins code for genes, which carry out the work of the cell.

○ **c.** Both genes and proteins control cell processes, regardless of type of cell.

○ **d.** Either genes or proteins control the cell, depending on the type of cell.

Gene Expression

Genes may or may not be expressed within a cell. Gene expression is the process by which the nucleotide sequence of a gene is transcribed to make an mRNA molecule. The mRNA can break down, or undergo translation to make a protein. Cells use protein synthesis to respond to particular needs and to react to changes in their environment.

 Collaborate With a partner, discuss the following questions: What does the term *expression* mean in everyday language? How does the meaning of this word relate to the concept of gene expression?

FIGURE 2: The instructions in DNA can be used to make a functional product, such as a protein.

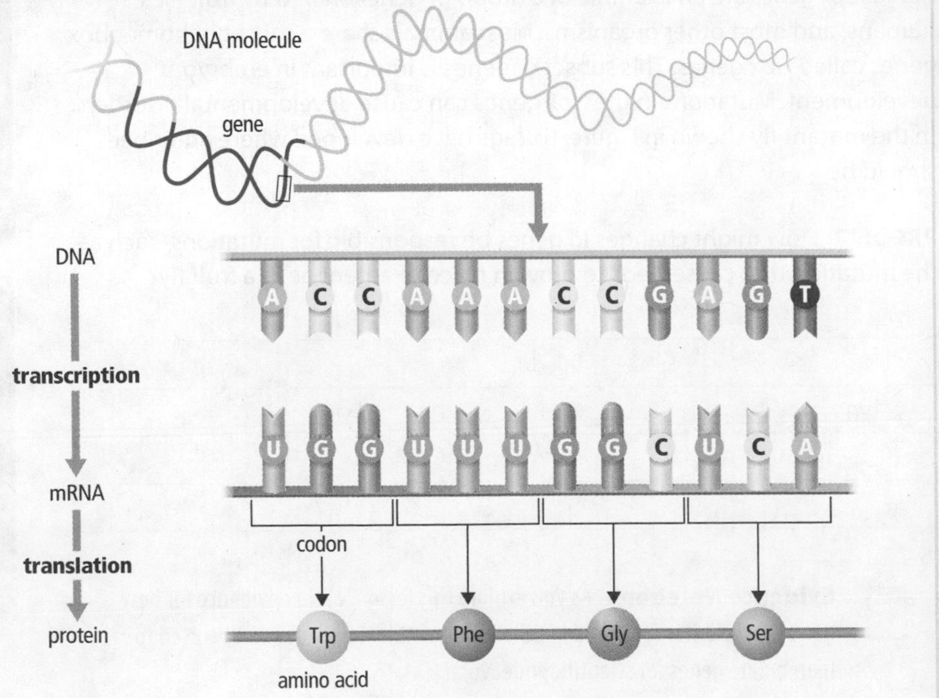

DNA molecule

gene

DNA

A C C A A A C C G A G T

transcription

U G G U U U G G C U C A

mRNA

codon

translation

protein

Trp   Phe   Gly   Ser

amino acid

Information always flows in one direction, from DNA to RNA to proteins. There are multiple steps along the way where gene expression and protein synthesis can be regulated, or controlled. Prokaryotic cells and eukaryotic cells regulate these processes differently.

Recall that prokaryotes are single-celled organisms such as bacteria. A prokaryotic cell does not have a nucleus or any other membrane-bound organelles. The DNA in a prokaryotic cell exists in a single chromosome in the center of the cell. Some prokaryotes also carry a smaller, circular segment of DNA. The DNA in a prokaryote carries far fewer genes than the DNA in a eukaryotic organism.

Eukaryotes range from single-celled amoebas and algae to multicellular orchids and antelopes. Most cells in a eukaryote have a nucleus and other membrane-bound organelles. The DNA in a eukaryotic cell is located on chromosomes within the nucleus. The number of chromosomes depends on each species. Humans have 46 chromosomes in each body cell. Dogs have 78.

In eukaryotes, regulation of gene expression and protein synthesis occurs at many different steps. In contrast, the ability of prokaryotes to regulate these processes is much simpler.

Gene Expression

FIGURE 3: In prokaryotic cells, transcription and translation both occur in the cytoplasm at about the same time. In eukaryotic cells, where DNA is located inside the nucleus, these processes are separated both in location and time.

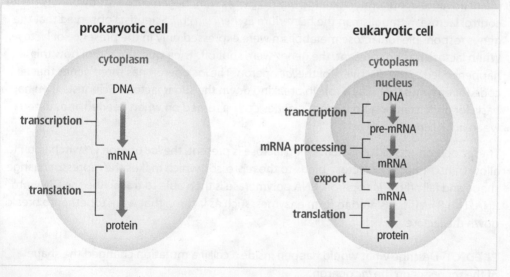

Structure and Function Write an explanation for how differences in cell structure are related to the differences in the ways gene expression and protein synthesis are regulated in prokaryotic and eukaryotic cells.

_____

_____

_____

_____

_____

Gene Regulation in Prokaryotes

Explore Online ▶

Hands-On Activity

Modeling Prokaryotic Operons Build a model of the *lac* operon. Then use your model to show how gene expression is regulated in prokaryotes.

Because transcription and translation occur at the same time in prokaryotic cells, gene expression in these cells is mainly regulated at the start of transcription. Prokaryotic cells control gene expression using operons to turn genes "on" or "off" during transcription. An *operon* is a region of DNA that includes a promoter, an operator, and one or more structural genes that code for all the proteins needed to do a specific task. Prokaryotes have much less DNA than eukaryotes, and their genes tend to be organized into operons.

ANALYZE What is the benefit of turning genes on and off? Select all correct answers.

☐ **a.** The cell needs to spend less energy when replicating DNA for cell division.

☐ **b.** The cell needs to use less energy and fewer resources on protein synthesis.

☐ **c.** The cell can alter the number of genes it carries to fit its role in the organism.

☐ **d.** The cell can take on specialized structures and functions.

The *promoter* is a segment of DNA that helps the enzyme RNA polymerase locate the starting point for transcription. The DNA segment that actually turns genes on or off is the *operator*. It interacts with proteins that increase the rate of transcription or block transcription from occurring.

The ability of a cell to switch certain genes on or off was first discovered in 1961. This major advance in our understanding of how genes work began with a study of how genes control lactose metabolism in the bacterium *Escherichia coli*. Scientists observed that the genes responsible for lactose metabolism were expressed only in the presence of lactose. When lactose was not present, the genes were shut off. Their questioning of how this happened led to the discovery of the *lac* operon. The *lac* operon has three genes that all code for enzymes that play a role in breaking down the sugar lactose. Scientists then had a basis for understanding how specific genes can be turned on when needed and turned off when not needed.

The *lac* operon acts like a switch. When lactose is present, the *lac* operon is switched on to allow transcription. The lactose binds to the repressor, which makes the repressor change shape and fall off the *lac* operon. RNA polymerase is then able to transcribe the DNA into RNA. This RNA is translated to form enzymes, such as lactase, that work together to break down the lactose.

PREDICT Describe what would happen inside a cell if a mutation changed the shape of the repressor on the *lac* operon.

_____

_____

_____

_____

_____

_____

When lactose is absent, the *lac* operon is switched off to prevent transcription of the *lac* genes, thus saving the cell's resources. Bacteria have a protein that can bind specifically to the operator. When lactose is absent, the protein binds to the operator, which blocks RNA polymerase from transcribing the genes. Because the protein blocks—or represses—transcription, it is called a repressor protein.

 Language Arts Connection Make an informational guide explaining how the *lac* operon helps prokaryotes to respond to changes in their environment. In your guide, explain the functions of the gene, promoter, operator, repressor, and RNA polymerase.

FIGURE 4: Lactose metabolism in *E. coli* is controlled by the *lac* operon. This is an example of gene regulation in prokaryotes.

Explore Online ▶

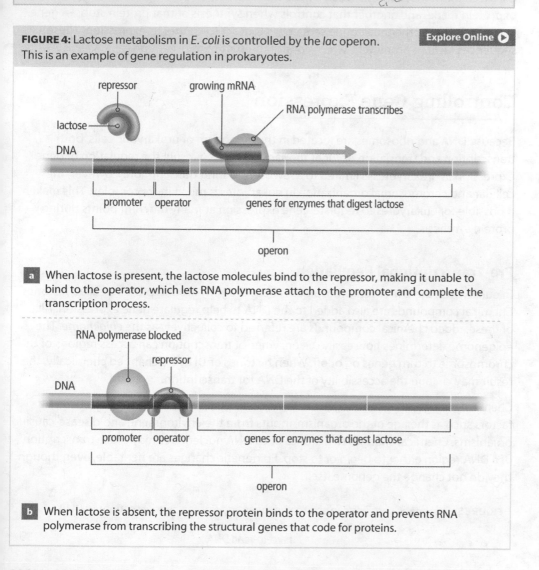

a When lactose is present, the lactose molecules bind to the repressor, making it unable to bind to the operator, which lets RNA polymerase attach to the promoter and complete the transcription process.

b When lactose is absent, the repressor protein binds to the operator and prevents RNA polymerase from transcribing the structural genes that code for proteins.

APPLY How does a bacterial cell benefit by using the *lac* operon to control transcription?

○ **a.** The cell does not waste energy making enzymes when lactose is not present.

○ **b.** The cell is able to maintain a constant level of lactase enzyme at all times.

○ **c.** The cell is able to maximize the amount of lactose that it uses for energy.

○ **d.** The cell is able to minimize the amount of lactose that it uses for energy.

 Evidence Notebook How is gene regulation generally related to gene expression and transcription in prokaryotes and other organisms?

Gene Regulation in Eukaryotes

Gene regulation is complex for a reason: the complexity ensures that the correct gene is expressed in the correct cell at the correct time. Cells rely on external information as well as information encoded in their DNA to regulate protein synthesis. In eukaryotes, there is a mechanism that controls when a gene is expressed, one that controls the amount of protein made, and another that controls when synthesis of that protein stops. A gene may also include other nucleotide sequences that act to control its expression. These sequences include promoters, which control the start of transcription.

Controlling Gene Expression

Because DNA and ribosomes are located in the cytoplasm of prokaryotic cells, both transcription and translation occur at the same time. As a result, the regulation of gene expression in prokaryotes is limited to a few steps during transcription. However, the cellular and chromosomal organization in eukaryotes is much more complex. This makes it possible for eukaryotes to regulate gene expression at many different points during protein synthesis.

Pre-Transcriptional Regulation

In eukaryotes, the DNA in chromosomes is bound tightly around proteins called histones. Chemical compounds are also added to the DNA to help regulate gene expression. All of these added chemical compounds are referred to collectively as the *epigenome*. The epigenome determines how easily the enzymes of transcription can access regions of the chromosome to turn genes on or off. When histones or DNA are changed chemically, the result may change the accessibility of the DNA for transcription.

Chemical changes that control gene activity, or epigenetic changes, can be caused by factors such as the age of the organism, inputs from the environment, and disease-causing organisms. Chemical changes to histones or to DNA nucleotides may cause transcription of a DNA region either to begin or to stop. Epigenetic changes are heritable, even though they do not change the genome itself.

FIGURE 5: Epigenetic changes can change histones and tighten certain sections of DNA.

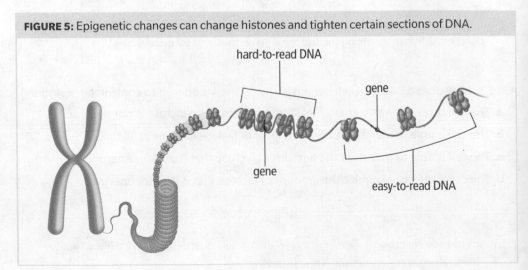

hard-to-read DNA

gene

gene

easy-to-read DNA

EXPLAIN Complete the statement by selecting the correct terms.

DNA that is wrapped tightly around histones is more | less | equally likely to be transcribed. DNA that is wrapped loosely around histones is more | less | equally likely to be transcribed. If DNA is not transcribed, a(n) DNA | RNA | protein molecule is not produced and a lipid | carbohydrate | protein cannot be made.

PREDICT What would happen to a multicellular organism if every gene were expressed in every cell all the time?

_____

_____

_____

Transcriptional Regulation

Recall that a promoter is a segment of DNA that helps RNA polymerase recognize the start site of a gene. In eukaryotic cells, each gene is controlled by a unique combination of promoters and other regulatory sequences. Most promoter sequences are unique to the gene, but some are repeated among many genes in many organisms. For example, most eukaryotic cells use a seven-nucleotide promoter with the sequence TATAAAA, called the TATA box.

Eukaryotic cells also have other types of promoters that are more specific to an individual gene. DNA sequences called *enhancers* speed up the transcription of a gene, while sequences called *silencers* act to slow down transcription. Transcription factors are proteins that bind to DNA sequences and control gene expression. Transcription factors may bind to a promoter, an enhancer, or other sections of DNA near a gene. When the correct transcription factors are present, RNA polymerase recognizes the start site of the gene, and transcription begins.

FIGURE 6: In eukaryotes, transcription factors bind to DNA sequences near a gene to help RNA polymerase recognize the start of the gene.

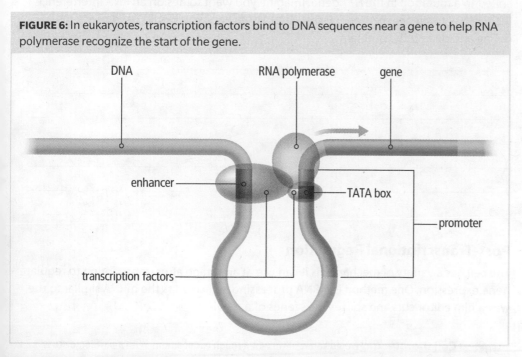

 Evidence Notebook Transcription factors occur in different combinations in different types of cells. How does this allow for variety in cell types?

Using RNA Interference to Fight Disease

FIGURE 7: Purple petunia flowers

In the early 1990s, scientists working on manipulating color in petunia plants saw something that was hard to explain. In an effort to increase the intensity of flower color, the scientists genetically modified petunia plants to overexpress the flower pigmentation gene for chalcone synthase (CHS), a plant enzyme. Some of the resulting flowers did indeed have the desired intense purple petals—but not all of them. Some flowers had purple and white petals, while others had completely white petals. Further investigation led to the discovery that both the introduced and naturally occurring forms of CHS had been turned off, or silenced, in some of these plants.

When the gene for the intense color was introduced to the plant, the cells used RNA interference to deactivate the gene. Small segments of double-stranded RNA began a series of reactions that degraded the mRNA molecules. RNA interference does not normally occur in healthy cells, but cells may use it to fight off infections or the effects of tissue damage. The study of RNA interference may lead to new treatments for a variety of diseases caused by harmful genes.

ASK Huntington's disease is an inherited disorder that affects the nervous system, resulting in loss of coordination and declining brain function. This disease has been linked to a mutation in the *HTT* gene. Imagine you want to design an RNA interference technology to silence this gene. Make a list of questions you would need to ask to define and delimit the problem.

_____

_____

_____

_____

_____

_____

Post-Transcriptional Regulation

The cell has a variety of mechanisms it can use at any stage after transcription to regulate gene expression. One method is mRNA processing, which edits the mRNA similar to the way a film editor cuts and splices the scenes of a movie.

 Collaborate Why would you want to edit a rough cut of a film? With a partner, discuss how this analogy relates to the transcription of a gene.

The cell makes many changes to mRNA after transcription. A specialized nucleotide is added to the beginning of each mRNA molecule, forming a cap. This cap helps the mRNA strand bind to a ribosome and prevents the strand from being broken down too fast. The end of the mRNA molecule gets a string of nucleotides called the tail that improves stability and helps the mRNA molecule exit the nucleus. The "extra footage" in the mRNA molecule takes the form of nucleotide segments, called *introns*, that are not included in the final protein. The nucleotide segments that code for parts of the protein are called *exons*. Introns occur between exons. They are removed from an mRNA molecule before it leaves the nucleus. The cut ends of the exons are then joined together by a variety of molecular mechanisms.

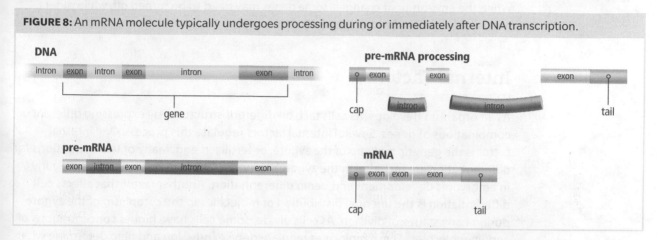

FIGURE 8: An mRNA molecule typically undergoes processing during or immediately after DNA transcription.

Introns are an example of what is called noncoding DNA, which are regions of DNA that do not code for proteins. Scientists are still determining the role of noncoding regions of the human genome. It is thought that noncoding regions may play a role in regulating gene expression and in chromosome pairing and condensation.

APPLY Which of the following affects the sequence of the protein that will be synthesized from an mRNA molecule?

○ **a.** introns

○ **b.** exons

○ **c.** cap

○ **d.** tail

Translational Regulation

Translation takes place after mRNA is moved into the cytoplasm, and it is this process that makes a protein from amino acids. In eukaryotes, gene expression may also be regulated by changes to the translation process. These changes depend mostly on the stability of the RNA molecule. For example, specific proteins help initiate the translation process. Changes in these proteins can prevent ribosomes from binding to mRNA, which slows or stops protein synthesis. These mechanisms let eukaryotic cells control protein production when conditions in the cell change rapidly.

 Evidence Notebook Make a graphic organizer to summarize the mechanisms that let eukaryotes such as fruit flies control gene expression at each stage of protein synthesis. How do these mechanisms compare to those in prokaryotes such as *E. coli* in terms of structure and function?

Factors That Influence Gene Expression

What determines whether a gene gets turned on or turned off? Factors both inside and outside cells can influence whether a gene is expressed. When an organism is developing, its cells take on different structures by expressing different sets of genes. Gene expression can also be responsible for changes that occur once the organism is fully developed. When the environment changes, some genes may need to be turned off, while others need to be expressed more frequently.

Internal Factors

As an organism develops, its cells take on different structures by expressing different combinations of genes. Several internal factors regulate this process. One internal factor is the genetic makeup of the zygote, or fertilized egg. Many of the instructions for differentiation are included in the zygote's genome. These genes are expressed early in embryonic development and begin differentiation. Another factor that affects cell differentiation is the unequal distribution of molecules in the cytoplasm of the zygote during early stages of division. As cells divide, some cells have higher concentrations of certain molecules. These molecules regulate gene expression and help determine what type of cell each one becomes.

Cells in a developing embryo also influence the cells around them by sending and receiving diffusible molecules that act as signals. Signals also come from proteins embedded in the cell membrane. Some of these proteins turn genes on and off to direct the developmental path of a cell. Still other molecules are enzymes that regulate gene expression by rapidly breaking down proteins made by translation.

FIGURE 9: During embryonic development, cell differentiation and growth form tissues and organs, such as the eye.

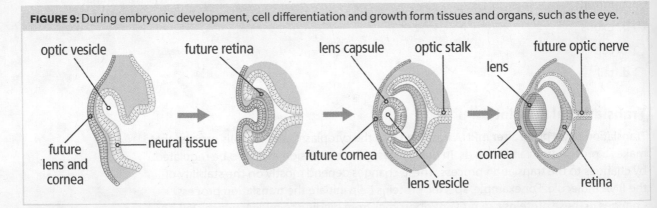

Structure and Function Make a claim for how the cells in an organism can take on different structures and functions even though they all have the same genetic material.

_____

_____

_____

_____

Epistasis

Polygenic traits are traits that are influenced by more than one gene. One polygenic trait is fur color in mice and other mammals. In mice, at least five different genes interact to produce the phenotype. Two genes give the mouse fur its general color. One gene affects the shading of the color, and another gene determines whether the fur will have spots. But the fifth gene involved in mouse fur color can overshadow all of the others. In cases such as this, one gene, called an epistatic gene, can interfere with the expression of other genes. Genes that modify the expression of another gene are said to show *epistasis*.

FIGURE 10: Albinism in this wallaby is caused by an epistatic gene that blocks the production of pigment.

 Cause and Effect

Genes for Eye Color

Another example of epistasis occurs in human eye color. Two genes thought to be responsible for eye color are called *OCA2* and *HERC2*, and both are located on chromosome 15. The dominant form of the *OCA2* gene codes for a protein involved in storing pigment in the iris. This protein helps cells store melanin, the pigment that affects eye coloration. More of the protein leads to darker eyes, which may appear brown. Less of the protein leads to lighter eyes, which may appear blue. The expression of the *OCA2* gene, however, can be turned on or off by a mutation in another gene. This gene, called *HERC2*, can reduce the expression of *OCA2*, causing less melanin to be stored in the iris, resulting in blue eyes. Several other genes are known to contribute to eye color, including those that lead to green eyes.

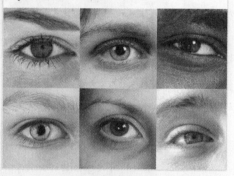

FIGURE 11: Several different genes interact to produce the range of human eye colors.

ANALYZE Use the information above to answer the following questions.

1. A child inherits a functional copy of the *OCA2* gene from his mother but a mutated version of this gene from his father. Predict his eye color. Explain your answer.

_____

_____

_____

2. Another child inherits two functional copies of the *OCA2* gene but also inherits two copies of the *HERC2* gene that suppress the expression of the *OCA2* genes. What would you predict about the color of this child's eyes? Explain your answer.

_____

_____

_____

External Factors

Factors in an organism's external environment can also affect gene expression. For example, a transcription factor called hypoxia-inducible factor, or HIF, is produced when oxygen concentrations are low. This transcription factor mediates important developmental processes such as blood vessel development. In tissues experiencing low oxygen concentrations, or hypoxia, HIF allows for the transcription of genes related to blood vessel development.

FIGURE 12: The Arctic fox expresses different colors of fur depending on the season.

Light and Temperature

Environmental factors, such as light and temperature, can affect gene expression. For example, an Arctic fox's fur color changes from white during the winter to gray-brown in the summer. This lets the fox better match its surroundings. This change in fur color is due to differences in melatonin secretion. In the winter, when day length is shorter, melatonin is secreted. The presence of melatonin prevents the pigment melanin from being produced and the fox's fur color becomes white. In the summer season, when daylight hours are longer, melatonin secretion is repressed. Melanin is then produced, and the fox's fur becomes gray-brown in color.

PREDICT Why might Arctic foxes that live closest to the Arctic Circle remain white longer than Arctic foxes that live at lower latitudes?

_____

_____

_____

Drugs and Chemicals

Pregnant women are strongly advised to avoid a variety of drugs and chemicals, including tobacco, alcohol, and many medications. These substances can disrupt the normal timing of gene expression in a developing fetus. For example, a drug called thalidomide was sometimes prescribed to treat morning sickness in the late 1950s and early 1960s. However, doctors discovered that it interfered with limb formation in the developing embryos. Children born to mothers who took this drug were often born with shortened and improperly formed limbs.

EXPLAIN Why is a developing fetus especially susceptible to chemicals that affect gene expression?

- ○ **a.** The genes of a fetus are especially diverse and complex.
- ○ **b.** The chemicals have no means of escaping the fetal body.
- ○ **c.** The fetus has a limited number of active genes at this time.
- ○ **d.** The chemicals can disrupt or block the expression of critical genes.

 Evidence Notebook What factors could influence the expression of *Hox* genes in different animals?

Isolating and Manipulating Genes

Huntington's disease causes nerve cells in the brain to break down. The onset of Huntington's often begins midlife, with no physical hints of the disease before symptoms arise. For those who have a parent with Huntington's disease, a Punnett square or pedigree analysis may provide a probability of having the disease but not a definitive diagnosis. For Huntington's and many other diseases, genetic material can be tested to determine whether a person has, or is a carrier of, a specific disease. Many people struggle with the decision to get tested and find out whether or not they may eventually get Huntington's disease.

EXPLAIN Would you undergo genetic tests to determine your likelihood of having certain diseases? Why or why not?

_____

_____

_____

Genetic Testing

Genetic testing is the analysis of a person's DNA to determine the risk of having or passing on a genetic disorder. Geneticists test for abnormalities in genetic material, from entire chromosomes down to individual genes. It is also possible to test for proteins that indicate a particular disease. Because proteins reflect the DNA patterns of genes, this is an indirect method of testing genetic material. Genetic testing is a powerful tool to screen for genetic disorders. However, not all diseases can be found through genetic testing.

APPLY Which disease would genetic testing be most likely to identify?

○ **a.** disease caused by improper diet or exercise

○ **b.** disease caused by bacteria or viruses

○ **c.** disease that is heritable

○ **d.** disease caused by environmental conditions

There are thousands of genetic tests available, each targeting a specific gene or genomic region. DNA microarrays are tools that allow scientists to study many genes, or their expression, at once. A microarray is a small chip that is dotted with the DNA sequences being studied. The genes are laid out in a grid pattern. Each block of the grid is so small that a one-square-inch chip can hold thousands of genes. Microarrays help researchers find which genes are expressed in which tissues and under what conditions.

FIGURE 13: DNA microarrays are used in genetic testing.

 Collaborate In a group, discuss the benefits, risks, and limitations of genetic testing. Why is it important to identify carriers of a genetic disease? How should genetic information be used and safeguarded?

Engineering Genes

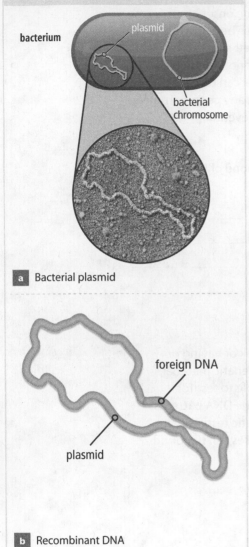

FIGURE 14: A bacterium that has been genetically modified has had foreign DNA inserted into its plasmid.

a Bacterial plasmid

b Recombinant DNA

Genetic engineering is the process of altering the genetic material of an organism. This means changing the organism's traits or introducing a new, desirable trait. Once a desirable trait has been successfully inserted into a genome, the new genome—and trait—can be passed on to future generations using cloning. An organism with one or more genes from another organism inserted into its genome is called a *transgenic* organism.

Genetic Engineering in Bacteria

A key element of genetic engineering is recombinant DNA technology, which combines genes from more than one organism. The organisms can be from the same species or from a different species. One method of producing recombinant DNA is to add foreign DNA to a plasmid, as shown in Figure 14. In bacteria, a plasmid is a small, circular segment of DNA that is separate from the bacterial chromosome. The foreign DNA that is inserted into the plasmid is then expressed by the bacterium. For example, when a gene from a bioluminescent jellyfish that codes for a green fluorescent protein is inserted into the plasmid of an *E. coli* bacterium, the *E. coli* will glow green under ultraviolet light.

Bacteria naturally recombine their DNA by absorbing plasmids from the environment or by exchanging plasmids between two bacteria. There can be multiple plasmids within a bacterium, and each one is able to replicate independently from the bacterial chromosome. Genetically modified bacteria are able to produce antibiotics, insulin, therapeutic proteins, and other types of proteins.

EXPLAIN Scientists commonly use bacteria in genetic engineering because bacteria

○ **a.** naturally make insulin.

○ **b.** infect viruses.

○ **c.** mutate quickly.

○ **d.** contain plasmids.

Consider the situation in which foreign DNA containing a gene for producing human insulin is inserted into a plasmid. Because plasmids self-replicate, numerous copies of a plasmid can exist within a bacterium. Plasmids are shared with daughter cells during binary fission, and bacteria divide at relatively fast speeds. A handful of bacteria with a plasmid coding for human insulin can quickly become a manufacturing center for the protein.

 Collaborate Genetically engineering bacteria to produce medicine can be less expensive than producing the medicine in a lab. This cost savings may be passed along to the consumer. Discuss the impacts less expensive medicines may have on society.

Editing Genes with CRISPR

Genetically engineering organisms requires the ability to cut DNA strands in specific places. Precisely cutting DNA can be difficult, time-consuming, and costly work. To solve this problem, genetic engineers needed to find an easier, faster, and cheaper method for precisely cutting DNA.

As it turns out, bacteria use a mechanism for precise DNA cuts called CRISPR, named for the clustered regularly interspaced palindromic repeats (CRISPRs) in bacterial DNA. These repeated sequences surround segments of viral DNA that bacteria have been exposed to. An enzyme uses the information in this viral library to target and cut viral DNA, preventing viral replication.

CRISPR is exciting for genetic engineers because it provides a very precise method for cutting DNA at a specific point. Cutting DNA easily and accurately simplifies the process of screening for genes that cause disease. It also improves the process of replacing defective genes with functional genes. This is one of the more difficult tasks in gene therapy, but one with the greatest potential benefits to humans. New ways to apply the CRISPR system to scientific problems are still being discovered. As with most genetic advances, the excitement surrounding the prospective benefits of CRISPR is tempered by the ethical concerns raised by such a powerful gene-editing tool.

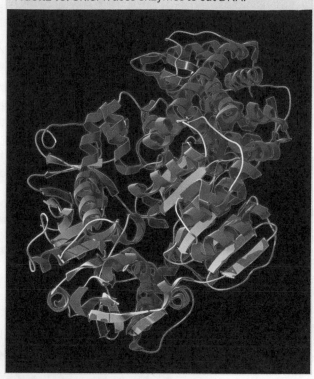

FIGURE 15: CRISPR uses enzymes to cut DNA.

PREDICT In what ways do you think CRISPR can advance the field of genetic engineering?

_____

_____

_____

_____

_____

EVALUATE What ethical concerns do you think people might have about CRISPR being used in gene therapy?

_____

_____

_____

_____

_____

Genetic Engineering in Plants

Genetic engineering has become a useful tool in agriculture. One of the most common methods for genetic modification in crop plants is the use of bacterial plasmids. A gene for a desired trait is inserted into a plasmid, and the plasmid is added to a plant cell. When the plant cell is infected, the recombinant DNA is inserted directly into the plant genome, modifying the plant. The plant expresses the bacterial DNA as well as its own.

EXPLAIN How does genetic engineering rely on a shared genetic code?

- **a.** Genes can only be inserted into organisms with the same DNA sequences.

- **b.** A gene's DNA sequence is translated into the same amino acid sequence across different organisms.

- **c.** Genetic engineering does not rely on a shared genetic code. This is why scientists insert new genes into organisms.

Genetically modified (GM) crops are becoming more widely used by farmers. If a farmer plants clones of GM crops, then he or she knows the desired trait is present in the entire population. However, this would also decrease genetic diversity, a necessary feature for a robust and flexible population.

Adoption of Genetically Engineered Crops in the United States, 1996–2016

FIGURE 16: This graph compares the usage of genetically engineered crops.

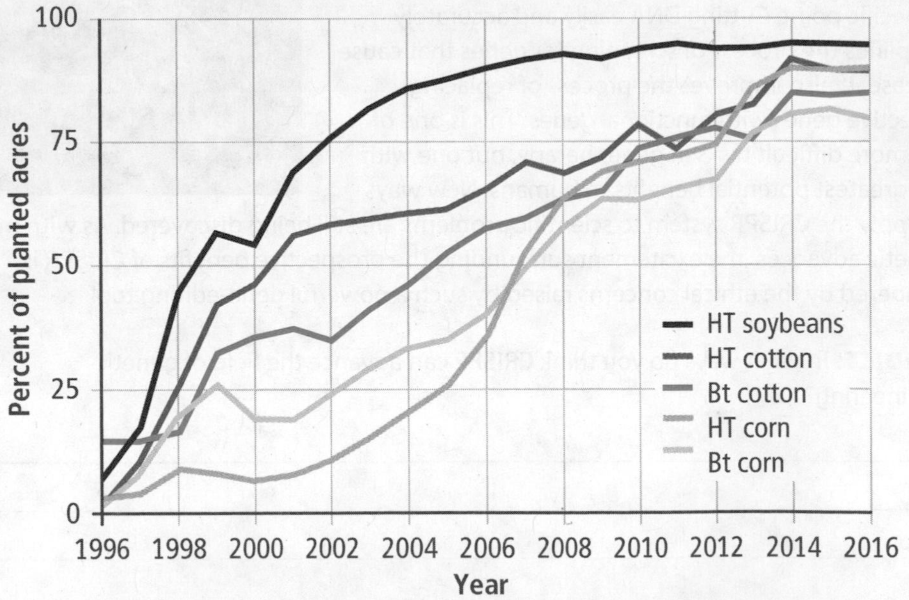

Sources: USDA, Economic Research Service using data from Fernandez-Comejo and McBride (2002) for the years 1996–99 and USDA, National Agricultural Statistics Service, *June Agricultural Survey* for the years 2000–16.

In the early 1990s, the FDA approved genetically engineered plants for human consumption in the United States. Insect resistance (Bt) and herbicide resistance (HT) are among the most common genetic modifications in crops, as shown Figure 16. Much of the genetically modified corn produced is fed to livestock, but GM corn does appear in the human food supply, in ingredients such as high-fructose corn syrup and corn starch. No long-term studies have found negative side effects from eating GM plants. However, some studies have identified negative environmental impacts from the use of these crops.

Genetic Engineering in Animals

Animal models of human diseases are valuable tools in medical research. These models allow scientists to study the disease process, from the genetic basis of a disease to how it responds to chemical substances. Through genetic engineering, scientists have been able to develop more and better models to study disease. They have also been able to develop organisms that can combat disease.

Consider the use of genetically modified mosquitoes to prevent the spread of disease. Mosquitoes act as vectors for many diseases. A vector can transmit disease-causing agents into another cell or organism. One species of mosquito, *Aedes aegypti,* is known to transmit the viruses for yellow fever, chikungunya, dengue, and Zika. Dengue is one of the leading causes of illness and death in tropical and subtropical regions. There is no vaccine for dengue, and the best way to minimize dengue cases is to minimize bites from infected mosquitoes.

To solve this problem, scientists engineered mosquitoes so that they require a manufactured drug to survive. When modified male mosquitoes are released into wild populations, they breed with wild females, passing the drug-dependency gene to their offspring. The affected males die soon after breeding, and, without access to the drug, any offspring die before maturity. Several field trials demonstrated that release of mosquitoes modified in this way can effectively control mosquito populations.

Explore Online

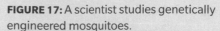

Hands-On Activity

Modeling Genetic Engineering
Simulate the techniques used by genetic engineers to modify genes in humans using recombinant DNA technology.

FIGURE 17: A scientist studies genetically engineered mosquitoes.

MODEL Draw a flow chart that demonstrates how genetically engineering mosquitoes can reduce the risk of illness in humans.

The possibility of unintended effects is a big constraint to this solution. The potential unintended effects of releasing genetically engineered mosquitoes into the wild are not fully understood. There may be tradeoffs for scientists and society between the risks of unintended effects and the benefits of smaller mosquito populations.

 Evidence Notebook Scientists learned about *Hox* genes by studying malformations in fruit flies. Why are fruit flies commonly used in genetic engineering experiments?

Engineering

Using Model Organisms to Study Human Diseases

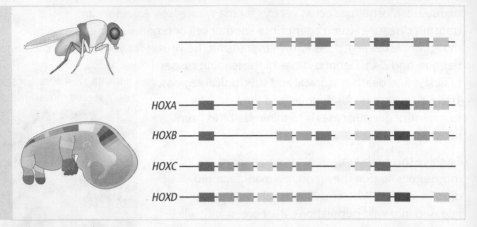

FIGURE 18: The genes that determine the body plan of a fruit fly are variations of the same genes that determine the body plan of a human, but they are expressed in different ways.

HOXA

HOXB

HOXC

HOXD

Geneticists work on the cutting edge of science and technology as they study genes, their functions, and their effects. They study not only how genes are inherited but also the role of genes in health, disease, and overall life span.

Genetically, humans and fruit flies are similar. They share many of the same genes and, in some cases, use them in the same way. Geneticists use the fruit fly as a model organism for studying genetics. The short lifespan and small size of the fruit fly, as well as the ease with which they can be grown and maintained in a lab, make them model organisms to study. Most importantly, their entire genome is contained on just four chromosomes. And, the genome of the fruit fly has now been completely mapped.

Some known human disease genes have a recognizable match in the genetic code of the fruit fly. Using a systems approach to research, scientists, including molecular biologists, geneticists, and mathematicians, can use the information gained from studying fruit flies to provide insight into these diseases and many others. This same approach can be used to determine the mechanisms responsible for a number of different birth defects. Studying fruit flies has led to many important discoveries. Observations of strange mutations in fruit flies, including legs where antennae should be or extra pairs of wings, led geneticists to the discovery of *Hox* genes.

Vertebrates, such as humans, also have *Hox* genes. However, they are a bit more complex. In a fly, each segment of its body expresses only one *Hox* gene. Therefore, a mutation to a single *Hox* gene directly affects the corresponding body segment. In vertebrates, however, each segment has at least two, and up to four, *Hox* genes involved in its development. So multiple *Hox* genes are responsible for the development of arms, hands, legs, feet, and other parts of a vertebrate's body. A mutation to any of these genes is likely to affect multiple parts of the developing vertebrate. However, the effects of the mutation are not likely to be as straightforward as the effects of a *Hox* gene mutation on a fruit fly.

Hox genes have a critical role in the regulation of cell differentiation. Some *Hox* genes also act as tumor suppressors, meaning they help control cell growth and prevent cells from growing or dividing too quickly.

Because we share common ancestry with other species, many other genes that humans have also exist in other organisms such as zebrafish and mice. This fact, along with their rapid life cycles, makes these organisms ideal models for the study of shared genes. Zebrafish have 70% of the same genes as humans, and they have bodies that are almost transparent as embryos. This feature allows for a better view of what is happening inside of their bodies. Zebrafish can also regenerate their spinal cords after injury, which makes them a promising model organism for studies on human spinal cord injuries.

FIGURE 19: Scientists often use model organisms such as zebrafish to learn more about human diseases.

Zebrafish have been used as a model organism for research on many human diseases, including muscle, kidney, heart, and nervous system disorders. Scientists use genetic manipulation techniques to induce mutations in the fish. By experimenting with mutant, or variant, forms of genes in this model organism, scientists can make predictions about how similar genes will function in humans. For example, a strain of mutant zebrafish called *breakdance* has been used for studies on arrhythmia, or abnormal heart rhythm, in humans.

In addition to sharing much of our genetic material, zebrafish also have eyes that are similar to the human eye in many ways. Several zebrafish mutants have been identified that display eye defects and visual impairment. These mutants have helped scientists better understand how different genes are involved in eye disorders. For example, two mutant strains called *grumpy* and *sleepy* have been vital in the study of certain disorders that affect the optic nerve.

Language Arts Connection Write an informational pamphlet about a different model organism that has been used in genetics research. Gather information on the organism from several sources, including articles and scientific journals. Be sure to properly cite your sources in your pamphlet. Use the following questions to guide your research:

1. What makes this organism a useful model for genetics research?
2. What kind of genetic information has been gathered from research using this model organism?

Biology in Your Community Scientists from diverse backgrounds are responsible for many of the advances in the field of genetics. Research a geneticist whose work has benefited our knowledge of human diseases.

IDENTIFY Make a list of criteria and constraints a researcher would need to consider when choosing a model organism for human disease study. Include factors related to the organism's development and life cycle, the genetic basis of the disease being studied, and any ethical considerations.

_____

_____

_____

_____

TWINS:
ARE THEY EXACTLY THE SAME?   **"JUNK" DNA**   **EPIGENETICS**   Go online to choose one of these other paths.

Lesson Self-Check

CAN YOU EXPLAIN IT?

FIGURE 20: Expression of *Hox* genes guides the development of body structures.

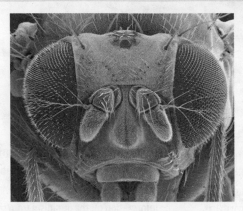

a Functional genes produce normal structures. (colored SEM)

b Mutant genes produce structural mutations, such as legs in place of antennae. (colored SEM)

Hox genes are shared by a wide array of animals, from fruit flies to jellyfish to humans. The expression of *Hox* genes defines the head-to-tail pattern of development in animal embryos. This helps explain why so many animals look the same during the embryonic stage. When expressed, *Hox* genes produce proteins that build segments in a larva or embryo that develop into specific organs and tissues.

A mutation in a homeobox gene leads to the development of a body structure in the wrong position. For example, the effect of a mutation in the gene *Antennapedia* determines whether an insect body segment will grow antennae or legs. In the wild-type fruit fly, antennae develop normally. In the fly with a mutation in this gene, legs develop where the antennae should be. However, the rest of the fly develops normally. Although the misplaced legs look normal in structure, they do not work properly. Flies with these mutations usually do not live very long.

 Evidence Notebook Refer to your notes in your Evidence Notebook to explain why a mutation in *Hox* genes results in structural malformations such as those that sometimes occur in fruit flies. In your explanation, answer the following questions:

1. Use the example of Hox genes to make a claim about gene expression. How is the expression of Hox genes related to body plan development?
2. What evidence supports your claim? For example, what happens when a Hox gene is expressed incorrectly?
3. How is genetic engineering related to gene expression and regulation, particularly in terms of genetically modified organisms (GMOs)?

CHECKPOINTS

Check Your Understanding

1. Which statement best explains why gene expression can be more complex and sophisticated in eukaryotic cells than in prokaryotic cells?
   - ○ a. Eukaryotic cells use a more complex genetic code.
   - ○ b. Eukaryotic cells use double-stranded DNA and single-stranded RNA.
   - ○ c. Transcription and translation occur in different places and at different times in eukaryotic cells.
   - ○ d. Gene expression in eukaryotic cells involves both transcription and translation.

2. Scientists have concluded that gene expression is responsible for the differentiation of the cells of a multicellular organism. Which two observations together most strongly support this conclusion?
   - ☐ a. All cells produce the enzymes needed for energy metabolism.
   - ☐ b. The DNA in each body cell of an organism is essentially identical.
   - ☐ c. Gene expression can be regulated by a wide variety of mechanisms.
   - ☐ d. Enzymes needed for digestion are made only by cells lining the digestive tract.

3. Which of the following is an example of mRNA processing?
   - ○ a. Non-coding segments of RNA are added to the beginning of an mRNA sequence.
   - ○ b. Double-stranded RNA initiates reactions that break apart RNA strands.
   - ○ c. Enzymes break down newly synthesized proteins.
   - ○ d. RNA polymerase attaches to a promoter near a gene cluster.

4. Determine whether each statement applies to prokaryotes, eukaryotes, or both.
   - a. RNA polymerase binds to the promoter to begin transcription. prokaryotes | eukaryotes | both
   - b. mRNA undergoes post-transcriptional processing. prokaryotes | eukaryotes | both
   - c. A repressor binds to the operator, preventing transcription of the gene. prokaryotes | eukaryotes | both
   - d. DNA sequences called silencers act to slow down transcription. prokaryotes | eukaryotes | both

5. Which of the following describes a trait that is most likely the result of epistasis?
   - ○ a. All mice in a population have smooth, brown fur.
   - ○ b. The fur of a weasel turns white in the winter months.
   - ○ c. The tissues of a soybean plant are resistant to an herbicide.
   - ○ d. One fraternal twin has blue eyes and the other has brown eyes.

6. Use the correct terms to complete the statement about the regulation of transcription.

   gene   promoter

   transcription factors   RNA polymerase

   A section of DNA which codes for a protein is called a _____ . An enzyme called _____ reads along the DNA and produces mRNA in a process called transcription. Special proteins called _____ help this enzyme bind to a segment of DNA called the _____ . When the correct factors are present in the nucleus, RNA polymerase can begin transcription.

7. How is CRISPR used in genetic engineering?
   - ○ a. It is used to clone cells.
   - ○ b. It is used to cut DNA.
   - ○ c. It is used to insert foreign DNA into a chromosome.
   - ○ d. It is used to test for genetic conditions.

CHECKPOINTS (continued)

8. Which of the following would most likely affect the structure and function of a protein: a mutation in an intron or a mutation in an exon? Explain your answer.

_____

_____

_____

_____

9. Some scientists have been studying the possibility of genetically engineering plants such as potatoes to express a vaccine for the norovirus. This virus can spread rapidly in humans and cause severe gastrointestinal illness. What could be one positive and one negative consequence if a vaccine were produced this way?

_____

_____

_____

_____

_____

10. The role of introns in newly transcribed mRNA is not yet determined. How might introns help increase genetic diversity without increasing the size of the genome?

_____

_____

_____

_____

MAKE YOUR OWN STUDY GUIDE

 In your Evidence Notebook, design a study guide that supports the main ideas from this lesson:

Gene expression and protein synthesis occur differently in prokaryotic and eukaryotic cells. Internal and external factors regulate gene expression.

The structure of DNA determines the structure of proteins, which carry out the essential functions of life through systems of specialized cells.

Genes can be engineered in other organisms to give them traits that benefit humans.

Remember to include the following information in your study guide:
- Use examples that model main ideas.
- Record explanations for the phenomena you investigated.
- Use evidence to support your explanations. Your support can include drawings, data, graphs, laboratory conclusions, and other evidence recorded throughout the lesson.

Consider how different factors influence the structure of genes and cause changes to gene expression.

Computer Science Connection

DNA Data Storage The amount of digital data in the world is growing at a fast rate. People need room to store their personal data, and institutions need room to store archives of information. Scientists have shown it is possible to code digital information into a strand of DNA and then re-create that information without errors. This technology is still being optimized, but there is real potential for DNA to be a solution for long-term data storage needs.

Research DNA data storage. Make a multimedia presentation that explains what it is and how information can be safely stored. Include a section in your presentation that anticipates end-user questions, such as "What barriers remain for this technology?"

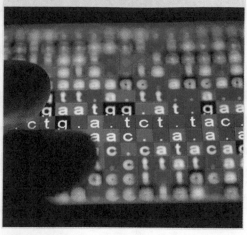

FIGURE 1: DNA could one day be used to store digital data.

Social Studies Connection

Contributors to Scientific Knowledge The race to discover the structure of DNA involved many scientists with varied backgrounds. The experiences and expertise of the scientists allowed them to approach the problem from different angles. The determination of the double-helix structure of DNA was a major accomplishment, but that wasn't the last discovery involving DNA. Since that time, there have been numerous advances in scientific knowledge related to the structure and function of DNA.

Prepare a short summary of the work of a current scientist in California who studies DNA. Describe their contributions to our understanding of the structure, function, or applications of DNA. Use appropriate resources and properly cite your sources.

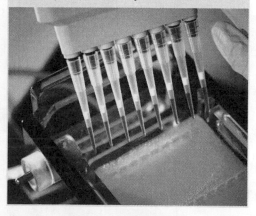

FIGURE 2: Many technologies, such as gel electrophoresis, have enhanced our ability to manipulate and study DNA.

Life Science Connection

Four-Stranded DNA The double-helix structure of DNA is very well known, so it may be surprising to learn that DNA can take on other structures. One example is four-stranded DNA, which is common in cancer genes. The four-stranded molecule arises from a different folding structure that is linked to sequences of DNA that are rich in guanine.

Make a 3D model of both the double-helix and four-stranded structures of DNA. Make a presentation that explains the differences in their structure and function, and includes potential uses for the four-stranded molecule.

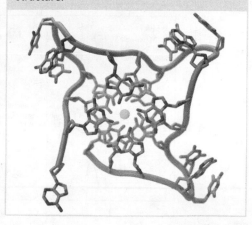

FIGURE 3: DNA can form a four-stranded structure.

A BOOK EXPLAINING
COMPLEX IDEAS USING
ONLY THE 1,000 MOST
COMMON WORDS

THING
EXPLAINER
COMPLICATED STUFF
IN SIMPLE WORDS

BOOKS INSIDE US

Why people's children are sort of like them but not exactly the same

You know that genetic material from two parents results in offspring with traits that follow a pattern of inheritance. Mendel found that these patterns can be predicted by using mathematical probabilities. Here's an overview.

MY NAME → RANDALL MUNROE
author of *What If?* and creator of *xkcd*

RANDALL MUNROE
XKCD.COM

THE STORY OF HIDDEN WRITING AND FAMILY TREES

LIVING THINGS MAKE MORE OF THEMSELVES.

THE THINGS THEY MAKE ARE A LOT LIKE THEM, BUT AREN'T EXACTLY THE SAME.

THERE ARE LOTS OF REASONS FOR THIS, BUT ONE OF THEM IS A KIND OF WRITING INSIDE LIVING THINGS.

-T-A-T-A-A-T-G-C-G-G-C-C-A-
-A-T-A-T-T-A-C-G-C-G-G-T-

THIS WRITING, WHICH IS STORED IN OUR BODIES AND IS TOO SMALL TO SEE, IS PASSED DOWN TO EVERY LIVING THING FROM THE LIVING THINGS IT CAME FROM.

WHEN THIS WRITING IS PASSED DOWN, LIKE WHEN TREES MAKE NEW TREES OR PEOPLE MAKE BABIES, THE WRITING GETS CHANGED AROUND AND PUT TOGETHER IN NEW WAYS.

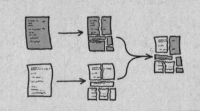

THERE ARE LOTS OF THINGS ABOUT THE WRITING THAT WE DON'T UNDERSTAND. BUT SOME THINGS, LIKE WHAT KIND OF BLOOD YOU HAVE OR WHICH THINGS MAKE YOU SICK, SEEM TO RUN IN FAMILIES IN THE SAME WAY. LOOKING AT HOW THE WRITING GETS CHANGED AROUND AND PUT TOGETHER IN EACH NEW LIVING THING CAN HELP US UNDERSTAND WHY.

CAN THAT MACHINE LET YOU SEE THE HIDDEN WRITING CARRIED WITHIN ALL LIVING THINGS?

NO, BUT IT DOES MAKE THEIR EYES LOOK REAL BIG!

WRITING INSIDE YOUR BODY

Living things are full of a kind of writing telling them how to grow. It's not written using letters and words; it uses four different tiny pieces, like letters, stuck together in long lines. We can think of them like words in a set of books, but remember, they're not really "words" like we're used to. People, like a lot of animals, have two different full sets of books in their bodies.

One set is from each parent. The two sets match; each book in a set has a matching book in the other set that is about the same size, as if they have the same number of pages, even if each page doesn't have the same words. We won't worry about how to read what the writing says. After all, in real life, we don't really know what most of the writing is for!

THE TWO SETS OF WRITING IN YOUR BODY THAT TELL IT HOW TO GROW

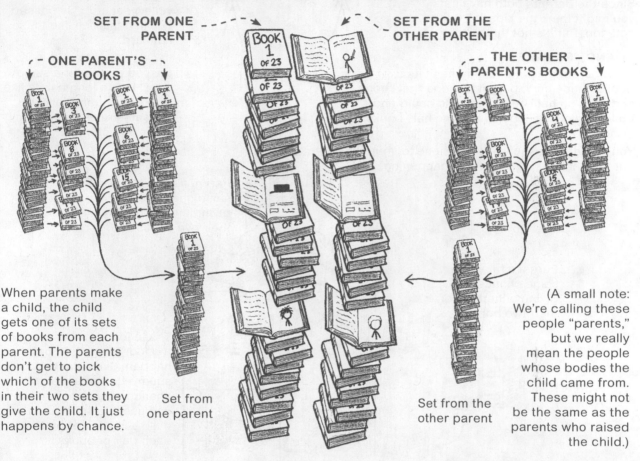

SET FROM ONE PARENT

SET FROM THE OTHER PARENT

ONE PARENT'S BOOKS

THE OTHER PARENT'S BOOKS

When parents make a child, the child gets one of its sets of books from each parent. The parents don't get to pick which of the books in their two sets they give the child. It just happens by chance.

Set from one parent

Set from the other parent

(A small note: We're calling these people "parents," but we really mean the people whose bodies the child came from. These might not be the same as the parents who raised the child.)

LEFT AND RIGHT

To learn a little more about how the left and right books come together, let's imagine that there's a piece of writing in a person's book that decides whether they will have a hat or not. (We'll pretend hats are part of our bodies.)

In the part of the book about hats, let's say some books have a piece of writing that means "HAT" and other books don't.

Here's the Hat Law: If either of your books says "HAT," then you will have a hat.

This person has a hat because there's a hat in one of their books.

This person has a hat because there's a hat in both of their books.

This person has a hat because there's a hat in one of their books.

This person doesn't have a hat because there's no hat in either one of their books.

WHY CHILDREN ARE DIFFERENT

TWO PARENTS WHO ARE THE SAME

Let's suppose two parents with hats have a baby. These parents both have the same thing in their books, as far as hats go—a hat in their left book and no hat in their right.

WHAT HAPPENS TO THE KIDS?

Since the parents both have hats, you might think the kids will have hats too. But it's not that simple.

CHANCE SQUARE

Each parent gives the child one of its two books. Since each parent has one "hat" book and one "no hat" book, the child could end up with two "hat" books, two "no hat" books, or one of each!

You can draw a square like this one to figure out the chances of each thing happening.

PARENT #1   +   PARENT #2

A NOTE ON HATS

In real life, hats aren't passed down in families like this, but lots of real things are.

Humans have yellow stuff in their ears, which is either wet or dry. "Having wet yellow ear stuff" is passed down in families like these hats are.

In cats, short hair is passed down in the same way. Having long hair is like having a hat and follows the same rules as hats do in these pictures.

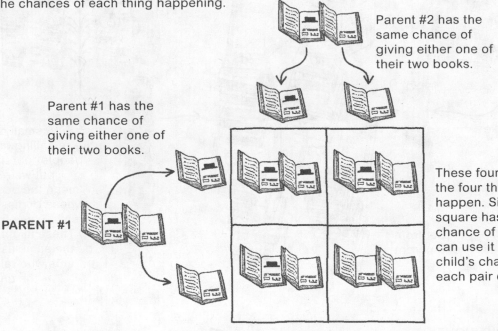

Parent #2 has the same chance of giving either one of their two books.

Parent #1 has the same chance of giving either one of their two books.

PARENT #1

These four squares show the four things that can happen. Since each square has an equal chance of happening, we can use it to figure out the child's chance of getting each pair of books.

The child has a one-in-four chance of getting the "no hat" book from both parents. If that happens, the child will not have a hat, even though both parents do.

The child has a two-in-four chance of getting the "no hat" book from one parent and the "hat" book from the other. That means the child will have one "hat" and one "no hat" book, just like both parents do. Like their parents, these children will have hats.

The child has a one-in-four chance of getting the "hat" book from both parents. This child will have a hat, and they are different from their parents because they don't have a "no hat" book.

25%

50%

25%

A HAT FAMILY TREE

Let's follow a pretend family tree to see how different branches end up with different sets of hat and no hat books.

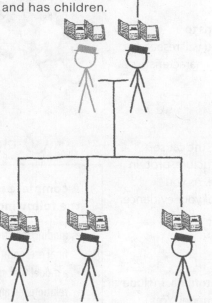

The family tree starts with two parents. Each has one hat book and one no hat book.

The parents have three children. Two of them have one hat book, like their parents (there's a two-in-four chance of this) and the third has no hat books (there's a one-in-four chance of this).

This person, who has one hat book like their parents, meets someone with no hat and has children.

This person, who has one hat book, meets someone else with one hat book and has children.

This person, who has no hat, meets someone else with no hat and has children.

This person has a hat, since they got the hat book from their hat-wearing parent. There was a one-in-two chance of this.

This person has no hat, which means hat books are gone from this branch of the family until someone with a hat shows up.

These people have one hat book and one no hat book, like their parents and grandparents.

This person got a hat book from both parents, which means all children this child has will have hats.

Since neither of the parents in this branch have hats, neither of the children have hats either, since no one has a hat book.

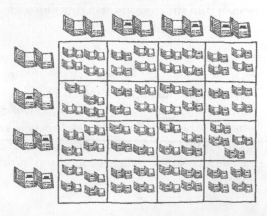

Investigating Phenylketonuria

Phenylketonuria (PKU) is a recessive disorder that is characterized by high levels of phenylalanine in the blood. Phenylalanine is an amino acid that is normally broken down for the body to use. In people with PKU, the phenylalanine is not broken down, and the amino acid accumulates in the blood. Buildup to harmful levels can lead to intellectual disability and other health problems. What causes the inability to break down phenylalanine in people suffering from PKU, and how does this change impact human health?

1. ASK A QUESTION

With your team, define a set of questions to be answered. Identify all the factors you will research to answer these questions. Outline the characteristics a complete answer should have.

2. CONDUCT RESEARCH

Investigate phenylketonuria to explore the cause-and-effect relationship among DNA structure, protein structure, and symptoms of the disease. As you research, cite specific texts as sources of your evidence, so others can easily locate your sources.

3. DEVELOP A MODEL

Develop a model to illustrate phenylketonuria. Include DNA, proteins, and symptoms in your model. You could draw a conceptual model, program a computer simulation, or build a physical model.

4. CONSTRUCT AN EXPLANATION

Use your answers to your questions to construct an explanation about the cause-and-effect relationship among DNA structure, protein structure, and symptoms of phenylketonuria.

5. COMMUNICATE

Present your findings as a researcher to a peer group. Describe phenylketonuria, the enzyme involved, why the enzyme malfunctions, and possible avenues for addressing the issue. Your presentation should include images and data to support and illustrate your research.

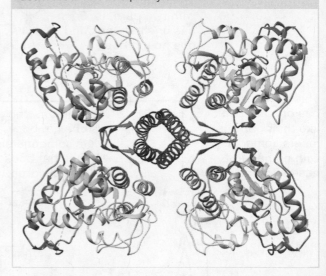

FIGURE 4: A special enzyme is responsible for breaking down the amino acid phenylalanine.

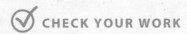 CHECK YOUR WORK

A complete presentation should include the following information:

- guiding questions that are answered in the final presentation
- a model that shows the cause-and-effect relationship among DNA structure, protein structure, and phenylketonuria symptoms
- an explanation about how the structure of DNA determines the structure of the proteins involved, and ultimately the traits associated, with phenylketonuria

Name _____ Date _____

SYNTHESIZE THE UNIT

In your Evidence Notebook, make a concept map, other graphic organizer, or outline using the Study Guides you made for each lesson in this unit. Be sure to use evidence to support your claims.

When synthesizing individual information, remember to follow these general steps:
- Find the central idea of each piece of information.
- Think about the relationships among the central ideas.
- Combine the ideas to come up with a new understanding.

DRIVING QUESTIONS

Look back to the Driving Questions from the opening section of this unit. In your Evidence Notebook, review and revise your previous answers to those questions. Use the evidence you gathered and other observations you made throughout the unit to support your claims.

PRACTICE AND REVIEW

1. What processes that occur during meiosis contribute to genetic diversity in offspring? Select all correct answers.
   - ☐ **a.** crossing over
   - ☐ **b.** cytokinesis
   - ☐ **c.** gametogenesis
   - ☐ **d.** independent assortment

2. What evidence do codons provide for the common ancestry of all organisms?
   - ○ **a.** Almost all living things use codons to transcribe RNA to proteins.
   - ○ **b.** Codons code for amino acids that are found in all living organisms.
   - ○ **c.** Codons in almost all living organisms code for the same amino acid.
   - ○ **d.** Codons are used to start and stop protein translation in almost all living things.

3. If meiosis produces four daughter cells, why does gametogenesis in females produce only a single egg cell?
   - ○ **a.** Egg cells contain four times the amount of DNA as sperm cells.
   - ○ **b.** Egg cells in females are not produced via meiosis.
   - ○ **c.** Gametogenesis involves steps in addition to meiosis, in which a single egg cell is retained.
   - ○ **d.** The process of meiosis does not fully complete when producing an egg cell.

4. The human genome contains roughly 1000 olfactory receptor genes, which allow us to detect and distinguish different odors. While only about one-third of these genes are functional, all of the genes may have arisen as duplications of a single ancestral gene. Put these steps in order to illustrate how this process could have occurred.
   - _____ **a.** Mutations accumulate over time in the duplicate copy of the gene.
   - _____ **b.** Chromosomes exchange uneven amounts of DNA.
   - _____ **c.** The duplicate gene encodes a protein with a slightly different function.
   - _____ **d.** Homologous chromosomes line up in the middle of the cell during meiosis.
   - _____ **e.** A chromosome obtains multiple copies of the same gene.

5. In what way can a recessive X-linked disease such as red-green color blindness be inherited by male offspring?
   - ○ **a.** from the father, but only if the father has the colorblind phenotype
   - ○ **b.** from the father, even if the father is unaffected
   - ○ **c.** from the mother, but only if the mother has the colorblind phenotype
   - ○ **d.** from the mother, even if the mother is unaffected

6. Explain how a point mutation at one location might affect an organism's phenotype but have no effect if it occurs at another location.

_____

_____

_____

_____

_____

_____

7. If you wished to replicate Mendel's experiments, how could you determine whether a potential parent plant was homozygous-dominant or heterozygous for a particular trait?

_____

_____

_____

_____

_____

_____

8. Explain the difference between haploid and diploid cells and how they function in human reproduction.

_____

_____

_____

_____

_____

_____

UNIT PROJECT

Return to your unit project. Prepare your research and materials into a presentation to share with the class. In your final presentation, evaluate the strength of your claim, data, analysis, and conclusions.

Remember these tips while evaluating:

- Look at the empirical evidence—evidence based on observations and data. Does the evidence

support your explanation of the cause or causes of Huntington's disease?

- Consider if the explanation is logical. Does it contradict any evidence you have seen?

- Is there enough evidence from credible sources to support your conclusions?

UNIT 6

Genetic Variation and Evolution

YOU SOLVE IT

What Evidence Supports Patterns of Evolution?

 To begin exploring this unit's concepts, go online to investigate ways to solve a real-world problem.

Dolphins communicate together to herd fish into balls from which they will feed.

FIGURE 1: The desert pupfish has unique adaptations that allow it to survive in the harsh conditions of Death Valley.

Death Valley was once a vast freshwater lake ecosystem that was home to mammoths, sloths, and the ancestors of modern pupfish. Today it is one of the hottest and driest deserts on Earth. The desert floor now only has scattered and remote water sources into which pupfish descendants have retreated. The differences between these niches are extreme. For example, Devil's Hole is a warm underground freshwater spring where the water temperature is a relatively steady 33 °C (92 °F), while Salt Creek is an ultra-salty stream with water temperatures ranging seasonally from near-freezing to almost 42 °C (108 °F). It is amazing that the original pupfish survived long enough to have diverged into distinct subspecies.

PREDICT What factors result in speciation, or the development of new species over time?

_____

_____

_____

_____

DRIVING QUESTIONS

As you move through the unit, gather evidence to help you answer the following questions. In your Evidence Notebook, record what you already know about these topics and any questions you have about them.

1. How do mutations affect genetic diversity?
2. What are some of the patterns we see in evolution of populations?
3. Can behaviors be inherited?

UNIT PROJECT

Go online to download the Unit Project Worksheet to help plan your project.

Investigating Water-Collecting Adaptations

Many species have adaptations that allow them to collect water. Darkling beetles have structures on their wings to trap tiny water droplets. The spines of some cactus species are covered with tapered microgrooves to channel water along their length, even against gravity. Explore one of these water-collecting adaptations, or another example of your choosing. Research how scientists are mimicking the adaptation for use in new technologies.

Language Development

Use the lessons in this unit to complete the chart and expand your understanding of the science concepts.

TERM: gene mutation

Definition	Example

Similar Term	Phrase

TERM: chromosomal mutation

Definition	Example

Similar Term	Phrase

TERM: gene pool

Definition	Example

Similar Term	Phrase

TERM: allele frequency

Definition	Example

Similar Term	Phrase

TERM: gene flow

Definition

Example

Similar Term

Phrase

TERM: speciation

Definition

Example

Similar Term

Phrase

TERM: stimulus

Definition

Example

Similar Term

Phrase

TERM: cultural behavior

Definition

Example

Similar Term

Phrase

Mutations and Genetic Diversity

A mutation causes red blood cells to have a "sickled," or bent, shape. (colored SEM)

CAN YOU EXPLAIN IT?

When you think of mutations, you may imagine enhanced, superhuman abilities, or you may think of negative effects on the body. Some mutations can be beneficial, while others can be quite harmful. For example, sickle cell anemia is a disease caused by a mutation that affects red blood cells. The result is anemia, or a shortage of healthy red blood cells in the body. Other symptoms include fatigue, pain, swelling of hands and feet, and delayed growth. The sickle cell anemia allele, HbS, causes the disease and can be passed on from parent to offspring.

Despite its damaging effects, the HbS allele persists in relatively high frequencies in some parts of the world. These areas include countries throughout Africa, especially those near the equator; the Middle East; India; and localized areas in the Mediterranean region. According to the Centers for Disease Control and Prevention, approximately 100 000 Americans have sickle cell disease. It is estimated that there are between 6500 and 7000 Californians living with sickle cell anemia or other forms of sickle cell disease.

PREDICT Why might the HbS allele be more common in some parts of the world than in others? What do you think causes this pattern?

_____

_____

_____

 Evidence Notebook As you explore the lesson, gather evidence for how mutations increase genetic diversity.

Gene Mutations

What you are made of and how your body functions begin with the instructions from your DNA. Your DNA carries the code from which all the proteins that give your body structure and help your body carry out life-maintaining processes are produced. Changes in DNA, or mutations, may result in diseases such as sickle cell anemia. How do mutations occur, and what causes them?

Causes of Mutations

Explore Online ▶

Hands-On Lab

Testing UV-Protective Fabrics Design a system to test UV-protective fabrics.

Mutations can be categorized as gene mutations or chromosomal mutations. Gene mutations are changes in the DNA sequence of a single gene. Typically, gene mutations happen during DNA replication. DNA polymerase has a built-in proofreading function that repairs mutations, but a small number of replication errors do not get fixed. They build up over time and can eventually affect how the cell works. Many studies suggest that mutations in somatic, or body cells, coupled with a decrease in the body's self-repairing ability, may contribute to the process of aging.

Mutagens are agents in the environment that can change DNA or increase the frequency of mutation in organisms. Some mutagens occur naturally, such as ultraviolet (UV) rays in sunlight. Some chemicals have also been linked to mutations. These mutagenic chemicals can be found in some kinds of food and cosmetics.

FIGURE 1: Mutagens can change DNA. The main types of mutagens include radiation, chemicals, and infectious agents.

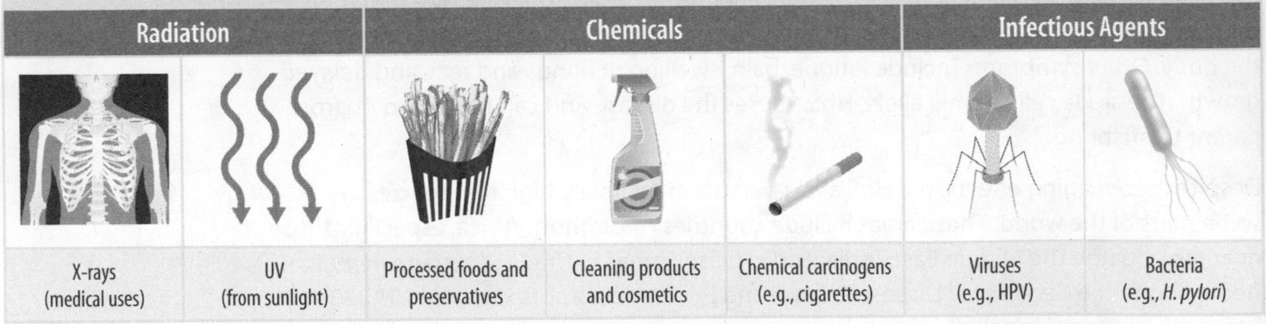

Radiation		Chemicals			Infectious Agents	
X-rays (medical uses)	UV (from sunlight)	Processed foods and preservatives	Cleaning products and cosmetics	Chemical carcinogens (e.g., cigarettes)	Viruses (e.g., HPV)	Bacteria (e.g., H. pylori)

APPLY When you get x-rays at the dentist, a lead vest is placed over your body. Why do you think this is necessary?

_____

_____

_____

Language Arts Connection Research a human health condition caused by a mutation, and write a blog post explaining how people are working to address the condition. What has been done to raise awareness of the condition? How are scientists approaching this condition? What kinds of treatments have been proposed so far, and which of them seems most promising?

Mutations Due to Radiation

One kind of mutation caused by a mutagen is a thymine dimer. In DNA, adenine pairs with thymine. UV light is a type of radiation that can cause neighboring thymine nucleotides to break their hydrogen bonds to adenine and bond together, forming a thymine dimer. The dimer causes the DNA to kink, which interferes with replication. Cells have a process for correcting these mutations. One enzyme removes the thymine dimer, another replaces the damaged section, and a third bonds the new segment in place. Sometimes, this process is not effective. When these mutations are not corrected, they may result in cancer. Fortunately, this type of mutation is not usually passed on to offspring.

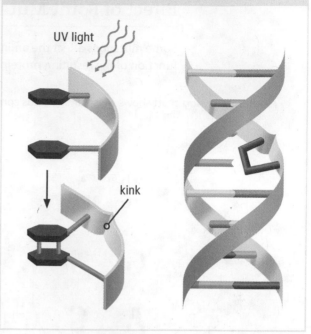

FIGURE 2: A thymine dimer occurs when UV light causes two thymine bases to bond to one another.

UV light

kink

 Collaborate Some drugs take advantage of mutagenic properties by damaging cancer cells. One drug wedges between nucleotides, causing so many mutations that cancer cells no longer function and reproduce. With a partner, discuss how you think this works.

Mutations Due to Chemicals

Some chemicals, such as those in some food, cleaning products, and cosmetics, have been linked to mutations. For example, companies that manufacture food products often add preservatives, such as sodium nitrate, to the food to prevent the food from spoiling. Or, they may smoke the food to give it more flavor. Studies show that ingesting these processed foods might increase the likelihood of developing cancer.

Mutations Due to Infectious Agents

Some infectious agents have also been linked to mutations that may cause cancer. Human papillomavirus (HPV) is a sexually transmitted disease that is known to cause several types of cancer. There are different strains of HPV, and scientists have identified 13 that cause cervical cancer. A vaccine has been developed to protect against HPV, thereby lowering the risk of cervical cancer.

Bacteria can also be mutagens. *Helicobacter pylori* is a bacterium that grows in the mucus layer that lines the inside of the human stomach. While most people do not become ill from an *H. pylori* infection, infections by this bacterium have been linked to an increased risk for stomach cancer.

FIGURE 3: Human papillomavirus (colored TEM)

Point Mutations

A point mutation is a mutation in which one nucleotide is substituted for another. In other words, an incorrect nucleotide takes the place of the correct nucleotide. Very often, such a mistake is caught and fixed by DNA polymerase. If not, the substitution may permanently change an organism's DNA.

Effect of Point Mutations on Protein Function

Some mutations affect the amino acid sequence, which can affect the structure and function of the resulting protein. Some mutations do not change the amino acid.

FIGURE 4: A codon chart shows which amino acids correspond to each possible combination of mRNA bases.

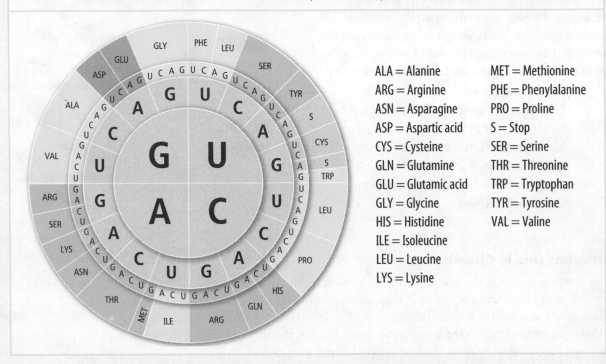

ALA = Alanine
ARG = Arginine
ASN = Asparagine
ASP = Aspartic acid
CYS = Cysteine
GLN = Glutamine
GLU = Glutamic acid
GLY = Glycine
HIS = Histidine
ILE = Isoleucine
LEU = Leucine
LYS = Lysine

MET = Methionine
PHE = Phenylalanine
PRO = Proline
S = Stop
SER = Serine
THR = Threonine
TRP = Tryptophan
TYR = Tyrosine
VAL = Valine

ANALYZE The table shows a normal sequence of nucleotides and three possible mutations in this sequence. Complete the table to show which amino acid corresponds to each mRNA codon.

| isoleucine | aspartic acid | glutamic acid | tryptophan |
| valine | proline | stop codon | serine |

	Normal sequence	Mutation 1	Mutation 2	Mutation 3
DNA	CTC	CAC	ATC	CTT
mRNA	GAG	GUG	UAG	GAA
amino acid	_____	_____	_____	_____

Mutations that change a codon, but not the identity of an amino acid in a protein, do not affect the amino acid sequence of that protein. This type of mutation is sometimes called a *silent mutation* because it does not change the structure and function of the protein. However, there are times when the substitution of a base results in a change in a codon and consequently in a new amino acid. This is called a *missense mutation*. If a mutation results in a stop codon being formed, the protein will not be complete. This is called a *nonsense mutation*. In both types, the amino acid sequence has changed, and the protein's structure and function may be altered.

Sickle cell anemia is caused by a point mutation that alters the gene that codes for the hemoglobin protein in red blood cells. Hemoglobin is made of four subunits with each of the subunits containing iron. This arrangement allows red blood cells to be efficient in transporting oxygen molecules from the lungs to the cells because oxygen molecules bind to the iron atoms.

In the point mutation that causes sickle cell anemia, glutamic acid is substituted by valine within the HbS alleles. The protein synthesized using the mutated gene as a template has a different structure than that of a typical hemoglobin protein. Glutamic acid is negatively charged and is attracted to positively charged amino acids. This interaction between amino acids helps the protein keep its shape. The substituted valine is not attracted to positively charged amino acids. Instead of grouping together to form the structure shown in Figure 5, the hemoglobin subunits form long, rigid chains. As a result, the red blood cells have a "sickle" shape.

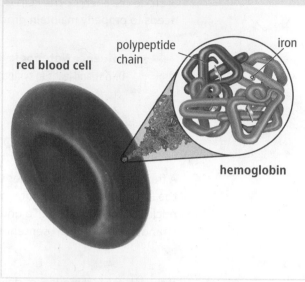

FIGURE 5: Hemoglobin has four subunits, each with an iron atom to which oxygen molecules attach.

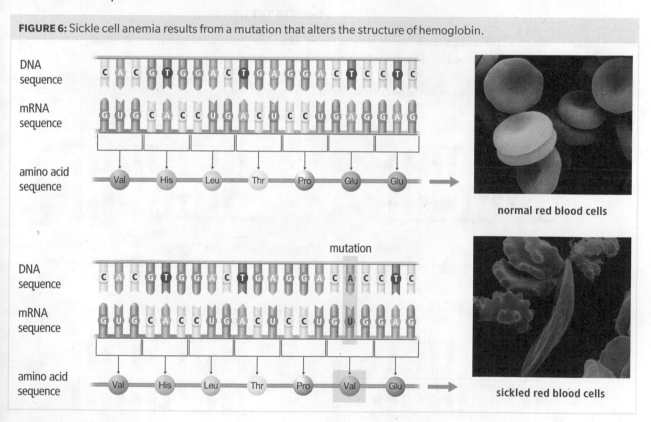

FIGURE 6: Sickle cell anemia results from a mutation that alters the structure of hemoglobin.

EXPLAIN Complete the following statement about mutations and sickle cell anemia.

Sickle cell anemia is caused by a silent | missense | nonsense mutation. This is a type of point mutation in which the substitution of a base results in a change in the codon | amino acid which affects the identify of the codon | amino acid. As a result, valine is substituted for glutamic acid, which restructures the hemoglobin protein and causes red blood cells to have a sickled shape.

When sickle-shaped red blood cells stack on top of each other, they can clog blood vessels. This mutation causes anemia and consequently fatigue and the other symptoms of sickle cell anemia. The cells do not get enough oxygen to produce the energy the body needs to properly maintain processes that keep the body healthy.

 Evidence Notebook Draw a flow chart to illustrate how a change in a nucleotide in a DNA strand leads to symptoms experienced by those with sickle cell anemia.

Frameshift Mutations

A frameshift mutation involves the insertion or deletion of one or more nucleotides in the DNA sequence. This mutation changes the reading frame, or the arrangement of nucleotides into codons. To understand how a frameshift mutation affects an mRNA strand, imagine a short sentence of three-letter "codons":

THE CAT ATE THE RAT

If the letter E is removed, or deleted, from the first "THE," all the letters that follow shift to the left. The sentence now reads:

THC ATA TET HER AT ...

The sentence no longer makes sense. The same would be true if a nucleotide was added, or inserted, and all the letters shifted to the right.

FIGURE 7: Frameshift mutations change the reading frame, which changes the amino acid sequence after the mutation.

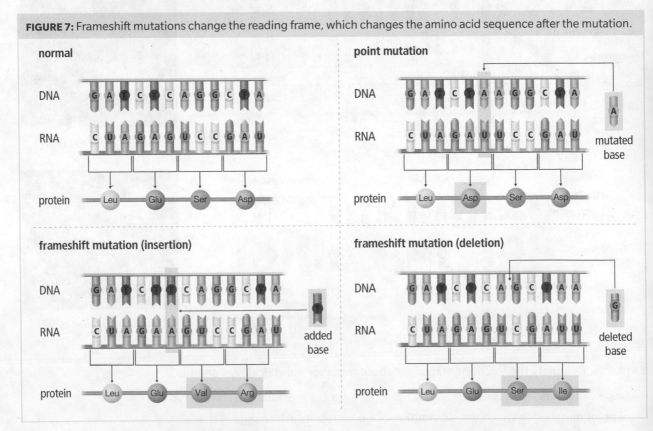

A nucleotide sequence loses its meaning when an insertion or deletion shifts all the codons by one nucleotide. This change throws off the reading frame, which results in codons that code for different amino acids.

Like other types of mutations, frameshift mutations cause changes in the genotype of individuals, often resulting in changes in phenotype. Cystic fibrosis is a genetic disease that may result from a frameshift mutation. A specific kind of mutation in a gene called the CF transmembrane conductance regulator (*CFTR*) gene can delete an entire amino acid. People with cystic fibrosis have thick rather than thin mucus, which builds up in the lungs and tubes of other organs.

Crohn's disease, which affects the lining of the digestive tract, has also been linked to a frameshift mutation. Although scientists have not identified the exact cause of Crohn's disease, they have found that a cytosine insertion within a specific gene is associated with the disease. They believe that Crohn's disease results from environmental factors that affect people who are genetically predisposed to the disease.

Trinucleotide Repeat Expansions

Frameshift mutations may also occur in sections of DNA that consist of repeating nucleotides, such as CAG CAG CAG. These repeating segments are known as trinucleotide repeats because they involve three nucleotides. During replication, DNA polymerase may "slip" and make duplicate copies of the repeated sequence. This forms a "hairpin" loop of DNA that sticks out from its complementary strand. When this strand is replicated, the loop becomes part of the DNA, resulting in a longer double strand of DNA. This expansion continues as cells divide and DNA is replicated.

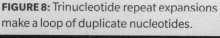

FIGURE 8: Trinucleotide repeat expansions make a loop of duplicate nucleotides.

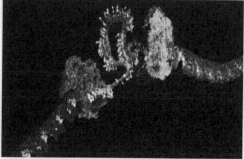

PREDICT Why do you think repeats of nucleotides cause DNA polymerase to "slip"?

_____

_____

_____

_____

Huntington's disease is an inherited condition caused by the mutation of a gene that provides instructions for making the protein huntingtin. The segment of DNA involved is a CAG trinucleotide repeat. Normally, this segment is repeated 10 to 35 times. In Huntington's disease, it is repeated 36 to over 120 times. People with Huntington's disease suffer from a range of neurological problems, including a decline in thinking and reasoning abilities.

Evidence Notebook People with sickle cell anemia have two copies of the gene for the disease. People with one copy are carriers and do not have the disease.

1. Is the sickle cell allele dominant or recessive? Explain how you know.
2. If two carriers have children, what is the probability of one of their children having the disease?

Chromosomal Mutations

Changes in either chromosome segments or whole chromosomes are called chromosomal mutations. These mutations may change the amount of genetic material or change the structure of a chromosome, and they usually occur during mitosis and meiosis.

Gene Duplication

During meiosis, homologous chromosomes exchange DNA segments through crossing over. If the chromosomes do not align with each other, they might exchange DNA segments of unequal size, resulting in one chromosome with two copies of a gene or genes. This process is called *gene duplication*. The chromosome that lost the segment has undergone gene deletion.

FIGURE 9: Mutations can have positive effects and result in genetic variation.

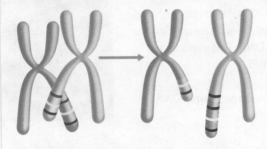

a When homologous chromosomes do not align properly during meiosis, gene duplication can occur.

b As a result of gene duplication, the douc langur evolved enzymes that allow them to digest leaves and fruit.

Mutations can have harmful effects, but they can also increase genetic variation, or the variety of traits among individuals within a population. Gene duplication has occurred many times in the evolution of eukaryotic organisms. When gene duplication occurs, multiple copies of a gene are present. As a result, one copy of the gene can encode functional proteins, while the other copies are "free" to accumulate mutations. Mutated genes may encode proteins with new structures, which may take on new functions in the organism.

MODEL Draw a model illustrating how gene duplication and mutations can lead to a gene with a new function over the course of several generations.

Polyploidy in Plants

Sometimes the entire genome is duplicated. This type of error can lead to polyploidy, or multiple copies of the genome. Genome duplication has occurred in the evolution of many crop plants, such as strawberry, wheat, and mustard plants.

Scientists can use chemicals to artificially induce polyploidy in cells. These chemicals interfere with the formation of microtubules, disrupting the separation of chromosomes during mitosis. As a result, one daughter cell receives a double set of chromosomes. This technique has been used to manipulate traits, such as flower size, making plants more desirable to customers.

FIGURE 10: Chromosome number in plants

Common Name	Chromosome Number
Banana	3N=33
Potato	4N=48
Common wheat	6N=42
Boysenberry	7N=49
Strawberry	8N=56

ASK Suppose you wanted to chemically induce polyploidy to make a plant with larger fruit. Write a list of questions you would ask to define and delimit the problem.

_____

_____

_____

_____

Gene Translocation

Translocation is another type of chromosomal mutation. In translocation, a segment of one chromosome moves to a nonhomologous chromosome. Translocations are often reciprocal, which means that the two nonhomologous chromosomes exchange segments with each other. In Figure 11, a translocation occurs between chromosome 1 and chromosome 17. This is known as a balanced translocation, because the swapping of segments did not break up any genes, and there was no gain or loss of material.

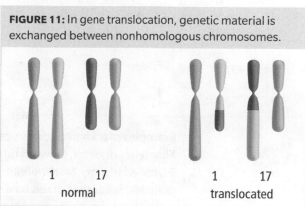

FIGURE 11: In gene translocation, genetic material is exchanged between nonhomologous chromosomes.

1   17
normal

1   17
translocated

ANALYZE Many people with balanced translocation mutations are not aware they have them until they try to have children. How is this possible? Select all correct answers.

☐ **a.** The person still has a full set of genes.

☐ **b.** There is no change in people's DNA until after they have children.

☐ **c.** Children inherit one chromosome from each parent, so they may not receive a full set of genes.

☐ **d.** Cells easily repair these types of mutations, so they should not cause health issues unless repair mechanisms are not functioning properly.

Nondisjunction Mutations

Nondisjunction mutations occur when one or more homologous chromosomes do not separate during anaphase of meiosis. The resulting gametes do not have the same number of chromosomes and can have more or fewer chromosomes than the parent cell.

FIGURE 12: A karyotype can be used to identify a nondisjunction mutation.

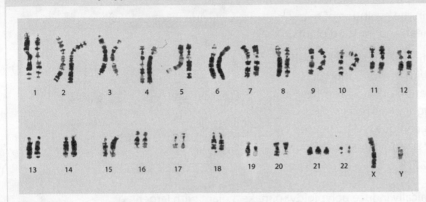

a This karyotype shows three copies of chromosome 21.

b People with Down syndrome have three copies of chromosome 21.

MODEL Draw a model to illustrate how a nondisjunction mutation could occur during either anaphase I or anaphase II of meiosis.

Examples of human disorders caused by nondisjunction include Down syndrome and Klinefelter disorder. Down syndrome occurs in people with three copies of chromosome 21, called trisomy 21. Klinefelter disorder is caused by an extra X chromosome in the cells of males. Recall that males have one X and one Y chromosome. A male with this disorder would have three chromosomes: XXY. This mutation affects the learning ability and sexual development of males. Turner syndrome is another example of a disorder caused by nondisjunction. Females with this syndrome have only one X chromosome instead of two. This missing X chromosome interferes with the development of secondary sexual characteristics in females.

 Evidence Notebook Make a chart to organize and describe the main types of mutations you have learned about so far. Then use your chart to help you write an explanation for these questions: When is a mutation likely to increase genetic variation? When is a mutation likely to have harmful effects, such as with sickle cell anemia?

Effects of Mutations

You have seen how HbS, the sickle cell anemia allele, can be passed on from parent to child. Whether or not a mutation is inherited depends on the type of cell in which the mutation occurs. If a mutation is transmitted, it may or may not affect the phenotype, or the physical expression of a trait, in the organism.

Effects on Offspring

There are two major types of cells in the body: somatic cells and germ cells. Germ cells are involved in the formation of gametes. Somatic cells include all other cells of the body. Mutations may occur in each type of cell, but only mutations in germ cells may be passed from parent to offspring. Mutations in the germ line affect the phenotype of offspring. Often, this effect is so harmful that offspring do not develop properly or die before they can reproduce. Other mutations, though less severe, often still result in less adaptive phenotypes. More rarely, a mutation results in a more beneficial phenotype.

FIGURE 13: Mutations can occur in gametes and in body cells.

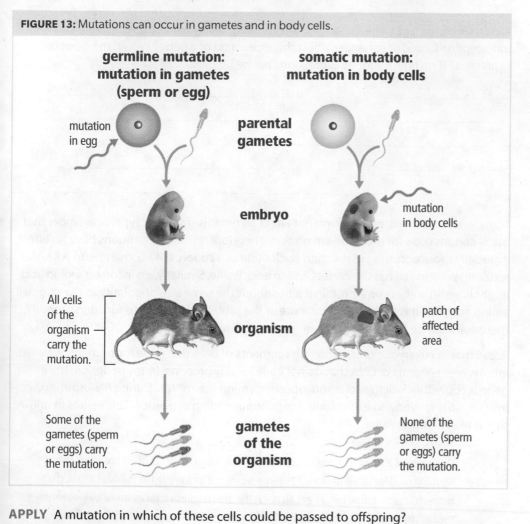

APPLY A mutation in which of these cells could be passed to offspring? Select all correct answers.

☐ **a.** muscle cell   ☐ **b.** sperm cell   ☐ **c.** skin cell   ☐ **d.** egg cell

Effects on Phenotype

Chromosomal mutations affect many genes and can have a major effect on the organism. A mutation may break up a gene, inactivating it, or make a new hybrid gene with a new function. Translocated genes may come under the control of new promoters.

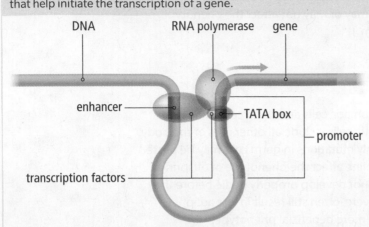

FIGURE 14: A promoter is a segment of DNA that binds to proteins that help initiate the transcription of a gene.

Gene mutations, though smaller in scale compared to chromosomal mutations, can also have a big effect on an organism. Although it is not as likely as with a coding region, even a mutation in a noncoding region can cause problems. Recall that noncoding sequences, such as promoters and enhancers, interact with transcription factors and RNA polymerase to start transcription. Therefore, a mutation that affects any one of these elements could also affect the expression of one or many genes. As with chromosomal mutations, the organism's phenotype could change significantly if many genes are affected.

PREDICT How might a mutation that affects a regulatory element, such as a promoter, transcription factor, or enhancer, affect the expression of a gene? Would the gene be expressed? If so, how might its expression change?

_____

_____

_____

_____

_____

Many gene mutations, however, do not affect an organism's phenotype. Remember that many codons code for the same amino acid. Therefore, some substitutions have no effect, especially those occurring in the third nucleotide of a codon. If AAG changes to AAA, the resulting protein still has the correct amino acid, lysine. Similarly, an incorrect amino acid might have little effect on a protein if it has about the same size or polarity as the original amino acid, or if it is far from an active site. If the protein is still able to function properly, there will likely be little to no effect on the organism's phenotype.

Recall that in eukaryotic cells, exons are segments of DNA that code for proteins, whereas introns are segments of DNA that do not code for any proteins. In transcription, the entire gene is copied, including exons and introns, forming pre-mRNA. During RNA splicing, introns are removed and exons form a continuous coding sequence. This results in mRNA that is ready for translation.

Cause and Effect If a mutation occurred in an intron, it would likely not affect the resulting protein. This is because the intron would not be included in the final mRNA strand. However, the mutation could have an effect if it affects splicing, for example by preventing the intron from being spliced out. The DNA sequence of the intron would be transcribed as part of the protein, which then would change the protein structure and probably its function.

Effects on Genetic Diversity

Genetic variation, or genetic diversity, is the variety of genes within a population. While genetic recombination via sexual reproduction is a major source of genetic diversity, mutations in germ cells are the ultimate source of genetic diversity in an organism's genome. Genetic diversity is essential for natural selection. Recall that in natural selection, environmental factors contribute to selection for phenotypes that allow organisms to better survive and reproduce.

For example, an individual might have a phenotype that allows the organism to attract more mates than other individuals. This individual would have more opportunities to pass on their genes, and over the course of many generations, this phenotype could evolve and become more prevalent in the population.

FIGURE 15: Mutations increase genetic diversity, which is the basis of natural selection.

ANALYZE Assume that in the lizard population shown in Figure 15, the brown phenotype results from a mutation. Why does this phenotype become more common in the population over time?

_____

_____

_____

_____

When less adaptive phenotypes result from mutations, natural selection typically removes these mutant alleles from the population. Less adaptive phenotypes may make it difficult for organisms to survive or reproduce. These traits are "selected against" by environmental factors and tend to become less prevalent in a population over time.

Another example of genetic variation due to a mutation is the ability to digest lactose. Two-thirds of the world's adult population cannot digest lactose, the main sugar in milk. The ability to digest lactose requires the production of the enzyme lactase. Typically, the production of lactase decreases significantly once a child is weaned off of their mother's milk. However, over 10 000 years ago, a mutation occurred in an individual that left the gene for lactase-production permanently switched on. This gene was passed on to subsequent generations, and now drinking milk throughout a person's life is possible for many people. This adaptation can be beneficial in parts of the world where milk from domesticated dairy animals is readily available. Over time, the adaptation for lactose tolerance is selected for and evolves within a population.

Using Beneficial Mutations to Develop New Medicines

FIGURE 16: A mutation in humans has been shown to protect against coronary artery disease.

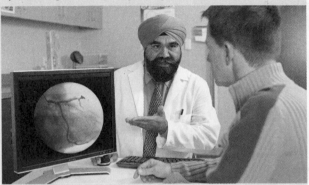

Sometimes, a mutation results in a more beneficial phenotype. These mutations are favored by natural selection. For example, one type of deletion mutation in humans has been shown to protect against coronary artery disease, a condition characterized by the hardening and thickening of artery walls. In this mutation, the deletion affects the compressed gene, called *ASGR1*, by rendering it unable to produce the normal structure and function of the asialoglycoprotein receptor. This receptor protein binds with certain sugars and plays a role in the metabolism of cholesterol and whether or not someone develops arteriosclerosis, a condition in which the arteries harden and thicken.

Surprisingly, researchers have discovered that people with the mutated *ASGR1* gene have lower levels of cholesterol in their blood and, therefore, have a 34% lower chance of developing arteriosclerosis. This discovery has led to further research of the mutation and how it might be applied to the development of medicines that help prevent the development of heart disease. One biotechnology company has already made several medical drugs that mimic the effects of the mutated gene.

Mutations in another gene called *PCSK9* are also proving to be an important model for the development of cholesterol-lowering medications. Mutations in this gene effectively eliminate a protein in the blood that has a significant role in the control of LDL cholesterol levels. Bioengineers and biomedical researchers are using this information to produce medications that inhibit the function of the *PCSK9* protein to dramatically reduce LDL cholesterol levels.

ANALYZE Why might scientists choose to study the genomes of healthy elderly people when searching for mutations that lead to a more beneficial phenotype?

_____

_____

_____

_____

_____

 Evidence Notebook In some cases, mutations that have some harmful effects continue to persist in certain human populations, such as sickle cell anemia. Why might a mutation with detrimental effects persist in a given population?

Data Analysis

The CCR5 Protein Mutation

Chemokines are small proteins in the human body that are secreted by cells in the immune system. These proteins allow for the movement of immune cells to a site of infection, so the immune cells can target and destroy agents such as harmful microbes. The function of chemokines is regulated by their gene-protein coupled receptors, or GPCRs.

The chemokine receptor CCR5 is found on the surface of white blood cells. CCR5 plays a role in the body's inflammatory responses to infections. In the 1990s, CCR5 was found to also be involved in the infection process of human immunodeficiency virus type 1 (HIV-1), acting as a co-receptor for the virus. According to researchers, HIV-1 uses CCR5 in the initial infection stages and an alternate co-receptor, CXCR4, in the latter stages of infection and the development of AIDS. In other words, CCR5 is essential for the cell entry of HIV-1, because the virus uses CCR5 as co-receptor for fusion with the cell.

A mutation exists in which the CCR5 allele has a 32 base pair deletion in the coding region, known as CCR5-Δ32. This mutation has a protein that cannot be detected on the cell surface. People who have two of the alleles for CCR5-Δ32 have been found to be highly resistant to HIV-1 infections.

Interestingly, the global distribution of people with the CCR5-Δ32 allele is greater in some areas than others. Although the first HIV transmission in the early 1900s has been traced back to Africa, the heaviest distribution of CCR5-Δ32 is found in European populations where contact with HIV-1 has been more recent.

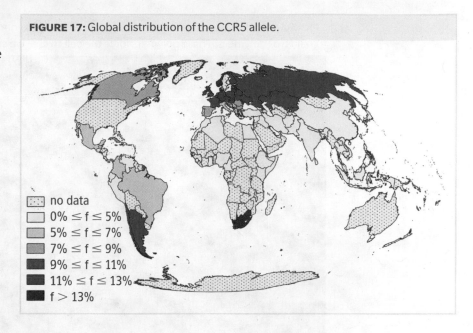

FIGURE 17: Global distribution of the CCR5 allele.

no data
0% ≤ f ≤ 5%
5% ≤ f ≤ 7%
7% ≤ f ≤ 9%
9% ≤ f ≤ 11%
11% ≤ f ≤ 13%
f > 13%

In fact, it is too recent to account for natural selection of individuals with the CCR5-Δ32 allele. Therefore, scientists theorize that other illnesses, such as the black plague or small pox, were involved in the selection for the CCR5-Δ32 allele.

Language Arts Connection Make a claim about the origin of the CCR5-Δ32 mutation. Carefully study the information about CCR5 and the map in Figure 17. Consider the following questions in your answer:

• Viruses like HIV-1 cannot enter the cell in people that lack the CCR5 protein receptor. Does this mutation provide clues for the development of an AIDS treatment or vaccine?

• Where is the greatest distribution of the CCR5 mutation?

• Why did the CCR5 mutation become so prevalent in these areas of the world?

Prepare a multimedia presentation of your analysis. Use evidence that supports your claim.

THE TUMOR SUPPRESOR GENE   MUTATIONS AND HUMAN HEALTH   INVESTIGATING MELANISM   Go online to choose one of these other paths.

Lesson Self-Check

FIGURE 18: "Sickling" of red blood cells occurs when deoxygenated HbS molecules form long chains, or polymers. These polymers force the cell to change shape.

The allele for sickle cell anemia is linked with resistance to malaria, a disease caused by a parasite transmitted from one infected person to another by mosquitoes. Individuals who have malaria may experience swelling of the brain, difficulty in breathing, liver and kidney failure, anemia, and low blood sugar. Although modern medical techniques can diagnose and cure malaria through early treatment, if untreated, the complications of malaria can lead to death.

Individuals who have malaria, but are also carriers of the sickle cell anemia gene (HbS), have been observed to not advance to the serious stage of malaria. Thus, in the absence of modern medical treatment, having an HbS allele helps protect them from the fatal consequences of malaria. According to the Centers for Disease Control and Prevention, HbS can provide 60% protection against malaria.

 Evidence Notebook Refer to your notes in your Evidence Notebook to explain why the HbS allele is more common in some populations than in others. Use what you know about genetic mutations as evidence to answer the following questions:

1. Make a claim about why the HbS allele is more common in some populations.
2. Support your claim with evidence. For example, is the phenotype that corresponds to the HbS allele harmful, beneficial, or both? How do changes in DNA lead to changes in the structure of red blood cells in people with the HbS allele?
3. Why is the frequency of the HbS allele higher in certain regions of the world, particularly in areas near Earth's equator?

CHECKPOINTS

Check Your Understanding

1. The results of a study on the effects of a mutagen on bacteria had the following results. Some bacterial cultures were exposed to the mutagen, some were not.

Culture	Number of mutant bacteria
A	0
B	350
C	10
D	4
E	3

Which culture was most likely exposed

to the mutagen? _____

2. *Epidermolysis bullosa* is a disease characterized by very delicate skin that easily blisters upon scratching or being exposed to the slightest friction. The disease is caused by a missense mutation. Which statement describes the mutation that causes this condition?

○ **a.** The mutation is a result of the premature completion of a protein.

○ **b.** The mutation is caused by a change in one of the amino acids.

○ **c.** This mutation is a result of the reading frame being shifted.

○ **d.** This mutation is caused by the duplication of the genome.

3. Before the genetic code could be understood, scientists needed to know that a codon is composed of three nucleotides. This is an example of the:

○ **a.** cumulative nature of scientific evidence.

○ **b.** scientists making inferences based on available data.

○ **c.** way that theories can lead to scientific laws.

○ **d.** ability of scientists to make hypotheses.

4. Individuals with trisomy X have three X chromosomes in their cells. Which statements can be used to describe this condition? Select all correct answers.

☐ **a.** This condition is caused by a chromosomal mutation called nondisjunction mutation.

☐ **b.** This condition is a result of the exchange of genetic material between two homologous chromosomes.

☐ **c.** This mutation is a result of chromosomes not separating during anaphase I of meiosis.

☐ **d.** This mutation is caused by balanced translocation, a type of chromosomal mutation.

5. What can change during meiosis? Select all correct answers.

☐ **a.** base sequence

☐ **b.** number of amino acids

☐ **c.** number of chromosomes

☐ **d.** gene sequence

6. Which processes are involved in the inheritance of mutated genes? Select all correct answers.

☐ **a.** meiosis

☐ **b.** fertilization

☐ **c.** mitosis

7. Watermelons are exposed to a mutagen to produce a variety that has four sets of chromosomes. The new variety is then crossed with a normal watermelon to produce seedless watermelons. What type of mutation is involved in the growing of seedless watermelon?

○ **a.** point mutation

○ **b.** gene duplication

○ **c.** frameshift mutation

○ **d.** trisomy 21

CHECKPOINTS (continued)

8. Explain what a frameshift mutation is and how it can have significant impacts on protein structure and function.

_____

_____

_____

9. Rachel Carson was one of the first ecologists to warn against the widespread use of pesticides and other potential mutagens and toxins. How might the presence of a chemical mutagen in the environment affect the genetic makeup and size of a population over time?

_____

_____

_____

10. How do mutations contribute to genetic diversity?

_____

_____

_____

_____

MAKE YOUR OWN STUDY GUIDE

In your Evidence Notebook, design a study guide that supports the main ideas from this lesson:

A mutation is a change in the sequence of an organism's DNA, and may occur spontaneously or as the result of exposure to a mutagen.

Mutations contribute to genetic diversity because as the genetic makeup of organisms changes through mutations, variety is produced.

Mutations may or may not affect an organism's phenotype.

Remember to include the following information in your study guide:
- Use examples that model main ideas.
- Record explanations for the phenomena you investigated.
- Use evidence to support your explanations. Your support can include drawings, data, graphs, laboratory conclusions, and other evidence recorded throughout the lesson.

Consider how mutations can lead to changes in DNA at both the cellular and organismal levels, and develop an explanation as to how each of these types of changes may or may not lead to changes in phenotype in real-world situations.

Evolution of Populations

Male ruffs differ in body size as well as in the size and color of the feathers on their heads and necks.

CAN YOU EXPLAIN IT?

Ruffs are shorebirds found mostly in parts of Europe and Asia. They typically make their homes in marshes and mudflats, where they feed primarily on insects and seeds. During breeding season, males gather in groups and participate in staged "fights" to attract females. In this courtship ritual, three types of males in the population are involved: the independents, the satellites, and the faeders.

About 84% of the male ruffs are "independent." These ruffs fight hard and use a lot of energy to establish a territory and attract female ruffs. They are the largest males and have large black and brown neck feathers. "Satellite" males are smaller and have white neck feathers. They move freely between independents' territories and do not fight. Though independent males may dominate them to attract a female into the territory, the satellites are often able to mate with the same females. The smallest males, called "faeders," look similar to females and generally mate with females by sneaking, often when independents and satellites are distracted or fighting.

PREDICT How can three different types of males evolve in one population?

_____

_____

_____

 Evidence Notebook As you explore this lesson, make a list of possible biotic or abiotic factors that may have contributed to the evolution of this population.

Genetic Variation in Populations

Adult Asian beetles are highly variable in color and pattern. These insect eaters are native to Asia but were introduced to the United States in the 1960s and 1970s by the U.S. Department of Agriculture to try to reduce agricultural pests. In autumn, the beetles cluster together to seek warm places to spend the winter. Often, these warm places are people's homes and offices, where the beetles become a pest.

FIGURE 1: Asian beetles

ANALYZE Record the similarities and differences you see between the Asian beetles in Figure 1. Why do you think traits vary between individuals in a population?

_____

_____

_____

_____

_____

_____

_____

Differences in the Gene Pool

Phenotypic differences are due to differences in genes that code for those traits. Certain differences may offer a competitive advantage compared to the rest of the population. A particular phenotype may allow individuals to survive longer and reproduce more efficiently, both of which increase the total number of offspring produced. As a result, the phenotype will become more prevalent over time. This gradual favoring of advantageous traits within a population is called natural selection, and it directly affects the population's gene pool. A gene pool is the collection of alleles found in all the individuals of a population.

Multiple alleles code for the Asian beetle color phenotype. Scientists think that this variation provides the beetles with a competitive advantage over other predators in certain habitats and seasons. For example, the darker-colored beetles might be able to absorb more heat from the sun in autumn, so they can survive outdoors longer as the weather cools, allowing them to eat more before they overwinter.

EXPLAIN Select the correct terms to complete the statement about genetic variation.

Genetic variation results from errors called mistakes | mutations | alterations that occur during DNA replication | transcription | translation. These errors can be passed on from parent to offspring through meiosis | mitosis | mutations, the process that produces gametes. In this process, there is an additional source of genetic variation. Alignment | Elongation | Recombination produces genetic variation when homologous chromosomes cross over and an exchange of genetic material occurs.

The different alleles in a gene pool ultimately result from mutations. When mutations occur during meiosis, the gametes that form may carry these mutations. Genetic variation may also be an outcome of crossing over and recombination, which occur during meiosis. During this process, chromosomes condense and homologous chromosomes align. Homologous chromosomes have the same genes but could have different alleles. During the alignment, an exchange of genetic material may take place. This exchange could alter the rearrangement of the linked genes in the chromosomes. As a result, the gametes are not genetically identical.

INFER How can mutations in gametes become widespread in the gene pool?

_____

_____

_____

_____

Variation in Alleles

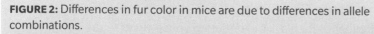

Different combinations of alleles in a gene pool can be formed when organisms mate and have offspring. Alleles are different forms, or versions, of genes. For example, mice with either one or two copies of the dominant *B* allele have brown fur, while mice with two recessive *b* alleles have black fur.

FIGURE 2: Differences in fur color in mice are due to differences in allele combinations.

EVALUATE Use the information in Figure 2 to answer the following questions.

1. How many total alleles for fur color are present in this gene pool? _____

2. How many of those alleles code for brown fur? _____

3. How many of those alleles code for black fur? _____

You can use the total number of alleles, the number of dominant alleles, and the number of recessive alleles to find the allele frequency in a population. Allele frequency is the proportion of one allele, compared with all the alleles for that trait, in the gene pool. To find the frequency of a particular allele, divide the number of times the allele is present by the total number of alleles in the population.

$$\text{Allele Frequency} = \frac{\text{Number of particular allele}}{\text{Total number of alleles}}$$

Allele frequency can also be expressed as a percentage by multiplying the frequency by 100. The frequencies of all the different alleles in a population should equal 1.0, or 100%.

Math Connection

SOLVE Use the information below and the allele frequency equation to answer the following questions.

- Total number of alleles = 12
- Number of dominant alleles (B) = 7
- Number of recessive alleles (b) = 5

1. What is the allele frequency for brown fur, B? Round your answer to the thousandths place. _____

2. What percentage of alleles are dominant B alleles? Round your answer to the tenths place. _____

3. What is the allele frequency for black fur, b? Round your answer to the thousandths place. _____

4. What percentage of alleles are recessive b alleles? Round your answer to the tenths place. _____

Allele frequency is used to track genetic variation in populations and detect changes in alleles. Imagine that periodic fires blacken the ground in the habitat where the mice with brown and black fur live. The black mice may be better camouflaged, providing more protection against predators. If they survive and reproduce more effectively than brown mice, the frequency of the b allele may increase over time relative to the B allele frequency.

Analyzing Population Evolution

Some chickens, ducks, and other birds can lay eggs that have either white or blue shells. Blue eggshells are dominant and are coded for by the allele O. White eggshells are recessive and are coded for by the allele o. The outcome of a heterozygous-heterozygous cross for eggshell color can be determined by making a Punnett square. We can make a Punnett square to represent any dominant or recessive allele in a population for this type of cross.

FIGURE 3: The Punnett square gives the possible genotypes of the offspring of parents heterozygous for eggshell color.

	O (p)	o (q)
O (p)	OO (p^2)	Oo (pq)
o (q)	Oo (pq)	oo (q^2)

a In some birds, blue eggshells are dominant to white eggshells.

b In this Punnett square, p represents the frequency of the dominant allele and q represents the frequency of the recessive allele.

In this simplified Punnett square, p represents any dominant allele and q represents any recessive allele. The Punnett square shows that the genotypic frequency of OO is represented as p^2, the frequency of Oo is represented as pq, and the frequency of oo is represented as q^2. The total frequency of all possible genotypes in a population must equal 1. Therefore, allele frequency can be found using the equation $p + q = 1$, and genotype frequency can be calculated from $p^2 + 2pq + q^2 = 1$. This equation is based on how many of each genotype are represented in the Punnett square. There is one p^2, there are two pq, and one q^2. Scientists use these equations to predict the genotypic frequencies in a population. Then they compare the predicted frequencies to the actual frequencies in a population.

ANALYZE What could a scientist conclude if the genotypic frequencies in a population are different from the predicted values?

_____

_____

_____

_____

The equation $p^2 + 2pq + q^2 = 1$ is known as the Hardy-Weinberg equation. A Hardy-Weinberg population is in equilibrium, meaning it is stable and not evolving. Five conditions must be met for a population to be in equilibrium: there are no genetic mutations, the population is very large, there is no occurrence of natural selection, there is no introduction of new genetic material into the population, and individuals are equally likely to mate with any other individual in the population.

For a population to be in equilibrium, the effects of any mutations have to be insignificant. The population must be large enough to avoid random changes in allele frequencies that come with small samples. Every individual has an equal chance of surviving, so there is no natural selection. Populations must be isolated, so there is no immigration or emigration of individuals or their genes, and individuals mate at random.

If you think about it, the Hardy-Weinberg equilibrium can be upset by many different things. These disruptions make the Hardy-Weinberg equilibrium nearly impossible in reality. Scientists use it as a model of an ideal population and compare real populations to it. This gives scientists a good idea of if a population is evolving and what the mechanism might be.

Data Analysis

Calculating Genotypic Frequencies

SAMPLE PROBLEM A population of chickens produces 840 blue eggs and 160 white eggs. Use the equation $p^2 + 2pq + q^2 = 1$ to determine the predicted genotypic frequencies for this population. Then compare those values with the actual genotypic frequencies in the population.

VARIABLES p = frequency of O (dominant allele)

q = frequency of o (recessive allele)

p^2 = frequency of eggs with OO (homozygous dominant genotype, blue shell)

$2pq$ = frequency of eggs with Oo (heterozygous genotype, blue shell)

q^2 = frequency of eggs with oo (homozygous recessive genotype, white shell)

STEP 1 Solve for q^2 by dividing the number of oo eggs by 1000.

$$q^2 = \frac{160}{1000} = 0.16$$

STEP 2 Solve for q by taking the square root of each side of the equation.

$$q = \sqrt{0.16} = 0.4$$

STEP 3 Determine p by substituting the value of q in the equation $p + q = 1$:

$$p + 0.4 = 1, p = 1 - 0.4 = 0.6$$

These are the predicted allele frequencies: $p = 0.6$ and $q = 0.4$.

STEP 4 Calculate the predicted genotypic frequencies from the predicted allele frequencies:

$$p^2 = (0.6)^2 = 0.36$$

$$2pq = 2\,(0.6)(0.4) = 0.48$$

$$q^2 = (0.4)^2 = 0.16$$

PRACTICE PROBLEMS **APPLY** What percentage of this population is expected to be OO, Oo, and oo? What do these values mean?

_____

_____

_____

INFER Through genetic analysis, scientists discovered the actual genotypic frequencies for the above population to be $OO = 0.60$, $Oo = 0.14$, and $oo = 0.26$. What can you infer by comparing these data to the values predicted above?

_____

_____

_____

Selection on Peppered Moth Populations

The peppered moth, *Biston betularia*, found in the English countryside, ranges in color from light (*Biston betularia typica*) to dark (*Biston betularia carbonaria*). Before the Industrial Revolution, light-colored moths were more prevalent than dark-colored moths. During the Industrial Revolution, trees became covered in dark soot from coal burned in factories. Over time, scientists observed that the number of dark moths increased relative to light moths. More recently, clean air laws returned the trees to their lighter coloring, and the dark-colored moths decreased in frequency.

Recent studies found bird predation was one possible driving force behind the population shift. When trees were covered with soot, birds preyed on light moths since they were easier to see. When the soot faded, birds preyed on dark moths. Other factors, such as migration, may have also influenced the population and require further study.

FIGURE 4: The two variations of the peppered moth, *Biston betularia*.

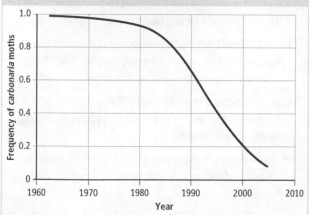

FIGURE 5: Frequency of dark moths around Leeds, England, from 1970 to 2000

Credit: Adapted from "The Rise and Fall of the Carbonaria Form of the Peppered Moth" by Laurence M Cook from *The Quarterly Review of Biology*, Vol. 78, No. 4, 399-417, https://doi.org/10.1086/378925. Copyright ©2003 by The University of Chicago Press. Adapted and reproduced by permission of The University of Chicago Press.

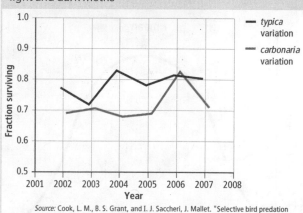

FIGURE 6: Effect of bird predation on the population of light and dark moths

Source: Cook, L. M., B. S. Grant, and I. J. Saccheri, J. Mallet. "Selective bird predation on the peppered moth: the last experiment of Michael Majerus." *Biol. Lett.* 2012. Published 8 February 2012. doi: 10.1098/rsbi.2011.1136.

ANALYZE Which statements correctly compare the frequencies of the *typica* and *carbonaria* moths? Select all correct answers.

☐ **a.** Before the Industrial Revolution, there were more *carbonaria* than *typica* moths.

☐ **b.** After clean air laws were implemented, the number of *typica* moths decreased.

☐ **c.** Before the Industrial Revolution, there were more *typica* than *carbonaria* moths.

☐ **d.** After clean air laws were implemented, birds preyed more on *carbonaria* moths.

☐ **e.** The number of *typica* and *carbonaria* moths has remained constant over time.

 Evidence Notebook How does the Hardy-Weinberg equilibrium equation use genetic variation and allele frequencies in a population to describe whether a population is evolving?

Selection on Populations

Though king penguins look similar, members of the population differ in some of their physical traits. Some penguins may be larger and some smaller. Some individuals may have long beaks, and some may have short beaks. The majority of penguins have characteristics somewhere between these two extremes.

Normal Distribution

If penguin beak lengths and their frequencies are graphed, the result is a bell-shaped curve like the one shown in Figure 7. The shape of the curve shows that the beak length of the majority of the individuals is close to the mean length. Mean, or average, beak length is determined by adding the beak lengths of all the individuals and then dividing the sum by the number of individuals. The graph also shows that there are not many individuals with extreme traits—that is, very short or very long beaks.

Normal Distribution

FIGURE 7: Most individuals in this population have traits that fall between two extreme phenotypes.

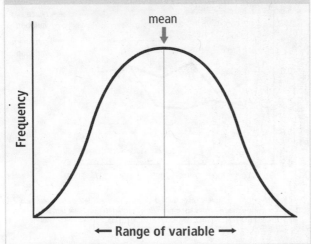

FIGURE 8: A colony of king penguins

EXPLAIN Why do few individuals have very extreme phenotypes, such as very long or very short beaks, and more individuals show a trait somewhere in between?

○ **a.** Extreme phenotypes are not as advantageous to the individual as are traits closer to the mean.

○ **b.** Individuals with phenotypes in between the extreme phenotypes do not survive and therefore cannot pass their traits to offspring.

○ **c.** A change in the environment must have occurred that resulted in the extreme phenotypes being favored over time.

○ **d.** The mean phenotypes are selected against, as those individuals do not survive long enough to reproduce.

A normal distribution shows an arrangement of data in which most of the values fall in the middle of the data set, represented by the mean. The frequency of occurrences of the variable is highest near the mean value and decreases toward each extreme end of the range. The curve that results is bell-shaped and symmetrical. This means that for a population showing a normal distribution, the alleles for the mean phenotype are more advantageous than the alleles associated with either extreme phenotype. Because individuals with average-sized beaks are more likely to survive and reproduce, king penguin beak size follows a normal distribution. Individuals with extremely short or extremely long beaks face disadvantages they must overcome if they are to survive and reproduce.

Changing Populations

King penguins live and breed on islands around Antarctica. Like other penguin species that live in cold areas, king penguins have features that allow them to live in this type of environment.

 Collaborate Suppose as a result of increasing temperatures, the trait for having a thicker layer of fat was selected against and the thinner layer of fat was selected for. With a partner, discuss how the normal distribution graph will be affected.

In populations, natural selection favors advantageous phenotypes that increase reproductive success. This results in favorable genes becoming more widespread in a population over time. This "favoring" results in observable changes in the allele frequencies in a population, and occurs in several ways. Microevolution is the observable change in the allele frequencies of a population over time. Microevolution occurs on a small scale—within a single population.

Stabilizing Selection

In humans, very low or very high birth weight can cause complications that affect a baby's health. Many infants with very low or very high birth weights do not survive to adulthood. Over many generations, these two phenotypes were selected against. More average birth weights, which had fewer weight-related complications, were selected for. Today, the frequency of individuals with an average birth weight is higher than those with extremely low or extremely high birth weights.

ANALYZE Which graph represents how natural selection has acted on birth weight? The original population is represented by the dotted line, and the solid line represents the population after selection.

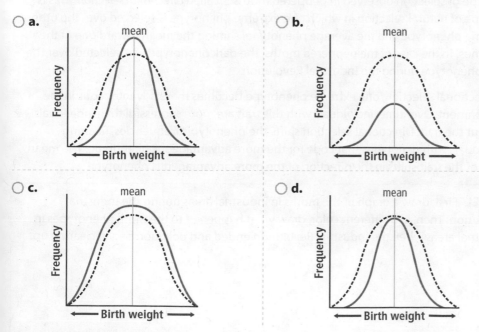

This type of selection is called *stabilizing selection*. In this selection type, intermediate phenotypes are selected over phenotypes at both extremes. Individuals that express the mean traits survive and reproduce more effectively than individuals without these traits. This results in an increase in the frequency of these phenotypes in the population.

Directional Selection

A different type of selection can be seen in the case of the peppered moth. Recall that before the Industrial Revolution, there were more sightings of light-colored (*typica*) moths and fewer sightings of dark-colored (*carbonaria*) moths. As factories were built during the Industrial Revolution, pollution increased. At this time, scientists observed that the number of *typica* moths decreased, while the number of the *carbonaria* moths increased and became more abundant in the population than the *typica* variety.

ANALYZE Which graph represents how natural selection acted on moth coloration during the Industrial Revolution? The dotted line represents the original population, and the solid line represents the population after selection.

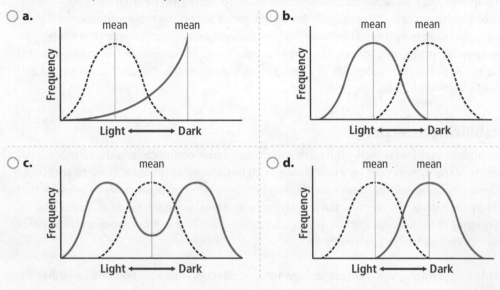

The type of selection observed in peppered moths is called *directional selection*. This is the type of natural selection in which one extreme phenotype is selected over the other extreme phenotype and the average phenotype, shifting the mean toward one of the extremes. In the case of the peppered moths, the dark phenotype was selected over the light phenotype during the Industrial Revolution.

In directional selection, one extreme phenotype becomes more advantageous in the environment. Over time, individuals with this trait are more successful than individuals without the trait. Directional selection shifts the phenotypic frequencies, favoring individuals with genotypes that code for the more advantageous phenotype. The mean value of the trait shifts in the direction of the more advantageous phenotype.

MODEL First, draw a graph of the moths in industrial areas during the Industrial Revolution. Then, in a different color, draw what happened to the moth phenotypes in industrial areas when the Industrial Revolution ended and pollution began clearing up.

Disruptive Selection

Lazuli buntings are birds found in the western part of the United States. The male birds have feathers with colors that range from brown to bright blue. The dominant adult males have the brightest blue feathers. They are the most successful in attracting mates and have the best territories. For young buntings, the brightest blue and the dullest brown males are more likely to win mates than males with bluish-brown feathers.

Research suggests that dominant adult males are aggressive toward young buntings they see as threats, including bright blue and bluish-brown males. The dullest brown birds can therefore attract a mate because the adult males leave them alone. Meanwhile, the bright blue birds attract mates simply because of their color.

APPLY Which graph represents how selective pressures will act upon male lazuli bunting feather coloration? The dotted line represents the original population, and the solid line represents the population after selection.

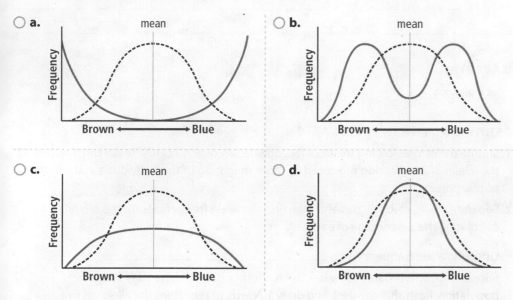

The type of selection observed in male lazuli bunting birds is called *disruptive selection*. This is the type of natural selection in which both extreme phenotypes are favored, while individuals with the intermediate phenotype (in between brown and blue) are selected against. The middle of the distribution graph is disrupted: individuals with genotypes that code for intermediate phenotypes are less successful than those with genotypes that code for extreme phenotypes. By favoring both extreme phenotypes, disruptive selection can lead to the formation of new species.

GATHER EVIDENCE Compare and contrast stabilizing, directional, and disruptive selection. Describe any patterns that can help to explain changes in populations.

_____

_____

_____

_____

_____

 Evidence Notebook Using evidence from this lesson, explain why populations, not individuals, evolve.

Hands-On Activity

Modeling Population Changes

Small populations are more likely to be affected by random events than large populations. Use a deck of cards to represent a lizard population. The four suits represent four different alleles for tail shape. The allele frequencies of the original population are 25% each of spade, heart, club, and diamond tail shapes.

MAKE A CLAIM

How can random chance affect the allele frequencies in a population?

_____

_____

MATERIALS

· deck of cards

CARRY OUT THE INVESTIGATION

1. Shuffle the cards. Holding the deck facedown, turn over 40 cards. These cards represent the alleles of 20 offspring produced by random mating of the individuals in the initial population.

2. Separate the 40 cards by suit and then find the allele frequencies for the offspring by calculating the percentage of each suit.

   Offspring allele frequency _____

3. Suppose a storm isolates a few lizards on another island where they start a new population. Reshuffle the deck and draw 10 cards to represent the alleles of five offspring produced in this smaller isolated population.

4. Repeat Step 2 to calculate the resulting allele frequencies.

   Offspring allele frequency _____

ANALYZE

1. Compare the original allele frequencies to those calculated in Steps 2 and 4. How did they change?

   _____

   _____

2. Does this activity demonstrate evolution? Why or why not? Does it demonstrate natural selection? Why or why not?

   _____

   _____

 Evidence Notebook Explain how the difference in gene flow between populations could cause them to evolve in different or similar ways.

Effects of Gene Flow

In addition to natural selection, two other mechanisms can cause changes in the alleles in a population: gene flow and genetic drift. Gene flow is the movement of genes into or out of a population, and can cause a population to evolve. Genetic drift is a change in allele frequencies due to chance. Without genetic drift, gene flow tends to make populations less diverse as compared to each other. If gene flow is restricted, populations tend to diverge and could eventually become separate species.

Genetic Drift

What you observed in the lizard population activity is genetic drift. Small populations are more likely to be affected by genetic drift than larger populations. The chance event causes some alleles to decrease in frequency, which may cause them to eventually disappear from the population altogether. It causes other alleles to increase in frequency and possibly become fixed in the population.

Bottleneck Effect

In the late 1800s, northern elephant seals were severely overhunted for their blubber, which was used in lamp oil. It is estimated that by 1890, there were fewer than 100 individuals left. After hunting ended, the population rebounded, and now there are more than 100 000 individuals.

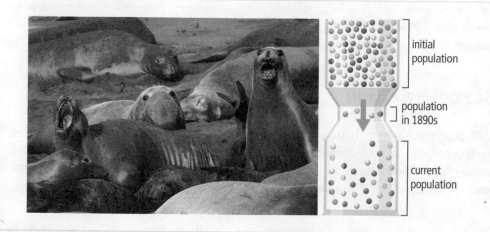

FIGURE 9: The hunting of northern elephant seals greatly depleted the species' numbers and genetic diversity.

initial population

population in 1890s

current population

ANALYZE Use the model in Figure 9 to explain the change in genetic variation between the initial elephant seal population and the population after it rebounded.

_____

_____

_____

The northern elephant seal suffered from the bottleneck effect. This is genetic drift that results from an event that reduces the size of a population. Through genetic drift, some alleles can be completely lost from the gene pool, which results in lower genetic diversity.

Founder Effect

Consider what would happen to a population of beetles that was nearly wiped out due to a natural disaster, such as the population shown in Figure 10. The original population had high levels of genetic diversity. After the disaster, two smaller populations of beetles survived, but there was no gene flow between the populations. The descendants of founding Population A would have a different gene pool from the descendants of Population B. For example, founding Population A had beetles with genes coding for black exoskeletons. The descendants of these individuals also had black exoskeletons. Founding Population B, however, had no individuals with genes for a black exoskeleton, so this gene was lost in Population B.

FIGURE 10: Genetic variation decreases when a small number of individuals colonize new areas.

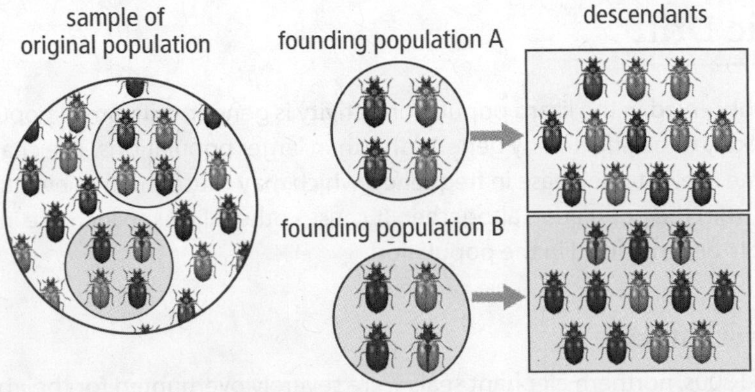

The founder effect is genetic drift that occurs when a small number of individuals become isolated from the original population and colonize a new area. Figure 10 demonstrates genetic drift due to the founder effect in a beetle population. The founding populations each represent a distinct gene pool observed in the original population. As a result, allele frequencies within the founding populations change from the original population, which reduces genetic variation.

Sexual Selection

Male peacocks have elaborate tails made of long, colorful feathers. These feathers not only make male peacocks easy targets for predators, they also make flying away from predators harder. Female peacocks, though, are a muted, brown color and do not possess long tail feathers like the males. These flashy colors and ornamental traits seem to be in contrast with what should have evolved from natural selection, so how did they evolve?

In general, mating is less costly to a male than a female. Males produce many sperm, so they can invest in mating without much cost. Females, on the other hand, produce a limited number of offspring. They tend to select males that will give their offspring the best chance of survival. This difference in reproductive costs can make females choosier than males about mates. Sexual selection occurs when certain traits increase reproductive success.

Prior to the mating season, male animals such as bighorn sheep, deer, elk, and sea lions fight other males. The winner in this competition establishes his dominance over other males or he solidifies his ownership of a territory. This type of competition among males to increase their access to females is known as intrasexual selection.

FIGURE 11: The winner of this fight increases his chances of mating with a female.

The superb bird of paradise, like other species of birds of paradise, engages in courtship behavior that increases mating success by attracting females. Superb males have feathers on their backs that are not used for flying. During courtship, the male birds use their back and chest feathers to form a funnel-like structure around their heads. This posture highlights their bright-colored breast feathers. They also flick their feathers and dance. Other birds of paradise have bright colors, large plumes, and long tail feathers and perform dances to attract the attention of females.

FIGURE 12: The male superb bird of paradise has bright feathers and large plumes to attract females.

Intersexual selection is a form of sexual selection in which males display certain traits that attract females. Males involved in intersexual selection are often more brightly colored, have larger features, or have other characteristics to attract females.

In birds of paradise, long feathers, bright plumes, and courtship behavior are due to intersexual selection. These traits are costly to develop, so males who possess them are usually healthier or stronger. Data show that, in some species, bright colors indicate parasite resistance. Sick males may have muted coloring and likely do not possess characteristics attractive to females. Females are able to pick the males in the best condition or those that have better genes for mating.

Stability and Change

A population is stable and in genetic equilibrium when its genetic makeup does not change over time. Because the conditions that lead to this genetic stability are rare in the natural world, evolution occurs.

APPLY Select the correct terms to identify each of the five mechanisms that can lead to evolution.

| Gene flow | Genetic drift | Mutations | Natural selection | Sexual selection |

1. _____ can lead to the formation of new alleles. These factors produce genetic variation.

2. _____ affects populations, acting on traits that increase an individual's ability to survive and reproduce.

3. _____ selects for traits that give members of a population a competitive advantage in mating and reproducing.

4. _____ affects small populations and is caused by random events that affect the population.

5. _____ occurs when individuals move in and out of populations. This movement introduces and removes alleles from the gene pool.

 Evidence Notebook Why is genetic drift more likely in small populations than in large populations? Consider the male ruffs from the beginning of this lesson. How could genetic drift or sexual selection explain the different types of males in the population? Use evidence from the lesson to support your claims.

Mechanisms of Speciation

FIGURE 13: These closely-related squirrels have different physical traits.

a Kaibab squirrel

b Abert's squirrel

In general, a species is a group of similar organisms that can breed and produce fertile offspring. The millions of species that live on Earth today emerged over time, with each new species arising from an already existing species. This diversification of one species from another is supported by genetic, developmental, and anatomical similarities among species. In addition, geological and fossil evidence show how species have changed over time.

 Collaborate Kaibab and Abert's squirrels live on opposite sides of the Grand Canyon. Though closely related, they do not share all of the same characteristics. How did these differences come about? Make a list with a partner to explain your reasoning.

Speciation

Where do new species come from? Speciation is the rise of two or more species from a single existing species. Experiments can be used to model speciation. In one such experiment, an existing population of fruit flies, *Drosophila melanogaster,* was divided into two groups. One group was given maltose-based food, and the other was given starch-based food. The goal of the experiment was to determine what changes would occur from the isolation of species and the presence of different food sources.

Many generations later, the mating preference of the flies was analyzed. The scientists found that the flies raised on maltose-based food, called maltose flies, preferred to mate with other maltose flies. The flies raised on starch-based food, called starch flies, preferred to mate with other starch flies. However, cross-breeding between the two groups could still occur. This experiment shows a distinct mating preference and the beginning of reproductive isolation within a species. If the two groups of fruit flies were eventually unable to breed successfully, then speciation would occur.

FIGURE 14: Changes in fruit flies can occur due to differing food sources.

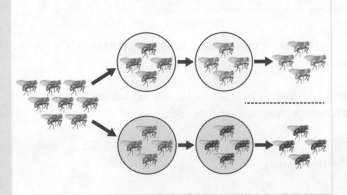

INFER What happened during the many generations that these flies were kept separated? How might this period of isolation have contributed to the mating preferences shown?

_____

_____

_____

Reproductive Isolation

If gene flow is interrupted between two populations of the same species, the populations are said to be isolated. Isolated populations are prevented from mating and exchanging genes. This means natural selection acts upon a different gene pool for each population. Different mutations will accumulate, different variations will be selected for or against, and eventually adaptations will occur that prevent mating between the two populations. Isolated populations that are in different environments, and therefore exposed to different selective pressures, will diverge from one another more quickly. It becomes more likely that reproductive isolation will occur as the two populations become more different. Even isolated populations in similar environments can undergo speciation if genetic drift takes the two gene pools in opposite directions.

Reproductive isolation occurs when members of different populations can no longer mate successfully. Sometimes members of the two populations are not physically able to mate with each other. In other cases, they cannot produce offspring that survive and reproduce. Reproductive isolation is the final step of becoming a separate species.

APPLY How might two populations of the same species become reproductively isolated from one another? Select all correct answers.

☐ **a.** A flock of birds stops migrating to its summer breeding grounds.

☐ **b.** A creek fills for the spring, separating mice on opposite banks for two months.

☐ **c.** A plant seed is carried from one population to a newly formed island.

Physical Separation

An isthmus is a strip of land with water on both sides that links two larger landmasses. The Isthmus of Panama formed through a combination of volcanic island formation and uplift of the ocean floor. These two geological factors made solid land where there was once an open passage between the Atlantic and Pacific Oceans.

Around 3 million years ago, the isthmus closed in, permanently separating populations of snapping shrimp. Once separated, each population of shrimp adapted to a different environment and became genetically different. Over time, the groups became different enough to be reproductively isolated and speciation occurred. The physical separation of two or more populations can lead to speciation through geographic isolation.

FIGURE 15: Speciation in snapping shrimp occurred due to geographic isolation.

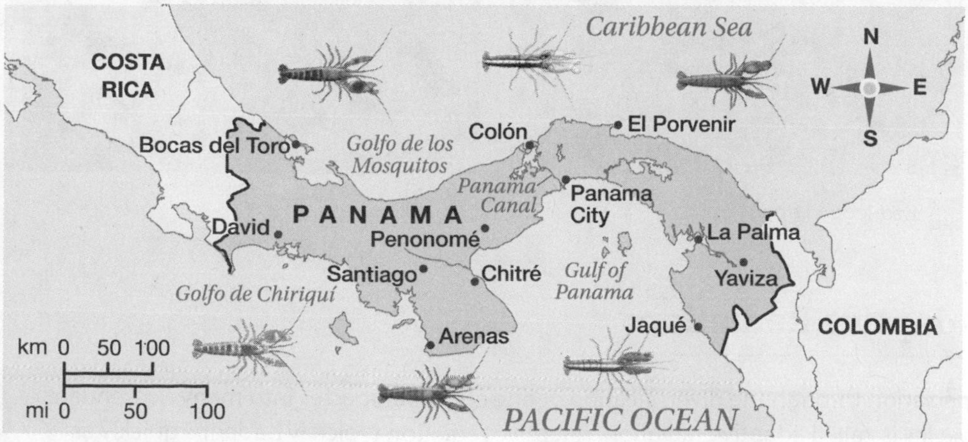

Credit: Adapted from *Allopatric Speciation* by Carl Hansen and Nancy Knowlton. Copyright © by The Smithsonian Institution. Adapted and reproduced by permission of The Smithsonian Institution.

FIGURE 16: These birds look similar but use different songs to attract mates.

a Eastern meadowlark

b Western meadowlark

Behavior and Timing

Behavioral isolation is caused by differences in courting or mating behaviors. If two populations do not use the same courting or mating behaviors, then mating, and therefore gene flow, between the two groups is unlikely to occur. When gene flow is interrupted, natural selection acts upon the different gene pools. Reproductive isolation and speciation may eventually occur.

Male songbirds sing to defend their territories and attract mates. An eastern meadowlark and a western meadowlark look almost exactly the same. The major difference between these species is their songs. The eastern and western meadowlarks use completely different songs to attract mates. This means eastern meadowlark males cannot successfully attract western meadowlark females, and western meadowlark females cannot give eastern meadowlark males the correct breeding cues. The two species have become behaviorally isolated.

The red-legged frog and the yellow-legged frog are closely related. The development of mating seasons that occur at different times caused these species to become temporally isolated. Temporal isolation occurs when timing prevents reproduction between populations. Red-legged frog populations breed from January to March while yellow-legged frog populations in the same area breed from late March to May. Speciation from a common ancestor occurred as the overlap in mating seasons shrank. The flow of genes between the two groups also shrank, and the two groups diverged.

ANNOTATE Highlight the text in the paragraph above to help you explain how the mating seasons of red-legged frogs and yellow-legged frogs differ. How does having different mating seasons lead to speciation within a population?

_____

_____

FIGURE 17: Red-legged frogs and yellow-legged frogs have different mating seasons.

a Red-legged frog   b Yellow-legged frog

Adaptive Radiation

Speciation through the diversification of one ancestral species into many descendant species is called adaptive radiation. Adaptive radiation typically happens quickly as species benefit from less competition, new niches, or specializations that give them a selective advantage.

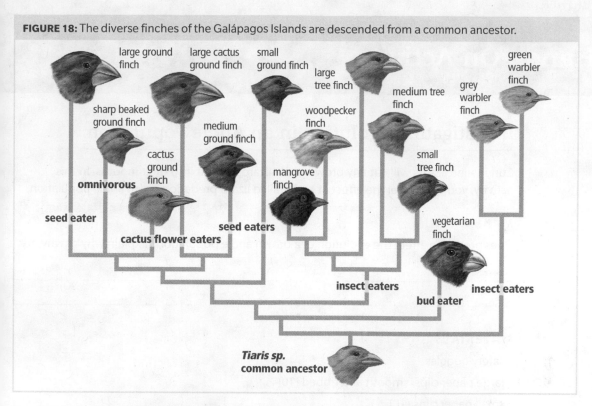

FIGURE 18: The diverse finches of the Galápagos Islands are descended from a common ancestor.

large ground finch

large cactus ground finch

small ground finch

large tree finch

medium tree finch

green warbler finch

grey warbler finch

sharp beaked ground finch

woodpecker finch

cactus ground finch

omnivorous

medium ground finch

small tree finch

mangrove finch

seed eater

seed eaters

cactus flower eaters

vegetarian finch

insect eaters

insect eaters

bud eater

Tiaris sp. common ancestor

Darwin's finches are an example of adaptive radiation that occurred on an island system. The 14 species of finch found on the Galápagos Islands came from a common ancestor. The descendants have diversified and specialized to take advantage of different niches. The many different finch species minimize competition among themselves by specializing in different food sources. For example, populations of finches with larger beaks can crack harder and larger seeds. Populations of finches with smaller, pointy beaks can catch insects. Darwin's finches are a classic example of changes in environmental conditions driving the adaptation and expansion of species.

EVALUATE Which factors support the idea that adaptive radiation occurred in the finches of the Galápagos Islands? Select all correct answers.

☐ **a.** Finches were exposed to a catastrophic event.

☐ **b.** Finches are closely related.

☐ **c.** Finches represent isolated populations.

☐ **d.** Finches focused on particular niches.

☐ **e.** Finches share a common ancestor.

☐ **f.** Finches share many of the same genes, with only minor differences.

For adaptive radiation to take place, there must be adaptation by a species that leads to speciation. For example, dinosaur extinctions led to more resources and fewer predators for mammals. The open niches left by dinosaurs may have been the trigger for adaptive radiation of mammals after dinosaurs became extinct. Mammals diversified and adapted to new niches, producing new species in many cases. This is an example of a catastrophic change in the environment leading to the expansion of an entire class of organisms.

 Evidence Notebook Which type of reproductive isolation could have led to the speciation of squirrels in the Grand Canyon? Use evidence to support your claim.

Hands-On Activity

Investigating Evolution in an Anole Population

Curly-tailed lizards will eat any brown anole lizards that fit into their mouths. In this activity, you will model the effect of curly-tailed lizard predation on an anole population.

MAKE A CLAIM

Does predation affect the evolution of a brown anole population? Explain why or why not.

MATERIALS

- safety goggles
- large paper clips, smooth and ribbed (10)
- small paper clips (10)
- "extras" cup containing 20 additional large paper clips (10 smooth, 10 ribbed)

SAFETY INFORMATION

- Wear safety goggles during the setup, hands-on, and takedown segments of the activity.
- Immediately pick up any items dropped on the floor so they do not become a slip/fall hazard.
- Wash your hands with soap and water immediately after completing this activity.

CARRY OUT THE INVESTIGATION

1. Obtain 10 large and 10 small paper clips to represent the initial population of anoles. Spread out the paper clips in front of your group. Large anoles may have genotype *BB* (large ribbed paper clip) or *Bb* (large smooth paper clip). Small anoles have genotype *bb* (small paper clip). Keep extra paper clips in the "extras" cup.

Effect of Curly-Tailed Lizard Predation on a Population of Brown Anole Lizards									
Population Stage	**Number of Anoles**				**Genotype Frequencies**			**Allele Frequencies**	
	Total	*BB*	*Bb*	*bb*	*BB*	*Bb*	*bb*	*B*	*b*
1 (Generation 1)									
2 (Generations 1+2)									
3 (Generation 1+2+3)									
4 (Generation 1+2+3+4)									

2. Fill out the table for Generation 1.

3. Three small brown anoles are eaten by curly-tailed lizards. Put three small paper clips in the "extras" cup.

4. Mix up the paper clips that remain in your population and randomly pull three aside. These represent the genotypes that get passed on to the next generation.

5. Take three paper clips from the cup—one to match each paper clip that you pulled aside in Step 4. The new paper clips represent the new generation. Join the three pairs with the rest of the population, bringing the population total back up to 20.

6. Fill in the information for this population stage in the second row of the table.

7. Repeat steps 3–6 until you have produced Generation 4.

8. Draw two line graphs, one each for each allele frequency—*B* and *b*. Put population stage (1 through 4) on the *x*-axis and allele frequency (from 0 to 1) on the *y*-axis.

ANALYZE

1. What happens to the frequency of each allele over the four generations?

2. Is this population evolving, or is it in Hardy-Weinberg equilibrium? Explain.

3. Which of the five conditions required for equilibrium are met and which are not?

EXAMINING SELECTION   SELECTION IN AFRICAN SWALLOWTAILS   RUNAWAY SELECTION   Go online to choose one of these other paths.

Lesson Self-Check

FIGURE 19: All three types of male ruffs can occur in the same population at the same time.

Scientists think that the independent males expend a lot of energy and face the risk of being injured in a fight when establishing a territory to attract females. The independents (85% of the population) attract females by showing dominance.

Types of males that pay fewer of these costs have also evolved within the population. The satellites (14% of the population) mate with the females in the independent males' territories. Though independent ruffs may mate with more females, they are at risk of being injured in territorial fights and are more vulnerable to predators because of their elaborate plumage and larger size. The faeder males (1% of the population) look like female ruffs. They generally mate with females sneakily while the other males are distracted or fighting. Faeder males are able to reproduce by sneaking into an independent male's territory and quickly mating with a female.

Interestingly, scientists have discovered that the behavior and physical traits that differentiate the three types are controlled at a single genetic location, which is referred to as a "supergene." Studies indicate that the faeders are a result of a chromosome inversion that occurred 3.8 million years ago. In a chromosome inversion, a chromosome segment breaks off and reattaches in reverse order. The satellite type was a result of a chromosomal rearrangement between the original sequence and the inverted sequence that happened about 500 000 years ago. The differences in traits and behavior among these types allow them all to be successful and persist in the population.

 Evidence Notebook Refer to your notes in your Evidence Notebook to explain how three different types of males can evolve in a single population.

1. Make a claim about which selection mechanism made it possible for all three males to be in the same population. How does that mechanism work? How does the selection mechanism influence the way traits are expressed?
2. What evidence do you have to support your hypothesis? Give an example.
3. What would happen if the three male forms did not all reproduce at the same time?

CHECKPOINTS

Check Your Understanding

Use the following information to answer the next two questions.

In a population of 900 pea plants, 530 are homozygous purple, 250 are heterozygous purple, and 120 are homozygous white. Purple (*P*) is dominant and white (*p*) is recessive.

1. Complete the table to describe the genotypic frequency in this population. Express the frequency as a percentage rounded off to the nearest whole number.

Genotype	Frequency (%)
PP	_____
Pp	_____
pp	_____

2. Using the information about pea plants above, answer the following questions about allele frequencies in the population. Express the frequencies as a decimal rounded to the nearest hundredths place.

Genotype	Frequency (%)
What is the total number of alleles in the pea plant gene pool?	_____
What is the allele frequency of *P*?	_____
What is the allele frequency of *p*?	_____

3. Order the events to model the evolutionary impact of the bottleneck effect on a population.

   _____ **a.** Many of the individuals die.

   _____ **b.** Population increases with less variation.

   _____ **c.** Random event acts on a population.

   _____ **d.** Surviving individuals reproduce.

4. Widow birds are found in the southeastern part of Africa. The males have black feathers, including tail feathers that measure an average of 41 cm long. Studies have shown that females prefer and choose to mate with males that have longer tails. Which outcome can be expected to occur in this scenario over time?

   ○ **a.** There will be more males with 41-cm tails.

   ○ **b.** There will be more males with tails longer than 41 cm.

   ○ **c.** There will be more males with tails shorter than 41 cm.

   ○ **d.** There will be more males with no tails.

5. Determine if the scenarios below will likely result in an increase or a decrease in genetic variation over time.

   increase   decrease

   Mosquitoes become resistant to pesticides.

   _____

   Arabian horses mate with wild horses.

   _____

   A smaller body is selected for in cheetahs.

   _____

6. Two tree species that grow in California are very closely related. However, they have different pollination periods. Which type of reproductive isolation do these two tree species exhibit?

   ○ **a.** adaptive radiation

   ○ **b.** geographic isolation

   ○ **c.** temporal isolation

   ○ **d.** physical isolation

7. Why are island systems favorable to adaptive radiation? Select all correct answers.

   ☐ **a.** Many islands are geologically young and have relatively few species.

   ☐ **b.** Islands are hard to access.

   ☐ **c.** Islands have fewer available ecological niches.

   ☐ **d.** An island may have fewer predators.

CHECKPOINTS (continued)

8. Explain how the process of genetic drift occurs completely by chance.

_____

_____

_____

9. What are the differences and similarities between natural selection and sexual selection?

_____

_____

_____

_____

10. Scientists observed a population of monkeys on an island. The monkeys had different average finger lengths. Some monkeys had long fingers, some had short fingers, but the majority of them had finger lengths that were closer to the short finger length. Explain how this trait in the population of monkeys would evolve over time if tree branches on the island grew thicker. Would this be an example of stabilizing, directional, or disruptive selection?

_____

_____

_____

_____

_____

MAKE YOUR OWN STUDY GUIDE

 In your Evidence Notebook, design a study guide that supports the main ideas from this lesson:

Changing allele frequencies can be an indication of the evolution of a population.

Selective pressures, such as competition and predation, can shift the distribution of traits in a population.

Small populations are more susceptible to genetic drift because large populations are able to lessen the impact of random events.

Remember to include the following information in your study guide:
- Use examples that model main ideas.
- Record explanations for the phenomena you investigated.
- Use evidence to support your explanations. Your support can include drawings, data, graphs, laboratory conclusions, and other evidence recorded throughout the lesson.

Consider how the evolution of populations relates to the assumption that natural laws operate today as they did in the past and will continue to do so in the future.

Adaptive Value of Behavior

Desert night lizards form family groups during winter.

CAN YOU EXPLAIN IT?

Desert night lizards (*Xantusia vigilis*) are born alive, not hatched from an egg. After birth, the lizards stay with their mother and other family members. This is unlike most other lizard species, which tend to hatch from eggs and live independently.

Desert night lizards live in the deserts of southern California and western Utah, Nevada, and Arizona. During winter, family members come together under fallen trees and leaf litter. Their tiny size and secretive habits make desert night lizards difficult to study. But patient scientists have uncovered interesting social behaviors. For example, young lizards stay with their family for years, although they care for themselves. Living together appears to give these lizards survival advantages.

PREDICT Why do you think desert night lizards join family groups? What advantages do you think they gain by living in a group?

_____

_____

_____

_____

 Evidence Notebook As you explore this lesson, gather evidence to explain how the social behavior of desert night lizards can help them to survive and reproduce.

Evolution of Behavior

Explore Online ▶

FIGURE 1: Normally motionless, this sea anemone will swim away when it detects a sea star.

a   Sea anemone, *Stomphia coccinea*

b   Sea star, *Dermasterias imbricata*

The sea anemone, *Stomphia coccinea*, has no brain or spinal cord and usually sits motionless. Yet, when it comes in contact with the sea star, *Dermasterias imbricata*—its predator—the anemone detaches itself from its perch and swims away to safety. At other times, with other organisms, the anemone will not swim away.

PREDICT   How do you think the sea anemone detects when it comes into contact with a sea star versus some other object?

_____

_____

_____

Responsive Behavior

Explore Online ▶

Hands-On Lab

Pill Bug Behavior   Design an experiment to determine how manipulating a variable changes the behavior of pill bugs.

The environment of every organism is constantly changing. In order to survive and thrive, organisms, such as the sea anemone, must respond to these changes. Anything that triggers a response is called a stimulus (plural *stimuli*). Internal stimuli trigger a response to a change in an organism's internal environment, such as a bacterial or viral infection. External stimuli are any changes in the external environment that causes a response, such as contact with a predatory sea star.

Sense organs have specialized cells with receptors that detect changes in the environment and communicate information through nerves to the brain. The brain then sends a message back to the appropriate system, telling it how to respond. This works well in organisms with complex nervous systems, such as monkeys and fish. However, this feedback mechanism also works in organisms such as the anemone, which only has a network of neurons with no centralized brain. Receptor cells on the outer surface of the anemone detect an external stimulus, which elicits an escape response. This response allows the anemone to swim away from danger and find another suitable environment. It can attach to a new perch and start gathering food in its new environment, until another threat comes along.

MODEL Draw a model of the process that occurs when you interact with an internal or external stimulus, such as touching something hot.

The sea anemone never learned to swim away from the sea star, but it can still respond and move to safety. This is an example of an *innate behavior*, sometimes called an *instinctive behavior*. Innate behaviors are passed from generation to generation without learning, so they are heritable behaviors. An innate behavior is performed correctly the first time an animal tries it, even when the animal has never been exposed to the stimulus that triggers the behavior.

EXPLAIN Complete the statement about responsive behavior.

Innate | Inherent | Learned behavior is hardwired into an organism and requires no prior experience or external cues. These behaviors are triggered by a stimulus in an organism's homeostasis | environment | development. An example of an internal stimulus | external stimulus | internal reaction would be an infection that causes the body to respond with a fever. Innate behaviors are passed from parent to offspring and are developmental | learned | heritable.

Innate behaviors are often found where mistakes can have severe consequences. A sea anemone that does not swim away from a sea star may be attacked. Set reactions to certain stimuli allow organisms to automatically respond in a life-or-death situation.

Function of Behavior

A lizard sunning itself on a rock is likely not just relaxing. If the rock becomes shaded, the lizard will shift its position to a warmer part of the rock. These behaviors actually help the lizard regulate its internal body temperature. Too hot? No problem. The lizard simply moves to a shadier spot. This behavior has developed over time in lizard populations to help them survive in a changing environment.

INFER Complete the statement about the function of behavior.

A behavior is anything an organism does in response to a stimulus | a command | an action. These behaviors evolved within a population to help the species relate | adapt | predict to a change in the environment. By responding to stimuli from the environment, the organism is able to maintain composure | growth | homeostasis, increasing its chances of survival | evolving | responding. Organisms with this type of behavior have a greater chance of producing offspring and passing on the behavior.

Maintaining a balanced internal state, or homeostasis, is critical to the health and functioning of an organism. When a bird's internal temperature drops too low, the bird responds by puffing up its feathers to stay warm. This is a behavioral response to both the environment (the cold) and an internal stimulus (low body temperature). These responses help support a balanced state, increasing the chance of the bird's survival.

Migration

FIGURE 2: Sandhill cranes migrate in spring and fall.

To survive and reproduce, animals need water, food, and shelter. For many species, this requires individuals to migrate, or move from one location to another. Each species has one or more triggers that cue migration. Certain species of birds often migrate from one area to another in a seasonal pattern. Each season brings changes in temperature, availability of food, and length of day.

Some migration cues are biological. In some species, depletion of energy reserves may signal a need to travel to available food sources. In others, changes in hormone levels or reproductive life cycles trigger mass movements. In the early spring, sandhill cranes in North America gather in huge numbers on the Platte River in Nebraska. These cranes feed and gain energy before heading north to nesting grounds in the tundra. When the seasons change, and food becomes less available, these birds travel back south to wintering grounds in California, Utah, Texas, Florida, and Mexico.

PREDICT How does a behavior evolve, such as mass migration of a species, where all individuals respond in the same way at the same time? Use evidence from natural selection and evolution to support your answer.

_____

_____

_____

Weighing the Costs of Behavior

Every behavior has benefits and costs. A swarm is a large, dense group of animals, such as insects. A swarm offers many advantages to living and traveling. Swarms confuse predators, which protects individual members. A swarm may be better at finding food than an individual. A swarm also provides many opportunities for mating. An individual that travels with a swarm may then be more likely to survive and reproduce, since it can find mates and food, and avoid being eaten.

FIGURE 3: Locusts swarm over a field.

A swarm has disadvantages too. The size of a swarm can actually attract predators, leaving individuals on the outer edges of the swarm particularly at risk. A group with more individuals requires greater resources, which must be shared. A swarm may also allow disease to travel more quickly through a population. Swarming behavior would have more costs than benefits in an area with many predators, a smaller food supply, and high disease rates.

Murmurations are a form of group behavior in which thousands of starlings flock together as shape-shifting clouds. The birds fly together almost as one, making incredible patterns as the flock twists and turns in the sky. Murmurations are often triggered by the presence of a predator, which is outmaneuvered by the rapid pattern changes. A murmuration may also attract predators, though. Birds on the edge could provide an easy meal for a hawk.

INFER When would swarming behavior be beneficial and when would it be too costly? How might a behavior such as swarming evolve among species?

_____

_____

_____

_____

_____

Costs of Behavior

Behavioral costs can be measured in terms of energy, risk, and opportunity. Energy costs describe the difference between the energy used in carrying out an activity and the energy used if the individual had done nothing. For example, it takes energy for a lizard to move from a shady spot to a sunny spot. However, it is worth that energy cost in order to maintain body temperature.

FIGURE 4: Fighting can result in serious injury or death.

Risk costs are the increased chance of being injured or killed by carrying out a certain behavior versus doing nothing. For example, wolves risk injury or even death by fighting with other wolves. However, they may gain access to mates or better territory if they win. Sometimes, the benefits outweigh the risks.

Opportunity costs result when an animal spends time doing one behavior and loses an opportunity to do a different behavior. For example, when a songbird defends its territory from rivals, it is using time that could have been spent foraging or mating.

 Evidence Notebook What might be some of the costs of gathering in family groups for the desert night lizard?

Benefits of Behavior

If a predator approaches an animal suddenly, the stimulus elicits a behavior that is meant to protect the animal, such as running away. This behavior increases survivorship, or the number of individuals that survive over time. A behavior that increases survivorship increases fitness. This is because individuals expressing this behavior reproduce more than those that do not express the behavior, and they pass the behavior on to their offspring. Over time, this behavior becomes common in the population. A behavior increases an individual's fitness if its benefits outweigh its costs. For example, if the benefit of maintaining homeostasis by basking in the sun outweighs the cost of a lizard exposing itself to predators, the behavior will spread through the population over time.

EXPLAIN Less visible spider webs catch more insects than more visible webs. However, some spiders build webs that include very visible zigzag lines. What benefits might the spider gain by building such a visible web? Select all correct answers.

☐ **a.** Webs with zigzag lines may be easier to build than those without the lines, saving the spider energy.

☐ **b.** The visible lines may keep larger animals from crashing into the web and destroying it, so the spider does not need to rebuild the web.

☐ **c.** The lines may help to camouflage the spider from potential predators.

☐ **d.** Spiders with lower fitness make webs with visible zigzag lines. Eventually this trait will be selected against by natural selection.

All organisms require food to survive. At times it is more beneficial for an individual to gather food alone. A solitary hunter only needs to find enough food for itself or its young. In other species, such as lions, group hunting is more beneficial. The division of labor reduces the energy cost and risk cost per individual. Group hunts increase the potential to take down bigger or more prey, and the group has greater protection. However, a group must find more food, and there is more competition for that food.

FIGURE 5: Dolphins work together to hunt fish.

In some group hunts, the pack works together to pursue and take down the prey. In other groups, such as bottlenose dolphins, individuals have specific roles. Bottlenose dolphins forage in groups of three to six. One individual acts as the driver to herd the fish towards other dolphins. These dolphins line up to form a barrier that prevents the fish from escaping. The driver slaps its tail, causing the fish to leap into the air. This makes it easier for the dolphins to catch the fish. The energy cost per individual and risk from predators is less for the group, which gathers far more fish than a solitary hunter. However, this type of hunt requires coordination. If any of the dolphins do not fulfill their role effectively, the fish may escape. The dolphins must also put aside any aggression within the group to work effectively. Any fighting would reduce the chance of success for the hunt.

INFER Complete the statement by selecting the correct terms.

In order for group hunting behaviors to evolve, the behavior must have increased | decreased | neutralized the benefits to the individuals and increased | decreased | neutralized the costs to the individuals. For example, an individual dolphin must catch more | less | equal amounts of food hunting with the group than hunting alone in order for the behavior to be beneficial.

Group behaviors, such as migration, swarming, protecting territory and mates, and hunting in groups, may appear to have high costs. But as long as the benefits of these behaviors outweigh the costs, these behaviors will increase the fitness of an individual. With increased fitness, these individuals can reproduce and pass the behavior on to the next generation. Over time, behaviors that increase individual fitness become more common.

 Evidence Notebook How would the benefits of gathering together in family groups outweigh the costs for desert night lizards?

Social Interactions

Explore Online ▶

FIGURE 6: When a predator is near, individuals in a group will move in unison for protection.

Similar to the flocking of birds, schooling in fish is a group activity that benefits the individual members. Fish school for several reasons, such as foraging for food, defending themselves from predators, and reproducing. Swimming in a group may also reduce the energy cost associated with traveling through water. In the absence of predators, schools will often break apart, or the fish will take cover when in danger.

ANALYZE How do you think schooling behavior evolved over time? How does it increase the fitness of individuals in the school?

_____

_____

_____

Living in a Group

FIGURE 7: A springbok pronking.

Sometimes, springboks hop on all four legs rather than run away when they spot a predator. This behavior, called pronking, alerts the rest of the herd but makes the individual visible to predators. Pronking gives the herd enough time to escape and signals to the predator that the herd already spotted it.

GATHER EVIDENCE Pronking carries with it high energy costs and high risk costs. Why would an individual put itself at risk to alert and protect the rest of the group? What are the potential benefits?

_____

_____

_____

_____

Social behaviors include all interactions between individuals of the same species. These behaviors help make interactions easier, and often involve special signals. Social groups interact in many ways, such as through communication, mate selection, and defense.

Explore Online ▶

FIGURE 8: Pant hooting is one form of communication among chimpanzees.

Communication

Communication is the sharing or exchange of information. It is critical to the survival of individuals and groups, as well as to the species itself. Animals use communication as a way to keep in contact with one another, raise alarm in the presence of danger, and attract a mate. Vocalizations, presentation of plumage in birds, mutual grooming, scent marking, and pheromone trails are all forms of animal communication.

Chimpanzees live in dense tropical rain forests, where it is easy to lose sight of others. They use a variety of vocalizations, such as pant hooting, to stay in touch and let each other know where they are located. Chimpanzees use other vocalizations to show excitement, greet group members, and alert the group to predators. Chimpanzees also communicate through facial expressions and body postures. They perform mutual grooming to build social ties.

Explore Online ▶

FIGURE 9: This blue-footed booby is performing a courtship dance.

Mate Selection

Courtship displays are behaviors most often used by male members of a species to attract females. Scientists theorize that females use courtship displays to judge the condition of their potential mate or the quality of his genes. Courtship displays often resemble intricate dances. These dances have certain features that can cue the female about the quality of the male. For example, blue-footed boobies high step and strut to show off their blue feet to potential partners. The pigment that gives the blue-footed booby its bright blue feet comes from its food. An individual that is more successful at finding food will have brighter feet. The courtship "dance" really just lets the female know that the male can provide food for offspring. Other courtship displays may show the quality of the male by showing his ability to build a sturdy nest, or his strength in fighting off other males.

Explore Online ▶

FIGURE 10: Penguins protecting their young from a petrel.

Defense

Defensive behaviors are responses to threatening stimuli from the environment. These various behaviors are meant to reduce harm or even death to the individual. Defensive behaviors can include fighting a predator, running away, or calling to others for help. Animals will often put themselves in harm's way to protect their young as well as themselves. For example, adult penguins will sometimes put themselves between their young and a petrel, which will eat young penguins. Groups of animals also will warn each other of danger with different vocalizations. Vervet monkeys, for example, use one call to indicate that a predator is a snake and different calls to indicate that it is a large cat or bird. This tells group members where to look and how to escape.

Language Arts Connection Choose a specific social behavior and write a short research paper explaining the function of the behavior, how the behavior benefits the individual, and how the behavior also benefits the group. How do you think this behavior evolved over time?

Cooperation

Lions hunt together in packs, called prides, to increase their chances of success. Most prey can outrun a single lion but not an entire hunting group. The group works together to stalk the prey and make a barrier to prevent its escape. Then, they pounce together to take down the prey. This behavior is an example of *cooperation*, which involves behaviors that improve the fitness of the individuals involved.

Reciprocity

Vampire bats live together in tightly-knit communities, providing protection and warmth to each other. A female vampire bat will donate food that she has collected from her hunt to a bat that is unable to hunt for its own food, voluntarily regurgitating and sharing part of her meal. This comes at a cost to the donor bat, because she has used energy to gather the food and is losing some energy by sharing.

FIGURE 11: Vampire bats share food with other bats in their community.

Vampire bats keep track of which bats share food and, in turn, will share food with those bats. This is an example of *reciprocity*, another form of cooperative behavior among animals. The idea is that one action, such as sharing food, will result in a future beneficial response, such as being the recipient of shared food. Research has shown that bats in need of food received more donations if they had previously shared food with other bats.

ANALYZE Which individuals within a larger community of bats would it be most beneficial to feed after they have missed a meal or two?

- ○ **a.** It does not matter; each individual should have an equal chance to survive.
- ○ **b.** It would be more beneficial to feed a bat that is genetically related.
- ○ **c.** It would be more beneficial to feed a bat that is not genetically related.
- ○ **d.** None of the weaker bats should be fed.

Altruism

Prairie dogs stand and watch for predators. When an individual sees a predator, it raises an alarm to the group. This signaling brings attention to itself and increases its own risk of being attacked, but may save other individuals. This type of behavior is known as altruism. Altruism is a kind of behavior in which an animal reduces its own fitness to help other members of its closely related social group. In other words, the animal appears to sacrifice itself for the good of the group.

Explore Online ▶

FIGURE 12: Prairie dogs show altruistic behaviors.

EXPLAIN Complete the statement by selecting the correct terms.

An individual in a group that sounds an alarm when it sees a predator is exhibiting altruism | reciprocity | cooperation. This individual has a higher chance of dying, but it protects others that most likely have different | the same genes. These genes will then be lost | passed down to future generations.

How can we explain the evolution of altruism if behavior is supposed to increase fitness? British evolutionary biologist William Hamilton realized that alleles can be transmitted and therefore spread in a population in two ways, either directly from an individual to its offspring (direct fitness) or indirectly by helping close relatives survive (indirect fitness). Inclusive fitness is an individual's total fitness, that is, the sum of its direct fitness and indirect fitness. When an animal reproduces, its offspring gets half of its alleles. But its relatives also share some of the same alleles, in the following proportions:

• Parents and siblings share 50% of the animal's alleles.
• Nephews and nieces share 25% of its alleles.
• First cousins share 12.5% of its alleles.

When natural selection acts on alleles that favor the survival of close relatives, it is called kin selection.

FIGURE 13: Each weaver ant has a job to do, but not all ants reproduce.

Eusocial Behavior

Within colonies of insects, such as wasps, bees, and ants, only a small number of reproductive females exist. Most individuals in a eusocial species are members of nonreproductive groups. In honey bee colonies, one queen produces a few male offspring along with thousands of sterile female workers. These worker bees cannot reproduce and spend their short lives maintaining and protecting the hive, gathering food, producing wax and honey, and feeding the young. They communicate with each other through buzzing displays that indicate where other workers can find the best food. The queen uses chemicals called pheromones to control the activity of workers. Pheromones control swarming by the workers and stop the development of their reproductive organs. Pheromones also signal the workers to take care of the queen. Worker bees live for about six weeks during the summer, while the queen can live for several years. Female offspring that will one day take the queen's place are raised in a separate cell and are fed a special diet.

INFER How is it possible for a behavior to evolve when there is only one reproductive female and the rest of the colony does not reproduce?

_____

_____

_____

_____

Many eusocial insect colonies are haplodiploid. This means their sex is determined by the number of chromosome sets in an individual. Males are haploid and females are diploid. Female social insects produce daughters through eggs fertilized by sperm. Unfertilized eggs produce sons. In these animals, daughters share half of their mother's alleles but all of their father's alleles. Sisters therefore share up to 75% of their alleles overall with one another, compared with 50% in humans and most other animals. The close relationship between sisters in a colony may influence the evolution of eusociality.

Evidence Notebook Compare and contrast individual behaviors and group behaviors. What requirements are there for these behaviors to evolve?

Learned Behaviors

The behavior of a worker bee as it gathers nectar from flowers is an innate behavior. The bee was born able to perform that behavior with no training. Some animals, however, learn new behaviors. Animals that are able to learn can modify, or change, their behavior to better adapt to new situations. This ability to learn can give animals an edge in survival and reproduction.

Learning

Young chimpanzees learn how to perform many tasks, some requiring the use of tools. Chimpanzees can learn to use leaves to drink water or to use rocks to crack open hard-shelled nuts and fruits. The chimpanzee in Figure 14 is using a twig to fish termites out of a mound. These are all examples of behaviors that must be learned. Chimpanzees are not born knowing how to use tools. They learn by watching and trying to imitate the behavior from their mother or other individuals in their social group.

Explore Online ▶

FIGURE 14: A chimpanzee uses a twig to fish for termites.

EXPLAIN Which of the following best describes a benefit of learning from another individual over learning by trial and error? Select all correct answers.

☐ **a.** Learning from another individual provides a model of the skill to follow.

☐ **b.** An organism can modify a learned behavior when the environment changes.

☐ **c.** Learning by trial and error stays with an individual longer than learning from others.

☐ **d.** Learning from others can lessen the amount of time it takes to learn a skill.

☐ **e.** Learning from others may be quicker than learning by trial and error.

Some aspects of behavior are influenced by genes, but many can be modified by experience. Learned behaviors are actions that change with experience. Learning takes many forms, ranging from changes in behaviors that are largely innate to problem-solving in new situations. In each case, learning involves the strengthening of nerve pathways. Most behaviors are not simple reactions to stimuli using already-existing pathways in the animal's brain. Instead, they represent a combination of innate tendencies influenced by learning and experience. Learning allows animals to quickly adapt to changes in their environment, increasing their ability to survive and reproduce.

Explore Online ▶

Hands-On Lab

Investigating Behavior Design your own investigation to collect and analyze data to determine how practice affects behavior.

ANALYZE Consider the example of the chimpanzee learning to use tools. Can the chimpanzee pass on what it has learned and can it pass on the ability to learn?

_____

_____

Animal Cognition

FIGURE 15: Scientists can use computer touchscreens to test animal cognition.

What does it mean when people say that a dog is smarter than a cat, or a parrot is smarter than a dog? When people make these statements, they are often thinking about how the intelligence of these animals relates to human intelligence. Scientists no longer compare an animal's intelligence level with that of a human. Instead, scientists study an animal's cognitive abilities. *Cognition* refers to the mechanisms by which animals acquire, process, store, and act on information from the environment. Animal cognition looks at which animals are better at learning, perceiving different situations, remembering, and making decisions. Researchers use computer touchscreens to test the cognition of many animals, such as dogs. By having animals solve problems or sequence images, scientists can learn more about the cognitive abilities of different animals.

PLAN How could you test the cognitive abilities of a dog?

_____

_____

_____

Cultural Behavior

Cultural behavior is behavior that is spread through a population largely through learning, rather than natural selection. The key to cultural behavior is that the behavior is taught to one generation by another, through a process known as *cultural transmission*.

Think about your own learning from childhood. You may speak a certain language or eat certain foods based on your cultural background. If you had grown up somewhere different in the world, you may have learned to like different kinds of foods, and learned to speak a different language. Although quite different, nonhuman populations show behaviors that are also clearly linked to cultural differences.

Explore Online ▶

FIGURE 16: Some orcas learn hunting strategies through cultural transmission.

The orca in Figure 16 intentionally beaches itself to hunt seals in shallow waters. Only orcas in certain parts of the world, and only in certain groups, exhibit this behavior. Orcas learn this from their mothers and other members in their group, and their offspring will learn it from them, as long as the behavior is advantageous.

The development of cultural behavior does not require living in complex societies. The transmission of birdsong in some taxonomic groups of birds is also an example of cultural behavior. However, living close together in social groups may help to enhance the transmission and expression of cultural behaviors.

 Evidence Notebook Construct an explanation as to how learned and cultural behaviors can increase an individual's fitness.

Language Arts

The Evolution of Play Behavior

The brown bear cubs in Figure 17 may look like they are fighting, but they are actually just playing. Play fighting carries the risk of injury and uses energy. Why risk so much just to play?

Determining what play behavior is can be tricky, as there is sometimes a fine line between what is play and what is genuine fighting. According to researchers, play involves behaviors that are an adaptation of normal behaviors, such as fighting, fleeing, or feeding. It also involves communications, such as postures or facial expressions, to let other individuals know that this is play.

Although play make look like it is just for fun, it is hypothesized that this activity also builds skills among juveniles that will be beneficial to them as adults. Play is observed in many forms, but can be understood under three main categories. Researchers classify play behavior as physical training, social training, and cognitive development.

Many young mammals engage in physical play as they wrestle and nip at each other with juvenile teeth. This physical play strengthens growing muscles. It also is thought to develop skills that may be needed later for hunting or protecting themselves or their own offspring as adults.

Social training involves learning from others. Think about behaviors that may be familiar in animals, such as interactions between wolves. Different postures signal different messages. One signal may be described as a "play bow," which sends a message that the wolves want to play. As juveniles, play provides the opportunity to learn social signals that may be used for other purposes, such as gaining attention, courting, or showing aggression. Cognitive development occurs as playful peers learn from one another.

Scientists are still researching why animals play and how the behavior evolved. They do know that the benefits of play, like other animal behaviors, outweigh the associated risks.

FIGURE 17: Play is often a juvenile form of adult behavior, such as fighting.

Language Arts Connection Write an explanatory blog post that supports the claim that play behavior has evolved because it benefits the individual by giving them practice for events later in life. As you write your argument, consider following these steps:

- Introduce your claim, or the point your argument makes.
- Develop your claim by providing strong, logical reasons and evidence.
- Link your ideas to show how your reasons relate to your claim.
- End with a conclusion that wraps up your argument.

EXAMPLES OF ANIMAL BEHAVIOR

USING AN ETHOGRAM

CAREER: ANIMAL BEHAVIORIST

Go online to choose one of these other paths.

Lesson Self-Check

CAN YOU EXPLAIN IT?

FIGURE 18: Social behavior has evolved in the desert night lizard, so it must provide them with advantages in their environment.

Scientists studying desert night lizards noticed that they lived together in groups during the winter, unlike many species of lizard. After performing DNA analysis on these lizards, scientists discovered that the lizards in each wintering group were related. What could be the advantages of gathering together with related individuals?

Scientists studying chameleons found that those raised in social groups were less submissive and better at finding food. Further research is needed on the social structure of desert night lizards, to understand exactly how living together could increase their fitness.

 Evidence Notebook Refer to your notes in your Evidence Notebook to explain how living in a family group could help increase the fitness of desert night lizards. Your explanation should include a discussion of the costs and benefits of social behavior for desert night lizards. Using this information, answer the following questions:

1. Make a claim about how the social behavior of the desert night lizard could have been selected for in a population.
2. What evidence supports your claim? How do the costs of social behavior in these lizards relate to the benefits?
3. What evidence did you gather that could support the idea that social behavior enhances the fitness of desert night lizards?

Check Your Understanding

1. Which of the following best explains how behaviors, such as swarming and flocking, help protect organisms?
   - ○ **a.** Individuals in swarms or flocks act as decoys to distract predators.
   - ○ **b.** The movement and size of the swarm or flock confuses predators.
   - ○ **c.** Working together in swarms or flocks requires less energy.
   - ○ **d.** The size of most swarms and flocks can overtake larger predators.

2. In a eusocial system, how does a worker bee increase her fitness by caring for young that has been produced by her father and the queen?
   - ○ **a.** The worker bee can produce young of her own after the queen's young leave the hive.
   - ○ **b.** The queen allows the worker bees that take care of her young to live longer.
   - ○ **c.** Worker bees are clones, so they share 100% of their alleles with these young.
   - ○ **d.** By making sure these young survive, the worker is passing up to 75% of her alleles to the next generation.

3. How does cooperative behavior contribute to the survival of animals?
   - ○ **a.** Cooperative behavior puts one individual at risk for the survival of the whole group.
   - ○ **b.** Cooperative behavior benefits one individual which may be reciprocated in the future.
   - ○ **c.** Cooperative behavior enables individuals to work together toward a common goal that will benefit the group.
   - ○ **d.** Cooperative behavior engages all members of a group to work together for the benefit of a few.

4. Which of the following best explains how a certain behavior may be more likely to be selected for and evolve as an innate behavior?
   - ○ **a.** The behavior is easily learned.
   - ○ **b.** The behavior has very low risk and opportunity costs.
   - ○ **c.** The benefits of the behavior for survival outweigh the costs.
   - ○ **d.** The behavior is in response to a stimulus.

5. Two separate groups of chimpanzees, living in separate regions, both use tools to gather honey. One group uses long sticks as tools to gather honey from a log and the other uses chewed leaves to collect the honey. Which of the following would best explain these two behaviors used for the same function?
   - ○ **a.** cultural transmission
   - ○ **b.** cooperation
   - ○ **c.** altruistic behavior
   - ○ **d.** migratory behavior

6. Classify each behavior using the terms below:

   | innate | learned |

Behavior	Classification
Chimpanzees use tools to fish for termites.	
Newly hatched sea turtles crawl into the sea.	
Bats fly out of caves at night to eat mosquitoes.	
Bears fish for salmon out of a running stream.	
Birds avoid eating monarch butterflies because they taste bad.	
Honey bees associate certain colors and fragrances with nectar.	

CHECKPOINTS (continued)

7. A female ground squirrel may send out a call warning her offspring that a predator is near. Sometimes, the mother sacrifices her own life since the predator can more easily locate her from the call. How does the mother benefit from giving the distress call?

_____

_____

_____

_____

_____

_____

8. An antelope is grazing on the savanna and feels thirsty. It takes a drink from a nearby watering hole. As the antelope drinks, another antelope in the herd signals danger. The antelope and herd members sprint away. After running, the antelope feels hot and goes to lie in the shade. Identify each stimulus and the response behavior in this paragraph.

_____

_____

_____

_____

_____

_____

MAKE YOUR OWN STUDY GUIDE

 In your Evidence Notebook, design a study guide that supports the main ideas from this lesson:

A behavior is anything an organism does in response to a stimulus to help the organism maintain homeostasis in a changing environment.

A behavior is selected for if the benefit of the behavior outweighs the cost or risk.

Behaviors may be classified as innate or learned. Innate behaviors are those that are instinctive and are heritable. Learned behaviors are acquired through observation, practice, and experience and may be culturally specific.

Remember to include the following information in your study guide:

- Use examples that model main ideas.
- Record explanations for the phenomena you investigated.
- Use evidence to support your explanations. Your support can include drawings, data, graphs, laboratory conclusions, and other evidence recorded throughout the lesson.

Consider how any behavior that causes an increase in the survival of an individual and its reproductive success will likely be passed from one generation to the next.

Earth Science

Color Blindness on Pingelap Catastrophic weather events can have significant impacts on populations for generations to come. In 1775, Typhoon Lengkieki struck the Micronesian atoll of Pingelap. Today, roughly 1 in 10 residents of Pingelap are entirely color-blind, compared with a rate of 1 in 40 000 individuals worldwide.

Research the link between color blindness in the residents of Pingelap and Typhoon Lengkieki. Prepare a report discussing your findings, including factors such as founder effect or genetic drift that may have contributed to the phenomenon.

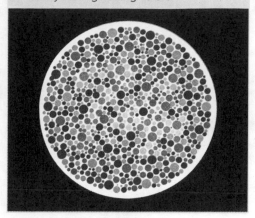

FIGURE 1: Color-blind individuals may have difficulty distinguishing colors.

Music Connection

Does Practice Make Perfect? Scientific studies have found that when it comes to musical talent, genetics may play an important role. For example, research by scientists at the University of California, San Francisco indicates that a particular region of genes on chromosome eight is related to perfect pitch. It's possible that some aspects of musical ability may be hardwired into our genes.

Research studies that have examined the role genetics may play in the development of musical talent. Form your own opinion about whether practice, genetics, or both are the key to becoming an expert musician. Write a blog post stating your opinion. Cite evidence and examples from credible sources to support your claim.

FIGURE 2: Musicians practice many hours every week.

Life Science Connection

Beneficial Mutations Small changes in DNA can result in new or modified phenotypes. If those mutations occur in germ cells, they may be passed on to future generations. Some scientists think that changes in environmental conditions, such as climate change, may also cause an increase in the rate of mutations. Scientists have found evidence that the DNA of several species is changing in response to higher temperatures.

Research three instances where changing environmental conditions appear to be affecting mutation rates. Make an infographic to explain what mutations are and why some scientists think they are helping some species survive higher temperatures. Include credible counterarguments you find, and explain why scientists might come to different conclusions.

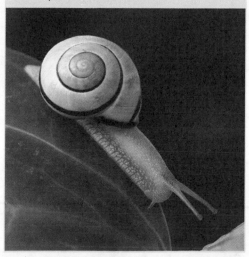

FIGURE 3: Shell color and banding pattern in brown-lipped snails are dependent on temperature.

RANDALL MUNROE
XKCD.COM

TREE OF LIFE

All living things as part of the same family

You've learned that organisms can be classified based on physical and genetic characteristics, which reveal their evolutionary relationships. Tree diagrams are used to describe the relationships between organisms, both living and extinct. Here's one that uses easy-to-understand language.

THE STORY OF LIVING THINGS, FROM THE BEGINNING

ALL LIFE (THAT WE KNOW OF) IS PART OF A FAMILY. WE ALL COME FROM ONE LIVING THING THAT APPEARED IN THE EARLY DAYS OF THE EARTH.

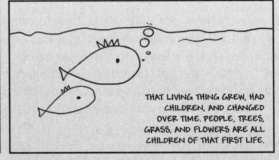

THAT LIVING THING GREW, HAD CHILDREN, AND CHANGED OVER TIME. PEOPLE, TREES, GRASS, AND FLOWERS ARE ALL CHILDREN OF THAT FIRST LIFE.

AS LIVING THINGS MAKE MORE LIVING THINGS, THE INFORMATION THEY PASS TO THEM CHANGES, MAKING THE NEW THINGS A LITTLE DIFFERENT FROM THE OLD.

OVER TIME, THESE SMALL CHANGES CAN LEAD TO VERY DIFFERENT KINDS OF LIVING THINGS GROWING FROM ONE.

FAMILY GET-TOGETHER!

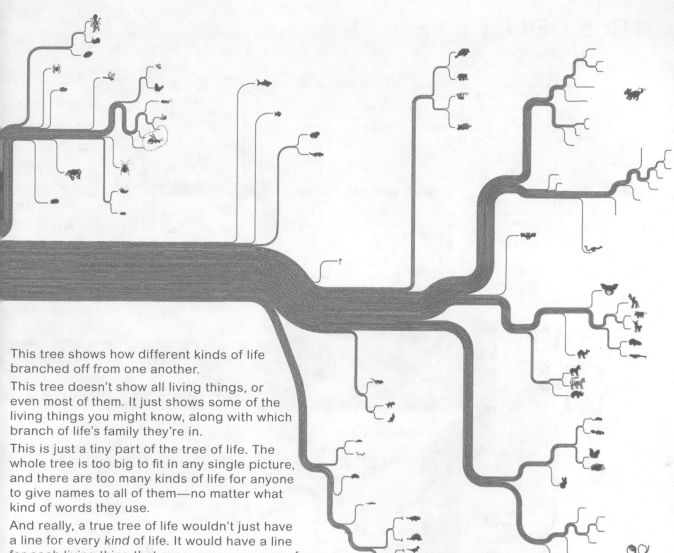

This tree shows how different kinds of life branched off from one another.

This tree doesn't show all living things, or even most of them. It just shows some of the living things you might know, along with which branch of life's family they're in.

This is just a tiny part of the tree of life. The whole tree is too big to fit in any single picture, and there are too many kinds of life for anyone to give names to all of them—no matter what kind of words they use.

And really, a true tree of life wouldn't just have a line for every *kind* of life. It would have a line for each living thing that ever was, every one of them crossing and joining and winding across the page, slowly changing from one kind of life to another, in a path that reaches all the way back, without a single break, to that very first life.

No one really knows how many living things there are in the world, but we can make some guesses, and they're big. Not only can we never find enough words to talk about all those lives, we have a hard time talking about the number itself.

Here's one way to think about how many things have lived on Earth: The world is covered in seas that are ringed with beaches of sand. One day, when you're walking on a beach, pick up some sand and look at it. Imagine that every tiny piece of sand under your feet is a whole world of its own, each one with its own seas and beaches, just like Earth.

The full tree of life has as many living things as there are bits of sand on all those beaches on all those tiny sand worlds put together.

Next to the world we're talking about, all our words are small.

ANIMAL THAT LIVES DEEP IN THE SEA AND HAS BEEN ON EARTH FOR A VERY LONG TIME

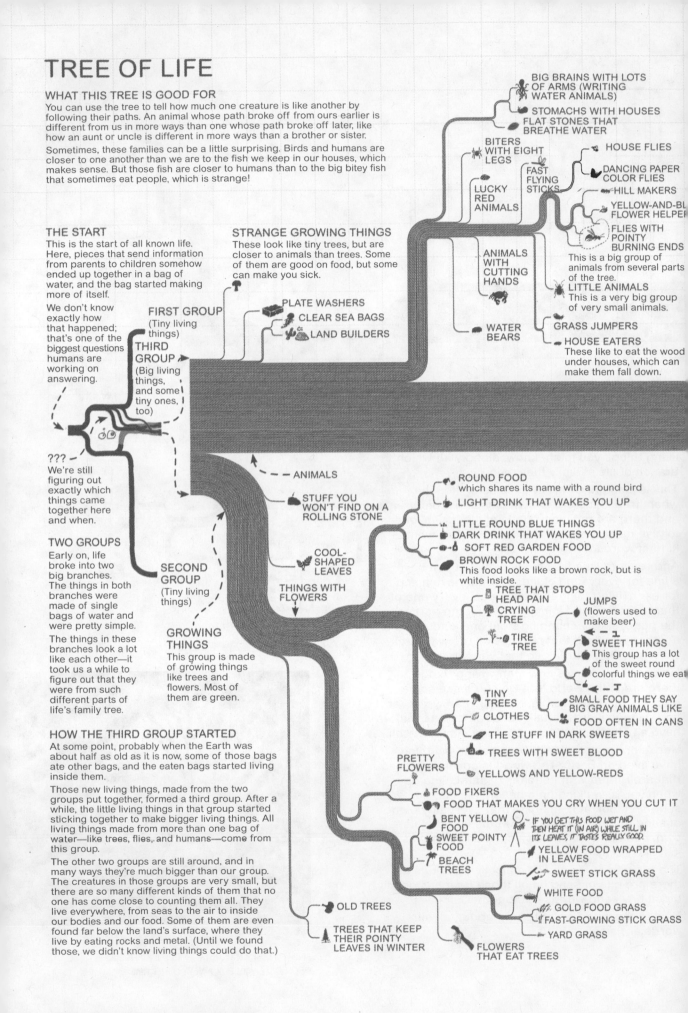

TREE OF LIFE

WHAT THIS TREE IS GOOD FOR

You can use the tree to tell how much one creature is like another by following their paths. An animal whose path broke off from ours earlier is different from us in more ways than one whose path broke off later, like how an aunt or uncle is different in more ways than a brother or sister.

Sometimes, these families can be a little surprising. Birds and humans are closer to one another than we are to the fish we keep in our houses, which makes sense. But those fish are closer to humans than to the big bitey fish that sometimes eat people, which is strange!

THE START

This is the start of all known life. Here, pieces that send information from parents to children somehow ended up together in a bag of water, and the bag started making more of itself.

We don't know exactly how that happened; that's one of the biggest questions humans are working on answering.

???
We're still figuring out exactly which things came together here and when.

TWO GROUPS

Early on, life broke into two big branches. The things in both branches were made of single bags of water and were pretty simple.

The things in these branches look a lot like each other—it took us a while to figure out that they were from such different parts of life's family tree.

HOW THE THIRD GROUP STARTED

At some point, probably when the Earth was about half as old as it is now, some of those bags ate other bags, and the eaten bags started living inside them.

Those new living things, made from the two groups put together, formed a third group. After a while, the little living things in that group started sticking together to make bigger living things. All living things made from more than one bag of water—like trees, flies, and humans—come from this group.

The other two groups are still around, and in many ways they're much bigger than our group. The creatures in those groups are very small, but there are so many different kinds of them that no one has come close to counting them all. They live everywhere, from seas to the air to inside our bodies and our food. Some of them are even found far below the land's surface, where they live by eating rocks and metal. (Until we found those, we didn't know living things could do that.)

STRANGE GROWING THINGS

These look like tiny trees, but are closer to animals than trees. Some of them are good on food, but some can make you sick.

FIRST GROUP (Tiny living things)

THIRD GROUP (Big living things, and some tiny ones, too)

PLATE WASHERS
CLEAR SEA BAGS
LAND BUILDERS

SECOND GROUP (Tiny living things)

GROWING THINGS
This group is made of growing things like trees and flowers. Most of them are green.

BIG BRAINS WITH LOTS OF ARMS (WRITING WATER ANIMALS)
STOMACHS WITH HOUSES
FLAT STONES THAT BREATHE WATER

BITERS WITH EIGHT LEGS
LUCKY RED ANIMALS
FAST FLYING STICKS
ANIMALS WITH CUTTING HANDS
WATER BEARS

HOUSE FLIES
DANCING PAPER COLOR FLIES
HILL MAKERS
YELLOW-AND-BL
FLOWER HELPER
FLIES WITH POINTY BURNING ENDS
This is a big group of animals from several parts of the tree.
LITTLE ANIMALS
This is a very big group of very small animals.
GRASS JUMPERS
HOUSE EATERS
These like to eat the wood under houses, which can make them fall down.

ANIMALS
STUFF YOU WON'T FIND ON A ROLLING STONE
COOL-SHAPED LEAVES
THINGS WITH FLOWERS

ROUND FOOD
which shares its name with a round bird
LIGHT DRINK THAT WAKES YOU UP
LITTLE ROUND BLUE THINGS
DARK DRINK THAT WAKES YOU UP
SOFT RED GARDEN FOOD
BROWN ROCK FOOD
This food looks like a brown rock, but is white inside.
TREE THAT STOPS HEAD PAIN
CRYING TREE
TIRE TREE

JUMPS (flowers used to make beer)
SWEET THINGS
This group has a lot of the sweet round colorful things we eat.
SMALL FOOD THEY SAY BIG GRAY ANIMALS LIKE
FOOD OFTEN IN CANS
THE STUFF IN DARK SWEETS
TREES WITH SWEET BLOOD
YELLOWS AND YELLOW-REDS

TINY TREES
CLOTHES

PRETTY FLOWERS
FOOD FIXERS
FOOD THAT MAKES YOU CRY WHEN YOU CUT IT
BENT YELLOW FOOD
SWEET POINTY FOOD
BEACH TREES

IF YOU GET THIS FOOD WET AND THEN HEAT IT (IN AIR) WHILE STILL IN ITS LEAVES, IT TASTES REALLY GOOD.
YELLOW FOOD WRAPPED IN LEAVES
SWEET STICK GRASS
WHITE FOOD
GOLD FOOD GRASS
FAST-GROWING STICK GRASS
YARD GRASS

OLD TREES
TREES THAT KEEP THEIR POINTY LEAVES IN WINTER
FLOWERS THAT EAT TREES

Go online for more about *Thing Explainer*.

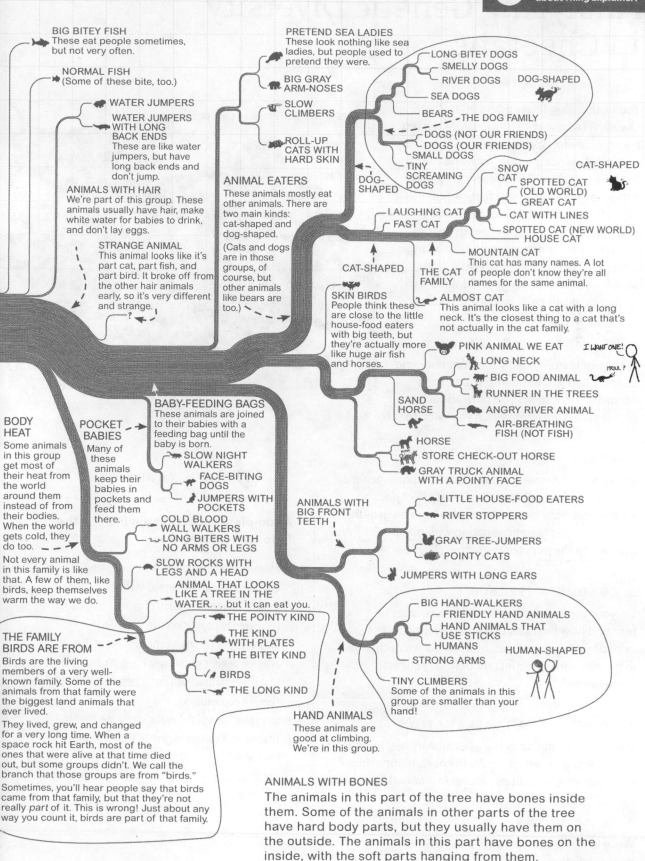

BIG BITEY FISH
These eat people sometimes, but not very often.

NORMAL FISH
(Some of these bite, too.)

WATER JUMPERS

WATER JUMPERS WITH LONG BACK ENDS
These are like water jumpers, but have long back ends and don't jump.

ANIMALS WITH HAIR
We're part of this group. These animals usually have hair, make white water for babies to drink, and don't lay eggs.

STRANGE ANIMAL
This animal looks like it's part cat, part fish, and part bird. It broke off from the other hair animals early, so it's very different and strange.

PRETEND SEA LADIES
These look nothing like sea ladies, but people used to pretend they were.

BIG GRAY ARM-NOSES

SLOW CLIMBERS

ROLL-UP CATS WITH HARD SKIN

ANIMAL EATERS
These animals mostly eat other animals. There are two main kinds: cat-shaped and dog-shaped.
(Cats and dogs are in those groups, of course, but other animals like bears are too.)

LONG BITEY DOGS
SMELLY DOGS
RIVER DOGS
SEA DOGS
BEARS
THE DOG FAMILY
DOGS (NOT OUR FRIENDS)
DOGS (OUR FRIENDS)
SMALL DOGS
TINY SCREAMING DOGS

DOG-SHAPED

DOG-SHAPED

LAUGHING CAT
FAST CAT

CAT-SHAPED

SNOW CAT
SPOTTED CAT (OLD WORLD)
GREAT CAT
CAT WITH LINES
SPOTTED CAT (NEW WORLD)
HOUSE CAT

CAT-SHAPED

THE CAT FAMILY

MOUNTAIN CAT
This cat has many names. A lot of people don't know they're all names for the same animal.

SKIN BIRDS
People think these are close to the little house-food eaters with big teeth, but they're actually more like huge air fish and horses.

ALMOST CAT
This animal looks like a cat with a long neck. It's the closest thing to a cat that's not actually in the cat family.

PINK ANIMAL WE EAT
LONG NECK
BIG FOOD ANIMAL
RUNNER IN THE TREES
ANGRY RIVER ANIMAL
AIR-BREATHING FISH (NOT FISH)

I WANT ONE!
MROW?

SAND HORSE

HORSE
STORE CHECK-OUT HORSE
GRAY TRUCK ANIMAL WITH A POINTY FACE

BODY HEAT
Some animals in this group get most of their heat from the world around them instead of from their bodies. When the world gets cold, they do too.
Not every animal in this family is like that. A few of them, like birds, keep themselves warm the way we do.

POCKET BABIES
Many of these animals keep their babies in pockets and feed them there.

BABY-FEEDING BAGS
These animals are joined to their babies with a feeding bag until the baby is born.

SLOW NIGHT WALKERS
FACE-BITING DOGS
JUMPERS WITH POCKETS

COLD BLOOD WALL WALKERS
LONG BITERS WITH NO ARMS OR LEGS
SLOW ROCKS WITH LEGS AND A HEAD
ANIMAL THAT LOOKS LIKE A TREE IN THE WATER. . . but it can eat you.

ANIMALS WITH BIG FRONT TEETH

LITTLE HOUSE-FOOD EATERS
RIVER STOPPERS
GRAY TREE-JUMPERS
POINTY CATS
JUMPERS WITH LONG EARS

THE FAMILY BIRDS ARE FROM
Birds are the living members of a very well-known family. Some of the animals from that family were the biggest land animals that ever lived.

They lived, grew, and changed for a very long time. When a space rock hit Earth, most of the ones that were alive at that time died out, but some groups didn't. We call the branch that those groups are from "birds."

Sometimes, you'll hear people say that birds came from that family, but that they're not really *part* of it. This is wrong! Just about any way you count it, birds are part of that family.

THE POINTY KIND
THE KIND WITH PLATES
THE BITEY KIND
BIRDS
THE LONG KIND

BIG HAND-WALKERS
FRIENDLY HAND ANIMALS
HAND ANIMALS THAT USE STICKS
HUMANS
STRONG ARMS

HUMAN-SHAPED

TINY CLIMBERS
Some of the animals in this group are smaller than your hand!

HAND ANIMALS
These animals are good at climbing. We're in this group.

ANIMALS WITH BONES
The animals in this part of the tree have bones inside them. Some of the animals in other parts of the tree have hard body parts, but they usually have them on the outside. The animals in this part have bones on the inside, with the soft parts hanging from them.

Analyzing Genetic Diversity in Cheetahs

Today, there are fewer than 20 000 African cheetahs (*Acinonyx jubatus*). Before the last ice age, cheetah species could be found in North America, Europe, Asia, and Africa. Around 10 000 to 12 000 years ago, a mass extinction event occurred that caused the extinction of almost 75% of the world's large mammals. A single cheetah species survived this extinction event, with a range limited to parts of eastern, central, and southern Africa. What effect did this mass extinction event have on cheetah diversity?

FIGURE 4: Modern cheetahs are not very genetically diverse.

1. DEFINE THE PROBLEM

With your team, write a statement outlining the problem you've been asked to solve. Record any questions you have about the problem and the information you need to solve it.

2. ANALYZE DATA

With your team, make a graph that compares genetic variation with population size. What effect does a sudden decrease in population size have on genetic variation? Does genetic variation within a species increase as the population recovers?

3. CONDUCT RESEARCH

On your own, use library or online resources to research how the mass extinction event affected genetic variation in cheetahs. How does this change in genetic variation affect modern-day cheetah populations?

4. CONSTRUCT AN EXPLANATION

Write an explanation of the evolutionary mechanism that affected genetic diversity in cheetah populations. Can cheetah populations recover lost genetic diversity?

5. COMMUNICATE

Write a report detailing your analysis and your predictions for what will happen to genetic variation in cheetah populations in the future.

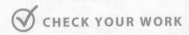

CHECK YOUR WORK

A complete report should include the following information:

- a clearly defined problem with supporting questions that are answered in the final report
- a graphical representation of genetic diversity compared to population size
- an analysis of the mass extinction event that affected genetic variation in cheetahs and how that event continues to impact modern-day cheetah populations
- an explanation of the evolutionary mechanism that led to a change in genetic variation in cheetahs
- predictions about future changes in genetic variation in cheetah populations

Name _____   Date _____

SYNTHESIZE THE UNIT

In your Evidence Notebook, make a concept map, other graphic organizer, or outline using the Study Guides you made for each lesson in this unit. Be sure to use evidence to support your claims.

When synthesizing individual information, remember to follow these general steps:

- Find the central idea of each piece of information.
- Think about the relationships among the central ideas.
- Combine the ideas to come up with a new understanding.

DRIVING QUESTIONS

Look back to the Driving Questions from the opening section of this unit. In your Evidence Notebook, review and revise your previous answers to those questions. Use the evidence you gathered and other observations you made throughout the unit to support your claims.

PRACTICE AND REVIEW

1. Bright green tree frogs are more common in tropical rain forests than in temperate areas, where leaf colors change seasonally. Why might this be true?
   - a. The frogs' numbers are similar in both environments but are easier to spot in green tropical rain forests.
   - b. The frogs' coloration provides better camouflage in temperate forests than in green tropical rain forests.
   - c. The frogs' coloration helps them stand out better in green tropical rain forests, compared with temperate forests.
   - d. The frogs' coloration provides better camouflage in green tropical rain forests than in temperate forests.

2. Some individuals in a particular species of butterfly display coloration that mimics that of a different, poisonous butterfly species living in the same habitat. Place the elements in order to model what may happen to the first butterfly species if the poisonous butterfly species is removed from the habitat.
   - _____ a. Predators will eat more butterflies with mimicking coloration than before.
   - _____ b. The proportion of individuals in the population with mimicking coloration will decrease.
   - _____ c. The pressure on predators to avoid eating poisonous butterflies will decrease.
   - _____ d. The survival advantage for mimicking butterflies will decrease.

3. Herring are small ocean fish that often swim together in large schools. Though this behavior uses significant energy and can increase competition for resources, what advantages might the evolution of schooling behavior provide for herring? Select all correct answers.
   - a. the ability for many individuals to spot predators
   - b. the possibility of diving deeper as a school
   - c. greater efficiency in searching for food together
   - d. confusing potential predators by appearing to be one large animal

4. Select the correct terms and phrases to complete the statement about adaptive radiation.

   Cichlids are a group of more than 2000 species of fish that live in African lakes and are thought to have evolved from adaptive radiation. It's likely that the different species originated from a(n) mass migration | population boom | common ancestor. Populations of cichlids may have adapted over time to occupy unique ecological niches | adaptive radiation | allele frequencies in the lakes, leading to the geographically distant | mostly unrelated | closely related species we see today.

5. In a certain species of sea snake, a single gene controls tongue shape. The forked-tongue allele (T) is dominant, while the non-forked-tongue allele (t) is recessive. In this population, 16 individuals are homozygous recessive, 36 individuals are homozygous dominant, and 48 individuals are heterozygous. Using this information, answer the following questions.

   a. How many total alleles for tongue shape are in this population? _____

   b. How many T alleles are in the population? _____

   c. How many t alleles are in the population? _____

   d. What is the frequency of the T allele? Express your answer as a percentage. _____

   e. What is the frequency of the t allele? Express your answer as a percentage. _____

6. Would you expect a mutation that deletes one base in a protein-coding region of DNA to be more or less harmful than a mutation that deletes three bases in a coding region? Explain your answer.

   _____

   _____

   _____

   _____

   _____

7. Natural selection favors organisms that are best adapted to their environment. There are three main selection patterns: stabilizing, directional, and disruptive. Discuss the differences and provide examples of each type of selection pattern.

   _____

   _____

   _____

   _____

   _____

   _____

   _____

UNIT PROJECT

Return to your unit project. Prepare your research and materials into a presentation to share with the class. In your final presentation, include an evaluation of your analysis and conclusions about water-collecting adaptations and their possible applications to human society.

Remember these tips while evaluating:

- Was your research based on an in-depth exploration of reliable sources?

- Is your claim focused on specific and relevant content?

- Are your claim and reasoning supported by evidence?

- Are your findings presented clearly in both written and oral formats?

Structure and Function in Living Things

YOU SOLVE IT

How Does Salt Intake Affect Blood Pressure?

To begin exploring this unit's concepts, go online to investigate ways to solve a real-world problem.

These living cells are in various stages of growth and division.

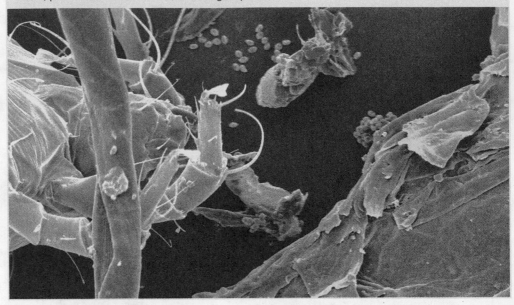

FIGURE 1: This scanning electron micrograph (SEM) of household dust shows skin flakes, fabric fibers, part of a dead dust mite, and fungal spores.

Your skin makes up roughly 16% of your body weight. Skin cells are easily shed, and as a result, we lose thousands of skin cells per hour. In fact, we lose so many skin cells that they can be found in the dust in our homes.

PREDICT How do you think multicellular organisms such as humans replace lost cells?

_____

_____

_____

_____

DRIVING QUESTIONS

As you move through the unit, gather evidence to help you answer the following questions. In your Evidence Notebook, record what you already know about these topics and any questions you have about them.

1. How do organisms balance the growth and division of their cells?
2. How do organisms with many cell types develop from a single cell?
3. How does the structure of cells relate to different functions and specialization?
4. How do systems in living things interact to maintain the organism?

UNIT PROJECT

Go online to download the Unit Project Worksheet to help plan your project.

Investigating Plant Systems

A seedling is a multicellular living system. How do seedlings survive and grow in changing conditions? How does the plant make new structures? Explain the levels of organization within a seedling and between the seedlings and the environment.

Language Development

Use the lessons in this unit to complete the chart and expand your understanding of the science concepts.

TERM: cell cycle

Definition	Example

Similar Term	Phrase

TERM: mitosis

Definition	Example

Similar Term	Phrase

TERM: cell

Definition	Example

Similar Term	Phrase

TERM: nucleus

Definition	Example

Similar Term	Phrase

TERM: organ system

Definition	Example

Similar Term	Phrase

TERM: cell differentiation

Definition	Example

Similar Term	Phrase

TERM: homeostasis

Definition	Example

Similar Term	Phrase

TERM: feedback loop

Definition	Example

Similar Term	Phrase

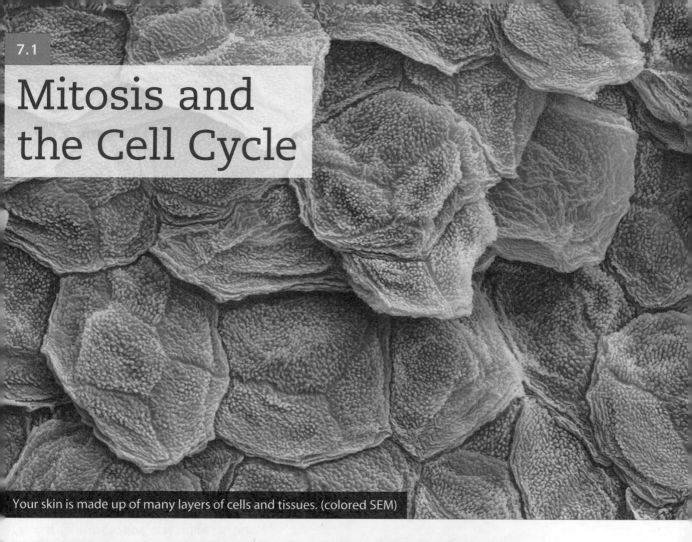

Mitosis and the Cell Cycle

Your skin is made up of many layers of cells and tissues. (colored SEM)

CAN YOU EXPLAIN IT?

Your skin may seem like it stays the same from day to day, but it is in a constant state of change. Like all organs, your skin is made up of cells. Skin cells have a lifespan of two to three weeks, so new cells are constantly forming to replace the old cells that die off. New skin cells form through the process of cell division. Existing cells divide to form two daughter cells. The new cells are genetically identical to the existing cells, which is why we don't notice massive changes in our skin when old cells die. However, we do see evidence of the process when we scrape off flaky, dead skin.

PREDICT Why aren't all organisms made of just one cell? Why do cells divide, instead of simply growing larger?

_____

_____

_____

_____

_____

 Evidence Notebook As you explore the lesson, gather evidence for how the cell cycle is related to the growth and maintenance of organisms.

Overview of the Cell Cycle

FIGURE 1: Cell division

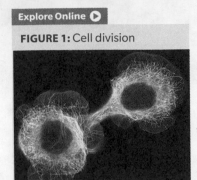

Living systems go through cycles of stable conditions and changing conditions. For example, when conditions in your outside environment change, mechanisms in your body help restore internal stability. Cells also cycle between phases of stability and change. Some cells stay in a relatively steady state, without dividing, for long periods of time. Other cells are constantly dividing.

INFER Which of these are situations in which an organism's cells would need to divide? Select all correct answers.

☐ **a.** The organism's tissue is in need of repair.

☐ **b.** The organism is storing energy.

☐ **c.** The organism is growing.

☐ **d.** The organism is in a dormant state.

Stages of the Cell Cycle

FIGURE 2: This diagram shows the stages of the cell cycle.

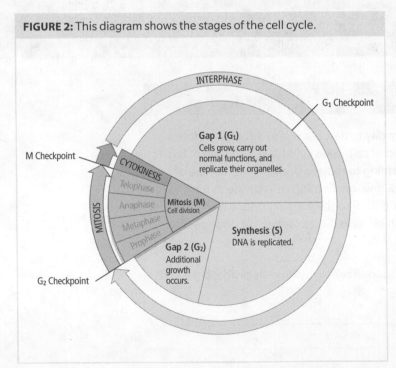

The life cycle of organisms involves birth, growth and development, reproduction, and eventually death. A cell also has a life cycle, and cell division is only one part of that cycle. The cell cycle is the regular pattern of growth, DNA replication, and cell division that occurs in eukaryotic cells, or cells with nuclei. This pattern can be divided into stages that get their names from the earliest studies of cell division, when scientists' observations were limited by the microscopes of the time.

Because these scientists were unable to observe activity in cells that were not actively dividing, they separated the cycle into two parts: a resting phase and a dividing phase. The resting phase was named *interphase*. The dividing phase was named mitosis. Mitosis includes a final step for complete cell division called *cytokinesis*.

Over time, scientists developed techniques and tools that let them detect the copying of DNA, or DNA synthesis. As a result, the description of the cell cycle was revised to include the DNA synthesis stage. At the time, scientists were still unable to observe activity between the stages of synthesis and mitosis, so the periods between these two stages were labeled gap 1 (G_1) and gap 2 (G_2). Eventually, scientists learned that cells in interphase undergo critical growth and preparation for cell division while they carry out normal cellular functions.

EXPLAIN Use the cell cycle diagram in Figure 2 to complete the statement.

In the G_1 phase, cells duplicate their DNA | organelles and carry out normal functions. In the S phase, cells duplicate their DNA | organelles. This ensures that each new cell receives a half | full | double set of DNA as compared to the original cell. In the G_2 phase, additional growth occurs, until the cell is ready to divide in the M phase. Cells spend most of their life in interphase | mitosis | cytokinesis.

Cell Cycle Checkpoints

Checkpoints in the cell cycle keep cells from moving to the next stage before certain conditions are met. During G_1, the cell must pass a critical checkpoint before it can proceed to the synthesis stage. This ensures that DNA is relatively undamaged and can be properly replicated. This checkpoint also lets other cells signal the cell when more cell division is needed. G_2 has its own critical checkpoint. Everything must be in order—adequate cell size, correct replication of DNA—before the cell goes through mitosis and division.

 Collaborate Discuss this question with a partner: If a cell has damaged DNA, what do you think happens during the G_2 checkpoint? Use evidence to support your claim.

G Zero (G_0) Stage

Not all cells need to divide regularly. Cells that divide rarely are thought to enter a gap phase called G_0. These cells continue to carry out everyday functions, but they do not undergo any of the processes necessary to prepare for division. Some cells, such as neurons, may remain in G_0 permanently. Other cells enter this stage temporarily until there is a need for them to divide. One such cell is a lymphocyte, which is a type of white blood cell that helps fight infections. Lymphocytes can remain dormant for years until they recognize an invading organism. Once the invading organism binds to a lymphocyte receptor, the lymphocyte goes through a series of rapid cell divisions to help fight infection.

INFER Heart muscle cells remain in the G_0 stage. Why might this be important for cardiac function?

_____

_____

_____

_____

 Evidence Notebook Make a claim for how the cell cycle relates to the growth and maintenance of organisms. Discuss the stages of the cell cycle, mechanisms that regulate it, and how this cycle is related to the growth and maintenance of organisms.

Mitosis and Cytokinesis

During interphase, the cell grows, replicates its DNA and organelles, and produces proteins needed for cell division. Interphase prepares the cell for the next stage in the cell cycle. Mitosis is the stage during which cell division takes place. At the end of mitosis, the process of cytokinesis divides the cell's cytoplasm. The result is two daughter cells that are genetically identical to the original, or parent, cell.

 Math Connection

Comparing Rates of Cell Division

FIGURE 3: Different cell types divide at different rates.

Cell Type	Approximate Life Span
Skin	2–3 weeks
Red blood cell	4 months
Liver	10–18 months
Intestine— internal lining	4–5 days
Intestine— muscle and other tissues	16 years

All cells in your body undergo cell division, but the rate at which they divide is linked to your body's need for that type of cell. In human cells, the S, G₂, and M stages together usually take about 12 hours. The length of the G₁ stage differs the most from cell type to cell type. The rate of cell division is greater in embryos and children than it is in adults. Children have a shorter cell cycle, and many of their organs are still developing. But the rate of cell division also varies within different tissues of the adult body. For example, the internal lining of the digestive tract receives a lot of wear and tear. The cells of the lining also encounter toxins that enter the body through the digestive tract. As a result, cells that line the stomach and intestine are replaced every few days. In contrast, cells that make up the rest of the intestine (mainly smooth muscle) and many of the internal organs, such as lungs, kidneys, and liver, divide only occasionally, in response to cell injury or death.

ANALYZE Why does a skin cell need to divide more frequently than a liver cell?

_____

_____

_____

There are about 25 trillion red blood cells in the human body. Red blood cells that are worn out and die are replaced by new cells produced in the bone marrow and stored in the spleen.

CALCULATE Use the data in the text and from Figure 3 to calculate the number of red blood cells the human body loses due to natural cell death each second. Assume there are 30 days in 1 month. Convert your answers to decimal form and round to the nearest tenth of a million (e.g., 1 500 000 = 1.5 million).

Calculate how many seconds a red blood cell lives. _____

How many red blood cells does the human body lose due to natural cell death each

second? _____

Mitosis in Detail

Specialized structures called *centrosomes* are involved in mitosis in animal cells. The centrosome is a small region of cytoplasm that produces protein fibers called *microtubules*. *Centrioles* are cylinder-shaped organelles made of short microtubules. Before an animal cell divides, the centrosome, including the centrioles, doubles and the two new centrosomes move to opposite ends of the cell. Microtubules grow from each centrosome, forming spindle fibers. These fibers attach to the DNA and help it divide between the two cells.

The combined processes of mitosis and cytokinesis produce two genetically identical daughter cells. Mitosis divides a cell's nucleus into two genetically identical nuclei, each with its own full set of DNA. This process occurs in all of your somatic, or body, cells and prepares them for cytokinesis. Although mitosis and cytokinesis are continuous processes, scientists have divided them into phases to make them easier to understand and discuss. The four main phases of mitosis are prophase, metaphase, anaphase, and telophase. Cytokinesis begins during late anaphase and ends in telophase.

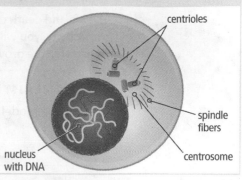

FIGURE 4: Centrosomes contain structures called centrioles. Spindle fibers are organized at the centrosome.

centrioles

spindle fibers

centrosome

nucleus with DNA

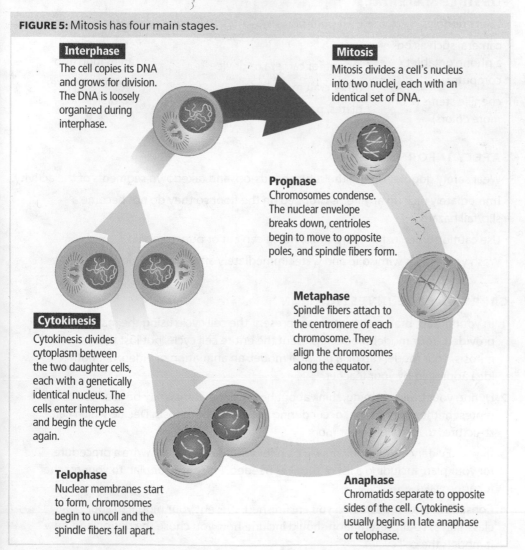

FIGURE 5: Mitosis has four main stages.

Interphase
The cell copies its DNA and grows for division. The DNA is loosely organized during interphase.

Mitosis
Mitosis divides a cell's nucleus into two nuclei, each with an identical set of DNA.

Prophase
Chromosomes condense. The nuclear envelope breaks down, centrioles begin to move to opposite poles, and spindle fibers form.

Metaphase
Spindle fibers attach to the centromere of each chromosome. They align the chromosomes along the equator.

Cytokinesis
Cytokinesis divides cytoplasm between the two daughter cells, each with a genetically identical nucleus. The cells enter interphase and begin the cycle again.

Telophase
Nuclear membranes start to form, chromosomes begin to uncoil and the spindle fibers fall apart.

Anaphase
Chromatids separate to opposite sides of the cell. Cytokinesis usually begins in late anaphase or telophase.

Hands-On Activity
Modeling the Cell Cycle

The life and death of cells is a continuous cycle that takes place in a living organism. In this activity, you will model the cell cycle and use the model to explain why this cycle is needed for the growth and development of living things.

MAKE A CLAIM

What does a model need to include in order to effectively demonstrate the stages of the cell cycle?

_____

_____

_____

_____

POSSIBLE MATERIALS

- safety goggles
- camera, such as on a phone or tablet computer
- chenille stems (2 or more colors)
- craft pom-poms
- glue
- mount for camera or device
- other craft materials
- plates, paper (8-10)
- scissors
- stop-motion animation app
- yarn (2 or more colors)

SAFETY INFORMATION

- Wear safety goggles during the setup, hands-on, and takedown segments of the activity.
- Immediately pick up any items dropped on the floor so they do not become a slip/fall hazard.
- Use caution when using sharp tools, which can cut or puncture skin.
- Wash your hands with soap and water immediately after completing this activity.

CARRY OUT THE INVESTIGATION

1. In your group, brainstorm ways to represent the cell cycle using the materials provided. Your model should represent the entire cell cycle, not just the stages of mitosis. Your model can be a physical model, an animation or video, or another idea approved by your teacher

2. During your brainstorming, think about how each material may be used to represent the changes that occur during the stages of mitosis. Decide which cell structures to include in your model.

3. In your Evidence Notebook,draw a plan for your model. Then, write a procedure for your plan, including a list of supplies needed. Present your plan to your teacher for approval.

4. Construct your model. When you are finished, present your model to your classmates. Your presentation should include how you chose the design and how it models the cell cycle.

ANALYZE

Answer the following questions in your Evidence Notebook.

1. What strengths and limitations did your model have? How could you improve your model with additional resources or time?

2. Human cells have 46 chromosomes. How could you modify your model to show how many chromosomes should be present during the G_2 phase of the cell cycle for human cells? How many chromosomes should be in each daughter cell after cytokinesis?

3. Explain why the process of mitosis is important to the growth and development of human embryos. Support your explanation with evidence you gathered.

CONSTRUCT AN EXPLANATION

Use your model to explain why the process of cell division and growth is best represented as a cycle instead of as a linear process.

_____

_____

_____

_____

DRAW CONCLUSIONS

Write a conclusion about your model that addresses each of the points below.

Claim What does a model of the cell cycle need to include in order to effectively demonstrate all of the stages of the process?

Evidence Support your claim using examples from your model. Remember that in science a negative result is also evidence. In other words, the result that your model did not effectively demonstrate some aspect of the cell cycle may still be useful evidence that supports your claim.

Reasoning Explain how the examples you gave support your claim. List specific parts of the model, what those parts of the model represent, and how those parts are effective at demonstrating the cell cycle.

_____

_____

_____

_____

_____

_____

_____

_____

Asexual Reproduction

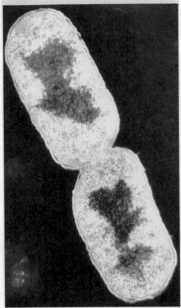

FIGURE 6: Asexual reproduction requires only one parent.

Reproduction is a process that makes new organisms from one or more parent organisms and can occur in one of two ways—sexually or asexually. Sexual reproduction involves the joining of gametes (eggs and sperm cells), one from each parent. Sexual reproduction requires two parents and takes longer, but it produces offspring that are genetically unique because they have a mixture of genes from both parents.

Asexual reproduction can occur relatively quickly, and the offspring are genetically identical to the parent organism. Prokaryotes and some eukaryotes reproduce asexually. Remember that prokaryotes do not have a nucleus. This typically allows prokaryotic cells to divide much faster. Because prokaryotes are single-celled, the resulting daughter cells are new single-celled organisms. The offspring that result are, for the most part, genetically identical to each other and to the original single-celled parent.

Binary Fission and Mitosis

Prokaryotes, such as bacteria, lack not only a nucleus but also membrane-bound organelles and spindle fibers. Prokaryotes also have much less DNA than most eukaryotes have. The DNA of most bacteria is in the form of a single circular chromosome, instead of the linear chromosomes found in your cells.

Bacteria reproduce through a process called binary fission, which differs from mitosis in several ways, as shown in Figure 7. Binary fission starts when the bacterial chromosome is copied. Both chromosomes are attached to the cell membrane on opposite sides of the cell. As the cell grows and gets longer, the chromosomes move away from each other. When the cell is about twice its original size, it undergoes cytokinesis. The membrane pinches inward, and a new cell wall forms between the two chromosomes, which completes the separation into two daughter cells.

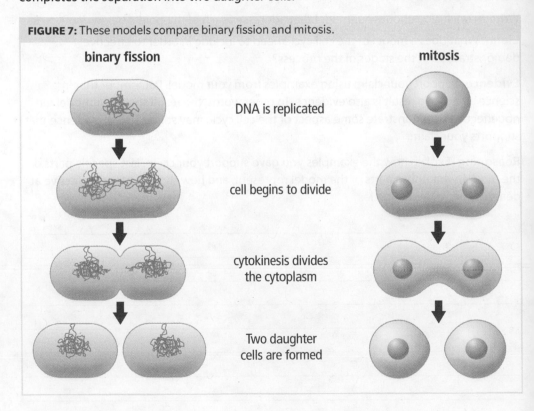

FIGURE 7: These models compare binary fission and mitosis.

binary fission

mitosis

DNA is replicated

cell begins to divide

cytokinesis divides the cytoplasm

Two daughter cells are formed

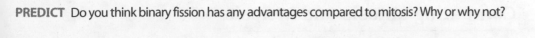

PREDICT Do you think binary fission has any advantages compared to mitosis? Why or why not?

_____

_____

_____

_____

Mitotic Reproduction

Some eukaryotes also reproduce asexually, through mitosis. Have you ever grown a new plant from a stem cutting? Or seen a new sea star growing from a separated arm of another? These new organisms are the result of mitotic reproduction and are therefore genetically the same as the parent organism. Mitotic reproduction is especially common in simpler plants and animals. It occurs in both multicellular and unicellular eukaryotes. Mitotic reproduction can take several forms, depending on the organism. Types of mitotic reproduction include budding, fragmentation, and vegetative reproduction.

FIGURE 8: Budding, vegetative reproduction, and fragmentation are three types of mitotic reproduction.

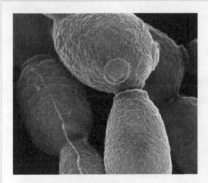  

a **Budding** A new genetically identical cell forms on the body of the parent cell.

b **Vegetative Reproduction** Multicellular structures from an organism develop into a new, genetically identical organism.

c **Fragmentation** A piece of an organism grows into a new genetically identical organism.

Both sexual and asexual reproduction are used in farming, industry, and scientific research. Food crops, such as strawberries and almonds, are pollinated by bees, which help plants carry out sexual reproduction and produce fruit. Horticulturists and home gardeners can use fragmentation and vegetative reproduction to grow new plants. For example, a piece of a leaf from an African violet plant can grow into an entirely new African violet plant. Planting a piece of potato that contains an "eye" can grow new potato plants in a garden.

 Collaborate If you wanted to grow a food crop for human consumption, which process do you think would be best—sexual or asexual reproduction? Write your argument and explain it to a partner.

Binary fission and budding are also widely used in industry. Many drugs, such as vaccines and insulin, are made by growing colonies of bacteria that have been genetically modified to produce the drug. Millions of people with diabetes use synthetic insulin, which is produced by genetically modified bacteria or yeast.

Comparing Mitosis and Meiosis

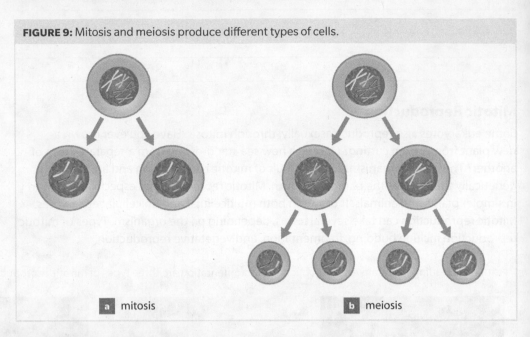

FIGURE 9: Mitosis and meiosis produce different types of cells.

a mitosis   b meiosis

ANALYZE Complete the table to compare mitosis and meiosis.

	Mitosis	Meiosis
How many cells are produced?		
Final cells: diploid or haploid?		
Final cells: genetically identical or unique?		
Involved in which type of reproduction?		

Sexually reproducing organisms go through the process of both meiosis and mitosis. Both processes involve the stages of interphase, prophase, metaphase, anaphase, and telophase. However, meiosis goes through two cycles of cell division while mitosis only has one. Both processes start with diploid cells, but mitosis results in two genetically identical, diploid daughter cells while meiosis results in four genetically different, haploid daughter cells.

EXPLAIN How would an error during mitosis cause a different effect on the body than an error during meiosis?

_____

_____

_____

_____

_____

 Evidence Notebook Develop a model to illustrate why mitosis is necessary for the repair and maintenance of healthy skin tissue. Your model should show how the process of mitosis relates to the skin as an organ.

Factors Affecting Cell Growth

Many factors influence cell growth and division, including cell size. A typical animal cell grows to a size of only 10–20 micrometers. Cell size is often expressed as a comparison of two quantities: surface area and volume. A cell's surface area-to-volume ratio is the relationship between the surface area of a cell's membrane and the inner volume of a cell.

PROBLEM SOLVING

Calculating Cell Size

A ratio is a comparison of two numbers. For example, suppose there are 25 students in a class—10 boys and 15 girls. The ratio of boys to girls is 10 to 15. We can express this ratio in one of three ways:

10 to 15   10:15 $\frac{10}{15}$

A ratio can be reduced, just like any other fraction, by determining the lowest common denominator. In the example above, the greatest common factor is 5.

$$\frac{10}{15} = \frac{2}{3} = 2:3$$

SAMPLE PROBLEM

Calculate the surface area-to-volume ratio for Cell A.

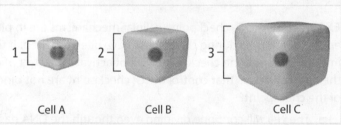

FIGURE 10: Cells are measured by their surface area and volume.

Cell A   Cell B   Cell C

1. Surface area = length × width × number of sides = 1 × 1 × 6 = 6.

2. Volume = length × width × height = 1 × 1 × 1 = 1.

3. Surface area-to-volume ratio = 6:1.

SOLVE

1. Calculate the surface area and volume for Cell B.

2. Calculate the surface area and volume for Cell C.

3. What is the correct surface area-to-volume ratio for Cell B?

  ○ **a.** 4:1   ○ **b.** 3:1   ○ **c.** 2:1   ○ **d.** 1:1

4. What is the correct surface area-to-volume ratio for Cell C?

  ○ **a.** 4:1   ○ **b.** 3:1   ○ **c.** 2:1   ○ **d.** 1:1

Cell Size

Explore Online ▶

Hands-On Lab

Modeling Cell Surface Area-to-Volume Ratio Use model cells to investigate how a cell's size affects its ability to transport materials across the membrane and maintain stable conditions.

ARGUE Make a claim for why cells must stay within a certain size range in order to maintain stable conditions. Explain how surface area and volume are related to this phenomenon.

_____

_____

_____

_____

Oxygen, nutrients, and wastes move across the cell membrane, or the surface of the cell. Some diffuse passively across the membrane, while others are transported actively via specialized proteins. No matter how materials move across the membrane, they must be transported in adequate amounts and with adequate speed to maintain stable conditions within the cell. If there is not enough surface area for materials to cross into and out of the cell, the cell may not be able to absorb materials or expel wastes effectively. To maintain a suitable cell size, growth and division must be coordinated.

Regulating Cell Division

Like other cellular processes, the cell cycle must be regulated. This is done by both internal and external factors that work together to control when and how often a cell divides. Internal factors come from inside the cell and include several types of molecules found in the cytoplasm. External factors come from outside the cell, either from nearby cells or from another part of the organism's body.

EXPLAIN At the G_2 checkpoint, cellular mechanisms are in place to make sure any DNA errors that formed during the S phase have been repaired. If they have not been repaired, internal factors at the checkpoint will not activate the start of mitosis. What might occur if the internal factors that control the G_2 checkpoint are not blocked in response to a failure of the checkpoint?

○ **a.** The cell will continue dividing even though the DNA has errors.

○ **b.** The cell will enter G_0 phase while the errors are repaired.

○ **c.** The cell will make a new copy of the DNA before mitosis.

○ **d.** The cell will continue in the G_2 phase indefinitely.

An external factor that regulates the cell cycle can be either a physical signal or a chemical signal. One example of a physical signal—cell-to-cell contact—can be observed in a single-layer culture of mammalian cells. Individual cells will divide to fill a gap of space, but when the cells touch other cells, they stop dividing. This process allows the body to determine when enough cells have been produced to fill in the gap. Scientists are not yet sure what causes this to happen. One hypothesis is that receptors on the surfaces of neighboring cells bind to each other, causing the cell's cytoskeletons to form structures that can block growth signals. Many cells also release chemical signals that can stimulate the growth of other cells. For example, growth factors are a broad group of proteins that stimulate cell division.

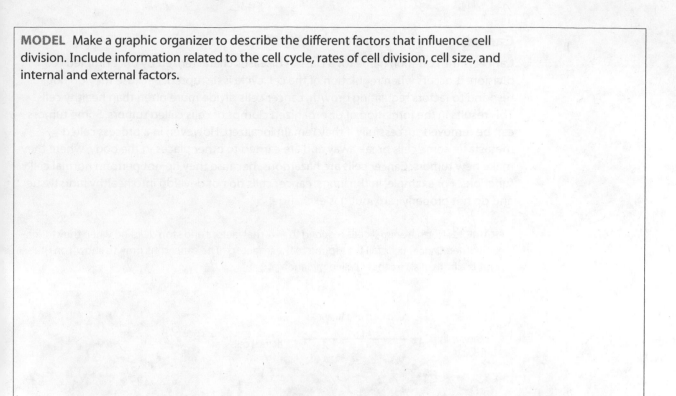

MODEL Make a graphic organizer to describe the different factors that influence cell division. Include information related to the cell cycle, rates of cell division, cell size, and internal and external factors.

When external factors bind to their receptors on a cell's surface, they can trigger internal factors that affect the cell cycle. Two well-studied kinds of internal factors are kinases and cyclins. A *kinase* is an enzyme that, when activated, increases the energy of the target molecule, changes its shape, or both. Your cells have many types of kinases. Those kinases that help control the cell cycle are activated by cyclins. *Cyclins* are a group of proteins that are rapidly made and destroyed at certain points in the cell cycle. These two factors help a cell advance to different stages of the cell cycle when they bind to each other. This cyclin-kinase interaction plays an important role in cell cycle checkpoints, ensuring that cells start and stop dividing at appropriate times.

Apoptosis

Some cells are programmed to die at a predetermined time in their life cycle or after a certain number of cell divisions. Programmed cell death is known as *apoptosis*. It occurs when internal or external signals activate genes that help produce self-destructive enzymes. Apoptosis may occur in cells with damaged DNA or in cells that are harmful to, or simply no longer needed by, the body. Normally immune system cells ignore other cells in the body, but some immune cells are specialized to recognize apoptotic cells. These cells very tidily gobble up the apoptotic cell and recycle its chemical parts for use in building other molecules. Apoptosis is also an important process in normal embryological development in animals, including humans.

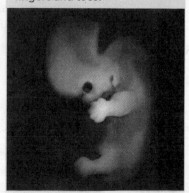

FIGURE 11: In early stages of development, human embryos have webbing between their fingers and toes.

 Collaborate With a partner, draw a model to show how apoptosis leads to changes in the structure of digits (fingers and toes) during later stages of human development.

Cancer

Cancer is the common name for a class of diseases characterized by uncontrolled cell division. It occurs when regulation of the cell cycle is disrupted. Because they do not respond to factors regulating growth, cancer cells divide more often than healthy cells. This results in the formation of disorganized clumps of cells called tumors. Some tumors can be removed successfully if they remain localized. However, in a process called metastasis, some cells break away and are carried to other places in the body, where they make new tumors. Cancer cells are hazardous, because they do not perform normal cell functions. For example, in the lungs, cancer cells do not develop into healthy lung tissue and do not properly carry out gas exchange.

FIGURE 12: Normal animal cells respond to external factors and stop dividing when they touch each other. Cancer cells fail to respond to these factors. The cancerous growth shown on the right is a form of skin cancer called melanoma.

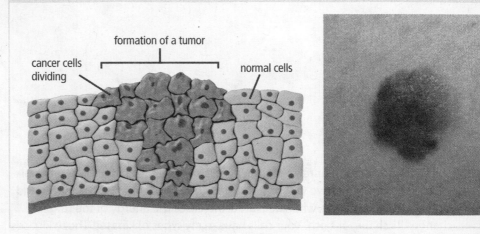

formation of a tumor

cancer cells dividing

normal cells

INFER Which of the following is evidence that cells no longer respond to external factors and may have turned cancerous?

○ **a.** New cells replace old or damaged cells.

○ **b.** Cell clumps form, crowding existing cells.

○ **c.** Dead cells are shed at a more rapid rate.

○ **d.** Dormant cells re-enter an active cell cycle.

Cells become cancerous when mutations occur in sections of DNA that code for regulatory factors. Some mutations are caused by radiation or chemical exposure while others are inherited. Substances that promote or produce cancerous growth are called carcinogens. These include tobacco smoke and certain air pollutants. Some cancers are inherited when the abnormal gene that causes the cancer is passed on from generation to generation.

Evidence Notebook A sensory neuron serving the toe of a giraffe has an average length of nearly 4.6 meters. Why is it important for giraffes to have specialized nerve cells? What role does cell division play in the development of these cells?

A Brief History of Cell Theory

To learn more about cells and how they function, scientists first relied on simple instruments. Over time, advancements in science and technology resulted in microscopes that allowed us to not only see cells, but also to observe processes occurring within them.

Before the 1600s, people had no idea that cells existed, so they had other explanations for the basis of life. That all began to change after the English scientist Robert Hooke first viewed cork under a microscope. He observed that cork is made of tiny, hollow compartments. The compartments reminded Hooke of small rooms found in a monastery, so he gave them the same name: cells. However, it took nearly 200 years before scientists made the connection between biological cells and life.

FIGURE 13: The cells viewed under Hooke's microscope are dead tissue from a cork tree. The cell viewed under the modern microscope is in the process of dividing.

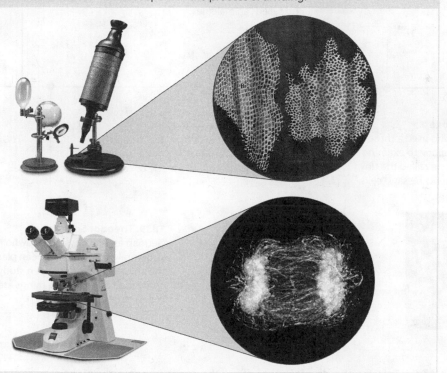

EXPLAIN How did advancements in technology help scientists better understand the process of cell division? What questions about cell division could future technologies help answer?

_____

_____

_____

_____

_____

Cell Theory

Almost all cells are too small to see without a microscope. Magnifying lenses had already been around for hundreds of years before Hooke developed his microscope, but their quality was limited by the lens-grinding technology of the times. Therefore, even though Hooke had designed a state-of-the-art microscope for his time, most likely he would not have seen anything inside the cork cells when he studied them, even if they had been alive. So how did scientists come to learn so much about cells, and how long did it take?

FIGURE 14: A timeline of the study of cells

1595: Zacharias Janssen
Dutch eyeglass maker who invented the compound microscope by placing two lenses in a tube.

1674: Antonie van Leeuwenhoek
Dutch tradesman who developed a more powerful microscope. He observed numerous single-celled organisms swimming in a drop of pond water, which he called "animalcules."

1855: Rudolf Virchow
German scientist who stated that all cells come from other cells. He also described the microscopic structure of cells such as nerve cells.

1665: Robert Hooke
English scientist who used a three-lens compound microscope to examine thin slices of cork. He called the tiny, hollow compartments he saw "cells."

1838: Matthias Schleiden
German botanist who used compound microscopes to study plant tissue and proposed that plants are made of cells.

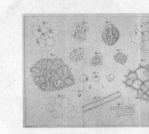

1839: Theodor Schwann
German animal physiologist who noticed structural similarities between plant cells and the animal cells he had been studying. He concluded that all living things are made of cells and cell products.

ARGUE Using the development of cell theory as an example, make a claim for how science influences technology and how technology influences science.

_____

_____

_____

_____

Theodor Schwann, influenced by the work of Matthias Schleiden and other scientists, published the first statement of the cell theory. Schwann's theory helped lay the groundwork for all biological research that followed. However, Schwann stated in his publication that cells form spontaneously by free-cell formation. As later scientists studied the process of cell division, they realized that this part of Schwann's idea was wrong.

The cell theory is one of the first unifying concepts developed in biology. The major principles of the cell theory are:

· All organisms are made of cells.

· All existing cells are made by other living cells.

· The cell is the most basic unit of life.

EXPLAIN Cell theory changed over time as new discoveries came to light. What does this say about a scientific theory? Select all correct answers.

☐ **a.** A theory is based on ideas that have been proven true and that are not subject to revision.

☐ **b.** A theory is a proposed explanation for a wide variety of observations and experimental results.

☐ **c.** New evidence that has been confirmed through observation and experiment may result in the modification of a theory.

☐ **d.** A theory is based on preliminary evidence but still needs to be confirmed with experiments.

 Engineering

Advances in Microscopy

Scientists can learn new things about cells using new technologies. An electron microscope can magnify images hundreds of thousands of times larger than their actual size. A transmission electron microscope (TEM) passes electrons through a specimen. Thick surfaces absorb more electrons than thinner areas, producing a black-and-white magnified image. In contrast, a scanning electron microscope (SEM) scans the surface of a sample. However, it can be used for larger specimens and produces a 3D image of the surface of a specimen.

FIGURE 15: Electron microscopes help scientists observe cells in new ways.

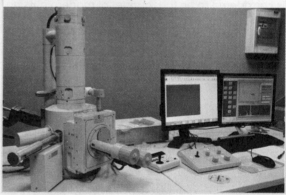

APPLY How have electron microscopes aided scientists' understanding of how cells function?

_____

_____

_____

_____

 Evidence Notebook Before the cell theory was developed, many people claimed that spontaneous generation was possible. In other words, that cells arose from nonliving matter, such as flies arising from rotting meat. Respond to that claim using the principles of cell theory.

Language Arts

Germ Theory and Disease Eradication

Today, it's common knowledge that infectious diseases such as the flu, strep throat, and malaria are caused by viruses, bacteria, and other pathogens that infect and reproduce inside the body. However, this understanding is a fairly recent discovery. Germ theory, first introduced in the 1860s, is a scientific theory that states that infectious diseases are caused by microscopic organisms that grow and reproduce inside the body.

An important contributor to germ theory was Louis Pasteur, a French scientist who developed the process of pasteurization and vaccines against rabies and anthrax. Around the same time, Florence Nightingale, a British nurse, recognized that basic hygiene and sanitation in hospitals was critical to patient recovery. Nightingale's experience helped her to develop the environmental theory of nursing that is still used today. She is considered to be the founder of modern nursing.

Another critical person in the development of germ theory was Robert Koch, a German scientist who discovered the bacterium that causes tuberculosis, *Mycobacterium tuberculosis* in 1882.

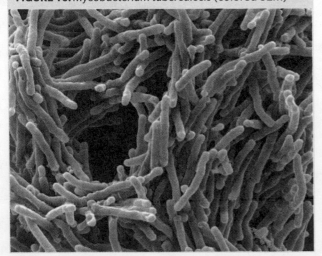

FIGURE 16: *Mycobacterium tuberculosis* (colored SEM)

M. tuberculosis is an unusual pathogen because it can stay dormant in the body for decades after the initial infection. Dormant means that the bacterial cells are not actively dividing at a rate that will cause an active infection. At least one-third of the world population is thought to be infected with the bacterium that causes tuberculosis.

The phrase "latent tuberculosis infection" is used to describe a dormant infection. During a latent infection, the person is not contagious, and they typically do not have any symptoms of the disease. Most healthy immune systems can control the bacteria and prevent the development of an active tuberculosis infection. The majority of active infection cases occur in people who have compromised immune systems, such as the very young and very old or people who are already under treatment for other infections or diseases.

During an active infection, the bacteria divide at a fast rate, killing healthy body cells in the process. People with active tuberculosis often develop a cough, chills, and excessive fatigue. They can also spread the bacteria to others. Without successful treatment, an active tuberculosis infection can be fatal.

Global death rates from tuberculosis have declined over time, but tuberculosis continues to kill approximately two million people each year. Most of these deaths occur in developing countries with limited medical facilities. *M. tuberculosis* is resistant to many antibiotics. Antibiotic resistance has evolved in response to modern medicinal use of such treatments. For *M. tuberculosis*, this resistance is due to changes in the bacterium's complex cell wall, which helps it to survive in the person's body. While this cell wall has a clear advantage, it also poses a challenge during reproduction because the bacterium needs to synthesize each layer of this cell wall while maintaining its rod-like shape. Further research into this mechanism can lead to new, successful treatments for the disease.

Evidence of tuberculosis infection has been found in mummies in ancient Egypt, which shows that the disease has been present for centuries. In the early 1800s, tuberculosis was a major cause of death in both the United States and Europe. You may actually already be familiar with this fact from the plotlines of books from your literature classes—back then, the disease was commonly referred to as *consumption*.

After Robert Koch identified the bacteria that caused the disease, he also discovered how it spread. In the 1900s, death rates declined due to improved sanitation methods and the development of antibiotics. In the 1920s, a vaccine was developed by French scientists Albert Calmette and Camille Guérin to combat the disease. Commonly referred to as Bacille-Calmette-Guérin, or BCG, this vaccine is most commonly administered to people living in developing countries, where the rate of tuberculosis infections remains high.

While tuberculosis rates have declined in general, it continues to be a major global health concern in many areas of the world. In all regions of the world, the incidence of antibiotic-resistant tuberculosis is also a growing threat.

Mortality from Tuberculosis in the United States

FIGURE 17: Deaths from tuberculosis have steadily declined in the U.S. since the 1900s.

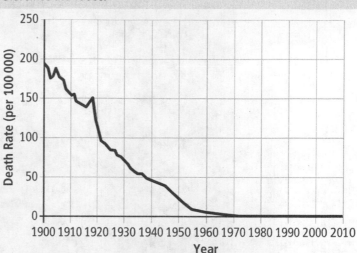

Credit: Adapted from "Explanations for 20th Century Tuberculosis Decline: How the Public Gets It Wrong" by Ray M. Merrill et. al from *Journal of Tuberculosis Research*, Vol 4, 111-121. doi: 10.4236/jtr.2016.43014 Copyright © 2016 by Ray M. Merrill and Scientific Research Publishing.

INFER How might improvements in sanitation have led to a decrease in mortality from tuberculosis?

_____

_____

_____

EXPLAIN Use germ theory to explain how the development of antibiotic-resistant tuberculosis is a threat even in regions where overall tuberculosis rates have declined.

_____

_____

_____

 Language Arts Connection Use online or library resources to find a poem or short novel that includes tuberculosis (typically referred to as "consumption") as a major theme or component of the plot. Write a short report about the literary work you chose and then make a digital presentation to share with your classmates.

STUDYING LIMB REGENERATION   **CAREER: CELL BIOLOGIST**   **MITOSIS UNDER THE MICROSCOPE**   Go online to choose one of these other paths.

Lesson Self-Check

FIGURE 18: Skin cells are replaced at a relatively rapid rate in the human body.

Did you know that you shed your entire outer layer of skin every two to four weeks? To do so, you shed 500 million skin cells every single day. How are you able to lose so many cells daily, and yet your body is still covered by skin? Thank the cell cycle.

Cells have a life cycle made up of periods of rest, growth, and division. When a multicellular organism develops, a single cell divides over and over to produce the trillions of cells that make up the organism. Throughout the organism's lifetime, internal and external signals regulate cell growth and cell division. These factors include physical and chemical signals, as well as limits on cell size. Even as your body is shedding skin cells by the hundreds of millions, plenty of new skin cells are ready to take their place due to the process of mitosis.

 Evidence Notebook Refer to your notes in your Evidence Notebook to explain why cells divide instead of simply growing larger. In your explanation, address the following questions:

1. Make a claim about the relationship between the cell cycle and the development, growth, and maintenance of both single-celled and multicellular organisms.
2. What evidence suggests that mitosis is necessary for the growth and reproduction of specialized cells, such as skin cells? Why is mitosis important for the repair of skin tissue?
3. Why is it important that the cell cycle is regulated? What can happen when regulation of the cell cycle is disrupted? Use reasoning and evidence to support your answer.

CHECKPOINTS

Check Your Understanding

1. Which events take place during mitosis but not during binary fission? Select all correct answers.
   - ☐ **a.** duplication of organelles
   - ☐ **b.** division of the cytoplasm
   - ☐ **c.** separation of chromosomes
   - ☐ **d.** formation of a mitotic spindle

2. Which of the following is not a principle of cell theory?
   - ○ **a.** The cell is the basic unit of life.
   - ○ **b.** All living things are made of cells.
   - ○ **c.** All organisms are made up of many cells.
   - ○ **d.** All cells come from other cells.

3. In their early embryonic stages, a human embryo has a tail, and a whale embryo has limb buds for hind legs. But when they are born, the human does not have a tail, and the whale does not have hind legs. Which process is responsible for these changes?
   - ○ **a.** apoptosis
   - ○ **b.** cytokinesis
   - ○ **c.** mitosis
   - ○ **d.** synthesis

4. Which of these statements best explains how advancements in technology influenced the development of the cell theory?
   - ○ **a.** Communication between scientists improved.
   - ○ **b.** Microscopes let scientists see cells.
   - ○ **c.** Increased knowledge allowed scientists to make predictions.
   - ○ **d.** Printing increased the number of books about the cell.

5. In which of these situations would cells most likely receive signals instructing them to enter the M phase of the cell cycle? Select all correct answers.
   - ☐ **a.** A tissue needs repairing.
   - ☐ **b.** Cells need to grow larger.
   - ☐ **c.** More cells are needed to defend the body.
   - ☐ **d.** Cells need to decrease in number during development.

6. Imagine a cell has six sides, each side measuring 4 micrometers (μm) in length. Use this information and the equations below to make the following calculations:

   Surface area = length × width × number of sides
   Volume = length × width × height

   a. What is the surface area of the cell? _____

   b. What is the volume of the cell? _____

   c. What is the surface area-to-volume ratio for the cell? _____

7. Complete the statement about cell size and conditions within a cell.

   As a cell grows in size, the transport of materials across the cell membrane may be affected. This is because as a cell increases in size, its surface area | volume increases more quickly than its surface area | volume. As a result, there may be too much | too little cell membrane for materials such as oxygen and nutrients to pass through, and stability within a cell may be disrupted.

8. Select the correct terms to complete the statement about factors that regulate cell growth and division.

   Different factors regulate cell growth and division. Cells are limited in size because they need a large growth area | volume | surface area as compared to their growth area | volume | surface area. This ensures that materials can move into and out of the cell at adequate rates. The cell cycle is also regulated by external factors such as growth factors | cyclins | cell shape and internal factors such as growth factors | cyclins | cell shape. These factors work together to make sure the cell enters the appropriate phase of the cell cycle at the correct time.

CHECKPOINTS (continued)

9. Suppose chromosomes in a skin cell are damaged by ultraviolet radiation. If the damaged genes do not affect cell cycle regulation, do you think the cell will become cancerous? Explain your answer.

_____

_____

_____

_____

_____

_____

_____

_____

10. How is mitosis involved in the healing of a wound?

_____

_____

_____

_____

_____

_____

_____

_____

_____

_____

MAKE YOUR OWN STUDY GUIDE

 In your Evidence Notebook, design a study guide that supports the main ideas from this lesson:

The cell cycle is a sequence of events in which cells grow and divide.

Mitosis and cytokinesis result in two daughter cells with identical genetic material.

This process is necessary for the growth and development of new body structures and the repair of damaged tissue.

Remember to include the following information in your study guide:

• Use examples that model main ideas.

• Record explanations for the phenomena you investigated.

• Use evidence to support your explanations. Your support can include drawings, data, graphs, laboratory conclusions, and other evidence recorded throughout the lesson.

Consider how models help scientists learn more about cells, the cell cycle, and cell division.

Organisms: Cells to Body Systems

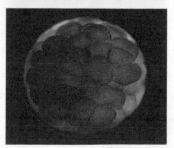

The underside of a glass frog is see-through, revealing its organ systems.

CAN YOU EXPLAIN IT?

Have you ever looked at an organism up close? If you were to look at tissue samples under a microscope, you would see that all organisms are composed of similar structures, called cells. All cells come from existing cells. This is easily observed in single-celled organisms, such as bacteria.

Multicellular organisms, such as a frog, begin as a single cell. That cell repeatedly divides to form a multicellular organism. As the cells divide, they begin to differentiate, or specialize, into different types of cells. These specialized cells, such as muscle cells, will work together to carry out specific tasks. Cells themselves are made up of parts that interact as a whole.

PREDICT How do cells become different types of tissues that work together in organ systems?

_____

_____

_____

_____

 Evidence Notebook As you explore the lesson, gather evidence to explain how systems within your body interact to regulate overall body functions.

Explore Online ▶

FIGURE 1: A single cell divides trillions of times to form a multicellular organism.

The Cell System

The most basic level of organization in living things is the cell. Organisms may be made of just one cell, or they may be made of many cells. Cells in multicellular organisms are specialized to perform different functions. Your body is made of trillions of cells of many different shapes, sizes, and functions. Long, thin, nerve cells transmit information while short, blocky, skin cells cover and protect the body. Despite this variety, the cells in your body share many characteristics with one another and with the cells of other organisms.

 Evidence Notebook Make a table to record the name of each organelle or cell structure, its role in the cell system, and a simple visual or analogy representing that organelle. Complete your table as you read each section.

Cell Structure

All cells are enclosed by a cell membrane that controls the movement of materials into and out of the cell. Inside the membrane, a cell is filled with cytoplasm. Cytoplasm is a jelly-like substance that contains dissolved materials such as proteins and sugars. These building blocks are used to make cell structures and can be broken down to release energy used by the cell to do work. Some types of cells also have organelles, which are specialized structures that perform distinct processes within a cell. Most organelles are surrounded by a membrane. In many cells, the largest and most visible organelle is the nucleus, which stores genetic information.

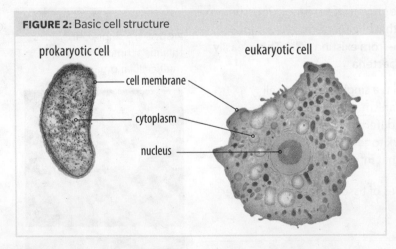

FIGURE 2: Basic cell structure

prokaryotic cell

eukaryotic cell

cell membrane

cytoplasm

nucleus

Prokaryotic and Eukaryotic Cells

Scientists classify cells into two broad categories based on their internal structures: prokaryotic cells and eukaryotic cells. Prokaryotic cells do not have a nucleus or other membrane-bound organelles. Instead, the cell's DNA is suspended in the cytoplasm. Most prokaryotes are microscopic, single-celled organisms. Eukaryotic cells have a nucleus and other membrane-bound organelles. Eukaryotes can be multicellular or single-celled organisms.

GATHER EVIDENCE Which characteristics do prokaryotic and eukaryotic cells share? Select all correct answers.

- ☐ **a.** cell membrane
- ☐ **b.** cytoplasm
- ☐ **c.** nucleus
- ☐ **d.** membrane-bound organelles

Animal Cell Structure

Like your body, eukaryotic cells are highly organized structures. They are surrounded by a protective membrane that receives messages from other cells. They have membrane-bound organelles that perform specific cellular processes, divide certain molecules into compartments, and help regulate the timing of key events.

FIGURE 3: Organelles in the animal cell interact to help the cell carry out functions.

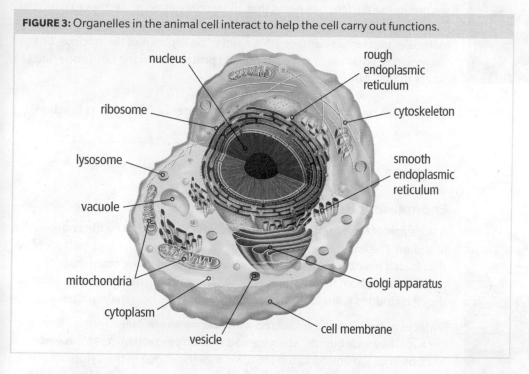

nucleus

ribosome

lysosome

vacuole

mitochondria

cytoplasm

vesicle

rough endoplasmic reticulum

cytoskeleton

smooth endoplasmic reticulum

Golgi apparatus

cell membrane

ASK What questions do you have about the organization of the eukaryotic cell or the role of organelles?

_____

_____

_____

_____

Cells come in numerous amounts of different shapes and sizes, yet they share many common structures. Cells are also not random jumbles of suspended organelles and molecules. Rather, certain organelles and molecules are anchored to specific sites, depending on the cell type. Cell structures serve many roles, including support, storage and waste removal, and cell division.

Cells have a cytoskeleton, which gives them their shape while at the same time maintaining flexibility. It is made of small subunits that form long threads, or fibers, that crisscross the entire cell. Cytoplasm also contributes to cell structure. In eukaryotes, cytoplasm fills the space between the nucleus and the cell membrane. The fluid portion, excluding the organelles, consists mostly of water. Water helps maintain the structure of the cell and provides a medium in which chemical reactions can occur.

Lysosomes are involved in waste removal. They are membrane-bound organelles scattered throughout the cytoplasm that contain special proteins called enzymes. These enzymes break down and recycle old, worn-out cell parts.

Nucleus

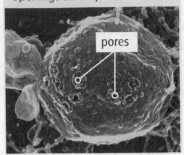

FIGURE 4: The nucleus has openings called pores.

pores

The nucleus is the storehouse for most of the DNA in your cells and consists of chromatin, a nucleolus, and a membrane. Chromatin is spread throughout the nucleus except when the cell is getting ready to divide. The nucleolus is a small region in the nucleus that contains ribosome precursors and rRNA, both of which are used during protein synthesis. The membrane that surrounds the nucleus has pores that allow only certain molecules to pass between the nucleus and cytoplasm. These specialized pores exist because molecules that would damage DNA need to be kept out of the nucleus, but the molecules that are involved in making proteins from the DNA code need access to the DNA.

ANALYZE How does the structure of the nuclear membrane contribute to its function?

_____

_____

Endoplasmic Reticulum and Ribosomes

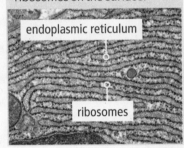

FIGURE 5: The rough ER is so named because it has ribosomes on the surface.

endoplasmic reticulum

ribosomes

A large part of the cytoplasm in most eukaryotic cells is filled by the endoplasmic reticulum. The endoplasmic reticulum, or ER, is an interconnected network of thin, folded membranes. Numerous processes, including the production of proteins, occur both on the surface of the ER and inside the ER. In some regions, the ER is studded with ribosomes, tiny organelles that help make proteins.

Surfaces of the ER that are covered with ribosomes are called rough ER because they look bumpy when viewed with an electron microscope. Not all ribosomes are bound to the ER; some are suspended in the cytoplasm. In general, proteins made on the rough ER are either incorporated into the cell membrane or secreted. In contrast, proteins made on suspended ribosomes are typically used in chemical reactions occurring within the cytoplasm. ER that does not have ribosomes on the surface is called smooth ER. Smooth ER performs a variety of specialized functions, such as breaking down drugs and alcohol.

EXPLAIN Neurons have special proteins in their cell membranes that control the flow of charged ions. Are these proteins most likely produced by ribosomes on the rough ER or ribosomes suspended in the cytoplasm? Explain your answer.

_____

_____

Golgi Apparatus

FIGURE 6: The Golgi apparatus is responsible for processing and delivering proteins.

After a protein has been made, part of the ER pinches off to form a vesicle surrounding the protein. Protected by the vesicle, the protein can be safely transported to the Golgi apparatus. The Golgi apparatus consists of stacks of membrane-enclosed spaces that process, sort, and deliver proteins. Its membranes contain structures called enzymes that make additional changes to proteins. The Golgi apparatus also packages proteins. Some of the packaged proteins are stored within the Golgi apparatus for later use. Some are transported to other organelles within the cell. Still others are carried to the membrane and secreted outside the cell.

Mitochondria

The mitochondrion (plural *mitochondria*) supplies energy to the cell. Mitochondria are bean shaped and have two membranes. Within the inner membrane, a series of chemical reactions (the electron transport chain) converts molecules from the food you eat into usable energy through the process of cellular respiration. Unlike most of the other organelles, mitochondria have their own ribosomes and DNA. This suggests that mitochondria were originally free-living prokaryotes that were taken in by larger cells.

INFER How is the structure of a mitochondrion important for its function? Select all correct answers.

☐ **a.** The outer membrane surrounds and acts as a gateway into the mitochondrion.

☐ **b.** The outer membrane is where the electron transport chain occurs.

☐ **c.** There are two membranes to generate twice the energy from respiration.

☐ **d.** The inner membrane has many folds to increase the surface area necessary for the electron transport chain to occur.

☐ **e.** The inner membrane is smooth so the electron transport chain can function efficiently.

FIGURE 7: Mitochondria provide energy to the cell.

Explore Online ▶

Hands-On Lab

Comparing Cells Use a microscope to investigate the similarities and differences between plant and animal cells.

Plant Cell Structure

Plant cells are also eukaryotic and have many of the same organelles as animal cells, but they also have distinct differences. Plant cells have structures that enable them to capture light energy from the sun and to have a more rigid support structure.

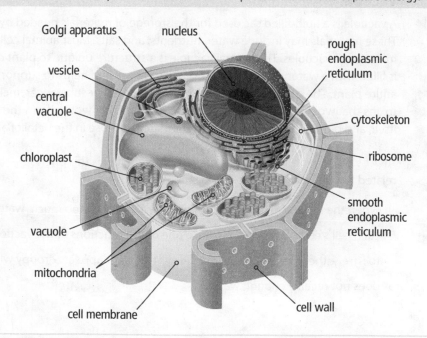

FIGURE 8: Plant cells have specialized structures that protect the cell and capture energy.

Golgi apparatus nucleus

vesicle

central vacuole

chloroplast

vacuole

mitochondria

cell membrane

rough endoplasmic reticulum

cytoskeleton

ribosome

smooth endoplasmic reticulum

cell wall

Collaborate With a partner, determine what organelles plant cells have that animal cells do not have. What do you think is the function of each of these organelles?

Cell Wall

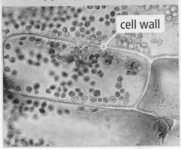

FIGURE 9: The cell wall protects and supports the cell.

cell wall

Plants, algae, fungi, and most bacteria have a cell wall that surrounds the cell membrane. The cell wall is a rigid layer that gives protection, support, and shape to the cell. The cell walls of multiple cells can adhere to each other to help support an entire organism. For instance, much of the wood in a tree trunk consists of dead cells whose cell walls continue to support the entire tree.

EXPLAIN The cell walls of plants and algae have openings, or channels. How is this structure most likely related to the functioning of a plant system?

○ **a.** It provides further support to the cell by making the cell wall more rigid.

○ **b.** It allows water and other molecules to enter and exit the system.

○ **c.** It ensures that all the organelles receive an equal amount of sunlight.

Chloroplast

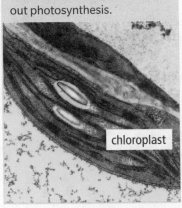

FIGURE 10: Chloroplasts carry out photosynthesis.

chloroplast

Recall that chloroplasts are organelles that carry out photosynthesis. Like mitochondria, chloroplasts are highly compartmentalized. For example, thylakoids in chloroplasts are organized in such a way as to maximize light absorption. Chloroplasts have both an outer membrane and an inner membrane. Chloroplasts have their own ribosomes and DNA. Scientists hypothesize that chloroplasts, like mitochondria, were originally free-living prokaryotes that were taken in by larger cells.

 Collaborate With a partner, answer the following question: Where do you think the most chloroplasts are found in the plant system—in leaves, the stem, or the root? Use evidence to support your answer.

Vacuole

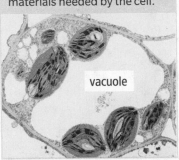

FIGURE 11: The vacuole stores materials needed by the cell.

vacuole

A vacuole is a fluid-filled sac used for the storage of materials needed by a cell. These materials may include water, nutrients, and salts. Most animal cells have many small vacuoles. The central vacuole is a structure unique to plant cells. It is filled with a watery fluid that strengthens the cell and helps to support the entire plant. The central vacuole also may contain other substances, including toxins that would harm predators, waste products that would harm the cell itself, and pigments that give color to cells, such as those in the petal of a flower.

ANALYZE When a plant wilts, its leaves shrivel. How is this phenomenon related to the function of the vacuole in the plant system?

When the leaves of a plant wilt, there is not enough | too much water in each cell's central vacuole. Because one of the functions of the vacuole is to strengthen the cell | capture energy, the plant appears droopy when it does not receive enough water.

 Evidence Notebook Make a claim for how the organization in eukaryotic cells allows cells to perform specialized functions within an organism, such as a frog. How do the components of the cell system interact to help it carry out specific tasks and interact with other systems in the body? Use evidence and examples to support your claim.

The Cell Membrane

The cell membrane, or plasma membrane, forms a boundary that separates the organelles within the cell from the environment outside of the cell. It also controls the passage of materials into and out of a cell to maintain stable conditions within the cell even when conditions in the surrounding environment change. The structure of the cell membrane also allows the cell to communicate with other cells.

FIGURE 12: The cell membrane is made of two phospholipid layers embedded with other molecules, such as proteins, carbohydrates, and cholesterol.

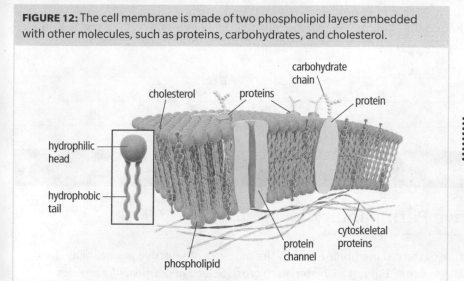

ANNOTATE Label the *inside* and the *outside* of the cell membrane in Figure 12.

PREDICT How do you think the structure of the cell membrane allows for some materials to move into the cell while other materials are kept out?

_____

_____

_____

Cell Membrane Structure

The cell membrane consists of a double layer of phospholipids. A phospholipid is a lipid with a "head" that is soluble in water, or hydrophilic, which means "water loving." Fatty acids make up the "tails." The nonpolar tails are insoluble in water, or hydrophobic, which means "water fearing." Lipids are carbon-based molecules that are nonpolar and generally insoluble in water. Fatty acids are the simplest type of lipid and consist of long chain hydrocarbons.

When phospholipids are placed in a watery environment, they arrange themselves into two layers, as shown in Figure 12. The hydrophilic heads of the phospholipids face the watery environment on both sides of the membrane (inside and outside of the cell), and the hydrophobic tails face the inside of the membrane. If the membrane were only composed of phospholipids, the types of substances that could pass through the membrane, and their rates of passage, would be quite limited. To solve this problem, the cell membrane also contains carbohydrates, proteins, and cholesterol.

A cell membrane needs multiple passageways for substances to enter and exit the cell. This task is accomplished by proteins. Some proteins embedded in the phospholipid bilayer transport materials across the membrane. Others, in the form of enzymes, speed up chemical reactions that take place on the membrane. Still others act as receptors for specific molecules, such as hormones.

Carbohydrates on the cell membrane serve as identification tags, which allow cells to distinguish one type of cell from another. They also let neighboring cells adhere to each other. Cholesterol gives strength to the cell membrane by limiting the movement of the phospholipids, which prevents the membrane from becoming too fluid. Cholesterol also protects the cell membrane at low temperatures by preventing it from becoming solid if the cell is exposed to cooler than normal temperatures.

APPLY How do the structures within the cell membrane help the cell function within a larger system?

_____

_____

_____

 Structure and Function

Selective Permeability

The structure of the cell membrane gives it the property of selective permeability. This means it allows some, but not all, materials to cross. Selective permeability enables a cell to maintain stable conditions in spite of unpredictable, changing conditions outside the cell. Molecules and other materials cross the membrane in several ways. Some of these methods require the cell to expend energy; others do not. How a particular molecule crosses the membrane depends on the molecule's size, polarity, and concentration inside versus outside the cell.

MODEL Draw a model to illustrate the concept of a selectively permeable membrane.

Passive Transport

Cells almost continually import and export substances across the cell membrane. If they had to expend energy to move every molecule, cells would require an enormous amount of energy to stay alive. Fortunately, some molecules enter and exit a cell without energy input from the cell in a process called *passive transport*. This type of transport results from the diffusion of molecules across a membrane.

Diffusion

Diffusion is the movement of molecules in a fluid or gas from a region of higher concentration to a region of lower concentration. It results from the natural motion of particles, which causes molecules to collide and scatter. Concentration is the number of molecules of a substance in a given volume. A concentration gradient is the difference in the concentration of a substance from one location to another. Molecules diffuse down their concentration gradient—that is, from a region of higher concentration to a region of lower concentration.

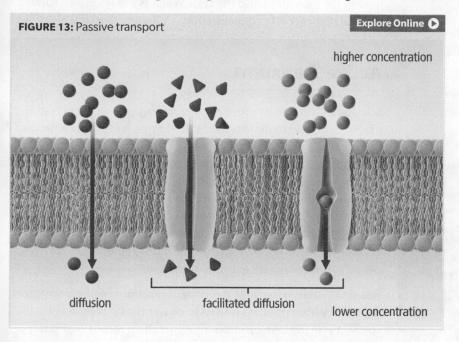

FIGURE 13: Passive transport

Explore Online ▶

higher concentration

diffusion   facilitated diffusion

lower concentration

ANALYZE Use the diagram to complete the statement about passive transport.

During diffusion, molecules move through the phospholipid bilayer, but in

active transport | facilitated diffusion | diffusion the molecules move through a protein.

Passive transport does not require an input of energy | lipids | proteins | water from the

cell in order to proceed. In both types of passive transport, molecules move from areas of

low | medium | high concentration to areas of low | medium | high concentration. Not all

molecules that undergo passive transport can interact easily with the phospholipid bilayer.

Some molecules cannot simply diffuse across a membrane. Facilitated diffusion is the diffusion of molecules across a membrane through transport proteins. Some proteins form openings, or pores, through which molecules can move. Other proteins bind to specific molecules to be transported on one side of the membrane. When the correct molecule binds, these proteins change their shape, and this allows the molecule to pass through the membrane to the other side. Each protein in the membrane is specific to a certain type of molecule or particle.

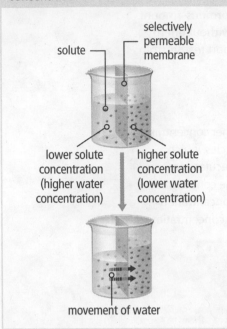

FIGURE 14: Osmosis is the movement of water toward areas of higher solute concentration.

selectively permeable membrane

solute

lower solute concentration (higher water concentration)

higher solute concentration (lower water concentration)

movement of water

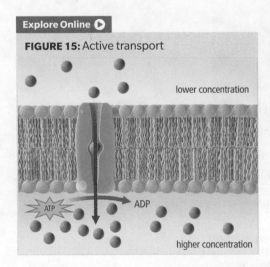

Explore Online ▶

FIGURE 15: Active transport

lower concentration

ATP   ADP

higher concentration

Osmosis

Water molecules also diffuse. They move across a semi-permeable membrane from an area of higher water concentration to an area of lower water concentration. They are also moving from an area of lower solution concentration to an area of higher solution concentration. This process is called *osmosis*. It is important to recognize that the higher the concentration of dissolved particles (solutes) in a solution, the lower the concentration of water molecules in the same solution. The membrane is only permeable to some solutes, so water must cross the membrane to equalize the concentrations of the two solutions.

Plants use osmosis to move water into the cells of their roots. Proteins in the cell membranes of root cells transport certain molecules into the cell. These molecules become more highly concentrated on the inside of the root cells than outside, and water follows the molecules into the cells. Water is always drawn toward areas of higher solute concentration.

Active Transport

Sometimes a cell must move a substance against a concentration gradient in order to remain stable. To do this, it must use a process called *active transport*. Active transport drives molecules across a membrane from a region of lower concentration to a region of higher concentration using transport proteins. Unlike facilitated diffusion, the activity of transport proteins must be powered by chemical energy. An input of energy is necessary because the transport proteins have to overcome the natural tendency of substances to move down a concentration gradient. ATP often provides the energy for active transport.

Recall that during the light-dependent reactions of photosynthesis, the energy from photons is used to power the conversion of $NADP^+$ to NADPH. An electron transport chain moves hydrogen ions across the thylakoid membrane into the lumen against the concentration gradient. A similar process happens in the electron transport chain during cellular respiration, where hydrogen ions are pumped across the inner mitochondrial membrane into the matrix.

ANALYZE Determine whether each characteristic describes active or passive transport.

Transport Characteristic	Mode of Transport
Particles move from low to high concentration.	
Energy is not required.	
Particles move from high to low concentration.	
Water moves through a membrane to areas of lower water concentration.	
Energy is required.	

Endocytosis

A cell may also use energy to move large substances or particles across the cell membrane using vesicles. *Endocytosis* is the process of taking liquids or fairly large molecules into a cell by engulfing them in a membrane. The cell membrane folds inward around the substance and pinches off inside the cell, forming a vesicle. The vesicle then fuses with a lysosome or similar vesicle. If necessary, the vesicle membrane and contents are broken down and released into the cell.

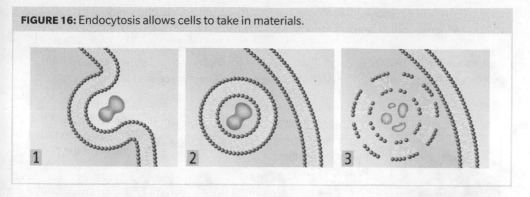

FIGURE 16: Endocytosis allows cells to take in materials.

Exocytosis

Exocytosis is the release of substances out of a cell by the fusion of a vesicle with the membrane. A vesicle forms around materials to be sent out of the cell. The vesicle then moves toward the surface of the cell, where it fuses with the membrane and releases its contents.

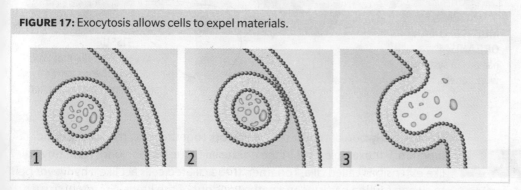

FIGURE 17: Exocytosis allows cells to expel materials.

APPLY Which would be more likely to carry out endocytosis: a white blood cell engulfing foreign materials or a cell that excretes hormones? Use evidence to support your answer.

_____

_____

_____

_____

_____

 Evidence Notebook Freshwater frogs absorb water and salts through their skin. Explain how a frog, which is saltier than its aquatic environment, might use diffusion to maintain water balance.

Interacting Systems in Organisms

Over the course of a day, you complete many different tasks. Whether you are eating, sleeping, or talking to a friend, systems within your body are interacting at different levels. Scientists organize multicellular organisms into five basic levels beginning with cells and moving to increasingly complex structures.

FIGURE 18: The systems of multicellular organisms are organized into different levels. Each system, such as the respiratory system, is made up of interacting components.

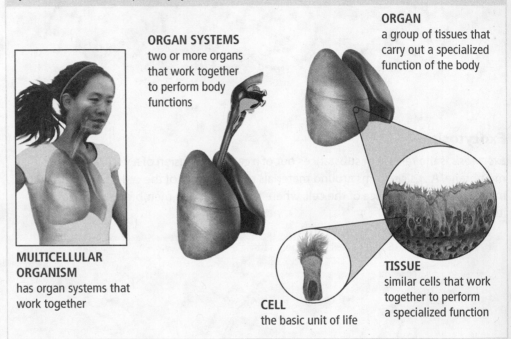

ORGAN SYSTEMS
two or more organs that work together to perform body functions

ORGAN
a group of tissues that carry out a specialized function of the body

MULTICELLULAR ORGANISM
has organ systems that work together

CELL
the basic unit of life

TISSUE
similar cells that work together to perform a specialized function

Explore Online ▶

Hands-On Lab

Connecting Form to Function
Examine a slice of the roots, stems, and leaves of a plant to explain how their structures relate to their functions.

A tissue is a group of similar cells that work together to carry out a specific function. For example, cells in the epithelial tissue of your lungs have tiny hair-like extensions called cilia. Together, these ciliated cells act like a conveyor belt to sweep foreign particles and pathogens out of the lungs. Groups of tissues form organs, such as the lungs, sinuses, and nose. Each of these organs has a specialized function in the body. Multiple organs interact to carry out whole-body functions. In the respiratory system, the nose and sinuses filter, moisten, and warm the air before it enters the lungs.

INFER According to the model of the human respiratory system, how do structures in the respiratory system interact to protect the lungs? How might a sinus infection affect the rest of the respiratory system?

_____

_____

_____

_____

Organ Systems and Organs

An organ system is two or more organs that work together to perform body functions. Organ systems interact to help the organism maintain internal stability, or homeostasis. For example, the muscular system interacts with the circulatory system to help pump your blood and deliver oxygen and nutrients to cells.

 Collaborate If a person's circulatory system did not function properly, how might other systems, such as the respiratory and digestive systems, be affected? How would homeostasis, or internal stability, be affected by these system imbalances? Discuss your answers with a partner.

Organ systems can carry out complex functions because they are made up of organs that work together within the system. An organ is a group of tissues that carry out a specialized function of the body. For example, the digestive system is made up of organs such as the mouth, esophagus, stomach, and liver.

The digestive system is a collection of organs that breaks down food into nutrients and energy that can be used by cells. When you eat, the mouth breaks down food mechanically by chewing, and proteins called enzymes in your saliva break down food chemically. Muscles in the esophagus contract to move the chewed food to the stomach. The stomach then uses both mechanical and chemical digestion to break down food into nutrient components that the body absorbs and uses. As muscles in the stomach churn food, it continues to be broken down by gastric juice, which consists of mucus, enzymes, and acid.

The partly digested food passes into the small intestine, where additional digestion takes place. Organs such as the liver and pancreas secrete chemicals into the upper small intestine. These chemicals break food particles into individual nutrients, which are absorbed through the walls of the small intestine and pass into the blood. Any food that remains undigested passes into the large intestine where excess water is absorbed before the solid waste is excreted from the body.

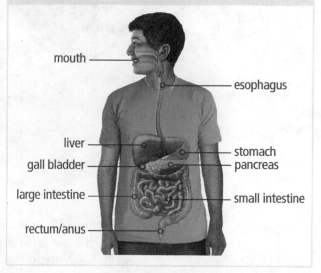

FIGURE 19: Organs make up a body system, such as the digestive system. In general, an organ system is made up of organs specific to the function of that system.

ANALYZE Place these steps in order to model how the organs of the digestive system interact to break down food and absorb nutrients.

_____ **a.** Excess water is absorbed through the large intestine and solid waste is excreted.

_____ **b.** The stomach churns food and gastric juice breaks down food into nutrients.

_____ **c.** Partially digested food passes into the small intestine. Chemicals secreted by the liver and the pancreas complete chemical digestion.

_____ **d.** Enzymes in saliva and chewing break down food.

_____ **e.** Chewed food is swallowed, and muscles in the esophagus contract to move food to the stomach.

_____ **f.** Nutrients pass through the walls of the small intestine and into the blood.

Tissues

For an organ such as the stomach to carry out its function of breaking down food, different types of tissues must work together. A tissue is a group of similar cells that work together to perform a specialized function, usually as part of an organ. In the human body, organs are made up of four general types of tissues—epithelial, connective, muscle, and nervous tissue.

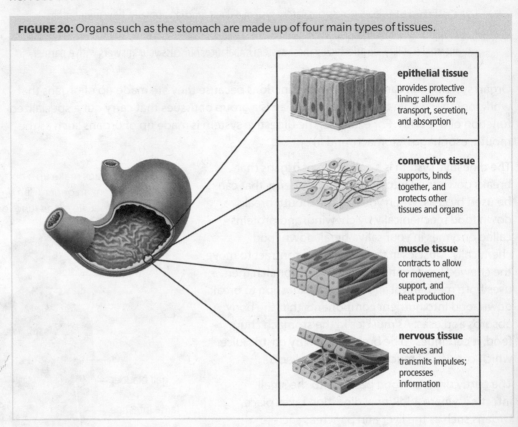

FIGURE 20: Organs such as the stomach are made up of four main types of tissues.

epithelial tissue
provides protective lining; allows for transport, secretion, and absorption

connective tissue
supports, binds together, and protects other tissues and organs

muscle tissue
contracts to allow for movement, support, and heat production

nervous tissue
receives and transmits impulses; processes information

Tissues in the stomach help it carry out its function in the body. Signals from nervous tissue stimulate muscle tissue in the stomach to contract. The walls of the stomach contain three layers of muscle tissue that contract about every 20 seconds. The muscle tissue in the stomach contracts involuntarily, without you having to think about it. The epithelial lining of the stomach is made up of cells that secrete stomach acid and absorb nutrients. The type of epithelial tissue that lines the stomach has column-shaped cells. This type of tissue provides a large amount of surface area for absorption and secretion.

INFER Which of these statements correctly describes how tissues interact to help the stomach churn food?

○ **a.** Connective tissue sends signals that cause nervous tissue to contract.

○ **b.** Nervous tissue sends signals that cause muscle tissue to contract.

○ **c.** Epithelial tissue sends signals that cause muscle tissue to contract.

○ **d.** Muscle tissue sends signals that cause connective tissue to contract.

Connective tissue provides support and protection for structures in the body. Some types of connective tissue are fibrous and tough. Other types, such as loose connective tissue, provide support to internal organs and the surrounding blood vessels. The connective tissue that surrounds blood vessels has the property of elasticity. This is important because as blood pumps through the circulatory system, the vessels within this system must stretch to accommodate blood flow.

Cells

Humans, like other multicellular organisms, are collections of specialized cells that work together. A cell is the most basic unit of life. The cells that make up a multicellular organism arise from a single cell that goes through many divisions to make new cells. *Cell differentiation* is the process by which cells become specialized in both structure and function.

The specialization enabled by differentiation is what allows different types of cells to have different functions. For example, sperm cells have a long tail called a flagellum that allows for movement. Some epithelial cells in the trachea have hair-like extensions called cilia. These structures provide a sweeping motion that helps clear small particles out of the trachea. Neurons have extensions that allow the cell to communicate with many other cells. This leads to the formation of complex, interconnected networks of neurons, such as those in the human brain. Your brain contains billions of neurons with trillions of connections to communicate with the cells of your body and to carry out higher functions, such as memory and learning.

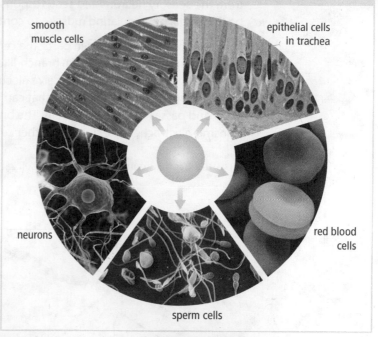

FIGURE 21: All cells in a multicellular organism arise from a single cell. As the organism develops, cells take on unique structures that help them carry out specialized functions.

smooth muscle cells

epithelial cells in trachea

neurons

red blood cells

sperm cells

Engineering

Scaling Down

Nanobots are microscopic robots built on the scale of a nanometer, which is the size of most of the molecules and structures inside living cells. Engineers are designing nanobots that can help deliver medicine, move through the bloodstream to hard-to-reach areas, and even destroy cancer cells. For example, red blood cells carry oxygen and nutrients to cells by binding oxygen and traveling through small blood vessels in the circulatory system called capillaries. Capillaries are so narrow that red blood cells must move through them "single file." For blood-related diseases, nanobots also need to be able to pass through capillaries to deliver medicine.

 Language Arts Connection Research a type of nanobot currently under development. How did the purpose of the nanobot affect its design? What structural features does the design have that help complete its purpose? What are the challenges of designing a nanobot? Present your research in a short blog post.

Neurons

The nervous system is a network of nerves and sensory organs that work together to process information and respond to the environment. The basic unit of the nervous system is the neuron. Neurons are specialized cells that are able to send electrical and chemical signals to help the organism sense information, coordinate a response, and carry out that response.

Humans and other organisms have three types of neurons: sensory neurons, interneurons, and motor neurons. Sensory neurons detect stimuli and send signals to the brain and the spinal cord. Interneurons in the brain and spinal cord receive and process the information from the sensory neurons and send response signals to motor neurons. Motor neurons act on the signal by stimulating muscles to contract.

Most neurons have three main parts: the cell body, one or more dendrites, and an axon, as shown in Figure 22. The short, branch-like extensions that extend from the cell body are called dendrites. Dendrites receive electrochemical messages from other cells. The axon is a long extension of the cell that carries electrochemical signals away from the cell body and passes them to other cells. The branched endings of the axon are specialized to transmit electrochemical signals to other cells.

FIGURE 22: The neuron is a specialized cell within the nervous system.

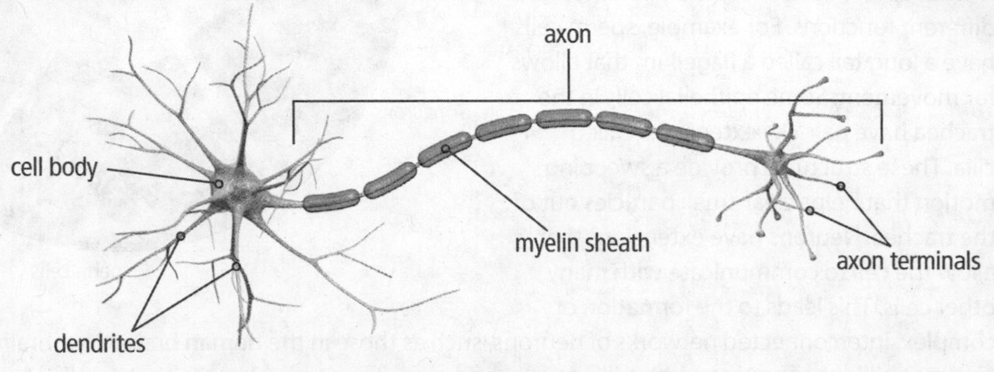

Just as most electric wires are wrapped in an insulating material, many axons are wrapped in a protective covering called a myelin sheath. This covering is formed from a collection of cells that is wrapped around the axon. The myelin sheath protects the axon and helps speed transmission of nerve impulses.

APPLY Multiple sclerosis is a disease that causes the myelin sheath to break down. How would the breakdown of myelin affect the functioning of a neuron?

_____

_____

_____

The nervous system interacts with all the other systems in the body. For example, when you eat, your brain signals your digestive system to start making chemicals and churning your food. Neurons also stimulate muscle tissue in the digestive system to contract, which helps the digestive system move and break down food.

Muscle Cells

Muscles consist of bundles of muscle cells that contract when they are stimulated by the nervous system. A contraction shortens the muscle, causing the bone or tissue to which the muscle is attached to move. Some muscles are under voluntary control, meaning you can choose to move the muscle. This type of muscle is called skeletal muscle. Some muscles are under involuntary control, meaning they move in response to nerve signals or hormones, but you do not choose to move them. Smooth muscle in internal organs and cardiac muscle in the heart are under involuntary control.

Collaborate With a partner, discuss why it is important that cardiac muscle is under involuntary control. Continue your discussion by describing an activity that would require muscles that are under voluntary control and another activity that would require muscles that are under involuntary control.

As shown in Figure 23, the specialized structure of muscle cells allows them to contract. Skeletal muscles are made up of long, cylindrical bundles that contain muscle fibers. Muscle fibers are bundles of single, thin muscle cells called myofibrils. Each myofibril is made up of several sarcomeres. A sarcomere is the contractile unit of the muscle cell.

FIGURE 23: Actin and myosin work together to help a muscle move. During contraction, myosin filaments pull actin filaments toward the center of the sarcomere.

Explore Online ▶

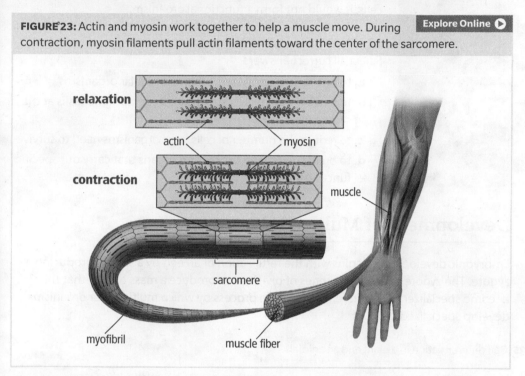

Sarcomeres contain thin filaments made of actin and thick filaments made of myosin. When a muscle cell is relaxed, actin and myosin are not connected to each other. In contraction, the myosin attaches to the actin and pulls the actin toward the center of the sarcomere. This in turn shortens the sarcomere, and the muscle cell contracts. The contraction of many muscle cells at once shortens the entire muscle.

EXPLAIN How does the structure of the muscle cell help it carry out its function?

When a muscle contracts, the actin | myosin | myofibrils | sarcomeres in the muscle shorten. To do this, the actin | myosin filaments pull the actin | myosin filaments toward the center of the sarcomere. When the muscle relaxes, the filaments move away from each other. Muscle cells can do this once | many times.

 Evidence Notebook Draw a model to illustrate how the nervous and digestive system interact when a frog catches and eats a fly. Which organs are most likely involved, and how do they interact?

Cell Differentiation

FIGURE 24: A sperm and egg fuse during fertilization, and a zygote is formed.

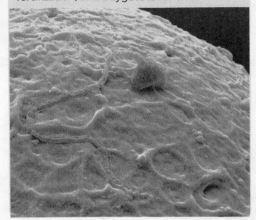

A skin cell can divide to make a new skin cell, or a single bacterium can generate another bacterium. But how does a complex organism like you develop? Your body began as a single fertilized egg, or zygote. If the egg simply divided to make lots of identical cells, it would not form a functional organism.

APPLY Why do multicellular organisms need specialized cells? Select all correct answers.

☐ **a.** to become larger systems than unicellular organisms

☐ **b.** to make many cells that can complete the same tasks at the same time

☐ **c.** to reduce the number of cells large organisms need to survive

☐ **d.** to build specialized tissues and organs that carry out specific functions

Development of Multicellular Organisms

Embryonic development begins with the fertilization of an egg by a sperm, producing a zygote. The zygote undergoes a series of divisions to produce a mass of cells that then become specialized. Cell differentiation is the process by which multicellular organisms develop specialized cells.

FIGURE 25: Cell differentiation in a plant and an animal.

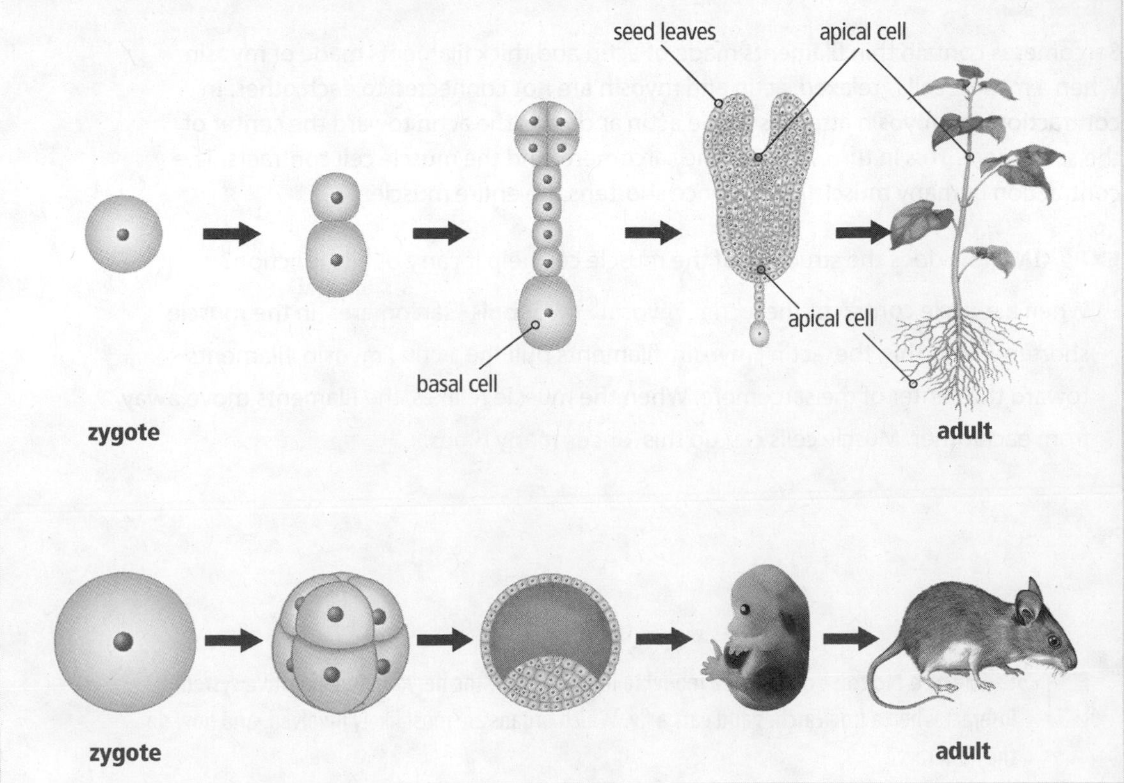

seed leaves   apical cell

apical cell

basal cell

zygote   adult

zygote   adult

A cell's location within an embryo helps determine how it will differentiate. In plant cells, the first division of a fertilized egg is unequal, or asymmetric, as shown in Figure 25. The apical, or topmost, cell forms most of the embryo, including the growth point for stems and leaves. The basal cell provides nutrients to the embryo and serves as the growth point for the roots. Plant cells cannot easily migrate because of their cell walls, but they adapt to changing conditions and continue to develop throughout their lifetime. As the plant grows, new cells continue to differentiate based on their location in the plant.

ANALYZE Compare the models of cell differentiation in the plant and animal shown in Figure 25. What are the differences, and what are the similarities?

_____

_____

_____

_____

In animals, an egg undergoes many divisions after it is fertilized. The resulting cells migrate to a specific area and begin to differentiate, forming a hollow ball. As the embryo develops, part of the ball folds inward, forming an inner layer called the endoderm. An opening is formed in the outer layer, called the ectoderm. Some animals, such as jellyfish, develop from only two cell layers. Vertebrates, including humans, develop a third layer of cells, called the mesoderm, between the inner and outer layers. This standard model of development varies from species to species.

FIGURE 26: Each cell layer in the gastrula of a human embryo produces cells that will form different tissues and organs.

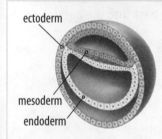
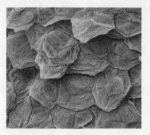
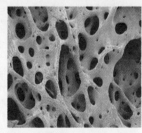

a The gastrula is the embryo stage that develops three layers of cells: the ectoderm, mesoderm, and endoderm.

b The ectoderm develops into the skin and the nervous system. It also forms the lining of organs, such as the mouth.

c The mesoderm develops into bone, muscle, blood, and connective tissue. It also forms organs, such as the kidneys.

d The endoderm forms the lining of organs in the digestive, respiratory, and excretory systems. It also forms some glands.

EXPLAIN Why is the high degree of regulation of the cell differentiation process especially important during the early stages of development? Select all correct answers.

☐ **a.** Regulation ensures that development is orderly.

☐ **b.** Regulation changes the size of the cell.

☐ **c.** Regulation ensures that specialized cells end up in the correct location within the organism.

☐ **d.** Regulation makes cells able to change into any other cell.

Stem Cells

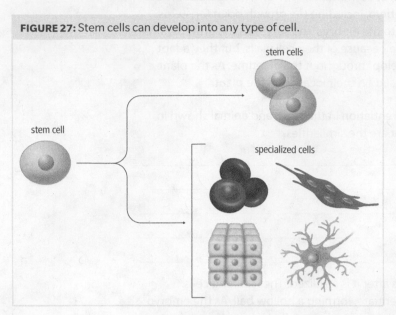

FIGURE 27: Stem cells can develop into any type of cell.

stem cells

stem cell

specialized cells

Specialized cells develop from a type of cell known as a *stem cell*. Stem cells are a unique type of body cell that can develop into specialized cells through differentiation. Stem cells are able to divide and renew themselves by mitosis for long periods of time, remaining undifferentiated until they are needed. When needed, they divide to form one new stem cell and one specialized cell. Stem cells are classified by their potential to develop into differentiated cell types. In general, the more differentiated a stem cell already is, the fewer the types of cells it can form.

Adult stem cells are located near the specialized cells of many organs and tissues. Their primary role is to maintain and repair the specialized cells in tissues and organs. Because adult stem cells are partially undifferentiated, they can only produce a limited variety of specialized cell types. Adult stem cells are found in small numbers all over the body in adults and children, as well as in umbilical cord blood.

EXPLAIN Label each of these statements as an advantage or disadvantage of using *adult stem cells* for research or medical purposes.

a. They can be taken from a patient, grown in culture, and put back into the patient, so risk of rejection by the immune system is low. _____

b. They can be difficult to isolate and grow. _____

c. They may contain DNA abnormalities. _____

d. They do not require the use of human embryos. _____

Embryonic stem cells can form any of the 200 cell types of the body. They may be obtained from donated three-to-five-day-old embryos that result from in vitro fertilization. During in vitro fertilization, eggs are fertilized outside a woman's body and go through several divisions in a culture.

EXPLAIN Label each of these statements as an advantage or disadvantage of using *embryonic stem cells* for research or medical purposes.

a. A patient's body might reject them as foreign material. _____

b. Their use raises many ethical questions. _____

c. They can form any of the 200 cell types of the body. _____

d. They can be grown indefinitely in culture. _____

Researchers are studying ways to use stem cells to treat many different medical conditions. Because stem cells can differentiate into other types of cells, they offer the potential to repair or replace damaged tissues or organs. For example, stem cells in bone marrow produce red and white blood cells. Bone marrow transplants are used to treat leukemia and lymphoma, cancers that affect white blood cells.

Scientists are also studying the use of stem cells to repair the pancreas of people with type 1 diabetes, so that they will produce normal amounts of insulin. A patient with a damaged heart could potentially have stem cells injected into the tissue to repair the damage and grow new capillaries, thus restoring normal heart function. However, there are many problems with these treatments that future research needs to solve.

 Language Arts Connection What tradeoffs might scientists consider when deciding whether to use stem cell treatments or traditional treatments to treat a disease such as diabetes? Research and develop an educational brochure about the tradeoffs of stem cell treatments.

Gene Expression

When a gene is "switched on," or expressed, the instructions within that segment of DNA are used to make a specific protein. When a gene is "switched off," or not expressed, its instructions are not used to make proteins. During development, genes are expressed differently in different types of cells. The set of genes expressed determines the type of cell and its location in the embryo or organism. By expressing some genes and not others, each cell generates the proteins it needs to function within the organism.

Structure and Function

Muscular Dystrophy

Muscular dystrophy is a group of 30 diseases that cause muscle weakness and increasing loss of skeletal muscle mass, affecting a person's ability to control his or her movements. It occurs in both males and females and in all races and ages. The most common variety is called Duchenne, and it emerges mostly in young boys.

Muscular dystrophies are caused by mutations in genes that code for proteins that make healthy muscles. Some of the mutations occur spontaneously in the egg or in the developing embryo, but many are inherited. The genes code for specific proteins that are often found in skeletal muscles, cardiac smooth muscles, and in the brain. These proteins are necessary for the repair of muscle fibers. If the proteins do not function properly, the muscle fibers are not regenerated, causing muscle loss. Over time, this can affect not just the individual muscle fibers, but entire organs, including the heart. This in turn affects all the organ systems that interact with them.

ANALYZE What conclusions can you draw about how muscular dystrophy might affect the respiratory, skeletal, and digestive systems?

_____

_____

_____

_____

 Evidence Notebook Make a model illustrating how a frog develops from a zygote to a fully grown adult. Include media and text to explain fertilization, cell division, and cell differentiation.

Engineering

Modeling Interacting Body Systems

Like muscular dystrophy, amyotrophic lateral sclerosis (ALS) is a neuromuscular disease. Although the exact cause of ALS is still unknown, it is thought to be caused by genetic mutations and environmental factors. ALS most often occurs in two forms: familial, or inherited, and sporadic, or noninherited.

ANNOTATE Circle the differences you see between the normal nerve cell and an ALS nerve cell.

normal nerve cell   ALS nerve cell

ALS causes the motor neurons that connect the brain to the spine and muscles to degenerate and eventually die. When they die, the brain cannot control the activity of voluntary muscles. This affects the ability to speak, eat, and move. In this activity, you will model how ALS affects the interactions among the muscular, skeletal, and neurological systems.

Conduct Research

Research how ALS affects the muscular, skeletal, and neurological systems. As you search for information, keep track of your sources to submit with your final model. Be sure to use sources that are reliable. For example, government and educational institutions are more reliable than personal websites. With your final model, submit a list of sources in the format specified by your teacher.

Define the System

Decide on a task that involves using your voluntary muscles, such as running, playing video games, or talking to a friend, that would be affected by ALS. Think about the body systems that are involved in completing that task. For example, reaching to pick up a cell phone requires having the thought, which transmits from your brain through your motor neurons and into your neck, eye, arm, and hand muscles. You simultaneously turn your head, find your phone, and take it. Your muscles contract, using the bones for leverage.

DESIGN Which task will you model, and which body systems interact to help you carry out this task?

_____

_____

_____

_____

Make a Model

Determine the type of model you will use to illustrate how ALS might affect the task you chose. Your model should demonstrate how ALS affects the relevant body systems at different levels, such as cells, tissues, organs, and organ systems. Your model should also demonstrate how energy, materials, and information flow within and between the systems. Finally, your model should be able to demonstrate how it could be used to design solutions to help a person with ALS complete the task you are modeling. The model could also highlight a potential complication for a person with ALS.

DESIGN Describe your model. What materials did you use to make your model?

_____

_____

_____

_____

_____

Test and Evaluate Your Model

Testing is an important part of the engineering process. Test the effectiveness of your model. Answer the following questions to help optimize your model design.

EVALUATE How well did your model demonstrate how ALS would affect the performance of the task you chose to model? Explain.

_____

_____

_____

_____

_____

REVISE What changes would you make to improve your model?

_____

_____

_____

_____

 Language Arts Connection Present your model to your peers. Explain how it illustrates the effect of ALS on the interactions between systems required to carry out the task you chose. Consider using illustrations, simulations, or demonstrations to clearly explain the processes involved.

| INVESTIGATING ORGAN SYSTEMS | | MODELING INDUCTION IN EMBRYOS | PLANT TISSUES AND CELLS | Go online to choose one of these other paths. |

Lesson Self-Check

CAN YOU EXPLAIN IT?

FIGURE 28: Many organ systems work together to allow the frog to conduct life processes.

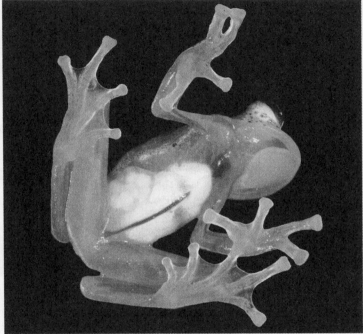

b All organisms begin with a single cell.

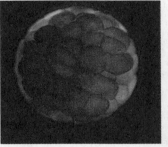

a Cells, tissues, organs, and organ systems work together to support the processes this frog needs to stay alive.

c Cell division occurs over and over again until an organism is fully formed.

Multicellular organisms have many trillions of cells that exist in an interdependent network that makes up the organism. At all different scales, the components work to fulfill the common goal of staying alive. Cells differentiate into new cells, and then divide to replace old cells or to repair damaged cells. Cells specialize to perform many functions and work together to form tissues. Organs are made of specialized tissues. Many organs work together to form organ systems.

 Evidence Notebook Refer to your notes in your Evidence Notebook to explain how body systems interact to regulate overall functions within a multicellular organism. Your explanation should include a discussion of cell structure and function, gene expression, and cell differentiation.

1. Make a claim about how systems within your body interact to regulate body functions.
2. What evidence supports your claim? For example, how do organs, tissues, and cells interact to carry out specific functions in an organism?
3. How do mitosis and differentiation produce and maintain multicellular organisms?

CHECKPOINTS

Check Your Understanding

1. Which of the following statements correctly describes the relationship between tissues and organs?

   ○ **a.** Several organs interact to help a tissue carry out a specialized function.

   ○ **b.** One type of specialized tissue is found in each organ.

   ○ **c.** Organs are made up of different types of tissues that work together.

   ○ **d.** Tissues compete with each other to carry out the main function of the organ.

2. Which of the following organ systems must work together to bring oxygen to the body's cells? Select all correct answers.

   ☐ **a.** digestive system

   ☐ **b.** skeletal system

   ☐ **c.** immune system

   ☐ **d.** respiratory system

   ☐ **e.** circulatory system

3. Number these levels of organization in the correct order. Number the largest system as number 1, and the smallest system as number 6.

   _____ **a.** cell   _____ **d.** tissue

   _____ **b.** organelle   _____ **e.** organism

   _____ **c.** organ system   _____ **f.** organ

4. In which processes do cell membranes help regulate the flow of materials into and out of the cell? Select all correct answers.

   ☐ **a.** photosynthesis

   ☐ **b.** respiration

   ☐ **c.** meiosis

   ☐ **d.** transcription

5. Select the correct terms to complete the statement.

   Stem cells are a unique type of body cell that can differentiate | fuse to form a variety of specialized cell types. A stem cell can either divide into two new stem cells or it can divide to produce one stem cell and one specialized cell, such as a(n) undifferentiated cell | identical cell | neuron. New advancements in science have allowed researchers to convert human skin cells to embryonic stem cells. This requires altering segments of DNA called proteins | genes | organelles. When these segments of DNA are expressed, the cell produces proteins | genes | organelles, which carry out specific functions within the cell.

6. Identify each of the following as either mitosis or cell differentiation.

   a. produces two identical daughter cells

   _____

   b. increases the number of tissues in an embryo

   _____

   c. produces a cell with a specific structure and function _____

   d. increases the number of cells in an embryo

   _____

7. Match these structures to their function within the larger plant system.

   | cell wall | chloroplast | vacuole |

   a. transfers light energy to high-energy molecules which plant cells can use for energy and growth

   _____

   b. provides support and protection for cells; can support entire plant system

   _____

   c. stores water and other materials; provides strength and support for plant system

   _____

CHECKPOINTS (continued)

8. The word *organ* comes from the Latin word *organum*, meaning "instrument" or "tool." How does this meaning relate to the definition of a living organ?

_____

_____

_____

_____

_____

9. Explain the relationship between embryonic cell layers, gene expression, proteins, and cell differentiation.

_____

_____

_____

_____

_____

10. Explain why stem cells are of great interest to researchers studying therapies for human diseases.

_____

_____

_____

_____

_____

_____

MAKE YOUR OWN STUDY GUIDE

 In your Evidence Notebook, design a study guide that supports the main ideas from this lesson:

Systems in organisms interact at different levels to carry out functions necessary for life.

Cell differentiation is a process in which cells take on specialized roles within the organism. Different genes are expressed in different types of cells.

Remember to include the following information in your study guide:
- Use examples that model main ideas.
- Record explanations for the phenomena you investigated.
- Use evidence to support your explanations. Your support can include drawings, data, graphs, laboratory conclusions, and other evidence recorded throughout the lesson.

Consider how interactions within and between systems at different levels help to support life functions and how cell differentiation affects the development of an organism.

Mechanisms of Homeostasis

Your body has control systems that keep its internal environment in balance.

CAN YOU EXPLAIN IT?

The complex tissues, organs, and organ systems in your body must respond to a wide variety of conditions. Your body temperature, for example, must remain within a certain range for you to survive. Consider how your body responds when you mountain bike down a trail on a hot day.

When you perform strenuous exercise, you might wear comfortable clothing that wicks away sweat. You might also drink ice water to help keep you cool. However, if you become too hot, your body's temperature control center jumps into action. Receptors in your skin send signals to the brain, which sets into motion cooling tactics, such as sweating. When you sweat, glands in your skin release salty water. This has a cooling effect when the water evaporates from the skin.

PREDICT Balancing on a bicycle requires subtle changes in muscle movements and body position. How is maintaining stable conditions in your body similar to balancing on a bicycle?

_____

_____

_____

 Evidence Notebook As you explore this lesson, gather evidence about the ways your body responds to changing environmental conditions.

Control Systems in Organisms

External and internal factors, such as temperature changes, infection, stress, and pollution challenge the stability of an organism. In the same way that a cell must maintain stable conditions, an organism must maintain stability despite changes in its internal state or within the environment in which it lives.

Control Systems

Fortunately, the body has many control systems that keep its internal environment stable. Together, these control systems are responsible for maintaining homeostasis. Homeostasis is the regulation and maintenance of the internal environment within the narrow ranges that are necessary to support life at the cellular level.

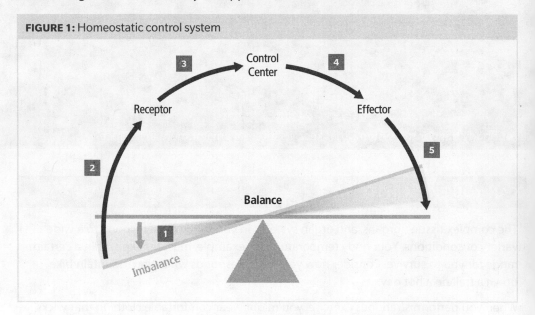

FIGURE 1: Homeostatic control system

As shown in Figure 1, homeostasis is maintained through the following steps:

1. A stimulus is anything from the internal or external environment that causes an imbalance in the internal conditions of a cell, organ, organ system, or organism.

2. Stimuli are detected by *receptors*. There are thousands of internal receptors, as well as specialized receptors that detect information about changes in the organism's external environment.

3. The receptor sends information to a control center, often in the central nervous system. The *control center* compares the information to set points. Set points are ideal values for the conditions at which the body functions best.

4. If the control center detects movement away from the set point, it responds by sending messages through one of the organism's communication systems. Messages sent by the control center are carried to *effectors* that carry out the response.

5. The response restores balance by returning internal conditions to their set points.

EXPLAIN Identify a change in the environment that might affect your balance on a bicycle. Explain how you would regain your balance using the terms *stimulus, control center, set point, receptors, effectors,* and *imbalance* in your answer.

_____

_____

_____

_____

Homeostasis depends on communication between the receptors, the control center, and the effectors. In the human body, communication is the joint responsibility of the nervous system and the endocrine system.

The nervous system sends messages along a direct route between the receptor and the control center, or between the control center and the effector. The control center in the human body is the central nervous system, which consists of the brain and the spinal cord. Some responses, such as sweating, are generated by the spinal cord and are called reflex responses. Information that requires more interpretation, such as visual or auditory input, is routed through the brain.

Unlike the nervous system, the endocrine system uses a more indirect—but still rapid—method of communication. *Hormones* are chemicals secreted into the bloodstream by endocrine glands. The hormones then travel throughout the body, acting only on cells that have receptors for those particular hormones.

To maintain homeostasis, receptors throughout the organism must constantly compare current conditions to the appropriate set points. Set points are actually narrow ranges of acceptable conditions in a cell or organism. If receptors detect a change in an internal condition causing it to stray outside the set point, the control center communicates instructions to the effector. The effector acts to restore the internal environment to its set point. This interaction between the receptor, the control center, and the effector is known as a feedback loop.

MODEL Refer to the control system diagram in Figure 1 to draw a model that shows how sweating can help body temperature return to normal.

Hands-On Activity

Modeling Feedback

FIGURE 2: Feedback will help you balance a book on your head.

Have you ever lost and recovered your balance? If so, you've experienced a feedback loop between your sense of balance and your skeletal muscles. In this activity, you will balance a book on your head while walking.

MAKE A CLAIM

How would you need to adjust your balance to keep the book on your head?

_____

_____

_____

MATERIALS

· hardcover book, at least 15 cm × 20 cm

· meterstick

CARRY OUT THE INVESTIGATION

1. Measure a space about 3 m long and clear it of obstacles.

2. Balance the hardcover book on your head.

3. Walk 3 m forward and then 3 m backward—first with your eyes open, and then with your eyes closed. Always walk with a partner when your eyes are closed. Try to keep the book on your head, but if it falls off, pick it up and put it back on your head

ANALYZE

1. What type of receptors provided you with information about the position of the book while you walked?

_____

_____

_____

_____

_____

2. How did you respond whenever the book changed position? Did you find it more or less difficult to maintain balance with your eyes closed? Explain your answer.

_____

_____

_____

_____

Negative Feedback Loops

Consider what happened in the book-balancing activity. You responded to a change in the book's position by changing your speed or moving your body in the opposite direction. You continued to make adjustments to maintain that balance until you removed the book from your head.

What you experienced was the result of a negative feedback loop. In a negative feedback loop, a stimulus causes an imbalance in one direction. This imbalance is detected by receptors that send information to the control center. The control center evaluates the information and sends a signal to the effectors to make an adjustment that is in the opposite direction from the stimulus, returning the system to balance.

Why is this process called a loop? The receptors also check the new conditions that result from the actions of the effector and then update the control center. The control center then signals any additional actions that the effector needs to take. These small changes cause conditions to hover around the set point and maintain homeostasis.

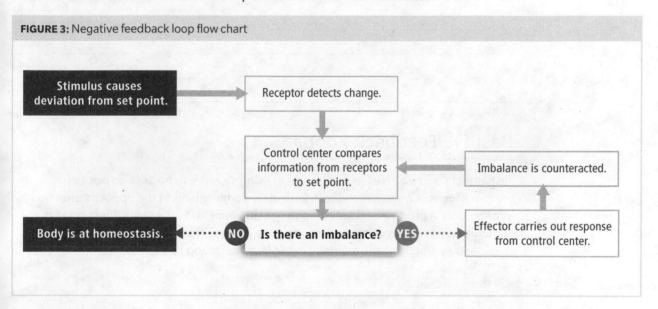

FIGURE 3: Negative feedback loop flow chart

EXPLAIN Use the correct terms to complete the statement about negative feedback loops.

control center   effectors   receptors   set point

Shivering and sweating are two parts of the same negative feedback loop, with

temperature as the stimulus that triggers its activity. When _____

in the skin and body core detect an imbalance in temperature, they send nerve

impulses to the _____. The information in these messages is

interpreted, and more nerve impulses are sent to the _____. If

body temperature is below the _____, these impulses are sent

to the muscles to stimulate shivering. If body temperature is too high, the messages

stimulate sweat glands to produce sweat.

The thermostat of a furnace is a nonliving example of a negative feedback loop. The thermostat contains a receptor (thermometer), a control center (microprocessor), and an effector (switch). The set point is the programmed temperature. When the thermometer detects that the air temperature is lower than the set point, it signals the thermostat's microprocessor, which responds by turning on the switch of the furnace.

While the heating system is running, the thermometer continues to measure air temperature and send updates to the microprocessor, which compares it to the desired temperature. Once the air temperature reaches the set point or just slightly above it, the control center turns off the furnace until the room temperature once again drops below the set point. As a result, the room temperature remains within a couple of degrees of the set point.

EXPLAIN Your body has its own internal thermostat. Humans need to maintain a body temperature between 36.7 °C and 37.1 °C. What are two mechanisms that help maintain this narrow temperature range in the human body? Explain how each mechanism affects body temperature.

_____

_____

_____

_____

Positive Feedback Loops

Just as there are negative feedback loops in living systems, there are also positive feedback loops. A negative feedback loop makes adjustments in the opposite direction of a stimulus. A positive feedback loop makes adjustments in the same direction as the stimulus. Scientists sometimes refer to positive feedback loops as reinforcing loops, because they amplify the stimulus instead of counteracting it.

FIGURE 4: Positive feedback loop flow chart

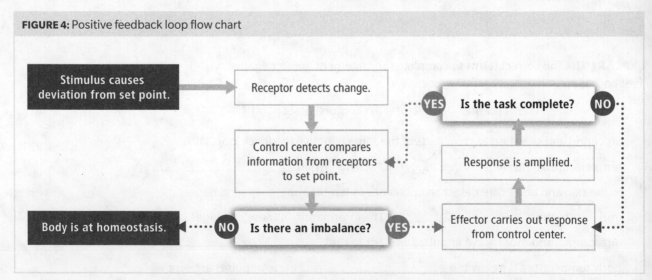

Have you ever experienced a loud screech coming from a loudspeaker in an auditorium or at a show? This is an example of a positive feedback loop. The sound from the microphone is amplified and sent through the loudspeaker. Sometimes, the microphone will pick up that sound again. It is amplified and sent through the speaker again. This loop continues over and over. Eventually, you hear the high-pitched screech from the loudspeaker.

Positive feedback is important when rapid change is needed, such as when you cut your finger. Your body depends on maintaining blood volume and blood pressure. A cut results in blood loss, so the body depends on a positive feedback loop to quickly generate a clot to stop the bleeding. This occurs as platelets and clotting factors stimulate the activation of more platelets and clotting factors at the wound. Once the cut has healed, a clot is no longer needed—and could be dangerous if it gets into the bloodstream. The body then uses another positive feedback loop to dissolve the clot.

FIGURE 5: A positive feedback loop is essential for preventing major blood loss during injuries.

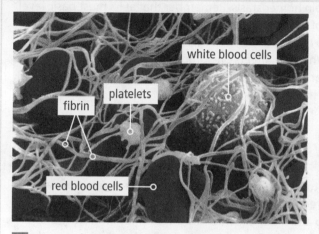
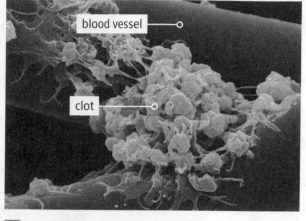

a Platelets cluster at the site of a wound.　　**b** A clot forms to stop the bleeding.

Positive feedback loops are not as common in the body as negative feedback loops, but they are important for maintaining homeostasis. For example, some hormones are regulated by positive feedback loops. The release of one hormone may stimulate the release or production of other hormones or substances, which stimulate further release of the initial hormone.

INFER Select the correct terms to complete the statement about positive feedback loops.

Another example of a positive feedback loop in the body is birth. When it is time

for a baby to be born, receptors | effectors in the mother's body stimulate the

hypothalamus in her brain. The hypothalamus acts as a control center | stimulus

| response, signaling cells in her pituitary gland to release the hormone oxytocin.

Oxytocin acts on the muscles in her uterus, causing contractions. Oxytocin also acts

on the placenta to cause the release of prostaglandins, which stimulate more uterine

contractions. This process causes the hypothalamus to signal the pituitary gland

to release less | more oxytocin, causing muscle contractions and prostaglandin

production to increase | decrease. Labor ends when the baby has been born and the

placenta has been expelled.

　Evidence Notebook The body relies on positive and negative feedback loops to maintain homeostasis. Identify a stimulus that could cause a change in homeostasis in your body. What type of feedback loop returns the body to the set point, and what body systems are included in the feedback loop? Use evidence from this lesson to support your answer.

Homeostasis in the Human Body

Negative and Positive Feedback Analyze data and generate graphs to determine whether a process is an example of a negative or positive feedback loop.

Homeostasis regulates many different things in organisms, such as temperature, water balance, salt levels, pH, nutrients, and gases. Because all of these things have set points, the body requires feedback loops for each one in order to maintain homeostasis. Remember that at its most basic level, the body is made up of many groups of specialized cells. These cells are further organized into tissues, then into organs, which in turn are organized into organ systems. Whatever affects one organ system affects the body as a whole. This means that whenever an imbalance occurs in one organ system, the imbalance affects the entire organism.

Interacting Organ Systems

All of your body systems interact to maintain homeostasis, much like a group of dancers interacts to perform a highly choreographed ballet. If one dancer misses a cue, it throws the rest of the dancers out of step and time. Consider the importance of healthy blood pressure to the body. Blood pressure is the force with which blood pushes against the walls of blood vessels. Receptors in the blood vessels and heart detect changes in blood pressure and then signal the brain. The brain stimulates the heart to beat faster or slower to help restore the blood pressure to its correct level.

Arteries are a type of blood vessel in the circulatory system that carry oxygen-rich blood throughout the body. If blood pressure is too low, the brain tells the heart to beat faster to increase the amount of blood in the arteries. This action increases the pressure exerted by the blood on the walls of the arteries. If the pressure is too high, the heart beats slower, reducing the amount of blood in the arteries and thus lowering the blood pressure. In this case, the systems working together to maintain blood pressure and homeostasis are the nervous system and the circulatory system.

⊶ Cause and Effect

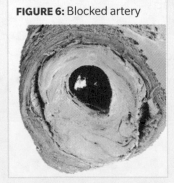

FIGURE 6: Blocked artery

Blood pressure depends on how elastic and unblocked the arteries are, as well as on the strength of the heart contraction. If the arteries are less elastic and there are blockages that reduce blood flow, the heart must pump harder. As a result, blood pressure rises. Blood pressure also rises naturally with activity, stress, and strong emotions, but it should drop again with rest. If blood pressure remains high, there could be a problem in the circulatory system.

ANALYZE If a person's blood pressure is too high or too low, how might the other organ systems in their body be affected?

_____

_____

_____

Maintaining Glucose Concentrations

The cells in the human body rely heavily on glucose to supply the energy needed to survive and grow. However, glucose concentrations in the blood must be maintained within a very narrow range for good health. Glucose needs can vary widely, depending on what activities the body is performing. A person's activity levels are always changing, so the body must work constantly to maintain the proper glucose level.

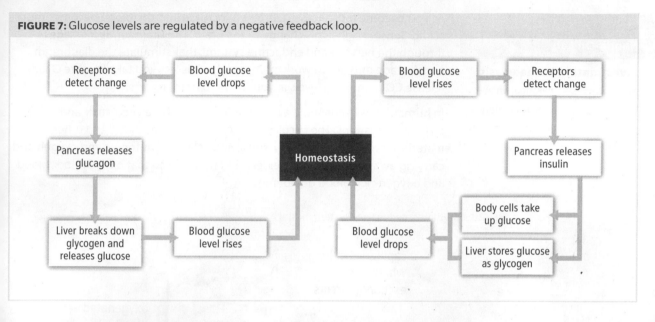

FIGURE 7: Glucose levels are regulated by a negative feedback loop.

EXPLAIN Why are the insulin and glucagon feedback loops examples of negative feedback loops?

○ **a.** The stimulus was a lower level of blood glucose.

○ **b.** The stimulus caused the insulin to take on a negative charge.

○ **c.** The effector caused a response in the opposite direction as the stimulus.

○ **d.** The effector caused a response in the same direction as the stimulus.

Blood glucose levels are controlled by two feedback loops, as shown in Figure 7. Each loop relies on the endocrine system to respond to changing levels. When blood glucose levels rise, such as when you eat a meal, the increase is detected by beta cells in the pancreas. The beta cells respond by releasing insulin, which stimulates cells to absorb glucose from the blood stream. It also causes the liver to store excess glucose in the form of glycogen. Once levels return to the set point, insulin secretion decreases. This feedback keeps blood glucose levels from going over the maximum set point.

The body has a second feedback loop that maintains a minimum blood glucose level. Blood glucose levels can drop after a long time passes without eating or during long periods of exercise. When the brain senses levels below the minimum set point, it signals pancreatic alpha cells to make glucagon. Glucagon stimulates the liver to convert glycogen to glucose and release it into the blood stream. If the liver cannot release glucose quickly enough, the brain signals a feeling of hunger to get additional glucose.

 Language Arts Connection Research the difference between hypoglycemia and hyperglycemia. What are the symptoms and treatments for each condition? Summarize your findings in a short 1–2 page paper. Be sure to cite your sources.

Maintaining Carbon Dioxide Concentrations

Every time you exercise, lie down to rest, or simply stand up, your needs for oxygen and nutrients change. Your heart speeds up or slows down and you breathe faster or slower, depending on your level of activity. The respiratory system interacts with the nervous system to maintain homeostasis. Control centers in the brain monitor dissolved gases in the blood, particularly carbon dioxide (CO_2) and oxygen (O_2) concentrations.

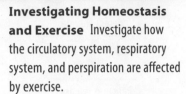

Explore Online

Hands-On Lab

Investigating Homeostasis and Exercise Investigate how the circulatory system, respiratory system, and perspiration are affected by exercise.

As you become more active, CO_2 levels increase and the blood becomes more acidic. Sensors signal this change to the brain. The brain sends messages through the nervous and endocrine systems that stimulate the diaphragm and rib cage muscles to work more rapidly. This lets you take in more O_2 and release CO_2, returning levels in your body to homeostasis.

In humans, gas exchange is a cooperative effort of the circulatory and respiratory systems. The circulatory system distributes blood and other materials throughout the body, supplying cells with nutrients and oxygen and carrying away wastes. Blood vessels are organized so that oxygen-poor blood and oxygen-rich blood do not mix.

FIGURE 8: Human circulatory system model

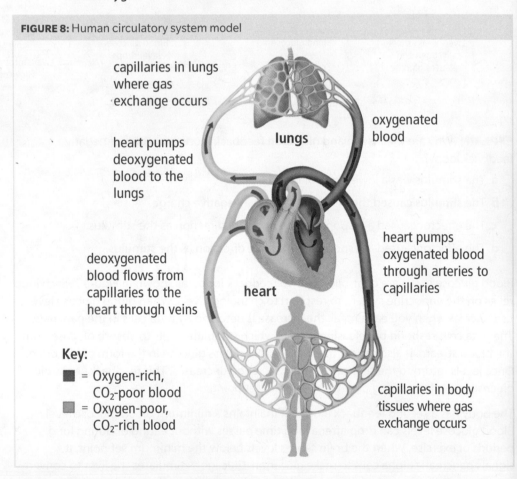

capillaries in lungs where gas exchange occurs

lungs

oxygenated blood

heart pumps deoxygenated blood to the lungs

deoxygenated blood flows from capillaries to the heart through veins

heart

heart pumps oxygenated blood through arteries to capillaries

Key:

■ = Oxygen-rich, CO_2-poor blood

■ = Oxygen-poor, CO_2-rich blood

capillaries in body tissues where gas exchange occurs

The circulatory system has three types of blood vessels: arteries, veins, and capillaries. Arteries carry oxygen-rich, or oxygenated, blood away from the heart. Veins are blood vessels that carry oxygen-poor, or deoxygenated, blood back to the heart. Capillaries are responsible for delivering O_2 directly to cells, and removing CO_2 and waste. These materials can diffuse through the capillary wall because the wall is only one cell thick. The capillary system serves as a connection between arteries and veins, ensuring a continuous path for blood flow throughout the body.

Once the veins deliver deoxygenated blood to the heart, it is immediately transported to the lungs, where gases can be exchanged with the air. When you inhale, the air flows from your nose or mouth through the trachea to the bronchi (singular *bronchus*). The air continues into smaller branches called bronchioles and finally into small, thin-walled air sacs called alveoli. A network of capillaries surrounds each alveolus, taking in O_2 and releasing CO_2. When you exhale, the CO_2 exits through your nose or mouth.

Gas homeostasis in the blood is maintained through diffusion. When you inhale, the air has a higher concentration of O_2 than the blood in the capillaries surrounding the alveoli. This allows O_2 to diffuse down a concentration gradient into the blood. From there, the blood is taken to the heart and pumped through the body. The concentration of O_2 in the blood is higher than in the cells, so it diffuses out of the blood. Carbon dioxide diffuses in the opposite direction—from the cells into the blood. The concentration of CO_2 is higher in the cells than in the blood because cells make CO_2 as a waste product. Once in the blood, it travels back to the heart and then into the lungs, where it diffuses into the alveoli and is exhaled out of the lungs.

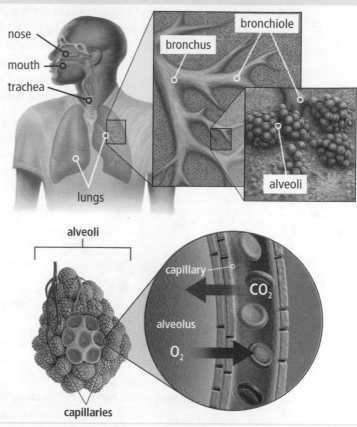

FIGURE 9: Diffusion of gases into and out of the alveoli maintains oxygen and carbon dioxide homeostasis.

ANALYZE In humans, the exchange of gases occurs across the cell membranes that make up the alveoli and the capillaries that surround them. Having numerous alveoli in the lungs makes more surface area that is exposed to these gases and more contact with the capillaries. Which of the choices below best describes the benefits of having a large amount of surface area in the lungs? Select all correct answers.

☐ **a.** It lets the blood move more quickly.

☐ **b.** It lets the lungs expand more slowly.

☐ **c.** It lets diffusion occur more quickly.

☐ **d.** It keeps gases from getting into the blood too quickly.

☐ **e.** It lets a high volume of gases diffuse at once.

☐ **f.** It limits the volume of blood flowing through the lungs.

MODEL Make a flow chart that shows how homeostasis is maintained at set points when you increase activity. How do systems interact to maintain appropriate CO_2 and O_2?

Disrupting Homeostasis

Homeostatic mechanisms usually work quickly, but sometimes a change in the environment can occur too rapidly or be of too great a magnitude to be controlled through feedback mechanisms. When this happens, homeostasis is disrupted. Disruptions can happen for several reasons, including failure of sensors to detect a change in the internal or external environment, sending or receiving the wrong message, serious injury, or disease-causing agents, such as bacteria or viruses.

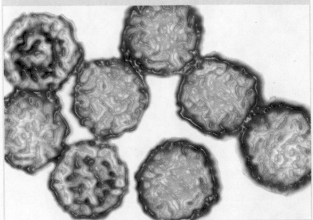

FIGURE 10: The common cold is caused by a rhinovirus.

A rhinovirus can change the body's internal chemistry to cause the common cold. This results in disruption of one or more homeostatic mechanisms. One commonly disrupted mechanism is body temperature, resulting in fever. A fever occurs when the hypothalamus raises the set point for internal temperature. This makes you feel cold, because your internal temperature is below the set point. Your body may shiver to raise your internal temperature closer to the new set point.

Short-Term Effects

Many disruptions in homeostasis are temporary. A cold is an excellent example of a short-term disruption in homeostasis. When the virus first enters your body, it may multiply too rapidly for your immune system to destroy it. When that happens, you may experience cold symptoms, such as a sore throat or runny nose. In only a few days, however, your immune system develops antibodies that mark the virus for destruction, restoring homeostasis. Lasting damage from the common cold is very rare.

Recall that shivering is the body's response to decreased body temperature. Shivering occurs when you are sick, not because you are experiencing cold environmental temperatures, but because your body is trying to adjust to a new, higher set point for body temperature. In other words, your body is shivering to produce a fever.

ARGUE Is your body's response to the common cold an example of negative or positive feedack? Use evidence to support your claim.

_____

_____

_____

_____

Long-Term Effects

Long-term disruptions of homeostasis can cause more damage than short-term disruptions. One form of long-term disruption is Cushing's syndrome. This disorder is caused by a long-term elevation of the hormone cortisol. Cushing's can result from tumors of the adrenal or pituitary gland, or from long-term cortisone treatment. Cortisol is one of the body's stress hormones. When it remains elevated for long periods of time, it disrupts glucose and fat metabolism, immune response, and sleep, and it causes blood pressure to increase. Each of these disruptions can lead to other disorders, such as hypertension, diabetes, strokes, and heart attacks.

Data Analysis

Understanding Diabetes

Recall that the regulation of blood glucose levels occurs through negative feedback loops. The insulin loop is stimulated by elevated blood glucose levels, and the glucagon loop is stimulated by lowered blood glucose levels.

Diabetes mellitus is a long-term disruption of the insulin feedback loop. Type 1 diabetes occurs when the body's immune system destroys the ability of beta cells in the pancreas to produce insulin. Type 2 diabetes is caused when pancreatic insulin production decreases or when insulin cannot move glucose from the blood into cells.

FIGURE 11: Blood glucose, insulin, and glucagon responses to a high-carbohydrate meal.

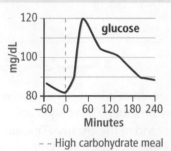 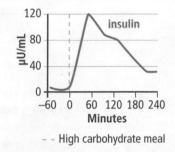 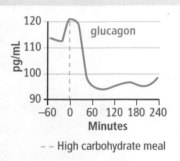

Two variables are inversely related if an increase in the value of one variable is associated with a decrease in the value of the other variable. For example, the levels of insulin and glucose increase and glucagon decreases shortly after a person eats. Therefore, insulin and glucose levels have an inverse relationship to glucagon levels. This relationship can be seen in the blood glucose, insulin, and glucagon graphs in Figure 11.

ANALYZE What is the relationship between blood sugar levels, insulin levels, and glucagon levels in the blood stream? Select all correct answers.

☐ **a.** Glucose is directly related to insulin.

☐ **b.** Glucose is inversely related to insulin.

☐ **c.** Insulin is directly related to glucagon.

☐ **d.** Insulin is inversely related to glucagon.

INFER Type 1 diabetes occurs when the body's immune system destroys the ability of the pancreas to produce insulin. How would these graphs look different in a person with type 1 diabetes? Select all correct answers.

☐ **a.** Glucose would remain low after eating.

☐ **b.** Glucose would continue to rise after 60 minutes.

☐ **c.** Insulin would remain low after eating.

☐ **d.** Insulin would continue to rise after 60 minutes.

☐ **e.** Glucagon would remain the same after eating.

☐ **f.** Glucagon would remain high after 60 minutes.

Enzymes and Homeostasis

One way to provide the necessary activation energy for a reaction is to increase the temperature of the system. However, chemical reactions in organisms must take place at the organism's body temperature, which must remain within a narrow range. In addition, the reactants of a chemical reaction are often present in low concentrations. To lower the activation energy and help molecular collisions be more efficient, cells use biological catalysts called enzymes. The optimal human body temperature for enzyme activity is 37 °C. Very high temperatures can denature, or unravel and unfold, enzymes.

INFER Why is having a very high fever dangerous for humans? Cite evidence related to enzyme structure and function.

_____

_____

_____

_____

_____

FIGURE 12: A change in temperature or pH can cause an enzyme to become denatured.

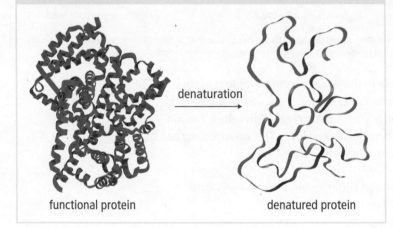

functional protein   denatured protein

Enzyme structure is important because each enzyme's shape lets only certain reactants bind to the enzyme. The specific reactants that an enzyme acts on are called substrates. In the same way that a key fits into a lock, substrates fit the active sites of enzymes. This is why, if an enzyme's structure changes, it may not work at all.

A change in pH can affect the hydrogen bonds in enzymes and thus cause denaturation. Many enzymes work best at the nearly neutral pH that is maintained within the body's cells. If the fluid becomes more acidic or basic as the pH changes, the reactions slow down. If the fluid becomes very acidic or basic, enzymes may stop working altogether. Not all enzymes have the same pH requirements. For example, enzymes in the stomach work best in acidic conditions. Alternatively, some enzymes in the small intestine work best under slightly basic conditions.

Because enzymes are proteins, changes in pH and adding heat can cause them to become denatured. For a catalyst to work properly, it must maintain the proper shape to accept the substrate molecule. Denaturation alters that shape and the catalyst no longer works properly. In some cases, denatured proteins can become renatured or regain their normal shape. However, many proteins are not able to regain normal function once they are denatured.

 Evidence Notebook Describe how a homeostatic variable, such as blood pressure, glucose concentration, or carbon dioxide concentration, can be disrupted. Explain whether this is the result of short-term or long-term disruption, and how the body can return to homeostasis.

Homeostasis in Other Organisms

Many of the homeostatic processes you have learned about in humans are the same in other organisms as well. However, some organisms use different mechanisms to maintain homeostasis. For example, not all mammals have sweat glands all over their skin and are therefore unable to rely on sweating to cool off. As sweat evaporates, heat is removed with it, cooling the skin. Dogs make up for the lack of sweat glands by panting. When they pant, the short, shallow breaths direct air flow over the moist linings of their upper respiratory tract. This has the same evaporative cooling effect as a breeze passing over your sweaty skin.

INFER What other organisms do you think would have different homeostasis mechanisms from humans? Why would this be an advantage in their environment?

_____

_____

_____

_____

Gas Exchange in Plants

Plants take in carbon dioxide for photosynthesis and give off oxygen as a waste product. In plants, as in humans, homeostatic mechanisms regulate gas exchange. Gases are exchanged through structures called stomata (singular *stoma*). Stomata are small openings, or pores, on the underside of leaves that are surrounded by cells called guard cells. Stomata can be open or closed, depending on the needs of the plant.

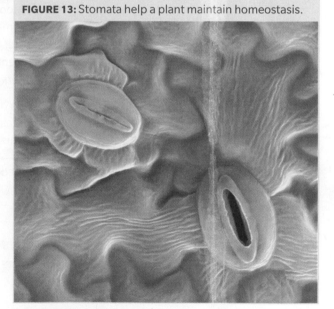

FIGURE 13: Stomata help a plant maintain homeostasis.

When the sun is out, a protein called phototropin absorbs certain wavelengths of light. This action stimulates a series of reactions that cause the guard cells to fill with water. The guard cells become more rigid, causing the stomata to open. While the stomata are open for photosynthesis, water vapor is given off. Giving off water vapor is not necessarily bad for the plant. In fact, it helps draw water into the plant at the roots. It also lets the plant get rid of the oxygen produced during photosynthesis.

Water vapor loss is not a problem for plants in moist environments. However, plants in dry or drought environments may struggle to maintain water balance because they lose water faster than they can replace it. This causes the plant to wilt and disrupts other homeostatic mechanisms that rely on nutrients that are drawn into the roots with water. To counteract this, many types of plants release a hormone called abscisic acid, or ABA, from the roots in response to decreased soil water levels. The buildup of ABA in leaves triggers the transport of water out of the guard cells. This causes the cells to relax, closing the stomata.

EXPLAIN Select the correct terms to complete the statement about homeostasis.

The maintenance of water homeostasis in a plant is the result of a negative | positive feedback loop. The stimulus for this feedback loop is low soil moisture. Unlike animals, plants do not have a central control center. In this case, the control center is the plant's leaves | stems | roots, which release ABA in response to the stimulus. The ABA is transported to the leaves | stems | roots, where it accumulates. When levels are high enough, it triggers guard cells to release | take in water, causing the stomata to close.

Stability and Change

Plant Response to Drought

FIGURE 14: The root growth of the plant on the right has been affected by drought.

How does a plant cope with long-term or repeated water stress? Again, the homeostatic mechanism begins with the roots. A drought changes the way roots grow in various plants. For example, when the plant maidenstears (*Silene vulgaris*) experiences moderate drought stress, its roots grow deeper into the soil in search of water. A larger percentage of the roots are thin, which lets them reach into tiny pores in the soil in search of every drop of water. In other plant species, such as myrtle (*Myrtus communis*), the percentage of thicker roots is greater in drought conditions. Scientists also discovered that roots in drought-stressed maidenstears have more branches than those grown under normal conditions.

Normal roots are relatively white and flexible. Drought stress tends to make roots become harder and turn brown. This is due to the presence of a waxy substance called suberin, the main component of cork. This forms a protective cap on the root tip as it enters a resting phase while soil moisture remains low.

Another change seen in drought-stressed plants is an increase in the thickness of the root cortex—the outer layer of root tissue. This helps protect the root from dehydration.

MODEL Make a model demonstrating how this feedback mechanism helps a plant maintain homeostasis during a drought.

Thermoregulation

Some feedback loops involve a behavioral response. Thermoregulation maintains a stable body temperature under a variety of conditions. Sometimes, the response to a temperature imbalance is a change in behavior. This type of feedback response is how cold-blooded animals, or ectotherms, manage their body temperature. Unlike warm-blooded animals, or endotherms, that use metabolic processes to manage internal body temperature, ectotherms do not have physiological mechanisms to maintain a constant body temperature. Instead, the surrounding environment determines their body temperature. When ectotherms become too cold, they move to a warmer environment. When they become too hot, they move to a cooler environment. This behavior helps them maintain homeostasis.

EXPLAIN Is thermoregulation an example of negative or positive feedback?

○ **a.** Negative, because it moves the temperature away from the set point.

○ **b.** Negative, because it moves the temperature back toward the set point.

○ **c.** Positive, because it moves the temperature away from the set point.

○ **d.** Positive, because it moves the temperature back toward the set point.

Osmoregulation

Organisms that live in a watery environment must have a strategy to maintain water and salt balances. Osmoregulation is a homeostatic process that balances the fluid and salt levels within the body.

If an organism lives in salt water, the environment has the potential to dehydrate the organism. If an organism lives in fresh water, its body acts like a permanently thirsty sponge. Saltwater and freshwater fish have developed strategies to cope with these problems. As part of those prevention strategies, both types of fish undergo osmoregulation to balance fluid and salt levels.

Saltwater fish, for example, have blood with a higher concentration of water than the surrounding seawater. Their kidneys secrete large amounts of salt and small amounts of water. In contrast, freshwater fish have blood with a lower concentration of water than the surrounding fresh water. Their kidneys secrete large amounts of water and small amounts of salt.

FIGURE 15: The type of water environment determines the osmoregulation strategy of fish.

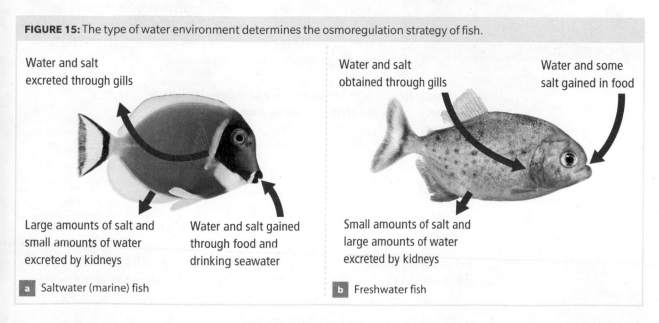

Water and salt excreted through gills

Large amounts of salt and small amounts of water excreted by kidneys

Water and salt gained through food and drinking seawater

Water and salt obtained through gills

Water and some salt gained in food

Small amounts of salt and large amounts of water excreted by kidneys

a Saltwater (marine) fish

b Freshwater fish

Fish in freshwater environments must retain as much salt as possible in order to maintain osmotic balance. Their kidneys reabsorb salt and excrete very dilute urine to rid them of as much excess water as they can. At the same time, they take in salt through the gills and in food, and drink very little water.

In contrast, when marine fish ingest salt water, their bodies actively excrete, or get rid of, as much of the salt as possible in order to maintain osmotic balance. The kidneys help extract salt from the body and concentrate it into very salty urine, which is then excreted from the body. The fish's gills actively excrete salt as well.

APPLY A saltwater fish swims into a river delta, where the salt concentration is lower than in normal salt water. This would disrupt its osmotic balance. How will the fish's body restore homeostasis? Select all correct answers.

- ☐ **a.** increase water intake
- ☐ **b.** decrease water intake
- ☐ **c.** increase salt excretion
- ☐ **d.** decrease salt excretion
- ☐ **e.** increase water excretion
- ☐ **f.** decrease water excretion

FIGURE 16: This giant kangaroo rat conserves water in its arid habitat by secreting concentrated urine.

Land animals, on the other hand, must maintain osmotic balance in a dry environment. Their primary goal for osmotic regulation is water conservation. The kidneys of land animals work more like those of a saltwater fish. That is, the necessary water is reabsorbed and excess salt ions are excreted.

The drier the climate and the more difficult it is to obtain water, the more concentrated the urine will be. Kangaroo rats, such as the giant kangaroo rat native to California's Central Valley, shown in Figure 16, are particularly well-known for the ability to conserve water by excreting super-concentrated urine.

The type of nitrogenous waste that land animals excrete also affects their ability to maintain osmotic balance. Fish excrete this waste as urea, which is water-soluble. Most mammals also excrete urea. This means they must take in enough water to maintain osmotic balance while excreting enough to flush the urea from their bodies. Reptiles, amphibians, birds, and insects excrete these wastes as insoluble uric acid. This lets them conserve water by producing highly concentrated urine.

EXPLAIN People traveling to Antarctica may be warned to watch for signs of dehydration. How could the arctic climate disrupt osmoregulation?

_____

_____

_____

_____

 Evidence Notebook Consider how homeostasis could be disrupted if a branch falls in your path while riding a bicycle. Make a flow chart modeling a homeostatic mechanism that could be involved when regaining your balance. In your flow chart, note the stimulus, receptor, control center response, and effector for the feedback loop.

Engineering

Organ Donation

Sometimes human organs fail due to disease or damage. A common example is heart disease in which the heart can no longer function properly and the body begins to fail. Fortunately, organ donation is a life-saving option for many people. A range of organs can be donated, and donors may be living or deceased. Living donor organs include one kidney, one lung, or a portion of the liver, intestine, or pancreas. Deceased donor organs include both kidneys, both lungs, the liver, heart, pancreas, intestines, eyes, and even hands and the face.

FIGURE 17: Maria Alvarez (center) received a kidney from her daughter, Rosario Proscia, and a part of a liver from her son, José Alvarez.

Engineering plays an important role in organ donation. For example, when a patient is a good candidate for receiving an organ, the patient is registered on a national computerized waiting list. When donor organs become available, a network called the Organ Procurement and Transplant Network makes a list of possible recipients. The list is based on certain criteria, depending on the organ that is to be transplanted. It is essential that organs be matched with recipients as efficiently as possible. The organ from a deceased donor will only last for a matter of hours, and the recipient is likely in poor health and needs the transplant done as soon as possible. The United Network for Organ Sharing (UNOS) is responsible for matching donors and recipients. They have built complex, multifaceted algorithms based on the criteria for each specific organ.

An algorithm compares factors such as blood type, medical urgency, and distance between the donor organ and recipient.

Despite the need for organs, and the technology available to make transplants more successful, there are problems that need solutions. One problem is lack of awareness. People do not fully understand the need for organ donors or how to join the registry. They are unaware that they can be living donors. According to U.S. Government Information on Organ Donation and Transplantation resources, 95% of U.S. adults support organ donation, but only 54% are actually signed up to donate.

Another issue is organ rejection. Sometimes the recipient's immune system rejects the organ tissues and the organ is destroyed. However, researchers have found that organ rejection could be avoided by transplanting the organ donor's stem cells to the recipient.

EXPLAIN Why does the demand for organ donations far outpace the organs available for donation? What are two ways that you might try to help the effort to increase organ donation?

Language Arts Connection There are several possible engineering solutions which could increase the number of organs and tissues available for transplant. Research some possible solutions, such as growing tissues from stem cells or 3D printing organs. Does any solution address all of the concerns surrounding organ donation? What are the advantages and disadvantages of each solution? Identify the important criteria and constraints for the problem and make a decision matrix evaluating each solution. Compare your matrix with those of your peers. How do your matrices differ?

DISORDERS OF THE ENDOCRINE SYSTEM **INVESTIGATING HOMEOSTASIS AND EXERCISE** **EXPLAINING HOMEOSTASIS** Go online to choose one of these other paths.

Lesson Self-Check

CAN YOU EXPLAIN IT?

FIGURE 18: The human body has control systems that maintain internal stability.

The human body must be able to respond to a wide variety of conditions to maintain internal balance. For example, when your body heats up during exercise it must respond in ways that keep your body within the normal temperature range.

The human body has many control systems that keep its internal environment stable. Together, these control systems are responsible for maintaining homeostasis. Homeostasis depends on communication between the receptors, the control center, and the effectors in various feedback loops.

 Evidence Notebook Refer to your notes in your Evidence Notebook to explain how maintaining stable conditions in your body is similar to balancing on a bicycle. Your explanation should include a discussion of the following:

1. Make a claim about how the human body maintains homeostasis.
2. What are some examples of the body's response to stimuli as a way to maintain homeostasis?
3. How do your examples explain why maintaining balance in the human body is like maintaining balance on a bicycle?

CHECKPOINTS

Check Your Understanding

1. How do stomata function in most plants relative to gas exchange?
   - a. Stomata close to prevent nitrogen from escaping.
   - b. Stomata close to allow photosynthesis to occur.
   - c. Stomata open to allow carbon dioxide in and oxygen and water out.
   - d. Stomata open to allow water to build up in the plant.

2. The circulatory and respiratory systems work together to provide cells with oxygen and nutrients and remove waste products, such as carbon dioxide. When you need more oxygen, how does the circulatory system respond?
   - a. More blood is sent to the lungs, and less blood is sent to the rest of the body.
   - b. The blood vessels to the arms and legs constrict to conserve oxygen.
   - c. The heart beats at a faster rate to match the rise in breathing rate.
   - d. Blood moves more slowly through the organs to carry away more wastes.

3. What would happen on a hot day if your brain did not receive input that your body was starting to heat up?
   - a. You would start to sweat.
   - b. You would start to overheat.
   - c. You would start to shiver.
   - d. You would not feel any effect at all.

4. Flatworms are invertebrates with soft bodies, and some live in freshwater environments. Based on this information, what can you predict about how this organism's body handles osmoregulation? Select all correct answers.
   - a. It excretes dilute urine.
   - b. It excretes concentrated urine.
   - c. It absorbs as much salt as possible from its surroundings.
   - d. It excretes as much salt as possible from its body.

5. During exercise, blood CO_2 levels increase as a result of muscle cell activity. This makes blood more acidic, which disrupts pH homeostasis. Place the following events in the regulation of gas exchange into the proper order.
   - _____ a. Blood pH returns to the set point.
   - _____ b. The brainstem signals muscles in the diaphragm and rib cage.
   - _____ c. The breathing rate increases.
   - _____ d. The blood becomes more acidic, and the pH decreases below the set point.
   - _____ e. The amount of CO_2 exhaled increases.
   - _____ f. The brainstem detects a pH change.
   - _____ g. Blood CO_2 levels increase.

6. How do temperature and pH affect an enzyme that a chemical reaction depends on?
   - a. They can break down the reactants.
   - b. They can break down the products.
   - c. They can change the shape of the enzyme.
   - d. They can cause the chemical reaction to reverse.

7. Complete the following statement about a feedback loop in the human body.

   A nursing baby makes a negative | positive feedback loop that causes the mother's body to lactate. Bottle-feeding eliminates the stimulus | control center | receptor of the feedback loop, so the mother will eventually stop producing milk.

CHECKPOINTS (continued)

8. People who experience severe blood loss go into a condition known as hemorrhagic shock. Shock occurs when the blood volume returning to the heart is reduced. The heart responds by trying to increase output, which can result in the patient bleeding to death if he or she is not treated in time. Is this an example of negative feedback or positive feedback? Explain your answer.

_____

_____

_____

_____

_____

9. How does a negative feedback loop differ from a positive feedback loop?

_____

_____

_____

_____

_____

10. How do ectothermic animals use behavior to maintain body temperature?

_____

_____

_____

_____

_____

MAKE YOUR OWN STUDY GUIDE

In your Evidence Notebook, design a study guide that supports the main idea from this lesson:

Homeostasis is the regulation and maintenance of the internal environment within a set range that is necessary to support life at the cellular level.

Remember to include the following information in your study guide:

- Use examples that model main ideas.
- Record explanations for the phenomena you investigated.
- Use evidence to support your explanations. Your support can include drawings, data, graphs, laboratory conclusions, and other evidence recorded throughout the lesson.

Consider the role positive and negative feedback loops play in maintaining homeostasis in an organism.

Life Science Connection

Modeling Apoptosis When infected with pathogens such as bacteria or viruses, our bodies mount an immune response to fight the invaders. Part of this response includes generating and activating a large number of immune cells specifically to counteract the current threat. Once the pathogens have been eliminated, the remaining immune cells must be destroyed, too.

> Research how the body destroys excess immune cells after a successful immune response. Make a model to show the role apoptosis plays, and predict possible outcomes if too many or too few Immune cells respond to apoptotic signals.

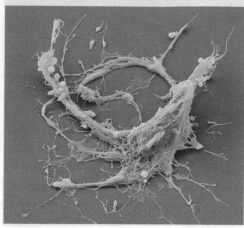

FIGURE 1: A cell undergoing apoptosis

Art Connection

Agar Art Since 2015, the American Society for Microbiology has sponsored a public competition called "Agar Art." Scientists from around the world submit artworks created by culturing one or more bacterial or fungal species in nutrient agar on petri dishes. The rate and color of the growth depend on the species, competition, and nutrients in the agar. With careful planning, the growth can result in an intricate work of art.

> Research art pieces made using agar. Design your own idea for an "agar art" piece. Include multiple colors and indicate, based on your research, which species would contribute each color. Provide an explanation for how growth and reproduction contribute to the work, and identify the factors to consider in growing multiple species together.

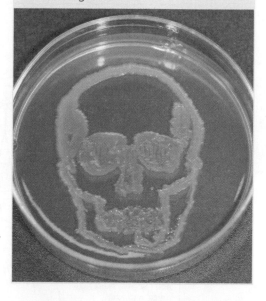

FIGURE 2: Agar art

Medical Science Connection

Heart Regeneration In your body, some cell types, such as skin, can regenerate through cell division to replace lost or dead cells. However, many other cell types lack this ability. Research has suggested for many years that heart muscle cannot regenerate after damage and that heart cells lose the ability to divide at a young age. Recent studies, including research by scientists at the University of California, Los Angeles, have challenged this idea, hinting that some heart muscle cells may be able to divide following tissue damage, though at a very slow rate.

> Locate and read three or more sources about heart regeneration research, with at least one source on either side of the debate. Summarize your findings in a report. State whether heart muscle cells can regenerate in adult humans, and support your claim with evidence.

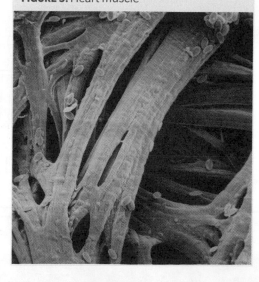

FIGURE 3: Heart muscle

A BOOK EXPLAINING
COMPLEX IDEAS USING
ONLY THE 1,000 MOST
COMMON WORDS

RANDALL MUNROE
XKCD.COM

BAGS OF STUFF INSIDE YOU

Parts of your body and how they work together

You know that an organ system is two or more organs working together to perform body functions. Here's a look at several organ systems in the human torso.

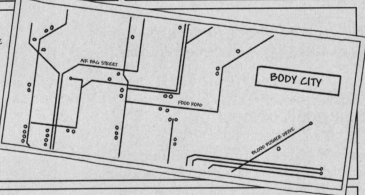

HOLE TO OUTSIDE

This hole is in your nose. It helps you breathe and lets you smell things.

HOLE TO OUTSIDE

This is the hole in your mouth. It's where air goes in and out, food goes in, and words come out.

Note: Some people don't like it when you make words come out while you're putting food in.

MOUTH WATER MAKER

This makes the water in your mouth that helps food fit down your neck.

THIS IS WHAT YOU THINK WITH.

When you read words (like these), this part of your body turns them into ideas.

By choosing the right words, you can take an idea that's happening in your head and try to make an idea like it happen in someone else's. That's what's happening right now.

YOU ARE HERE

THINKING BAG

BLOOD

(to your arms and the rest of your head)

This pushes on your blood about once a second to send it around your body.

AD
RTS

EST
RTS

AIR BAG

AIR BAG

BLOOD PUSHER

These add air to your blood. They get bigger and smaller to pull and push air in and out.

PART BREAKER

Sometimes, blood gets stuck in here.
That's one of the biggest reasons people's bodies stop working.

BLOOD CLEANER

BLOOD

(from other body parts)

This bag breaks tiny things into even smaller, simpler parts they're made of. Your body uses it in many ways, like to get rid of the stuff in wine that makes you feel strange (which keeps you from feeling strange forever). It also makes water for your hallways. If this bag has a problem, your eyes turn yellow and your body stops working.

BLOOD HALLWAYS

These carry blood around your body. If you get a hole in them, the blood starts to fall out. If this starts happening, it can be a big problem, and you should fix it fast.

BAGS OF STUFF INSIDE YOU

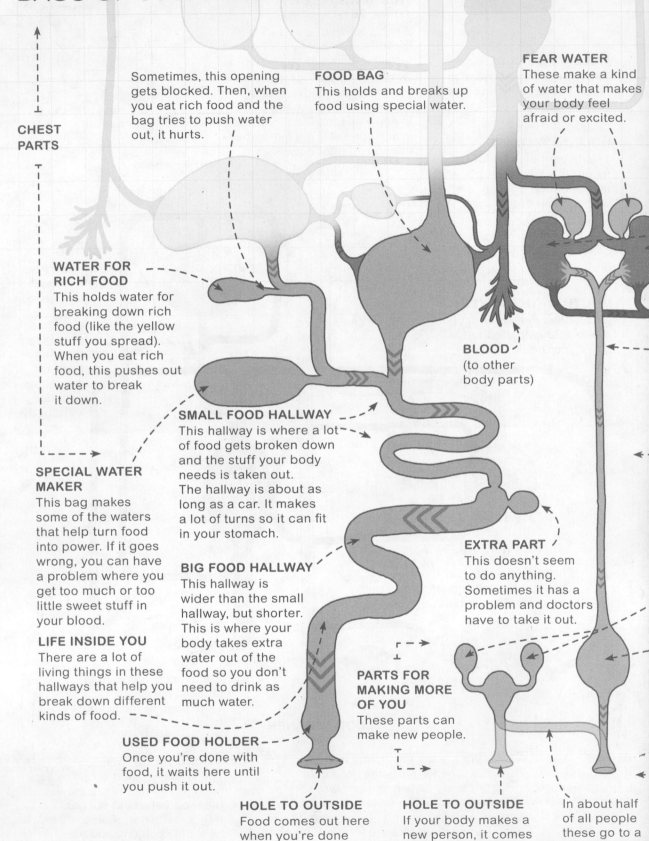

CHEST PARTS

Sometimes, this opening gets blocked. Then, when you eat rich food and the bag tries to push water out, it hurts.

FOOD BAG
This holds and breaks up food using special water.

FEAR WATER
These make a kind of water that makes your body feel afraid or excited.

WATER FOR RICH FOOD
This holds water for breaking down rich food (like the yellow stuff you spread). When you eat rich food, this pushes out water to break it down.

BLOOD
(to other body parts)

SMALL FOOD HALLWAY
This hallway is where a lot of food gets broken down and the stuff your body needs is taken out. The hallway is about as long as a car. It makes a lot of turns so it can fit in your stomach.

SPECIAL WATER MAKER
This bag makes some of the waters that help turn food into power. If it goes wrong, you can have a problem where you get too much or too little sweet stuff in your blood.

LIFE INSIDE YOU
There are a lot of living things in these hallways that help you break down different kinds of food.

BIG FOOD HALLWAY
This hallway is wider than the small hallway, but shorter. This is where your body takes extra water out of the food so you don't need to drink as much water.

EXTRA PART
This doesn't seem to do anything. Sometimes it has a problem and doctors have to take it out.

PARTS FOR MAKING MORE OF YOU
These parts can make new people.

USED FOOD HOLDER
Once you're done with food, it waits here until you push it out.

HOLE TO OUTSIDE
Food comes out here when you're done eating it.

HOLE TO OUTSIDE
If your body makes a new person, it comes out of here. About half of all people have this.

In about half of all people these go to a single opening

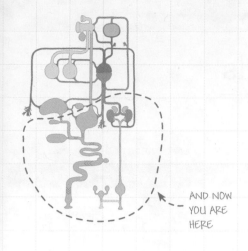

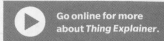

Go online for more
about *Thing Explainer*.

AND NOW
YOU ARE
HERE

WHITE BLOOD
PIECES

RED BLOOD
PIECES

BLOOD CLEANERS

These look for stuff in your blood that you're
done with or have too much of—like extra
sweet stuff, or stuff from the doctor that you
ate to feel better—and send it to be pushed
out of your body.

YELLOW WATER HALLWAY

Most of the time, the water from your blood
cleaners is yellow, but eating certain colorful
foods can make it change color for a while.

(If it turns dark or red, it may mean
you're sick.)

PUSHED TOGETHER

In real life, these parts are all pushed
together inside your chest like this.

BODY PLAN HOLDERS

These parts hold lots of plans for
new people. Each plan is made from
pieces of the plans used to make you.

These parts also control how your
voice, hair, and body grow.

YELLOW WATER HOLDER

This holds yellow water until
you push it out.

HOLE TO OUTSIDE

The yellow water from your
blood comes out here.

LOWER
PARTS

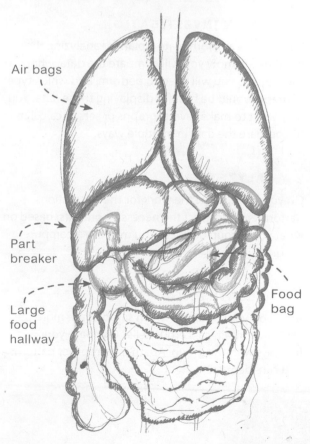

Air bags

Part
breaker

Large
food
hallway

Food
bag

Identifying Cancerous Cells

FIGURE 4: For each tissue sample, the number of cells in each phase of the cell cycle were counted and recorded.

	Sample 1	Sample 2	Sample 3	Sample 4	Sample 5	Sample 6
Interphase	33	34	34	35	33	35
Metaphase	2	2	1	1	2	2
Anaphase	1	3	2	0	2	4
Telophase	1	3	1	1	3	3

Cancer arises in cells due to abnormal genetic changes and can lead to other genetic, structural, and molecular alterations. Typically, the cell cycle of cancerous cells is disrupted compared with that of normal cells from the same tissue. The data shown in Figure 4 are from six different tissue samples. The samples were collected to determine whether the tissue in question contains cancerous cells. In this activity, your task is to analyze the data and make a claim for which samples are most likely to contain cancerous cells.

1. PLAN AN INVESTIGATION

With your team, formulate a plan for analyzing the data. Decide how you will compare the data, what calculations you will need to perform, and which type of graph would be best for displaying these data. You may want to make several graphs or sets of calculations to compare the data in multiple ways.

2. ANALYZE DATA

On your own, show the work for the calculations performed. Construct the necessary graph(s) based on what your group decided. You may use a computer program if necessary.

3. EVALUATE DATA

Based on your findings, which samples are more likely to contain cancerous cells? Compare your findings with the group. Are there any other patterns you can identify?

4. COMMUNICATE

Write a report that clearly states your claim and explains your conclusions. Your claim should state which samples are most likely to contain cancerous cells, and you should explain, in detail, how your analysis of the data supports your claim. In addition, describe some of the factors that might have caused the cancerous cells to become cancerous. How is the cell cycle related to the development of these types of cells? How is a person's genetic material and external environment related to the development of cancer?

 CHECK YOUR WORK

A complete report should include the following information:

- a clearly defined plan for analyzing and evaluating the data
- a clear conclusion based on evidence and supporting analysis
- one or more graphs displaying the data you evaluated in your investigation
- an explanation of which cells are most likely to be cancerous, using evidence to support your claim

Name _____ Date _____

In your Evidence Notebook, make a concept map, other graphic organizer, or outline using the Study Guides you made for each lesson in this unit. Be sure to use evidence to support your claims.

When synthesizing individual information, remember to follow these general steps:
- Find the central idea of each piece of information.
- Think about the relationships among the central ideas.
- Combine the Ideas to come up with a new understanding.

Look back to the Driving Questions from the opening section of this unit. In your Evidence Notebook, review and revise your previous answers to those questions. Use the evidence you gathered and other observations you made throughout the unit to support your claims.

1. How does organization make it possible for the human body to carry out the wide range of interactions necessary for survival?
   - a. Cells are the foundation of the human body, and each cell can carry out all interactions necessary for survival.
   - b. Tissues are the highest level of organization in the human body, and tissues are capable of carrying out specialized tasks necessary for survival.
   - c. Levels of organization make it possible for cells, tissues, organs, and organ systems to specialize and take on specific functions.
   - d. There is no overlap in the organization and interaction of organ systems, making it possible for the body to fulfill a wide range of life functions.

2. What are some of the advantages for organisms that undergo mitotic reproduction, as opposed to sexual reproduction? Select all correct answers.
   - a. Mitotic reproduction can occur without a partner.
   - b. Mitotic reproduction leads to offspring with greater genetic diversity.
   - c. Mitotic reproduction requires less energy than sexual reproduction.
   - d. Mitotic reproduction can allow a new organism to grow from a fragment of its parent organism.

3. In adults, the liver does not normally grow larger or regenerate cells. Based on this knowledge, most adult liver cells would be expected to
   - a. regularly undergo mitosis.
   - b. have highly condensed chromosomes.
   - c. often replicate the cells' DNA.
   - d. be in the interphase, or resting phase.

4. Apoptosis, or programmed cell death, is triggered during which biological processes? Select all correct answers.
   - a. DNA damage suffered by a cell
   - b. response of a lymphocyte to an active infection
   - c. differentiation of a stem cell into a specialized cell
   - d. removal of certain tissues during embryonic development

5. Which of the following best explains why stem cells can be used to treat some diseases such as leukemia, a cancer of white blood cells?
   - a. Stem cells do not age, and they can divide indefinitely.
   - b. Certain types of stem cells can differentiate into any type of cell.
   - c. Stem cells are able to adhere to damaged cells and initiate a repair sequence.
   - d. Stem cells contain a full set of chromosomes, unlike other cells in the body.

6. How is the cell cycle related to the growth and maintenance of an organism? What role does differentiation play?

_____

_____

_____

_____

_____

7. As a cell grows larger, what happens to its surface area-to-volume ratio? How does this affect a cell's ability to grow further?

_____

_____

_____

_____

_____

8. Explain the connection between the cell cycle and cancer development.

_____

_____

_____

_____

_____

9. Must the cell cycle always proceed in the same direction, or is it possible for the cell cycle to proceed in the opposite direction? Explain your reasoning.

_____

_____

_____

_____

_____

UNIT PROJECT

Return to your unit project. Prepare your research and materials into a presentation to share with the class. In your final presentation, evaluate the strength of your hypothesis, data, analysis, and conclusions.

Remember these tips while evaluating:

- Look at the empirical evidence—evidence based on observations and data. Does the evidence support the explanation? Does the evidence support your claim regarding the processes involved in the formation of a new plant?

- Consider if the explanation is logical. Does it contradict any evidence you have seen?

- Think of tests you could do to support and contradict the ideas.

Ecosystem Stability and the Response to Climate Change

YOU SOLVE IT

**How Can You Control the Spread
of an Invasive Fish Species?**

 To begin exploring this unit's concepts,
go online to investigate ways to solve a
real-world problem.

Transportation networks cover Earth,
representing the extent of human
development.

FIGURE 1: This device collects trash floating in the ocean.

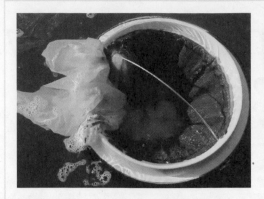
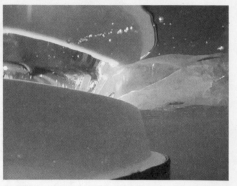

Millions of tons of trash enter oceans and other bodies of water every year. Many animals mistake plastic objects for food and die after eating them. Other animals may become trapped in plastic pieces and other trash. As plastics accumulate in the water, human and animal health suffers. Currently, there are many ways different groups are trying to keep plastics and other trash out of the oceans. Cleaning beaches, increasing public education about the problem, decreasing plastic use, and creating more opportunities to recycle plastic material are some ways people are trying to prevent more trash from entering the ocean. Engineers are developing technology to capture and remove plastic and trash already in the ocean.

PREDICT How can humans cause and solve the same environmental problems?

_____

_____

_____

_____

DRIVING QUESTIONS

As you move through the unit, gather evidence to help you answer the following questions. In your Evidence Notebook, record what you already know about these topics and any questions you have about them.

1. How does human population growth affect the environment?
2. How can humans mitigate the effects of human development on biodiversity?
3. Why do solutions to environmental impacts need to consider a range of criteria, including societal needs?

UNIT PROJECT

Go online to download the Unit Project Worksheet to help plan your project.

To Dam or Not to Dam

Dams provide humans with energy and water but also negatively impact the environment. How can we reduce the negative impacts and restore ecosystem function in landscapes affected by dams? Investigate the tradeoffs to understand how these structures can both help and harm the modern world.

Language Development

Use the lessons in this unit to complete the chart and expand your understanding of the science concepts.

TERM: energy budget

Definition	Example

Similar Term	Phrase

TERM: greenhouse gas

Definition	Example

Similar Term	Phrase

TERM: habitat fragmentation

Definition	Example

Similar Term	Phrase

TERM: sustainable development

Definition	Example

Similar Term	Phrase

TERM: invasive species

Definition	Example
Similar Term	**Phrase**

TERM: extinction

Definition	Example
Similar Term	**Phrase**

TERM: renewable resource

Definition	Example
Similar Term	**Phrase**

TERM: nonrenewable resource

Definition	Example
Similar Term	**Phrase**

Human Impacts on Climate

As climate warms, sea level rise is a growing concern for coastal communities in California.

CAN YOU EXPLAIN IT?

Over the past three decades, scientists have noticed that the total area covered by Arctic sea ice has been steadily shrinking. In September 1984, the ice covered 6.206 million square kilometers, but in September 2016, it covered only 4.14 million square kilometers. In addition, the portion of ice that is more than a year old has decreased. In the 1980s, about 45% of the ice was permanent. In 2016, only about 20% of the ice was permanent. This is a sign that the ice is not just covering a smaller area but is also becoming thinner.

PREDICT How could melting sea ice affect the coastline and beaches of California?

_____

_____

_____

_____

_____

_____

Evidence Notebook As you explore the lesson, gather evidence to help explain the factors that influence climate, why climate has changed in the past, and why it is changing today.

Explore Online ▶

FIGURE 1: Between 1984 and 2016, both the total area covered by sea ice and the portion of sea ice that was more than a year old decreased significantly in the Arctic.

a September 1984

b September 2016

Earth's Energy

All processes within Earth and on its surface involve the flow of energy and the cycling of matter. The energy that Earth emits into space comes from Earth's surface, which is heated by the sun, with a small contribution from the hot rocks and metal beneath Earth's crust.

Earth's Energy Sources

Explore Online ▶

Hands-On Lab

Energy Transfer Measure the results of conduction between metal and water.

Energy moves through Earth's systems in three different ways—by radiation, conduction, and convection. Energy from the sun reaches Earth through *radiation*, the movement of energy as visible light, ultraviolet rays, and other types of electromagnetic waves. Radiation is the only way that energy can travel through outer space.

EXPLAIN Select the correct phrases and terms to complete the statement about solar radiation.

Figure 2 shows that approximately half of the incoming radiation from the sun is absorbed by Earth's surface | reflected by the atmosphere | absorbed by the atmosphere. Earth's atmosphere only absorbs | only reflects | absorbs and reflects some of the sun's radiation. If Earth had a much thinner atmosphere, the percentage of the sun's electromagnetic radiation that reaches Earth's surface would increase | decrease | stay the same. This would cause minimal | significant | no changes to Earth's climate.

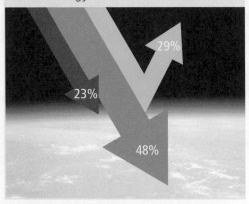

FIGURE 2: Earth's atmosphere absorbs and reflects energy.

29%

23%

48%

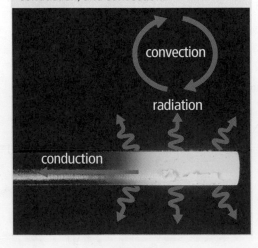

FIGURE 3: Energy exits the hot steel bar into the surrounding air via radiation, conduction, and convection.

convection

radiation

conduction

Conduction is the transfer of energy between objects or atoms and molecules in contact. When you walk barefoot on warm ground, for example, heat moves by conduction from the ground to the soles of your feet. Air touching hot ground also is warmed when heat transfers by conduction from the ground to the air.

Convection is the movement of energy caused by motion in matter. The motion in matter is a result of a difference in density. Convection often moves thermal energy through a liquid or gas. For example, in a pot of simmering water, the water at the bottom of the pot is heated by conduction and becomes less dense. Because it is less dense, it rises and is replaced by downward-flowing water that is colder and denser. Energy is transferred by convection within Earth's atmosphere, hydrosphere, and geosphere.

Earth's interior contains more thermal energy than the surface and atmosphere, but the energy is released more slowly. The flow of Earth's internal energy does not have a direct effect on Earth's climate, but it is responsible for important processes, such as volcanic eruptions that can affect the atmosphere, and earthquakes that shape surface features.

Based on available evidence, scientists estimate that the temperature at the center of Earth is about 5500 °C. Some of Earth's internal energy is left over from Earth's formation. The rest is a result of radioactive decay, which is occurring all the time.

INFER Where is the flow of energy from Earth's interior observable and measurable without sensitive scientific equipment?

_____

_____

_____

_____

_____

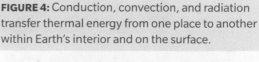

FIGURE 4: Conduction, convection, and radiation transfer thermal energy from one place to another within Earth's interior and on the surface.

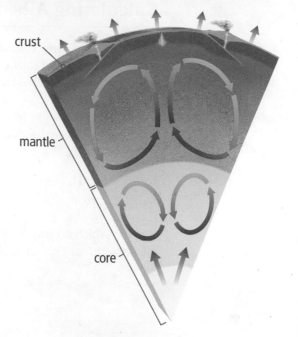

crust

mantle

core

Energy flows differently within Earth's interior, depending on the physical properties of the layers. For example, energy flows by convection in part of the mantle and in the liquid outer core. Energy flows by conduction through the solid inner core and the rigid surface. All materials radiate energy, but within Earth, this energy is absorbed almost immediately by the surrounding materials.

Earth's Energy Budget

Solar energy is constantly reaching the uppermost reaches of Earth's atmosphere. On average, the same amount of energy leaves Earth's surface and atmosphere each second and moves out into space. For Earth's surface temperature to remain stable, the total amount of incoming and outgoing radiation must be balanced. The balance of incoming and outgoing energy is Earth's energy budget.

When sunlight reaches rock, plants, ocean water, and ice on Earth's surface, some of it is reflected while the rest is absorbed. Albedo is a measure of the amount of light that a particular surface will reflect. It is most often expressed as a value between 0 and 1. For example, Earth's average albedo is 0.39. However, different areas can have different albedos. Ice has a high albedo—more light is reflected than is absorbed. Forests have a low albedo—more energy is absorbed than is reflected.

 Collaborate With a partner, consider what happens to Earth's surface temperature when the amount of incoming energy exceeds the amount of outgoing energy. What about when the amount of outgoing energy exceeds the amount of incoming energy?

Calculating Albedo

The albedo of a surface is a measure of how reflective it is. To calculate the albedo, divide the amount of solar energy reflected by the surface by the total amount of solar energy that reaches Earth.

SOLVE There are approximately 100 units of total incoming solar radiation, and 30 units are reflected. Calculate Earth's albedo. Express your answer as a decimal and as a percentage.

Earth's albedo is about _____. This means that about _____ % of solar radiation striking Earth is reflected back into space.

APPLY Which do you think would have a higher albedo, a planet with water or a planet with ice? Explain your reasoning.

_____

_____

_____

You can tell whether a surface has a high or low albedo just by looking at it. Surfaces with a high albedo are light or brightly colored, because they reflect a relatively high amount of light. Surfaces with a low albedo are dark, because they reflect very little light. For example, some clouds have a high albedo and appear white from above, while others absorb more light and are grayer in color.

Heating Imbalances

Because Earth is a sphere, the amount of radiation any given part of the surface receives at any given time differs with latitude. As the diagram shows, this occurs because the lower the sun is in the sky, the more the solar energy is spread out on the surface. For this reason, the amount of incoming radiation falling on any given area is greatest in the equatorial regions, where the sun can be straight overhead, and is least in the polar regions, where the sun is lower in the sky.

FIGURE 5: The amount of energy that strikes the surface differs from place to place.

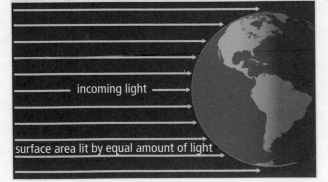

incoming light

surface area lit by equal amount of light

EXPLAIN If Earth is unevenly heated, why don't temperatures at the equator become too hot to support life? What happens to the energy that Earth receives?

_____

_____

_____

_____

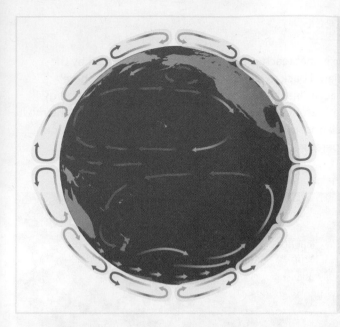

FIGURE 6: Ocean currents circulate thermal energy. Convection cycles in the atmosphere also redistribute energy in a similar pattern.

PREDICT How might surface temperatures on Earth be different if there were no oceans and no wind?

_____

_____

_____

Water is a better heat conductor than air. For this reason, most of the transfer of thermal energy between the equator and the poles takes place through surface ocean currents. Water in equatorial regions is heated as solar radiation is absorbed. Thus, as currents flow from equatorial regions toward the poles, thermal energy moves with the currents. Some of this energy is eventually radiated directly to space. The rest is released to the atmosphere through conduction and radiation. From there, it eventually moves out to space but from a higher latitude than where it came in.

Wind also moves solar energy toward the poles. The global wind system is driven by the unequal heating of Earth's surface. Because Earth's surface is not heated evenly, the air is warmer in some places than in others. Cool, dry air is denser than warm, humid air, so it sinks, pushing warmer air upward. In an atmospheric convection cell, warm air rises and cools. It then travels horizontally toward the poles until it is cool and dense enough to sink. When it gets near Earth's surface, the cooler air flows back toward the equator. This general pattern of circulation moves energy away from the equatorial regions toward the poles, partially evening out the imbalance of energy.

EXPLAIN Select the correct terms to complete the statement about sunlight on Earth.

Polar regions receive more | less solar radiation than equatorial regions. Polar ice also absorbs | reflects much of the incoming sunlight. This produces an imbalance of energy between the equator and the poles. In addition, polar regions radiate more energy than they absorb from the sun (they have an energy deficit), while equatorial regions have an energy surplus. Conduction | Convection | Radiation in the ocean and the atmosphere, driven by the imbalance in incoming solar radiation, moves energy from one place to another. This flow of air and water decreases | increases the difference in temperature between the equator and the poles.

The Greenhouse Effect

Overall, the amount of solar energy that reaches Earth from space is balanced by the amount that is reflected and radiated back to space. However, Earth's atmosphere contains greenhouse gases that act as insulators and slow down the escape of energy that radiates from Earth's surface. Water vapor, carbon dioxide, and methane are the most common greenhouse gases. The atmosphere absorbs some of the outgoing radiation, which raises Earth's surface temperature. This process is called the *greenhouse effect*.

FIGURE 7: The greenhouse effect helps to maintain Earth's surface temperature.

2 Energy from the sun is absorbed by Earth's surface and then radiated into the atmosphere as heat, some of which escapes into space.

3 Greenhouse gases also absorb some of the sun's energy and radiate it back toward the lower atmosphere and Earth's surface.

1 Solar radiation passes through the atmosphere and warms Earth's surface.

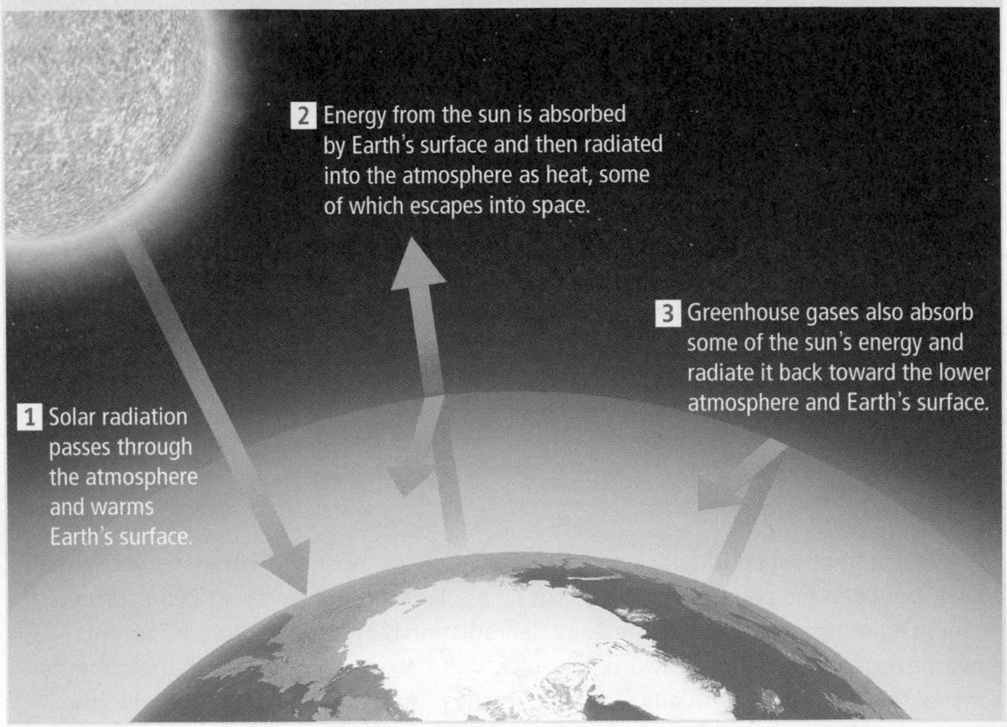

Without the greenhouse effect, much of Earth's heat would be lost almost immediately to outer space. Earth's average surface temperature (about 15 °C) would be about 33 °C cooler than it is now. The greenhouse effect has helped Earth thrive as a planet. Recently, however, there has been such a significant increase in the levels of carbon dioxide in the atmosphere that Earth's energy budget may be out of balance. Many scientists warn of the effects of global climate change.

APPLY The greenhouse effect on Venus makes the average surface temperature on the planet 464 °C. What does this tell you about the composition of the atmosphere on Venus?

_____

_____

_____

_____

_____

 Evidence Notebook Light moves differently through different materials. What are some factors that could change the amount of sunlight absorbed by Earth's surface and atmosphere?

Understanding Earth's Climate

Weather is defined as the current state of the atmosphere. Climate, on the other hand, is the characteristic weather patterns over a long period of time. A description of a region's climate includes average temperature and total precipitation as well as ranges of temperature and precipitation. Because many parts of the world experience seasonal variations, complete descriptions of climate also include monthly averages.

Factors That Influence Climate

Earth's global climate changes for various reasons and on many different scales of time. Periods of global climate change can range from several years to millions of years. Climate change can involve a small portion of Earth's surface or the entire globe.

 Collaborate With a partner, explain how fossils could be used to show how the climate in a region has changed over time.

Changes in Earth's Motion

Based on evidence from rock, fossils, and ice cores, we know that Earth's global climate has gone through much cooler periods, in which more of Earth's surface was covered in ice. The climate has also gone through much warmer periods, in which the surface was virtually free of ice. For the most part, these long-term patterns can be explained by patterns of change in Earth's motion in space. Over thousands of years, the elongation of Earth's orbit changes, the tilt of its axis increases and decreases, and the direction that its axis points in space moves. The combination of these factors causes changes in the total amount of solar energy that reaches Earth's surface.

Another factor that affects the amount of solar energy reaching Earth is the amount of energy given off by the sun. The sun's energy output increases and then decreases over the course of 11 years. This cycle, called a *sunspot cycle*, repeats every 11 years and causes slight changes in global temperatures.

EXPLAIN Earth has gone through many cycles of ice ages followed by periods of warmer climate. How might these cycles be related to patterns of solar output and patterns of change in Earth's motion in space?

_____

_____

_____

_____

_____

_____

_____

Continental Motion

The continents have not always been located where they are today. Millions of years ago, all the continents were once connected as one large land mass. Due to the movement of the tectonic plates, the land masses separated and drifted apart. This movement had drastic effects on local climates and the overall climate of Earth.

FIGURE 8: Landmasses form and break apart as tectonic plates move across the surface of Earth.

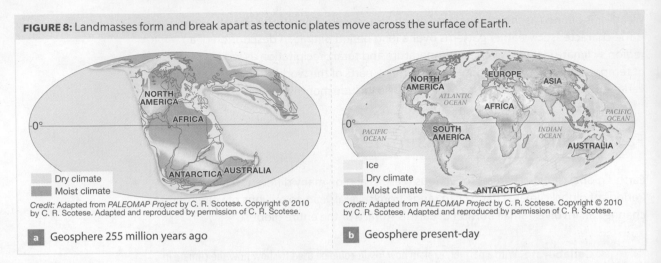

Credit: Adapted from *PALEOMAP Project* by C. R. Scotese. Copyright © 2010 by C. R. Scotese. Adapted and reproduced by permission of C. R. Scotese.

a Geosphere 255 million years ago

Credit: Adapted from *PALEOMAP Project* by C. R. Scotese. Copyright © 2010 by C. R. Scotese. Adapted and reproduced by permission of C. R. Scotese.

b Geosphere present-day

Approximately 85 million years ago, Australia began to separate from Antarctica. Around 34 million years ago, Australia and South America separated from Antarctica, leaving Antarctica isolated in a newly formed ocean basin. This led to the formation of a cold oceanic surface current, which flows clockwise around the continent, and the westerly flow of winds. The ocean current and winds stopped the flow of warm, tropical air and water from the South Atlantic Ocean to Antarctica. Warm water was no longer able to reach the South Pole, which triggered the first Antarctic glaciation.

INFER Suppose rising sea levels separate the continents of North and South America. Choose one of Earth's spheres, and explain how it might interact differently with another of Earth's spheres because of this change.

_____

_____

_____

_____

_____

_____

Over geologic time, oceans grow and shrink, continents move, and mountains form and erode. Global air and ocean circulation patterns also change. This alters the cycling of energy through Earth's systems and affects global climate. Periods of mountain building can also affect global climate by increasing rates of weathering. During weathering, CO_2 reacts with rocks and is removed from the atmosphere.

Atmospheric Composition

Many factors can influence the concentration of greenhouse gases in the atmosphere. Plants remove CO_2 from the atmosphere through photosynthesis. Respiration and decomposition release CO_2 back into the atmosphere. When ocean water temperature increases, more CO_2 moves out of ocean water and into the atmosphere. When water temperature decreases, more CO_2 moves from the atmosphere into the ocean. Relatively small amounts of CO_2 move from Earth's interior into the atmosphere during volcanic eruptions. Human activities such as burning fossil fuels and making cement release CO_2. Although CO_2 and methane (CH_4) make up less than 0.04% of the atmosphere, they, along with water vapor (H_2O), have a significant effect on air temperature.

 Collaborate Volcanoes release CO_2 and water vapor into the atmosphere, but the overall effect of volcanic activity is to cool the planet. How can volcanoes have a cooling effect even though they release greenhouse gases? Discuss your ideas with a partner.

Changes in Temperature

Earth's climate changes continuously between periods of relatively warm and cool global temperatures. Currently, we are in a relatively cool period of geologic history. Therefore, it seems reasonable that global temperatures would be rising. In the past, temperatures have been much higher as a result of natural causes. The difference today is the rate of temperature increase. Compared with the temperature changes throughout geologic history, the warming we are expected to experience in the next century is at least 20 times greater than any other global warming event in the past two million years.

Global Temperature Changes

FIGURE 9: Average global temperature has changed throughout geologic history.

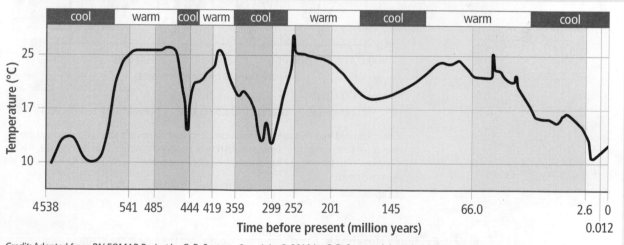

Credit: Adapted from *PALEOMAP Project* by C. R. Scotese. Copyright © 2010 by C. R. Scotese. Adapted and reproduced by permission of C. R. Scotese.

 Stability and Change Do the following two statements contradict one another? Explain why or why not.

1. The climate undergoes periodic natural variations, and we are currently in a relatively cool period in geologic history.
2. Humans are causing global average temperature to rise through the burning of fossil fuels.

Stability and Change

Analyzing Climate Data

One method to detect and measure climate change is to compare the amount of atmospheric CO_2 present in the past to the amount in the atmosphere now. To infer CO_2 levels in the past, scientists use ice cores. Ice cores are long tubes of ice drilled from glaciers or ice sheets. As snow falls to Earth, the snow carries chemicals that are in the air at the time. The substances contained in snow are buried with the snow, one layer on top of another, over time. Air bubbles between snowflakes and grains become trapped when the snow is compacted. These air bubbles can provide information about the composition of the atmosphere. Scientists can also analyze ice cores to infer global temperature over time.

FIGURE 10: An ice core is extracted in Antarctica.

Carbon Dioxide Levels and Temperature Change

FIGURE 11: Ice cores provide information about past temperature and CO_2 levels.

Explore Online ▶

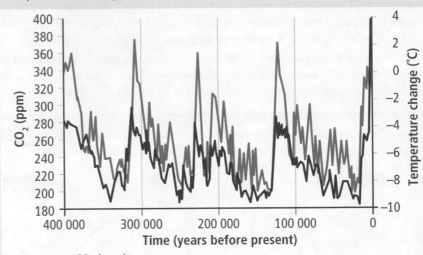

— CO_2 (ppm)
— Temperature change (°C) compared to present-day temperature

Credit: Adapted from "Climate and Atmospheric History of the Past 420,000 Years from the Vostok Ice Core, Antarctica" by Jean-Robert Petit et. al. from *Nature*, Volume 399, 429–436. Copyright © by Macmillan Magazines Ltd. Adapted and reproduced by permission of SpringerNature.
Source: NOAA

Evidence Notebook Answer these questions about the data in the graph.

1. Describe patterns you see in the CO_2 and temperature data.

2. The CO_2 concentration in Earth's atmosphere has now reached 400 parts per million. How do you think this will affect average temperatures on Earth? Explain your answer.

3. What additional evidence would you need to support the claim that changes in CO_2 levels cause changes in average global temperatures?

Evidence Notebook How could the trend in CO_2 levels and temperatures affect the ecosystems along the coast of California?

Climate Change

Human activity can affect global systems, including climate. For example, the use of fossil fuels for energy increases the amount of carbon dioxide and other greenhouse gases in the atmosphere, causing average global temperatures to rise. Since the Industrial Revolution began around 1750, human activities have been adding significant amounts of greenhouse gases to the atmosphere. These activities include burning fossil fuels such as coal, oil, and gas; making concrete; and practicing agriculture.

Climate Models

To understand the causes of today's temperature increase, scientists model the effects on climate of various factors such as volcanism, sunspots, and burning fossil fuels. Because so many factors are interacting, climate models can be very complicated. But with the help of computers, it is now possible to make models that accurately simulate real conditions and help predict future conditions.

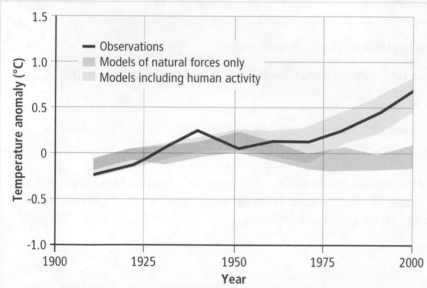

Credit: Adapted from "Climate Change 2007" by Denman et al. from *IPCC Fourth Assessment Report*, WG1, SPM. Copyright © 2007 by Intergovernmental Panel on Climate Change. Adapted and reproduced by permission of IPCC.

Climate Models

FIGURE 12: Climate models provide scenarios to help scientists better understand climate change. The blue region models global temperatures if climate was influenced only by natural factors. The orange region models global temperatures if climate was influenced by human activity. The red line models observations of actual global temperatures. The term *temperature anomaly* refers to the difference between the long-term average temperature and the actual temperature.

ANALYZE What patterns do you notice in this model? What conclusions can you make about climate change based on the data displayed in this model?

_____

_____

_____

_____

_____

_____

Greenhouse Gas Emissions

When carbon dioxide and methane are added to the atmosphere, they cause the atmosphere to retain thermal energy. The table shows the properties of the main greenhouse gases, including their Global Warming Potentials (GWP). GWP is a comparative measure of how much heat a gas may absorb.

Math Connection

FIGURE 13: The Global Warming Potential of some of the main greenhouse gases is shown in parts per million.

Greenhouse gases	Concentration in 2016	Global Warming Potential (GWP) over 100 years	Duration in the atmosphere
Carbon dioxide	399.5 ppm	1	~100 to 300 years
Methane	1.8 ppm	28	12 years
Nitrous oxide	0.3 ppm	265	121 years
Chlorofluorocarbons	0.9 ppm	4670 to 10 200	45 to 100 years

Source: Carbon Dioxide Information Analysis Center. Recent Greenhouse Gas Concentrations. DOI: 10.3334/CDIAC/atg.032.

SOLVE Use the table to answer these questions:

1. How many times greater is the GWP for nitrous oxide than for methane?

   _____

2. How much longer is the duration in the atmosphere for nitrous oxide than for methane? _____

3. Which of these gases—methane or nitrous oxide—is most likely to have the greatest warming effect on Earth's climate? What other factors might need to be considered to form a valid conclusion?

   _____

   _____

   _____

   _____

   _____

As more energy is stored in Earth's atmosphere and oceans, the cycling of matter and energy among ecosystems is altered. Studies suggest that hurricanes, for example, are becoming more intense on average. Scientists think this is because there is more energy stored as heat in Earth's oceans, and this energy provides the fuel for these destructive storms. As global temperatures rise, glaciers and ice caps have been observed decreasing in size, and the water contained in them is added to oceans. This causes average global sea level to rise, which affects ecosystems and human societies. In addition, a warmer atmosphere also means warmer water. Water expands as it warms. This is a major contributor to sea-level rise.

Today, we are releasing more CO_2 than any other greenhouse gas into the atmosphere. Billions of tons of CO_2 are released into the atmosphere each year from electrical plants that burn coal or oil and from cars that burn gasoline. Millions of trees are burned in tropical rain forests to clear the land for farming. Thus, the amount of CO_2 in the atmosphere increases. We are also releasing other greenhouse gases, such as methane and nitrous oxide, in significant amounts.

ANALYZE Where on Earth are CO_2 concentrations highest? What does the uneven distribution of CO_2 in the atmosphere indicate?

_____

_____

_____

_____

_____

_____

_____

Explore Online ▶

FIGURE 14: This image from the GEOS-5 computer model shows the concentration of CO_2 in the atmosphere on January 1, 2006. Areas in orange indicate high CO_2 concentrations, while those in blue are low. Carbon monoxide concentrations appear in gray.

The majority of human CO_2 emissions come from burning fossil fuels, such as oil, gas, and coal. Fossil fuels are still a major source of energy for powering cars, trucks, trains, planes, and ships; for heating homes and cooking food; and for generating electricity. In 2015, CO_2 accounted for more than 80% of all greenhouse gases emitted from human activities.

MODEL Draw a model to show how burning fossil fuels can cause sea level to change along the California coastline.

Feedback Effects of Climate Change

Earth's climate is a system of interacting feedback cycles. The effects of a global increase in temperature are complicated in part because of feedback effects. Negative feedback reduces the effect of a change. In the case of climate change, a negative feedback would decrease or slow down the rise in temperatures. Scientists are most concerned with positive feedback effects, that is, effects of temperature increase that result in an even greater temperature increase.

Albedo has an important effect on climate. Surfaces with low albedo generally warm up more easily than those with high albedo. On a local scale, asphalt and other building materials with low albedo contribute to urban heat islands—city areas that have warmer temperatures than surrounding rural areas. As Earth's albedo decreases, global temperature will increase.

 Engineering One way engineers are trying to reduce the effects of climate feedback is through carbon storage. Research the pros and cons of carbon storage. Gather evidence from multiple sources. Be sure to cite your sources. For more information on citing sources, see the ELA Handbook or ask your teacher. Consider the following when conducting your research:

1. How deep must CO_2 be buried?
2. How does CO_2 move underground?
3. How much CO_2 can be stored at a single site?
4. What is the cost of storing CO_2?

Come up with two questions of your own to guide your research.

FIGURE 15: Positive feedback loops affect Earth's temperature.

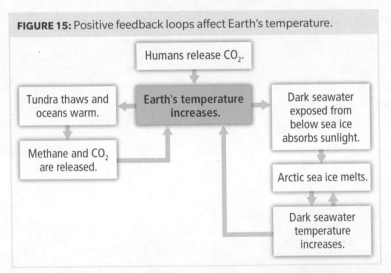

EXPLAIN Describe one example of a positive feedback in the climate system.

_____

_____

_____

_____

_____

_____

_____

_____

_____

Scientists and engineers are developing methods for removing carbon that is already in the atmosphere. The most obvious way is to plant trees and encourage the growth of phytoplankton that remove CO_2 from the air through photosynthesis. Scientists are also developing machines, sometimes referred to as "artificial trees," that remove CO_2 from the air. Similar devices can capture CO_2 on its way out of a pollution source such as a coal-fired power plant before it enters the atmosphere.

 Evidence Notebook As scientists continue to research climate change, they could discover other positive and negative feedback effects on global temperatures. Explain why researching both types of feedback effects are important to protecting California from the harmful effects of climate change.

Effects of Global Climate Change

The most obvious effect of global climate change is an increase in average annual global surface temperature. Because current climate change involves an increase in average global temperatures, it is often referred to as *global warming*. However, this does not mean that every region will experience the same increase in average temperature. Some regions may warm at a greater rate than others. Some may not change significantly at all. Because so many factors affecting regional climates interact with each other, some regions may become cooler.

Glaciers and Sea Ice

Current trends of increasing global temperatures will melt ice in glaciers and polar regions and expand seawater volume, which will impact islands and coastlines around the world. A major cause of sea-level rise today is the addition of water to the oceans as glaciers, sea ice, and ice sheets melt. Increasing temperature also causes sea levels to rise because water expands as it warms. As ocean water warms, the water molecules move apart. The water becomes less dense and takes up more space. This is known as *thermal expansion*.

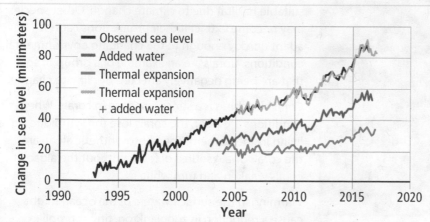

Climate Change and Global Sea-Level Rise

FIGURE 16: The graph shows the observed change in sea level since 1993. Additional data show the estimated change in sea level due to thermal expansion, added water from glacier melt and other sources, and the estimated change in sea level due to both.

Credit: Adapted from "2017: Sea level variability and change" by Thompson, et. al., from *State of the Climate* in 2016, 98 (8), S80. Copyright © by American Meteorological Society. Adapted and reproduced by permission of American Meteorological Society.

Source: NOAA, Climate Change: Global Sea Level

ANALYZE Using evidence from the graph, what is likely causing the change in sea level?

_____

_____

_____

_____

The exact rate of sea-level change varies from place to place as a result of local and regional factors. Some areas of the ocean are warming up and expanding faster. Wind systems can push water from one part of the ocean to another. Earth's gravitational pull varies across the oceans. Land itself can rise or fall. For example, land that has been covered in ice can slowly rise upward (rebound) as the weight of ice is reduced.

One of the most dramatic effects of global climate change is sea-level rise. Measurements from tide gauges show that over the past 100 years, global mean sea level has been rising at a rate of about 1.3–1.7 mm/year. Satellite and tide gauge measurements show that since 1993, the rate has doubled to about 2.6–3.5 mm/year. Current climate change models suggest that sea level could rise another 1 to 2 meters by 2100.

One meter over 100 years might not seem like a lot, but keep in mind that many coastlines consist of gently sloping land, not sheer cliffs. An increase in sea level of 1 meter can flood many kilometers inland. In addition, sea-level rise increases the frequency of flooding during extreme weather events such as hurricanes.

EXPLAIN Complete the statement by selecting the correct terms.

The rise in sea levels will most likely increase | decrease the rate of erosion along affected coastlines and beaches. These rising sea levels will also likely increase | decrease flooding in low-lying areas and wetlands. This will increase | decrease the salinity of coastal freshwater aquifers, which will increase | decrease the quality of fresh water.

Aquatic Ecosystems

FIGURE 17: Coral bleaching is a stress response in corals.

Climate change is causing rapid changes to environments, from increasing temperatures to rising sea levels. Some species may find an increase in suitable habitat due to climate change. Other species may become extinct if their populations cannot adapt quickly enough to the changing environmental conditions. Corals are an example of a group of species that are being negatively affected by climate change.

Coral bleaching is a stress response in corals. When conditions are poor, the corals lose the symbiotic algae living inside of them. The photosynthetic algae are the corals' main source of food. Without the algae, the corals weaken and turn white.

Warming in the surface waters of the ocean might cause a reduction in zooplankton, tiny shrimplike animals that many marine animals depend on for food. In addition, because bacteria thrive in warmer temperatures, bacterial growth in ocean waters may impact organisms living in coastal tide pools and elsewhere in the marine environment.

PREDICT What might happen if a coral species that is well adapted to higher temperature was introduced into a coral reef habitat?

_____

_____

_____

_____

_____

_____

Ocean acidification occurs when carbon dioxide is absorbed by seawater. The reaction between carbon dioxide and seawater also uses dissolved carbonate ions, which results in a decreased concentration of carbonate ions in the water. As carbon dioxide levels in the atmosphere increase, the amount of carbonic acid in the hydrosphere also increases.

Scientists can determine how acidic a solution is by measuring its pH. An acid is a compound that releases hydrogen ions (H^+) when it dissolves in water. So, an acidic solution will have a higher concentration of H^+ ions. On the pH scale, which is measured between 0 and 14, a *more* acidic solution has a *lower* number. For example, stomach acid, which is very acidic, has a pH between 1 and 3. Seawater, which is not very acidic, has a pH around 8. The pH scale is an important tool scientists use to measure the impact of ocean acidification over time.

Carbon Dioxide and pH

FIGURE 18: This graph shows changes in atmospheric carbon dioxide concentrations, seawater carbon dioxide concentrations (pCO_2), and seawater pH for the past few decades. A decrease in water pH indicates an increase in acidity.

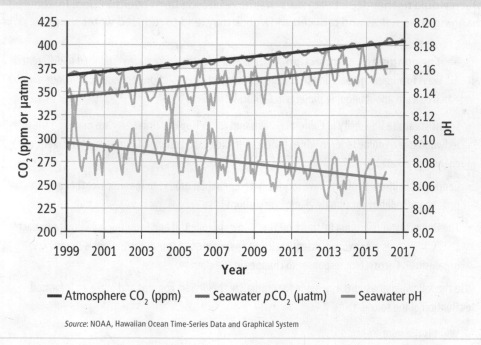

Source: NOAA, Hawaiian Ocean Time-Series Data and Graphical System

EXPLAIN How does the amount of carbon dioxide in the atmosphere relate to the amount of carbon dioxide in seawater? How does the amount of carbon dioxide in dissolved seawater relate to its pH?

_____

_____

_____

_____

This rise in acidification is particularly problematic for marine animals, such as coral and oysters, that build their shells using carbonate molecules found in seawater. Increasing carbon in the ocean produces a higher quantity of bicarbonate molecules, which the marine life can no longer use for building shells. Large increases in carbonic acid can even break down part of an animal's existing shell. Since ocean acidification can cause environmental changes at rates much faster than aquatic life can adapt, marine life and existing ecosystems are increasingly vulnerable.

Changes in Global Weather Patterns

With climate change comes changes in the weather, and not just in terms of temperature. With an increase in temperature, evaporation rates increase, changing precipitation patterns. Current models show, for example, that the tropical rain forests are likely to be wetter, with the subtropical dry areas becoming even drier.

Scientists also predict that with an increase in ocean temperatures, there will likely be an increase in the maximum wind speeds and rainfall rates of hurricanes. In addition, some scientists are also concerned that global warming will cause a change in ocean current patterns, such as shutting off the Gulf Stream. Such a change could cause some regions to have more rainfall than normal, whereas other regions might have less.

Agriculture would be most severely impacted by global climate change if extreme weather events such as droughts became more frequent. Higher temperatures could result in decreased crop yields. Warmer winters may alter crop growth cycles and require new agriculture and management practices. The demand for irrigation could increase, which would further deplete aquifers that have already been overpumped. In addition, changing stream flow and reduced snowpack may lead to reduced water supplies.

Language Arts Connection Citizens and scientists alike have responded in different ways to address global climate change. Choose from the solutions provided or do your own research to learn about ongoing projects in California.

- Scientists at the University of California, Davis and Johns Hopkins University are mapping the redwood tree genome to learn which traits can make coastal redwood forests more resilient in a changing climate.

- Concerned California citizens have formed different action groups to monitor weather and air quality and to lobby for climate change resolutions.

- The University of California Institute for the Study of Ecological and Evolutionary Climate Impacts (ISEECI) oversees a network of scientists using environmental sensor technologies to monitor organism and ecosystem responses to changes in the climate.

Use the following questions as a guide to summarize the project concept and make an informed evaluation of the solution.

- What is the solution?
- What impact does the solution have on the environment and society?
- What costs, benefits, and tradeoffs did you consider in your evaluation?
- Would you support this project? Why or why not?
- Could the project address extreme weather patterns?

Air Pollution

Anything added to the environment that has a negative effect on the environment or its organisms is called pollution. Pollutants, the substances that cause pollution, can take the form of chemicals, particulates, or microorganisms.

 Collaborate Have you seen any evidence of human impacts on the air in your town? Make a list of the types of evidence you think would indicate air pollution. Compare your evidence and your list with a partner.

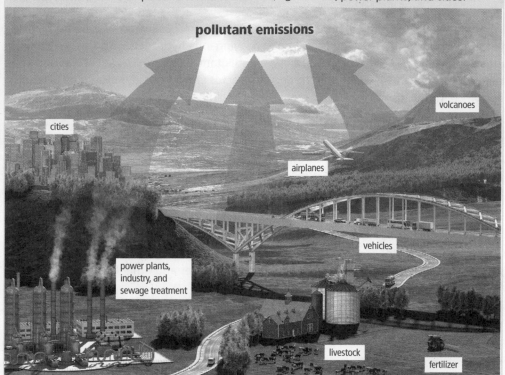

FIGURE 19: Sources of air pollution include vehicles, agriculture, power plants, and cities.

pollutant emissions

volcanoes

cities

airplanes

vehicles

power plants, industry, and sewage treatment

livestock

fertilizer

Smog is a type of air pollution caused by the interaction of sunlight with pollutants produced by fossil fuel emissions. Smog is composed of particulates and ground-level ozone. Particulates are microscopic bits of dust, metal, and unburned fuel. Some particulates may stay in the atmosphere for weeks before settling to the ground.

 Engineering Smog is a major health concern in many major cities, including Los Angeles, California and Beijing, China. Engineers in China are working on an anti-smog bike, which will take in air, remove pollutants, and release cleaner air. What social and cultural impacts of this solution need to be considered?

_____

_____

_____

When fossil fuels are burned, nitrogen oxides are produced. When these substances react with oxygen in the air in the presence of light, they produce ozone (O_3) that tends to stay close to the ground. This is called ground-level ozone, which can be harmful to ecosystems and human health. However, O_3 does play an important role in Earth's upper atmosphere by protecting the biosphere from harmful UV rays in sunlight.

EXPLAIN Some cities have "Ozone Action Days" when carpooling or taking public transportation is encouraged. These days tend to be scheduled when it is hot and sunny outside. Why is ground-level ozone worse on hot, sunny days?

○ **a.** Energy from the sun increases the production of nitrogen oxides.

○ **b.** Ground-level ozone production is driven by the presence of sunlight.

○ **c.** Sunlight reacts with oxygen in the upper atmosphere to form ozone.

Acid Precipitation

When water falls to Earth as rain, sleet, or snow, water molecules react with carbon dioxide to form carbonic acid. This acid breaks apart, leaving lone hydrogen ions. This gives precipitation a pH level of about 5.6. When air pollutants such as nitrogen oxides and sulfur oxides react with water, sulfuric and nitric acids are produced, making the pH drop below 5.6. Thus, the precipitation becomes more acidic and is called acid rain.

Acid precipitation can have negative effects on soil. As pH decreases, reactions occur that cause metal ions to be released into the soil. These ions prevent plants from absorbing calcium, a nutrient that enhances plant growth and development. Aluminum can leach out of the soil and be carried to bodies of water. This can cause the deaths of fish and fish eggs.

Aquatic animals are adapted to live in an environment with a particular pH range. If acid precipitation falls on a lake and changes the water's pH, acid can kill fish and other aquatic animals. The effects of acid precipitation are worst in the spring, when acidic snow that accumulated during the winter melts and rushes into lakes and other bodies of water.

Human Health

Climate change can affect human health in a variety of ways. Pollution threatens air and water quality, and even the quality of some food resources such as fish. Changes in weather can alter environmental landscapes and the communities where people live.

 Engineering

Biomass and Human Health

It is estimated that about a third of the world's population burns wood or other biomass for heating and cooking. This produces carbon dioxide that pollutes indoor air, which can cause respiratory disease. But in many countries around the world, other sources of energy are not easily accessible. Cleaner, more efficient stoves are needed to reduce these impacts on the environment and human health.

 Evidence Notebook Research some of the current solutions being proposed to fix this problem. Make a list of the proposed solutions, and evaluate each based on how well it addresses the problem.

ASK Come up with at least two specific questions about climate change and human health that could be answered through scientific research.

_____

_____

_____

 Evidence Notebook Over a long period, how might living things adapt to increased carbon dioxide levels and global warming?

Data Analysis

Is Your Diet Efficient?

A carbon footprint is the estimated total amount of carbon released into the atmxosphere by any entity that produces carbon dioxide. Have you ever considered how much carbon dioxide is released during the production of the things you eat? Record everything you eat and drink for three days and enter your meals into an online tracker to determine the nutritional content of your diet. Find an online food carbon calculator to calculate the carbon footprint of your diet. Conduct research using credible online or library sources to find ways to modify your diet to meet your nutrient needs and minimize your carbon footprint.

FIGURE 20: How do our dietary choices affect the environment?

EXPLAIN How can you alter your diet to reduce your carbon footprint but maintain a healthy diet? Calculate the change in carbon footprint for at least three actions.

_____

_____

_____

_____

APPLY What compromises could you make to reduce your carbon footprint but still possibly eat the things you like?

_____

_____

_____

 Language Arts Connection Gather evidence to make an informational pamphlet that describes the differences between a meat-based diet and a vegetarian diet. Consider the following while conducting your research:

• What can you conclude about the relative energy efficiency when comparing diet options? Describe the resources necessary to maintain the average U.S. meat-based diet and the average vegetarian diet.

• Include an energy pyramid that represents a meat-based diet and another that represents a plant-based diet.

• Would there be an environmental benefit for a large population of humans to follow a vegetarian diet as opposed to a meat-based diet?

• What effort would be necessary to convince people to switch from a meat-based diet in a large enough number that it would greatly reduce the carbon footprint in the ecosystem in which the people lived?

| POLLUTION AND HUMAN HEALTH | DESIGNING CLIMATE CHANGE SOLUTIONS | CLIMATE EFFECT ON PIKAS | Go online to choose one of these other paths. |

Lesson Self-Check

CAN YOU EXPLAIN IT?

FIGURE 21: Rising sea levels and a decline in polar sea ice over time are two pieces of evidence that support the concept of climate change.

 a Coastal communities in California are vulnerable to climate change.

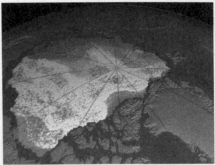

b Arctic sea ice in September 1984

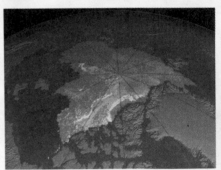

c Arctic sea ice in September 2016

While both natural forces and human activity can impact climate, substantial scientific evidence shows that modern-day climate change is primarily caused by human activity. The burning of fossil fuels for energy increases the amount of greenhouse gases in the atmosphere. Over time, this has led to a steady rise in global temperatures. Some evidence for climate change is rising sea levels and a decline in polar sea ice over time.

Evidence Notebook Refer to your notes in your Evidence Notebook to explain how rising sea levels affect the coastline and beaches of California. Your explanation should include a discussion of how human activity affects the natural cycles that control climate.

1. Make a claim about the effect of global climate change on the California coastline and beaches.
2. Based on evidence that you have gathered, make a feedback loop to explain the relationship between atmospheric CO_2, sea ice melt, and coastal erosion.
3. How can this evidence be used to design solutions to protect the California coastline and beaches?

CHECKPOINTS

Check Your Understanding

1. Which of the following statements about studying climate change is true?
   - ○ **a.** With modern technology, it is possible to measure climate change almost instantly.
   - ○ **b.** Air bubbles trapped in ice cores help scientists estimate the temperature of the air hundreds of thousands of years ago.
   - ○ **c.** Most fossils do not provide any information about past climates.
   - ○ **d.** Satellites are useful for studying weather but not climate.

2. Select the correct terms to complete the statement about feedback mechanisms and climate change.

   Scientists are most concerned about positive | negative | neutral feedback effects of climate change that will intensify or increase the rate of rising temperatures. A positive | negative | neutral feedback effect for climate change will minimize or slow down the rate of rising temperatures.

3. Which statement bests explains how greenhouse gases in the atmosphere affect global temperatures?
   - ○ **a.** Greenhouse gases reflect infrared energy into space.
   - ○ **b.** Greenhouse gases absorb infrared energy that is heading back into space.
   - ○ **c.** Greenhouse gases reduce infrared energy that is sent back to Earth's surface.
   - ○ **d.** Greenhouse gases ensure that all the sun's infrared energy reaches the Earth's surface.

4. Select the correct terms to complete the statement about the potential effects of climate change.

   Climate change is expected to increase | decrease the intensity of hurricanes. This will occur because there will be more | less | no energy stored as heat in the oceans. Rising global temperatures will also lead to an increase | decrease in sea levels around the world. This change in sea levels will likely increase | decrease the rate of erosion along California beaches.

5. Use the correct terms to complete the table to explain the convection of ocean water between the poles and the equator.

denser	less dense	warm
cold	sinking	rising

	Water At Equator	Water At Poles
Density	_____	_____
Temperature	_____	_____
Movement of Water	_____	_____

6. Which of the following is an accurate description of Earth's global climate? Select all correct answers.
   - ☐ **a.** 100 cm average annual precipitation
   - ☐ **b.** 15 °C and sunny
   - ☐ **c.** average annual temperature of 15 °C
   - ☐ **d.** average annual temperature of -18 °C
   - ☐ **e.** average weather conditions over the entire Earth over many years

CHECKPOINTS (continued)

7. California has some of the most productive farm regions in the world because its farmers are capable of growing a wide assortment of fruits and vegetables. Explain one threat that rising global temperatures could have on the productivity of California agriculture.

_____

_____

_____

_____

8. What is a greenhouse gas? What are the main greenhouse gases in Earth's atmosphere? How are they related to climate change?

_____

_____

_____

_____

9. Briefly explain how changes in technology and changes in human activity can affect climate change. Give a specific example to support your claim.

_____

_____

_____

_____

_____

_____

MAKE YOUR OWN STUDY GUIDE

In your Evidence Notebook, design a study guide that supports the main ideas from this lesson:

Global climate is affected by several interacting factors, including Earth's motion in space, solar output, continental motion, and atmospheric composition.

Earth's climate changes on various scales of time and space.

Earth's current climate change is thought to be a result of an increase in greenhouse gas concentration caused by human activities.

Remember to include the following information in your study guide:
- Use examples that model main ideas.
- Record explanations for the phenomena you investigated.
- Use evidence to support your explanations. Your support can include drawings, data, graphs, laboratory conclusions, and other evidence recorded throughout the lesson.

Consider how trends in climate change data can be used to analyze stability and change in Earth's systems.

Human Impacts on Biodiversity

These monarch butterflies have migrated to Santa Cruz, California for the winter.

CAN YOU SOLVE IT?

Those aren't flowers on this tree—they are orange-and-black monarch butterflies. During the summer months, monarch butterfly populations are found throughout the United States. But in the fall, millions of monarchs travel thousands of miles to gather at wintering grounds in Mexico and California. During their migration, monarchs depend on milkweed and other flowering plants for nectar. Milkweed is also critical for monarch reproduction. When monarchs arrive at their wintering grounds, they depend on trees such as eucalyptus, cypress, and fir for shelter. The butterflies also need particular climate conditions, so they won't freeze. Unfortunately, the needs of monarchs during their life cycle are being threatened by various human activities.

PREDICT How do human activities affect monarch butterfly populations? How might this problem be solved?

FIGURE 1: Forests at this monarch wintering ground in Mexico have been cleared to make farmland.

Evidence Notebook As you explore this lesson, gather evidence to explain the impact of human activity on biodiversity, and what can be done to reduce this impact.

Human Population Growth

The human population has changed over time as a result of many factors. Increased use of natural resources, along with improvements in areas such as transportation, agriculture, health, and sanitation, has allowed the human population to grow.

 Data Analysis

Analyzing Human Population Growth

This graph shows how the human population has changed over time. Although humans existed long before 1750, we will focus on more recent data for this analysis.

Human Population Growth Projected to 2050

FIGURE 2: This graph shows that human population has grown over time.

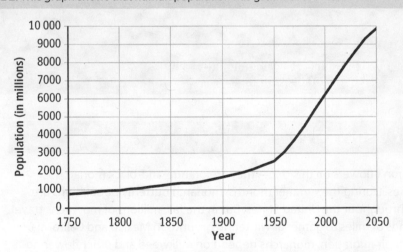

Credit: Adapted from World Population Prospects 2017 by United Nations, Population Division. Copyright © 2017 by United Nations. Adapted and reproduced by permission of the United Nations.
Credit: Adapted from Historical Population data by Netherlands Environmental Assessment Agency. Copyright © 2018 by Netherlands Environmental Assessment Agency. Adapted and reproduced by permission of Netherlands Environmental Assessment Agency.

ANALYZE What type of growth is the human population experiencing? Explain.

_____

_____

EXPLAIN What are some of the factors that allowed the human population to grow this way?

_____

_____

_____

_____

Earth's Carrying Capacity

As the human population continues to grow, we might ask the following questions: Will the human population ever start shrinking? Will there ever be a time when Earth is not able to support human life? Human use of Earth's resources has changed the planet's environment in many ways. Some of these changes support the growth of the human population on Earth. In other words, human activities overall have increased Earth's carrying capacity for humans.

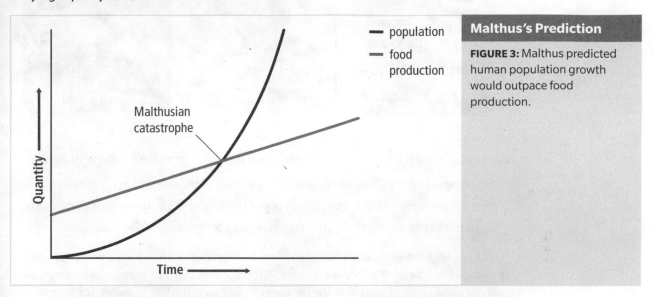

— population
— food production

Malthus's Prediction

FIGURE 3: Malthus predicted human population growth would outpace food production.

What is Earth's carrying capacity, or maximum number, for humans? This value can only be estimated, because human population growth is affected by so many factors. In the late 1700s, Thomas Malthus wrote in a controversial essay that the human population was growing faster than Earth's resources could support. Furthermore, he said that if the human population continued to grow unchecked, poverty and famine would result. According to Malthus, these would be natural ways to halt human population growth.

INFER Which of the following factors did Malthus not account for when he wrote his essay about human population growth? Consider what changes have occurred since the 1700s that have allowed the human population to avoid a "Malthusian catastrophe." Select all correct answers.

☐ **a.** improved sanitation

☐ **b.** development of vaccines

☐ **c.** increased crop productivity

☐ **d.** increased antibiotic resistance

☐ **e.** increased number of droughts

Factors That Affect Population Growth

Malthus did not consider that the carrying capacity of an environment can change as the environment changes. In modern times, the environment has changed due to technological advancements, such as industrial farming equipment, pesticides, and genetic modifications of crops. Food that is grown more efficiently and abundantly can support a larger population. Improvements in sanitation have reduced disease rates. These improvements in drinking water quality and food safety have reduced the number of people who die from water- or foodborne diseases such as cholera and salmonella. Advances in medicine have also greatly increased the human lifespan.

FIGURE 4: Better sanitation practices have allowed the human population to grow.

EXPLAIN Select the correct terms to complete the statement about hand-washing.

Washing your hands causes | prevents the spread of disease and may contribute to the decrease | increase in the human population. Washing your hands is particularly important after eating | using the restroom and before cooking | going to bed.

It was not until the mid-1800s that physicians began to wash their hands before surgery to reduce the spread of infectious disease. Although this concept seems obvious now, it was not so obvious to people at the time—even doctors. The link between the spread of disease-causing agents and sanitation was less clear. Many years passed before this idea was fully accepted. When it was, it revolutionized health and medicine.

New technologies and new knowledge about human health and disease have allowed the human population to grow exponentially. In 2011, the global human population reached the 7 billion mark. Just six years later, it was estimated to be around 7.6 billion. At the current rate of growth, scientists predict that the population will be around 9.5 billion in 2050. Poverty and famine, due to changing climate and political factors, may cause that rate to slow, however.

Language Arts Connection Research the following question: How might changes in society, science, and economics influence the future growth rate of the human population? There are many opinions and a variety of informational text related to this question. As you do your research be sure to:

- Use specific examples to support your claim and reasoning.
- Gather your information from relevant and credible sources. Cite your sources as directed by your teacher or following the ELA Handbook.
- Use your own words to summarize your research, drawing from multiple sources.
- Revise your summary as needed, using only relevant evidence to focus on your claim and reasoning.

Present your findings to the class. Your poster should include a summary of your research as well as graphics, such as graphs or illustrations, that support your findings.

Evidence Notebook How could human population growth affect North American ecosystems? How could a change in these habitats affect monarch butterfly populations?

Habitat Loss

Earth is currently experiencing a significant loss of biodiversity that is increasingly being recognized as the sixth mass extinction. Habitat loss is the most common cause of the decline and extinction of species. Human development activities such as agriculture, deforestation, and urbanization, all lead to habitat loss and fragmentation.

ANALYZE How can agricultural practices lead to a decrease in biodiversity? Include an explanation of how agricultural practices affect ecosystem function in your answer.

_____

_____

_____

_____

FIGURE 5: Habitat loss threatens orangutan survival.

Clearing Land

The island of Borneo, located in southeast Asia, was once widely covered by lowland and mountainous rain forests. Today the island is losing rain forest habitat at an unsustainable rate due to logging, fires, and land clearing for commercial crops. One such crop is oil palms.

Palm oil is made from the fruits of the oil palm. It is the most used vegetable oil on the planet and is found in products ranging from cosmetics to packaged foods. The market for palm oil is growing quickly even as the negative effects of palm plantations reach a critical level.

The biggest threat to biodiversity on Borneo is habitat loss. Species such as the Bornean orangutan need rain forest habitat

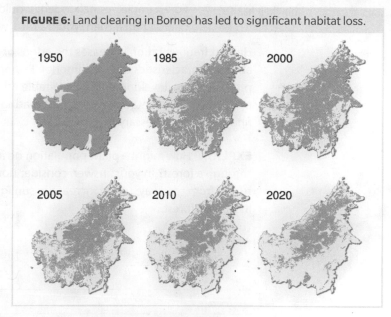

FIGURE 6: Land clearing in Borneo has led to significant habitat loss.

1950   1985   2000

2005   2010   2020

to survive and are therefore particularly sensitive to habitat loss. The number of Bornean orangutans has decreased by over 60% since 1950. Figure 6 shows the change in forest cover in Borneo since 1950. It is expected that this habitat loss will continue into the near future. Conservation scientists estimate that if the current rate of deforestation continues, the total forest cover in Borneo will be reduced to only 24% by 2020. Poaching also threatens orangutans' survival. The Bornean orangutan is critically endangered and may become extinct if enough suitable habitat is not preserved. This species has reached the point that is known as an extinction threshold. If habitat loss continues, the population of Bornean orangutans will not be able to recover, and they will become extinct.

Habitat Fragmentation

FIGURE 7: Roads cause habitat fragmentation.

Habitat is fragmented as land is cleared for human developments. Habitat fragmentation occurs when a barrier, such as a road or cleared landscape, divides a larger habitat into smaller sections, preventing individuals or populations of species from accessing their full home ranges. Roads, such as the one shown in Figure 7, form a physical barrier to dispersal for many species. Agriculture and urban sprawl are also barriers to dispersal, as they are not welcoming habitats for many species.

ANALYZE Which of these human activities is likely to cause habitat fragmentation? Select all correct answers.

- ☐ **a.** planting of pollinator habitats
- ☐ **b.** deforestation of mountain slopes
- ☐ **c.** preservation of habitat in a nature reserve
- ☐ **d.** construction of a high speed railway system
- ☐ **e.** an increase in coffee plantations

Explore Online ▶

Hands-On Activity

Modeling Habitat Fragmentation Explore how building a shopping center affects animal species within their habitat.

Habitat fragmentation is a process that decreases suitable habitat for living organisms. This decrease in habitat, in turn, leads to a decrease in carrying capacity for most species. Some species may become locally extinct if a habitat patch is not large enough to support a breeding population. Fragmentation also isolates smaller patches of habitat, which can prevent immigration and gene flow depending on the degree of isolation and the species involved. For example, a small rodent would have a harder time moving to an isolated habitat patch than would a bird, which can fly from one place to another.

Habitat fragmentation increases the edges of a habitat, which have different biotic and abiotic characteristics than the interior. Examples of edge effects include increased predation, the development of unsuitable microclimates, and greater exposure to pollutants. Fragmentation can disrupt mating and breeding patterns or make it difficult to find resources necessary for survival.

EXPLAIN How might a plant population be affected by the construction of a road through a forest? In your answer, consider how things such as pollution from automobiles, runoff from roadways, or an increase in sunlight might affect the plant populations that live in the forest.

_____

_____

_____

_____

_____

_____

_____

_____

Building Wildlife Corridors

FIGURE 8: These wildlife corridors reduce habitat fragmentation.

a Highway overpass   b Highway underpass   c Canal overpass

Wildlife corridors connect isolated patches of habitat. The goal of a wildlife corridor is to help individuals move freely throughout their entire range. This movement helps to maintain gene flow and genetic diversity between populations of a species.

Wildlife corridors can be natural, such as riparian corridors along river systems that link populations of species that live in isolated wetlands. They can also be artificial, such as the construction of highway underpasses or overpasses that let wildlife safely cross the roadways that fragment their habitat. A canal overpass allows aquatic animals to move over a barrier. Fish ladders let fish navigate past barriers in a waterway, such as dams or waterfalls. Each artificial crossing must be carefully designed, with the specific situation and animals in mind.

Every year, monarch butterflies migrate between Canada and Mexico. These butterflies depend on nectar from wildflowers to sustain them on their long journey. Milkweed is an important food source for monarch butterfly larvae. Monarch butterflies depend on nectar corridors, or a series of habitat patches that contain plants that flower during the spring and fall monarch butterfly migration. It is particularly important that these patches be protected within urban and agricultural zones that are vulnerable to development. Habitat destruction and the use of agricultural chemicals can threaten these patches.

Developing wildlife crossings requires an understanding of both engineering and conservation. Some of the criteria include the needs of people, the logistics of building the crossing, and the habitat and behavior of the animals targeted for the crossing. Each crossing is unique. The problem that each crossing is trying to solve should be looked at from different perspectives.

PLAN Why is cooperation between public agencies and private landowners important when selecting the path of a wildlife corridor?

_____

_____

_____

_____

_____

_____

Habitat Management

FIGURE 9: President Theodore Roosevelt (left) and naturalist John Muir (right), shown here in California's Yosemite National Park, advocated for the preservation of wild spaces.

Resources are often overexploited for economic reasons. In contrast, sustainable development uses natural resources in a way that meets current needs without causing permanent damage. Widespread adoption of sustainable development depends on convincing people that nature has a cultural and aesthetic value as well as an economic one.

Collaborate With a partner, make a list of three locations in your city or state that protect habitat.

Setting aside areas of public land to be preserved in a natural state is one way that governments can protect ecosystems. The Yosemite Grant of 1864 was the first federal legislation in the United States aimed at protecting nature from development. The bill designated Yosemite Valley and the Mariposa Grove of sequoia trees as protected wilderness areas. Yellowstone National Park was established as the country's first national park in 1872. The writings of naturalist John Muir were influential in convincing Americans that nature was worth protecting, in part because of its inspirational value. The next step in the preservation of U.S. public lands was the Antiquities Act of 1906, signed by President Theodore Roosevelt. It let presidents designate historic landmarks, structures, and other objects of interest as national monuments. In 1916, the National Park Service (NPS) was established with the mandate to preserve and protect natural environments for the enjoyment of future generations. Now, more than 100 years later, the NPS oversees 59 national parks and many other areas of natural and historical significance.

Today, federal conservation and management of public lands includes rangelands managed by the Bureau of Land Management, forests managed by the U.S. Forest Service, and wildlife refuges managed by the U.S. Fish and Wildlife Service. State, regional, and city governments also protect natural lands through parks and nature preserves. Many protected areas are managed with the dual purpose of human recreation and conservation of natural habitat.

ARGUE Construct an argument to convince an elected official that protecting wild spaces is important.

_____

_____

_____

_____

_____

 Evidence Notebook How could habitat management protect migrating and overwintering monarch butterflies?

Introduced Species

A native species is one that lives in its historical range. Non-native species, also called introduced species, are species that have been introduced into new areas that have not historically been part of their native range. Introduced species are commonly brought to an ecosystem as a result of human activity.

Introduced and Invasive Species

FIGURE 10: Since their introduction in the 1980s, zebra and quagga mussels have spread to more than 30 states.

Explore Online ▶

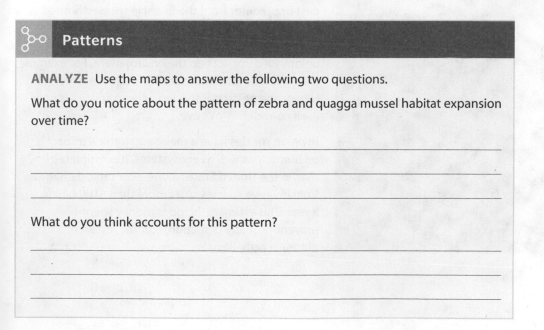

1986

2016

⸽⚬ Patterns

ANALYZE Use the maps to answer the following two questions.

What do you notice about the pattern of zebra and quagga mussel habitat expansion over time?

_____

_____

_____

What do you think accounts for this pattern?

_____

_____

_____

Over human history, people have relocated many species around the world. Some introductions were accidental, such as the release of rodents into many island ecosystems from ships. Other introductions were deliberate. For example, in the late 19th century, a group determined to bring every species mentioned by the English playwright William Shakespeare into the United States successfully released European starlings in New York. Starlings are now found across the country.

FIGURE 11: Zebra mussels attach to mollusks and can kill them. They can also clog water intake pipes.

When an introduced species causes economic or environmental harm or poses a threat to human health, it is called an invasive species. These species can act as predators, cause disease, or outcompete native species. The zebra mussel and the quagga mussel are examples of invasive species. The zebra mussel is native to Russia, and the quagga mussel is native to Ukraine. It is suspected that these invasive mussels were introduced into the Great Lakes from the wastewater of transatlantic cargo ships in the 1980s. Not long after, the invasive mussels spread into nearby river drainages. Today, more than 30 states have invasive mussel infestations. The mussels compete with native mollusks for food and decrease phytoplankton and zooplankton populations in habitats they invade. They may also attach to native mollusks in numbers that are large enough to kill them.

Invasive Species Management

Physical removal, chemical herbicides, burning, and grazing are all methods that can be used to control invasive plants. For animals, physical removal through hunting, fishing, or trapping may be effective. Many successful programs for invasive species management combine several different methods.

FIGURE 12: Park volunteers remove invasive garlic mustard.

Biological controls are a particularly useful option for invasive plants. A biological control agent is a pest or predator from the invasive species' home range. Potential biological controls must be studied extensively before they are introduced to prevent unintended impacts on the environment. For example, the cane toad was introduced in Australia to control sugar cane pests, but this introduced species is now itself considered invasive.

Invasive species have a major economical impact on humans as well as ecosystems. It is estimated that, in the United States alone, economic damage from invasive species costs more than $100 billion a year. This estimate includes money spent on prevention, early detection, control, research, and outreach activities.

 Evidence Notebook What types of invasive species could threaten monarch butterfly populations during their migration?

Overharvesting Species

Humans use many plant and animal species for food, clothing, medicine, and other purposes. In this context, plants and animals are considered natural resources. Overharvesting occurs when individual organisms are removed from an ecosystem faster than a population can replace them. The American bison is one such example.

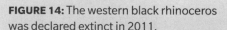

FIGURE 13: American bison were hunted to the verge of extinction in the mid-1800s.

Figure 13 shows a massive pile of American bison skulls. While Native American populations used the bison as a source of food and clothing, the arrival of the transcontinental railroad in the 1860s led to the popularization of hunting bison for sport by travelers from the East Coast. The species was hunted nearly to extinction. It was only saved by the establishment of Yellowstone National Park in 1872, which was at the time home to the last surviving herd of bison.

Overhunting

Hunting, trapping, and collecting can be used to manage a population of animals. However, if more individuals are continually removed from a population than can be replaced by normal population growth, the population will decline and eventually become extinct. Overhunting impacts biodiversity in two ways. If extinction occurs, species richness—the number of species present in a given area—will decrease. Reducing the population of any species to very small numbers reduces genetic diversity of that species and may cause a genetic bottleneck. Species richness and genetic diversity are measurements of biodiversity. Decreases in these two values will lead to a decrease in biodiversity.

FIGURE 14: The western black rhinoceros was declared extinct in 2011.

APPLY Which components of biodiversity are negatively impacted by overhunting? Select all correct answers.

☐ **a.** speciation

☐ **b.** genetic diversity

☐ **c.** number of individuals

☐ **d.** extinction

☐ **e.** species richness

The western black rhinoceros was one of four subspecies of black rhinoceroses that once ranged across central and western Africa. Three factors led to the demise of this subspecies. First, sport hunting decimated many populations in the early 20th century. Second, the clearing of land for agriculture destroyed rhinoceros habitat. Third, the rise in popularity of traditional Chinese medicine in the 1950s, in which powdered rhinoceros horn plays a major part, led to a massive increase in poaching. By the early 1990s, less than 2% of the original population of black rhinoceroses was left in the wild. The last remaining western black rhinoceroses—just five of them—were observed in 2001. A decade later, with no further observations, the International Union for Conservation of Nature formally declared the western black rhinoceros extinct.

Data Analysis

Californian Sardine Fishery Collapse

FIGURE 15: Overfishing has affected the California sardine industry.

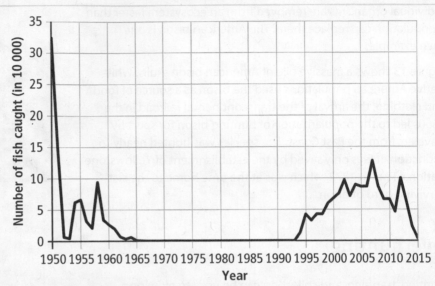

Credit: Adapted from Global Capture Production database, http://www.fao.org/fishery/statistics/global-capture-production/en. Copyright © 2018 by Food and Agriculture Organization of the United Nations. Adapted and reproduced by permission of Food and Agriculture Organization of the United Nations. Reproduced with permission.

The California pilchard (*Sardinops caeruleus*) is a type of sardine fish. Populations span from southern Alaska to Baja California. Historically, California pilchard schools have been known to contain up to 10 million individuals. These small, oily fish are canned and used as food. The California pilchard fishery produced hundreds of thousands of tons of sardines each year in the early to mid-20th century. The fishery collapsed in the 1960s. Fishing California pilchard was banned in the U.S. until the mid-1990s. The graph shows population trends before and after this ban.

ANALYZE What has been the largest annual catch since the fishery collapsed?

_____

_____

INFER What factors may have led to the apparent collapse of the fishery in 2015?

_____

_____

ARGUE What actions would you recommend for the California pilchard fishery at this point in time and why?

_____

_____

Overfishing

Fishing is defined as the harvesting of aquatic species. Fisheries can be overharvested if more individuals are removed than the population can produce. In other words, the reproduction rates of a fishery must be equal to or higher than the harvesting rates, or overharvesting will occur. Overharvesting can cause the collapse of a fishery if it is widespread and populations are harvested to the point of extremely low numbers, particularly in terms of females. If fisheries continue to be harvested after a collapse, the harvested species could become extinct.

In California, 34 species and subspecies of fish have been identified as threatened or endangered. These include many subspecies of salmon, steelhead, and trout, which are significant food and sport fish. Oceanic fisheries are particularly vulnerable to overharvesting because no single nation owns the open oceans. To maintain sustainable fisheries, countries must cooperate together to ensure that populations are not overharvested. Some countries may prefer to act on their own, and there are few laws to stop them. These countries may experience short-term economic benefits, but at a long-term cost to fish species.

Sustainable Hunting and Fishing Practices

Humans have found solutions to overharvesting, such as sustainable fishing practices. Many fisheries now have regulations for catch size, season length, and the type of equipment that can be used for fishing. These regulations aim to keep fish populations at sustainable levels, while also providing a food source that humans depend on. Regulations also help reduce *bycatch*, which refers to any species captured during commercial fishing that is not the target species. Bycatch is a threat to many vulnerable species, such as sea turtles and dolphins. For example, fine-meshed nets used for catching shrimp now must be equipped with turtle excluder devices. The devices prevent turtles and other large species from becoming trapped in the nets.

EVALUATE Which of the following statements explains how a sustainable fishing method can help protect fish populations and aquatic biodiversity? Select all correct answers.

☐ **a.** Regulating catch size can protect genetic diversity.

☐ **b.** Regulating types of nets used can protect non-fish species.

☐ **c.** Regulating season length can change the timing of reproduction.

☐ **d.** Regulating size of fish that can be kept can protect fish that are reproducing.

Similar to fishing, wildlife managers regulate hunting seasons, the age and sex of animals that can be hunted, and the equipment that can be used. Money collected from hunting licenses and stamps is often used to improve habitat for the species being hunted. In this way, hunters can help to increase populations.

 Evidence Notebook What type of overexploitation is likely to affect overwintering monarch butterflies?

Expansion and Extinction of Species

Natural environmental changes, such as droughts, can lead to the expansion of a species' range. For example, a long-lasting drought can change an ecosystem to make it more suitable for plants adapted to dry conditions. These plants could expand into the ecosystem and outcompete plants that are not as well adapted to the dry conditions. Humans can also cause environmental changes that lead to the expansion of species.

Climate Change and Species Expansion

FIGURE 16: Grizzly bears have expanded their range into polar bear habitat.

Climate change is affecting different areas on Earth in different ways, from rising water levels in the oceans to an increase in summer temperatures in Australia. As areas warm, they may become more suitable for organisms that were previously kept out due to uninviting habitat conditions.

EXPLAIN How can climate change lead to an expansion of a species?

_____

_____

_____

Polar bear habitat in northern Canada was once too cold and inaccessible for grizzly bears. As this area has warmed, it has become more suitable habitat for the bears. Because of these new environmental changes, grizzlies have expanded their range into polar bear habitat. This movement could lead to a wider expansion of grizzly bear populations in the long term.

The expansion of species into new territories can lead to hybridization. Hybridization occurs when two distinct, but closely related, species are able to successfully mate. Sometimes, the features shown by the hybridized species fall within the range of characteristics shown by one or both of the original populations. Over time, as the two species continue to interact with one another, they may become a single species.

In the case of grizzly bears, as climate change lets them expand their territories northward, they are interacting more and more with polar bears. Because both bear species are closely related, they are able to successfully mate and produce viable offspring. Some scientists worry that this inbreeding may result in the disappearance of the polar bear as a separate species, particularly as it is already being threatened by habitat loss due to climate change.

Territory Expansion

Historically, the barred owl lived in the eastern United States. The Great Plains served as a barrier to the westward expansion of many species that lived in forests, including the barred owl. The Great Plains were maintained in part due to regular burning by Native Americans and the disturbance caused by massive herds of bison. Much has changed in these ecosystems over the past 150 years. The plains are no longer burned, herds of bison no longer shape the landscape, wildfires are put out, and the climate has warmed.

These environmental changes are a potential cause for the barred owl range expansion across British Columbia in Canada and into Washington, Oregon, and Northern California in the Pacific Northwest region of the United States. The warming climate could have made Canada's northern boreal forests more suitable for the barred owl. The owls may have used this habitat as a bridge to reach the Pacific Northwest. Another possibility is that the barred owl worked its way across the plains as settlers planted trees and encouraged tree growth along streams. The owls could have used these intermediate habitats to journey from eastern forests to western forests.

 Collaborate Consider the two possible ways that the barred owl made it to the Pacific Northwest from the eastern United States. Decide which way you think was more likely, and discuss your ideas with a partner. Use evidence in the text and the map below to support your conclusion.

The territory expansion has been good for the barred owl, as evidenced by its increasing success and growing population numbers. Unfortunately, the appearance of the barred owl in the forests of the Pacific Northwest has negatively affected a closely related species—the northern spotted owl. This bird is listed as a threatened species under the Endangered Species Act. Historically, the northern spotted owl has been most threatened by habitat loss due to logging, land development, and natural disasters. Now the small amount of northern spotted owl habitat that remains is being invaded by the barred owl.

FIGURE 17: The northern spotted owl is being displaced by the larger barred owl.

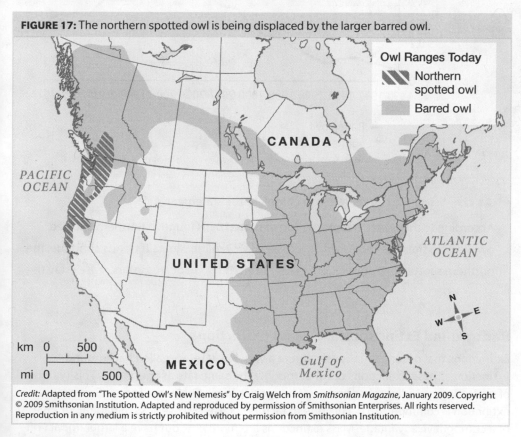

Credit: Adapted from "The Spotted Owl's New Nemesis" by Craig Welch from *Smithsonian Magazine*, January 2009. Copyright © 2009 Smithsonian Institution. Adapted and reproduced by permission of Smithsonian Enterprises. All rights reserved. Reproduction in any medium is strictly prohibited without permission from Smithsonian Institution.

INFER Barred owls and northern spotted owls use old-growth forests for food and nesting. Which of the following characteristics of the barred owl would give it a competitive advantage over the northern spotted owl? Select all correct answers.

☐ **a.** larger body

☐ **b.** aggressive behavior

☐ **c.** ability to roost in trees

☐ **d.** better breeding success

☐ **e.** ability to eat a wide range of prey

Extinction

Just as birth and death are natural events in the life of an individual, the rise and fall of species are natural processes of evolution. The elimination of a species from Earth is called extinction. Extinction often occurs when a species as a whole cannot adapt to a change in its environment. Extinctions have occurred throughout time, as shown in the fossil record. Natural events such as droughts and floods can cause extinctions if species are unable to adapt to the new environment.

Northern Spotted Owl and Barred Owl Population Changes

FIGURE 18: The graph shows the proportion of spotted owl nesting sites in which barred owls and northern spotted owls were detected.

a Northern spotted owl

b Barred owl

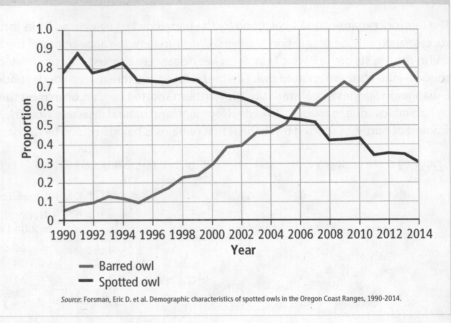

Source: Forsman, Eric D. et al. Demographic characteristics of spotted owls in the Oregon Coast Ranges, 1990-2014.

ANALYZE Select the correct terms to complete the statement.

According to the graph, the proportion of barred owls found in northern spotted owl nesting sites has increased | decreased | stayed the same. If trends continue, the northern spotted owl population is likely to continue to decrease | increase | stay the same.

Background Extinctions and Mass Extinctions

Extinctions that occur continuously, but at a very low rate, are called background extinctions. These extinctions occur at roughly the same rate as speciation. This type of extinction typically affects one or a few species in relatively small areas. Background extinction is common and occurs due to factors such as disease, loss of habitat, or loss of a competitive advantage. Mass extinctions are more rare, but have a larger impact on Earth's biodiversity. Entire orders or families may be wiped out by mass extinction events.

Mass extinctions are thought to occur suddenly in geologic time, usually because of a catastrophic event such as an ice age or asteroid impact. An example of a mass extinction is the K-T event that occurred at the end of the Cretaceous period 65 million years ago, when a large meteor crashed onto Earth. This meteor strike caused the extinction of 70% of Earth's species. The fossil record confirms that there have been at least five mass extinctions in the past 600 million years.

Comparing Extinction Rates

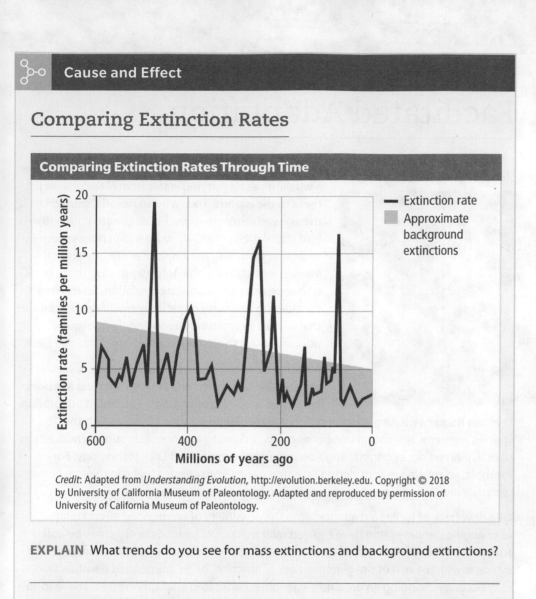

Comparing Extinction Rates Through Time

Credit: Adapted from *Understanding Evolution*, http://evolution.berkeley.edu. Copyright © 2018 by University of California Museum of Paleontology. Adapted and reproduced by permission of University of California Museum of Paleontology.

EXPLAIN What trends do you see for mass extinctions and background extinctions?

_____

_____

_____

_____

Preventing the Extinction of Species

Both the U.S. Fish and Wildlife Service and the National Oceanic and Atmospheric Administration manage the species listed under the Endangered Species Act (ESA) of 1973. The ESA is designed to protect individual species that are near extinction by providing protection for the species and its habitat. Protection under the ESA comes in many forms, including habitat conservation and captive breeding programs. The ESA recognizes the ecological, historical, educational, aesthetic, and scientific value of threatened species.

When a single species within an ecosystem is placed on a list of endangered species, other species within the ecosystem may benefit as well. For example, when the northern spotted owl was listed as threatened in 1990, logging practices in the owls' habitat were changed to leave more old-growth forest. The northern spotted owls benefited from the conservation of habitat, as did all plant, animal, fungal, and microbial organisms living in the same habitat.

Facilitated Adaptation

FIGURE 19: The 'i'wi is going extinct in Hawaii.

Hawaii had no mosquitoes until the early 1800s, when a whaling vessel carrying water from Mexico brought them to the islands. Today, avian malaria, carried by these invasive mosquitoes, has decimated the native bird population. The 'i'iwi, or Hawaiian honeycreeper, and other birds native to Hawaii are going extinct. Many scientists think the only way to save these birds is to wipe out the mosquito population. Scientists are considering releasing genetically modified mosquitoes that will die prematurely, reducing the mosquito population and hopefully saving Hawaii's native birds.

For species threatened by climate change or low genetic diversity, scientists are investigating a process known as *facilitated adaptation*. Facilitated adaptation involves humans guiding adaptations in threatened populations by changing the species' genome. Advantageous genes can be added to a genome through hybridization, selective breeding, or genetic engineering using recombinant DNA technology. For example, scientists are considering inserting genes from species that can tolerate higher temperatures into different species suffering from global warming.

One drawback of facilitated adaptation is the possibility of unintended effects related to changing genomes that have evolved over millions of years. Scientists may be able to identify the main function of a gene, but they cannot determine all the ways a gene interacts with the rest of the genome. Loss of function, or an unintended new function, may occur by changing an organism's genome. Facilitated adaptation could also lead to an unintended loss of genetic diversity. If the genetically engineered individuals are much more successful than normal individuals, that single gene could become widespread in the population.

ARGUE What role could genetic engineering play in solving the problem of extinction? Use evidence to support your claims.

_____

_____

_____

EVALUATE What are the tradeoffs related to facilitated adaptation? What criteria would you evaluate to determine if these tradeoffs are worth the risk?

_____

_____

_____

 Evidence Notebook How could listing the monarch butterfly as threatened under the Endangered Species Act help it to survive?

Language Arts

Rethinking the Value of Non-native Species

There is a distinct bias against non-native species in both scientific and public communities. In some ways, this means scientists have effectively educated the public about the dangers of invasive species.

This distrust of non-native species seems to be well-founded. Managers dealing with kudzu or zebra mussel infestations can give firsthand accounts about how destructive invasive species can be. Many scientists think that it is both fair and necessary to be critical of non-native species. Invasive non-native species take over landscapes and often outcompete other species for precious resources.

The harm caused by invasive species is not always immediate. A wait-and-see approach will not always work, as a once-harmless species can quickly turn into an invasive nightmare. For example, the Brazilian pepper tree was introduced to the United States as an ornamental plant and originally did not seem to be invasive. Today, it is an invasive threat to mangrove communities in Florida.

However, some scientists have begun to challenge the "native or bust" ideals that dominate current science. They quickly point out that some non-native species provide important ecosystem services. For example, honey bees are not native to North America. They were introduced by early European settlers in 1622. Today they are invaluable pollinators of crops and producers of honey.

Non-native plants often provide habitat for native species. Salt cedar, introduced to control erosion, is particularly invasive in the southwestern United States but has become a critical nesting habitat for the endangered southwestern willow flycatcher. An attempt to remove salt cedar populations was accompanied by a decline in the flycatcher population.

Other issues to consider in the debate are how the term *native* is defined and what should happen to non-

FIGURE 20: Non-native honey bees pollinate many flowering plants, including important agricultural crops.

native species that are now threatened in their home ranges. Native defines a species' home range during a certain period of time. Most species were non-native at some point, meaning they arrived in their current home ranges from elsewhere. Further confusing the difference between native and non-native species is that climate change is causing species to move into new ranges on their own.

Cold-adapted species are moving to higher elevations for more suitable temperature ranges. Warm-adapted species are expanding their ranges as they move into previously unsuitable habitat. Climate change, habitat loss, and other human impacts can mean that a non-native species may be threatened in its home range. Should these species be removed from their new ranges if they may not survive in their home ranges?

Both sides of the debate want to maintain biodiversity and ecosystem function. The difference is how non-native species fit into the picture: as potential beneficial contributors or as a potential destructive force.

Language Arts Connection Write a short position paper focused on whether all non-native species should be targeted for removal from new environments. Support your position and claims with evidence from the passage. You and your classmates will discuss your positions in a classroom debate.

 **DESIGN A PRESERVE IN YOUR COMMUNITY** **PROTECTING BIODIVERSITY** **KILLER KITTIES** Go online to choose one of these other paths.

Lesson Self-Check

CAN YOU SOLVE IT?

FIGURE 21: Monarch butterflies require certain plant species and climatic conditions at their wintering grounds.

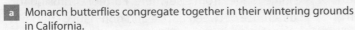

 a Monarch butterflies congregate together in their wintering grounds in California.

b Many of the monarch butterflies' wintering grounds are threatened by habitat destruction.

Monarch butterflies face many threats throughout their life cycle. Their reproduction depends completely on milkweed plants. But these plants are considered to be weeds by many people, so areas of milkweed are often treated with herbicides. Increased development removes monarch butterfly habitat in their summering grounds and along their migration route. Deforestation and development threaten their wintering grounds. In California, monarch butterfly wintering grounds often contain Australian eucalyptus trees. These trees are useful to the butterflies, but they are not native to California. Many of these trees are removed during ecological restoration efforts.

Evidence Notebook Refer to your notes in your Evidence Notebook to explain how human activities affect monarch butterfly populations and how this problem might be solved. Your explanation should include a discussion of the resources monarch butterflies need during breeding, migration, and overwintering. It should also include ways that humans could ensure that those resources are available to the butterflies throughout their life cycle. Use this information to answer the following questions.

1. Make a claim about the impact humans have on monarch butterfly populations. How could human activities harm the butterflies during their life cycle?
2. How could habitat management help monarch butterflies during their life cycle? Use evidence to support your claim.
3. How could habitat fragmentation be reduced to allow monarch butterflies to migrate successfully to their wintering grounds?

CHECKPOINTS

Check Your Understanding

1. Which of these fishing practices is likely to help increase Pacific salmon populations? Select all correct answers.

   ☐ **a.** regulations to increase bycatch

   ☐ **b.** use of nets with turtle excluders

   ☐ **c.** reduced fishing season length

   ☐ **d.** limits on catch size

2. Why is monitoring an important part of controlling invasive species?

   ○ **a.** Monitoring can prevent the spread of invasive species.

   ○ **b.** Monitoring can identify new populations of invasive species while they are still small.

   ○ **c.** Monitoring can maintain the historic state of a landscape.

   ○ **d.** Monitoring can assess the impacts an invasive species could have on a new environment.

3. Which of the following is an example of a barrier in a fragmented habitat? Select all correct answers.

   ☐ **a.** road or pipeline

   ☐ **b.** commercial development between habitat patches

   ☐ **c.** open land that connects habitat patches

   ☐ **d.** housing developments throughout the home range of a species

4. Select the correct terms or phrases to complete the statement about biodiversity and habitat loss.

   In general, the level of biodiversity in an ecosystem is inversely related | directly related to the amount of habitat loss. When the amount of habitat loss increases, the degree of biodiversity decreases | increases. Habitat connectivity is inversely related | directly related to genetic diversity in a population. When habitat connectivity increases in a fragmented landscape, genetic diversity decreases | increases.

5. Which of the following have contributed to the increase of human population growth? Select all correct answers.

   ☐ **a.** discovery of penicillin

   ☐ **b.** increase in antibiotic-resistant bacteria

   ☐ **c.** transportation that allows food distribution

   ☐ **d.** administration of vaccines

   ☐ **e.** availability of all types of fast food

6. In a scenario where the human population has nearly reached Earth's carrying capacity, what kind of growth would the human population experience?

   ○ **a.** exponential

   ○ **b.** logistic

   ○ **c.** linear

   ○ **d.** non-restricted

7. Which of these methods for the management of an invasive plant species could result in the development of more invasive species?

   ○ **a.** biological control

   ○ **b.** herbicide use

   ○ **c.** burning

   ○ **d.** grazing

8. Select the correct terms to complete the statement about genetic diversity and facilitated adaptation.

   Climate change is most likely to threaten populations that have high | low genetic diversity. Scientists are exploring facilitated adaptation to change the diversity | genome of a species through genetic engineering using breeding | recombinant DNA technology. The technology aims to add | remove genes that will be advantageous to populations, and potentially reduce the likelihood of extinction.

CHECKPOINTS (continued)

9. Why are species with low reproductive rates more sensitive to extinction due to overexploitation than those with higher reproductive rates?

_____

_____

_____

_____

_____

_____

10. In what ways can an introduced species impact an ecosystem it has colonized? Use a specific example in your answer.

_____

_____

_____

_____

_____

_____

MAKE YOUR OWN STUDY GUIDE

 In your Evidence Notebook, design a study guide that supports the main ideas from this lesson:

Human activities can have a negative impact on biodiversity.

As a global society, humans need to find a way to balance the economic benefits of development with the cultural and environmental benefits of biodiversity.

Changes in the environment can lead to the expansion of some species and the extinction of some species.

Remember to include the following information in your study guide:
- Use examples that model main ideas.
- Record explanations for the phenomena you investigated.
- Use evidence to support your explanations. Your support can include drawings, data, graphs, laboratory conclusions, and other evidence recorded throughout the lesson.

Consider how human impacts are changing the stability of ecosystems. Think about specific causes and effects related to declining biodiversity that could be linked to human activities.

Engineering Solutions to Environmental Impacts

Green roofing can reduce the impacts of urbanization.

CAN YOU SOLVE IT?

According to the 2010 U.S. Census, over 80% of the population in the United States lives in urban areas. There are environmental costs to this urbanization. For example, the high concentration of dark-colored building materials and asphalt in urban areas absorbs heat and radiates it back into the environment. This increases the temperature of many cities. The water cycle is disrupted because there is not enough soil and ground cover to absorb precipitation, which leads to increased runoff and flooding. Urban areas can also fragment habitats for many organisms.

Green roofs are one way to lessen many of the effects of urbanization. The green roof atop the California Academy of Sciences in San Francisco, for example, helps control the interior temperature of the building. This living roof is ringed by solar panels and features many hills with venting skylights linked to an automatic ventilation system. The roof is over 10 000 square meters in size and covered by 15 centimeters of soil that is planted with over a million native plants. These plants help the roof absorb excess water, which helps reduce the amount of pollution carried in water runoff.

PREDICT How might green roofing solve some of the impacts of urbanization? What additional positive effects might a green roof have on a building and its occupants?

_____

_____

_____

 Evidence Notebook As you explore the lesson, identify how green spaces and other solutions help both society and the environment.

Engineering Sustainable Solutions

Natural resources exist freely in nature and are drawn upon by humans for survival, pleasure, and economic gain. Water, air, land, fossil fuels, wildlife, and vegetation are all examples of natural resources. Each natural resource is part of an environmental web. The use of one resource can affect other resources in positive or negative ways. For example, burning fossil fuels may be cost effective, but their emissions increase atmospheric CO_2 levels, contributing to global warming.

Natural Resources and Climate Change

U.S. Energy Consumption by Energy Source

FIGURE 1: Primary energy sources for the United States in 2014

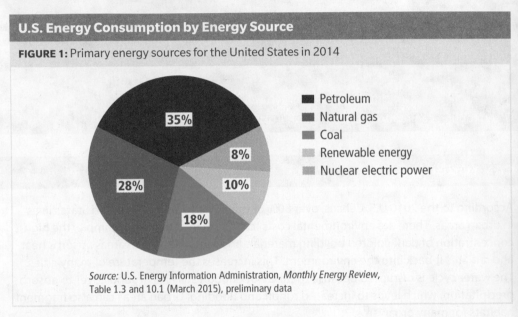

Legend:
- Petroleum
- Natural gas
- Coal
- Renewable energy
- Nuclear electric power

35%
8%
10%
28%
18%

Source: U.S. Energy Information Administration, *Monthly Energy Review*, Table 1.3 and 10.1 (March 2015), preliminary data

Natural resources are generally materials that occur in a natural state and have economic value. They are typically either renewable or nonrenewable.

Renewable Resources

A renewable resource regenerates at about the same rate that it is consumed, or is so vast that it is considered inexhaustible. Even though renewable resources can be replaced at the same rate they are consumed, using these resources can still have impacts on the environment and human health. Examples of renewable resources include wind, solar, and geothermal energy. Renewable energy is used for both electric power and transportation and does not emit greenhouse gases.

Nonrenewable Resources

A nonrenewable resource is used faster than the rate at which it forms. The primary sources of energy in the United States in 2014 are shown in Figure 1. Petroleum products are mostly used as fuel for transportation. Natural gas is used to produce electric power and to heat buildings. Most coal is burned to produce electric power. All three fuels emit greenhouse gases when burned.

Nuclear power plants use nuclear fission to produce electricity. Its main environmental impact is the production of nuclear waste, which must be stored properly for thousands of years. The process of finding and extracting fossil fuels and nuclear material can result in habitat destruction, fragmentation, and pollution.

FIGURE 2: Nonrenewable natural resources include fossil fuels, nuclear materials, and minerals.

a Fossil fuels, such as petroleum and natural gas, can be accessed through drilling.

b Nuclear reactions release heat, which can be converted into electrical energy.

c Minerals, such as limestone, granite, and marble can be used as building materials.

Fossil Fuel and Mineral Extraction

When fossil fuels and minerals are mined, parts of the ecosystem, including rocks, soil, plants, and animals, are disturbed. There are two main types of mining. Subsurface mining, shown in Figure 3a, is the extraction of materials from below Earth's surface. Drilling for oil and gas is an example of subsurface mining. Surface mining involves the removal of rocks and soil from Earth's surface to expose and extract minerals, as shown in Figure 3b.

FIGURE 3 : There are two types of mining—subsurface mining and surface mining.

a Subsurface mining.

b Surface mining

ANALYZE What are some of the negative impacts mining can have on the environment? Select all correct answers.

☐ **a.** Minerals can be extracted for use by humans.

☐ **b.** Surface mining may cause habitat destruction for plants, animals, and other living organisms.

☐ **c.** The soil that plants and fungi rely on may be removed from the mining area.

☐ **d.** Accessing fossil fuels through subsurface mining is a renewable practice.

☐ **e.** Noisy mining equipment may disturb local wildlife.

Mining can damage land, air, and water. For example, when water runs through mines, it can become acidic, causing metals to be released from the surrounding rock. This mixture of acidic water and metals, called acid mine drainage, is very harmful to living things. It can contaminate drinking water and corrode metal structures, such as bridges. Mining may also release harmful chemicals into the atmosphere. Additionally, mining disturbs soil, and therefore can cause erosion and land damage.

 Engineering

Reclaiming Mined Land

FIGURE 4: A reclaimed mining site

Mine reclamation is the restoration of a previously mined area to a natural or economically usable state. The goal is to return the area to its previous natural state, while minimizing environmental impacts. There are many factors to consider when reclaiming a mined site. The resource that was mined, the mining method, the current stage of the mining operation, and the available budget of time and money are all parts of the equation. The restoration goal itself has to be tailored to fit the individual site.

The people and government of California have taken a proactive approach to mine reclamation. Plans are being put in place to reclaim sites that were mined before 1976. These mines go back to the legacy gold and silver strikes of the 1800s. California is also planning for the retirement of current and recent mining operations.

IDENTIFY List criteria and constraints that engineers might need to consider when considering whether a former mine should be reclaimed.

_____

_____

_____

_____

_____

Nuclear Energy

Nuclear energy is derived from radioactive minerals. Nuclear materials such as uranium are mined in much the same way as other minerals. Nuclear energy can be considered clean energy because carbon dioxide is not released into the atmosphere from its use. The heat from the nuclear reactions is used to make steam, and the steam is used to spin turbines, which produces energy.

Nuclear reactions result in radioactive waste, which must be disposed of using very strict procedures. Eventually, the waste will return to the same radioactivity levels as the originally mined ore, but this may take 1000 to 10000 years. Some people still consider nuclear energy to be a viable alternative energy, but others feel its potential hazards outweigh its benefits.

Alternative Energy Sources

The use of alternative energy sources can help to reduce our output of greenhouse gases by reducing the amount of carbon dioxide emitted into the atmosphere.

Biofuel

Biomass can be converted to liquid fuel called *biofuel*. Unlike fossil fuels, biofuels are considered renewable because their sources can quickly regenerate. Burning biofuel gives off smaller amounts of carbon dioxide than fossil fuels. The plants grown to replace the used fuel also consume some of the CO_2 that is produced. Algae are another source of biofuel. These photosynthetic organisms consume CO_2 during the biofuel production process, making them an ideal alternative energy source.

FIGURE 5: Some waste can be converted into biofuel.

Some waste products can be converted into biofuel. Used cooking oil from restaurants can be processed into biodiesel. Ethanol can be made from agricultural waste, used paper products, or commercial crops such as corn. However, growing crops for biofuels can have negative environmental impacts, such as increased water use.

Solar Energy

Solar power plants produce renewable energy, reducing our dependence on fossil fuels. When designing solar power plants, engineers must take cost and efficiency into consideration. The power plants must be able to provide enough energy on a consistent basis. Engineers must also consider the added cost, required time, and potential environmental impact of building solar plants.

FIGURE 6: Ivanpah Solar Electric Generating System in California's Mojave Desert is a solar plant.

Ivanpah is a large solar power plant in California. The plant provides area residents with electricity during peak hours of the day, and claims that it will dramatically reduce CO_2 emissions. However, there have been reports of underproduction, significant bird deaths caused by the plant, and disruptions to many desert-dwelling organisms.

APPLY How do solar energy plants meet the needs of society and the environment? Select all correct answers.

☐ **a.** Solar energy reduces our dependence on fossil fuels.

☐ **b.** Solar energy is the major energy source for urban environments.

☐ **c.** Solar energy is the cheapest energy source.

☐ **d.** Solar energy plants convert light energy, an abundant and renewable energy source, into electrical energy.

☐ **e.** Solar energy plants produce fewer greenhouse gases than fossil fuels.

Wind Energy

Wind turbines can be used to harvest wind energy. Planning the location of a wind farm is important because wind speed and duration must be fairly consistent. Although wind farms occupy a large physical footprint, the area between the windmills can safely serve many other purposes—including raising crops and livestock.

Wind farms can be a danger to bird and bat species, which may fly into the turbines. Engineers have designed solutions to lessen the impact on these species. For example, ultrasonic deterrents emit high-frequency sounds. These sounds interfere with bat echolocation, causing the bats to avoid the area. The deterrents can also emit distress sounds that frighten birds away.

FIGURE 7: Wind farms can cover several acres, but the area between the windmills can be used for many purposes.

PLAN Make a list of criteria that engineers might consider when developing a plan to test the effectiveness of an ultrasonic deterrent for a wind farm. What other solutions might be effective in protecting bird and bat species?

_____

_____

_____

_____

Geothermal Energy

Geothermal energy is energy derived from the thermal energy of Earth's interior. A geothermal power plant uses steam produced from superheated water to rotate a turbine. The turbine activates a generator to produce electrical energy. The United States is a global leader in installed geothermal capacity. Eighty percent of this capacity is located in California, where more than 40 geothermal plants provide nearly 7% of the state's electrical energy. In 2015, geothermal power plants in the United States accounted for 0.4% of the country's energy needs.

FIGURE 8: California is a leader in geothermal energy.

Geothermal energy is a clean, renewable resource. Unlike wind and solar energy, it is virtually unlimited and can be used to heat and cool buildings. Geothermal energy requires no fuel and is almost emission free. This means it produces a low carbon footprint. One drawback to geothermal energy is the limited number of locations where the energy can be accessed. As shown in Figure 9, plants can only be built where the subsurface temperatures are sufficient to produce energy. Since long-distance transmission tends to be inefficient, geothermal probably has to be considered a local energy resource. Other drawbacks to the geothermal process are its use of large amounts of water and the high cost of construction of geothermal plants.

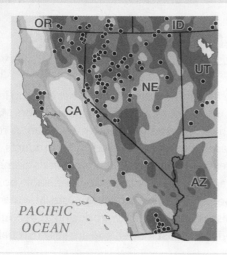

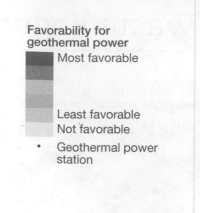

Favorability for
geothermal power

Most favorable

Least favorable
Not favorable

• Geothermal power
station

Source: National Renewable Energy Laboratory

Collaborate Discuss this question with a partner: How could a map, such as the map shown in Figure 9, be used to plan for future geothermal facilities? What other information might be needed to choose a location for a geothermal plant?

Sustainable Solutions

Sustainability is the ability of natural systems and human needs to remain in balance for an extremely long time. There is concern, however, that many human activities are unsustainable and that a limit may be reached one day. Resources once considered renewable, such as fresh water and timber, can become nonrenewable when used at a rate faster than they form. Likewise, through pollution and overuse, human activities can weaken many of the important functions vital to sustaining life on Earth, called ecosystem services. Some of the services ecosystems naturally perform that benefit humans include supplying food for organisms, filtering water, and forming soil.

ANALYZE Why is lumber from trees considered a potential nonrenewable resource?

○ **a.** Lumber is always used up more quickly than it is replenished.

○ **b.** Lumber can be replenished at the same rate it is consumed.

○ **c.** Lumber is replaced more quickly than it is consumed.

○ **d.** The rate of consumption is continually increasing.

Influence of Science, Engineering, and Technology Every energy source currently available poses some threat to the environment. In response, engineers develop new technologies to increase energy use efficiency and reduce energy demands. For example, electronically switchable glass and roof tiles transition from black to white, absorbing heat when outdoor temperatures are cool and reflecting heat when temperatures are warm. On hot summer days, this mechanism keeps heat from entering buildings and decreases the need for air conditioning. Design solutions can also harness untapped naturally existing energy sources to heat buildings and homes. In Paris, the movement of people in underground metro stations is being used to heat large tanks of water that is then piped into nearby homes.

Waste Reduction Solutions

FIGURE 10: Discarded items can find new uses.

FIGURE 11: Recycled plastic can be used to make many items, such as this park bench.

MADE OF RECYCLED MATERIALS

Reducing the amount of waste that ends up in landfills is an important aspect of sustainable living. Many materials that are often thrown away can be re-purposed. For example, used paper products, plastics, and textiles can be used as art materials. Some items, such as rechargeable batteries or refillable bottles, can be used many times, reducing waste. Manufacturers can also reduce waste by producing items with less material, that last longer, and are easy to repair.

DEFINE Imagine you are an engineer trying to reduce waste produced by a small town. What is one engineering problem that could be defined?

_____

_____

_____

_____

Many materials that are thrown away can be recycled to make something new. Making products from recycled materials usually saves energy, water, and other resources. If more people buy products made from recycled materials, the increased demand encourages manufacturers to supply recycled products. Making items out of materials that can be recycled easily, such as glass, cardboard, or aluminum, can increase the impact of recycling.

PLAN What are some engineering-based ways that you might increase the impact of recycling in your community?

_____

_____

_____

_____

Recycling other common household products into new, usable products could also help reduce waste. For example, telephone books, magazines, and catalogs can be recycled to make building materials. Used aluminum beverage cans can be recycled to make new beverage cans, lawn chairs, aluminum siding for houses, and cookware. Plastic beverage containers can be recycled to make nonfood containers, insulation, carpet yarn, textiles, fiberfill, scouring pads, toys, plastic lumber, and crates.

Evidence Notebook How might an increase in green spaces contribute to sustainability? Provide an example to support your claim.

Reducing Impacts on Land

As the human population grows, more land is needed for homes, agriculture, and the extraction of natural materials. Building, agriculture, and mining activities often affect organisms by disrupting local ecosystems and causing pollution. This has led to deforestation, soil erosion, and desertification.

Preventing Deforestation

Deforestation is the removal of trees and other vegetation from an area. Deforestation affects the plant, animal, and human communities living in direct contact with the forest. It also affects the rest of the planet because forests are large carbon sinks, as they store carbon as biomass. When the trees are removed, the stored carbon is eventually released into the environment, which contributes to climate change. Deforestation also causes a loss of plant and animal habitat and a loss of plants that could be used for medicine. It reduces biodiversity, interrupts the water cycle, reduces water quality, and reduces oxygen production. All of these changes impact global communities. The deforestation map in Figure 12 shows how forests have been lost and gained from 2000 to 2012.

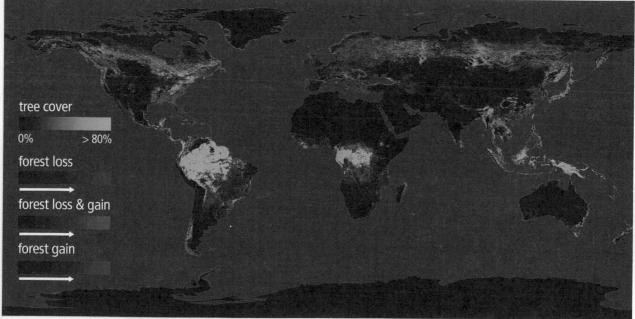

FIGURE 12: Forest cover extent, loss, and gain from 2000–2012

tree cover

0%   > 80%

forest loss

forest loss & gain

forest gain

GATHER EVIDENCE What evidence does the deforestation map provide that the rate of deforestation from 2000 to 2012 is unsustainable?

○ **a.** The areas of forest loss are smaller than the areas of forest gain.

○ **b.** The areas of forest gain are smaller than the areas of forest loss.

○ **c.** The areas of forest loss and regain are larger than the areas of forest gain.

○ **d.** Most of the forest cover loss occurred in the northern hemisphere.

The current overall rate of deforestation is unsustainable—the rate of deforestation is greater than the rate of new tree growth—which makes forests a nonrenewable resource. The demand for wood is one cause of deforestation. To solve this problem, scientists are developing wood alternatives to take the place of traditional wood materials.

FIGURE 13: Wood alternatives can be used in place of newly harvested wood products.

a Reclaimed wood **b** Wood by-products **c** Alternative plants **d** Recycled paper

Collaborate What products do you use, or could you use, that come from wood alternatives? Check the labels of items in your classroom or at home. Are any of them made from wood alternatives? Compare your results to a partner's.

Wood alternatives are often satisfactory replacements for newly harvested wood, lessening the economic pressures driving deforestation. Wood alternatives include reclaimed wood, wood shavings, alternative plants, and recycled paper products.

Reclaimed wood from pallets and old buildings is often used for detail work and home items. Wood shavings, often waste from lumber mills, can be turned into paper products. Fibers from plants other than trees, such as bamboo, hemp, and flax, can be used to make paper products and fabrics. Using alternative plants to meet wood demands can lessen the effects of deforestation because some alternative tree species are more sustainable and grow faster than traditional species. Recycled paper can be reprocessed to produce new paper products, which also keeps a large amount of waste out of landfills.

Engineering

Finding Wood Alternatives

Wood is typically thought of as a building material, but it also is used in hundreds of products, some of which may surprise you. For example, wood products are used to make table tennis balls, chewing gum, and eyeglass frames. The use of wood in such a wide variety of products is one of the reasons deforestation is so problematic. It also is the reason that finding wood alternatives is so important.

DEFINE What criteria would be important to research before using a wood alternative for hardwood flooring?

_____

_____

_____

Soil Erosion

Human activities such as clear-cutting forests, building structures, raising livestock, and growing crops can damage land. These activities often involve the removal of plants from their natural habitat, which leaves the soil exposed. Additionally, the loss of plant cover can lead to less absorption of rainwater. With sufficient plant loss, soil may be transported away by moving water, wind, and other agents in a process called soil erosion.

Soil erosion can reduce the fertility of land, thereby reducing crop production. It can also damage infrastructure and change the quality of water in rivers and streams. Soil can carry with it disease-causing organisms called pathogens. These pathogens may be transported into bodies of water, negatively affecting the health of humans and other species.

The field of soil and water engineering applies science and technology to design solutions that conserve water and soil resources. Engineers can help farmers and agricultural operations conserve valuable topsoil and more precisely apply water to crops. Figure 14 shows an example of soil terracing, a technique that has been used for centuries to reduce soil erosion caused by rainfall. Farmers can also prevent soil erosion by leaving field residues on the ground after a crop has been harvested. Field residues are the stems, leaves, and other plant parts that are not harvested. Leaving these materials on the soil surface reduces soil and water loss. It also helps the soil retain important nutrients.

FIGURE 14: Terracing prevents soil erosion and water loss by using ridges to capture rainwater that would otherwise flow down the slopes after rainfall.

ASK Imagine you are a soil engineer called upon to help a farmer prevent soil erosion. Write a list of questions you would ask to define the problem.

_____

_____

_____

_____

_____

Desertification

Continuously growing the same crops on the same land is another way that nutrients are removed from soil. The use of fertilizers to replace these nutrients can lead to other negative outcomes. Artificial eutrophication, or the buildup of nutrients, can occur in bodies of water that receive runoff from overfertilized soil. Soil can also be compacted, or pressed together, by heavy farm equipment or during construction. When soil is compacted, it does not absorb water as readily, and plant roots cannot grow normally. If soil is damaged enough, a process called desertification can occur. This makes land in dry areas become more desert-like over time. Many factors, including drought, deforestation, and poor farming techniques, increase the likelihood of desertification.

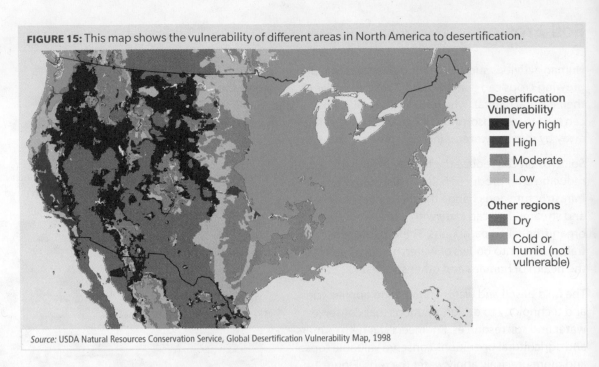

FIGURE 15: This map shows the vulnerability of different areas in North America to desertification.

Desertification Vulnerability
- Very high
- High
- Moderate
- Low

Other regions
- Dry
- Cold or humid (not vulnerable)

Source: USDA Natural Resources Conservation Service, Global Desertification Vulnerability Map, 1998

ANALYZE According to the map, which areas are most at risk of desertification and why?

○ **a.** Areas near cold regions are most at risk, because water freezes so plants cannot grow there.

○ **b.** Areas near humid regions are most at risk, because water stays in the atmosphere so plants cannot grow well there.

○ **c.** Areas near icy regions are most at risk, because water stays frozen so plants cannot thrive there.

○ **d.** Areas near dry regions are most at risk, because water is scarce and plants need water to grow.

Climate change can lead to enhanced desertification and vice versa. Climate change alters patterns in temperature and rainfall, which affects wind patterns and creates a positive feedback loop. In times of drought, with less surface water to evaporate, more of the sun's energy is available to heat the land, which turns the soil to dust. The wind picks dust up into the atmosphere, disrupting the temperature differences that trigger rainfall in the water cycle. Less rainfall makes the land drier and the cycle continues. Improved agricultural practices can help reverse the problem. Farmers can diversify their crops, use more sustainable irrigation and fertilization practices, and integrate animals as natural fertilization sources or tractor alternatives into their operation.

EXPLAIN There are many locations in California that are in danger of desertification. What steps could be taken to reverse this trend?

_____

_____

_____

_____

 Evidence Notebook How might green roofs and other green spaces help reduce the effect that humans have on the environment with respect to deforestation, soil erosion, and desertification?

Engineering Lab

Designing a Green Roof

Humans have a long history of using sod roofs. In the past, sod roofs were used because the materials were readily available and they provided insulation for buildings. Modern green roofs are still used for their insulating properties, which reduce heating and cooling bills, but they are also used to control water runoff, reduce temperatures, and provide habitat for wildlife.

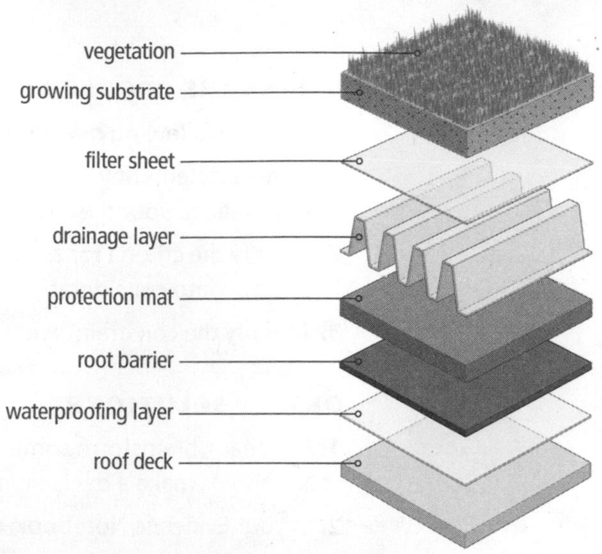

Each layer of the green roof serves a specific function.

- The roof deck is the basic roofing substrate that provides support for the entire green roof.
- The waterproofing layer ensures water does not enter the building.
- The drainage layer stores water and moves it away from the growing substrate.
- The filter sheet prevents the growing substrate from clogging the drainage layer.
- The growing substrate provides nutrients and a water source for the vegetation.
- Vegetation anchors the growing substrate and provides green biomass.

FIGURE 16: Green roofs are made of several layers of different materials.

vegetation
growing substrate
filter sheet
drainage layer
protection mat
root barrier
waterproofing layer
roof deck

Your team has been selected to design a green roof for the new city hall in the town of William's Beach. Average temperatures in William's Beach are increasing, as are the amounts of pollution in waterways and the occurrences of flash floods. The William's Beach city council thinks green roofs might be the best solution to their problems, but they would like to see evidence that green roofs can work. The city council would like a green roof that reduces the surface temperature of the roof and decreases the runoff during light rain events by 50%.

MATERIALS

- safety goggles, nonlatex apron, nonlatex gloves
- container, plastic (to collect runoff)
- pan or box

Possible Materials measurement tools (ruler, thermometer, stopwatch), wax paper, aluminum foil, tar paper, plastic wrap, large pebbles, pea gravel, peat moss, sand, marbles, cotton balls, chenille stems, fabrics, carpet pieces, polystyrene foam, shredded paper, cardboard, loose soil, live plants

SAFETY INFORMATION

- Wear safety goggles, a nonlatex apron, and nonlatex gloves during the setup, hands-on, and takedown segments of the activity.
- Use caution when using sharp tools or materials, which can cut or puncture skin.
- Immediately wipe up any spilled water on the floor so it does not become a slip/fall hazard.
- Wash your hands with soap and water when you are finished handling soil and plant samples and immediately after completing this activity.

CONDUCT RESEARCH

What do you think is the best design, including materials, for this green roof?

_____

_____

_____

DEFINE THE PROBLEM

Answer the following questions in your Evidence Notebook.

1. Write a statement identifying the problem you are designing a solution for. How will you evaluate your design?

2. Identify the criteria for a successful solution. Should the model's appearance or "looks" be taken into consideration?

3. Identify the constraints that will impact a successful solution.

DESIGN SOLUTIONS

1. As a team, brainstorm some possible solutions to the problem. In your Evidence Notebook, make a decision matrix to choose the solution that best meets the criteria.

2. In your Evidence Notebook, make a conceptual model of your design that includes the problem your green roof will solve, the components of your green roof, and the materials you will use to build your prototype.

3. In your Evidence Notebook, develop a plan for building your prototype. As you develop the plan, make sure to include the steps for constructing your prototype and the materials and technology that you will use.

4. Consult with your teacher and build your prototype.

TEST

1. In your Evidence Notebook, develop a plan for testing your prototype. Write out a description of your plan and make sure to include the following:

   • materials and technology you will need

   • necessary safety procedures

   • how you will test the system components

   • the total amount of water you will apply to your prototype to simulate a light rain event

   • the amount of water your prototype will need to absorb to reach the runoff reduction goal

   • how you will collect and analyze your data

   Note: The maximum rate of rainfall during a light rain event is 0.025 cm in 6 minutes over an area equal to 8.56 cm^2. For the purpose of this lab, evenly distribute 2.5 mL of water per square centimeter of area your green roof prototype covers over a period of 6 minutes to replicate a light rain event.

2. Consult with your teacher to make sure that the conditions you have chosen are appropriate. Then test your prototype to determine whether it meets the most important criteria for an effective solution.

OPTIMIZE

Share your model with other teams. Demonstrate your prototype and explain how it meets the criteria for success. Elicit other teams' feedback on your design. Use their comments and critique to improve your prototype. Test it again as many times as necessary.

1. What tradeoffs can you make to meet the criteria more fully?

_____

_____

_____

2. Draw a labeled diagram of your final optimized design in your Evidence Notebook.

ANALYZE

1. In your Evidence Notebook, graph the data you collected. In the space provided below, record any trends or patterns in your data.

_____

_____

_____

2. How did you measure success, and how successful was your design?

_____

_____

_____

_____

3. How could your design be optimized to better meet the goals of the project?

_____

_____

_____

_____

4. If your green roof was duplicated on over 50% of William's Beach buildings, what effect would this have on the temperatures, runoff rates, and flooding in the city?

_____

_____

_____

_____

 Evidence Notebook How can green roofs help to reduce the human effect on local ecosystems?

Human Impacts on Water

Water pollution and water shortages are endangering access to clean, fresh water for humans and other organisms. Chemical runoff from pesticides, herbicides, and fertilizers is one of the many causes of water pollution. Water shortages are caused by increasing population sizes, high water usage rates for personal and agricultural needs, and long periods of drought. Engineers are developing ways to solve the problems related to water access, water usage, and water pollution in order to ensure water is available in the future.

ANALYZE Part of the engineering process is to take a larger problem and break it down into smaller problems. How could you break down the problem of obtaining clean water into smaller problems that can be addressed more easily?

_____

_____

_____

Reducing Water Usage

The availability of fresh water, population sizes, and economic conditions affect how people use water. Worldwide, agriculture accounts for about 67% of water usage, industry accounts for more than 19%, and household activities—such as drinking and washing—account for about 10% of water usage.

Fresh water availability is one of the most important factors affecting human activity. Conflicts over water use, rights, and management are common where there is high demand but limited water availability. An example involves the early part of the 20th century, when the population in the city of Los Angeles increased and additional water sources were needed.

FIGURE 17: The Los Angeles aqueduct and a map of Owens Valley

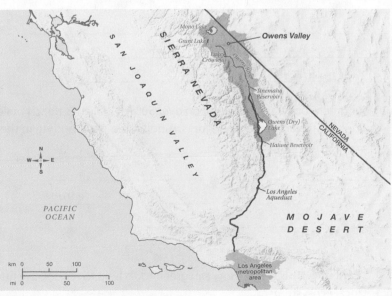

City leaders at the time looked north to the Owens River to meet the city's water needs. Farmers in Owens Valley knew that diverting water to the growing city would threaten their livelihood, but they were unable to stop the city from purchasing farmland and acquiring the water rights. Los Angeles city officials were eventually able to build an aqueduct system that brought water from Owens Valley to Los Angeles. Once water was available, the city could grow.

The long-term effects of the Los Angeles aqueduct construction are still being studied. Water is available to city residents, but studies have shown that the output of water is greater than the input to the Owens Valley water system. According to some studies, Owens Valley will eventually become more desert-like. This will affect the people, agriculture, and industry in the region.

Rainwater Harvesting Systems

Rainwater harvesting systems allow people to collect rainwater for household and commercial use instead of relying on freshwater sources that are in danger of being depleted. A simple rainwater harvesting system consists of a barrel to store the water, a conveyance system to direct the water to the barrel, a screen or lid to keep out insects and debris, a runoff pipe to allow excess water to escape, and a spigot to access the water. More advanced harvesting systems use large reservoirs instead of a barrel for water storage, pumps to move the water through a building, and even filtration systems to make the water safe to drink.

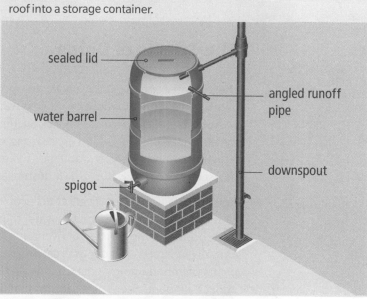

FIGURE 18: Many rainwater harvesting systems divert water from a roof into a storage container.

sealed lid

water barrel

spigot

angled runoff pipe

downspout

Small rainwater harvesting systems are often used to meet the personal water needs of a household, or to water a garden. Farmers or small towns may use ponds to store rainwater for agricultural or human needs.

EXPLAIN How could a rainwater harvesting system lessen the stress on a water supply, even if the water collected is not safe to drink?

○ **a.** by filtering the water to increase the quality to human consumption standards

○ **b.** by reducing the amount of water people need for daily activities

○ **c.** by increasing the amount of precipitation in an area

○ **d.** by providing water for uses that have lower water quality standards

To maximize efficiency, rainwater harvesting systems should be designed to meet the specific needs of the people using it. Small harvesting systems can be scaled up to store larger amounts of water to meet agricultural needs or the needs of a larger community. Engineers understand that changes in scale can affect a system's structure and performance. For example, an uncovered rainwater harvesting system that did not have problems with evaporation on a small scale may suffer high levels of evaporation when built on a larger scale. A potential solution to this problem could be to store the water in underground tanks, lowering the amount of evaporation.

Explore Online ▶

Hands-On Lab

Design a Rainwater Harvesting System Design, construct, and evaluate a rainwater harvesting system to determine what makes a successful system.

Greywater Reuse

In addition to collecting rainwater, water can be reused for other residential activities. Greywater is water that has been "gently" used in your home. It may contain trace amounts of hair, dirt, food, and some household cleaning products. With proper treatment, greywater can be used for toilet flushing, to launder clothes, and to irrigate plants. If green cleaning products are used in the home, then greywater is especially useful for indoor plants or outside irrigation, making the home an essential link in the natural water cycle.

EXPLAIN Some states and municipalities exclude water from kitchen sinks from the list of acceptable sources of greywater. Explain why this water source would not be reusable.

_____

_____

_____

The Effects of Dams

The potential energy of moving water is powerful and can be harnessed by building dams. The energy produced by moving water is called hydroelectric power. This energy source is beneficial because it is a clean, renewable energy resource that does not pollute the air, water, or land. During dry seasons, water from dams may be released to irrigate agricultural lands for crop production. Water in dams can also be redirected to homes to be used as drinking water, or to industrial areas for industrial purposes.

However, dams can negatively affect ecosystems. Releasing excess water from dams can cause flooding downstream. The water that dams hold contains silt that otherwise would be deposited along beaches or riverbanks. This can result in changes in the formation of natural landscapes. Silt deposits can increase soil fertility, and a lack of silt may deprive plants of important nutrients. Changes in the water quality in the dam reservoir may impact the populations of organisms that live in a local ecosystem.

FIGURE 19: These images compare a region before and after the construction of a dam.

EXPLAIN In what ways could building the dam have affected the river and the ecosystems in the region shown in Figure 19? Select all correct answers.

☐ **a.** Building the dam flooded some upstream habitats, possibly disrupting or killing plants and animals that lived there.

☐ **b.** Building the dam had no effect on the landscape.

☐ **c.** Building the dam had no effect on the flow of the river downstream.

☐ **d.** Building the dam might affect aquatic species above and below the dam.

The Beaver: Nature's Engineer

Beavers are one of only a few organisms that are able to greatly alter the landscape. Many people found beavers and their dams to be a nuisance, and sought to remove them from many areas. By the early 20th century, the beaver population in the United States dropped dramatically from overhunting. Because of these actions, many ecosystems began to suffer due to changes in the water table. Local agencies began turning to engineers to design human-made solutions to raise water levels. Engineers, though, realized that beavers would be much better at engineering a solution.

Beaver wetlands support maximal plant and animal diversity, allow toxins and sediments to settle out of streams, and temper the effects of heavy precipitation events. Groundwater movement is also changed by beaver dams. It no longer follows the stream channel, but rather flows outward, raising the water table throughout the valley. Over time, this results in healthier ecosystems.

EXPLAIN How do beavers contribute to stability and change in ecosystems?

_____

_____

_____

FIGURE 20: Beavers are an important part of their ecosystem.

Water Pollution

Nearly every way that humans use water contributes to water pollution, and human population growth is amplifying the problem. Contaminated water can have negative impacts on ecosystems and on human health. Water pollution comes from two types of sources. Point source pollution is pollution that originates and is discharged from a single source. An example of point source pollution is a waste-release pipe from a factory manufacturing plastic products. Nonpoint source pollution comes from many different sources that are often difficult to identify. One example of nonpoint source pollution is excess fertilizer and other contaminants that drain down the banks into rivers. Another nonpoint source example is the water from storm drains. Although the point of entry into the polluted water body is a single physical location, the water is collected along the entire length of the pipe.

> **Collaborate** With a partner, choose a body of water in your community and identify any potential point and nonpoint sources of pollution. Are any of them more or less concerning, and why?

FIGURE 21: Pollution may come from one or many sources.

a A waste-release pipe is an example of point source pollution.

b Water collected by a storm drain is an example of nonpoint source pollution.

FIGURE 22: Oil from a spill covers a beach in Santa Barbara County, California.

Oil Spills

Oil spills are any release into the environment of liquid petroleum—crude oil, refined petroleum, or even waste oil. The causes of oil spills can range from human error and equipment breakdown to natural disasters. Oil quickly coats the skin and feathers of wildlife, which results in hypothermia. Oil is also toxic through direct physical contact, ingestion, and inhalation for many aquatic organisms. Due to biomagnification, this toxicity can travel up the food chain and affect organisms that did not have direct contact with the oil.

Oil spills may have long-term effects on ecosystems. Oil can reach the beach and cover sand and rocks. Oil may also enter wetland ecosystems and destroy plants that absorb the oil. Some oil in the ocean may sink into underwater ecosystems, harming organisms that rely on clean water for survival.

ASK Imagine you are an engineer that has been tasked with cleaning up an oil spill. What questions would you ask before you begin designing a solution?

_____

_____

_____

There are many methods to clean up oil spills. Plants that are covered in oil can be removed by hand. Certain chemicals can break the oil down into small droplets, which are more easily absorbed by aquatic systems. However, these chemicals can be harmful to the ecosystems and are not used for every spill. Bioremediation is a process that uses microbes and other living things to break down pollutants. Some types of bacteria can digest oil. Workers spray oil-polluted beaches with a fertilizer that helps the bacteria grow. These bacteria can change the toxin to another form that is not dangerous, they can break the compound into smaller parts, or they can completely degrade it into inorganic molecules such as carbon dioxide and water.

 Stability and Change

Impacts of Oil Spills

The California Refugio spill in 2015 released over 100 000 gallons of crude oil into the Pacific Ocean. The spill caused extensive wildlife fatalities in the area, which has a lasting negative impact on the health of the ecosystem. The oil damaged a rare coastal area where diverse wildlife normally flourishes.

 Language Arts Connection Research the effects of the Refugio oil spill, or another oil spill that affected California. How did the oil spill affect the local ecosystem? What steps were taken to clean up the spill? Write a newspaper article to present your research.

 Evidence Notebook How might green spaces help reduce the negative impact that humans have on Earth's water supply?

Careers in Engineering

Energy Engineer

The ability to access energy is critical to modern life. We depend on energy to heat and cool our homes, office buildings, and even our vehicles. Energy is also needed to power our appliances, computers, phones, and numerous other devices. Looking at the variety of energy resources—fossil fuels, biofuels, solar, wind, water, geothermal, and nuclear—gives a sense of the opportunity provided by a career path in energy engineering.

A primary role of an energy engineer is to find ways to save energy and make residential and commercial spaces more energy efficient. They begin by evaluating the current energy use and demands for a particular client. The engineers inspect, analyze, and model thermal, mechanical, and electrical energy flow within the building. The primary goal is to reduce the amount of energy that goes into the building, while still meeting the energy demands of those who use the building. Sometimes energy engineers are brought onto projects from the beginning, such as when a developer builds a new housing community. Other times, energy engineers help remodel existing buildings.

Depending on criteria and constraints, energy engineers recommend many kinds of solutions. For example, he or she may recommend installing a solar-paneled roof on a home or office building as a way to reduce the use of fossil fuels. In fact, there is a subgroup of energy engineers who focus on using renewable energy sources including solar, wind, geothermal, and hydropower.

Energy engineers also work on designing energy-efficient machinery, as well as maintaining and improving the equipment that is currently in use.

FIGURE 23: Energy engineers are part of a team responsible for maintaining energy plants, such as this geothermal plant.

Language Arts Connection Ardenberg is a new co-housing community in the planning stages for a 200-acre property in California. Their intent is to be eco-friendly and largely energy-independent. Your firm has been asked to consult in their energy planning process.

Using the given information, make a presentation about what information an energy engineer would need to collect in order to complete the task for the co-housing community. Using your knowledge of the engineering design process, be sure to define the problem and include criteria and constraints that may need to be considered.

Biology in Your Community Research and write a two-page article about California's energy efficiency and clean energy initiatives. What programs are available to ensure all citizens have access to affordable and efficient energy sources? If possible, consult a local energy engineer about programs that support energy equity for diverse populations in your community.

 BUILDING SOLAR CELLS   **CLEANING UP OIL SPILLS**   **REDUCING YOUR CARBON FOOTPRINT**   Go online to choose one of these other paths.

Lesson Self-Check

CAN YOU SOLVE IT?

FIGURE 24: A living roof offers an aesthetic approach as well as a solution to some of the problems of urbanization.

Widespread urbanization to meet human needs has had many negative consequences on the environment. For example, the high concentration of dark-colored building materials and asphalt in urban areas has had a heating effect, increasing the temperature of many cities. Removal of soil and vegetation disrupts the water cycle because there is not enough soil and ground cover to absorb precipitation, leading to increased runoff and flooding. Clearing areas for urbanization destroys the natural habitats of countless organisms. Increasing green areas can reduce the effects that humans have on the environment. Engineers have designed multiple solutions, including green roofs, but the criteria and constraints of each solution must be carefully considered.

 Evidence Notebook Refer to your notes in your Evidence Notebook to explain how green spaces, and green roofs in particular, can help both society and the environment.

1. Make a claim about how the engineering design process is used to plan sustainable solutions to the problem of human impact on the environment, such as the construction of green roofs.
2. What evidence supports your claim? For example, how can green roofs reduce the amount of energy required to heat and cool a building?
3. How can green roofs be further optimized to help society and the environment?

Name _____   Date _____

Check Your Understanding

1. A drought leads to the loss of much of the local vegetation. Which measure would be best for preventing soil erosion?

   ○ **a.** plant more bushes and trees

   ○ **b.** water remaining plants daily

   ○ **c.** cover soil with stones or rocks

   ○ **d.** add more soil to the ground

2. How does deforestation affect climate change?

   ○ **a.** It decreases the amount of carbon dioxide in the atmosphere.

   ○ **b.** It increases the amount of carbon dioxide in the atmosphere.

   ○ **c.** It decreases the amount of ozone in the atmosphere.

   ○ **d.** It increases the amount of ozone in the atmosphere.

3. Which of the following is *not* an example of point source pollution?

   ○ **a.** oil that is escaping from a damaged tanker

   ○ **b.** heavy metals that are leaching out of an underground mine

   ○ **c.** water runoff from residential lawns

   ○ **d.** untreated sewage that is accidentally released from a wastewater treatment plant

4. What are the advantages of collecting rainwater for human consumption and other uses? Select all correct answers.

   ☐ **a.** It lowers stress on freshwater resources.

   ☐ **b.** It improves access to water.

   ☐ **c.** It frees time usually spent collecting water.

   ☐ **d.** It reduces the occurrence of acid rain.

   ☐ **e.** It reduces runoff and flooding.

5. What are the environmental benefits of building green roofs? Select all correct answers.

   ☐ **a.** They have a reduced warming effect.

   ☐ **b.** They increase the demand for energy.

   ☐ **c.** They are built with nonrenewable resources.

   ☐ **d.** They reduce water runoff rates.

6. Which project would be best suited for each type of wood alternative? List one wood alternative per project.

   | alternative wood species | recycled paper |
   | reclaimed wood | alternative plant fiber |

Project	Wood alternative
commercial paper products	
fabric	
new building	
wood crafts	

7. One solution for reducing soil erosion is for farmers to leave field residues on the ground after a crop has been harvested. What are some advantages of this solution? Select all correct answers.

   ☐ **a.** It does not require extra time when harvesting the crops.

   ☐ **b.** It is an inexpensive solution.

   ☐ **c.** It makes the landscape more visually appealing.

   ☐ **d.** It creates new green spaces.

   ☐ **e.** It helps soil retain nutrients.

8. Wheatgrass is the young stalk of the wheat plant, and it is used to feed livestock. What kind of resource is wheatgrass?

   ○ **a.** renewable and biomass

   ○ **b.** nonrenewable and biomass

   ○ **c.** renewable and fossil fuel

   ○ **d.** nonrenewable and fossil fuel

CHECKPOINTS (continued)

9. Suppose you are an environmental engineer. You have been hired by a manufacturing plant to help it conserve natural resources and save money. What suggestions would you give to achieve these goals?

_____

_____

_____

_____

_____

_____

10. Human-made dams can be used to generate hydroelectric power, but there are negative impacts. How might dams negatively affect ecosystems?

_____

_____

_____

_____

_____

_____

_____

MAKE YOUR OWN STUDY GUIDE

In your Evidence Notebook, design a study guide that supports the main idea from this lesson:

Engineering solutions are used to lessen human impacts on the environment. For example, energy alternatives, soil erosion prevention, and water treatment solutions can reduce pollution and other negative environmental effects.

Remember to include the following information in your study guide:

- Use examples that model main ideas.
- Record explanations for the phenomena you investigated.
- Use evidence to support your explanations. Your support can include drawings, data, graphs, laboratory conclusions, and other evidence recorded throughout the lesson.

Consider how engineering solutions can influence the way humans interact with the environment.

Earth Science Connection

Landsat 8 NASA's Landsat 8 is the latest in a series of Landsat satellites that have been providing crucial information about Earth's resources for over 40 years. Data gathered by Landsat 8 helps enhance our understanding of climate, the carbon cycle, and ecosystems. Visible trends linked to the growing human population, such as changes in forest cover over time, are shown by Landsat imagery and help inform resource management decisions.

Research Landsat 8 and develop a multimedia presentation that explains this Earth Science Mission. Describe the technology that is used and how the gathered data is applied to a particular problem, such as deforestation or change in ocean temperatures. Your presentation should also include information on the types of maps Landsat 8 provides.

FIGURE 1: Landsat 8 provides valuable information about Earth's surface.

Social Studies Connection

Working Dogs With their excellent sense of smell and tracking abilities, a dog's skills can be highly useful in the field. Dogs have been used in anti-poaching efforts, to find particular species, and to sniff out illegally imported animals and artifacts. In California, dogs are an important tool used by search-and-rescue teams. A specific breed called Karelian bear dogs are also used to chase away troublesome bears in places such as Yosemite National Park.

With a group, research ways that dogs are used in California to reduce human impacts on the environment. Then write and perform a short skit that describes the impact on the environment, why it is a problem, and how dogs can help lessen the impact.

FIGURE 2: Trained dogs are useful in many areas of conservation biology.

Art Connection

Environmental Awareness Through Art Art can be used as a medium for raising awareness about ecological issues. For example, some artists paint murals in public spaces that highlight environmental and social issues and the interconnectivity between humans and nature. Another example is artists who upcycle, or use recycled items or trash items, to make art that is visually engaging while making a statement about human consumption and waste.

Create your own artwork to raise environmental awareness. Hold an art exhibit with your class. Individuals should describe how their art is linked to environmental awareness, why the selected materials were chosen to complete the artwork, and the message the artist would like to communicate with their art.

FIGURE 3: This elephant was made from recycled plastic bottles.

A BOOK EXPLAINING
COMPLEX IDEAS USING
ONLY THE 1,000 MOST
COMMON WORDS

STUFF IN THE EARTH WE CAN BURN

How we get things we need out of the ground

You've explored rock, mineral, and energy resources that are essential to life on Earth. What methods have humans devised to find and extract those valuable resources from deep inside Earth?

RANDALL MUNROE
XKCD.COM

THE STORY OF HOW LIVING THINGS GET POWER

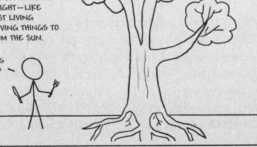

ALMOST ALL LIVING THINGS ARE POWERED BY THE SUN. SOME LIVING THINGS GET THEIR POWER STRAIGHT FROM THE SUN'S LIGHT—LIKE TREES, AND SOME THINGS THAT GROW IN THE SEA. MOST LIVING THINGS THAT DON'T EAT THE SUN'S LIGHT EAT OTHER LIVING THINGS TO GET THEIR POWER. IN THE END, THE POWER COMES FROM THE SUN.

LOOKS PRETTY DRY. I'M GOING TO NEED A LOT OF WATER TO EAT THE WHOLE THING!

WHEN THINGS DIE, SOME OF THAT POWER IS LEFT IN THEIR REMAINS, WHICH IS WHY YOU CAN GET POWER OUT OF DEAD TREES BY BURNING THEM. SOMETIMES, IF DEAD THINGS DON'T BURN OR GET EATEN, THEY GO INTO THE GROUND WITH THAT POWER STILL INSIDE THEM.

SO WHEN DO I GET THE POWER?

OVER A LONG TIME, UNDER THE WEIGHT AND HEAT OF THE EARTH, HUGE NUMBERS OF THESE REMAINS CAN CHANGE INTO DIFFERENT KINDS OF ROCKS, WATER, OR AIR . . . BUT EVEN AS THEY CHANGE, THEY HOLD ON TO THEIR POWER. WHEN WE FIND THESE REMAINS, WE CAN BURN THEM, AND GET ALL THAT POWER—GATHERED FROM THE SUN OVER HUGE STRETCHES OF TIME—AT ONCE.

— HOW DO I GET IT?

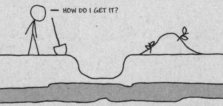

WHEN WE FIRST BUILT MACHINES POWERED BY FIRE, WE BURNED WOOD FROM THE FORESTS OF OUR TIME. WHEN THOSE WEREN'T ENOUGH, WE STARTED BURNING THE FORESTS OF THE PAST. ONE DAY, THOSE WILL RUN OUT, TOO, AND WE'LL HAVE TO GET POWER SOMEWHERE NEW— LIKE STRAIGHT FROM THE SUN, OR THE EARTH'S HEAT.

THAT CAN'T BE RIGHT . . .

BUT WE MAY HAVE TO CHANGE THE KIND OF POWER WE USE SOON, BEFORE WE FINISH BURNING ALL THE STUFF IN THE GROUND. IT TURNS OUT BURNING THAT STUFF IS CHANGING OUR AIR, IN A WAY THAT'S MAKING THE WORLD HOTTER. IF WE USE UP ALL THE BLACK ROCKS, FIRE WATER, AND FIRE AIR, THE PROBLEM IT MAKES MAY BE TOO BIG FOR US.

IS THAT POWER?

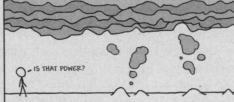

HOW WE GET BLACK ROCKS OUT OF THE GROUND

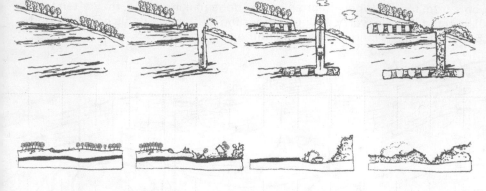

If the rocks aren't very deep, we can make holes under the ground and carry them up with machines. This is how we used to get most of the rocks we burned.

As we built bigger earth-moving machines, we learned to just move all the trees and land out of the way to get the rocks.

THEY DO THIS IN THE MOUNTAINS NEAR WHERE I PLAYED AS A KID.

Some rocks are inside mountains, so some companies have started blowing up the tops of the mountains so they can get the rocks out more easily.

HOW WE GET FIRE WATER AND FIRE AIR OUT OF THE GROUND

FIRE WATER

FIRE AIR

We make holes looking for places where lots of things died. When we find a pool, we push a stick down and pull up all the fire air and fire water.

Over time, some dead things slowly turn to fire water and fire air.

These are both lighter than rocks and rise up through tiny holes. When they reach a rock with no holes, they form pools, with the lighter air on top.

STUFF IN THE EARTH WE CAN BURN

This kind of work leaves pools full of heavy metals and strange kinds of water that was used to get the black rocks out. Sometimes you can notice the bright colors of these pools from the air. When companies are done making holes, they often leave the pools behind. People worry about whether the stuff in the pools could be bad for us. Sometimes birds land in the pools and die.

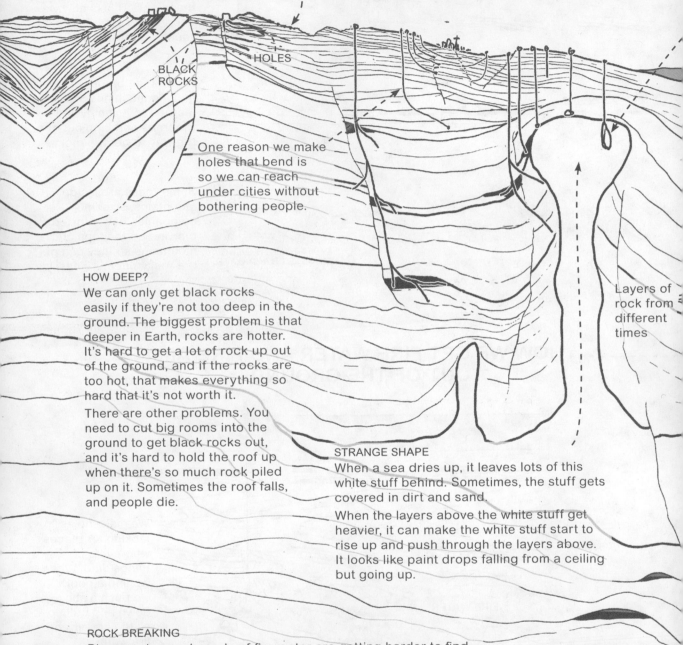

BLACK ROCKS

HOLES

One reason we make holes that bend is so we can reach under cities without bothering people.

Layers of rock from different times

HOW DEEP?

We can only get black rocks easily if they're not too deep in the ground. The biggest problem is that deeper in Earth, rocks are hotter. It's hard to get a lot of rock up out of the ground, and if the rocks are too hot, that makes everything so hard that it's not worth it.

There are other problems. You need to cut big rooms into the ground to get black rocks out, and it's hard to hold the roof up when there's so much rock piled up on it. Sometimes the roof falls, and people die.

STRANGE SHAPE

When a sea dries up, it leaves lots of this white stuff behind. Sometimes, the stuff gets covered in dirt and sand.

When the layers above the white stuff get heavier, it can make the white stuff start to rise up and push through the layers above. It looks like paint drops falling from a ceiling but going up.

ROCK BREAKING

Big, easy-to-reach pools of fire water are getting harder to find, so we've been trying new ideas for getting it from the ground. We've found that sometimes, rock has fire water or air you can burn stuck in it. To get it out, we push water into the ground so hard that it makes the rocks break. Then we push in small rocks or glass to hold the breaks open, and the fire water and fire air come out through the openings.

Making all these holes in the rock might mean that when we drink water, we'll also drink whatever stuff they use to get fire water out, since everything can run through the new holes in the rock.

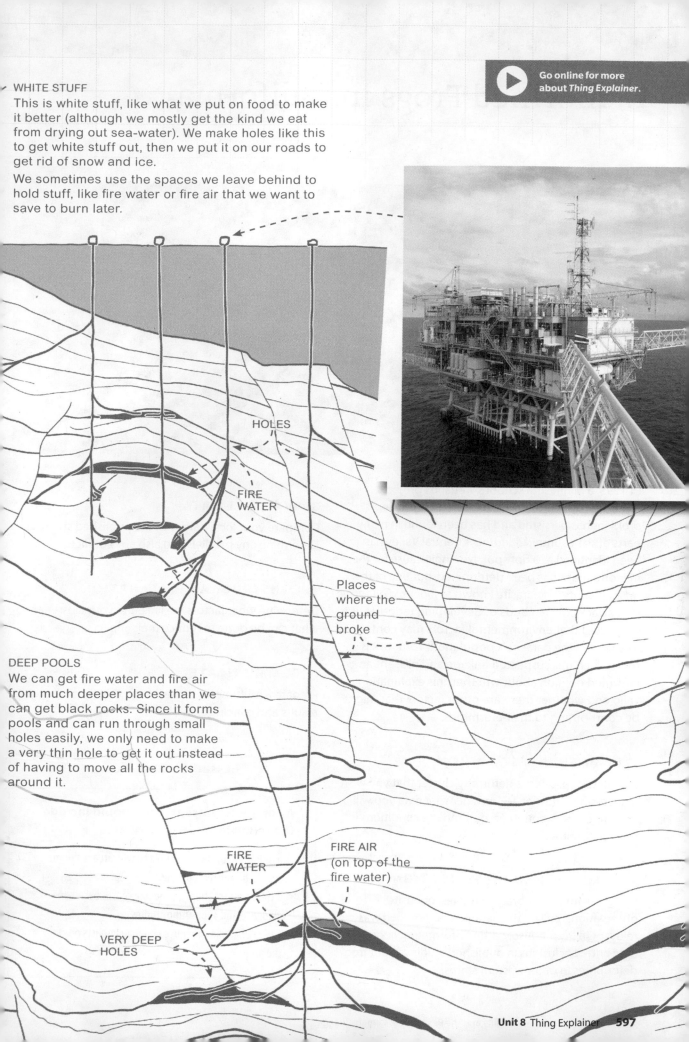

WHITE STUFF

This is white stuff, like what we put on food to make it better (although we mostly get the kind we eat from drying out sea-water). We make holes like this to get white stuff out, then we put it on our roads to get rid of snow and ice.

We sometimes use the spaces we leave behind to hold stuff, like fire water or fire air that we want to save to burn later.

Go online for more about *Thing Explainer*.

HOLES

FIRE WATER

Places where the ground broke

DEEP POOLS

We can get fire water and fire air from much deeper places than we can get black rocks. Since it forms pools and can run through small holes easily, we only need to make a very thin hole to get it out instead of having to move all the rocks around it.

FIRE WATER

FIRE AIR (on top of the fire water)

VERY DEEP HOLES

Malformed Frogs in California

FIGURE 4: This frog has limb deformities.

In 1995, a Minnesota school's wetlands project reported high numbers of deformed frogs. The problem has persisted and has been found in many parts of the country. California's Central Valley has been identified as a hot spot. No single cause for these malformations has been determined, but one of the major culprits is a parasite known as *Ribeiroia ondatrae* that attacks the leg buds of developing tadpoles. It is suspected that environmental factors may contribute to spikes in the parasite's population. Your task is to research this suspected linkage and present an informed opinion about whether this explanation is valid and whether there are other factors that might be contributing to the deformities.

1. PLAN AN INVESTIGATION

In your group, select a deformity cluster that you wish to investigate further. Determine what data you will need to collect about the frogs and the conditions in their environment.

2. CARRY OUT AN INVESTIGATION

Using the Internet, library materials, or onsite observations, collect the data you determined was relevant in Step 1. Also, gather information about data and conclusions in published studies about frog deformities in other western states.

3. EVALUATE DATA

Compare your local data with the published studies. Determine any parallels and also any conflicts.

4. CONSTRUCT AN EXPLANATION

Determine what factors are linked to your cluster and what can be done to reduce their impacts.

5. COMMUNICATE

Prepare a multimedia presentation that presents your results and conclusions.

 CHECK YOUR WORK

A complete presentation should include the following:

- a definition of the problem and why area residents should be concerned
- a clear presentation of probable causes based on evidence and supporting studies
- a plan of action to reduce negative impacts on the area

Name _____   Date _____

In your Evidence Notebook, make a concept map, other graphic organizer, or outline using the Study Guides you made for each lesson in this unit. Be sure to use evidence to support your claims.

When synthesizing individual information, remember to follow these general steps:
- Find the central idea of each piece of information.
- Think about the relationships among the central ideas.
- Combine the ideas to come up with a new understanding.

Look back to the Driving Questions from the opening section of this unit. In your Evidence Notebook, review and revise your previous answers to those questions. Use the evidence you gathered and other observations you made throughout the unit to support your claims.

PRACTICE AND REVIEW

1. Why is engineering important for conservation efforts? Select all correct answers.

   ☐ **a.** Engineering can provide solutions that enable human populations to grow while minimizing impacts to the environment and biodiversity.

   ☐ **b.** Engineering solutions can involve shared facilities, such as wastewater treatment or the generation of energy, that can be designed to minimize impacts on the environment.

   ☐ **c.** Conservation is not possible without engineering.

   ☐ **d.** Many conservation problems can be addressed using engineering solutions, such as monitoring illegal logging activity through satellite images.

2. What role does adaptation play in how species respond to human disturbances? Select all correct answers.

   ☐ **a.** Species that do not adapt quickly enough may decline, or even become locally extinct, in a changed environment.

   ☐ **b.** Species that adapt quickly enough may survive, or even thrive, in a changed environment.

   ☐ **c.** Adaptation does not play a role in how species are affected by human disturbances.

   ☐ **d.** The adaptation level in species is equal to the disturbance level in an ecosystem.

3. What would need to occur for a "potentially renewable" resource to be considered renewable?

   ○ **a.** The resource is used at a slower rate than it is replenished.

   ○ **b.** The resource is used at a faster rate than it is replenished.

   ○ **c.** People use the resource to generate electricity.

   ○ **d.** People decide to renew the resource.

4. Which factor is *not* a benefit of high biodiversity levels on Earth?

   ○ **a.** inspirational value of landscapes

   ○ **b.** ecosystem stability

   ○ **c.** ecosystem services and functions

   ○ **d.** homogeneous ecosystems

5. An increase in human density in a formerly natural area typically causes what type of change in biodiversity?

   ○ **a.** an increase

   ○ **b.** a decrease

   ○ **c.** no change

   ○ **d.** a decrease followed by an immediate increase

6. How would an increase in atmospheric greenhouse gases contribute to an increase in average global temperature?

_____

_____

_____

_____

_____

_____

_____

7. How might climate change impact biodiversity in a given area?

_____

_____

_____

_____

_____

_____

_____

8. What are three ways that climate change could affect the people and ecosystems of California?

_____

_____

_____

_____

_____

_____

_____

_____

UNIT PROJECT

Return to your unit project. Prepare your materials and models into a final presentation to share with the class. Include an evaluation of your investigation into the uses and environmental impacts of dams.

Remember these tips while evaluating:

- Was your research based on an in-depth exploration of reliable sources?

- Are your claims supported by detailed evidence?
- Does your model clearly demonstrate the pros and cons of building a dam?
- Are your findings presented clearly in both written and oral formats?

Index

Page numbers for definitions are printed in **boldface** type.
Page numbers for illustrations, maps, and charts are printed in *italics*.

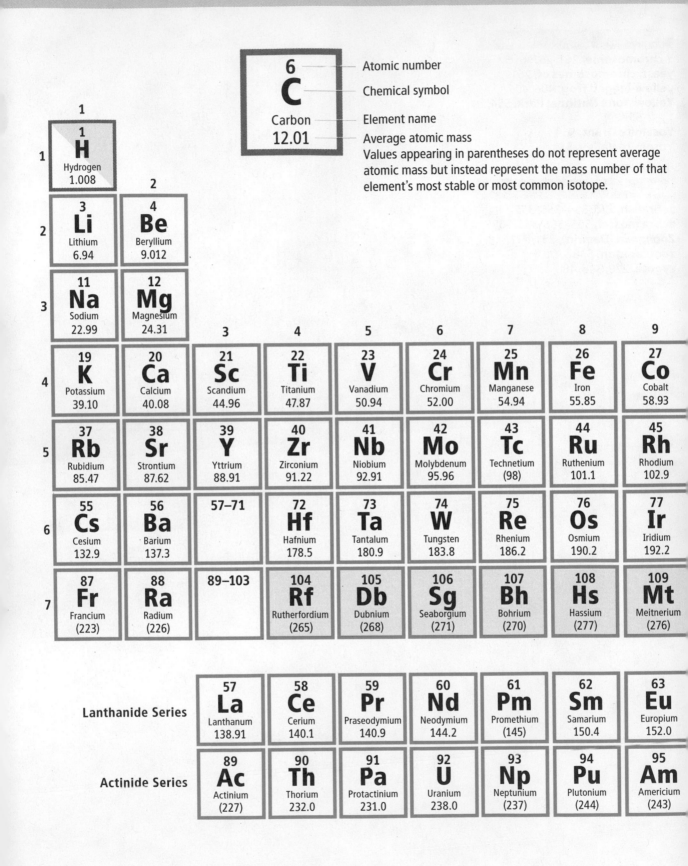

6
C
Carbon
12.01

Atomic number
Chemical symbol
Element name
Average atomic mass

Values appearing in parentheses do not represent average atomic mass but instead represent the mass number of that element's most stable or most common isotope.

1

1
1 H Hydrogen 1.008

2

2
3 Li Lithium 6.94 | **4 Be** Beryllium 9.012

3
11 Na Sodium 22.99 | **12 Mg** Magnesium 24.31

| | | **3** | **4** | **5** | **6** | **7** | **8** | **9** |

4
19 K Potassium 39.10 | **20 Ca** Calcium 40.08 | **21 Sc** Scandium 44.96 | **22 Ti** Titanium 47.87 | **23 V** Vanadium 50.94 | **24 Cr** Chromium 52.00 | **25 Mn** Manganese 54.94 | **26 Fe** Iron 55.85 | **27 Co** Cobalt 58.93

5
37 Rb Rubidium 85.47 | **38 Sr** Strontium 87.62 | **39 Y** Yttrium 88.91 | **40 Zr** Zirconium 91.22 | **41 Nb** Niobium 92.91 | **42 Mo** Molybdenum 95.96 | **43 Tc** Technetium (98) | **44 Ru** Ruthenium 101.1 | **45 Rh** Rhodium 102.9

6
55 Cs Cesium 132.9 | **56 Ba** Barium 137.3 | **57–71** | **72 Hf** Hafnium 178.5 | **73 Ta** Tantalum 180.9 | **74 W** Tungsten 183.8 | **75 Re** Rhenium 186.2 | **76 Os** Osmium 190.2 | **77 Ir** Iridium 192.2

7
87 Fr Francium (223) | **88 Ra** Radium (226) | **89–103** | **104 Rf** Rutherfordium (265) | **105 Db** Dubnium (268) | **106 Sg** Seaborgium (271) | **107 Bh** Bohrium (270) | **108 Hs** Hassium (277) | **109 Mt** Meitnerium (276)

Lanthanide Series
57 La Lanthanum 138.91 | **58 Ce** Cerium 140.1 | **59 Pr** Praseodymium 140.9 | **60 Nd** Neodymium 144.2 | **61 Pm** Promethium (145) | **62 Sm** Samarium 150.4 | **63 Eu** Europium 152.0

Actinide Series
89 Ac Actinium (227) | **90 Th** Thorium 232.0 | **91 Pa** Protactinium 231.0 | **92 U** Uranium 238.0 | **93 Np** Neptunium (237) | **94 Pu** Plutonium (244) | **95 Am** Americium (243)

Metals   **Metalloids**   **Nonmetals**

State of Element at STP

☐ Solid   ◰ Liquid

◰ Gas   ☐ Not yet known

18

2
He
Helium
4.003

13	**14**	**15**	**16**	**17**	
5	6	7	8	9	10
B	**C**	**N**	**O**	**F**	**Ne**
Boron	Carbon	Nitrogen	Oxygen	Fluorine	Neon
10.81	12.01	14.007	15.999	19.00	20.18
13	14	15	16	17	18
Al	**Si**	**P**	**S**	**Cl**	**Ar**
Aluminum	Silicon	Phosphorus	Sulfur	Chlorine	Argon
26.98	28.085	30.97	32.06	35.45	39.95

10	**11**	**12**							
28	29	30	31	32	33	34	35	36	
Ni	**Cu**	**Zn**	**Ga**	**Ge**	**As**	**Se**	**Br**	**Kr**	
Nickel	Copper	Zinc	Gallium	Germanium	Arsenic	Selenium	Bromine	Krypton	
58.69	63.55	65.38	69.72	72.63	74.92	78.96	79.90	83.80	
46	47	48	49	50	51	52	53	54	
Pd	**Ag**	**Cd**	**In**	**Sn**	**Sb**	**Te**	**I**	**Xe**	
Palladium	Silver	Cadmium	Indium	Tin	Antimony	Tellurium	Iodine	Xenon	
106.4	107.9	112.4	114.8	118.7	121.8	127.6	126.9	131.3	
78	79	80	81	82	83	84	85	86	
Pt	**Au**	**Hg**	**Tl**	**Pb**	**Bi**	**Po**	**At**	**Rn**	
Platinum	Gold	Mercury	Thallium	Lead	Bismuth	Polonium	Astatine	Radon	
195.1	197.0	200.6	204.38	207.2	209.0	(209)	(210)	(222)	
110	111	112	113	114	115	116	117	118	
Ds	**Rg**	**Cn**	**Nh**	**Fl**	**Mc**	**Lv**	**Ts**	**Og**	
Darmstadtium	Roentgenium	Copernicium	Nihonium	Flerovium	Moscovium	Livermorium	Tennessine	Oganesson	
(281)	(280)	(285)	(284)	(289)	(288)	(293)	(294)	(294)	

64	65	66	67	68	69	70	71
Gd	**Tb**	**Dy**	**Ho**	**Er**	**Tm**	**Yb**	**Lu**
Gadolinium	Terbium	Dysprosium	Holmium	Erbium	Thulium	Ytterbium	Lutetium
157.3	158.9	162.5	164.9	167.3	168.9	173.1	175.0
96	97	98	99	100	101	102	103
Cm	**Bk**	**Cf**	**Es**	**Fm**	**Md**	**No**	**Lr**
Curium	Berkelium	Californium	Einsteinium	Fermium	Mendelevium	Nobelium	Lawrencium
(247)	(247)	(251)	(252)	(257)	(258)	(259)	(262)

Elements with atomic numbers of 95 and above are not known to occur naturally, even in trace amounts. They have only been synthesized in the lab. The physical and chemical properties of elements with atomic numbers 100 and above cannot be predicted with certainty.